The first**writer**.com

Writers' Handbook

2017

The firstwriter.com

Writers' Handbook

2017

EDITOR
J. PAUL DYSON

Published in 2016 by JP&A Dyson
Copyright JP&A Dyson

https://www.firstwriter.com

ISBN 978-1-909935-13-6

Registered with the IP Rights Office
Copyright Registration Service
Ref: 3052237699

Foreword

The firstwriter.com Writers' Handbook returns for its 2017 edition with over 1,300 listings of literary agents, publishers, and magazines, updated in firstwriter.com's online databases between 2014 and 2016, including revised and updated listings from the previous edition and over 40% new entries.

Previous editions of this handbook have been bought by writers across the United States, Canada, and Europe; and ranked in the United Kingdom as the number one bestselling writing and publishing directory on Amazon. The 2017 edition continues this international outlook, giving writers all over the English-speaking world access to the global publishing markets.

Readers of this edition can also benefit from insights from Andrew Lownie, of the Andrew Lownie Literary Agency Ltd, who describes a week in the life of a literary agent.

The handbook also provides free online access to the entire current firstwriter.com databases, including over 2,000 magazines, over 650 literary agencies, over 1,800 book publishers that don't charge fees, and constantly updated listings of current writing competitions, with typically more than 50 added each month.

For details on how to claim your free access please see the back of this book.

Included in the subscription

A subscription to the full website is not only free with this book, but comes packed with all the following features:

Advanced search features

- Save searches and save time – set up to 15 search parameters specific to your work, save them, and then access the search results with a single click whenever you log in. You can even save multiple different searches if you have different types of work you are looking to place.
- Add personal notes to listings, visible only to you and fully searchable – helping you to organise your actions.
- Set reminders on listings to notify you when to submit your work, when to follow up, when to expect a reply, or any other custom action.
- Track which listings you've viewed and when, to help you organise your search – any listings which have changed since you last viewed them will be highlighted for your attention.

Daily email updates

As a subscriber you will be able to take advantage of our email alert service, meaning you can specify your particular interests and we'll send you automatic email updates when we change or add a listing that matches them. So if you're interested in agents dealing in romantic fiction in the United States you can have us send you emails with the latest updates about them – keeping you up to date without even having to log in.

User feedback

Our agent, publisher, and magazine databases all include a user feedback feature that allows our subscribers to leave feedback on each listing – giving you not only the chance to have your say about the markets you contact, but giving a unique authors' perspective on the listings.

Save on copyright protection fees

If you're sending your work away to publishers, competitions, or literary agents, it's vital that you first protect your copyright. As a subscriber to firstwriter.com you can do this through our site and save 10% on the copyright registration fees normally payable for protecting your work internationally through the Intellectual Property Rights Office (https://www.Copyright RegistrationService.com).

firstwriter.magazine

firstwriter.magazine showcases the best in new poetry and fiction from around the world. If you're interested in writing and want to get published, the most important thing you can do is read contemporary writing that's getting into print now. Our magazine helps you do that.

Half price competitions

As well as saving money on copyright registration, subscribers to firstwriter.com can also make further savings by entering writing competitions at a special reduced rate. Subscribers can enter the firstwriter.com International Poetry Competition and International Short Story Contest for half price.

Monthly newsletter

When you subscribe to firstwriter.com you also receive our monthly email newsletter – described by one publishing company as "the best in the business" – including articles, news, and interviews for writers. And the best part is that you can continue to receive the newsletter even after you stop your paid subscription – at no cost!

For details on how to claim your free access please see the back of this book.

Contents

Publishers

Free Access

Glossary of Terms

This section explains common terms used in this handbook, and in the publishing industry more generally.

Academic

Listings in this book will be marked as targeting the academic market only if they publish material of an academic nature; e.g. academic theses, scientific papers, etc. The term is not used to indicate publications that publish general material aimed at people who happen to be in academia, or who are described as academic by virtue of being educated.

Adult

In publishing, "adult" simply refers to books that are aimed at adults, as opposed to books that are aimed at children, or young adults, etc. It is not a euphemism for pornographic or erotic content. Nor does it necessarily refer to content which is unsuitable for children; it is just not targeted at them. In this book, most ordinary mainstream publishers will be described as "adult", unless their books are specifically targeted at other groups (such as children, professionals, etc.).

Advance

Advances are up-front payments made by traditional publishers to authors, which are off-set against future royalties.

Agented

An *agented* submission is one which is submitted by a literary agent. If a publisher accepts only *agented* submissions then you will need a literary agent to submit the work on your behalf.

Author bio

A brief description of you and your life – normally in relation to your writing activity, but if intended for publication (particularly in magazines) may be broader in scope. May be similar to *Curriculum Vitae* (CV) or résumé, depending on context.

Bio

See *Author bio*.

Curriculum Vitae

A brief description of you, your qualifications, and accomplishments – normally in this context in relation to writing (any previous publications, or awards, etc.), but in the case of nonfiction proposals may also include relevant experience that qualifies you to write on the subject. Commonly abbreviated to "CV". May also be referred to as a résumé. May be similar to *Author bio*, depending on context.

CV

See *Curriculum Vitae*.

International Reply Coupon

When submitting material overseas you may be required to enclose *International Reply Coupons*, which will enable the recipient to send a response and/or return your material at your cost. Not applicable/available in all countries, so check with your local Post Office for more information.

IRC
See *International Reply Coupon*.

Manuscript
Your complete piece of work – be it a novel, short story, or article, etc. – will be referred to as your manuscript. Commonly abbreviated to "ms" (singular) or "mss" (plural).

MS
See *Manuscript*.

MSS
See *Manuscript*.

Professional
Listings in this book will be marked as targeting the professional market if they publish material serving a particular profession: e.g. legal journals, medical journals, etc. The term is not used to indicate publications that publish general material aimed at a notional "professional class".

Proposal
A proposal is normally requested for nonfiction projects (where the book may not yet have been completed, or even begun). Proposals can consist of a number of components, such as an outline, table of contents, CV, marketing information, etc. but the exact requirements will vary from one publisher to another.

Query
Many agents and publishers will prefer to receive a query in the first instance, rather than your full *manuscript*. A query will typically consist of a cover letter accompanied by a *synopsis* and/or sample chapter(s). Specific requirements will vary, however, so always check on a case by case basis.

Recommendation
If an agent is only accepting approaches by recommendation this means that they will only consider your work if it comes with a recommendation from an established professional in the industry, or an existing client.

RoW
Rest of world.

SAE
See *Stamped Addressed Envelope*. Can also be referred to as SASE.

SASE
Self-Addressed Stamped Envelope. Variation of SAE. See *Stamped Addressed Envelope*.

Stamped Addressed Envelope
Commonly abbreviated to "SAE". Can also be referred to as Self-Addressed Stamped Envelope, or SASE. When supplying an SAE, ensure that the envelope and postage is adequate for a reply or the return of your material, as required. If you are submitting overseas, remember that postage from your own country will not be accepted, and you may need to provide an *International Reply Coupon*.

Simultaneous submission
A simultaneous submission is one which is sent to more than one market at the same time. Normally you will be sending your work to numerous different magazines, agents, and publishers at the same time, but some demand the right to consider it exclusively – i.e. they don't accept simultaneous submissions.

Synopsis
A short outline of your story. This should cover all the main characters and events, including the ending. It is not the kind of "teaser" found on a book's back cover. The length of synopsis required can vary, but is generally between one and three pages.

TOC
Table of Contents. These are often requested as part of nonfiction proposals.

Unagented
An unagented submission is one which is not submitted through a literary agent. If a publisher accepts unagented submissions then you can approach them directly.

Unsolicited mss

A manuscript which has not been requested.
Many agents and publishers will not accept
unsolicited mss, but this does not necessarily
mean they are closed to approaches – many
will prefer to receive a short *query* in the first
instance. If they like the idea, they will
request the full work, which will then be a
solicited manuscript.

Youth

The term "Youth" in this book is used to
indicate the Young Adult market.

*Claim your free access to **www.firstwriter.com**: See p.423*

The Writer's Roadmap

With most objectives in life, people recognise that there is a path to follow. Whether it is career progression, developing a relationship, or chasing your dreams, we normally understand that there are foundations to lay and baby steps to take before we'll be ready for the main event.

But for some reason, with writing (perhaps because so much of the journey of a writer happens in private, behind closed doors), people often overlook the process involved. They often have a plan of action which runs something like this:

1. Write novel.

2. Get novel published.

This is a bit like having a plan for success in tennis which runs:

1. Buy tennis racket.

2. Win Wimbledon.

It misses out all the practice that is going to be required; the competing in the minor competitions and the learning of the craft that will be needed in order to succeed in the major events; the time that will need to be spent gaining reputation and experience.

In this roadmap we'll be laying out what we think is the best path to follow to try and give yourself the best shot of success in the world of writing. You don't necessarily have to jump through all the hoops, and there will always be people who, like Pop Idol or reality TV contestants, get a lucky break that propels them to stardom without laying any of the foundations laid out below, but the aim here is to limit your reliance on luck and maximise your ability to shape your destiny yourself.

1: Write short material

Writers will very often start off by writing a novel. We would advise strongly against this. It's like leaving school one day and applying for a job as a CEO of an international corporation the next. Novels are the big league. They are expensive to produce, market, and distribute. They require significant investment and pose a significant financial risk to publishers. They are not a good place for new writers to try and cut their teeth. If you've already written your novel that's great – it's great experience and you'll have learned a lot – but we'd recommend shelving it for now (you can always come back to it later) and getting stuck into writing some short form material, such as poetry and short fiction.

This is what novelist George R. R. Martin, author of *A Game of Thrones*, has to say on the subject:

> "I would also suggest that any aspiring writer begin with short stories. These days, I meet far too many young writers who try to start off with a novel right off, or a trilogy, or even a nine-book series. That's like starting in at rock climbing by tackling Mt Everest. Short stories help you learn your craft."

You will find that writing short material will improve your writing no end. Writing short fiction allows you to play with lots of different stories and characters very quickly. Because you will probably only spend a few days on any given story you will quickly gain a lot of experience with plotting stories and will learn a lot about what works, what doesn't work, and what you personally are good at. When you write a novel, by contrast, you may spend years on a single story and one set of characters, making this learning process much slower.

Your writing will also be improved by the need to stick to a word limit. Writers who start their career by writing a novel often produce huge epics, the word counts of which they wear as a badge of honour, as if they demonstrate their commitment to and enthusiasm for writing. What they actually demonstrate is a naivety about the realities of getting published. The odds are already stacked against new writers getting a novel published, because of the cost and financial risk of publishing a novel. The bigger the novel, the more it will cost to print, warehouse, and distribute. Publishers will not look at a large word count and be impressed – they will be terrified. The longer the novel, the less chance it has of getting published.

A lengthy first novel also suggests that the writer has yet to learn one of the most critical skills a writer must possess to succeed: brevity. By writing short stories that fit the limits imposed by competitions and magazines you will learn this critical skill. You will learn to remove unnecessary words and passages, and you will find that your writing becomes leaner, more engaging, and more exciting as a result. Lengthy first novels are often rambling and sometimes boring – but once you've been forced to learn how to "trim the fat" by writing short stories, the good habits you've got into will transfer across when you start writing long form works, allowing you to write novels that are pacier and better to read. They will stand a better chance of publication not just because they are shorter and cheaper to produce, but they are also likely to be better written.

2: Get a professional critique

It's a good idea to get some professional feedback on your work at some point, and it's probably better to do this sooner, rather than later. There's no point spending a long time doing something that doesn't quite work if a little advice early on could have got you on the right track sooner. It's also a lot cheaper to get a short story critiqued than a whole novel, and if you can learn the necessary lessons now it will both minimise the cost and maximise the benefit of the advice.

Should you protect the copyright of short works before showing them to anyone?

This is a matter of personal preference. We'd suggest that it certainly isn't as important to register short works as full novels, as your short works are unlikely to be of much financial value to you. Having said that, films do sometimes get made which are based on short stories, in which case you'd want to have all your rights in order. If you do choose to register your short works this can be done for a relatively small amount online at https://www.copyrightregistrationservice.com/register.

3: Submit to competitions and magazines, and build a list of writing credits

Once you have got some short works that you are happy with you can start submitting them to competitions and small magazines. You can search for competitions at https://www.firstwriter.com/competitions and magazines at https://www.firstwriter.com/magazines. Prize money may not be huge, and you probably won't be paid for having your work appear in the kind of small literary magazines you will probably be approaching at first, but the objective here is to build up a list of writing credits to give you more credibility when approaching agents and publishers. You'll be much more likely to grab their attention if you can reel off a list of places where you have already been published, or prizes you have won.

4: Finish your novel and protect your copyright

Okay – so you've built up a list of writing credits, and you've decided it's time to either write a novel, or go back to the one you had already started (in which case you'll probably find yourself cutting out large chunks and making it a lot shorter!). Once you've got your novel to the point where you're happy to start submitting it for publication you should get it registered for copyright. Unlike the registration of short works, which we think is a matter of personal preference, we'd definitely recommend registering a novel, and doing so before you show it to anybody. That *includes* family and friends. Don't worry that you might want to change it – as long as you don't rewrite it to the point where it's not recognisable it will still be protected – the important thing is to get it registered without delay. You can protect it online at https://www.copyrightregistrationservice.com/register.

If you've already shown it to other people then just register it as soon as you can. Proving a claim to copyright is all about proving you had a copy of the work before anyone else, so time is of the essence.

5: Editing

These days, agents and publishers increasingly seem to expect manuscripts to have been professionally edited before being submitted to them – and no, getting your husband / wife / friend / relative to do it doesn't count. Ideally, you should have the whole manuscript professionally edited, but this can be expensive. Since most agents and publishers aren't going to want to see the whole manuscript in the first instance you can probably get away with just having the first three chapters edited. It may also be worth having your query letter and synopsis edited at the same time.

6: Submit to literary agents

There will be many publishers out there who will accept your submission directly, and on the face of it that might seem like a good idea, since you won't have to pay an agent 15% of your earnings.

However, all the biggest publishers are generally closed to direct submissions from authors, meaning that if you want the chance of getting a top publisher you're going to need a literary agent. You'll also probably find that their 15% fee is more than offset by the higher earnings you'll be likely to achieve.

To search for literary agents go to https://www.firstwriter.com/Agents. Start by being as specific in your search as possible. So if you've written a historical romance select "Fiction", "Romance", and "Historical". Once you've approached all the agents that specifically mention all three elements broaden your search to just "Fiction" and "Romance". As long as the new results don't specifically say they don't handle historical romance, these are still valid markets to approach. Finally, search for just "Fiction", as there are many agents who are willing to consider all kinds of fiction but don't specifically mention romance or historical.

Don't limit your approaches to just agents in your own country. With more and more agents accepting electronic queries it's now as easy to approach agents in other countries as in your own, and if you're ignoring either London or New York (the two main centres of English language publishing) you're cutting your chances of success in two.

7: Submit directly to publishers

Once you're certain that you've exhausted all potential agents for your work, you can start looking for publishers to submit your work directly to. You can search for publishers at https://www.firstwriter.com/publishers. Apply the same filtering as when you were searching for agents: start specific and gradually broaden, until you've exchausted all possibilities.

8: Self-publishing

In the past, once you got to the point where you'd submitted to all the publishers and agents who might be interested in your book, it would be time to pack away the manuscript in the attic, chalk it up to experience, and start writing another. However, these days writers have the option to take their book directly to market by publishing it themselves.

Before you decide to switch to self-publishing you must be sure that you've exhausted all traditional publishing possibilities – because once you've self-published your book you're unlikely to be able to submit it to agents and publishers. It will probably take a few years of exploring the world of traditional publishing to reach this point, but if you do then you've nothing to lose by giving self-publishing a shot. See our guide to self-publishing for details on how to proceed.

Why Choose Traditional Publishing

When **firstwriter.com** first started, back in 2001, there were only two games in town when it came to getting your book published: traditional publishing, and vanity publishing – and which you should pick was a no-brainer. Vanity publishing was little more than a scam that would leave you with an empty bank account and a house full of unsold books. If you were serious about being a writer, you had to follow the traditional publishing path.

Since then, there has been a self-publishing revolution, with new technologies and new printing methods giving writers a genuine opportunity to get their books into the market by themselves. So, is there still a reason for writers to choose traditional publishing?

The benefits of traditional publishing

Despite the allure and apparent ease of self-publishing, the traditional path still offers you the best chance of making a success of being a writer. There are rare cases where self-published writers make staggering fortunes and become internationally renowned on the back of their self-published books, but these cases are few and far between, and a tiny drop in the rapidly expanding ocean of self-published works. The vast majority of successful books – and the vast majority of successful writers – have their homes firmly in the established publishing houses. Even those self-published authors who find success usually end up moving to a traditional publisher in the end.

This is because the traditional publishers have the systems, the market presence, and the financial clout to *make* a book a bestseller. While successful self-published authors often owe their success in no small part to a decent dose of luck (a social media comment that goes viral; the right mention on the right media outlet at the right time), traditional publishers are in the business of engineering that success. They might not always succeed, but they have the marketing budgets and the distribution channels in place to give themselves, and the book they are promoting, the best possible chance.

And it's not just the marketing and the distribution. Getting signed with a traditional publisher brings a whole team of people with a wealth of expertise that will all work towards the success of the book. It will provide you with an editor who may have experience of working on previous bestsellers, who will not only help you get rid of mistakes in your work but may also help you refine it into a better book. They will help make sure that the quality of your content is good enough to make it in the marketplace.

The publishers will source a professional cover designer who will make your book look the part on the shelves and on the pages of the bookselling websites. They will have accountants who will handle the technicalities of tax regimes both home and abroad. They will have overseas contacts for establishing foreign publishing rights; translations; etc. They may even have contacts in the film industry, should there be a prospect of a movie adaptation. They will have experts working on every aspect of your book, right down to the printing and the warehousing and the shipping of the physical products. They will have people to manage the ebook conversion and the electronic distribution. As an author, you don't need to worry about any of this.

This means you get more time to simply be a writer. You may have to go on book tours, but even these will be organised for you by PR experts, who will also be handling all the press releases, etc.

And then there's the advances. Advances are up-front payments made by traditional publishers to authors, which are off-set against future royalties. So, an author might receive a $5,000 advance before their book is published. When the royalties start coming in, the publisher keeps the first $5,000 to off-set the advance. The good news for the author is that if the book flops and doesn't make $5,000 in royalties they still get to keep the full advance. In an uncertain profession, the security of an advance can be invaluable for an author – and of course it's not something available to self-published authors.

The drawbacks of traditional publishing

The main downside of traditional publishing is just that it's so hard to get into. If you choose to self-publish then – provided you have enough perseverance, the right help and advice, and perhaps a little bit of money – you are guaranteed to succeed and see your book in print and for sale. With traditional publishing, the cold hard fact is that most people who try will not succeed.

And for many of those people who fail it may not even be their fault. That aspect of traditional publishing which can bring so many benefits as compared to self-publishing – that of being part of a team – can also be part of its biggest drawback. It means that you have to get other people to buy into your book. It means that you have to rely on other people being competent enough to spot a bestseller. Many failed to spot the potential of the Harry Potter books. How many potential bestsellers never make it into print just because none of the professionals at the publishers' gates manage to recognise their potential?

So if you choose traditional publishing your destiny is not in your own hands – and for some writers the lack of exclusive control can also be a problem. Sometimes writers get defensive when editors try to tinker with their work, or annoyed when cover artists don't realise their vision the way they expect. But this is hardly a fair criticism of traditional publishing, as most writers (particularly when they are starting out) will benefit from advice from experienced professionals in the field, and will often only be shooting themselves in the foot if they insist on ignoring it.

The final main drawback with traditional publishing is that less of the sale price of each copy makes it to the writer. A typical royalty contract will give the writer 15%. With a self-published book, the author can expect to receive much more. So, all other things being equal, the self-published route can be more profitable – but, of course, all things are not equal. If self-publishing means lower sales (as is likely), then you will probably make less money overall. Remember, it's better to have 15% of something than 50% of nothing.

Conclusion

In conclusion, our advice to writers would be to aim for traditional publishing first. It might be a long shot, but if it works then you stand a much better chance of being successful. If you don't manage to get signed by an agent or a publisher then you still have the option of self-publishing, but make sure you don't get tempted to resort to self-publishing too soon – most agents and publishers won't consider self-published works, so this is a one-way street. Once you've self-published your work, you probably won't be able to change your mind and go back to the traditional publishers with your book unless it becomes a huge hit without them. It's therefore important that you exhaust all your traditional publishing options before making the leap to self-publishing. Be prepared for this to take perhaps a few years (lots of agents and publishers can take six months just to respond), and make sure you've submitted to everyone you can on *both* sides of the Atlantic (publishing is a global game these days, and you need to concentrate on the two main centres of English-language publishing (New York and London) equally) before you make the decision to self-publish instead.

Formatting Your Manuscript

Before submitting a manuscript to an agent, magazine, or publisher, it's important that you get the formatting right. There are industry norms covering everything from the size of your margins to the font you choose – get them wrong and you'll be marking yourself out as an amateur. Get them right, and agents and editors will be far more likely to take you seriously.

Fonts

Don't be tempted to "make your book stand out" by using fancy fonts. It *will* stand out, but not for any reason you'd want. Your entire manuscript should be in a monospaced font like Courier (not a proportional font, like Times Roman) at 12 points. (A monospaced font is one where each character takes up the same amount of space; a proportional font is where the letter "i" takes up less space than the letter "m".)

This goes for your text, your headings, your title, your name – everything. Your objective is to produce a manuscript that looks like it has been produced on a simple typewriter.

Italics / bold

Your job as the author is to indicate words that require emphasis, not to pick particular styles of font. This will be determined by the house style of the publisher in question. You indicate emphasis by underlining text; the publisher will decide whether they will use bold or italic to achieve this emphasis – you shouldn't use either in your text.

Margins

You should have a one inch (2.5 centimetre) margin around your entire page: top, bottom, left, and right.

Spacing

In terms of line spacing, your entire manuscript should be double spaced. Your word processor should provide an option for this, so you don't have to insert blank lines manually.

While line spacing should be double, spaces after punctuation should be single. If you're in the habit of putting two spaces after full stops this is the time to get out of that habit, and remove them from your manuscript. You're just creating extra work for the editor who will have to strip them all out.

Do not put blank lines between paragraphs. Start every paragraph (even those at the start of chapters) with an indent equivalent to five spaces. If you want a scene break then create a line with the "#" character centred in the middle. You don't need blank lines above or below this line.

*Claim your free access to **www.firstwriter.com**: See p.423*

Word count

You will need to provide an estimated word count on the front page of your manuscript. Tempting as it will be to simply use the word processor's word counting function to tell you exactly how many words there are in your manuscript, this is not what you should do. Instead, you should work out the maximum number of characters on a line, divide this number by six, and then multiply by the total number of lines in your manuscript.

Once you have got your estimated word count you need to round it to an approximate value. How you round will depend on the overall length of your manuscript:

- up to 1,500 words: round to the nearest 100;
- 1,500–10,000 words: round to the nearest 500;
- 10,000–25,000 words: round to the nearest 1,000;
- Over 25,000 words: round to the nearest 5,000.

The reason an agent or editor will need to know your word count is so that they can estimate how many pages it will make. Since actual pages include varying amounts of white space due to breaks in paragraphs, sections of speech, etc. the formula above will actually provide a better idea of how many pages will be required than an exact word count would.

And – perhaps more importantly – providing an exact word count will highlight you immediately as an amateur.

Layout of the front page

On the first page of the manuscript, place your name, address, and any other relevant contact details (such as phone number, email address, etc.) in the top left-hand corner. In the top right-hand corner write your approximate word count.

If you have registered your work for copyright protection, place the reference number two single lines (one double line) beneath your contact details. Since your manuscript will only be seen by agents or editors, not the public, this should be done as discreetly as possible, and you should refrain from using any official seal you may have been granted permissions to use. (For information on registering for copyright protection see "Protecting Your Copyright", below.)

Place your title halfway down the front page. Your title should be centred and would normally be in capital letters. You can make it bold or underlined if you want, but it should be the same size as the rest of the text.

From your title, go down two single lines (or one double line) and insert your byline. This should be centred and start with the word "By", followed by the name you are writing under. This can be your name or a pen name, but should be the name you want the work published under. However, make sure that the name in the top left-hand corner is your real, legal name.

From your byline, go down four single lines (or two double lines) and begin your manuscript.

Layout of the text

Print on only one side of the paper, even if your printer can print on both sides.

In the top right-hand corner of all pages except the first should be your running head. This should be comprised of the surname used in your byline; a keyword from your title, and the page number, e.g. "Myname / Mynovel Page 5".

Text should be left-aligned, *not* justified. This means that you should have a ragged right-hand edge to the text, with lines ending at different points. Make sure you don't have any sort of hyphenation function switched on in your word processor: if a word is too long to fit on a line it should be taken over to the next.

Start each new chapter a third of the way down the page with the centred chapter number / title, underlined. Drop down four single lines (two double lines) to the main text.

At the end of the manuscript you do not need to indicate the ending in any way: you don't need to write "The End", or "Ends", etc. The only exception to this is if your manuscript happens to end at the bottom of a page, in which case you can handwrite the word "End" at the bottom of the last page, after you have printed it out.

Protecting Your Copyright

Protecting your copyright is by no means a requirement before submitting your work, but you may feel that it is a prudent step that you would like to take before allowing strangers to see your material.

These days, you can register your work for copyright protection quickly and easily online. The Intellectual Property Rights Office operates a website called the "Copyright Registration Service" which allows you to do this:

- *https://www.CopyrightRegistrationService.com*

This website can be used for material created in any nation signed up to the Berne Convention. This includes the United States, United Kingdom, Canada, Australia, Ireland, New Zealand, and most other countries. There are around 180 countries in the world, and over 160 of them are part of the Berne Convention.

Provided you created your work in one of the Berne Convention nations, your work should be protected by copyright in all other Berne Convention nations. You can therefore protect your copyright around most of the world with a single registration, and because the process is entirely online you can have your work protected in a matter of minutes, without having to print and post a copy of your manuscript.

What is copyright?

Copyright is a form of intellectual property (often referred to as "IP"). Other forms of intellectual property include trade marks, designs, and patents. These categories refer to different kinds of ideas which may not exist in a physical form that can be owned as property in the traditional sense, but may nonetheless have value to the people who created them. These forms of intellectual property can be owned in the same way that physical property is owned, but – as with physical property – they can be subject to dispute and proper documentation is required to prove ownership.

The different types of intellectual property divide into these categories as follows:

- **Copyright:** copyright protects creative output such as books, poems, pictures, drawings, music, films, etc. Any work which can be recorded in some way can be protected by copyright, as long as it is original and of sufficient length. Copyright does not cover short phrases or names.

- **Trade marks:** trade marks cover words and/or images which distinguish the goods or services of one trader from another. Unlike copyright, trade marks can cover names and short phrases.

*Claim your free access to **www.firstwriter.com**: See p.423*

- **Designs:** designs cover the overall visual appearance of a product, such as its shape, etc.

- **Patents:** patents protect the technical or functional aspects of designs or inventions.

The specifics of the legal protection surrounding these various forms of intellectual property will vary from nation to nation, but there are also generally international conventions to which a lot if not most of the nations of the world subscribe. The information provided below outlines the common situation in many countries but you should be aware that this may not reflect the exact situation in every territory.

The two types of intellectual property most relevant to writers are copyright and trade marks. If a writer has written a novel, a short story, a poem, a script, or any other piece of writing then the contents themselves can be protected by copyright. The title, however, cannot be protected by copyright as it is a name. An author may therefore feel that they wish to consider protecting the title of their work by registering it as a trade mark, if they feel that it is particularly important and/or more valuable in itself than the cost of registering a trade mark.

If a writer wants to register the copyright for their work, or register the title of their work as a trade mark, there are generally registration fees to be paid. Despite the fact that copyright covers long works that could be hundreds of thousands of words long, while trade marks cover single words and short phrases, the cost for registering a trade mark is likely to be many times higher than that for registering a work for copyright protection. This is because trade marks must be unique and are checked against existing trade marks for potential conflicts. While works to be registered for copyright must also not infringe existing works, it is not practical to check the huge volume of new works to be registered for copyright against the even larger volume of all previously copyrighted works. Copyright registration therefore tends to simply archive the work in question as proof of the date at which the person registering the work was in possession of it.

In the case of both copyright and trade marks the law generally provides some protection even without any kind of registration, but registration provides the owner of the intellectual property with greater and more enforceable protection. In the case of copyright, the creator of a work usually automatically owns the copyright as soon as the work is recorded in some way (i.e. by writing it down or recording it electronically, etc.), however these rights can be difficult to prove if disputed, and therefore many countries (such as the United States) also offer an internal country-specific means of registering works. Some countries, like the United Kingdom, do not offer any such means of registration, however an international registration is available through the Intellectual Property Rights Office's Copyright Registration Service, and can be used regardless of any country-specific provisions. This can help protect copyright in all of the nations which are signatories of the Berne Convention.

In the case of trade marks, the symbol "™" can be applied to any mark which is being used as a trade mark, however greater protection is provided if this mark is registered, in which case the symbol "®" can be applied to the mark. It is often illegal to apply the "®" symbol to a trade mark which has not been registered. There are also options for international registrations of trade marks, which are administered by the World Intellectual Property Organization, however applications cannot be made to the WIPO directly – applications must be made through the relevant office of the applicant's country.

Copyright law and its history

The modern concept of copyright can be traced back to 1710 and the "Statute of Anne", which applied to England, Scotland, and Wales. Prior to this Act, governments had granted monopoly rights to publishers to produce works, but the 1710 Act was the first time that a right of ownership was acknowledged for the actual creator of a work.

From the outset, the attempt to protect the creator's rights was beset with problems due to the local nature of the laws, which applied in Britain only. This meant that lots of copyrighted works were reproduced without the permission of the author in Ireland, America, and in European countries. This not only hindered the ability of the London publishers to sell their legitimate copies of their books in these territories, but the unauthorised reproductions would also find their way into Britain, harming the home market as well.

A natural progression for copyright law was therefore its internationalisation, beginning in 1846 with a reciprocal agreement between Britain and Prussia, and culminating in a series of international treaties, the principal of which is the Berne Convention, which applies to over 160 countries.

Traditionally in the United Kingdom and the United States there has been a requirement to register a work with an official body in order to be able to claim copyright over it (Stationers Hall and the US Library of Congress respectively), however this has been changed by the Berne Convention, which requires signatory countries to grant copyright as an automatic right: i.e. the creator of a work immediately owns its copyright by virtue of creating it and recording it in some physical way (for instance by writing it down or making a recording of it, etc.). The United Kingdom and the United States have both been slow to fully adopt this approach. Though the United Kingdom signed the Berne Convention in 1887, it took 100 years for it to be fully implemented by the Copyright Designs and Patents Act 1988. The United States did not even sign the convention until 1989.

In the United States the US Library of Congress continues to provide archiving services for the purposes of copyright protection, but these are now optional. US citizens no longer need to register their work in order to be able to claim copyright over it. It is necessary, however, to be able to prove when the person who created it did so, and this is essentially the purpose of the registration today. In the United Kingdom, Stationers Hall has ceased to exist, and there is no longer any state-run means of registering the copyright to unpublished works, leaving the only available options as independent and/or international solutions such as the copyright registration service provided by the IP Rights Office.

Registering your work for copyright protection

Registering your work for copyright protection can help you protect your rights in relation to your work. Generally (particularly if you live in a Berne Convention country, as most people do) registration will not be compulsory in order to have rights over your work. Any time you create a unique original work you will in theory own the copyright over it, however you will need to be able to prove when you created it, which is the purpose of registering your work for copyright protection. There are other ways in which you might attempt to prove this, but registration provides better evidence than most other forms.

There are a range of different options for protecting your copyright that vary depending on where you live and the kind of coverage you want. Some countries, like the United States, provide internal means of registering the copyright of unpublished works, however the scope of these will tend to be restricted to the country in question. Other countries, like the United

Kingdom, do not offer any specific government-sponsored system for registering the copyright of unpublished works. An international option is provided by the Intellectual Property Rights Office, which is not affiliated to any particular government or country. As long as you live in a Berne Convention country you should be able to benefit from using their Copyright Registration Service. You can register your work with the Intellectual Property Rights Office regardless of whether or not there are any specific arrangements in your home country (you may even choose to register with both to offer your work greater protection). Registration with the Intellectual Property Rights Office should provide you with protection throughout the area covered by the Berne Convention, which is most of the world.

Registering your work for copyright protection through the Intellectual Property Rights Office is an online process that can be completed in a few minutes, provided you have your file in an accepted format and your file isn't too large (if your file is too large and cannot be reduced you may have to split it and take out two or more registrations covering it). There is a registration fee to pay ($45 / £25 / €40 at the time of writing) per file for registration, however if you are a subscriber to **firstwriter.com** you can benefit from a 10% discount when you start the registration process on our site.

When registering your work, you will need to give some consideration to what your work actually consists of. This is a straightforward question if your work is a novel, or a screenplay, but if it is a collection of poetry or short stories then the issue is more difficult. Should you register your collection as one file, or register each poem separately, which would be more expensive? Usually, you can answer this question by asking yourself what you propose to do with your collection. Do you intend to submit it to publishers as a collection only? Or do you intend to send the constituent parts separately to individual magazines? If the former is the case, then register the collection as a single work under the title of the collection. If the latter is the case then this could be unwise, as your copyright registration certificate will give the name of the collection only – which will not match the names of the individual poems or stories. If you can afford to, you should therefore register them separately. If you have so many poems and / or stories to register that you cannot afford to register them all separately, then registering them as a collection will be better than nothing.

Proper use of the copyright symbol

The first thing to note is that for copyright there is only one form of the symbol (©), unlike trade marks, where there is a symbol for registered trade marks (®) and a symbol for unregistered trade marks (™).

To qualify for use of the registered trade mark symbol (®) you must register your trade mark with the appropriate authority in your country, whereas the trade mark symbol (™) can be applied to any symbol you are using as a trade mark. Use of the copyright symbol is more similar to use of the trade mark symbol, as work does not need to be registered in order to use it.

You can place the copyright symbol on any original piece of work you have created. The normal format would be to include alongside the copyright symbol the year of first publication and the name of the copyright holder, however there are no particular legal requirements regarding this. While it has historically been a requirement in some jurisdictions to include a copyright notice on a work in order to be able to claim copyright over it, the Berne Convention does not allow such restrictions, and so any country signed up to the convention no longer has this requirement. However, in some jurisdictions failure to include such a notice can affect the damages you may be able to claim if anyone infringes your copyright.

A similar situation exists in relation to the phrase "All Rights Reserved". This phrase was a requirement in order to claim international copyright protection in countries signed up to the 1910 Buenos Aires Convention. However, since all countries signed up to the Buenos Aires Convention are now also signed up to the Berne Convention (which grants automatic copyright) this phrase has become superfluous. The phrase continues to be used frequently but is unlikely to have any legal consequences.

The Berne Convention

The Berne Convention covers 162 of the approximately 190 countries in the world, including most major nations. Countries which are signed up to the convention are compelled to offer the same protection to works created in other signatory nations as they would to works created in their own. Nations not signed up to the Berne Convention may have their own arrangements regarding copyright protection.

You can check if your country is signed up to the Berne Convention at the following website:

- *https://www.CopyrightRegistrationService.com*

The status of your country should be shown automatically on the right side of the screen. If not, you can select your country manually from the drop-down menu near the top right of the page.

A Week in the Life of a Literary Agent

Andrew Lownie outlines the range of activities he is involved with in a "typical" agency week.

Monday

A raft of submissions have come in overnight. One author writes, "At this time I respectfully request you unsheathe your sharpened red pen and engage me. In good faith that you are up for the challenge, let us dance." Afraid I'm not really up to such frenetic activity first thing on a Monday.

Other submissions include "a 130 page essay on Roberto Bolaño's poetry", the "historical origins and cultural significance of Jamaica's national dish", "a Short Social History of the Clitoris" and something describing itself as "erotica-tinged space and techno-fantasy fiction". A clever submission where Bible stories have been written as Cockney rhyming slang, in broad Yorkshire, in SMS Text, in Egyptian Hieroglyphics., for Toddlers etc. Difficult to assess and I suspect not something which will sustain reader interest.

Film enquiry from US and I pass it on to my film agent.

The monthly newsletter has gone out and various requests have come in for titles, especially from scouts, foreign agents and publishers. I send it on to various editors, serial buyers, film producers who I know don't subscribe to the newsletter, or probably don't read it if they do. I get a bounceback saying it was "blocked by MailMarshal: Because it may contain unacceptable language, or inappropriate material". I wonder which bit of the newsletter this refers to.

Meeting with Daily Mail journalist to throw around ideas for a possible book.

Eleven pages of monthly stats for website visits for the previous month are in from Jing Dong who runs the website, and I share these with David Haviland. It shows visits are pretty constant – in some months a particular article will go viral and cause a spike in views. As usual, new visitors constitute about 80% of the hits and Twitter is the most important feed. We'll look at the referral sources, how long visitors stay on the site and what they look at.

Give feedback to author on manuscript which I've read over the weekend.

Lunch with editor. He's keener to discuss changes in publishing than the authors I'm pitching but still enjoyable.

Chase some film monies on behalf of an author.

Claim your free access to www.firstwriter.com: See p.423

Invitation from a university for the launch of their creative writing course anthology.

Liaise with editor on cover design for an inspirational memoir.

Receive a "warm invitation to you to participate in the 2nd Summit on Child Abuse & Human Trafficking". Is this as participant or delegate I wonder, and how did they get my details?

Rework proposal with author in light of publisher's feedback.

Meeting with ghost writer brought in by publisher to work on TV tie-in. She's seeing several agents in a beauty parade. I give her biscuits with her coffee.

Reworked version of a diet book proposal from author which is ready to go and I pitch to various editors.

Discuss titles with author and his ghost. Publishers don't like the original title and we don't like their suggestion. Eventually we come up with something which is not ideal, but the author and publisher like it.

Sort out details of an audio deal.

Leave office at 6:00 to give talk to a writing group.

Tuesday

I go through the overnight submissions which include "a recipe book with Dadaist overtones, elements of satire, and a number of puns, and is a reaction to celebrity chef cookbooks in general", "a Placenta Recipes Cook Book aimed at pregnant mothers and birth support workers/doulas/midwives", "a critical verse by verse analysis of the gospel of John", and "a picture book reading series, entitled Dandan The Drilling Man And His Drilling Caravan! This is a unique storyline that acquaints children and their parents with the Natural Gas / Oil drilling industry".

Other submissions amidst the usual suspects of memoir and fiction include an illustrated humour book about the ukulele, a "simple, concise pocket sized directory of public toilets, supermarkets, pharmacies, laundry services, post offices and police stations in every district of the Eternal City", a police memoir of catching a serial killer and something which categorises itself as "Young Adult/Substance Abuse/Political Fiction/Humor". Not sure where the bookshops will put that.

Publisher rings and asks my view of an editor who applied for a job with him.

Meeting with ghost writer who has not had representation before. We discuss what I can do for her and how I market my ghost writers. I'm aware I have to be careful about taking on too many ghost writers and then not being able to find work for them.

One writer emails claiming to have found the agency from doing a google search for UK agents publishing erotic fiction / biographies – not a joint category I was aware I hitherto specialised in nor even existed.

Mid-morning post brings a book which editor wants sent on to one of my authors asking to give a jacket quote.

Invoice for a publication advance and chase an editor for a delivery payment.

The Publishers Lunch round-up of sales for the week arrives and I forward links to the agency authors whose deals have been announced.

Chase some editors for a submission whose deadline was Friday.

A not untypical turn down from an editor: 'I've just come out the acquisitions meeting and sadly I'm not emailing with good news. The sales team said that our list is quite full at the moment for real-life stories and that […]'s story wasn't stand-out enough to push in another title on the schedule. I massively disagree and there is a wealth of topical subjects found within her life story that it really is remarkable, but as they sell in to the supermarkets (and we would need the supermarkets' support) I lost the fight and I'm incredibly disappointed. I think her book could be fantastic and wish her all the best. Thanks for giving me the opportunity to read the material."

If it's hard selling books to publishers, it's equally difficult for the editor selling projects to their colleagues. The collegiate approach make sense but it does mean books that don't tick all the boxes are having trouble finding publishers.

Author alerts me to forthcoming appearances on Australian and New Zealand radio so check with UK publisher that copies of book have arrived and available locally.

Someone has kindly but curiously endorsed me on LinkedIn for Poetry – a genre I neither represent nor write. I wonder how valid all my other endorsements are.

Forward some foreign royalty statements to author and to my royalties person Hazel Hill for checking.

Seek some contract advice on film contract from my contracts expert Stephen Aucutt.

Publisher turns down a biography: "I am afraid I don't think we could make the figures work for this one. It is such a shame as it has been such an extraordinary life spanning the twentieth century."

Nice review in Publishers Weekly for an author's book which I add to website and agency's social media.

Reader's report back which I forward to the author.

US publisher chases about an offer they've made. I'm hoping for a better one elsewhere, stall him and nudge other editor. One appears to now be on holiday for next two weeks and after the deadline.

Forward news of a Dutch sale to author and Chinese royalty statement to another.

Bestseller lists for the week announced and gratifying to see several agency authors in top twenty.

To book launch for an author at a bookshop and then back to catch up on reading and emails.

Wednesday

A screenwriter from South Africa says they "would like to submit script personally". Tell them email is probably easier for all concerned.

Other submissions include a "Self help guide to street performing", an author who hopes "to create a niche for myself with historical Jewish warrior fiction" and author asking "if I'm interested in representing gay erotic comics?" I explain the list is eclectic but that's not an area of agency expertise.

Other submissions include a "Field Guide to American Barns", "a novel with a naturist theme", a "200,000 word short story", a submission from someone using the pen name Stephen Spielberg, two physics books from a professor in Bangladesh, an urban fantasy novel with a Christian slant, the offer of a 320,000 word travelogue set in South America which has been translated from the original Estonian version, a book charting the history of the great ocean liners, a memoir of an army officer in the Middle East in the 1960s–1980s and something which does sound intriguing: an account of "the very dark side of the Home Furnishings Industry".

Sort out VAT payment for ghost who is not part of the publishing contract.

Author updates me on research on a biography after an introduction I gave him.

Lunch with editor, where I pitch a couple of authors, but he explains they have so many existing authors delivering a new book each year that there are very few gaps in the list.

Serial offer on title from *The Sun*. Try to push them up.

Discuss trying to fix some more speaking engagements for a business writer.

Update author on their submissions, even though I've forwarded rejections as they've come in.

Forward contract to author with my comments and seeking theirs.

Marsh Agency chase me for Romanian Certificate of Residency, which I forward to author.

Pitch a book on Royal Family to a dozen editors.

Nudge other editors who have not responded to an initial email pitch last week.

Forward a radio enquiry to an author to let them deal directly.

Meeting with author and freelance publicists brought in to promote her book. Put forward some ideas and pass on some contacts at literary festivals.

Finally agree clause with US publisher allowing author to offer new book once they have delivered rather than wait until the book is published.

Liaise with a freelance editor who an author has paid to polish his manuscript. I send her copies of my reader's reports to brief her.

Liaise with another US publisher on Publisher Quit Claim for a film contract.

Author writes to say they are "Happy to be connected with a liked-minded Tweep!" Me too.

Go to a presentation at a publishing house with other agents where they take us through their commissioning process. Very useful. If only authors realised how much care and time was taken in assessing submissions.

Thursday

The overnight submissions bring an author who has "written a good number of manuscripts – friction and non friction. I am yet to find a nice literary agent who could them published internationally". I like the idea of "friction" as a genre.

Other submissions include a memoir "Something Is Wrong With My Penis", a "humorous coffee table cartoon book that cleverly and comically combines two popular themes: Penguins and Superheroes" the offer of "the synopsis of a novel (300 pgs, in Portuguese) that maybe can interest you" (I only wish I was like continental agents moving effortlessly from one language to another), "an Autobiography of the Universe" and an email from my old friend crazypants1986.

There's also an email saying "I have visited your company website, glad to know that you're on the market for plastic/rubber mold and products". I wonder which bit of the agency website suggests that?

Meeting at a film company who are interested in drawing on research by an author for biography. We dance around each other neither wanting to give much away.

Chase publishing royalties department who forgotten to pay VAT on recent royalty payment.

Invoice publisher with signature advance and return the signed contract.

Discuss various options with author after publisher tries to cancel contract on a memoir because a family member has decided to now withhold co-operation. We take legal advice and marshal our arguments to try and save the deal as book is about to be published.

Meeting with reference book author I'm taking on.

Send out proposal for reader's report.

Seek advice from my accountants about new VAT rules on commission for British-based authors on monies from abroad.

Lunch with editor of the Bookseller where we discuss publishing changes and I give him some material for an article on the current publishers' rights grab.

Accompany author writing on pregnancy to meeting with interested editor.

Answer series of email questions about pitching, the state of the market etc. from a journalist putting together an article for a writing magazine.

Chase yet again permissions department of a US publisher for overdue permission payment. The promised bank transfer has never materialised, and nor did the promised check. Saga has been going on since September.

Update from my Polish sub-agent on submissions. Reminds me to pitch some new possible books to my Asian sub-agents.

Meeting with film producer.

Go on to dinner of a literary dining club. Back to emails and reading manuscript which has just been delivered.

Friday

The overnight submissions include: a book about Israeli Cinema; another on "Holistic Microneedling"; "The Memoir of a Bi-Polar/Alcoholic/Superman/Ginger"; a "Southern Gothic novel with literary ambitions"; a 41 page romance/paranormal manuscript "of a woman who falls in love with a weresnake"; a proposal for a book on 19th Century Maltese Filigree Jewellery; an "African-American Romantic Vampire Thriller" and "Confessions of a Las Vegas Hair Stylist" which the author compares to Joseph Conrad's Heart of Darkness.

Go into local school to talk to pupils about a career in publishing. Love doing so as it reminds me why I went into publishing over thirty years ago. A cluster of pupils at the end keen to discuss their creative writing. What a shame few schools encourage creative writing after the age of thirteen.

Pass on enquiry to an author from an historian researching 16th Century Spanish shipyards.

Send out some sample proposals to a new author to help him produce his own.

The mid-morning post brings, alongside the customary scripts, contracts, payments, finished books etc. an invitation addressed to "Dear Friends and Colleagues, It is our great pleasure to invite you to participate at the 2011 World Congress on Human Trafficking, Prostitution and Sex Work." Am I a friend or colleague and what exactly does participation mean? Has a disgruntled author or rival agent passed on my contact details?

A small publisher asks if I can sell film and US rights in their list. I look at a couple of their books but decide they are too marginal.

Send out statements and payments for authors which have come in from my foreign rights agency.

Lunch with editor cancelled at last moment as he's busy. A relief as finding it especially hard to keep up with succession of telephone calls and emails this morning.

Serial contract from newspaper which I check and forward to author for signature.

Meeting with new author I've just taken on and her editor. The book will be a highly illustrated gift book and we discuss format, price and direct sales outlets.

My film agent brings me up to speed on contract negotiations for a film based on one of the agency's biographies.

Fix an author tour with publishers for an author for next week. There's a lot of juggling to co-ordinate editors' availability with a sensible route around town.

Put forward some writers to the new editor of Newsweek who is looking for current affairs specialists.

US author emails some jacket endorsements he's gathered.

An author kindly writes "You have published many memoirs, some of which I have enjoyed reading".

It's 7:00pm. Time for a break but I'll return to my desk to catch up on emails and finish the recently-delivered manuscript.

Saturday

The overnight submissions include: a book "aimed at the under-tens, this book hopes to introduce a whole new generation to the joys of alcohol abuse, chain-smoking, questionable morals and hanging out with a bunch of arseholes"; a novel "about killer babies"; a submission from someone describing themselves as "a literary phenomenon"; an autobiography of working life in the world of various IT departments; "a travel book with sausages as the common factor" and a "one hundred and twenty word mystery following the adventures of four charming ex-battery hens as they discover a free-range life as pampered pets"; a "self-help book on alcohol misuse" – presumably to prevent rather than encourage this; something which describes itself as an "Interactive Autobiography"; a submission which claims "I found your agency when I typed the genre of politically incorrect nonfiction, and since my book may be viewed as politically incorrect, I thought you might be the right agent for my work" and a general email clearly sent to lot of agents. "The submission outline is generic and may not comply with your specific format. I appreciate your mandated requirements. For reasons I shall not include herein, I am unable to follow these at present, and so I fully understand and respect your rejection on this basis alone." I reject it. Time for filing and a bit more reading...

The Andrew Lownie Literary Agency Ltd, founded in 1988, is one of the UK's leading boutique literary agencies, with some two hundred nonfiction and fiction authors handled respectively by Andrew Lownie and David Haviland. It prides itself on its personal attention to its clients and specialises both in launching new writers and taking established writers to a new level of recognition. Andrew Lownie remains the top selling agent worldwide, according to Publishers

Marketplace, and was short-listed for Literary Agent of the Year at the 2013, 2014, and 2015 Bookseller Awards.

Books represented have included: The Cambridge Guide to Literature in English; The Oxford Classical Dictionary; The Penguin Companion to the European Union; Norma Major's history of Chequers; the memoirs of Sir John Mills, Alan Whicker, Gloria Hunniford, David Hasselhoff, Emily Lloyd, Kerry Katona and Patrick MacNee; the best-selling fostering series by Cathy Glass and Casey Watson; Sam Faiers' Living Life the Essex Way; Daniel Tammet's international best-seller Born on a Blue Day; Laurence Gardner'sThe Magdalene Legacy and The Shadow of Solomon, the literary estates of Joyce Cary and Julian MacLaren-Ross; the historians Juliet Barker, Roger Crowley, Tom Devine, Robert Hutchinson, Sean McMeekin, Linda Porter, Geoff Roberts ,Desmond Seward, David Stafford and Christian Wolmar; the wine writer Michael Schuster; crime writers, such as Mei Trow and David Roberts, and thriller writers such as Duncan Falconer.

Should You Self-Publish?

Over recent years there has been an explosion in self-published books, as it has become easier and easier to publish your book yourself. This poses writers with a new quandary: continue to pursue publication through the traditional means, or jump into the world of self-publishing? As the rejections from traditional publishers pile up it can be tempting to reach for the control and certainty of self-publishing. Should you give into the temptation, or stick to your guns?

Isn't it just vanity publishing?

Modern self-publishing is quite different from the vanity publishing of times gone by. A vanity publisher would often pose or at least seek to appear to be a traditional publisher, inviting submissions and issuing congratulatory letters of acceptance to everyone who submitted – only slowly revealing the large fees the author would have to pay to cover the cost of printing the books.

Once the books were printed, the vanity publisher would deliver them to the author then cut and run. The author would be left with a big hole in their pocket and a mountain of boxes of books that they would be unlikely to ever sell a fraction of.

Modern self-publishing, on the other hand, is provided not by shady dealers but by some of the biggest companies involved in the publishing industry, including Penguin and Amazon. It doesn't have the large fees that vanity publishing did (depending on the path you choose and your own knowledge and technical ability it can cost almost nothing to get your book published); it *does* offer a viable means of selling your books (they can appear on the biggest bookselling websites around the world); and it *doesn't* leave you with a house full of unwanted books, because modern technology means that a copy of your book only gets printed when it's actually ordered.

That isn't to say that there aren't still shady characters out there trying to take advantage of authors' vanity by charging them enormous fees for publishing a book that stands very little chance of success, but it does mean that self-publishing – done right – can be a viable and cost effective way of an author taking their book to market.

The benefits of self-publishing

The main benefit of self-publishing, of course, is that the author gets control of whether their book is published or not. There is no need to spend years submitting to countless agents and publishers, building up countless heartbreaking rejection letters, and possibly accepting in the end that your dreams of publication will never come true – you can make them come true.

And this need not be pure vanity on the author's part. Almost every successful book – even such massive hits as *Harry Potter* – usually build up a string of rejections before someone finally accepts them. The professionals that authors rely on when going through the traditional publishing process – the literary agents and the editors – are often, it seems, just not that good at spotting what the public are going to buy. How many potential bestsellers might languish forever in the slush pile, just because agents and editors fail to spot them? What if your book is one of them? The traditional publishing process forces you to rely on the good judgment of others, but the self-publishing process enables you to sidestep that barrier and take your book directly to the public, so that readers can decide for themselves.

Self-publishing also allows you to keep control in other areas. You won't have an editor trying to change your text, and you'll have complete control over what kind of cover your book receives.

Finally, with no publisher or team of editors and accountants taking their slice, you'll probably get to keep a lot more of the retail price of every book you sell. So if you can sell the same amount of books as if you were traditionally published, you'll stand to make a lot more money.

The drawbacks of self-publishing

While self-publishing can guarantee that your book will be available for sale, it cannot guarantee that it will actually sell. Your self-published book will probably have a much lower chance of achieving significant sales than if it had been published traditionally, because it will lack the support that a mainstream publisher could bring. You will have no marketing support, no established position in the marketplace, and no PR – unless you do it yourself. You will have to arrange your own book tours; you will have to do your own sales pitches; you will have to set your own pricing structure; and you will have to manage your own accounts and tax affairs. If you're selling through Amazon or Smashwords or Apple (and if you're not, then why did you bother self-publishing in the first place?) you're going to need to fill in the relevant forms with the IRS (the US tax office) – whether you're a US citizen or not. If you're not a US citizen then you'll have to register with the IRS and complete the necessary tax forms, and potentially other forms for claiming treaty benefits so that you don't get taxed twice (in the US and your home country). And then of course you'll also have to register for tax purposes in your home nation and complete your own tax return there (though you would also have to do this as a traditionally published author).

It can all get very complicated, very confusing, and very lonely. Instead of being able to just be a writer you can find yourself writing less and less and becoming more and more embroiled in the business of publishing a book.

And while it's great to have control over your text and your cover, you'd be ill advised to ignore the value that professionals such as editors and cover designers can bring. It's tempting to think that you don't need an editor – that you've checked the book and had a friend or family member check it too, so it's probably fine – but a professional editor brings a totally different mindset to the process and will check things that won't have even occurred to you and your reader. Without a professional editor, you will almost certainly end up publishing a book which is full of embarrassing mistakes, and trust me – there is no feeling quite as deflating as opening up the first copy of your freshly printed book to see an obvious error jump out – or, even worse, to have it pointed out in an Amazon review, for all to see.

The cover is also incredibly important. Whether for sale on the shelf or on a website, the cover is normally the first point of contact your potential reader has with your book, and will cause them to form immediate opinions about it. A good cover can help a book sell well, but a bad one can kill its chances – and all too often self-published books have amateurish covers that will have readers flicking past them without a second glance.

Finally, the financial benefits of self-publishing can often be illusory. For starters, getting a higher proportion of the retail price is pretty irrelevant if you don't sell any copies. Fifty per cent of nothing is still nothing. Far better to have 15% of something. And then there's the advances. Advances are up-front payments made by traditional publishers to authors, which are off-set against future royalties. So, an author might receive a $5,000 advance before their book is published. When the royalties start coming in, the publisher keeps the first $5,000 to off-set the advance. The good news for the author is that if the book flops and doesn't make $5,000 in royalties they still get to keep the full advance. In an uncertain profession, the security of an advance can be invaluable for an author – and of course it's not something available to self-published authors.

Conclusion

Self-publishing can seem like a tempting shortcut to publication, but in reality it has its own challenges and difficulties. For the moment at least, traditional publishing still offers you the best shot of not only financial success, but also quality of life as a writer. With other people to handle all the other elements of publishing, you get to concentrate on doing what you love.

So we think that writers should always aim for traditional publishing first. It might be a long shot, but if it works then you stand a much better chance of being successful. If you don't manage to get signed by an agent or a publisher then you still have the option of self-publishing, but make sure you don't get tempted to resort to self-publishing too soon – most agents and publishers won't consider self-published works, so this is a one-way street. Once you've self-published your work, you probably won't be able to change your mind and go back to the traditional publishers with your book unless it becomes a huge hit without them. It's therefore important that you exhaust all your traditional publishing options before making the leap to self-publishing. Be prepared for this to take perhaps a few years (lots of agents and publishers can take six months just to respond), and make sure you've submitted to everyone you can on *both* sides of the Atlantic (publishing is a global game these days, and you need to concentrate on the two main centres of English-language publishing (New York and London) equally) before you make the decision to self-publish instead.

However, once you have exhausted all options for traditional publishing, modern self-publishing does offer a genuine alternative path to success, and there are a growing number of self-published authors who have managed to sell millions of copies of their books. If you don't think traditional publishing is going to be an option, we definitely think you should give self-publishing a shot.

For directions on your path through the traditional publishing process see our Writers' Roadmap, above.

If you're sure you've already exhausted all your options for traditional publishing then see below for our quick guide to the self-publishing process.

The Self-Publishing Process

Thinking about self-publishing your book? Make sure you go through all these steps first – and in the right order! Do them the wrong way round and you could find yourself wasting time and/or money.

1. Be sure you want to self-publish

You need to be 100% sure that you want to self-publish, because after you've done it there is no going back. Publishers and literary agents will not normally consider books that have been self-published, so if you wanted to get your book to print the old fashioned way you should stop now and rethink. Make absolutely sure that you've exhausted every possible opportunity for traditional publishing before you head down the self-publishing path.

For more information, see "Why choose traditional publishing?" and "Should you self-publish?", above.

2. Protect your copyright

Authors often wonder about what stage in the process they should protect their copyright – often thinking that it's best to leave it till the end so that there are no more changes to make to the book after it is registered.

However, this isn't the case. The key thing is to protect your work before you let other people see it – or, if you've already let other people see it, as soon as possible thereafter.

Don't worry about making small changes to your work after registering it – as long as the work is still recognisable as the same piece of work it will still be protected. Obviously, if you completely change everything you've written then you're going to need another registration, as it will effectively be a different book, but if you've just edited it and made minor alterations this won't affect your protection.

You can register you copyright online at https://www.copyrightregistrationservice.com.

3. Get your work edited

Editing is a vital step often overlooked by authors who self-publish. The result can often be an amateurish book littered with embarrassing mistakes. Any professionally published book will go through an editing process, and it's important that the same applies to your self-published book. It's also important to complete the editing process before beginning the layout, or you could find yourself having to start the layout again from scratch.

4. Choose your self-publishing path

Before you can go any further you are going to need to choose a size for your book, and in order to do that you are going to need to choose a self-publishing path.

There are various different ways of getting self-published, but in general these range from the expensive hands off approach, where you pay a company to do the hard work for you, to the cheap DIY approach, where you do as much as you can yourself.

At the top end, the hands off approach can cost you thousands. At the bottom end, the DIY approach allows you to publish your book for almost nothing.

5. Finalise your layout / typesetting

Before you can finalise your layout (often referred to in the industry as "typesetting") you need to be sure that you've finalised your content – which means having your full work professionally edited and all the necessary changes made. If you decide to make changes after this point it will be difficult and potentially costly, and will require you to go through many of the following steps all over again.

You also need to have selected your path to publication, so that you know what page sizes are available to you, and what page margins you are going to need to apply. If you create a layout that doesn't meet printing requirements (for instance, includes text too close to the edge of the page) then you will have to start the typesetting process all over again.

6. Organise your ISBN

Your book needs to have an ISBN. If you are using a self-publishing service then they may provide you with one of their own, but it is likely to come with restrictions, and the international record for your book will show your self-publishing service as the publisher.

You can acquire your own ISBNs directly from the ISBN issuer, but they do not sell them individually, so you will end up spending quite a lot of money buying more ISBNs than you need. You will, however, have control of the ISBN, and you will be shown as the publisher.

Alternatively, you can purchase a single ISBN at a lower price from an ISBN retailer. This should give you control over the ISBN, however the record for the book will show the ISBN retailer as the publisher, which you may not consider to be ideal.

Whatever you choose, you need to arrange your ISBN no later than this point, because it needs to appear in the preliminary pages (prelims) of your book.

7. Compile your prelims

Your prelims may include a variety of pages, but should always include a title page, a half title page, and an imprint/copyright page. You might then also include other elements, such as a foreword, table of contents, etc. You can only compile your table of contents at this stage, because you need to know your ISBN (this will be included on the copyright/imprint page) and the page numbers for your table of contents. You therefore need to make sure that you are happy with the typesetting and have no further changes to make before compiling your prelims.

8. Create your final press proof

Depending on the self-publishing path you have chosen, you may be able to use a Word file as your final document. However, you need to be careful. In order to print your book it will have to be converted into a press-ready PDF at some point. If a self-publishing service is doing this for you then you will probably find that they own the PDF file that is created, meaning you don't have control over your own press files. Some services will impose hefty charges (hundreds or even more than a thousand dollars) to release these press files.

It might also be the case that you won't get to see the final PDF, and therefore won't get chance to check it for any errors introduced by the conversion process. If it's an automated system, it may also be difficult to control the output you get from it.

We'd suggest that it's best to produce your own PDF files if possible. To do this you will need a copy of Adobe Acrobat Professional, and you will need to be familiar with the correct settings for creating print ready PDFs. Be careful to embed all fonts and make sure that all images are at 300 DPI.

9. Create your cover

Only once your press proof is finalised can you complete your cover design. That's because your cover includes not only the front cover and the back cover, but also (critically) the spine – and the width of the spine will vary according to the number of pages in your final press proof. In order to complete your cover design you therefore need to know your page size, your page count (including all prelims), and your ISBN, as this will appear on the back cover. You also need to get a barcode for your ISBN.

10. Produce your book

Once your cover and press proof are ready you can go through whichever self-publishing path you have chosen to create your book. With some pathways the production of a print proof can be an optional extra that is only available at an extra cost – but we'd recommend standing that cost and getting a print version of your book to check. You never know exactly how it's going to come out until you have a physical copy in your hand.

If you're happy with the proof you can clear your book for release. You don't need to do anything to get it on online retailers like Amazon – they will automatically pick up the ISBN and add your book to their websites themselves.

11. Create an ebook version

In the modern day, having an ebook version of your book is imperative. Ebooks account for a significant proportion of all book sales and are a particularly effective vehicle for unknown and self-published authors.

There are various different file formats used by the different platforms, but .epub is emerging as a standard, and having your book in .epub format should enable you to access all the platforms with a single file.

12. Distribute your ebook

Unlike with print books, you will need to act yourself to get your ebooks into sales channels. At a minimum, you need to ensure that you get your ebook available for sale through Amazon, Apple, and Google Play.

US Magazines

For the most up-to-date listings of these and hundreds of other magazines, visit http://www.firstwriter.com/magazines

*To claim your **free** access to the site, please see the back of this book.*

The Alembic

Providence College
English Department
Attn: The Alembic Editors
1 Cunningham Square
Providence, RI 02918-0001
Email: Alembic@providence.edu
Website: http://www.providence.edu/english/
creative-writing/Pages/alembic.aspx

Publishes: Fiction; Poetry; Scripts; *Areas:*
Drama; Short Stories; *Markets:* Adult;
Treatments: Literary

Publishes poetry, drama, and fiction –
including short stories and self-contained
excerpts of novels. Send up to 5 poems or
prose up to 6,000 words by post with return
postage if return of material required.
Accepts submissions from August 1 to
November 30 annually.

A New Heart

PO Box 4004
San Clemente, CA 92474-4004
Email: HCFUSA@gmail.com
Website: http://www.hcfusa.com

Publishes: Articles; Nonfiction; Poetry;
Areas: Health; Religious; *Markets:*
Professional

Editors: Aubrey Beauchamp

Magazine aimed at healthcare workers,
publishing articles with a Christian message.
Also some limited space for poetry. Submit
by email or by post with SASE. See website
for full writers' guidelines.

A&U

Main Office
25 Monroe Street, Suite 205
Albany, New York 12210
Tel: +1 (518) 426-9010
Fax: +1 (518) 436-5354
Email: mailbox@aumag.org
Website: http://www.aumag.org

Articles; Essays; Fiction; Interviews; News;
Nonfiction; Poetry; Reviews; *Areas:* Culture;
Health; Medicine; Politics; Short Stories;
Markets: Adult

Editors: David Waggoner

Publishes material covering the medical,
cultural, and political responses to AIDS
only. Does not publish material unconnected
to AIDS so please do not send any. For
fiction, and poetry, send complete MS. For
nonfiction send query with published clips.
Accepts approaches by email.

American Indian Art Magazine

7314 East Osborn Drive
Scottsdale, AZ 85251
Tel: +1 (480) 994-5445

Fax: +1 (480) 945-9533
Email: editorial@aiamagazine.com
Website: http://www.aiamagazine.com

Publishes: Articles; Nonfiction; *Areas:* Arts;
Markets: Adult; Professional

Publishes articles covering the art of all
native Americans. Articles should be of
interest to both casual readers and
professionals. See website for full guidelines.

Able Muse

467 Saratoga Avenue, #602
San Jose, CA 95129
Email: submission@ablemuse.com
Website: http://www.ablemuse.com

Publishes: Essays; Fiction; Interviews;
Nonfiction; Poetry; Reviews; *Areas:* Short
Stories; Translations; *Markets:* Adult;
Treatments: Light; Literary

Editors: Alex Pepple

Publishes mainly metrical poetry and poetry
in translation. All forms of formal poetry
welcome. Also publishes fiction, and
nonfiction relating to metrical poetry,
including book reviews and interviews.
Accepts electronic submissions only –
preferably using online submission system,
but will also accept submissions by email.
Welcomes humorous and light poetry. See
website for full details.

The Adirondack Review

Email: editors@theadirondackreview.com
Website: http://adirondackreview.
homestead.com

Publishes: Fiction; Nonfiction; Poetry;
Reviews; *Areas:* Arts; Photography; Short
Stories; Translations; Markets

Editors: Angela Leroux-Lindsey

Publishes poetry, fiction, translation, art,
photography, and book reviews. Submit
through online system via website.

Adventure Cyclist

150 East Pine Street
Missoula, MT 59802
Tel: +1 (406) 532-2762
Email: mdeme@adventurecycling.org
Website: http://www.adventurecycling.org/
adventure-cyclist

Publishes: Articles; Essays; Features;
Nonfiction; *Areas:* How-to; Technology;
Travel; *Markets:* Adult

Editors: Mike Deme

Magazine dedicated to bicycle travel and
adventure. See website for full submission
guidelines, and submit using online
submission system.

African-American Career World

Equal Opportunity Publications, Inc.
445 Broad Hollow Road, Suite 425
Melville, NY 11747
Tel: +1 (631) 421-9421
Fax: +1 (631) 421-1352
Email: info@eop.com
Website: http://www.eop.com

Publishes: Articles; Nonfiction; Reference;
Areas: How-to; Self-Help; *Markets:* Adult;
Professional

Careers magazine aimed at African
Americans.

Akron Life

1653 Merriman Road, Suite 116
Akron OH 44313
Tel: +1 (330) 253-0056
Fax: +1 (330) 253-5868
Email: editor@bakermediagroup.com
Website: http://www.akronlife.com

Publishes: Articles; Features; Interviews;
Nonfiction; *Areas:* Arts; Beauty and
Fashion; Culture; Entertainment; Gardening;
Health; Historical; How-to; Humour;
Leisure; Lifestyle; Travel; *Markets:* Adult

Editors: Abby Cymerman

Monthly regional lifestyle publication

committed to providing information that enhances and enriches the experience of living in or visiting Akron and the surrounding region of Summit, Portage, Medina and Stark Counties.

Alebrijes
Email: alebrijesliterature@gmail.com
Website: http://www.alebrijeslit.org

Publishes: Essays; Fiction; Nonfiction; Poetry; *Markets:* Adult; *Treatments:* Experimental; Literary

Editors: Franco Strong; Anna Torres; Tiffany Ameline Zhu; Tyler Grinham

Publishes fiction, poetry, and lyrical essays. Particularly interested in pieces that play with form and structure, and surreal themes. In each reading period send up to one piece of fiction, one essay, or up to three poems, as Word file attachments. See website for full submission guidelines.

Alimentum
PO Box 210028
Nashville, TN 37221
Email: editor@alimentumjournal.com
Website: http://www.alimentumjournal.com

Publishes: Essays; Fiction; Nonfiction; Poetry; Reviews; *Areas:* Cookery; Short Stories; *Markets:* Adult; *Treatments:* Literary

Editors: Peter Selgin, fiction and nonfiction editor; Cortney Davis, poetry editor

Publishes poetry, fiction, creative nonfiction, book reviews, and art, related to food. Send submissions by post with SAE in specific submission windows. See website for more details.

The Allegheny Review
Allegheny College Box 32
520 North Main Street
Meadville, PA 16335
Email: review@allegheny.edu
Website: https://alleghenyreview.
wordpress.com

Publishes: Fiction; Nonfiction; Poetry; *Areas:* Short Stories; *Markets:* Adult; *Treatments:* Literary

National magazine publishing the work of enrolled undergraduate students. Submit fiction or creative nonfiction up to 20 double-spaced pages, or up to five poems. Submissions via online form only. See website for details.

Allegory
Email: submissions@allegoryezine.com
Website: http://www.allegoryezine.com

Publishes: Articles; Fiction; Nonfiction; *Areas:* Fantasy; Horror; Humour; Sci-Fi; Short Stories; *Markets:* Adult

Editors: Ty Drago

Online magazine specialising in science fiction, fantasy and horror, but also willing to consider humour and general interest fiction. No specific length restrictions for fiction, but stories under 500 words or over 5,000 may be hard sells. Also publishes articles up to 2,000 words on the art or business of writing. All submissions must be as attachments by email. See website for full guidelines.

Alligator Juniper
Prescott College
220 Grove Avenue
Prescott, AZ 86301
Email: alligatorjuniper@prescott.edu
Website: http://www.alligatorjuniper.org

Publishes: Fiction; Nonfiction; Poetry; *Areas:* Short Stories; *Markets:* Adult; *Treatments:* Literary

Annual magazine publishing winners and finalists from its annual competitions only. $18 entry fee. Open August 15 – October 15 each year. Submit through online submission system. Winner in each category receives $1,000. Submit up to 5 poems, or a piece of fiction or creative nonfiction up to 30 pages. No children's literature or strict genre work. All entrants receive a copy of the magazine.

American Careers

6701 West 64th Street, Suite 210
Overland Park, KS 66202
Tel: +1 (800) 669-7795
Email: ccinfo@carcom.com
Website: http://www.carcom.com

Publishes: Articles; Nonfiction; *Areas:*
How-to; Self-Help; *Markets:* Children's

Publishes career information for middle and
high school students. Send query with
sample and CV in first instance.

American Turf Monthly

747 Middle Neck Road
Great Neck, NY 11024
Tel: +1 (516) 773-4075
Fax: +1 (516) 773-2944
Email: editor@americanturf.com
Website: http://www.americanturf.com

Publishes: Articles; Nonfiction; *Areas:*
Sport; *Markets:* Adult

Editors: Joe Girardi

Horse racing magazine aimed at
horseplayers, focusing on handicapping and
wagering. Not aimed at owners or breeders.
Send query in first instance.

Analog Science Fiction & Fact

44 Wall Street, Suite 904
New York, NY 10005-2401
Email: analog@dellmagazines.com
Website: http://www.analogsf.com

Publishes: Articles; Fiction; Poetry; *Areas:*
Science; Sci-Fi; Short Stories; *Markets:*
Adult

Editors: Trevor Quachri

Publishes short stories with few restrictions:
the story must have some aspect of science
or technology as an integral part of it (i.e. the
story can't happen without it), and the
characters must be believable (though not
necassarily human), regardless of how
fantastic the setting. For fiction, between
2,000 and 7,000 words for shorts is
preferred, 10,000–20,000 words for
novelettes, and 40,000–80,000 for serials.
For serials, send query in first instance,
otherwise send complete MS.

Also publishes articles of current and future
interest (i.e. at the cutting edge of research).
Though subscribers tend to have a high level
of technical knowledge they come from a
wide variety of backgrounds, and therefore
specialised jargon should be kept to a
minimum. Contributors should also
remember that the magazine is read largely
for entertainment, and your style should
reflect this.

Submit using online submission system on
website. If absolutely necessary, accepts
submissions by post with return postage. No
submissions by fax or email. See website for
full guidelines.

Ancient Paths

Email: skylarburris@yahoo.com
Website: http://www.editorskylar.com/
magazine/table.html

Publishes: Fiction; Poetry; *Areas:* Religious;
Short Stories; *Markets:* Adult; *Treatments:*
Literary

Editors: Skylar Hamilton Burris

Contains writing and art that makes the
reader both think and feel. The poems,
stories, and art celebrate God, depict the
consequences of sin, and explore man's
struggle with faith. The editor favors works
that convey a message subtly without
directly telling the reader what to think. This
magazine is a Christian publication, but
works by non-Christian authors will be
considered provided that the themes, values,
and issues explored are appropriate in a
Christian context.

As of 2012, this publication is online only.

Angus Beef Bulletin

3201 Frederick Avenue
St Joseph, MO 64506-2997
Tel: +1 (816) 383-5270
Email: shermel@angusjournal.com
Website: http://www.angusbeefbulletin.com

Publishes: Articles; Interviews; Nonfiction; *Areas:* Business; How-to; Nature; Technology; *Markets:* Professional; *Treatments:* Commercial

Editors: Shauna Rose Hermel

Publishes material aimed at commercial cattle owners of Angus bulls.

Another Chicago Magazine (ACM)

Email: editors@anotherchicagomagazine.net
Website: http://www.anotherchicagomagazine.net

Publishes: Fiction; Nonfiction; Poetry; *Areas:* Short Stories; *Markets:* Adult; *Treatments:* Literary

Literary magazine publishing work by both new and established writers. Send up to 5 poems; fiction up to 7,500 words; or nonfiction up to 25 pages. Submit via website using online submission system only. $3 fee per submission.

Apalachee Review

PO Box 10469
Tallahassee, FL 32302
Email: ARsubmissions@gmail.com
Website: http://apalacheereview.org

Publishes: Fiction; Nonfiction; Poetry; *Areas:* Short Stories; *Markets:* Adult; *Treatments:* Literary

Editors: Michael Trammell; Jenn Bronson

Publishes fiction, poetry, and creative nonfiction. Send one story (or more, if very short), or 3-5 poems, with SASE. Will consider chapters of novels if they work by themselves, but no short story collections or novels. Accepts simultaneous submissions. Aims to reply within four months. Send query by email for details of submissions policies for writers outside the US. See website for full details.

Appalachian Heritage

Borea College

101 Chestnut Street
Berea, KY 40403
Email: appalachianheritage@berea.edu
Website: http://appalachianheritage.net

Publishes: Essays; Fiction; Nonfiction; Poetry; Reviews; *Areas:* Short Stories; *Markets:* Adult; Youth; *Treatments:* Literary

Strives to be a literary sanctuary for the finest contemporary writing. Publishes previously unpublished fiction, creative nonfiction, poetry, writing for young adults, literary craft essays, book reviews, and visual art. No genre fiction.

Apple Valley Review

Email: editor@leahbrowning.net
Website: http://applevalleyreview.com

Publishes: Essays; Fiction; Nonfiction; Poetry; *Areas:* Short Stories; *Markets:* Adult; *Treatments:* Literary; Positive

Editors: Leah Browning

Online literary journal, publishing poetry, short fiction, and essays. Prose should be between 100 and 4,000 words. Preference is given to non-rhyming poetry under two pages in length. No genre fiction, scholarly, critical, inspirational, children's, erotica, explicit, violent, or depressing. Submit up to three prose pieces or up to six poems, by email. See website for full submission guidelines.

Aquatics International

6222 Wilshire Boulevard, Suite 600
Los Angeles, CA 90048
Tel: +1 (972) 536-6439
Email: etaylor@hanleywood.com
Website: http://www.aquaticsintl.com

Publishes: Articles; Interviews; Nonfiction; *Areas:* Business; How-to; Technology; Theatre; *Markets:* Professional

Editors: Erika Taylor, Editorial Director

Magazine aimed at professionals in the commercial and public swimming pool industries. Send query with published clips.

Aries

c/o Dr. Price
McMurray, General Editor
Texas Wesleyan University
Department of Languages and
Literature
1201 Wesleyan
Fort Worth, TX 76105-1536
Email: aries@txwes.edu
Website: http://ariesjournal.wix.com/aries

Publishes: Essays; Fiction; Nonfiction;
Poetry; Scripts; *Areas:* Drama; Short Stories;
Theatre; *Markets:* Adult; *Treatments:*
Literary

Editors: Dr Price McMurray (General
Editor); Rolanda West (Managing Editor)

Literary journal inviting submissions of
original, unpublished poetry (including
poetry written by the author in Spanish and
then translated to English); fiction; essays;
one-act plays; and black-and-white
photography and art. Submit up to 5 poems
or one piece of prose up to 4,000 words,
between August 15 and December 15
annually. See website for full submission
guidelines.

Arms Control Today

1313 L Street, NW, Suite 130
Washington, DC 20005
Tel: +1 (202) 463-8270
Fax: +1 (202) 463-8273
Email: aca@armscontrol.org
Website: https://www.armscontrol.org

Publishes: Articles; Nonfiction; *Areas:*
Military; *Markets:* Adult; Professional

Publishes articles providing information and
ideas to solve global nuclear, biological,
chemical, and conventional weapons-related
security challenges. Articles should be aimed
at both experts and non-experts. Send query
with outline in first instance.

Arsenic Lobster Poetry Journal

Email: lobster@magere.com
Website: http://arseniclobster.magere.com

Publishes: Poetry; *Markets:* Adult;
Treatments: Literary

Send 3-5 poems of any length in the body of
an email. No attachments. One submission
per year. See website for more details.

Artifact Nouveau

Delta College, Shima 310
5151 Pacific Avenue
Stockton, CA 95207
Tel: +1 (209) 954-5533
Email: artifactsjdc@gmail.com
Website: https://www.deltacollege.edu/org/
wrtrsgld/pubinfo.htm

Publishes: Essays; Fiction; Nonfiction;
Poetry; *Areas:* Adventure; Arts;
Autobiography; Criticism; Culture; Current
Affairs; Drama; Entertainment; Erotic;
Fantasy; Horror; Humour; Leisure; Lifestyle;
Literature; Media; Music; Mystery; Nature;
New Age; Philosophy; Photography;
Politics; Romance; Sci-Fi; Short Stories;
Spiritual; Suspense; Theatre; Thrillers; TV;
Westerns; Women's Interests; *Markets:*
Academic; Adult; *Treatments:*
Contemporary; Experimental; In-depth;
Literary; Popular; Progressive; Satirical;
Serious; Traditional

A magazine of works by students, faculty,
alumni, and employees of the college and
Writers' Guild. Currently in its first year of
publication, it is a re-branding of a previous
publication (2007-2014). With a new
advisor, officers, and editors, the magazine
was re-booted to reflect its new beginnings.
Its current format is 5.5 x 8.5 in a full color
presentation. Works by writers and artists
unaffiliated with the College may be selected
for publication for up to 15% of the overall
content. We accept submissions year round.
All genres and mediums are welcome.
Submit by email.

Asinine Poetry

Email: editor@asininepoetry.com
Website: http://www.asininepoetry.com

Publishes: Fiction; Poetry; *Areas:* Humour;
Short Stories; *Markets:* Adult; *Treatments:*
Satirical

Editors: Shay Tasaday

Online quarterly publishing humorous poetry and prose. Submit by email with material included in the body of the email. No attachments.

Astronomy
Kalmbach Publishing
21027 Crossroads Circle
PO Box 1612
Waukesha, WI 53187-1612
Tel: +1 (800) 533-6644
Fax: +1 (262) 798-6468
Website: http://www.astronomy.com

Publishes: Articles; *Areas:* Hobbies; How-to; Science; *Markets:* Adult

Magazine publishing articles on the science and hobby of astronomy. Send query by post or via form on website.

ATV Rider Magazine
GrindMedia, LLC
1733 Alton Parkway
Irvine, CA 92606
Tel: +1 (763) 383-4499
Website: http://www.atvrider.com

Publishes: Articles; Features; Interviews; Nonfiction; *Areas:* Hobbies; Technology; Travel; *Markets:* Adult

Editors: John Prusak

Magazine for all-terain vehicle enthusiasts. Send query with published clips.

Autograph Collector
Odyssey Publications
510-A South Corona Mall
Corona, CA 92879
Email: editorev@telus.net
Website: http://autographmagazine.com

Publishes: Articles; Interviews; Nonfiction; *Areas:* Historical; Hobbies; How-to; *Markets:* Adult

Magazine for collectors of autographs.

The Avalon Literary Review
PO Box 780696
Orlando, FL 32878
Email: submissions@ avalonliteraryreview.com
Website: http://www. avalonliteraryreview.com

Publishes: Essays; Fiction; Nonfiction; Poetry; *Areas:* Short Stories; *Markets:* Adult; *Treatments:* Literary

Quarterly literary review. Submit up to three poems; one piece of fiction up to 2,500 words; up to two pieces of flash fiction up to 500 words each; or one personal essay up to 1,000 words, by email only. No query necessary. See website for full details.

B'nai B'rith Magazine
2020 K Street, NW, 7th Floor
Washington, DC 20006
Tel: +1 (202) 857-6539
Email: bbmag@bnaibrith.org
Website: http://www.bnaibrith.org

Publishes: Articles; Features; Interviews; Nonfiction; *Areas:* Culture; Current Affairs; Historical; Lifestyle; Politics; Religious; Sociology; Travel; *Markets:* Adult

Jewish magazine focussing on the North American and Isreali Jewish communities. Send query with published clips.

Backpacker
2520 55th Street, Suite 210
Boulder, CO 80301
Email: dlewon@backpacker.com
Website: http://www.backpacker.com

Publishes: Articles; Essays; Features; Interviews; Nonfiction; *Areas:* Hobbies; How-to; Travel; *Markets:* Adult

Editors: Dennis Lewon, Editor-in-Chief

Hiking magazine covering destinations, personality, skills, and gear. Send query by email (preferred) or by post with SASE, with published clips. See website for full guidelines.

Baltimore Magazine
1000 Lancaster Street, Suite 400 Baltimore,
MD 21202
Tel: +1 (410) 752-4200
Fax: +1 (410) 625-0280
Email: frontdesk@baltimoremagazine.net
Website: http://www.baltimoremagazine.net

Publishes: Articles; Features; News;
Nonfiction; *Markets:* Adult

Editors: Max Weiss; Suzanne Loudermilk;
Ken Iglehart; John Lewis; Amy Mulvihill

Regional magazine serving the Baltimore
metropolitan area, focussing on local people,
events, trends, and ideas. See website for
writer's guidelines.

The Baltimore Review
Email: editor@baltimorereview.org
Website: http://baltimorereview.org

Publishes: Essays; Fiction; Nonfiction;
Poetry; *Areas:* Short Stories; *Markets:* Adult;
Treatments: Literary

Editors: Barbara Westwood Diehl

Quarterly online literary journal. Submit 1-3
poems, or fiction or creative nonfiction up to
5,000 words, via online submission system.
Also publishes annual collection in print.
Reading periods are between August 1 and
November 30, and February 1 and May 31.

Barbaric Yawp
3700 County Route 24
Russell, NY 13684
Website: http://www.
boneworldpublishing.com

Publishes: Fiction; *Areas:* Adventure;
Fantasy; Historical; Horror; Religious;
Science; Sci-Fi; Short Stories; *Markets:*
Adult; *Treatments:* Experimental; Literary;
Mainstream

Send submissions by post, with SASE for
reply.

Bartleby Snopes
Website: http://www.bartlebysnopes.com

Publishes: Fiction; *Areas:* Short Stories;
Markets: Adult; *Treatments:* Literary

Publishes short stories between 1,000 and
3,000 words, and flash fiction up to 1,200
words (stories between 1,000 and 1,200 can
be either). Submit online via website
submission system.

Bayou Magazine
Department of English
University of New Orleans
2000 Lakeshore Drive
New Orleans, LA 70148
Email: bayou@uno.edu
Website: http://bayoumagazine.org

Publishes: Essays; Fiction; Nonfiction;
Poetry; *Areas:* Short Stories; *Markets:* Adult;
Treatments: Literary

Editors: Joanna Leake

National literary magazine. Publishes short
stories, including flash fiction and short
shorts; literary nonfiction, creative personal
essays and lyric essays; and poetry. No
gothic, horror, juvenile fiction, or scholarly
articles. Submit a maximum of five poems at
a time. Submit online via web system or by
post with SASE for response only – mss will
not be returned.

Bee Culture
PO Box 706
Medina, OH 44256-0706
Tel: +1 (330) 725-6677
Fax: +1 (330) 725-5624
Email: info@BeeCulture.com
Website: http://www.beeculture.com

Publishes: Articles; Interviews; Nonfiction;
Areas: Hobbies; Nature; Science;
Technology; *Markets:* Adult; Professional;
Treatments: In-depth

Magazine of beekeeping. See website for
writers' guidelines.

Bellevue Literary Review

NYU Langone Department of Medicine
550 First Avenue, OBV-A612
New York, NY 10016
Tel: +1 (212) 263-3973
Email: info@BLReview.org
Website: http://blr.med.nyu.edu

Publishes: Essays; Fiction; Nonfiction;
Poetry; *Areas:* Short Stories; *Markets:* Adult;
Treatments: Literary; Traditional

Publishes fiction, creative nonfiction, and
poetry. Submit up to three poems maximum
per submission. $5 reading fee for non-
subscribers. Submit online using online
submission system. Closed to submissions
during July and August.

Berkeley Fiction Review

102 Hearst Gym MC: #4500
Berkeley, CA 94720
Email: berkeleyfictionreview@gmail.com
Website: http://berkeleyfictionreview.com

Publishes: Fiction; *Areas:* Short Stories;
Markets: Adult; *Treatments:* Literary

Annual magazine of short fiction, inviting
submissions from around the world. Send
submissions as email attachments in .doc or .
pdf format, double-spaced and up to 30
pages maximum. Do not paste stories into
the body of the email. No hard copy
submissions. Accepts multiple submissions,
and also simultaneous submissions, provided
notification is given of acceptance
elsewhere. Response time varies between
about three months and a year.

Best New Writing

PO Box 11
Titusville, NJ 08560
Email: info@bestnewwriting.com
Website: http://www.bestnewwriting.com

Publishes: Essays; Fiction; Nonfiction;
Areas: Short Stories; *Markets:* Adult

Accepts unpublished fiction and creative
nonfiction under 10,000 words. No
simultaneous submissions. Maximum one
submission per quarter.

Bible Advocate

PO Box 33677
Denver, CO 80233
Tel: +1 (303) 452-7973
Email: bibleadvocate@cog7.org
Website: http://baonline.org

Publishes: Articles; Features; Nonfiction;
Poetry; *Areas:* Current Affairs; Lifestyle;
Religious; Sociology; *Markets:* Adult

Christian magazine publishing articles on
Bible doctrine, current social and religious
issues, Christian living, Bible topics, textual/
biblical book studies, prophecy, personal
experience, and poetry (traditional, free, and
blank verse). Prefers email submissions. See
website for full guidelines.

Big Bridge

Email: walterblue@bigbridge.org
Website: http://www.bigbridge.org

Publishes: Essays; Fiction; Nonfiction;
Poetry; *Areas:* Short Stories; *Markets:* Adult;
Treatments: Literary

Editors: Michael Rothenberg and Terri
Carrion

Publishes poetry, fiction, nonfiction, essays,
journalism, and art of all kinds. Only open to
submissions at specific times – see website
for current status.

Big Pulp

Email: editors@bigpulp.com
Website: http://www.bigpulp.com

Publishes: Fiction; Poetry; *Areas:*
Adventure; Fantasy; Horror; Mystery;
Romance; Sci-Fi; Short Stories; *Markets:*
Adult

Quarterly magazine of genre fiction and
poetry, including horror, fantasy, science
fiction, mystery and romance.

Bilingual Review

Hispanic Research Center
Arizona State University
PO Box 875303

Tempe, AZ 85287-5303
Tel: +1 (480) 965-3867
Fax: +1 (480) 965-0315
Email: brp@asu.edu
Website: https://www.asu.edu/brp/bilin/
bilin.html

Publishes: Articles; Fiction; Nonfiction;
Poetry; Reviews; Scripts; *Areas:* Criticism;
Drama; Literature; Short Stories; *Markets:*
Academic; Adult; *Treatments:* Literary

Scholarly/literary journal on the linguistics
and literature of bilingualism and bilingual
education. Publishes scholarly articles,
literary criticism, book reviews, and creative
literature: poetry, short stories, essays, and
short theatre. Accepts material in English or
Spanish. No previously published work. US
Hispanic themes only. Response time is 2-3
months.

BirdWatching Magazine
25 Braintree Hill Office Park, Suite 404
Braintree, MA 02184
Tel: +1 (617) 706-9098
Email: mail@birdwatchingdaily.com
Website: http://www.birdwatchingdaily.com

Publishes: Essays; Features; Interviews;
Nonfiction; *Areas:* Hobbies; How-to;
Nature; Photography; Travel; *Markets:* Adult

Editors: Matt Mendenhall

Magazine for bird watchers. Send query with
published clips.

Blackbird
VCU Department of English
PO Box 843082
Richmond, VA 23284-3082
Email: blackbird@vcu.edu
Website: http://www.blackbird.vcu.edu

Publishes: Essays; Fiction; Nonfiction;
Poetry; *Areas:* Short Stories; *Markets:* Adult;
Treatments: Literary

Publishes, poetry, short stories, novel
excerpts (if self-contained), personal essays,
and memoir excerpts (if self-contained).
Send up to six poems maximum at a time.

Reading period runs from November 1 to
April 15. Will consider long works, but
query before submitting prose over 8,000
words or poems over 10 pages. No
unsolicited books reviews or criticism.
Prefers to receive submissions through
online submission system.

Blueline
120 Morey Hall, SUNY Potsdam
Potsdam, NY 13676
Email: blueline@potsdam.edu
Website: http://bluelinemagadk.com

Publishes: Essays; Fiction; Nonfiction;
Poetry; *Areas:* Nature; Short Stories;
Markets: Adult; *Treatments:* Literary

Publishes poems, stories and essays about
the Adirondacks and regions similar in
geography and spirit, focussing on nature's
shaping influence. Accepts submissions from
July to November. Submit by post, or by
email with Word file attachments. See
website for full details.

Bluestem
Email: info@bluestemmagazine.com
Website: http://www.bluestemmagazine.com

Publishes: Essays; Fiction; Nonfiction;
Poetry; *Areas:* Short Stories; *Markets:* Adult;
Treatments: Literary

Editors: Charlotte Pence

Submit one short story or creative nonfiction
essay, or up to five poems at a time, via
online submission system.

Bow & Arrow Hunting
Beckett Media LLC
22840 Savi Ranch Parkway, Suite 200
Yorba Linda, CA 92887
Tel: +1 (714) 200-1900
Fax: +1 (800) 249-7761
Email: editorial@bowandarrowhunting.com
Website: http://www.
bowandarrowhunting.com

Publishes: Articles; Features; News;
Nonfiction; Reviews; *Areas:* Nature; Sport;

Markets: Adult

Editors: Joe Bell

Magazine for bow-hunting enthusiasts. Send complete ms.

Boys' Quest
Fun For Kidz Magazines
ATTN: Submissions
PO Box 227
Bluffton, OH 45817
Tel: +1 (419) 358-4610
Website: http://funforkidzmagazines.com

Publishes: Articles; Fiction; Nonfiction; Poetry; *Areas:* Cookery; Entertainment; Hobbies; Nature; Science; Short Stories; Sport; *Markets:* Children's

Magazine aimed at boys aged 6-13 (focussing on ages 8-10), publishing articles, fiction, nonfiction, and poetry that deal with timeless topics, such as pets, nature, hobbies, science, games, sports, careers, simple cooking, and anything else likely to interest a 10-year-old boy. No submissions by email. All issues are themed – see website for upcoming themes.

Bread for God's Children
PO Box 1017
Arcadia, FL 34265
Tel: +1 (863) 494-6214
Email: bread@breadministries.org
Website: http://www.breadministries.org

Publishes: Articles; Features; Fiction; Nonfiction; *Areas:* Religious; *Markets:* Children's; Youth

Christian magazine aimed at children and young adults. Looks for teaching stories that portray Christian lifestyles without preaching.

Brew Your Own
PO Box 469121
Escondido, CA 92046
Tel: +1 (800) 900-7594
Fax: +1 (760) 738-4805
Email: edit@byo.com

Website: http://byo.com

Publishes: Articles; Interviews; Nonfiction; *Areas:* Cookery; Hobbies; How-to; Technology; *Markets:* Adult

Magazine for home brewing enthusiasts. Send query with published clips, or details of brewing expertise, in first instance.

Brilliant Corners
Lycoming College
700 College Place
Williamsport, PA 17701
Email: feinstein@lycoming.edu
Website: http://www.lycoming.edu/brilliantcorners

Publishes: Fiction; Nonfiction; Poetry; *Areas:* Literature; Music; *Markets:* Adult; *Treatments:* Literary

Editors: Dr Sascha Feinstein

Publishes fiction, poetry, and nonfiction related to jazz. Send submissions by post with SASE. No fax or email submissions. Reading period runs from September 1 to May 15 annually.

Bryant Literary Review
Faculty Suite F
Bryant University
1150 Douglas Pike
Smithfield, RI 02917
Email: blr@bryant.edu
Website: http://bryantliteraryreview.org

Publishes: Fiction; Poetry; *Areas:* Short Stories; *Markets:* Adult; *Treatments:* Literary

Publishes poetry and fiction. Submit one story up to 5,000 words or up to five poems by post only with SASE. No submissions by email. Reading period runs from September 1 to December 1 annually.

Bugle
Rocky Mountain Elk Foundation
5705 Grant Creek
Missoula, MT 59808

Tel: (800) 225-5355
Email: bugle@rmef.org
Website: http://www.rmef.org/
NewsandMedia/BugleMagazine.aspx

Publishes: Articles; Essays; Fiction;
Nonfiction; Poetry; *Areas:* Adventure;
Historical; Hobbies; Humour; Nature;
Markets: Adult

Editors: PJ DelHomme

Magazine of elk hunting and conservation.
Publishes relevant articles, essays, and also
fiction and poetry on the subject.

Burnside Review
Portland, Oregon
Email: sid@burnsidereview.org
Website: http://burnsidereview.org

Publishes: Fiction; Poetry; *Areas:* Short
Stories; *Markets:* Adult

Editors: Sid Miller

Publishes poetry and fiction. Send 3-5 poems
and brief bio, or fiction up to 5,000 words
(can be collections of flash fiction or a single
story), using online submission system only.
$3 fee.

Business NH Magazine
55 South Commercial Street
Manchester, NH 03101

Tel: +1 (603) 626-6354
Fax: +1 (603) 626-6359
Email: edit@BusinessNHmagazine.com
Website: http://millyardcommunications.com

Publishes: Articles; Features; Interviews;
News; Nonfiction; *Areas:* Business; How-to;
Markets: Professional

Editors: Matthew J. Mowry

New Hampshire business magazine aimed at
the business owners and managers of New
Hampshire.

Bust
253 36th Street, Suite C307
Brooklyn, NY 11232
Email: submissions@bust.com
Website: http://bust.com

Publishes: Articles; Features; Fiction; News;
Nonfiction; *Areas:* Beauty and Fashion;
Cookery; Crafts; Culture; Erotic; Health;
Music; Travel; Women's Interests; *Markets:*
Adult

Editors: Debbie Stoller

Magazine for women, publishing a variety of
nonfiction, plus erotic fiction. No poetry or
other forms of fiction considered. See
website for full details and submission
guidelines.

Cadet Quest
PO Box 7259
Grand Rapids, MI 49510-7259
Tel: +1 (616) 241-5616
Email: submissions@calvinistcadets.org
Website: http://www.calvinistcadets.org

Publishes: Articles; Fiction; Nonfiction;
Areas: Adventure; Hobbies; Humour;
Religious; Short Stories; *Markets:* Children's

Editors: G. Richard Broene

Publishes fiction and nonfiction for boys
aged 9-14, presenting Christian life and
helping boys relate to Christian values in
their own lives. Issues are themed. View
website for details or send request with
SASE. Submit complete ms. Do not query
first.

The Cafe Irreal
Email: editors@cafeirreal.com
Website: http://www.cafeirreal.com

Publishes: Fiction; *Areas:* Short Stories;
Markets: Adult; *Treatments:* Literary

Quarterly webzine publishing fantastic
fiction resembling the work of writers such
as Franz Kafka and Jorge Luis Borges. Send
stories up to 2,000 in the body of an email.
No simultaneous submissions.

California Lawyer
44 Montgomery Street, Suite 500
San Francisco, CA 94104
Tel: +1 (415) 296-2400
Fax: +1 (415) 296-2440
Email: Chuleenan_Svetvilas@
dailyjournal.com
Website: http://www.callawyer.com

Publishes: Articles; Features; News;
Nonfiction; *Areas:* Legal; *Markets:*
Professional

Editors: Chuleenan Svetvilas

Magazine aimed at professionals working in
the Californian legal market.

Callaloo
249 Blocker Hall, 4212 TAMU
College Station, TX 77843-4212
Tel: +1 (979) 458-3108
Fax: +1 (979) 458-3275
Email: callaloo@tamu.edu
Website: http://callaloo.tamu.edu

Publishes: Articles; Essays; Fiction;
Interviews; Nonfiction; Poetry; Reviews;
Areas: Arts; Culture; Literature; Short
Stories; *Markets:* Academic; Adult;
Treatments: Literary

Editors: Charles H. Rowell

Literary journal devoted to creative work by
and critical studies of the work of African
Americans and peoples of African descent
throughout the African Diaspora. Submit via
online submission system.

Camas
Email: camas@mso.umt.edu
Website: http://www.camasmagazine.org

Publishes: Essays; Fiction; Nonfiction;
Poetry; *Areas:* Nature; *Markets:* Adult;
Treatments: Literary

Publishes fiction, essays, and poetry that
examines the relationships between
individuals, communities, and the natural
world in the American West. Issues are

themed: see website for current theme and to
submit via online submission system.

Cape Cod Life
13 Steeple Street
Mashpee, MA 02649
Tel: +1 (508) 419-7381
Fax: +1 (508) 477-1225
Email: info@capecodlife.com
Website: http://capecodlife.com

Publishes: Articles; Features; Interviews;
Nonfiction; *Areas:* Business; Culture;
Historical; Lifestyle; Nature; Travel;
Markets: Adult

Lifestyle magazine covering the area of Cape
Cod, sold locally, nationally, and
internationally. Freelances have a good
chance of publication. Send query with wide
selection of writers' clips in first instance.

Carbon Culture Review
PO Box 1643
Moriarty, NM 87035
Email: editorial@carbonculturereview.com
Website: http://www.
carbonculturereview.com

Publishes: Articles; Essays; Features;
Fiction; Interviews; Nonfiction; Poetry;
Reviews; *Areas:* Adventure; Anthropology;
Architecture; Arts; Business; Crafts; Crime;
Criticism; Culture; Design; Drama;
Entertainment; Fantasy; Film; Gothic;
Hobbies; Humour; Literature; Media;
Medicine; Military; Mystery; Philosophy;
Photography; Radio; Science; Sci-Fi; Short
Stories; Sociology; Suspense; Technology;
Thrillers; Translations; *Markets:* Adult;
Treatments: Commercial; Contemporary;
Dark; Experimental; Literary; Mainstream;
Niche; Popular

Editors: Jessica Housand-Weaver

A journal at the intersection of technology
and literature and art. Available in
bookstores in the United States, we feature
monthly creative work, literature and art as
well as articles and reviews on exciting new
tech online alongside our annual print
edition.

For more information, please visit our website or Submittable page.

The Carolina Quarterly
510 Greenlaw Hall
CB# 3520
The University of North Carolina at Chapel Hill
Chapel Hill, NC 27599-3520
Tel: +1 (919) 408-7786
Email: carolina.quarterly@gmail.com
Website: http://thecarolinaquarterly.com

Publishes: Essays; Fiction; Nonfiction; Poetry; *Areas:* Autobiography; Short Stories; Travel; *Markets:* Adult; *Treatments:* Literary

Publishes poetry, fiction, nonfiction, and visual art. Submit by post or through online submission system from September to May. Send up to 6 poems, or one piece of prose. As well as fiction, increasingly looking for nonfiction, including personal essays, travel writing, memoirs, and other forms of creative nonfiction. Novel excerpts acceptable if self-contained.

Carve Magazine
PO Box 701510
Dallas, TX 75370
Email: managingeditor@carvezine.com
Website: http://carvezine.com

Publishes: Fiction; *Areas:* Short Stories; *Markets:* Adult; *Treatments:* Literary

Editors: Kristin S. vanNamen, PhD

Publishes literary fiction up to 10,000 words, and poetry/fiction crossovers: poetry that tells a story; or flash fiction that has a lyrical feel, etc. No genre fiction or previously published fiction. Submit by post for free, or via online submission system for $3. See website for full guidelines.

Cat Fancy
I-5 Publishing
PO Box 6050
Mission Viejo, CA 92690
Tel: +1 (949) 855-8822
Fax: +1 (949) 855-3045

Email: query@catfancy.com
Website: http://www.catfancy.com

Publishes: Articles; Features; Nonfiction; *Areas:* Health; How-to; Lifestyle; Nature; Markets

Magazine covering the subjects of cats and cat ownership. No unsolicited mss. Send query by post or email between January and May only.

Caveat Lector
400 Hyde St. #606
San Francisco, CA 94109
Email: caveatlectormagazine@gmail.com
Website: http://www.caveat-lector.org

Publishes: Essays; Fiction; Nonfiction; Poetry; *Areas:* Arts; Criticism; Literature; Short Stories; *Markets:* Adult; *Treatments:* Literary

Online magazine dedicated to literature, social and cultural criticism, philosophy, and the arts. Send poetry submissions by post only, between February 1 and June 30. Prose, art, and multimedia accepted year-round by post or by email (up to 5MB). Postal submissions should include brief bio and SASE.

Cemetery Moon
Email: cemeterymoon@yahoo.com
Website: http://www. fortresspublishinginc.com

Publishes: Fiction; Poetry; *Areas:* Gothic; Horror; Short Stories; Suspense; *Markets:* Adult

Editors: Chris Pisano

Publishes horror, suspense, and/or gothc short stories and poetry. Send submissions as Word documents by email.

The Chaffin Journal
Department of English
467 Case Annex
Eastern Kentucky University
Richmond, KY 40475

Email: robert.witt@eku.edu
Website: http://english.eku.edu/chaffin-journal

Publishes: Fiction; Poetry; *Areas:* Short Stories; *Markets:* Adult; *Treatments:* Literary

Editors: Robert W. Witt

Annual literary journal, open to all forms, subjects, schools, and styles. Send 3-5 poems, or short fiction up to 10,000 words, by post.

Chamber Music Magazine
12 West 32nd Street, 7th Floor
New York, NY 10001-3813
Tel: +1 (212) 242-2022
Fax: +1 (212) 967-9747
Email: egoldensohn@chamber-music.org
Website: http://www.chamber-music.org

Publishes: Articles; Essays; Nonfiction; *Areas:* Music; *Markets:* Adult

Editors: Ellen Goldensohn

Magazine publishing material on chamber music. Send query with published clips in first instance.

Chantarelle's Notebook
Email: chantarellesnotebook@yahoo.com
Website: http://www.
chantarellesnotebook.com

Publishes: Poetry; *Markets:* Adult;
Treatments: Literary

Poetry ezine. Submit 3-5 poems per reading period, pasted into the body of an email (no attachments) with cover letter and bio, up to 75 words.

The Chattahoochee Review
Georgia State University's Perimeter College
555 North Indian Creek Drive
Clarkston, GA 30021
Email: gpccr@gpc.edu
Website: http://thechattahoocheereview.gpc.edu

Publishes: Essays; Fiction; Interviews; Nonfiction; Poetry; Reviews; *Areas:* Arts; Short Stories; Translations; *Markets:* Adult; *Treatments:* Literary

Editors: Anna Schachner

Publishes fiction, poetry, reviews, essays, interviews, translations, and visual art. See website for details and for online submission system. No paper submissions.

Chef Magazine
704 North Wells Sreet, 2nd Floor
Chicago, IL 60654
Tel: +1 (312) 849-2220
Fax: +1 (312) 849-2174
Email: cjohnson@talcott.com
Website: http://www.chefmagazine.com

Publishes: Articles; Features; News; Nonfiction; *Areas:* Business; Cookery; How-to; Technology; *Markets:* Professional

Editors: Claire Johnson

Magazine aimed at foodservice professionals, providing food and equipment articles; industry news; case studies; business solutions, etc.

Chicago Quarterly Review
517 Sherman Avenue
Evanston, IL 60202
Email: cqr@icogitate.com
Website: http://www.
chicagoquarterlyreview.com

Publishes: Essays; Fiction; Nonfiction; Poetry; *Areas:* Short Stories; *Markets:* Adult; *Treatments:* Literary

Editors: S. Afzal Haider; Elizabeth McKenzie

Submit fiction or personal essays up to 5,000 words, or 3-5 poems, via online submission system.

Chicago Review
935 East 60th Street
Chicago, IL 60637

Email: chicagoreviewmail@gmail.com
Website: http://chicagoreview.org

Publishes: Essays; Fiction; Nonfiction; Poetry; Reviews; *Areas:* Criticism; Literature; Short Stories; *Markets:* Adult; *Treatments:* Literary

Send fiction up to 5,000 words, or poetry of any length (prefers to see at least three pages). Also publishes critical essays, books reviews, and review essays, but query by email before submitting nonfiction.

The Christian Century
104 S. Michigan Ave., Suite 1100
Chicago, IL 60603-5901
Tel: +1 (312) 263-7510
Fax: +1 (312) 263-7540
Email: submissions@christiancentury.org
Website: http://www.christiancentury.org

Publishes: Articles; Essays; Interviews; Nonfiction; Poetry; Reviews; *Areas:* Culture; Humour; Politics; Religious; *Markets:* Adult

Christian magazine seeking to apply religious traditions to modern questions such as poverty, human rights, international relations, etc. For articles, send query by email. For poetry, submit poetry by email to separate address on website. See website for full submission guidelines.

Cimarron Review
205 Morrill Hall
English Department
Oklahoma State University
Stillwater, OK 74078
Email: cimarronreview@okstate.edu
Website: https://cimarronreview.com

Publishes: Fiction; Poetry; *Areas:* Short Stories; *Markets:* Adult; *Treatments:* Literary

Editors: Toni Graham

Submit 3-6 poems or one piece of fiction by post or through online submission system. No fixed length restrictions, but rarely publishes short shorts or fiction over 25

pages. See website for full submission guidelines.

Cincy
30 Garfield Place, Suite 440 Cincinnati OH 45202
Tel: +1 (513) 421-2533
Fax: +1 (513) 421-2542
Email: cminard@cincymagazine.com
Website: http://www.cincymagazine.com

Publishes: Articles; Features; Interviews; News; Nonfiction; *Areas:* Business; Health; Lifestyle; Travel; *Markets:* Professional

Editors: Corinne Minard, Managing Editor

Magazine aimed at business professionals both at work and away from work, publishing features and news related to business, as well as lifestyle pieces on dining, shopping, health, home, travel, etc.

Cloud Rodeo
Email: submit@cloudrodeo.org
Website: https://cloudrodeo.org

Publishes: Fiction; Nonfiction; Poetry; *Markets:* Adult; *Treatments:* Experimental; Literary

Editors: Jake Syersak

Describes itself as a journal of the irregular. Send 3-5 short pieces or one longer piece of fiction, nonfiction, or poetry, as a Word or PDF attachment by email.

Cloudbank
PO Box 610,
Corvallis, OR 97339-0610
Tel: +1 (877) 782-6762
Email: michael@cloudbankbooks.com
Website: http://www.cloudbankbooks.com

Publishes: Fiction; Poetry; *Areas:* Short Stories; *Markets:* Adult; *Treatments:* Literary

Editors: Michael Malan

Publishes poetry and flash fiction. Submit up

to five poems or up to five pieces of flash fiction by post or via online submission system. Online submissions require payment of a $3 fee.

Coal City Review

English Department
University of Kansas
Lawrence KS, 66045
Email: briandal@ku.edu
Website: https://coalcitypress.com

Publishes: Fiction; Poetry; *Areas:* Short Stories; *Markets:* Adult; *Treatments:* Literary

Editors: Brian Daldorph

Publishes poetry, short stories, and flash fiction. Send up to 6 poems, or one story up to 4,000 words, per year. Submissions by post only, with SASE for reply.

Cold Mountain Review

Attn: Poetry/Nonfiction/Fiction/Art
Submission
Department of English
ASU Box 32052
Boone, NC 28608-2052
Email: coldmountain@appstate.edu
Website: http://coldmountain.appstate.edu

Publishes: Essays; Fiction; Interviews; Nonfiction; Poetry; *Areas:* Autobiography; Short Stories; *Markets:* Adult; *Treatments:* Literary

Send up to five poems, creative nonfiction up to 6,000 words, interviews up to five double-spaced pages, or fiction up to 6,000 words, by post or via online submission system. See website for full details and to submit.

The Collagist

Email: fiction@thecollagist.com
Website: http://thecollagist.com

Publishes: Essays; Fiction; Nonfiction; Poetry; Reviews; *Areas:* Literature; Short Stories; *Markets:* Adult; *Treatments:* Literary

Editors: Gabriel Blackwell (fiction and excerpts); Matthew Olzmann (poetry and nonfiction)

Online journal publishing short fiction, poetry, essays, book reviews, and excerpts from novels. Reads submissions from March 1-August 31 and from October 1-January 31. Poetry and nonfiction submissions closed until summer 2016.

Colorado Review

9105 Campus Delivery
Department of English
Colorado State University
Fort Collins, CO 80523-9105
Tel: +1 (970) 491-5449
Fax: +1 (970) 491-0283
Email: creview@colostate.edu
Website: http://coloradoreview.colostate.edu/colorado-review/

Publishes: Essays; Fiction; Nonfiction; Poetry; Reviews; *Areas:* Short Stories; *Markets:* Adult; *Treatments:* Literary

Send full MSS with cover letter through online submission system ($3 charge) or by post with SASE. Poetry and fiction read between August 1 and April 30 only. Nonfiction read year-round. No specific word limit, but generally publishes short stories and essays between 15 and 25 manuscript pages. Submit up to five poems in any style at one time. No unsolicited book reviews" query first. Simultaneous submissions are accepted if immediate notification is given of acceptance elsewhere. No previously published material.

Columbia: A Journal of Literature and Art

Email: info@columbiajournal.org
Website: http://columbiajournal.org

Publishes: Essays; Fiction; Poetry; *Areas:* Arts; Film; Music; Short Stories; Translations; *Markets:* Adult; *Treatments:* Literary

Publishes poetry, fiction, nonfiction, translations, art, film, and music. Submit via online submission system. Send up to 5 pages of poetry, or up to 7,500 words of prose. See website for details of specific reading periods for print and online editions.

Common Ground Review
H-5132
Western New England University
1215 Wilbraham Road, Springfield, MA 01119
Tel: +1 (413) 782-1729
Email: submissions@cgreview.org
Website: http://www.cgreview.org

Publishes: Fiction; Nonfiction; Poetry; *Areas:* Short Stories; *Markets:* Adult; *Treatments:* Literary

Editors: Janet Bowdan

Publishes two issues a year, with deadlines of August 31 and March 31. Submit up to three poems per issue. Publishes one piece of creative nonfiction in the Autumn/Winter issue, and one short story in the Spring/Summer issue. Prose may be up to 12 double-spaced pages. Accepts submissions by post or by email. See website for full guidelines.

Compose
Email: editor@composejournal.com
Website: http://composejournal.com

Publishes: Articles; Fiction; Interviews; Nonfiction; Poetry; *Areas:* How-to; Literature; Short Stories; *Markets:* Adult; *Treatments:* Literary

Online journal publishing fiction, poetry, creative nonfiction, articles on the craft of writing (both practical and inspirational), interviews with established writers, literary agents, editors, etc. excerpts from traditionally published works, photography and artwork. Submit online via website.

Confrontation Magazine
English Department
LIU Post
Brookville, NY 11548
Email: confrontationmag@gmail.com
Website: http://confrontationmagazine.org

Publishes: Essays; Fiction; Nonfiction; Poetry; *Areas:* Autobiography; Culture; Politics; Short Stories; *Markets:* Adult; *Treatments:* Literary

Editors: Jonna G. Semeiks

Submit fiction up to 7,500 words; up to six pieces of flash fiction up to 500 words per piece; up to six poems up to two pages each; or cultural, political, or other types of essays or self-contained sections of memoirs up to 5,000 words. Will consider genre fiction if it has literary merit. Accepts email submissions from writers outside the US only.

Consumer Goods Technology
4 Middlebury Boulevard
Randolph, NJ 07869
Tel: +1 (973) 607-1300
Fax: +1 (973) 607-1395
Email: aackerman@edgellmail.com
Website: http://consumergoods.edgl.com

Publishes: Articles; Features; Interviews; News; Nonfiction; *Areas:* Business; Technology; *Markets:* Professional

Editors: Alliston Ackerman Orr

Publishes material aimed at businesses in the consumer good sector and techologies used by the industry. Always on the lookout for freelances. Send query with published clips.

Cosmopolitan
Hearst Corporation
300 West 57th Street
New York, NY 10019-3791
Tel: +1 (212) 649-2000
Email: inbox@cosmopolitan.com
Website: http://www.cosmopolitan.com

Publishes: Articles; Essays; Features; Nonfiction; *Areas:* Beauty and Fashion; Entertainment; Health; Lifestyle; Women's Interests; *Markets:* Adult

Women's lifestyle magazine. This is the largest magazine in the world, and generally a hard market to break into – however, is looking to build a "network of talented and eager contributors" and is looking for personal essays up to 800 words on college experiences, or what you did instead of college, etc. Submit online via website. For other areas of the magazine, approach by email with published clips and "story pitch" in the subject line.

Creating Keepsakes

Creative Crafts Group, LLC
14850 Pony Express Road
Bluffdale, UT 84065
Tel: +1 (801) 984-2070
Email: editorial@CreatingKeepsakes.com
Website: http://www.creatingkeepsakes.com

Publishes: Articles; Nonfiction; *Areas:* Crafts; Hobbies; *Markets:* Adult

Magazine for scrapbook enthusiasts. Send query with two images to illustrate your topic.

Cruising Outpost Magazine

Box 100,
Berry Creek, 95916
Tel: +1 (510) 900-3616
Email: submissions@cruisingoutpost.com
Website: http://cruisingoutpost.com

Publishes: Articles; Essays; Interviews; Nonfiction; *Areas:* Cookery; How-to; Technology; Travel; *Markets:* Adult

Magazine covering boats/cruising. Submit via form on website.

Cura – A Literary Magazine of Art and Action

Email: curamag@fordham.edu
Website: http://curamag.com

Publishes: Articles; Essays; Fiction; Nonfiction; Poetry; *Areas:* Short Stories; Markets

Publishes prose and poetry based in some way on the theme: Borderlands. Accepts online submissions only. Reading period runs from October to March. See website for full guidelines and to submit via online submission system.

Current Nursing in Geriatric Care

Freiberg Press, Inc.
PO Box 612
Cedar Falls, IA 50613
Tel: +1 (319) 553-0642
Fax: +1 (319) 553-0644
Email: kfreiberg@cfu.net
Website: http://www.care4elders.com

Publishes: Articles; Nonfiction; *Areas:* Health; *Markets:* Professional

Magazine for geriatric care professionals. Query in first instance.

Dance Teacher

Email: khildebrand@dancemedia.com
Website: http://www.dance-teacher.com

Publishes: Articles; Nonfiction; *Areas:* Business; Health; How-to; Legal; Music; *Markets:* Professional

Editors: Karen Hildebrand

Magazine for professional teachers of dance. Send query in the first instance.

Dime (Designs in Machine Embroidery)

2517 Manana Drive
Dallas, TX 75220
Tel: +1 (888) 739-0555
Fax: +1 (214) 352-3102
Email: dholguin@dzgns.com
Website: http://www.dzgns.com

Publishes: Articles; Interviews; Nonfiction; *Areas:* Crafts; Hobbies; How-to; *Markets:* Adult

Editors: Denise Holguin

Project-based magazine covering embroidery. Send submissions by post or by email. See website for more details.

Dollars & Sense

One Milk Street
Boston, MA 02109
Tel: +1 (617) 447-2177

Fax: +1 (617) 447-2179
Email: dollars@dollarsandsense.org
Website. http://www.dollarsandsense.org

Publishes: Articles; Features; Nonfiction;
Reviews; *Areas:* Finance; *Markets:* Adult;
Treatments

Magazine explaining economics in a popular
way. Send queries in the first instance, by
post or by email.

Drunken Boat
Email: editor@drunkenboat.com
Website: http://www.drunkenboat.com

Publishes: Fiction; Nonfiction; Poetry;
Areas: Arts; Short Stories; Translations;
Markets: Adult; *Treatments:* Literary

Online journal of art and literature,
publishing fiction, poetry, and creative
nonfiction. Submit online via website
submission system ($3 charge).

Early American Life
Firelands Media Group LLC
Post Office Box 221228
Shaker Heights, OH 44122-0996
Tel: +1 (440) 543-8566
Email: queries@firelandsmedia.com
Website: http://www.ealonline.com

Publishes: Articles; Nonfiction; *Areas:*
Antiques; Architecture; Crafts; Historical;
Markets: Adult

Magazine aimed at people with an interest in
the style of the period 1600-1840 in
America, and its use in their modern homes
and lives. Covers architecture, antiques, etc.
Will consider unsolicited mss but prefers
initial queries by email.

El Restaurante
Maiden Name Press, LLC
PO Box 2249
Oak Park, IL 60303-2249
Tel: +1 (708) 267-0023
Email: kfurore@restmex.com
Website: http://elrestaurante.com

Publishes: Articles; Features; Nonfiction;
Areas: Business; Cookery; *Markets:*
Professional

Editors: Kathleen Furore

Magazine for the owners and operators of
restaurants interested in Mexican, Tex-Mex,
Southwestern, and Latin cuisine. Send query
with published clips.

Electrical Apparatus
Barks Publications, Inc.
500 North Michigan Avenue, Suite 901
Chicago, IL 60611-4299
Tel: +1 (312) 321-9440
Fax: +1 (312) 321-1288
Email: eamagazine@barks.com
Website: http://www.barks.com/eacurr.html

Publishes: Articles; Features; Nonfiction;
Areas: Technology; *Markets:* Professional

Magazine for professionals working with and
maintaining electronic machinery including
motors, transformers, etc. technical expertise
required. Send query with CV and article
outline.

Epoch
251 Goldwin Smith Hall
Cornell University
Ithaca, NY 14853
Website: http://english.arts.cornell.edu/
publications/epoch

Publishes: Essays; Fiction; Nonfiction;
Poetry; Scripts; *Areas:* Drama; Film; Short
Stories; TV; *Markets:* Adult; *Treatments:*
Literary

Editors: Michael Koch

Publishes literary fiction, poetry, essays,
screenplays, cartoons, graphic art, and
graphic fiction. Previously unpublished
material only. Accepts submissions between
September 15 and April 15 annually. Submit
up to 5 poems, one short story, or upt to
three short short stories. Submit by post
only. See website for full details.

Equal Opportunity
445 Broad Hollow Road, Suite 425
Melville, NY 11747
Tel: +1 (631) 421-9421
Fax: +1 (631) 421-1352
Email: jschneider@eop.com
Website: http://www.eop.com

Publishes: Articles; Nonfiction; *Areas:*
Business; Finance; How-to; Self-Help;
Markets: Academic; Professional

Editors: James Schneider (Director, Editorial
& Production)

Career-guidance and recruitment magazine
aimed at minority college students and
professionals in career disciplines. Send
complete ms.

Escapees Magazine
100 Rainbow Drive
Livingston, TX 77351
Tel: +1 (888) 757-2582
Fax: +1 (936) 327-4388
Email: editor@escapees.com
Website: http://escapees.com

Publishes: Articles; Nonfiction; *Areas:*
Lifestyle; Travel; *Markets:* Adult

Editors: Allyssa Dyson

Magazine covering the RV community and
lifestyle.

Evansville Living
Tucker Publishing Group
223 NW Second Street, Suite 200
Evansville, IN 47708
Tel: +1 (812) 426-2115
Email: webmaster@evansvilleliving.com
Website: http://www.evansvilleliving.com

Publishes: Articles; Features; Nonfiction;
Areas: Design; Gardening; Historical;
Lifestyle; Sport; Travel; *Markets:* Adult

Regional magazine covering Evansville,
Indiana, and the greater area. Send query
with published clips.

The Fabricator
833 Featherstone Road
Rockford, IL 61107
Tel: +1 (815) 227-8281
Email: dand@thefabricator.com
Website: http://www.thefabricator.com

Publishes: Articles; News; Nonfiction;
Areas: How-to; Technology; *Markets:*
Professional

Editors: Dan Davis

Magazine covering metal forming and the
fabricating industry. Publishes news,
technical articles, and case histories. Send
query with published clips.

Fast Company
7 World Trade Center
New York, NY 10007-2195
Tel: +1 (212) 389-5300
Fax: +1 (212) 389-5496
Email: pr@fastcompany.com
Website: http://www.fastcompany.com

Publishes: Articles; Nonfiction; *Areas:*
Business; Design; Finance; Technology;
Markets: Professional

Publishes business articles, with a focus on
innovation in technology, ethonomics
(ethical economics), leadership, and design.
See website for submission guidelines.

Fence
Science Library 320
University at Albany
1400 Washington Avenue
Albany, NY 12222
Tel: +1 (518) 591-8162
Email: peter.n.fence@gmail.com
Website: http://www.fenceportal.org

Publishes: Fiction; Nonfiction; Poetry;
Areas: Arts; Criticism; Literature; Short
Stories; *Markets:* Adult; *Treatments:*
Literary

Biannual journal of poetry, fiction, art, and
criticism. Submit online using web-based
submission system. Submit no more than

five poems at any one time, and up to twenty-five pages of fiction.

Field & Stream
Email: fsletters@bonniercorp.com
Website: http://www.fieldandstream.com

Publishes: Articles; Essays; Nonfiction; *Areas:* Hobbies; How-to; Leisure; Nature; Sport; *Markets:* Adult

Magazine aimed at hunters and fishermen. Send query by email to propose article ideas.

Film Comment
70 Lincoln Center Plaza
New York, NY 10023
Tel: +1 (212) 875-5610
Email: editor@filmlinc.com
Website: http://www.filmlinc.com/fcm

Publishes: Articles; Essays; Interviews; Nonfiction; *Areas:* Criticism; Film; Historical; *Markets:* Adult

Editors: Gavin Smith

Magazine of film criticism and history. Publishes good writing relating about films the writer feels passionately about, rather than focusing currently popular stars or upcoming blockbusters. No unsolicited submissions. Accepts queries, but cannot guarantee a response.

FineScale Modeler
21027 Crossroads Circle
PO Box 1612
Waukesha, WI 53187
Website: http://www.finescale.com

Publishes: Articles; Nonfiction; *Areas:* Crafts; Hobbies; How-to; *Markets:* Adult

Magazine for modeling enthusiasts. Most articles come from modelers, rather than professional writers. Prefers queries describing proposed article in first instance. See website for full guidelines.

Food Product Design
Tel: +1 (480) 990-1101 ext. 1241

Email: lkuntz@vpico.com
Website: http://www.foodproductdesign.com

Publishes: Articles; News; Nonfiction; *Areas:* Business; Cookery; How-to; *Markets:* Professional

Editors: Lynn A. Kuntz

Magazine for professionals working in the food processing industry.

Freelance Writer's Report (FWR)
CNW Publishing, Editing & Promotion Inc.
PO Box A
North Stratford, NH 03590
Tel: +1 (603) 922-8338
Email: info@writers-editors.com
Website: http://www.writers-editors.com

Publishes: Articles; Nonfiction; *Areas:* Business; How-to; *Markets:* Professional

Magazine for freelance writers. Publishes how-to articles. No articles on freelancing basics. Submit complete ms by email.

Fruit Growers News Magazine
Great American Media Services
PO Box 128
Sparta, Michigan 49345
Tel: +1 (616) 887-9008
Fax: +1 (616) 887-2666
Email: fgnedit@fruitgrowersnews.com
Website: http://fruitgrowersnews.com

Publishes: Articles; Interviews; News; Nonfiction; *Areas:* Business; Nature; *Markets:* Professional

Magazine for commercial growers of fruit.

Girlfriendz Magazine
6 Brookville Drive
Cherry Hill, NJ 08003
Tel: +1 (856) 751-2997
Email: tobi@girlfriendzmag.com
Website: http://www.girlfriendzmag.com

Publishes: Articles; *Areas:* Beauty and Fashion; Business; Health; Historical; How-to; Humour; Self-Help; Women's Interests; *Markets:* Adult

Editors: Tobi Schwartz-Cassell, Editor-in-Chief

Publishes well-researched articles for the thinking woman, from credentialed professionals. Aimed at women born between 1946 and 1964. Prefers not to be pitched ideas, but interested in baby-boom women writers who can be assigned to write articles, make-over tips, business articles, and fitness programmes. No poetry, personal essays, or community calendar announcements. Send query by email including published clips. No queries by fax. See website for full guidelines.

Golf News Magazine

PO Box 1040
Rancho Mirage, CA 92270
Tel: +1 (760) 321-8800
Fax: +1 (760) 328-3013
Email: dan@golfnewsmag.com
Website: http://golfnewsmag.com

Publishes: Articles; Features; Interviews; News; Nonfiction; *Areas:* Health; How-to; Sport; *Markets:* Adult

Magazine covering the sport of golf. Send query with published clips.

Grain Journal

Country Journal Publishing Co.
3065 Pershing Court
Decatur, IL 62526
Tel: +1 (800) 728-7511
Email: ed@grainnet.com
Website: http://www.grainnet.com

Publishes: Articles; Interviews; Nonfiction; *Areas:* Business; How-to; Technology; *Markets:* Professional

Editors: Ed Zdrojewski

Trade magazine for the North American grain industry.

GuestLife

303 North Indian Canyon Drive
Palm Springs, CA 92262
Tel: +1 (760) 325-2333
Fax: +1 (760) 325-7008
Email: Sales@GuestLife.com
Website: http://www.guestlife.com

Publishes: Articles; Features; Nonfiction; *Areas:* Culture; Entertainment; Historical; Leisure; Travel; *Markets:* Adult

Magazine placed in hotel rooms, covering activities, attractions, and history of the specific area being covered. See website for details.

Gyroscope Review

Website: http://www.gyroscopereview.com

Publishes: Poetry; *Markets:* Adult; *Treatments:* Contemporary; Literary

Publishes fine contemporary poetry in a variety of forms and themes. Welcomes both new and established writers. Submit online via website submission system.

Hard Hat News

PO Box 121
Palatine Bridge, NY 13428
Tel: +1 (717) 497-7616
Fax: +1 (518) 673-2381
Email: jcasey@leepub.com
Website: http://hardhat.com

Publishes: Articles; Interviews; News; Nonfiction; *Markets:* Professional

Editors: Jon Casey

Magazine for construction workers. Send complete ms.

Hill Country Sun

Email: melissa@hillcountrysun.com
Website: http://www.hillcountrysun.com

Publishes: Articles; Nonfiction; *Areas:* Travel; *Markets:* Adult

Editors: Melissa Maxwell Ball

Magazine covering interesting people, places, and things to do in Central Texas Hill Country from Austin to Leakey, from San Antonio to Burnet. Aimed at both residents and visitors. All topics must be pre-approved by editor. Send query by email.

Home Energy Magazine
1250 Addison Street, Suite 211B
Berkeley, CA 94702
Tel: +1 (510) 524-5405
Fax: +1 (510) 981-1406
Email: contact@homeenergy.org
Website: http://www.homeenergy.org

Publishes: Articles; Nonfiction; *Areas:*
Architecture; Design; *Markets:* Professional

Editors: Jim Gunshinan

Magazine for the construction industry, publishing articles that disseminate objective and practical information on residential energy efficiency, performance, comfort, and affordability. Send query with published clips.

The Horn Book Magazine
300 The Fenway
Palace Road Building, Suite P-311
Boston, MA 02115
Tel: +1 (617) 628-0225
Fax: +1 (617) 628-0882
Email: magazine@hbook.com
Website: http://www.hbook.com

Publishes: Articles; Nonfiction; *Areas:*
Criticism; Literature; *Markets:* Academic;
Professional

Magazine aimed at professionals and academics involved with children's literature, publishing critical articles on the same. No fiction or work by children.

Houston Press
2603 La Branch Street
Houston, TX 77004
Tel: +1 (713) 280-2400
Fax: +1 (713) 280-2444
Website: http://www.houstonpress.com

Publishes: Articles; News; Nonfiction;
Areas: Arts; Entertainment; *Markets:* Adult

Covers news, arts, and entertainment specific to Houston.

Hyde Park Living
179 Fairfield Avenue
Bellevue, KY 41073
Tel: +1 (859) 291-1412
Email: hydepark@livingmagazines.com
Website: http://www.livingmagazines.com/
Hyde_Park_Living/Hyde_Park_Living.html

Publishes: Articles; Essays; Features;
Interviews; Nonfiction; Poetry; Reviews;
Areas: Historical; Humour; Travel; *Markets:*
Adult

Editors: Grace DeGregorio

Publishes material related to Hyde Park, Ohio, only. Query in first instance.

Indianapolis Monthly
1 Emmis Plaza
40 Monument Circle Suite 100
Indianapolis, IN 46204
Tel: +1 (317) 237-9288
Fax: +1 (317) 684-2080
Email: khannel@indianapolismonthly.com
Website: http://www.
indianapolismonthly.com

Publishes: Articles; Essays; Features;
Interviews; Nonfiction; *Areas:* Lifestyle;
Markets: Adult

Editors: Kim Hannel

Regional magazine publishing material related to Indiana. No fiction or poetry. Send query with published clips.

InTents
Industrial Fabrics Association International
1801 County Road, B W
Roseville MN 55113
Email: editorial@ifai.com
Website: http://intentsmag.com

Publishes: Interviews; Nonfiction; *Areas:*

How-to; Technology; *Markets:* Professional

Magazine covering event tents, providing information on renting tents and staging tented events. Query in first instance.

Interweave Knits
201 East Fourth Street
Loveland, CO 80537
Website: http://www.knittingdaily.com

Publishes: Articles; Features; Nonfiction; *Areas:* Beauty and Fashion; Crafts; Design; Hobbies; How-to; *Markets:* Adult

Knitting magazine. Send query by post.

Iron Horse Literary Review
Texas Tech University
English Department
Mail Stop 43091
Lubbock, TX 79409-3091
Tel: +1 (806) 742-2500
Fax: +1 (806) 742-0989
Email: ihlr.mail@gmail.com
Website: http://www.ironhorsereview.com

Publishes: Essays; Fiction; Nonfiction; Poetry; *Areas:* Short Stories; *Markets:* Adult; *Treatments:* Literary

Publishes stories, poetry, and essays. Pays for published pieces, but submission fee charged. Subject matter, length restrictions, and submission fees vary from issue to issue. See website for details for upcoming issues.

The Journal of Adventist Education
12501 Old Columbia Pike
Silver Spring, MD 20904-6600
Tel: +1 (301) 680-5069
Fax: +1 (301) 622-9627
Email: mcgarrellf@gc.adventist.org
Website: http://jae.adventist.org

Publishes: Articles; Nonfiction; *Areas:* Religious; *Markets:* Professional

Editors: Faith-Ann McGarrell

Magazine aimed at Seventh-day Adventist

teachers and educational administrators. See website for full submission guidelines.

Kashrus Magazine
PO Box 204
Brooklyn, NY 11204
Tel: +1 (718) 336-8544
Fax: +1 (718) 336-8550
Email: editorial@kashrusmagazine.com
Website: http://www.kashrusmagazine.com

Publishes: Articles; Nonfiction; *Areas:* Health; Religious; Travel; *Markets:* Adult

Magazine publishing information on Kosher.

KNOWAtlanta
9040 Roswell Road, Suite 210
Atlanta, GA 30350
Tel: +1 (770) 650-1102
Fax: +1 (770) 650.2848
Email: lindsay@knowatlanta.com
Website: http://www.knowatlanta.com

Publishes: Articles; Interviews; Nonfiction; *Areas:* Business; Culture; Finance; Health; How-to; Lifestyle; Self-Help; Travel; *Markets:* Adult; Professional

Magazine for businesses and individuals looking to relocate to Atlanta.

Lakeland Boating
O'Meara-Brown Publications
630 Davis Street, Suite 301
Evanston, IL 60201
Tel: +1 (312) 276-0610
Email: ljohnson@lakelandboating.com
Website: http://www.lakelandboating.com

Publishes: Articles; Essays; Features; Interviews; Nonfiction; *Areas:* Historical; How-to; Leisure; Technology; Travel; *Markets:* Adult

Editors: Lindsey Johnson

Magazine covering boating in the Great Lakes.

Leisure Group Travel
621 Plainfield Road, Suite 406

Willowbrook, IL 60527
Tel: +1 (630) 794-0696
Fax: +1 (630) 794-0032
Email: editor@ptmgroups.com
Website: http://leisuregrouptravel.com

Publishes: Articles; News; Nonfiction;
Areas: Business; Travel; *Markets:*
Professional

Magazine aimed at group travel buyers. Send
query with published clips in first instance.

Little Patuxent Review
PO Box 6084
Columbia, MD 21045
Email: editor@littlepatuxentreview.org
Website: http://littlepatuxentreview.org

Publishes: Fiction; Nonfiction; Poetry;
Areas: Short Stories; *Markets:* Adult;
Treatments: Literary

Editors: Steven Leyva

A community-based publication focused on
writers and artists from the Mid-Atlantic
region, but will consider work originating
from anywhere in the United States. Submit
fiction up to 5,000 words; creative nonfiction
up to 3,500 words, or up to three poems of
up to 100 lines. No submissions from writers
outside the US. Submit online using website
submission system.

Lost Treasure, Inc.
PO Box 451589
Grove, OK 74345
Tel: +1 (918) 786-2182
Email: managingeditor@losttreasure.com
Website: http://new.losttreasure.com

Publishes: Articles; Nonfiction; *Areas:*
Hobbies; *Markets:* Adult

Editors: Carla Nielsen

Magazine for treasure hunting hobbyists.

Media Inc.
PO Box 24365
Seattle, WA 98124-0365

Tel: +1 (206) 382-9220
Fax: +1 (206) 382-9437
Email: ksauro@media-inc.com
Website: http://media-inc.com

Publishes: Articles; Features; News;
Nonfiction; *Areas:* Business; Media;
Markets: Professional

Editors: Katie Sauro

Magazine serving professionals in the US
Northwest working in the media, including
marketing, advertising, and creative services.
Send query or complete ms.

Ms. Magazine
433 South Beverly Drive
Beverly Hills, CA 90212
Tel: +1 (310) 556-2515
Fax: +1 (310) 556-2514
Email: mkort@msmagazine.com
Website: http://www.msmagazine.com

Publishes: Articles; Fiction; News;
Nonfiction; Poetry; Reviews; *Areas:* Arts;
Culture; Legal; Nature; Politics; Short
Stories; Sociology; Women's Interests;
Markets: Adult

Editors: Michel Cicero

Publishes articles focussing on politics,
social commentary, popular culture, law,
education, art and the environment, through
a feminist lens. Also publishes original
fiction and poetry, but publishes these
infrequently. See website for full submission
guidelines.

Main Line Today
4645 West Chester Pike
Newtown Square, PA 19073
Tel: +1 (610) 325-4630
Fax: +1 (610) 325-4636
Email: hrowland@mainlinetoday.com
Website: http://www.mainlinetoday.com

Publishes: Articles; Features; Interviews;
Nonfiction; *Areas:* Arts; Historical; How-to;
Humour; Lifestyle; Travel; *Markets:* Adult

Editors: Hobart Rowland (Editorial Director)

Monthly magazine covering Philadelphia's main line and western suburbs. Send query with published clips.

The Maine Review

Email: editor@themainereview.com
Website: http://www.themainereview.com

Publishes: Essays; Fiction; Nonfiction; Poetry; *Areas:* Short Stories; *Markets:* Adult; *Treatments:* Literary

Editors: Katherine Mayfield

Publishes creative nonfiction, poetry, short fiction, essays, and prose. See website for full details.

Massage & Bodywork

25188 Genesee Trail Road, Suite 200
Golden, CO 80401
Tel: +1 (800) 458-2267
Email: editor@abmp.com
Website: http://www.
massageandbodywork.com

Publishes: Articles; Interviews; Nonfiction; *Areas:* Health; How-to; Medicine; *Markets:* Professional

Editors: Leslie Young

Magazine aimed at professional massage therapists and bodyworkers. Send query with published clips.

Metro Parent

Metro Parent Publishing Group
22041 Woodward Avenue
Ferndale, MI 48220
Email: jelliott@metroparent.com
Website: http://www.metroparent.com

Publishes: Articles; Features; News; Nonfiction; *Areas:* Lifestyle; *Markets:* Adult

Editors: Julia Elliott

Regional lifestyle magazine aimed at Southeast Michigan. Publishes pieces on trends, local people, products of interest to parents / kids, child behaviour, etc. Must

have a local focus. See website for full guidelines.

Midwest Meetings

Hennen Publishing
302 Sixth Street West
Brookings, SD 57006
Email: editor@midwestmeetings.com
Website: http://www.midwestmeetings.com

Publishes: Articles; News; Nonfiction; Reference; *Areas:* Business; *Markets:* Professional

Editors: Randy Hennen

Magazine for convention and meeting planners in the Midwest. Always looking for content from new authors, bloggers, industry experts and everyday professionals. Submit via online form on website.

Military Vehicles Magazine

700 East State Street
Iola, WI 54990-0001
Tel: +1 (888) 457-2873
Fax: +1 (715) 445-4087
Email: john.adams-graf@fwpubs.com
Website: http://www.militarytrader.com

Publishes: Articles; News; Nonfiction; *Areas:* Historical; How-to; Military; Technology; *Markets:* Adult

Editors: John Adams-Graf

Magazine aimed at people who own, restore, and collect historic military vehicles.

Mobile Bay

PMT Publishing
P.O.Box 66200
Mobile, AL 36660
Tel: +1 (251) 473-6269
Fax: +1 (251) 479-8822
Email: jculbreth@pmtpublishing.com
Website: http://www.mobilebaymag.com

Publishes: Articles; Nonfiction; *Areas:* Arts; Beauty and Fashion; Cookery; Culture; Historical; Lifestyle; *Markets:* Adult

Editors: Judy Culbreth, Editorial Director

Lifestyle magazine aimed at residents of Mobile and Baldwin counties. Send query with published clips. Material must have local relevance.

Model Engineer
MyTimeMedia Ltd
Enterprise House
Enterprise Way
Edenbridge
Kent
TN8 6HF
Email: diane.carney@mytimemedia.com
Website: http://www.model-engineer.co.uk

Publishes: Articles; Nonfiction; *Areas:* Hobbies; How-to; Technology; *Markets:* Adult

Editors: Diane Carney

Magazine for model making enthusiasts.

More
Email: More@meredith.com
Website: http://www.more.com

Publishes: Articles; Features; Nonfiction; *Areas:* Beauty and Fashion; Entertainment; Finance; Health; Lifestyle; Women's Interests; *Markets:* Adult

Editors: Lesley Jane Seymour

Women's lifestyle magazine celebrating women of style and substance who influence others. Aimed at sophisticated and accomplished readers.

Nails Magazine
Tel: +1 (310) 533-2552
Email: Erika.Kotite@bobit.com
Website: http://www.nailsmag.com

Publishes: Articles; Features; Interviews; News; Nonfiction; *Areas:* Business; Health; How-to; *Markets:* Professional

Editors: Erika Kotite

Magazine for nail salon professionals.

The National Jurist
7670 Opportunity Road, #105
San Diego, CA 92111
Tel: +1 (858) 300-3201
Email: Jack@cypressmagazines.com
Website: http://www.nationaljurist.com

Publishes: Articles; Interviews; News; Nonfiction; *Areas:* How-to; Legal; *Markets:* Academic

Editors: Jack Crittenden (Editor-In-Chief)

Magazine for law students. Contact by email.

New Mobility Magazine
United Spinal Association
120-34 Queens Boulevard #320
Kew Gardens, NY 11415
Email: info@unitedspinal.org
Website: http://www.spinalcord.org/new-mobility-magazine/

Publishes: Articles; Features; Interviews; News; Nonfiction; *Areas:* Health; Medicine; *Markets:* Adult; Professional

Editors: Ian Ruder

Magazine for people affected by spinal cord injuries and disorders, including sufferers, carers, and professionals in the field.

News Photographer
6677 Whitemarsh Valley Walk
Austin, TX 78746-6367
Email: magazine@nppa.org
Website: https://nppa.org/magazine

Publishes: Articles; Interviews; News; Nonfiction; *Areas:* Current Affairs; Historical; How-to; Photography; Technology; *Markets:* Professional

Editors: Donald R. Winslow

Magazine aimed at professional photo-journalists.

NFPA Journal

Tel: +1 (617) 770-3000
Email: nfpajournal@nfpa.org
Website: http://www.nfpa.org

Publishes: Articles; Features; News;
Nonfiction; *Markets:* Professional

Association magazine covering fire
protection and suppression.

Niche

3000 Chestnut Avenue, Suite 104
Baltimore, MD 21211
Tel: +1 (410) 889-3093
Email: info@nichemagazine.com
Website: http://www.nichemagazine.com/

Publishes: Articles; Nonfiction; *Areas:* Arts;
Business; Crafts; Finance; *Markets:*
Professional

Editors: Hope Daniels

Trade magazine aimed at craft gallery
retailers. Send query with published clips.

Nob Hill Gazette

Fairmont Hotel
950 Mason Street, Mezzanine Level
San Francisco, CA 94108
Tel: +1 (415) 227-0190
Email: fred@nobhillgazette.com
Website: http://www.nobhillgazette.com

Publishes: Articles; Nonfiction; *Areas:* Arts;
Beauty and Fashion; Cookery; Design;
Finance; Health; Historical; Lifestyle;
Travel; *Markets:* Adult

Editors: Fred Albert

Upscale lifestyle magazine for the San
Francisco Bay area. Send query with
published clips.

Northwest Quarterly Magazine

Hughes Media Corp.
728 North Prospect Street
Rockford, IL 61107
Tel: +1 (815) 316-2301
Email: clinden@northwestquarterly.com

Website: http://www.northwestquarterly.com

Publishes: Articles; Features; Interviews;
Nonfiction; *Areas:* Business; Culture;
Gardening; Health; Historical; Humour;
Leisure; Lifestyle; Nature; *Markets:* Adult

Lifestyle magazine aimed at Northern
Illinois, Southern Wisconsin, and Kane and
McHenry counties.

Nostalgia Magazine

PO Box 8466
Spokane, WA 99203
Email: editor@nostalgiamagazine.net

Publishes: Essays; Nonfiction; *Areas:*
Historical; *Markets:* Adult

Publishes nostalgic personal essays,
illustrated with interesting photographs. At
least one photo per 400 words. Accepts
submissions in any format, but prefers stories
and photos by email.

Nurseweek

Email: editor@nurse.com
Website: http://www.nurse.com

Publishes: Articles; Nonfiction; *Areas:*
Medicine; *Markets:* Professional

Magazine provided free to registered nurses
living in the United States.

O'Dwyer's

271 Madison Ave., #600
New York, NY 10016
Tel: +1 (212) 679-2471
Email: john@odwyerpr.com
Website: http://www.odwyerpr.com

Publishes: Articles; News; Nonfiction;
Areas: Business; Legal; Technology;
Markets: Professional

Editors: John O'Dwyer, Associate Publisher/
Editor

Magazine aimed at PR professionals.

OfficePro
10502 N Ambassador Drive, Suite 100
Kansas City, MO 64153
Tel: +1 (816) 891-6600
Fax: +1 (816) 891-9118
Email: john.naatz@iaap-hq.org
Website: http://www.iaap-hq.org/page/
OfficeProMagazine

Publishes: Articles; News; Nonfiction;
Areas: Business; *Markets:* Professional

Editors: John Naatz

Publishes stories related to office life, from
office politics to new software. Send query
by email.

Onion World
Columbia Publishing
8405 Ahtanum Road
Yakima, WA 98903
Email: dkeller@columbiapublications.com
Website: http://www.onionworld.net

Publishes: Articles; Interviews; Nonfiction;
Areas: Business; Nature; *Markets:*
Professional

Editors: Denise Keller

Magazine for potential onion growers and
sellers.

Opera News
70 Lincoln Center Plaza, 6th Floor
New York, NY 10023-6593
Tel: +1 (212) 769-7080
Fax: +1 (212) 769-8500
Email: info@operanews.com
Website: http://www.operanews.com

Publishes: Articles; News; Nonfiction;
Areas: Music; *Markets:* Adult; Professional

Editors: Kitty March

Magazine for opera professionals and
enthusiasts. Send queries, proposals, and
unsolicited mss with published writing clips
by email.

Oregon Coast
4969 Highway 101 N, Suite 2
Florence, OR 97439
Tel: +1 (541) 997-8401
Email: edit@nwmags.com
Website: http://www.
oregoncoastmagazine.com

Publishes: Articles; Nonfiction; *Areas:*
Historical; Leisure; Nature; *Markets:* Adult;
Family

Publishes articles of regional interest. Send
query or submit complete ms by email or by
post. No fiction or poetry. See website for
full details.

Organic Life
400 South 10th Street
Emmaus, PA 18049
Email: ROLsubmissions@rodale.com
Website: http://www.rodalesorganiclife.com

Publishes: Articles; Nonfiction; *Areas:*
Gardening; Health; Lifestyle; Nature;
Markets: Adult

Publishes articles that address some aspect of
the magazine's focus on living naturally in
the modern world.

Orson Scott Card's InterGalactic Medicine Show
Website: http://www.
intergalacticmedicineshow.com

Publishes: Fiction; *Areas:* Fantasy; Sci-Fi;
Short Stories; *Markets:* Adult; Youth

Online magazine publishing fantasy and
science fiction of any length. Submit via
online submission form.

The Ottawa Object
Email: threwlinebooks@gmail.com
Website: https://theottawaobject.
wordpress.com

Publishes: Fiction; *Areas:* Short Stories;
Markets: Adult; *Treatments:* Literary

Editors: Joshua Hjalmer Lind

Print literary journal with a particular interest in speculative fiction. Submit online through website.

Overtones
808 W. Melrose Avenue #802
Findlay, OH 45840
Email: jrsmith@handbellmusicians.org
Website: http://handbellmusicians.org/music-resources/overtones/

Publishes: Articles; Features; Interviews; News; Nonfiction; *Areas:* How-to; Music; *Markets:* Adult

Editors: J.R. Smith

Magazine for handbell musicians.

Painted Bride Quarterly
Drexel University
Department of English and Philosophy
3141 Chestnut Street
Philadelphia, PA 19104
Email: pbq@drexel.edu
Website: http://pbq.drexel.edu

Publishes: Essays; Fiction; Nonfiction; Poetry; *Areas:* Short Stories; *Markets:* Adult; *Treatments:* Literary

Submit up to 5 poems; fiction up to 5,000 words; or essays up to 3,000 words, via online submission system.

Painted Cave
Email: paintedcavesubmissions@gmail.com
Website: http://paintedcave.net

Publishes: Fiction; Nonfiction; Poetry; *Areas:* Short Stories; *Markets:* Adult; *Treatments:* Literary

Online literary magazine publishing submissions from community college students. Submit up to three pieces of flash fiction or flash creative nonfiction up to 750 words; one piece of fiction or creative nonfiction up to 5,000 words; or 3-5 poems up to 50 lines each. Include short, third-person biography. See website for full submission guidelines.

Palm Springs Life
303 North Indian Canyon Drive
Palm Springs, CA 92262
Tel: +1 (760) 325-2333
Website: http://www.palmspringslife.com

Publishes: Articles; Essays; Features; Interviews; Nonfiction; *Areas:* Arts; Beauty and Fashion; Culture; Design; Entertainment; Lifestyle; *Markets:* Adult

Editors: Kent Black

Magazine covering the Palm Springs-area desert resort communities. Send query with published clips.

Parents
805 3rd Ave #22
New York, NY 10022
Tel: +1 (212) 499-2000
Website: http://www.parents.com

Publishes: Articles; Features; Nonfiction; *Areas:* Beauty and Fashion; Health; Lifestyle; Women's Interests; *Markets:* Adult

Magazine aimed at mothers with small children. Query in first instance.

Pediatric Annals
Healio.com, c/o SLACK Incorporated
6900 Grove Road, Thorofare, NJ 08086
Tel: +1 (856) 848-1000
Fax: +1 (800) 257-8290
Email: editor@healio.com
Website: http://www.healio.com/pediatrics/journals/pedann

Publishes: Articles; News; Nonfiction; *Areas:* Medicine; *Markets:* Professional

Monthly online medical journal providing pediatricians and other clinicians with practical information on the diagnosis and treatment of pediatric diseases and disorders.

Pentecostal Evangel
1445 N. Boonville Avenue
Springfield, MO 65802
Email: pe@ag.org
Website: http://www.pe.ag.org

Publishes: Articles; Nonfiction; *Areas:* Religious; *Markets:* Adult

Christian magazine publishing inspirational articles. Prefers submissions by email. See website for full guidelines.

Pentecostal Messenger
701 Brown Trail
Bedford, TX 76021
Email: Communications@pcg.org
Website: http://www.pcg.org

Publishes: Articles; Essays; Nonfiction; *Areas:* Religious; *Markets:* Adult

Christian magazine acting as the official voice of the Pentecostal Church.

Perfume River Poetry Review
Tourane Poetry Press
PO Box 2192
Cupertino, CA 95015-2192
Website: http://touranepoetrypress.
wordpress.com/about-4/

Publishes: Poetry; *Markets:* Adult;
Treatments: Literary

Submit 3-5 poems during specific reading periods only, relating to the subject of the upcoming issue (see website for details). No email submissions, unless outside of the US (in which case query by email in first instance).

Pest Management Professional
North Coast Media
1360 E. 9th Street, Suite 1070
Cleveland, OH 44114
Tel: +1 (216) 706-3766
Fax: +1 (216) 706-3712
Email: mwhitford@northcoastmedia.net
Website: http://www.mypmp.net

Publishes: Articles; News; Nonfiction; *Areas:* Nature; *Markets:* Professional

Editors: Marty Whitford, Publisher & Editorial Director

Magazine for professionals working in the pest management industry. Send query by email with news or ideas for stories.

Philly Weekly
1617 JFK Boulevard, Suite 1005
Philadelphia, PA 19103
Tel: +1 (215) 563-7400
Fax: +1 (215) 563-6799
Email: mail@phillyweekly.com
Website: http://philadelphiaweekly.com

Publishes: News; Nonfiction; *Areas:* Arts; Current Affairs; Entertainment; *Markets:* Adult

Editors: Anastasia Barbalios

Local magazine publishing arts and entertainment news, dining reviews, and provocative current affairs coverage relating to Philadelphia.

Phoenix Magazine
15169 North Scottsdale Road, Suite 310
Scottsdale, AZ 85254
Website: http://www.phoenixmag.com

Publishes: Articles; Features; News; Nonfiction; *Areas:* Beauty and Fashion; Cookery; Finance; Health; Lifestyle; Travel; *Markets:* Adult

Publishes material of interest to the local area only. Send query by email with published clips.

Photonics & Imaging Technology
Tech Briefs Media Group
261 Fifth Avenue, Suite 1901
New York, NY 10016
Tel: +1 (212) 490-3999
Website: http://www.
techbriefsmediagroup.com

Publishes: Articles; Nonfiction; *Areas:* Science; Technology; *Markets:* Academic; Professional

Technical magazine for the photonics /

optics industry. Send query or submit complete ms.

Pizza Today

908 South 8th Street, Suite 200
Louisville, KY 40203
Tel: +1 (502) 736-9500
Email: jwhite@pizzatoday.com
Website: http://www.pizzatoday.com

Publishes: Articles; Features; News; Nonfiction; *Areas:* Business; Cookery; *Markets:* Professional

Editors: Jeremy White

Magazine aimed at the pizza industry. Send query by email, post, or fax.

Plain Truth Magazine

Plain Truth Ministries
Pasadena, CA 91129
Tel: +1 (800) 309-4466
Email: managing.editor@ptm.org
Website: http://www.ptm.org

Publishes: Articles; Interviews; Nonfiction; *Areas:* Religious; *Markets:* Adult

Christian magazine promoting a direct relationship with God, disintermediated by religion. Send query with SASE and published clips.

Play & Playground Magazine

Playground Professionals, LLC
10 North Bridge Street
Saint Anthony, ID 83445
Tel: +1 (208) 569-9189
Website: http://www.
playgroundprofessionals.com

Publishes: Articles; Features; News; Nonfiction; *Areas:* Design; How-to; Leisure; Technology; *Markets:* Professional

Trade journal publishing material of relevance to the play and playground industry.

PN (Paraplegia News)

PVA Publications
2111 East Highland Avenue, Suite 180
Phoenix, AZ 85016-4702
Tel: +1 (602) 224-0500
Fax: +1 (602) 224-0507
Email: richard@pvamag.com
Website: http://pvamag.com/pn/

Publishes: Articles; Nonfiction; *Areas:* Health; Leisure; Lifestyle; Sport; *Markets:* Adult

Editors: Richard Hoover

Monthly magazine for people with spinal-cord injuries, family members and caregivers.

Police and Security News

1208 Juniper Street
Quakertown, PA 18951-1520
Tel: +1 (215) 538-1240
Fax: +1 (215) 538-1208
Email: dyaw@policeandsecuritynews.com
Website: http://policeandsecuritynews.com

Publishes: Articles; News; Nonfiction; *Areas:* How-to; Legal; *Markets:* Professional

Magazine for law enforcement professionals, covering new technology; training and tactics; new weaponry; management ideas; and more. Send query by email or through online form.

Popular Science

2 Park Avenue, 9th Floor
New York, NY 10016
Email: queries@popsci.com
Website: http://www.popsci.com

Publishes: Articles; News; Nonfiction; *Areas:* Science; Technology; *Markets:* Adult; *Treatments:* Popular

Magazine covering science and technology for a general adult readership. Welcomes queries by email. Send pitch with brief summary and links to past work, if available. No submission by post.

Postcard Poems and Prose
Website: https://postcardpoemsandprose.
wordpress.com

Publishes: Fiction; Poetry; *Areas:* Short
Stories; *Markets:* Adult

Publishes postcard-sized combinations of
images and poems (12-20 lines) or prose (up
to 190 words). Text and images should be
sent as separate attachments. Will consider
text without images.

PracticeLink Magazine
415 2nd Avenue
Hinton, WV 25951
Tel: +1 (800) 776-8383
Email: HelpDesk@PracticeLink.com
Website: http://www.practicelink.com

Publishes: Nonfiction; *Areas:* Medicine;
Markets: Professional

Career advancement resource for physicians.

Preservation in Print
The Leeds-Davis Building
923 Tchoupitoulas Street
New Orleans, LA 70130
Tel: +1 (504) 636-3043
Email: ddelsol@prcno.org
Website: http://www.prcno.org

Publishes: Articles; Essays; Interviews;
Nonfiction; *Areas:* Architecture; Historical;
Markets: Adult

Editors: Danielle Del Sol

Louisiana publication covering architectural
preservation and neighbourhood
revitalisation issues.

The Produce News
800 Kinderkamack Road, Suite 100
Oradell, NJ 07649
Tel: +1 (201) 986-7990
Fax: +1 (201) 986-7996
Email: groh@theproducenews.com
Website: http://www.theproducenews.com

Publishes: Articles; News; Nonfiction;

Markets: Professional

Editors: John Groh

Magazine for professionals in the fresh fruits
and vegetables industry.

Properties Magazine
3826 W. 158th St.
Cleveland, OH 44111
Tel: +1 (216) 251-0035
Fax: +1 (216) 251-2655
Email: mwatt@propertiesmag.com
Website: http://www.propertiesmag.com

Publishes: Articles; News; Nonfiction;
Areas: Architecture; Business; Design;
Markets: Professional

Editors: Mark Watt, Managing Editor/Art
Director

Monthly publication dedicated to realty,
construction and architecture in Northeast
Ohio.

QSR
Tel: +1 (919) 945-0703
Email: sam@qsrmagazine.com
Website: https://www.qsrmagazine.com

Publishes: Articles; News; Nonfiction;
Areas: Business; Cookery; *Markets:*
Professional

Editors: Sam Oches

Magazine for the limited-service restaurant
industry.

Rappahannock Review
University of Mary Washington
1301 College Avenue
Fredericksburg, VA 22401
Tel: +1 (540) 654-1033
Fax: +1 (540) 654-1569
Email: editor@rappahannockreview.com
Website: http://www.
rappahannockreview.com

Publishes: Essays; Fiction; Nonfiction;
Poetry; *Areas:* Short Stories; *Markets:* Adult;

Treatments: Experimental; Literary

Editors: Avery Kopp; Sarah Palmer

Online literary journal publishing poetry of any length (submit up to five poems), plus creative nonfiction and fiction up to 8,000 words (or three pieces up to 1,000 words each). Encourages experimental pieces. See website for reading periods and any special topics.

The Realm Beyond

Email: realm.beyond@yahoo.com
Website: http://www.fortresspublishinginc.com

Publishes: Fiction; *Areas:* Horror; Sci-Fi; Short Stories; Suspense; *Markets:* Adult; Youth

Editors: Brian Koscienski

Magazine publishing exciting and suspenseful stories of science fiction, fantasy and horror. Send submissions by email as Word file attachments. No profanity or graphic scenes.

Red Paint Hill Poetry Journal

Email: submissions@redpainthill.com
Website: http://redpainthill.com

Publishes: Essays; Nonfiction; Poetry; Reviews; *Markets:* Adult; *Treatments:* Literary

Editors: Stephanie Bryant Anderson

Send 3-5 poems in a single Word document by email. No PDF files. Work must be unpublished. Simultaneous submissions accepted, provide immediate notification given of acceptance elsewhere. No rhyming poetry, poetry about poems or the writing process, or melodramatic love poems. Also publishes reviews, essays, and interviews. See website for full submission guidelines.

Sequestrum

Email: sequr.info@gmail.com
Website: http://www.sequestrum.org

Publishes: Articles; Essays; Features; Fiction; Nonfiction; Poetry; *Areas:* Arts; Criticism; Culture; Drama; Fantasy; Horror; Literature; Mystery; Philosophy; Sci-Fi; Short Stories; *Markets:* Adult; Youth; *Treatments:* Commercial; Contemporary; Literary; Mainstream; Progressive; Satirical

Editors: Ralph Cooper

Founded by graduates of creative writing programs. This magazine has faithfully published award-winning writers and new voices alike for its 1,000+ monthly readership since its advent.

We accept and publish manuscripts on a rolling basis, and maintain our archives for the public free of charge. We only accept submissions through our online submission system. Hard copy or otherwise emailed submissions will not be read.

Sixpenny Magazine

Email: elizabeth@sixpenny.org
Website: http://www.sixpenny.org

Publishes: Fiction; *Areas:* Arts; Literature; Short Stories; *Markets:* Adult; *Treatments:* Contemporary; Dark; Experimental; Literary; Popular; Progressive; Satirical; Serious; Traditional

Editors: Elizabeth Leonard, Kate Thomas

A digital and print magazine of illustrated short stories. Our stories will be classified as literary fiction, but they'll also be entertaining as a rule. Each issue has six stories that take six minutes to read: three by established authors, and three by emerging authors.

Sling Magazine

Email: SlingMag@gmail.com
Website: http://www.slingmag.com

Publishes: Essays; Fiction; Interviews; Poetry; *Areas:* Short Stories; *Markets:* Adult; *Treatments:* Literary

Editors: Hope Johnson; Bonita Lee Penn; Kaela Danielle McNeil

Publishes essays, fiction, poetry, art / photography and interviews. See website for current requirements and deadlines. Submit one piece of prose, or up to two poems, by email.

St Petersburg Review

Email: annejjames@gmail.com
Website: http://www.stpetersburgreview.com

Publishes: Essays; Fiction; Nonfiction; Poetry; Scripts; *Areas:* Short Stories; Theatre; *Markets:* Adult; *Treatments:* Literary

Send submissions of up to four poems, fiction, essays, or creative nonfiction up to 7,500 words, or plays up to 30 pages, via online submission system. Accepts submissions between September 1 and January 1 annually.

Star 82 Review

Email: editor@star82review.com
Website: http://star82review.com

Publishes: Essays; Fiction; Nonfiction; *Areas:* Short Stories; *Markets:* Adult; *Treatments:* Literary

Publishes short fiction, creative fiction, mini essays, and work that combines words with visual art. Especially looks for humanity, humility and humour. Submit through website via online submission system.

Straylight

English Department
University of Wisconsin-Parkside
900 Wood Road
Kenosha, WI 53141
Email: submissions@straylightmag.com
Website: http://www.straylightmag.com

Publishes: Fiction; Poetry; *Areas:* Short Stories; *Markets:* Adult; *Treatments:* Literary

Literary magazine with separate print and online editions, with different content. Accepts stories of 1,000-5,000 words for the print edition (but prefers 1,500-3,000), and

up to 1,000 for online. Also publishes novellas up to 45,000 words online only. Poems may be submitted for both print and online editions. See website for specific submission guidelines.

Struggle

Box 28536
Detroit, MI 48228
Email: timhall11@yahoo.com
Website: http://www.strugglemagazine.net

Publishes: Fiction; Poetry; Scripts; *Areas:* Drama; Politics; Short Stories; *Markets:* Adult; *Treatments:* Literary; Progressive

Magazine publishing progressive and revolutionary literature and art expressing the "anti-establishment struggles of the working class and oppressed people in the U. S. and worldwide". Publishes poems, songs, stories, short plays, drawings, cartoons. See website for full details.

The Summerset Review

25 Summerset Drive
Smithtown, New York 11787
Email: editor@summersetreview.org
Website: http://www.summersetreview.org

Publishes: Essays; Fiction; Nonfiction; Poetry; *Areas:* Short Stories; *Markets:* Adult; *Treatments:* Literary

Editors: Joseph Levens

Submit literary fiction and nonfiction up to 8,000 words or up to five poems. Prefers to receive submissions by email. Will accept prose by post but no hard copy poetry submissions. See website for full details.

The Sun

107 N. Roberson Street
Chapel Hill, NC 27516
Tel: +1 (919) 942-5282
Fax: +1 (919) 932-3101
Website: http://thesunmagazine.org

Publishes: Essays; Fiction; Interviews; Nonfiction; Poetry; *Areas:* Culture; Philosophy; Politics; Short Stories; *Markets:*

Adult; *Treatments:* Literary

Publishes essays, interviews, fiction, and poetry. Favours personal writing, but also looking for thoughtful, well-written essays on political, cultural, and philosophical themes. No journalistic features, academic works, or opinion pieces.

Suspense Magazine
26500 Agoura Road, #102-474
Calabasas, CA 91302
Email: editor@suspensemagazine.com
Website: http://www.suspensemagazine.com

Publishes: Fiction; Nonfiction; Reviews; *Areas:* Horror; Mystery; Short Stories; Suspense; Thrillers; *Markets:* Adult

Magazine of suspense, mystery, horror, and thriller fiction. Send stories up to 5,000 words in the body of an email. No attachments. Response not guaranteed unless story is accepted.

T. Gene Davis's Speculative Blog
Email: tgenedavis@gmail.com
Website: http://tgenedavis.com/submission-guidelines/

Publishes: Fiction; *Areas:* Fantasy; Gothic; Horror; Sci-Fi; Short Stories; *Markets:* Adult; Family; *Treatments:* Dark; Experimental; Light; Literary; Mainstream; Popular; Satirical; Serious

Editors: T. Gene Davis

A web-based magazine releasing a family-friendly speculative story every Monday, mostly by guest authors. Speculative stories include horror, fantasy, science fiction and other related genres.

The stories accepted are for adults with mature themes, but safe to read out loud with children in the room. All stories MUST be written so that adults will enjoy them.

Stories can be of any length. This includes flash fiction, short stories, novelettes, and novellas. Preference is given to flash fiction

and short stories. Formatting should be in standard manuscript format.

Payment for accepted stories is made upon my receipt of the signed author agreement.

Tales of the Talisman
Hadrosaur Productions
PO Box 2194
Mesilla Park, NM 88047-2194
Email: hadrosaur@zianet.com
Website: http://www.talesofthetalisman.com

Publishes: Fiction; Poetry; *Areas:* Fantasy; Horror; Sci-Fi; Short Stories; *Markets:* Adult

Editors: David L. Summers

Publishes Science Fiction, fantasy, and horror short stories up to 6,000 words and poems up to 50 lines. Accepts submissions by post and by email. See website for full guidelines.

Talking River
Lewis-Clark State College
500 8th Avenue
Lewiston, ID 83501
Email: talkingriver@lcmail.lcsc.edu
Website: http://www.lcsc.edu/talking-river/

Publishes: Fiction; Nonfiction; Poetry; Reviews; *Areas:* Short Stories; *Markets:* Adult; *Treatments:* Literary

Submit fiction or creative nonfiction up to 4,000 words, or up to five poems at a time. Also publishes reviews between 500 and 1,000 words. Accepts submissions between August 1 and April 1. Include cover letter, email address for correspondence, and SASE for return of material. See website for full guidelines.

Tattoo Highway
Email: submissions@tattoohighway.org
Website: http://www.tattoohighway.org

Publishes: Fiction; Poetry; *Areas:* Short Stories; *Markets:* Adult; *Treatments:* Literary

Online magazine publishing fiction and poetry. Submit by email as RTF attachments, or as plain text in the body of your email.

The Teacher's Voice
PO Box 150384
Kew Gardens, NY 11415
Email: editor@the-teachers-voice.org
Website: http://www.the-teachers-voice.org

Publishes: Fiction; Nonfiction; Poetry; Scripts; *Areas:* Drama; Short Stories; *Markets:* Professional; *Treatments:* Experimental; Literary

Literary magazine for poets and writers in education. Publishes poems, flash fiction, flash creative nonfiction, flash plays, and flash experimental. Simultaneous submissions accepted if immediate notification of acceptance elsewhere is given. Send query with up to 5 pages of poetry, or prose pieces no longer than 1,500 words. Prefers shorter work. See website for full submission guidelines, and/or to submit using online submission system.

The Health Journal
4808 Courthouse Street, Suite 204
Williamsburg, VA 23188
Tel: +1 (757) 645-4475
Email: editorial@thehealthjournals.com
Website: http://www.thehealthjournals.com

Publishes: Articles; Nonfiction; *Areas:* Health; *Markets:* Adult

Health magazine focussing on Virginia, but willing to publish articles of both local and national interest.

The Write Place at the Write Time
Email: submissions@
thewriteplaceatthewritetime.org
Website: http://www.
thewriteplaceatthewritetime.org

Publishes: Essays; Fiction; Nonfiction; Poetry; *Areas:* Short Stories; *Markets:* Adult; *Treatments:* Literary

Editors: Nicole M. Bouchard

Online magazine publishing fiction, poetry, and personal essays in a memoir style. Send up to three short stories, up to five poems, or up to three essays per issue. Send submissions in the body of an email – no attachments. See website for full guidelines.

34th Parallel
Email: 34thParallel@gmail.com
Website: http://www.34thparallel.net

Publishes: Essays; Fiction; Nonfiction; Poetry; Scripts; *Areas:* Short Stories; *Markets:* Adult; *Treatments:* Literary

Editors: Tracey Boone Swan; Martin Chipperfield

Publishes fiction, creative nonfiction, essays, scripts, poetry, and artwork. Submit via online submission system. $6 fee includes download of latest digital edition.

Timber
Email: timberjournal@gmail.com
Website: http://www.timberjournal.com

Publishes: Fiction; Nonfiction; Poetry; *Areas:* Short Stories; *Markets:* Adult; *Treatments:* Literary

Editors: Matthew Treon

Publishes innovative fiction, flash fiction, poetry, nonfiction, visual art and webcomics. Accepts prose up to 5,000 words and 3-5 poems. One submission per reading period (August to March) only. Submit using submission system on website.

Toad Suck Review
Email: toadsucksubmit@gmail.com
Website: http://www.toadsuckreview.org

Publishes: Fiction; Interviews; Nonfiction; Poetry; Reviews; Scripts; *Areas:* Autobiography; Culture; Literature; Nature; Politics; Short Stories; *Markets:* Adult

Editors: Mark Spitzer

Publishes a wide range of fiction, nonfiction, and poetry. Offers open and ambiguous guidelines: "Don't send us too much and don't make it too long". See website for more details.

Toasted Cheese Literary Journal

Email: submit@toasted-cheese.com
Website: http://www.toasted-cheese.com

Publishes: Fiction; *Areas:* Short Stories; *Markets:* Adult; *Treatments:* Literary

Quarterly e-zine. Submit flash fiction up to 500 words; fiction up to 5,000 words; creative nonfiction up to 5,000 words; or up to five poems. See website for full submission guidelines.

Trail of Indiscretion

Email: realm.beyond@yahoo.com
Website: http://www.fortresspublishinginc.com

Publishes: Fiction; *Areas:* Short Stories; *Markets:* Adult; Youth

Editors: Brian Koscienski

Magazine publishing short stories and graphic novel storytelling in the genres of science fiction, fantasy, and horror. No profanity or graphic scenes. Send submissions as Word documents by email.

Trajectory

PO Box 655
Frankfort, KY 40602
Tel: +1 (502) 330-4746
Email: adobechris@hotmail.com
Website: http://www.trajectoryjournal.com

Publishes: Fiction; Interviews; Nonfiction; Poetry; Reviews; *Areas:* Autobiography; Short Stories; *Markets:* Adult; Literary

Editors: Chris Helvey

Publishes fiction, poetry, creative nonfiction, memoirs, book reviews, and author interviews. No fiction or poetry for young

children, young adult, fantasy, romance, sci-fi, or horror. Send submissions by post with SASE and 25-75 word bio. No electronic submissions.

Transition Magazine

Hutchins Center for African & African American Research
Harvard University
104 Mount Auburn Street, 3R
Cambridge, MA 02138
Tel: +1 (617) 495-8508
Fax: +1 (617) 495-8511
Email: HutchinsCenter@fas.harvard.edu
Website: http://hutchinscenter.fas.harvard.edu/transition

Publishes: Essays; Fiction; Interviews; Nonfiction; Poetry; Reviews; *Areas:* Culture; Short Stories; *Markets:* Adult; *Treatments:* Literary

Magazine publishing material from and about Africa and the Diaspora. Publishes short stories, novel extracts, poetry, creative nonfiction, essays, reviews, and interviews. See website for full submission guidelines and online submission system.

TriQuarterly

Email: triquarterly@northwestern.edu
Website: http://www.triquarterly.org

Publishes: Essays; Features; Fiction; Interviews; Nonfiction; Poetry; Reviews; Scripts; *Areas:* Drama; Literature; *Markets:* Adult; *Treatments:* Literary

University online literary magazine. Accepts submissions of fiction, creative nonfiction, poetry, short drama, video essays and hybrid work from established and emerging writers between October 15 and July 15 only. Accepts interviews, reviews and other features year-round. See website for full submission guidelines and online submission manager.

Tulane Review

122 Norman Mayer
Tulane University
New Orleans, LA 70118

Email: litsoc@tulane.edu
Website: http://www.tulane.edu/~litsoc/
ueview.html

Publishes: Fiction; Poetry; *Areas:* Arts;
Literature; Short Stories; *Markets:* Adult;
Treatments: Literary

Literary arts journal publishing poetry, prose,
and artwork. Submit up to five poems or
prose up 4,000 words by email, or by post
with SASE. See website for full guidelines.

US Catholic
205 West Monroe Street
Chicago, IL 60606
Email: submissions@uscatholic.org
Website: http://www.uscatholic.org

Publishes: Articles; Essays; Features;
Fiction; Nonfiction; Poetry; Reviews; *Areas:*
Religious; Short Stories; Spiritual; *Markets:*
Adult

Religious magazine aimed at Catholics. See
website for detailed submission guidelines
and separate email address for submissions
of short stories and poetry.

Vanillerotica
Email: talentdripseroticpublishing@
yahoo.com
Website: http://eroticatalentdrips.
wordpress.com

Publishes: Fiction; *Areas:* Erotic; Romance;
Markets: Adult

Editors: Kimberly Steele

Print and electronic magazine publishing
erotic and romantic short fiction between
10,000 and 15,000 words, plus poetry up to
30 lines.

Verse
English Department, University of
Richmond, Richmond, VA 23173
Website: http://versemag.blogspot.com

Publishes: Fiction; Nonfiction; Poetry;
Areas: Short Stories; *Markets:* Adult;

Treatments: Literary

Editors: Brian Henry and Andrew Zawacki

Magazine publishing poetry, fiction,
nonfiction, and visual art. Originally founded
in England in 1984, it moved to its current
US home in 2005. Submissions should be
chapbook-length (20-40 pages long), and
entirely unpublished. Current subscribers
may submit for free; non-subscribers must
pay a $10 reading fee.

Washington Square Review
Creative Writing Program
New York University
58 West 10th St.
New York, NY 10011
Email: washingtonsquarereview@gmail.com
Website: http://washingtonsquarereview.com

Publishes: Fiction; Poetry; *Areas:* Short
Stories; Translations; *Markets:* Adult;
Treatments: Literary

Nationally distributed literary journal
publishing fiction and poetry by emerging
and established writers. Submit fiction up to
50 pages, or up to 5 poems up to 10 pages
total. Reading periods run August 1 to
October 15 and December 15 to February 1.
Accepts submissions by post or online using
website submission system.

Wesleyan Life
PO Box 50434
Indianapolis, IN 46250
Tel: +1 (317) 774-7900
Email: info@wesleyan.org
Website: http://www.wesleyanlifeonline.com

Publishes: Articles; Nonfiction; *Areas:*
Religious; *Markets:* Adult

Magazine publishing inspirational and
religious articles. No poetry. Send complete
ms.

Whole Life Times
Whole Life Media, LLC
23705 Vanowen Street, #306
West Hills, CA 91307

Tel: +1 (877) 807-2599
Fax: +1 (310) 933-1693
Email: abigail@wholelifemagazine.com
Website: http://www.wholelifemagazine.com

Publishes: Articles; Interviews; Nonfiction; *Areas:* Finance; Health; Lifestyle; Medicine; Nature; New Age; Sociology; Spiritual; *Markets:* Adult

Publishes stories that deal with a progressive, healthy lifestyle, including stories on natural health, alternative healing, green living, sustainable and local food, social responsibility, conscious business, the environment, spirituality and personal growth. Relies heavily on freelances. See website for full submission guidelines.

Willow Review

19351 West Washington Street
Grayslake, IL 60030-1198
Tel: +1 (847) 543-2956
Email: com426@clcillinois.edu
Website: http://www.clcillinois.edu/campus-life/arts/literary-arts/willow-review

Publishes: Fiction; Nonfiction; Poetry; *Areas:* Short Stories; *Markets:* Adult; *Treatments:* Literary

Send up to five poems, or short fiction or creative nonfiction up to 7,000 words, with SASE. Prize money for the best poetry and prose in the issue. See website for full details.

Windhover

UMHB Box 8008
900 College Street
Belton, TX 76513
Email: windhover@umhb.edu
Website: http://undergrad.umhb.edu/english/windhover-journal

Publishes: Fiction; Nonfiction; Poetry; *Areas:* Religious; Short Stories; Spiritual; *Markets:* Adult

Editors: Dr Nathaniel Hansen

Magazine publishing poetry, fiction, and creative nonfiction that considers Christian and spiritual perspectives and themes. Submit via online submission system between Feb 1 and Aug 1 annually.

Wine Press Northwest

333 West Canal Drive
Kennewick, WA 99336
Tel: +1 (509) 582-1443
Email: gmcconnell@winepressnw.com
Website: http://www.winepressnw.com

Publishes: Articles; Features; Interviews; Nonfiction; *Areas:* Historical; Travel; *Markets:* Adult

Editors: Gregg McConnell

Wine magazine focusing on wines of Washington, Oregon, Idaho and British Columbia.

Wine Spectator

M. Shanken Communications
387 Park Avenue South
New York, NY 10016
Tel: +1 (212) 684-4224
Email: wsonline@mshanken.com
Website: http://www.winespectator.com

Publishes: Articles; Features; Interviews; News; Nonfiction; *Areas:* Hobbies; Travel; *Markets:* Adult

Consumer magazine publishing news, interviews, features, and articles aimed at wine enthusiasts. Send query in first instance.

Wisconsin Review

University of Wisconsin Oshkosh
800 Algoma Boulevard
Oshkosh, WI 54901
Tel: +1 (920) 424-2267
Email: wisconsinreview@uwosh.edu
Website: http://www.uwosh.edu/wisconsinreview

Publishes: Essays; Fiction; Nonfiction; Poetry; *Areas:* Short Stories; *Markets:* Adult; *Treatments:* Literary

Publishes fiction, poetry, and essays. Submit

3-5 poems or up to 15 double-spaced pages of fiction or nonfiction. Submit by post or online for $3 fee (free for subscribers).

Witches & Pagans
BBI Media
PO Box 687
Forest Grove, OR 97116
Tel: +1 (503) 430-8817
Email: editor2@bbimedia.com
Website: http://www.witchesandpagans.com

Publishes: Articles; Essays; Fiction;
Interviews; Nonfiction; Poetry; Reviews;
Areas: Religious; Short Stories; Spiritual;
Markets: Adult

Magazine of pagan spirituality. Submit by email. See website for full details.

Woodshop News
10 Bokum Road
Essex, CT 06426
Tel: +1 (860) 767-8227
Fax: +1 (860) 767-1048
Email: editorial@woodshopnews.com
Website: http://www.woodshopnews.com

Publishes: Articles; Features; Interviews;
News; Nonfiction; *Areas:* Business; Crafts;
How-to; *Markets:* Professional

Magazine for professional woodworkers.
Send query or complete ms.

The Worcester Review
1 Ekman St
Worcester, MA 01602
Email: twr.diane@gmail.com
Website: http://www.theworcesterreview.org

Publishes: Articles; Fiction; Nonfiction;
Poetry; *Areas:* Literature; Short Stories;
Markets: Adult; *Treatments:* Literary

Editors: Diane Mulligan

Publishes poetry, fiction, and literary
articles. No submissions by email. Submit by
post only, including email address and
telephone number for response. Do not send

SASE, as responses will be electronic only
See website for full guidelines.

Word Riot
PO Box 414
Middletown, NJ 07748-3143
Email: wr.submissions@gmail.com
Website: http://www.wordriot.org

Publishes: Fiction; Interviews; Nonfiction;
Poetry; Reviews; *Areas:* Short Stories;
Markets: Adult; *Treatments:* Experimental;
Literary

Online magazine publishing short stories,
flash fiction, novel excerpts, creative
nonfiction, poetry, reviews, and interviews.
Likes edgy and experimental material.
Maximum one entry per writer per quarter
across all genres. Submit online via website.

Wordpeace
Email: editors.wordpeace@gmail.com
Website: http://wordpeace.co

Publishes: Articles; Fiction; Interviews;
Nonfiction; Poetry; *Areas:* Short Stories;
Markets: Adult; *Treatments:* Literary

Editors: Monica A. Hand, Poetry; Joanna
Eleftheriou, Nonfiction; Oonagh C. Doherty,
Fiction

Online journal of literary response to world
events in the spirit of promoting peace and
hope for all people. Seeks poems, stories and
articles or interviews that reflect or are in
conversation with world events. Submit
using online submission system.

Workers Write
Blue Cubicle Press
PO Box 250382
Plano, TX 75025-0382
Email: coliseum@workerswritejournal.com
Website: http://www.
workerswritejournal.com

Publishes: Fiction; Poetry; *Areas:* Short
Stories; *Markets:* Adult

Magazine publishing stories and poems from

the world of work. Each issue concentrates on one specific industry – see website for current focus, submission deadlines, and details on how to submit.

Writer's Bloc

MSC 162, Fore Hall 110
700 University Boulevard
Texas A&M University-Kingsville
Kingsville, Texas 78363
Email: WritersBlocLitMag@hotmail.com
Website: http://www.tamuk.edu/artsci/
langlit/index4.html

Publishes: Essays; Fiction; Interviews; Nonfiction; Poetry; Scripts; *Areas:* Drama; Short Stories; Translations; *Markets:* Adult; *Treatments:* Literary

Editors: Dr Octavio Quintanilla

Publishes poetry, short fiction, flash fiction, one-act plays, interviews, and essays from around the world. Publishes in multiple languages, with or without translation. All work must be submitted by February. No new work accepted February to May. See website for more details and for submission form.

The Writing Disorder

PO Box 93613
Los Angeles, CA 90093-0613
Email: submit@thewritingdisorder.com
Website: http://www.thewritingdisorder.com

Publishes: Articles; Nonfiction; Poetry; Reviews; *Areas:* Short Stories; *Markets:* Adult; *Treatments:* Experimental; Literary; Traditional

Editors: C.E. Lukather

Publishes: Fiction, Poetry, Nonfiction, Art, Reviews, Comic Art, Experimental. Send prose or poetry to appropriate email addresses (see website) as MS Word attachments, or submit by post or via online form. No specific guidelines regarding subject matter, and no length limits. Traditional accepted as well as experimental.

Written By

7000 West Third Street
Los Angeles, CA 90048
Tel: +1 (323) 782-4699
Website: http://www.wga.org/writtenby/
writtenby.aspx

Publishes: Articles; Essays; Features; Interviews; Nonfiction; *Areas:* Business; Film; TV; *Markets:* Professional

Magazine for screen and TV writers, aimed at those already inside the industry rather than those trying to break in.

Xavier Review

Xavier University of Louisiana
1 Drexel Drive Box 89
New Orleans, LA 70125
Email: radamo@xula.edu
Website: http://www.xula.edu/review

Publishes: Essays; Fiction; Nonfiction; Poetry; *Areas:* Criticism; Religious; Short Stories; Spiritual; *Markets:* Adult; *Treatments:* Literary

Editors: Ralph Adamo

Publishes poetry, fiction, translations, personal essays, and critical essays. Willing to consider all themes, but particularly interested in African American, Caribbean and Southern literature, as well as works that touch on issues of religion and spirituality. Rarely publishes mss over 20 pages. Send complete ms by post with SASE. No simultaneous submissions. See website for full guidelines.

Yachting Magazine

55 Hammarlund Way
Middletown, RI 02842
Fax: +1 (401) 845-5180
Email: letters@yachtingmagazine.com
Website: http://www.yachtingmagazine.com

Publishes: Articles; Nonfiction; *Areas:* Hobbies; Travel; *Markets:* Adult

Magazine on yachting, aimed at an experienced and knowledgeable audience.

Send query with published clips in first instance.

Zeek

125 Maiden Lane, 8th Floor
New York, NY 10038
Email: zeek@zeek.net
Website: http://zeek.forward.com

Publishes: Articles; Essays; Fiction; Nonfiction; Poetry; *Areas:* Arts; Culture; Religious; Spiritual; *Markets:* Adult; *Treatments:* Progressive

Editors: Erica Brody

Jewish online magazine launched in 2001 and relaunched in 2013 as a hub for the domestic Jewish social justice movement. Publishes first-person essays, commentary, reporting, fiction, and poetry. Send query by email in first instance. Not accepting fiction submissions as at January 2015.

Zink

Email: fashion@zinkmediagroup.com
Website: http://www.zinkmagazine.com

Publishes: Articles; Features; Nonfiction; *Areas:* Beauty and Fashion; *Markets:* Adult

Editors: Leila Cole; Jennifer Stevens

Fashion magazine. Like edgy material. Submission must be in line with the theme of the issue. See website for upcoming themes and detailed submission guidelines.

ZYZZYVA

57 Post Street, Suite 604
San Francisco, CA 94104
Tel: +1 (415) 752-4393
Fax: +1 (415) 752-4391
Email: editor@zyzzyva.org
Website: http://www.zyzzyva.org

Publishes: Fiction; Nonfiction; Poetry; *Areas:* Short Stories; Translations; *Markets:* Adult; *Treatments:* Literary

Publishes material by writers living on the West Coast, in Alaska and Hawaii only. Submit one piece of fiction or nonfiction or up to five poems at a time, with SASE for response. No restrictions as to length of item or number of items submitted. Accepts simultaneous submissions, but notify if accepted elsewhere. No submissions by email. Accepts submissions from January 1 to May 31 and from August 1 to November 30 only. See website for full guidelines.

UK Magazines

For the most up-to-date listings of these and hundreds of other magazines, visit http://www.firstwriter.com/magazines

*To claim your **free** access to the site, please see the back of this book.*

Acumen

6 The Mount
Higher Furzeham
Brixham
South Devon
TQ5 8QY
Tel: +44 (0) 1803 851098
Email: patriciaoxley6@gmail.com
Website: http://www.acumen-poetry.co.uk

Publishes: Articles; Features; Interviews; Nonfiction; Poetry; Reviews; *Areas:* Criticism; Literature; *Markets:* Adult; *Treatments:* Literary

Editors: Patricia Oxley

Magazine publishing poetry and articles, features, and reviews connected to poetry. Send submissions with SAE and author details on each page, or submit by email as Word attachment. See website for full submission guidelines.

Aesthetica: A Review of Contemporary Artists

PO Box 371
York
YO23 1WL
Tel: +44 (0) 1904 629137
Email: info@aestheticamagazine.com
Website: http://www.aestheticamagazine.com

Publishes: Articles; Essays; Features; Fiction; Interviews; News; Nonfiction; Poetry; Reviews; *Areas:* Arts; Culture; Current Affairs; Drama; Film; Humour; Literature; Music; Short Stories; Theatre; Women's Interests; *Markets:* Adult; *Treatments:* Literary

Editors: Cherie Federico

I am the founder and editor of a literary and arts magazine that I actually began with my MA fee money (I eventually paid the fees and received my MA). I started the magazine because I believe that there are too many closed doors in the literary and art world. I believe in making the arts accessible and available for all. My convictions are deep because I believe that in this modern, some say, post-modern world that we live in it is important to remember the essentials about being human. There are too many reality TV shows that mock existence. As a culture we are slipping away from the arts. Writing has too many stigmas attached and people believe that there are too many rules. My aim was to bring a magazine to life that would challenge some of these notions and make a difference.

This writing and artistic platform is spreading across the UK and making it to places like Israel, Italy, Ireland, New Zealand, Australia, America, Canada, Bulgaria, and Switzerland. We started in

York and are now selling at Borders in York, Leeds, Brighton, Islington, and Oxford Street as well as in some local York bookshops and direct either from the website or by post.

I believe that art and literature is something that is found within all of us. We need to believe in ourselves and see the beauty of the moment to take this concept further. With my literary magazine I have created a space for new ideas and fresh opinions. I believe in creativity, diversity, and equality.

Africa Confidential

37 John's Mews
London
WC1N 2NS
Tel: +44 (0) 20 7831 3511
Email: andrew@africa-confidential.com
Website: http://www.africa-confidential.com

Publishes: Articles; News; Nonfiction; *Areas:* Finance; Politics; *Markets:* Adult

Editors: Andrew Weir, Deputy Editor

Magazine publishing news and articles on African politics and economics. Welcomes unsolicited mss.

Africa-Asia Confidential

73 Farringdon Road
London
EC1M 3JQ
Tel: +44 (0) 20 7831 3511
Fax: +44 (0) 20 7831 6778
Email: editorial@africa-asia-confidential.com
Website: http://www.africa-asia-confidential.com

Publishes: Articles; Features; News; Nonfiction; *Areas:* Current Affairs; *Markets:* Adult

Editors: Clare Tauben

Publishes news articles and features focussing on the Africa-Asia axis. Welcomes unsolicited mss, but must be unpublished and offered exclusively.

African Business

IC Publications Ltd
7 Coldbath Square
EC1R 4LQ
London
Tel: +44 (0) 20 7841 3210
Fax: +44 (0) 20 7841 3211
Email: editorial@icpublications.com
Website: http://africanbusinessmagazine.com

Publishes: Articles; Nonfiction; *Areas:* Business; Finance; *Markets:* Professional

Editors: Anver Versi

Bestselling pan-African business magazine. Special reports profile a wide range of sectors and industries including transport, energy, mining, construction, aviation and agriculture.

Agenda

The Wheelwrights
Fletching Street
Mayfield
East Sussex
TN20 6TL
Tel: +44 (0) 1435 873703
Email: submissions@agendapoetry.co.uk
Website: http://www.agendapoetry.co.uk

Publishes: Essays; Poetry; Reviews; *Areas:* Criticism; Literature; *Markets:* Adult; *Treatments:* Literary

Editors: Patricia McCarthy

Publishes poems, critical essays, and reviews. Send up to five poems or up to two essays / reviews with email address, age, and short bio. No previously published material. Submit by email only, with each piece in a separate Word attachment. Accepts work only during specific submission windows – see website for current status.

All Out Cricket

TriNorth Ltd
Fourth Floor
Bedser Stand
Kia Oval
Kennington
London

SE11 5SS
Tel: +44 (0) 20 3696 5732
Email: comments@alloutcricket.com
Website: http://www.alloutcricket.com

Publishes: Articles; Interviews; News;
Nonfiction; *Areas:* Sport; *Markets:* Adult

Editors: Phil Walker

Cricket magazine. Send query by email in
first instance.

Ambit

Staithe House
Main Road
Brancaster Staithe
Norfolk
PE31 8BP
Tel: +44 (0) 7503 633601
Email: info@ambitmagazine.co.uk
Website: http://ambitmagazine.co.uk

Publishes: Fiction; Poetry; *Areas:* Arts;
Short Stories; *Markets:* Adult; *Treatments:*
Literary

An international magazine. Potential
contributors are advised to read a copy
before submitting work to us. Send up to 5
poems, a story up to 5,000 words, or flash
fiction up to 1,000 words. Submit via online
portal on website, or by post (see website for
full details). No submissions by email. Two
reading periods per year. For poetry: Feb 1 to
April 1; and Sep 1 to Nov 1. For fiction: Feb
1 to March 1; and Sep 1 to Oct 1.

Android Magazine

Richmond House
33 Richmond Hill
Bournemouth
Dorset
BH2 6EZ
Tel: +44 (0) 1202 586200
Email: enquiries@imagine-publishing.co.uk
Website: http://www.littlegreenrobot.co.uk

Publishes: Articles; Features; News;
Nonfiction; Reviews; *Areas:* How-to;
Technology; *Markets:* Adult

Magazine covering the Android operating

system, including news, features, reviews,
and tips. Send query by email. No
unsolicited mss.

Angler's Mail

Pinehurst 2
Pinehurst Road
Farnborough Business Park
Farnborough
Hampshire
GU14 7BF
Tel: +44 (0) 1252 555055
Email: anglersmail@timeinc.com
Website: http://www.anglersmail.co.uk

Publishes: Features; News; Nonfiction;
Areas: Hobbies; Sport; *Markets:* Adult

Publishes pictures, stories, and features
relating to angling news and matches.

Aquila

Studio 2
67A Willowfield Road
Eastbourne
East Sussex
BN22 8AP
Tel: +44 (0) 1323 431313
Fax: +44 (0) 1323 731136
Email: info@aquila.co.uk
Website: https://www.aquila.co.uk

Publishes: Features; Fiction; Nonfiction;
Areas: Short Stories; *Markets:* Children's

Magazine for children aged 8-13. Publishes
fiction 1,000-1,150 words; serials 1,050-
1,150 words per episode; and features
between 600 and 800 words. See website for
full submission guidelines.

Arc

c/o New Scientist
Lacon House
84 Theobald's Road
London
WC1X 8NS
Tel: +44 (0) 20 7611 1205
Email: simon.ings@arcfinity.org
Website: http://www.arcfinity.org

Publishes: Essays; Features; Fiction;

Nonfiction; *Areas:* Science; Sci-Fi; Short
Stories; *Markets:* Adult

Editors: Simon Ings

"Journal of the future". Publishes features,
essays, and speculative fiction about the
world to come. Most work is commissioned.

Architecture Today
34 Pentonville Road
London
N1 9HF
Tel: +44 (0) 20 7837 0143
Email: editorial@architecturetoday.co.uk
Website: http://www.architecturetoday.co.uk

Publishes: Articles; Features; Nonfiction;
Areas: Architecture; *Markets:* Professional

Monthly magazine for architects, presenting
the most important current projects in the
UK and the rest of Europe.

Artificium
Email: editor@artificium.co.uk
Website: http://www.artificium.co.uk

Publishes: Fiction; Poetry; *Areas:* Short
Stories; *Markets:* Adult; *Treatments:*
Literary

Publishes short fiction between 2,000 and
6,000 words; three-part serials up to a total
of 12,000 words; very short fiction between
400 and 1,250 words; and poetry of any
length. All work must be in English and
submitted by email during open reading
periods: see website for details.

ArtReview
1 Honduras Street
London
EC1Y 0TH
Tel: +44 (0) 20 7490 8138
Email: artreview@abacusemedia.com
Website: http://artreview.com

Publishes: Articles; News; Nonfiction;
Reviews; *Areas:* Arts; Criticism; *Markets:*
Adult; *Treatments:* Contemporary

International contemporary art magazine,
dedicated to expanding contemporary art's
audience and reach.

Assent
Room E701
Kedelston Road
University of Derby
Derby
DE22 1GB
Email: editorassent@gmail.com
Website: http://assentpoetry.com

Publishes: Essays; Interviews; Nonfiction;
Poetry; Reviews; *Areas:* Criticism;
Literature; *Markets:* Adult; *Treatments:*
Literary

Editors: Julia Gaze

A leading small press magazine with a world
wide circulation and readership. Publishes
poetry, critical essays, interviews and
reviews of contemporary collections.

Athletics Weekly
Athletics Weekly Limited
PO Box 614
Farnham
Surrey
GU9 1GR
Tel: +44 (0) 1733 808531
Fax: +44 (0) 1733 808530
Email: jason.henderson@
athleticsweekly.com
Website: http://www.athletics-weekly.com

Publishes: Features; News; Nonfiction;
Areas: Sport; *Markets:* Adult

Editors: Jason Henderson

Publishes features, news, and fixtures
relating to track and field, race walking,
sport politics, etc. Send query in writing in
first instance.

Attitude
Attitude Media Ltd
33 Pear Tree Street
London
EC1V 3AG

Email: matthew.todd@attitude.co.uk
Website: http://attitude.co.uk

Publishes: Articles; Features; News;
Nonfiction; *Areas:* Beauty and Fashion;
Entertainment; Lifestyle; Men's Interests;
Travel; *Markets:* Adult

Editors: Matthew Todd (Editorial Director)

Magazine for gay men.

The Author

84 Drayton Gardens
London
SW10 9SB
Tel: +44 (0) 207 7373 6642
Email: theauthor@societyofauthors.org
Website: http://www.societyofauthors.org

Publishes: Articles; Nonfiction; *Areas:*
Business; How-to; Legal; *Markets:*
Professional

Editors: James McConnachie

Magazine covering all aspects of the writing
profession, including legal, technical, and
commercial considerations. Query in writing
in first instance.

Banipal

1 Gough Square
London
EC4A 3DE
Tel: +44 (0) 20 7832 1350
Fax: +44 (0) 20 8568 8509
Email: editor@banipal.co.uk
Website: http://www.banipal.co.uk

Publishes: Features; Fiction; Poetry;
Reviews; *Areas:* Short Stories; Translations;
Markets: Adult

Editors: Margaret Obank

Contemporary Arab authors in English
translations. Publishes new and established
writers, and diverse material including
translations, poetry, short stories, novel
excerpts, profiles, interviews, appreciations,
book reviews, reports of literary festivals,
conferences, and prizes.

Bare Fiction Magazine

177 Copthorne Road
Shrewsbury
Shropshire
SY3 8NA
Email: info@barefiction.co.uk
Website: http://www.
barefictionmagazine.co.uk

Publishes: Essays; Fiction; Interviews;
Nonfiction; Poetry; Reviews; Scripts; *Areas:*
Drama; Literature; Short Stories; Theatre;
Markets: Adult; *Treatments:* Literary

Publishes poetry, fiction and plays, literary
review, interviews and commentary. Does
not accept submissions at all times – check
website for current status and sign up to
newsletter to be notified when submissions
next open.

The Beano

185 Fleet Street
London
EC4A 2HS
Tel: +44 (0) 1382 575580
Fax: +44 (0) 1382 575413
Email: beano@dcthomson.co.uk
Website: http://www.beano.com

Publishes: Fiction; *Areas:* Humour; Short
Stories; *Markets:* Children's

Publishes comic strips for children aged 6-
12. Accepts artwork and scripts.

The Big Issue

43 Bath Street
Glasgow
G2 1HW
Tel: +44 (0) 1413 527280
Email: editorial@bigissue.com
Website: http://www.bigissue.com

Publishes: Articles; Features; Interviews;
News; Reviews; *Areas:* Arts; Culture;
Sociology; *Markets:* Adult

General interest magazine focusing on social
issues, culture, the arts, etc. No short stories
or poetry.

Bizarre

Dennis Publishing
30 Cleveland Street
London
W1T 4JD
Tel: +44 (0) 20 7907 6000
Email: bizarre@dennis.co.uk
Website: http://www.bizarremag.com

Publishes: Articles; Features; Interviews;
News; Nonfiction; *Markets:* Adult

Describes itself as one of the most shocking
magazines in the world. Publishes features,
interviews, and uncensored photos of the
weird, freakish, and outrageous. No fiction.

Black Static

TTA Press
5 Martins Lane
Witcham
Ely
Cambs
CB6 2LB
Website: http://ttapress.com

Publishes: Fiction; *Areas:* Fantasy; Horror;
Short Stories; *Markets:* Adult; *Treatments:*
Dark

Editors: Andy Cox

Publishes short stories of horror and dark
fantasy. See website for full guidelines and
online submission system.

British Birds

4 Harlequin Gardens
St Leonards on Sea
East Sussex
TN37 7PF

EDITORIAL
Spindrift
Eastshore
Virkie
Shetland
ZE3 9JS
Tel: +44 (0) 1424 755155
Fax: +44 (0) 1424 755155
Email: editor@britishbirds.co.uk
Website: https://britishbirds.co.uk

Publishes: Articles; Nonfiction; *Areas:*
Nature; *Markets:* Adult

Editors: Roger Riddington

Magazine for birdwatchers, publishing
articles on behaviour, conservation,
distribution, identification, status and
taxonomy.

British Journal of Photography

Apptitude Media Ltd
Unit A, Zetland House
5-25 Scrutton Street
Shoreditch
London
EC2A 4HJ
Tel: +44 (0) 20 8123 6873
Email: bjp.editor@bjphoto.co.uk
Website: http://www.bjp-online.com

Publishes: Articles; News; Nonfiction;
Reviews; *Areas:* Arts; Beauty and Fashion;
Photography; Technology; *Markets:*
Professional

Editors: Simon Bainbridge

Magazine for professional photographers,
publishing articles and reviews.

British Journalism Review

SAGE Publications
1 Oliver's Yard
55 City Road
London
EC1Y 1SP
Tel: +44 (0) 20 7324 8500
Fax: 20 7324 8600
Email: editor@bjr.org.uk
Website: http://www.bjr.org.uk

Publishes: Articles; Nonfiction; *Areas:*
Media; *Markets:* Academic

Editors: Kim Fletcher

Quarterly peer-reviewed academic journal
covering the field of journalism. Welcomes
letters and articles, by post or by email.

Building

Ludgate House
245 Blackfriars Road
London
SE1 9UY
Tel: +44 (0) 20 7560 4000
Email: sarah.richardson@ubm.com
Website: http://www.building.co.uk

Publishes: Articles; News; Nonfiction;
Areas: Architecture; Business; *Markets:*
Professional

Editors: Sarah Richardson

Magazine for the construction industry.

Bunbury Magazine

Email: submissions@bunburymagazine.com
Website: https://bunburymagazine.com

Publishes: Articles; Fiction; Nonfiction;
Poetry; Reviews; *Areas:* Short Stories;
Markets: Adult; *Treatments:* Literary

Online literary magazine. Publishes anything
from poetry to artwork, flash fiction to
graphic story, life writing to photography,
plus reviews and articles. Send submissions
by email. See website for full guidelines, and
for current issue theme.

Buses

PO Box 14644
Leven
KY9 1WX
Tel: +44 (0) 1780 755131
Fax: +44 (0) 1780 751323
Email: buseseditor@btconnect.com
Website: http://www.busesmag.com

Publishes: Articles; Nonfiction; *Areas:*
Travel; *Markets:* Adult; Professional

Editors: Alan Millar

The UK's highest circulation magazine
covering the bus and coach industries.
Aimed at both industry professionals and
interested enthusiasts. Query in first instance.

Cambridge Magazine

Winship Road
Milton
Cambridge
Cambridgeshire
CB24 6BQ
Tel: +44 (0) 01223 434419
Email: alice.ryan@cambridge-news.co.uk
Website: http://www.cambridge-news.co.uk/
CambridgeMagazine.html

Publishes: Features; Interviews; Nonfiction;
Areas: Arts; Beauty and Fashion; Culture;
Gardening; Lifestyle; Technology; *Markets:*
Adult

Editors: Alice Ryan

Magazine covering Cambridge, including
food and drink, arts and culture, homes and
gardens, fashion and beauty, and gears and
gadgets.

Caravan Magazine

Warners Group Publications
The Maltings
Bourne
Lincs
PE10 9PH
Tel: +44 (0) 1778 392450
Email: johns@warnersgroup.co.uk
Website: http://www.caravanmagazine.co.uk

Publishes: Articles; Nonfiction; *Areas:*
Hobbies; Leisure; Travel; *Markets:* Adult

Editors: John Sootheran

Magazine for those interested in
caravanning.

Carousel

The Saturn Centre
54-76 Bissell Street
Birmingham
B5 7HP
Tel: +44 (0) 1216 227458
Email: carousel.guide@virgin.net
Website: http://www.carouselguide.co.uk

Publishes: Articles; Interviews; Nonfiction;
Reviews; *Areas:* Literature; *Markets:*
Children's

Editors: David Blanch

Magazine publishing reviews of fiction, poetry, and nonfiction books for children. Also publishes articles, author profiles, and interviews.

The Casket of Fictional Delights
Email: joanna@thecasket.co.uk
Website: http://www.thecasket.co.uk

Publishes: Fiction; *Areas:* Short Stories; *Markets:* Adult

Editors: Joanna Sterling

Online magazine. Publishes flash fiction up to 300 words and short stories between 1,200 and 3,000 words. No children's stories, science fiction, excessive swearing, sex or violence. See website for full guidelines and to submit online.

The Caterer
Travel Weekly Group Ltd
52 Grosvenor Gardens
London
SW1W 0AU
Tel: +44 (0) 20 7881 4803
Email: info@thecaterer.com
Website: https://www.thecaterer.com

Publishes: Articles; News; Nonfiction; *Areas:* Business; *Markets:* Professional

Editors: Amanda Afiya

Magazine for hotel, restaurant, foodservice and pub and bar operators.

The Catholic Herald
Herald House
15 Lamb's Passage
Bunhill Row
London
EC1Y 8TQ
Tel: +44 (0) 20 7448 3607
Fax: +44 (0) 20 7448 3603
Email: editorial@catholicherald.co.uk
Website: http://www.catholicherald.co.uk

Publishes: Articles; News; Nonfiction; *Areas:* Religious; *Markets:* Adult

Editors: Luke Coppen

Weekly magazine publishing articles and news for Catholics.

Central and Eastern European London Review
Email: ceel.org@gmail.com
Website: http://ceel.org.uk

Publishes: Articles; Nonfiction; Reviews; *Areas:* Arts; Culture; Film; Literature; Music; Theatre; Travel; *Markets:* Adult

Editors: Robin Ashenden

Online magazine covering all aspects of Central and Eastern European life in London. Send submissions by email.

Ceramic Review
63 Great Russell Street
London
WC1B 3BF
Tel: +44 (0) 20 7183 5583
Fax: +44 (0) 20 3137 0924
Email: editorial@ceramicreview.com
Website: http://www.ceramicreview.com

Publishes: Articles; Features; Nonfiction; Reviews; *Areas:* Crafts; *Markets:* Adult

Magazine covering ceramics and clay art. See website for full submission guidelines.

Chapman
4 Broughton Place
Edinburgh
EH1 3RX
Tel: +44 (0) 131 557 2207
Email: chapman-pub@blueyonder.co.uk
Website: http://www.chapman-pub.co.uk

Publishes: Articles; Essays; Features; Fiction; Nonfiction; Poetry; Reviews; *Areas:* Arts; Criticism; Culture; Literature; Short Stories; Theatre; *Markets:* Adult; *Treatments:* Literary

Editors: Joy Hendry

Describes itself as Scotland's leading literary magazine, publishing new creative writing – poetry, fiction, discussion of cultural affairs, theatre, reviews and the arts in general, plus critical essays. It publishes international as well as Scottish writers and is a dynamic force for artistic and cultural change and development. Always open to new writers and ideas.

Fiction may be of any length, but average is around 3,000 words. Send one piece at a time. Poetry submissions should contain between four and ten poems. Single poems are not usually published.

Articles and reviews are usually commissioned and ideas should be discussed with the editor in advance.

All submissions must include an SAE or IRCs or email address for response. No submissions by email.

Classic Boat
The Chelsea Magazine Company
Jubilee House
2 Jubilee Place
London
SW3 3TQ
Tel: +44 (0) 20 7349 3700
Fax: +44 (0) 20 7349 3701
Email: Dan.Houston@
chelseamagazines.com
Website: http://www.classicboat.co.uk

Publishes: Articles; Features; News; Nonfiction; Reviews; *Areas:* Crafts; Historical; Hobbies; Travel; *Markets:* Adult

Editors: Dan Houston

Showcases classic yachts and traditionally designed workboats, plus news, opinions and reviews. Read at least three previous issues then query for guidelines if appropriate.

Classic Cars
Bauer
Lynch Wood
Peterborough Business Park
Peterborough
Cambridgeshire
PE2 6EA
Tel: +44 (0) 1733 468582
Email: classic.cars@bauermedia.co.uk
Website: http://www.
classiccarsmagazine.co.uk

Publishes: Articles; Nonfiction; *Areas:* Historical; Technology; Travel; *Markets:* Adult

Publishes articles on classic cars and related events.

Closer
Tel: +44 (0) 20 7859 8463
Email: closer@closermag.co.uk
Website: http://www.closeronline.co.uk

Publishes: Articles; Features; News; Nonfiction; *Areas:* Beauty and Fashion; Entertainment; Health; Lifestyle; Women's Interests; *Markets:* Adult

Women's lifestyle magazine publishing news, articles, and features on style and beauty, body and wellbeing, celebrities, and real life stories.

Commando
185 Fleet Street
London
EC4A 2HS
Email: webmaster@commandocomics.com
Website: http://www.commandocomics.com

Publishes: Fiction; *Areas:* Adventure; Military; Short Stories; *Markets:* Adult; Children's; Youth

Publishes stories of action and adventure set in times of war, told in graphic novel format. May be wars of the modern age or ancient wars, or even occasionally wars of the future. Encourages new writers. Send synopsis in first instance.

Cook Vegetarian
25 Phoenix Court
Hawkins Road
Colchester

Essex
CO2 8JY
Tel: +44 (0) 1206 508627
Email: fae@cookveg.co.uk
Website: http://www.
vegetarianrecipesmag.com

Publishes: Nonfiction; *Areas:* Cookery;
Markets: Adult

Editors: Fae Gilfillan

Publishes recipes for meat-free cooking.

craft&design Magazine
PO Box 5
Driffield
East Yorkshire
YO25 8JD
Tel: +44 (0) 1377 255213
Email: info@craftanddesign.net
Website: http://www.craftanddesign.net

Publishes: Articles; Features; News;
Nonfiction; *Areas:* Crafts; Design; *Markets:*
Adult

Editors: Angie Boyer

Publishes material for those interested in
crafts and design. Ideas for articles and
features welcome.

Crafts
44a Pentonville Road
Islington
N1 9BY
Tel: +44 (0) 20 7806 2538
Email: editorial@craftscouncil.org.uk
Website: http://www.craftsmagazine.org.uk

Publishes: Articles; Features; News;
Nonfiction; Reviews; *Areas:* Crafts;
Markets: Adult

Magazine covering crafts. Send query by
email with brief outline and example of
previous work. Response not guaranteed.

Critical Quarterly
Newbury
Crediton

Devon
EX17 5HA
Email: CQpoetry@gmail.com
Website: http://onlinelibrary.wiley.com/
journal/10.1111/(ISSN)1467-8705

Publishes: Essays; Fiction; Nonfiction;
Poetry; *Areas:* Criticism; Culture; Literature;
Short Stories; *Markets:* Adult; *Treatments:*
Literary

Editors: Colin MacCabe

Publishes literary criticism, cultural studies,
poetry and fiction. Send submissions by
email. See website for separate email address
for submissions of criticism.

Crystal Magazine
3 Bowness Avenue
Prenton
Birkenhead
CH43 0SD
Tel: +44 (0) 1516 089736
Email: christinecrystal@hotmail.com
Website: http://www.christinecrystal.
blogspot.com

Publishes: Articles; Fiction; Nonfiction;
Poetry; *Areas:* Drama; Fantasy; Humour;
Literature; Mystery; Nature; Romance; Sci-
Fi; Short Stories; Suspense; Thrillers; Travel;
Westerns; *Markets:* Adult; *Treatments:*
Light; Literary; Mainstream; Popular;
Positive; Traditional

Editors: Christine Carr

A Popular Publication for Creative Writers.

Your poems, your stories, your articles and
more. The editor only considers work from
subscribers.

A4. Spiral-bound and easy to lie open
40 pages. Bi-monthly. Part colour
Stories (true and fiction), articles, poems

Submissions from subscribers can be any
length and theme except erotica.
Work can be sent by email or post.
Handwritten material is acceptable.
Under normal circumstances you will not
have to wait weeks and weeks for a reply.

Readers' Letters (usually pages and pages). Subscribers' News. Wordsmithing – Titters, Tips, Titillations. Each issue the writer of the most popular piece will win £10.

There has been a lot of positive feedback over the years. Here are just two comments:

"The magazine is good value for money and worth every penny."   Alan Jones

"Thanks for providing us with such a great and friendly magazine."   Heather Buswell

Cycle Sport

IPC Focus Network
Leon House
233 High Street
Croydon
CR9 1HZ
Tel: +44 (0) 20 8726 8453
Email: cyclesport@ipcmedia.com
Website: http://www.cyclesportmag.com

Publishes: Articles; Features; Interviews; News; Nonfiction; *Areas:* Sport; *Markets:* Adult; Professional

Editors: Robert Garbutt

Magazine on professional cycle racing. Includes coverage of events such as the Tour de France, and interviews with the big names in the field. Most material commissioned, but will consider unsolicited materia. Welcomes ideas for articles and features.

Dare

Ground Floor
16 Connaught Place
London
W2 2ES
Tel: +44 (0) 20 7420 7000
Email: info@therivergroup.co.uk
Website: http://www.therivergroup.co.uk

Publishes: Articles; Features; Nonfiction; *Areas:* Beauty and Fashion; Women's Interests; *Markets:* Adult

Free magazine published on behalf of high street chain.

Decanter

Blue Fin Building
110 Southwark Street
SE1 0SU
Tel: +44 (0) 20 3148 5000
Email: editor@decanter.com
Website: http://www.decanter.com

Publishes: Articles; Features; News; Nonfiction; *Areas:* Cookery; Travel; *Markets:* Adult

Magazine on wines publishing articles, features, and news relating to wine and related subjects of food, cookery, etc. Welcomes ideas by post or fax.

Decanto

PO Box 3257
Littlehampton
BN16 9AF
Email: masque_pub@btinternet.com
Website: http://www.masquepublishing.eu.pn

Publishes: Poetry; *Markets:* Adult

Editors: Lisa Stewart

On hiatus as of January 2015. Check website for current status.

Send up to six original poems, of which 1-3 may be published, by post with SAE or by email in the body of the message (no attachments). Poems of any subject or style are considered.

The Dickensian

The School of English
Rutherford College
University of Kent
Canterbury
Kent
CT2 7NX
Email: M.Y.Andrews@kent.ac.uk
Website: http://www.dickensfellowship.org/dickensian

Publishes: Articles; Nonfiction; *Areas:* Biography; Criticism; Historical; Literature; *Markets:* Adult

Editors: Professor Malcolm Andrews

Publishes articles on the life and works of Dickens. Send articles as hard copy by post with SAE and electronic copy in .doc format (not .docx). See website for full guidelines.

Digital Camera World
Quay House
The Ambury
Bath
BA1 1UA
Tel: +44 (0) 1225 442244
Website: http://www.
digitalcameraworld.com

Publishes: Articles; Features; Nonfiction; Reviews; *Areas:* How-to; Photography; *Markets:* Adult

How-to magazine for photographers, including reviews of equipment and software, etc.

Dogs Today
The Old Print House
62 The High Street
Chobham
Surrey
GU24 8AA
Tel: +44 (0) 1276 858880
Fax: +44 (0) 1276 858860
Email: enquiries@dogstodaymagazine.co.uk
Website: http://www.
dogstodaymagazine.co.uk

Publishes: Articles; Features; Interviews; Nonfiction; *Areas:* Entertainment; Health; Hobbies; Nature; Travel; *Markets:* Adult

Glossy monthly magazine for dog lovers. Send submissions by post with SAE, or by email with "Editorial Submission" in the subject line.

Dragon's Haul
Tel: +44 (0) 1303 720155
Email: editors@dragonshaul.com
Website: http://dragonshaul.com

Publishes: Fiction; *Areas:* Fantasy; *Markets:* Adult; Youth; *Treatments:* Commercial;

Contemporary; Cynical; Dark; Experimental; Light; Literary; Mainstream; Popular; Progressive; Satirical; Serious; Traditional

Editors: Andy Coughlan and David Winstanley

A Fantasy Fiction short story anthology, and sister publication to a Sci-Fi anthology. Published bimonthly exclusively through Apple's Newsstand app and Google's Play Store, it will be available to billions of iOS and Android users.

The aim of the anthology is to bring cutting-edge fiction to an eager and discerning global Fantasy Fiction audience.

We welcome fiction submissions from around the globe (please refer to our submissions guidelines), and we look forward to publishing brilliant and astounding Fantasy Fiction to a worldwide readership.

Drapers
Telephone House
69-77 Paul St
London
EC2A 4NQ
Tel: +44 (0) 20 3033 2600
Email: eric.musgrave@emap.com
Website: http://www.drapersonline.com

Publishes: Articles; Nonfiction; *Areas:* Beauty and Fashion; Business; Design; *Markets:* Professional

Editors: Eric Musgrave

Magazine for fashion retailers and suppliers.

Dream Catcher
Stairwell Books
161 Lowther Street
York
YO31 7LZ
Tel: +44 (0) 1904 733767
Email: rose@stairwellbooks.com
Website: http://www.
dreamcatchermagazine.co.uk

Publishes: Fiction; Interviews; Nonfiction;

Poetry; Reviews; *Areas:* Short Stories; Translations; *Markets:* Adult; *Treatments:* Literary

Editors: Paul Sutherland

Send submissions by post, following guidelines on website.

East Lothian Life
1 Beveridge Row
Belhaven
Dunbar
East Lothian
EH42 1TP
Tel: +44 (0) 1368 863593
Fax: +44 (0) 1368 863593
Email: info@eastlothianlife.co.uk
Website: http://www.eastlothianlife.co.uk

Publishes: Articles; Features; Nonfiction; *Markets:* Adult

Editors: Pauline Jaffray

Publishes articles and features relating to East Lothian.

The Edge
Unit 138
22 Notting Hill Gate
London
W11 3JE
Tel: +44 (0) 8454 569337
Email: enquiries@theedgemagazine.co.uk
Website: http://www.theedgemagazine.co.uk

Publishes: Features; Fiction; Interviews; Nonfiction; Reviews; *Areas:* Crime; Entertainment; Erotic; Fantasy; Gothic; Horror; Sci-Fi; *Markets:* Adult; *Treatments:* Contemporary; Experimental

Editors: Dave Clark

Not accepting submissions as at May 2014. See website for current status.

Education Journal
The Education Publishing Company
Devonia House
4 Union Terrace
Crediton
EX17 3DY
Tel: +44 (0) 1363 774455
Fax: +44 (0) 1363 776592
Email: ejw@educationpublishing.com
Website: http://www.educationpublishing.com

Publishes: Articles; Features; News; Nonfiction; *Markets:* Professional

Magazine for education professionals, including news, features, analysis, conference and parliamentary reports, reviews of major documents and research reports on schools, colleges, universities and the full range of educational issues.

Energy Engineering
Media Culture
Office 46
Pure Offices
Plato Close
Leamington Spa
Warwickshire
CV34 6WE
Tel: +44 (0) 1926 671338
Email: info@energyengineering.co.uk
Website: http://www.energyengineering.co.uk

Publishes: Articles; Features; News; Nonfiction; *Areas:* Design; Technology; *Markets:* Professional

Magazine covering the products and processes, innovation, technology and management of renewable energy and sustainability.

The English Garden
The Chelsea Magazine Company
Third Floor Offices
Cumberland House
Oriel Road
Cheltenham
GL50 1BB
Email: theenglishgarden@chelseamagazines.com
Website: http://www.theenglishgarden.co.uk

Publishes: Articles; Features; Nonfiction; *Areas:* Gardening; How-to; *Markets:* Adult

Editors: Stephanie Mahon

Publishes features on gardens across the UK and Ireland, as well as gardening advice.

Envoi

Meirion House
Glan yr afon
Tanygrisiau
Blaenau Ffestiniog
LL41 3SU
Tel: +44 (0) 1766 832112
Email: jan@envoipoetry.com
Website: http://www.cinnamonpress.com/envoi

Publishes: Articles; Nonfiction; Poetry; Reviews; *Areas:* Literature; Translations; *Markets:* Adult; *Treatments:* Literary

Editors: Dr Jan Fortune-Wood

Magazine of poems, poetry sequences, reviews, and competitions, now more than 50 years old. Occasional poetry related articles and poetry in translation. Submit up to 6 poems up to 40 lines each or one or two longer poems by email only (in the body of the email; attachments will not be read). No submissions by post.

What others say:

"Probably the best poetry magazine currently available" – The Writers' College

"Without a grant and obviously well read, this poetry magazine excels itself." – Ore

"The policy of giving poets space to show their skills is the right one." – Haiku Quarterly

"Good quality, lots of bounce, poems, comps, reviews, reader comeback" – iota

"If you haven't tried it yet, do so, you'll get your money's worth." – New Hope International

Erotic Review

Email: editorial@ermagazine.org
Website: http://eroticreviewmagazine.com

Publishes: Articles; Features; Fiction; Nonfiction; Reviews; *Areas:* Erotic; Lifestyle; Short Stories; *Markets:* Adult

Editors: Jamie Maclean

Literary lifestyle publication about sex and sexuality aimed at sophisticated, intelligent and mature readers. Print version has been retired and is now online only. Publishes features, articles, short stories, and reviews. See website for full submission guidelines.

Esquire

Hearst Magazines UK London
72 Broadwick Street
London
W1F 9EP
Tel: +44 (0) 20 7439 5000
Email: alex.bilmes@hearst.co.uk
Website: http://www.esquire.co.uk

Publishes: Articles; Features; Nonfiction; *Areas:* Beauty and Fashion; Culture; Lifestyle; Men's Interests; Technology; *Markets:* Adult

Editors: Alex Bilmes

Men's general interest magazine. Publishes features and articles on style, tech gadgets, food and drink, culture, and women.

Evergreen

The Lypiatts
Lansdown Road
Cheltenham
Gloucestershire
GL50 2JA
Tel: +44 (0) 1242 225780
Email: editor@evergreenmagazine.co.uk
Website: https://www.thisengland.co.uk

Publishes: Articles; *Areas:* Culture; Historical; Nature; Travel; *Markets:* Adult

Magazine which "takes readers on a gentle journey around the highways and byways of Britain", covering British history, culture, people, and places. Publishes articles and poetry.

Family Law Journal
Jordan Publishing Limited
21 St Thomas Street
Bristol
BS1 6JS
Tel: +44 (0) 1179 230600
Fax: +44 (0) 1179 250486
Email: sales@jordanpublishing.co.uk
Website: http://www.jordanpublishing.co.uk

Publishes: Articles; Nonfiction; *Areas:*
Legal; *Markets:* Professional

Editors: Elizabeth Walsh

Legal journal publishing articles in the area
of family law.

Feminist Review
c/o Women's Studies,
London Metropolitan University
166-220 Holloway Road
London
N7 8DB
Email: feminist-review@londonmet.ac.uk
Website: http://www.feminist-review.com

Publishes: Articles; Essays; Fiction;
Interviews; Nonfiction; *Areas:* Politics;
Sociology; Women's Interests; *Markets:*
Academic; Adult; *Treatments:* Experimental

Editors: Joanna Hoare, Assistant Editor

Peer reviewed, interdisciplinary feminist
journal. Publishes academic articles,
experimental pieces, visual and textual
media and political interventions, including,
for example, interviews, short stories, poems
and photographic essays. Submit via online
submission system.

Fire Magazine
Ground Floor
Rayford House
School Road
Hove
BN3 5HX
Tel: +44 (0) 1273 434951
Email: andrew.lynch@pavpub.com
Website: http://www.fire-magazine.com

Publishes: Articles; Nonfiction; *Markets:*

Professional

Editors: Andrew Lynch

Publishes expert articles and fire fighting and
prevention. No unsolicited mss; query in first
instance.

Fishing News
11th Floor
Nexus Place
25 Farringdon Street
London
EC4A 4AB
Tel: +44 (0) 1434 607375
Email: editor@fishingnews.co.uk
Website: http://fishingnews.co.uk

Publishes: Articles; News; Nonfiction;
Areas: Business; Legal; Nature; *Markets:*
Professional

Editors: Dave Linkie

Magazine for the fishing industry.

Flash: The International Short-Short Story Magazine
Department of English
University of Chester
Parkgate Road
Chester
CH1 4BJ
Email: flash.magazine@chester.ac.uk
Website: http://www.chester.ac.uk/flash.
magazine

Publishes: Fiction; *Areas:* Short Stories;
Markets: Adult; *Treatments:* Literary

Editors: Dr Peter Blair; Dr Ashley Chantler

Publishes flash fiction up to 360 words,
including the title. Send up to four pieces per
issue. Attach submissions to a single email.
See website for full submission guidelines.

Forage
Email: foragepoetry@gmail.com
Website: https://foragepoetry.com

Publishes: Essays; Nonfiction; Poetry;

Reviews; *Markets:* Adult; *Treatments:*
Literary

Publishes poetry, essays / creative
nonfiction, reviews, art and photography.
Submit up to five poems per issue. See
website for upcoming issues and submit
appropriate work by email.

France
Archant House
3 Oriel Road
Cheltenham
GL50 1BB
Tel: +44 (0) 1242 216050
Email: editorial@francemag.com
Website: http://www.francemag.com

Publishes: Articles; Features; Interviews;
Nonfiction; *Areas:* Cookery; Culture; Film;
Historical; Literature; Travel; *Markets:*
Adult

Editors: Carolyn Boyd

Magazine about France, including articles on
weekend getaways, destinations and holiday
ideas, food and wine section, history and
culture, guide to improving your French,
book and film reviews, interviews with A-list
French stars and France-loving celebrities.

The Friend
173 Euston Road
London
NW1 2BJ
Tel: +44 (0) 20 7663 1010
Email: editorial@thefriend.org
Website: https://thefriend.org

Publishes: Articles; Features; Nonfiction;
Areas: Arts; Humour; Nature; Politics;
Religious; Sociology; *Markets:* Adult

Unofficial magazine of Quaker interest
intended to propogate their religious
teaching, and promote interest in their work.

Gay Times (GT Magazine)
Millivres Prowler Group
Unit M, Spectrum House
32-34 Gordon House Road

London
NW5 1LP
Tel: +44 (0) 20 7424 7400
Email: edit@gaytimes.co.uk
Website: http://www.gaytimes.co.uk

Publishes: Articles; Features; Interviews;
Nonfiction; *Areas:* Arts; Beauty and
Fashion; Culture; Current Affairs;
Entertainment; Film; Health; Lifestyle;
Music; Technology; *Markets:* Adult

Editors: Darren Scott

Lifestyle magazine aimed at gay men.

Glamour
6-8 Old Bond Street
London
W1S 4PH
Tel: +44 (0) 20 7499 9080
Fax: +44 (0) 20 7491 2551
Email: glamoureditorialmagazine@
condenast.co.uk
Website: http://www.glamourmagazine.co.uk

Publishes: Articles; Features; Nonfiction;
Areas: Beauty and Fashion; Health;
Lifestyle; Women's Interests; *Markets:* Adult

Editors: Jo Elvin; Rachel Pask (Features
Editor)

Women's magazine publishing features on
beauty, fashion, health, celebrities, love and
relationships, gossip, etc. Send query to
Features Editor with synopsis of idea. No
unsolicited MSS.

The Good Book Guide
4A All Hallows Road
Bispham
Blackpool
Lancs
FY2 0AS
Tel: +44 (0) 1213 143539
Fax: +44 (0) 20 3070 0343
Email: enquiries@thegoodbookguide.com
Website: http://www.thegoodbookguide.com

Publishes: Nonfiction; Reviews; *Areas:*
Literature; *Markets:* Adult

Publishes reviews of books published in the UK.

Governance + Compliance
The Institute of Chartered Secretaries and Administrators
Saffron House
6–10 Kirby Street
London
EC1N 8TS
Tel: +44 (0) 20 7580 4741
Fax: +44 (0) 20 7323 1132
Email: ajones@icsa.org.uk
Website: https://www.icsa.org.uk/products-and-services/governance-and-compliance

Publishes: Articles; News; Nonfiction; *Areas:* Business; How-to; Legal; *Markets:* Professional

Editors: Alexandra Jones, Supervising Editor

Magazine publishing news, views and practical advice on the latest developments in the area of corporate governance and compliance.

Graffiti Magazine
Email: graffiti.magazine@yahoo.co.uk
Website: https://www.facebook.com/pages/Graffiti-Magazine/63653000411

Publishes: Fiction; Interviews; Poetry; Reviews; *Areas:* Short Stories; *Markets:* Adult; *Treatments:* Literary

Editors: Rona Laycock

Magazine produced by a writers group to help showcase local writing, and to publish commissioned items and competition winners. Publishes fiction, poetry, reviews, and interviews.

Granta
12 Addison Avenue
Holland Park
London
W11 4QR
Tel: +44 (0) 20 7605 1360
Fax: +44 (0) 20 7605 1361
Email: editorial@granta.com

Website: http://www.granta.com

Publishes: Fiction; Nonfiction; *Areas:* Autobiography; Culture; Politics; Short Stories; *Markets:* Adult; *Treatments:* Contemporary; Literary

Editors: Sigrid Rausing; Yuka Igarashi; Rachael Allen

Publishes fiction, memoirs, reportage, and photography. Issues tend to be themed and aim to be high-brow, diverse, and contemporary. No essays, book reviews, articles or news items that are topical and therefore transitory, genre fiction, poetry, or travel writing that does not have a particular focus. Accepts submissions between October 1 and April 1 only. No length limits, but pieces are generally between 3,000 and 6,000 words. Submit online through website submission system.

The Grocer
William Reed Business Media Ltd
Broadfield Park
Crawley
RH11 9RT
Tel: +44 (0) 1293 610263
Email: adam.leyland@wrbm.com
Website: http://www.thegrocer.co.uk

Publishes: Articles; News; Nonfiction; *Areas:* Business; *Markets:* Professional

Editors: Adam Leyland

Magazine for professionals in the grocery trade.

Grow Your Own
25 Phoenix Court
Hawkins Road
Colchester
Essex
CO2 8JY
Tel: +44 (0) 1206 505979
Email: lucy.halsall@aceville.co.uk
Website: http://www.growfruitandveg.co.uk

Publishes: Articles; Features; News; Nonfiction; *Areas:* Gardening; How-to; *Markets:* Adult

Editors: Lucy Halsall

Magazine covering the growing of fruit and veg.

Guitarist Magazine
Future Publishing Limited Quay House
The Ambury
Bath
BA1 1UA
Tel: +44 (0) 1225 442244
Email: futurenet-webmaster@
futurenet.co.uk
Website: http://www.musicradar.com/
guitarist

Publishes: Articles; Nonfiction; *Areas:*
How-to; Music; *Markets:* Adult

Editors: Jamie Dickson

Magazine for guitar players, offering advice on what to buy and how to play. Welcomes ideas for articles.

Gutter Magazine
Email: info@guttermag.co.uk
Website: http://www.guttermag.co.uk

Publishes: Fiction; Poetry; Scripts; *Areas:*
Drama; Short Stories; *Markets:* Adult;
Treatments: Literary

Editors: Robbie Guillory; Colin Begg

Publishes poetry, short stories, and drama, by writers born or living in Scotland. Send up to five poems up to 120 lines total, or prose up to 3,500 words. Submit by email as Word attachment. See website for full guidelines.

Health Club Management
The Leisure Media Company Ltd
Portmill House
Portmill Lane
Hitchin
Hertfordshire
SG5 1DJ
Tel: +44 (0) 1462 431385
Fax: +44 (0) 1462 433909
Email: lizterry@leisuremedia.com
Website: http://www.

healthclubmanagement.co.uk
Publishes: Articles; News; Nonfiction;
Areas: Business; Health; Leisure; *Markets:*
Professional

Editors: Liz Terry

Professional magazine for those involved in the running of health clubs, sports centres, etc.

Homes and Gardens
IPC Media Limited
Blue Fin Building
110 Southwark Street
London
SE1 0SU
Tel: +44 (0) 20 3148 5000
Email: housetohome@ipcmedia.com
Website: http://www.housetohome.co.uk/
homesandgardens

Publishes: Articles; Nonfiction; *Areas:*
Design; Gardening; How-to; *Markets:* Adult

Publishes articles on domestic design, both inside and out.

Hortus
The Bryansground Press
Bryan's Ground
Stapleton (Nr Presteigne)
Herefordshire
LD8 2LP
Tel: +44 (0) 1544 260001
Email: all@hortus.co.uk
Website: http://www.hortus.co.uk

Publishes: Articles; Nonfiction; Reviews;
Areas: Design; Gardening; Historical;
Literature; *Markets:* Adult

Privately published quarterly journal aimed at intelligent and lively-minded gardeners throughout the English-speaking world. Publishes articles on gardens, plants, people and books; history design and ornament.

Housebuilder
Housebuilder Media Ltd
Ground Floor

HBF House
27 Broadwall
London
SE1 9PL
Tel: +44 (0) 20 7960 1630
Email: info@house-builder.co.uk
Website: http://www.house-builder.co.uk

Publishes: Articles; Nonfiction; *Areas:*
Design; Technology; *Markets:* Professional

Professional journal for builders. Best to
make initial contact in writing before
submitting.

Icon Magazine
Tel: +44 (0) 20 3225 5200
Email: christopher@icon-magazine.co.uk
Website: http://www.iconeye.com

Publishes: Articles; Interviews; Reviews;
Areas: Architecture; Arts; Design; *Markets:*
Adult

Editors: Christopher Turner

Magazine of architecture and design.
Includes interviews with architects and
designers, visits to the best new buildings,
analysis of new cultural movements and
technologies, and reviews of an eclectic
range of exhibitions, books, products and
films.

Index on Censorship
92-94 Tooley Street
London
SE1 2TH
Email: rachael@indexoncensorship.org
Website: https://www.indexoncensorship.org

Publishes: Articles; Nonfiction; *Areas:*
Politics; *Markets:* Adult

Editors: Rachael Jolley

Magazine publishing material on censorship
and the right to the freedom of expression.

International Affairs
Email: csoper@chathamhouse.org
Website: http://www.chathamhouse.org/

publications/ia

Publishes: Articles; Nonfiction; Reviews;
Areas: Current Affairs; Politics; *Markets:*
Academic

Editors: Caroline Soper

Publishes peer-reviewed articles on
international current affairs and relevant
book reviews. Send submissions by email as
Word documents with abstract summarising
the main points of the article and a note
about the author. See website for full
guidelines.

Interzone
TTA Press
5 Martins Lane
Witcham
Ely
Cambs
CB6 2LB
Website: http://ttapress.com

Publishes: Fiction; *Areas:* Fantasy; Sci-Fi;
Short Stories; *Markets:* Adult

Editors: Andy Cox

Publishes science fiction and fantasy short
stories up to about 10,000 words. See
website for full guidelines and online
submission system.

Irish Pages
129 Ormeau Road
Belfast
BT7 1SH
Tel: +44 (0) 2890 434800
Email: editor@irishpages.org
Website: http://www.irishpages.org

Publishes: Essays; Fiction; Nonfiction;
Poetry; Reviews; *Areas:* Autobiography;
Historical; Nature; Science; Short Stories;
Translations; *Markets:* Adult; *Treatments:*
Literary

Editors: Chris Agee

Non-partisan and non-sectarian literary
journal publishing writing from the island of

Ireland and elsewhere in equal measure. Publishes work in English, and in the Irish Language or Ulster Scots with English translations or glosses. Welcomes submissions throughout the year by post only with SAE or IRCs. See website for more details.

Jamie Magazine

Email: contact@jamiemagazine.com
Website: http://www.jamiemagazine.com

Publishes: Articles; Features; Nonfiction; *Areas:* Cookery; How-to; Markets

Cookery magazine publishing recipes, features, tips, etc.

Jewish Quarterly

28 St Albans Lane
London
NW11 7QE
Email: editor@jewishquarterly.org
Website: http://www.jewishquarterly.org

Publishes: Essays; Fiction; News; Nonfiction; Poetry; *Areas:* Arts; Culture; Current Affairs; Film; Historical; Literature; Music; Philosophy; Politics; Religious; Short Stories; *Markets:* Adult; *Treatments:* Literary

Says of itself it "leads the field in Jewish writing, covering a wide spectrum of subjects including art, criticism, fiction, film, history, Judaism, literature, poetry, philosophy, politics, theatre, the Shoah, Zionism and much more". Submissions welcomed by email or post with SAE.

Kalyna Review

Email: editor@kalynareview.com
Website: http://www.kalynareview.com

Publishes: Fiction; Poetry; *Areas:* Short Stories; Translations; *Markets:* Adult; *Treatments:* Literary

Free online journal publishing poetry and fiction (including translations), photography, prints and art. Send submissions by email in the body of the email.

Kent Life

Apple Barn
Hythe Road, Smeeth
Ashford
Kent
TN25 6SS
Tel: +44 (0) 1303 817000
Email: sarah.sturt@archant.co.uk
Website: http://www.kent-life.co.uk

Publishes: Articles; Features; Nonfiction; *Areas:* Entertainment; Historical; Leisure; Lifestyle; Travel; *Markets:* Adult

Editors: Sarah Sturt

Local lifestyle magazine for Kent. Publishes articles and features on local people, events, walks, and heritage, etc. Send query with ideas for articles and features in first instance.

Kids Alive!

The Salvation Army
101 Newington Causeway
London
SE1 6BN
Tel: +44 (0) 20 7367 4911
Fax: +44 (0) 20 7367 4710
Email: kidsalive@salvationarmy.org.uk
Website: http://www.salvationarmy.org.uk/kidsalive

Publishes: Fiction; Nonfiction; *Areas:* Religious; *Markets:* Children's

Editors: Justin Reeves

Christian children's magazine publishing puzzles, comic strips, etc.

The Lancet

125 London Wall
London
EC2Y 5AS
Tel: +44 (0) 20 7424 4922
Email: editorial@lancet.com
Website: http://www.thelancet.com

Publishes: Articles; Features; Nonfiction; *Areas:* Health; Medicine; Science; *Markets:* Professional

Journal of health and medical science and practice, with offices in London, Newy York, and Beijing. Publishes articles, commentaries, and research papers. See website for submission guidelines.

Legal Week
Incisive Media
Haymarket House
28-29 Haymarket
London
SW1Y 4RX
Tel: +44 (0) 20 7316 9755
Email: georgina.stanley@incisivemedia.com
Website: http://www.legalweek.com

Publishes: Articles; Features; News; Nonfiction; *Areas:* Business; Legal; *Markets:* Professional

Editors: Georgina Stanley

Magazine dedicated exclusively to commercial lawyers in the UK and major international jurisdictions.

Leopard Magazine
24 Cairnaquheen Gardens
Aberdeen
AB15 5HJ
Email: editor@leopardmag.co.uk
Website: http://www.leopardmag.co.uk

Publishes: Articles; Fiction; News; Nonfiction; Poetry; *Areas:* Culture; Historical; Short Stories; *Markets:* Adult

Editors: Judy Mackie

Magazine celebrating the people, places, history, and heritage of North-East Scotland. For articles, send query in first instance. For poetry and fiction, send complete ms.

Litro Magazine
1-15 Cremer Street
Studio 213
E2 8HD
Tel: +44 (0) 20 3371 9971
Email: editor@litro.co.uk
Website: http://www.litro.co.uk

Publishes: Features; Fiction; Nonfiction; Poetry; Reviews; *Areas:* Arts; Autobiography; Literature; Short Stories; Travel; *Markets:* Adult

Independent magazine distributing around 100,000 copies for free, across the UK and France. Publishes fiction and creative nonfiction; features; reviews; interviews; columns, and more. See website for upcoming themes and to submit using online submission system. Also publishes poetry and novel extracts, but no unsolicited submissions accepted for these.

Little White Lies
TCOLondon
71A Leonard Street
London
EC2A 4QS
Email: hello@tcolondon.com
Website: http://www.littlewhitelies.co.uk

Publishes: Articles; Features; Interviews; News; Reviews; *Areas:* Film; *Markets:* Adult

Publishes material relating to films, including articles, interviews, and reviews.

Living France Magazine
Archant House
Oriel Road
Cheltenham
Glos
GL50 1BB
Tel: +44 (0) 1242 216050
Email: karen.tait@archant.co.uk
Website: http://www.livingfrance.com

Publishes: Articles; Features; Interviews; Nonfiction; *Areas:* Culture; How-to; Leisure; Lifestyle; Travel; *Markets:* Adult

Editors: Karen Tait

Magazine for poeple looking to relocate to France. Includes advice on buying property, starting a business, and stories from ex-pats.

London Review of Books
28 Little Russell Street

London
WC1A 2HN
Tel: +44 (0) 20 7209 1101
Fax: +44 (0) 20 7209 1102
Email: edit@lrb.co.uk
Website: http://www.lrb.co.uk

Publishes: Articles; Essays; Nonfiction;
Poetry; Reviews; *Areas:* Arts; Culture; Film;
Literature; Politics; Science; *Markets:* Adult;
Treatments: Literary

Editors: Mary-Kay Wilmers

Contact editor in writing in first instance,
including SAE. Publishes mainly reviews,
essays, and articles, but also publishes
poetry. Welcomes unsolicited contributions
over 2000 words.

Lunar Poetry

Email: editor@lunarpoetry.co.uk
Website: http://www.lunarpoetry.co.uk

Publishes: Articles; Nonfiction; Poetry;
Reviews; *Areas:* Criticism; Literature;
Markets: Adult; *Treatments:* Literary

Publishes poems of any kind or style, articles
on poetry up to 1,000 words, and reviews.
Send up to six poems in the body of an email
or as attachments, with 50-word bio. See
website for full submission guidelines.

Methodist Recorder

122 Golden Lane
London
EC1Y 0TL
Tel: +44 (0) 20 7793 0033
Fax: +44 (0) 20 7793 3459
Email: editorial@methodistrecorder.co.uk
Website: http://www.
methodistrecorder.co.uk

Publishes: Articles; News; Nonfiction;
Areas: Religious; *Markets:* Adult

Methodist newspaper with limited
opportunities for freelances. Potential
contributors are advised to query in first
instance.

Military Modelling Magazine

Email: kelvin.barber@mytimemedia.com
Website: http://www.militarymodelling.com

Publishes: Articles; Nonfiction; *Areas:*
Crafts; Hobbies; How-to; Military; *Markets:*
Adult

Editors: Kelvin Barber

Magazine for military model enthusiasts.
Contact the editor in first instance.

Mixmag

Development Hell Ltd
90-92 Pentonville Road
London
N1 9HS
Tel: +44 (0) 20 7078 8400
Fax: +44 (0) 20 7833 9900
Email: mixmag@mixmag.net
Website: http://www.mixmag.net

Publishes: Articles; Features; Interviews;
News; Nonfiction; Reviews; *Areas:* Music;
Markets: Adult

Dance music and clubbing magazine,
publishing news, features, reviews, and
interviews.

Mother & Baby Magazine

Bauer Consumer Media Ltd
1 Lincoln Court
Lincoln Road
Peterborough
PE1 2RF
Email: team@motherandbaby.co.uk
Website: http://www.motherandbaby.co.uk

Publishes: Articles; Features; Nonfiction;
Areas: Health; How-to; Lifestyle; Women's
Interests; *Markets:* Adult

Publishes articles and features offering
advice on pregnancy, birth, and babycare.

Mslexia

PO Box 656
Newcastle upon Tyne
NE99 1PZ
Tel: +44 (0) 1912 048860

Email: postbag@mslexia.co.uk
Website: http://www.mslexia.co.uk

Publishes: Articles; Essays; Features;
Fiction; Interviews; News; Nonfiction;
Poetry; Reference; Reviews; *Areas:*
Autobiography; Short Stories; Women's
Interests; *Markets:* Adult

By women, for women who write, who want
to write, who teach creative writing or who
have an interest in womens' literature and
creativity. It is a mixture of original work,
features, news, views, advice and listings.
The UK's only magazine devoted to women
writers and their writing.

See website for themes of upcoming issues /
competitions.

Publishes features, columns, reviews, flash
fiction, and literature listings. Email
submissions for themed new writing from
overseas writers only. Email submissions for
other contributions accepted from anywhere.
See website for full details.

Musical Opinion

1 Exford Road
London
SE12 9HD
Tel: +44 (0) 20 8857 1582
Email: musicalopinion@hotmail.co.uk
Website: http://www.musicalopinion.com

Publishes: Articles; Features; Nonfiction;
Reviews; *Areas:* Music; *Markets:* Adult

Editors: Robert Matthew-Walker

Magazine publishing articles, features, and
reviews on classical music. No unsolicited
MSS, but welcomes ideas by phone or email.

The Musical Times

7 Brunswick Mews
Hove
East Sussex
BN3 1HD
Email: mted@gotadsl.co.uk
Website: http://themusicaltimes.
blogspot.com

Publishes: Articles; Nonfiction; *Areas:*
Music; *Markets:* Adult

Editors: Antony Bye

Publishes articles on a wide variety of
subjects pertaining to "classical" music,
between 2,000 and 8,000 words. Send
articles by email. See website for full
submission guidelines.

New Fairy Tales

Email: editor@newfairytales.co.uk
Website: http://www.newfairytales.co.uk

Publishes: Fiction; Poetry; *Areas:* Short
Stories; *Markets:* Adult; Children's; Family;
Youth

Editors: Claire Massey

**Note: Closed to submissions as at January
2016**

Publishes new original fairy tales, suitable
for adults and children. Not looking for
retellings or reimaginings of existing fairy
tales. Send submissions and queries by
email; see website for full guidelines.

New Humanist

Merchants House
5-7 Southwark Street
London
SE1 1RQ
Tel: +44 (0) 20 3117 0630
Email: editor@newhumanist.org.uk
Website: http://www.newhumanist.org.uk

Publishes: Articles; Nonfiction; *Areas:* Arts;
Current Affairs; Historical; Literature;
Philosophy; Religious; Science; *Markets:*
Adult

Editors: Daniel Trilling; Samira Shackle

Publishes humanist articles on current
affairs, history, humanism, human rights,
literature, philosophy, and science. No
fiction. Pitch articles by email.

New London Writers
Flat 34
6 / Hatton Garden
London
EC1N 8JY
Tel: +44 (0) 07913 373870
Email: publish@newlondonwriters.com
Website: http://newlondonwriters.com

Publishes: Articles; Fiction; Reviews; *Areas:*
Fantasy; Mystery; Philosophy; Sci-Fi; Short
Stories; Suspense; *Markets:* Adult; Youth;
Treatments: Commercial; Contemporary;
Dark; Experimental; Literary; Mainstream;
Niche; Satirical

Editors: Alice Wickham

A platform for new writing. We act as
publisher and literary agent for emerging
novelists. Work is published and promoted to
our network of over 500 literary agents and
publishers in the UK and overseas, mainly
USA. Work published on our site is noticed
by the people who count.

New Musical Express (NME)
Time Inc. (UK)
The Blue Fin Building
110 Southwark Street
London
SE1 0SU
Tel: +44 (0) 20 3148 5000
Website: http://www.nme.com

Publishes: Articles; News; Nonfiction;
Reviews; *Areas:* Film; Music; *Markets:*
Adult; *Treatments:* Popular

Editors: Conor McNicholas

Publishes articles, news, and reviews on
popular music, plus coverage of film.

New Welsh Review
PO Box 170
Aberystwyth
SY23 1WZ
Tel: +44 (0) 1970 628410
Email: submissions@newwelshreview.com
Website: http://www.newwelshreview.com

Publishes: Features; Fiction; Nonfiction;

Poetry; Reviews; *Areas:* Short Stories;
Markets: Adult; *Treatments:* Literary

Editors: Gwen Davies

Focus is on Welsh writing in English, but
has an outlook which is deliberately diverse,
encompassing broader UK and international
contexts. For feature articles, send 300-word
query by email. Submit fiction or up to 6
poems by email or by post with cover letter
and SAE. Full details available on website.

**Note: Not accepting fiction submissions as
at November 2015 due to high volume of
submissions. Poetry submissions open
from December 1, 2015. See website for
current status.**

newbooks
1 Vicarage Lane
Stubbington
PO14 2JU
Email: info@newbooksmag.com
Website: http://www.newbooksmag.com

Publishes: Nonfiction; Reviews; *Areas:*
Entertainment; Literature; *Markets:* Adult

Editors: Sheila Ferguson (Managing Editor)

Magazine aimed at readers and reading
groups. Welcomes books for review from all
publishers.

Nursery World
MA Education
St Jude's Church
Dulwich Road
London
SE24 0PB
Tel: +44 (0) 20 7501 6693
Email: liz.roberts@markallengroup.com
Website: http://www.nurseryworld.co.uk

Publishes: Articles; News; Nonfiction;
Markets: Professional

Editors: Liz Roberts

Magazine aimed at professionals dealing
with the care of children in nurseries,
primary schools, childcare, etc.; nannies and

foster parents; and those involved with caring for expectant mothers, babies, and young children.

Opera
36 Black Lion Lane
London
W6 9BE
Tel: +44 (0) 20 8563 8893
Fax: +44 (0) 20 8563 8635
Email: editor@opera.co.uk
Website: http://www.opera.co.uk

Publishes: Articles; Nonfiction; Reviews; *Areas:* Culture; Entertainment; *Markets:* Adult

Editors: John Allison

Review of the contemporary opera scene. Virtually all articles are commissioned so no unsolicited MSS. Approach in writing in first instance.

Peace News
5 Caledonian Road
London
N1 9DY
Tel: +44 (0) 20 7278 3344
Email: editorial@peacenews.info
Website: http://peacenews.info

Publishes: Articles; News; Nonfiction; *Areas:* Politics; *Markets:* Adult

Newspaper covering peace and justice issues, focussing on non-violence. Draws on the traditions of pacifism, feminism, anarchism, socialism, human rights, animal rights and green politics.

The People's Friend
80 Kingsway East
Dundee
DD4 8SL
Tel: +44 (0) 1382 462276
Fax: +44 (0) 1382 452491
Email: peoplesfriend@dcthomson.co.uk
Website: http://www.thepeoplesfriend.co.uk

Publishes: Articles; Features; Fiction; Nonfiction; Poetry; *Areas:* Adventure;

Cookery; Crafts; Crime; Hobbies; Mystery; Nature; Romance; Short Stories; Thrillers; Travel; Women's Interests; *Markets:* Adult; Family; *Treatments:* Traditional

Publishes complete short stories (1,200-3,000 words (4,000 for specials)) and serials, focusing on character development rather than complex plots. Also considers nonfiction from nature to nostalgia and from holidays to hobbies. Send request with SAE for guidelines.

People's Friend Pocket Novels
80 Kingsway East
Dundee
DD4 8SL
Tel: +44 (0) 1382 223131
Email: tsteel@dcthomson.co.uk
Website: http://www.thepeoplesfriend.co.uk

Publishes: Fiction; *Areas:* Romance; *Markets:* Adult; Family

Editors: Tracey Steel

Publishes romance and family fiction between 40,000 and 42,000 words, aimed at adults aged over 30. Send query by post or by email (preferred) with synopsis and first two chapters in first instance. See website for more information.

The Photographer
The British Institute of Professional Photography
The Coach House
The Firs
High Street
Whitchurch
Aylesbury
Buckinghamshire
HP22 4SJ
Tel: +44 (0) 1296 642020
Fax: +44 (0) 1296 641553
Email: editor@bipp.com
Website: http://www.bipp.com

Publishes: Articles; News; Nonfiction; Reviews; *Areas:* Photography; *Markets:* Professional

Photography magazine for professional photographers.

Planet
PO Box 44
Aberystwyth
Ceredigion
SY23 3ZZ
Tel: +44 (0) 1970 611255
Fax: +44 (0) 1970 611197
Email: emily.trahair@planetmagazine.org.uk
Website: http://www.planetmagazine.org.uk

Publishes: Articles; Features; Fiction; Nonfiction; Poetry; Reviews; *Areas:* Arts; Current Affairs; Literature; Music; Politics; Short Stories; Theatre; *Markets:* Adult; *Treatments:* Literary

Editors: Emily Trahair

Publishes one story and between eight and ten poems per issue. A range of styles and themes are accepted, but postal submissions will not be considered unless adequate return postage is provided. Submit 4-6 poems or fiction up to 2,750 words. Submissions are accepted by email.

Most articles, features, and reviews are commissioned, however if you have an idea for a relevant article send a query with brief synopsis.

PN Review
St John's College
Cambridge
CB2 1TP

4th Floor
Alliance House
Cross Street
Manchester
M2 7AP
Tel: +44 (0) 161 834 8730
Fax: +44 (0) 161 832 0084
Email: schmidt@carcanet.co.uk
Website: http://www.pnreview.co.uk

Publishes: Articles; Features; Interviews; News; Poetry; Reviews; *Areas:* Translations; *Markets:* Adult

Editors: Michael Schmidt

Send query with synopsis and sample pages, after having familiarised yourself with the magazine. Accepts prose up to 20 pages and poetry up to 10 pages.

Bimonthly magazine of poetry and poetry criticism. Includes editorial, letters, news, articles, interviews, features, poems, translations, and a substantial book review section. No short stories, children's prose / poetry, or non-poetry related work (academic, biography etc.). Accepts electronic submissions from individual subscribers only – otherwise only hard copy submissions are considered.

The Poetry Box
The Poetry Box
Ramshackles
2 Downview
Nyewood
Nyewood Road
Petersfield
Hampshire
GU31 5JA
Tel: +44 (0) 1730 821030
Email: FairyTaleRhymes@aol.com
Website: http://www.thepoetrybox.co.uk

Publishes: Poetry; *Areas:* Romance; *Markets:* Adult; *Treatments:* Literary

Poetry magazine publishing Romantic and Epic poetry in rhyming form. Also runs annual poetry award and live poetry events.

Poetry London
The Albany
Douglas Way
Deptford
London
SE8 4AG
Tel: +44 (0) 20 8691 7260
Email: ahren@poetrylondon.co.uk
Website: http://www.poetrylondon.co.uk

Publishes: Features; Nonfiction; Poetry; Reviews; *Areas:* Translations; *Markets:* Adult; *Treatments:* Contemporary; Literary

Editors: Ahren Warner; Martha Kapos

Send up to six poems with SASE or adequate return postage. Considers poems by both new and established poets. Also publishes book reviews. No submissions by email.

The Poetry Review

The Poetry Society
22 Betterton Street
London
WC2H 9BX
Tel: +44 (0) 20 7420 9880
Fax: +44 (0) 20 7240 4818
Email: poetryreview@poetrysociety.org.uk
Website: http://www.poetrysociety.org.uk

Publishes: Essays; Nonfiction; Poetry; Reviews; *Markets:* Adult

Editors: Sophie Kirk

Describes itself as "one of the liveliest and most influential literary magazines in the world", and has been associated with the rise of the New Generation of British poets – Carol Ann Duffy, Simon Armitage, Glyn Maxwell, Don Paterson... though its scope extends beyond the UK, with special issues focusing on poetries from around the world. Poets from the UK must submit by post; those from elsewhere in the world may submit using online system. See website for details. Send up to 6 unpublished poems.

Poetry Wales

57 Nolton Street
Bridgend
CF31 3AE
Tel: +44 (0) 1656 663018
Email: info@poetrywales.co.uk
Website: http://poetrywales.co.uk

Publishes: Poetry; *Markets:* Adult

Editors: Nia Davies

Send up to six poems in one .doc file with your name, contact details, and short bio up to 50 words, via online submission system (see website).

Post

Incisive Financial Publishing Ltd

28-29 Haymarket
London
SW1Y 4RX
Tel: +44 (0) 20 7316 9134
Email: stephanie.denton@incisivemedia.com
Website: http://www.postonline.co.uk

Publishes: Articles; News; Nonfiction; *Areas:* Business; *Markets:* Professional

Editors: Stephanie Denton

Industry journal for insurance professionals.

Poultry World

Quadrant House
The Quadrant
Sutton
Surrey
SM2 5AS
Tel: +44 (0) 20 8652 4921
Fax: +44 (0) 20 8652 4005
Email: poultry.world@rbi.co.uk
Website: http://www.fwi.co.uk/poultry

Publishes: Articles; News; Nonfiction; *Areas:* Business; Nature; *Markets:* Professional

Monthly magazine, catering for the whole poultry sector: eggs, broilers, turkeys, ducks and geese.

PR Week

Tel: +44 (0) 20 8267 4429/4428
Email: prweek@haymarket.com
Website: http://www.prweek.com

Publishes: Articles; Features; News; Nonfiction; *Areas:* Business; *Markets:* Professional

Editors: Daniel Farey-Jones

Magazine publishing news and features on public relations and communications.

Practical Photography

Bauer Consumer Media Limited
Media House
Peterborough
PE2 6EA

Email: photoanswers@bauermedia.co.uk
Website: http://www.photoanswers.co.uk

Publishes: Articles; Features; Nonfiction;
Areas: How-to; Photography; *Markets:*
Adult

Magazine for photography enthusiasts. Send
query in first instance.

Prima
33 Broadwick Street
London
W1F 9EP
Tel: +44 (0) 20 7439 5000
Email: prima@hearst.co.uk
Website: http://www.allaboutyou.com/prima/

Publishes: Articles; Features; Nonfiction;
Areas: Beauty and Fashion; Cookery; Crafts;
Health; Travel; Women's Interests; *Markets:*
Adult

Women's magazine publishing articles and
features on food, diet and wellbeing, fashion
and beauty, homes, crafts, and country and
travel.

Private Eye
6 Carlisle Street
London
W1D 3BN
Tel: +44 (0) 20 7437 4017
Fax: +44 (0) 20 7437 0705
Email: strobes@private-eye.co.uk
Website: http://www.private-eye.co.uk

Publishes: Articles; Features; News;
Nonfiction; *Areas:* Current Affairs; Humour;
Politics; *Markets:* Adult; *Treatments:*
Satirical

Editors: Ian Hislop

Satirical and investigative magazine
publishing news stories, features, and
cartoons.

Prole
Prolebooks
15 Maes-y-Dre
Abergele
Conwy
LL22 7HW
Email: admin@prolebooks.co.uk
Website: http://www.prolebooks.co.uk

Publishes: Fiction; Nonfiction; Poetry;
Areas: Short Stories; *Markets:* Adult;
Treatments: Literary

Publishes accessible literature of high
quality, including poetry, short fiction, and
creative nonfiction. Seeks to appeal to a wide
audience and avoid literary elitism (obscure
references and highly stylised structures and
forms are unlikely to find favour). No
previously published material or
simultaneous submissions. Submit one piece
of prose or up to five poems in the body of
an email, with your name, contact details,
word count and third person author bio up to
100 words. See website for appropriate email
addresses for prose and poetry submissions,
and full submission guidelines. No
attachments.

Prospect
25 Sackville Street
London
W1S 3HQ
Tel: +44 (0) 20 7255 1281
Fax: +44 (0) 20 7255 1279
Email: editorial@prospect-magazine.co.uk
Website: http://www.prospect-
magazine.co.uk

Publishes: Essays; Features; Fiction;
Nonfiction; Reviews; *Areas:* Arts; Culture;
Current Affairs; Literature; Politics; Short
Stories; *Markets:* Adult

Editors: David Goodhart

Intelligent magazine of current affairs and
cultural debate. No news features. Almost all
articles are commissioned from regular
writers, but will consider unsolicited
nonfiction submissions if suitable for the
magazine, but no unsolicited fiction
submissions. Does not publish any poetry.
No postal submissions or telephone pitches.
Submit by email only.

Q Magazine

Endeavour House
189 Shaftesbury Avenue
London
WC2H 8JG
Tel: +44 (0) 20 7437 9011
Email: qmail@qthemusic.com
Website: http://www.qthemusic.com

Publishes: Articles; Features; Interviews;
News; Nonfiction; *Areas:* Music; *Markets:*
Adult

UK's biggest selling music monthly
magazine.

Rail

Media House
Lynch Wood
Peterborough
PE2 6EA
Email: rail@bauermedia.co.uk
Website: http://www.railmagazine.com

Publishes: Articles; Features; News;
Nonfiction; *Areas:* Technology; Travel;
Markets: Adult

Editors: Nigel Harris

Magazine of the modern railway. No fiction
or accounts of personal journeys.

Reach

IDP
24 Forest Houses
Halwill
Beaworthy
Devon
EX21 5UU
Email: publishing@indigodreams.co.uk
Website: http://www.indigodreams.co.uk/
reach-poetry/4563791643

Publishes: Poetry; *Markets:* Adult;
Treatments: Literary

Editors: Ronnie Goodyer

Publishes quality poetry from both
experienced and new poets. Formal or free
verse, haiku.. everything is considered.
Subscribers can comment on and vote for
poetry from the previous issue, the winner
receiving £50, plus regular in-house
anthologies and competitions. Receives no
external funding and depends entirely on
subscriptions. Priority for inclusion goes to
subscribers.

Reform

86 Tavistock Place
London
WC1H 9RT
Tel: +44 (0) 20 7916 8630
Email: reform@urc.org.uk
Website: http://www.reform-magazine.co.uk

Publishes: Articles; Features; News;
Nonfiction; *Areas:* Current Affairs;
Religious; Sociology; Spiritual; *Markets:*
Adult

Describes itself as a magazine for thinking
people "who enjoy reading about Christian
ideas from a range of viewpoints".

Resurgence & Ecologist

The Resurgence Trust
Ford House
Hartland
Bideford
Devon
EX39 6EE
Tel: +44 (0) 1237 441293
Fax: +44 (0) 1237 441203
Email: info@resurgence.org
Website: http://www.resurgence.org

Publishes: Articles; Features; News;
Nonfiction; Poetry; Reviews; *Areas:* Arts;
Humour; Nature; Philosophy; Spiritual;
Markets

Publishes articles, features, news, book
reviews, recipe columns, humour, poetry,
and profiles, covering ecology, social justice,
philosophy, spirituality, sustainable
development and the arts. Send proposal in
first instance.

Retail Week

EMAP Publishing Limited
Telephone House
69 – 77 Paul Street

London
EC2A 4NQ
Email: chris brook carter@cmap.com
Website: http://www.retail-week.com

Publishes: Articles; Features; News;
Nonfiction; *Areas:* Business; *Markets:*
Professional

Magazine for the retail industry.

The Rialto
PO Box 309
Aylsham
Norwich
NR11 6LN
Email: info@therialto.co.uk
Website: http://www.therialto.co.uk

Publishes: Articles; Nonfiction; Poetry;
Reviews; *Markets:* Adult

Editors: Michael Mackmin

Send up to six poems with SASE or adequate
return postage, or submit through online
submission system. No submissions by
email. Reviews and articles commissioned.

Royal Academy of Arts (RA) Magazine
Royal Academy of Arts
Burlington House
Piccadilly
London
W1J 0BD
Tel: +44 (0) 20 7300 5820
Fax: +44 (0) 20 7300 5032
Email: ramagazine@royalacademy.org.uk
Website: https://www.royalacademy.org.uk/
ra-magazine

Publishes: Articles; News; Nonfiction;
Areas: Architecture; Arts; Culture; *Markets:*
Adult

Publishes articles relating to the academy, or
to the wider British and international arts
scene. No unsolicited MSS. Freelances who
can write about art in an accessible way
should approach by email or telephone.
Articles are usually tied in to upcoming
exhibitions, projects, or books.

Sarasvati
24 Forest Houses
Halwill
Beaworthy
Devon
EX21 5UU
Email: dawnidp@gmail.com
Website: http://www.indigodreams.co.uk/
sarasvati/4563791846

Publishes: Fiction; Poetry; *Areas:* Short
Stories; *Markets:* Adult

Editors: Dawn Bauling

Showcases poetry and prose. Each
contributor will have three to four pages
available to their poetry, up to 35 lines per
page, or prose up to 1,000 words.

Scientific Computing World
Europa Science Ltd
9 Clifton Court
Cambridge
CB1 7BN
Tel: +44 (0) 1223 275464
Fax: +44 (0) 1223 211107
Email: editor.scw@europascience.com
Website: http://www.scientific-
computing.com

Publishes: Articles; Features; Interviews;
News; Nonfiction; *Areas:* Science;
Technology; *Markets:* Professional

Editors: Beth Harlen

Describes itself as "the only global
publication dedicated to the computing and
information technology needs of scientists
and engineers". Covers computing for
engineering, science, and technology.
Publishes news, comment, feature articles,
product news, white papers and webcasts.
No research papers. Send submissions by
email only. See website for full submission
guidelines.

Scots Heritage Magazine
496 Ferry Road
Edinburgh
EH5 2DL
Tel: +44 (0) 1315 511000

Fax: +44 (0) 1315 517900
Email: editor@scotsheritagemagazine.com
Website: http://www.
scotsheritagemagazine.com

Publishes: Articles; Features; Nonfiction;
Areas: Historical; *Markets:* Adult

Editors: Richard Bath

Magazine of Scottish history, aimed at
people of Scottish descent all over the world.

Scottish Memories
Celebrate Scotland
5th Floor
31-32 Park Row
Leeds
LS1 5JD
Email: matthewh@warnersgroup.co.uk
Website: https://www.celebrate-
scotland.co.uk

Publishes: Articles; Features; Nonfiction;
Areas: Historical; Military; *Markets:* Adult

Editors: Matthew Hill

Magazine of Scottish nostalgia, focussing on
the period 1940-1980. War stories also
considered if a Scottish connection.

SelfBuild & Design
151 Station Street
Burton on Trent
DE14 1BG
Tel: +44 (0) 1584 841417
Email: ross.stokes@sbdonline.co.uk
Website: http://www.selfbuildanddesign.com

Publishes: Articles; Nonfiction; *Areas:*
Design; How-to; *Markets:* Adult

Editors: Ross Stokes

Magazine aimed at those intending to build
or manage the build of their own home, or
any major building project.

Shooter Literary Magazine
Email: shooterlitmag@gmail.com
Website: https://shooterlitmag.com

Publishes: Essays; Fiction; Nonfiction;
Poetry; *Markets:* Adult; *Treatments:* Literary

Publishes literary fiction, poetry, creative
nonfiction and narrative journalism relating
to specific themes for each issue. Send one
piece of prose between 2,000 and 7,500
words or up to three poems per issue, by
email. See website for current theme and full
submission guidelines.

Shooting Times
Tel: +44 (0) 20 3148 4741
Email: steditorial@ipcmedia.com
Website: http://www.shootinguk.co.uk

Publishes: Articles; Nonfiction; *Areas:*
Nature; Sport; *Markets:* Adult

Editors: Alistair Balmain

Magazine covering shooting and the
countryside.

Shoreline of Infinity
8 Craiglockhart Bank
Edinburgh
EH14 1JH
Email: editor@shorelineofinfinity.com
Website: https://www.
shorelineofinfinity.com

Publishes: Fiction; Interviews; Nonfiction;
Reviews; *Areas:* Literature; Music; Sci-Fi;
Short Stories; *Markets:* Adult; Family;
Youth

Editors: Noel Chidwick

Science Fiction magazine from Scotland. We
want stories that explore our unknown
future. We want to play around with the big
ideas and the little ones. We want writers to
tell us stories to inspire us, give us hope,
provide some laughs. Or to scare the stuffing
out of us. We want good stories: we want to
be entertained. We want to read how people
cope in our exotic new world, we want to be
in their minds, in their bodies, in their souls.

ShortStorySunday.com
27 Old Gloucester Street

London
WC1N 3AX
Email: submissions@shortstorysunday.com
Website: http://www.shortstorysunday.com

Publishes: Fiction; *Areas:* Adventure;
Crime; Fantasy; Gothic; Historical; Horror;
Humour; Literature; Mystery; Nature; New
Age; Philosophy; Romance; Sci-Fi; Short
Stories; Suspense; Thrillers; Westerns;
Markets: Adult; Children's; Family; Youth;
Treatments: Commercial; Contemporary;
Dark; Experimental; Light; Literary;
Mainstream; Niche; Popular; Positive;
Progressive; Satirical; Traditional

A home for short stories and flash fiction
online.

Launched in November 2014, this is a new
'boutique' experience for readers, authors,
agents and publishers interested in reading
and contributing world-class short stories.
We wanted to create an experience for the
reader so that every Sunday they can take
half an hour and visit with a cup of tea and
read through that week's story on their
mobile, tablet or desktop either at home, at a
coffee shop or on their lunch break.

To ensure we have the best stories we put
together an editorial panel with an eye for a
good story to pick the most interesting and
original stories for our readers each Sunday.

Shropshire Magazine
Shropshire Newspapers Ltd
Ketley
Telford
TF1 5HU
Tel: +44 (0) 1952 241455
Email: neil.thomas@shropshirestar.co.uk
Website: http://www.
shropshiremagazine.com

Publishes: Articles; Features; News;
Nonfiction; Reviews; *Areas:* Beauty and
Fashion; Entertainment; Historical; Leisure;
Lifestyle; *Markets:* Adult

Glossy lifestyle magazine publishing
features, profiles, news and reviews relating
to the county.

Sky at Night Magazine
Immediate Media Co,
Vineyard House
44 Brook Green
Hammersmith
London
W6 7BT
Tel: +44 (0) 20 7150 5000
Email: skyatnight@bbcmagazines.com
Website: http://www.
skyatnightmagazine.com

Publishes: Articles; Features; News;
Nonfiction; Reviews; *Areas:* How-to;
Science; Technology; *Markets:* Adult

Magazine for those interested in space,
publishing space science stories and tips and
advice for astronomers.

Smallholder
3 Falmouth Business Park
Bickland Water Road
Falmouth
Cornwall
TR11 4SZ
Tel: +44 (0) 1326 213340
Fax: +44 (0) 1326 212084
Email: elizabeth.perry@packetseries.co.uk
Website: http://www.smallholder.co.uk

Publishes: Articles; Features; Nonfiction;
Areas: Business; Nature; *Markets:* Adult;
Professional

Editors: Elizabeth Perry

Magazine aimed at small-scale farmers.
Publishes articles and features on poultry,
livestock, bees, machinery, conservation, and
will consider items on the countryside more
generally. Send email for guidelines.

Snooker Scene
Hayley Green Court
130 Hagley Road
Halesowen
B63 1DY
Tel: +44 (0) 1215 859188
Fax: +44 (0) 01215 857117
Email: info@snookerscene.co.uk
Website: http://www.snookerscene.co.uk

Publishes: Articles; News; Nonfiction; *Areas:* Sport; *Markets:* Adult

Editors: Clive Everton

Magazine covering the sports of snooker and billiards.

The Squash Player

Email: info1@squashplayer.co.uk
Website: http://www.squashplayer.co.uk

Publishes: Articles; Features; Nonfiction; *Areas:* Sport; *Markets:* Adult

Magazine covering all aspects of the game of squash. Query editor with ideas in first instance.

Stand Magazine

School of English
Leeds University
Leeds
LS2 9JT
Tel: +44 (0) 113 233 4794
Fax: +44 (0) 113 233 2791
Email: stand@leeds.ac.uk
Website: http://standmagazine.org

Publishes: Fiction; Poetry; *Areas:* Short Stories; Translations; *Markets:* Adult; *Treatments:* Literary

A well established magazine of poetry and literary fiction. Has previously published the work of, among others, Samuel Beckett, Angela Carter, Seamus Heaney, Geoffrey Hill, and Andrew Motion. No electronic submissions. See website for submission guidelines and alternative US address for American submissions.

Stuff

Teddington Studios
Broom Road
Teddington
Middlesex
TW11 9BE
Tel: +44 (0) 20 8267 5036
Email: stuff@haymarket.com
Website: http://www.stuff.tv

Publishes: Articles; News; Nonfiction; Reviews; *Areas:* Lifestyle; Technology; *Markets:* Adult

Magazine publishing articles on technology, gadgets, lifestyle, news, and reviews.

Style at Home

Time Inc. (UK) Ltd
Blue Fin Building
110 Southwark Street
London
SE1 0SU
Tel: +44 (0) 20 3148 7112
Email: elizabeth.hudson@timeinc.com
Website: http://www.timeincuk.com/brands/style-at-home/

Publishes: Articles; Nonfiction; *Areas:* Design; How-to; Women's Interests; *Markets:* Adult

Editors: Elizabeth Hudson

Magazine offering practical advice for women taking a hands-on approach to styling, decorating, and revamping their homes on a budget.

Taxation

LexisNexis
Quadrant House
The Quadrant
Brighton Road
Sutton
SM2 5AS
Tel: +44 (0) 20 8212 1949
Email: taxation@lexisnexis.co.uk
Website: http://www.taxation.co.uk

Publishes: Articles; Nonfiction; *Areas:* Finance; Legal; *Markets:* Professional

Editors: Mike Truman

Publishes articles on tax for accountants and tax experts. All articles are written by professionals in the field. Send query by email – see website for full guidelines.

Television

Royal Television Society

3 Dorset Rise
London
FC4Y 8FN
Tel: +44 (0) 20 7822 2810
Email: info@rts.org.uk
Website: https://rts.org.uk

Publishes: Articles; Nonfiction; *Areas:*
Technology; TV; *Markets:* Professional

Editors: Steve Clarke

Magazine covering the technical aspects of
television and audio-visual equipment.

Tempo: A Quarterly Review of New Music

PO Box 171
Herne Bay
CT6 6WD
Email: tempoeditor@cambridge.org
Website: http://journals.cambridge.org/
action/displayJournal?jid=TEM

Publishes: Articles; Nonfiction; Reviews;
Areas: Music; *Markets:* Adult; *Treatments:*
Contemporary

Editors: Christopher Fox; Juliet Fraser

Publishes articles and reviews on the new
music scene. Emphasises musical
developments of the 21st century, and
developments of the late 20th century that
have not yet received the deserved attention.
Submit articles up to 5,000 words and
reviews as Word format documents (no
PDFs) with 100-word bio. See website for
full guidelines.

10th Muse

c/o October Books
243 Portswood Road
Southampton
SO17 2NG
Website: http://www.nonism.org.uk/muse.
html

Publishes: Articles; Nonfiction; Poetry;
Humour; *Markets:* Adult; *Treatments:*
Literary
Editors: Andrew Jordan

Looking for poetry, prose, and b&w artwork,
combining lyrical with pastoral and
experimental. Poetry is accepted in any style
or form.

The Voice

GV Media Group Ltd
The Elephant & Castle Shopping Centre
Unit 236
London
SE1 6TE
Tel: +44 (0) 20 7510 0383
Email: newsdesk@gvmedia.co.uk
Website: http://voice-online.co.uk

Publishes: Articles; Features; Interviews;
News; Nonfiction; *Areas:* Arts; Business;
Culture; Entertainment; Politics; Sport;
Markets: Adult

Weekly newspaper aimed at black Britons,
publishing a mixture of news, features,
sports and celebrity interviews.

The Times Literary Supplement (TLS)

1 London Bridge Street
London
SE1 9GF
Tel: +44 (0) 20 7782 5000
Fax: +44 (0) 20 7782 4966
Email: queries@the-tls.co.uk
Website: http://www.the-tls.co.uk

Publishes: Articles; Features; News;
Nonfiction; Poetry; Reviews; *Areas:* Arts;
Film; Historical; Literature; Philosophy;
Science; Theatre; *Markets:* Adult

Editors: Peter Stothard

Publishes coverage of the latest and most
important publications, as well as current
theatre, opera, exhibitions and film. Also
publishes letters to the editor and poetry.
Send books for review by post. For poetry,
submit up to six poems with SASE. Letters
to the Editor may be sent by post or by email
to the address provided on the website.

Today's Golfer

Media House

Peterborough
PE2 6EA
Tel: +44 (0) 1733 468243
Fax: +44 (0) 1733 468843
Email: editorial@todaysgolfer.co.uk
Website: http://www.todaysgolfer.co.uk

Publishes: Articles; Features; Nonfiction;
Reviews; *Areas:* How-to; Sport;
Technology; *Markets:* Adult

Editors: Chris Jones

Publishes articles, features, and reviews on
golf equipment, technique, and courses.

Top Sante

Bauer Media
Media House
Lynch Wood
Peterborough
PE2 6EA
Tel: +44 (0) 1733 468938
Email: nikki.dutton@bauermedia.co.uk
Website: http://www.topsante.co.uk

Publishes: Articles; Features; News;
Nonfiction; *Areas:* Beauty and Fashion;
Health; Women's Interests; *Markets:* Adult

Magazine publishing articles, features, and
news on health and beauty.

Total Off-Road

Assignment Media Ltd
Repton House G34
Bretby Business Park
Burton on Trent
Staffordshire
DE15 0YZ
Tel: +44 (0) 1283 741311
Email: alan.kidd@assignment-media.co.uk
Website: http://toronline.co.uk

Publishes: Articles; Features; Nonfiction;
Areas: Hobbies; Sport; Technology;
Markets: Adult

Editors: Alan Kidd

Publishes items on off-roading, including
competitions, events, and vehicles. Send
query by email in first instance.

Truck & Driver

Sixth Floor, Chancery House
St Nicholas Way
Sutton
SM1 1JB
Tel: +44 (0) 20 8912 2131
Email: pip.dunn@roadtransport.com
Website: http://truckanddriver.co.uk

Publishes: Articles; Features; News;
Nonfiction; *Areas:* Travel; *Markets:*
Professional

Editors: Pip Dunn

Magazine for truck drivers.

Unthology

Unthank Submissions (Unthology)
PO Box 3506
Norwich
NR7 7QP
Email: unthology@unthankbooks.com
Website: http://www.unthankbooks.com

Publishes: Essays; Fiction; Nonfiction;
Areas: Short Stories; *Markets:* Adult;
Treatments: Experimental; Literary;
Traditional

Publishes the work of new or established
writers and can include short stories of any
length, reportage, essays or novel extracts
from anywhere in the world. Allows space
for stories of different styles and subjects to
rub up against each other, featuring classic
slice-of-life alongside the experimental, the
shocking and strange. Submit by post with
SAE and personal contact details, or by
email.

Vegan Life

Prime Impact Events & Media
Park House
The Business Centre
Earls Colne Business Park
Earls Colne
Colchester
CO6 2NS
Tel: +44 (0) 1787 224040
Email: info@veganlifemag.com
Website: http://www.veganlifemag.com

Publishes: Articles; Features; News;
Nonfiction; *Areas:* Cookery; Health;
Leisure; Lifestyle; Travel; *Markets:* Adult

Editors: Maria Chiorando

Vegan consumer magazine, aiming to bring
about a change in attitudes by encouraging
the adoption of a plant based diet.

Viz
30 Cleveland Street
London
W1T 4JD
Tel: +44 (0) 20 7907 6000
Fax: +44 (0) 20 7907 6020
Email: viz@viz.co.uk
Website: http://www.viz.co.uk

Publishes: Articles; Fiction; *Areas:* Humour;
Markets: Adult

Editors: Russell Blackman

Magazine of adult humour, including
cartoons, spoof articles, etc.

Wanderlust Magazine
PO Box 1832
Windsor
Berkshire
SL4 1YT
Tel: +44 (0) 1753 620426
Fax: +44 (0) 1753 620474
Email: submissions@wanderlust.co.uk
Website: http://www.wanderlust.co.uk

Publishes: Articles; Features; Nonfiction;
Areas: Travel; *Markets:* Adult

Magazine covering all aspects of
independent, semi-independent and special-
interest travel. Particularly interested in local
culture. No unsolicited mss. Send query by
email with one-paragraph proposal.

Wasafiri
1-11 Hawley Crescent
Camden Town
London
NW1 8NP
Tel: +44 (0) 20 7556 6110

Fax: +44 (0) 20 7556 6187
Email: wasafiri@open.ac.uk
Website: http://www.wasafiri.org

Publishes: Articles; Essays; Fiction;
Interviews; Nonfiction; Poetry; Reviews;
Areas: Criticism; Culture; Literature; Short
Stories; *Markets:* Adult; *Treatments:*
Literary

Editors: Susheila Nasta

The indispensable journal of contemporary
African, Asian Black British, Caribbean and
transnational literatures.

In over fifteen years of publishing, this
magazine has changed the face of
contemporary writing in Britain. As a literary
magazine primarily concerned with new and
postcolonial writers, it continues to stress the
diversity and range of black and diasporic
writers world-wide. It remains committed to
its original aims: to create a definitive forum
for the voices of new writers and to open up
lively spaces for serious critical discussion
not available elsewhere. It is Britain's only
international magazine for Black British,
African, Asian and Caribbean literatures. Get
the whole picture, get the magazine at the
core of contemporary international literature
today.

The Week
30 Cleveland Street
London
W1T 4JD
Tel: +44 (0) 20 7907 6000
Email: holden_frith@dennis.co.uk
Website: http://www.theweek.co.uk

Publishes: News; Nonfiction; *Markets:*
Adult

Editors: Holden Frith

Weekly magazine condensing the best of the
British and international news from the week
into 35 succinct pages.

What Car?
Teddington Studios
Teddington

Middlesex
TW11 9BE
Tel: +44 (0) 20 8267 5688
Fax: +44 (0) 20 8267 5750
Email: editorial@whatcar.com
Website: http://www.whatcar.com

Publishes: Articles; Features; News;
Nonfiction; Reviews; *Areas:* Technology;
Travel; *Markets:* Adult

Magazine providing new, reviews, articles
and features on cars.

The White Review
243 Knightsbridge
London
SW7 1DN
Email: editors@thewhitereview.org
Website: http://www.thewhitereview.org

Publishes: Essays; Fiction; Nonfiction;
Poetry; Reviews; *Areas:* Arts; Culture;
Literature; Short Stories; *Markets:* Adult;
Treatments: Literary; Serious

Print and online quarterly arts and literature
magazine. Publishes cultural analysis,
reviews, and new fiction and poetry. See
website for guidelines and submit by email.

Woman & Home Feel Good Food
Email: wandhmail@ipcmedia.com
Website: http://www.womanandhome.com

Publishes: Articles; Nonfiction; *Areas:*
Cookery; Women's Interests; *Markets:* Adult

Editors: Jane Curran

Magazine covering cookery, recipes,
ingredients, etc.

Woman's Own
Time Inc. (UK) Ltd
Blue Fin Building
110 Southwark Street
London
SE1 0SU
Tel: +44 (0) 20 3148 6530
Email: womansown@timeinc.com

Website: http://www.timeinc.com/brands/
womans-own/

Publishes: Articles; Features; Nonfiction;
Areas: Beauty and Fashion; Entertainment;
Lifestyle; Women's Interests; Markets

Editors: Karen Livermore

Magazine aimed at women aged 40 and
older.

Woman's Weekly
IPC Media Ltd
Blue Fin Building
110 Southwark Street
London
SE1 0SU
Tel: +44 (0) 20 3148 5000
Email: womansweeklypostbag@
timeinc.com
Website: http://www.womansweekly.com

Publishes: Features; Fiction; News;
Nonfiction; *Areas:* Beauty and Fashion;
Cookery; Crafts; Gardening; Health; Short
Stories; Travel; Women's Interests; *Markets:*
Adult; *Treatments:* Contemporary

Editors: Diane Kenwood; Sue Pilkington
(Features); Gaynor Davies (Fiction)

Publishes features of interest to women over
forty, plus fiction between 1,000 and 2,000
words and serials in three, four, or five parts
of 3,300 words each. Only uses experienced
journalists for nonfiction. No submissions by
email. Submit by post with SAE.

Woman's Weekly Fiction Special
IPC Media Ltd
The Blue Fin Building
110 Southwark Street
London
SE1 0SU
Tel: +44 (0) 20 3148 6600
Email: womansweeklypostbag@
timeinc.com
Website: http://www.womansweekly.com
Publishes: Fiction; *Areas:* Short Stories;
Women's Interests; *Markets:* Adult

Editors: Gaynor Davies

Publishes short stories for women between 1,000 and 8,000 words. Send stories by post – no correspondence by email.

The World Today
The Royal Institute of International Affairs
Chatham House
10 St James's Square
London
SW1Y 4LE
Tel: +44 (0) 20 7957 5700
Fax: +44 (0) 20 7957 5710
Email: contact@chathamhouse.org
Website: http://www.theworldtoday.org

Publishes: Articles; News; Nonfiction; *Areas:* Current Affairs; Politics; *Markets:* Adult; *Treatments:* Serious

Bimonthly magazine providing authoritative analysis and commentary on current topics.

Writing Short Fiction
Email: bruceharris241@btinternet.com
Website: http://writingshortfiction.org

Publishes: Articles; Fiction; Nonfiction; *Areas:* Adventure; Architecture; Arts; Autobiography; Crime; Culture; Current Affairs; Entertainment; Historical; Humour; Leisure; Literature; Media; Nature; Politics; Short Stories; Travel; *Markets:* Adult; Youth; *Treatments:* Contemporary; Literary; Mainstream

Editors: Bruce Harris

The magazine offers advice, questionnaires and resources to new and established writers, and also publishes stories which have won prizes, commendations or listings in UK fiction competitions in its 'Champion Fiction' section.

Yachts & Yachting
Email: Georgie.Corlett-Pitt@ chelseamagazines.com
Website: http://www.yachtsandyachting.com

Publishes: Articles; Nonfiction; *Areas:*

Hobbies; How-to; Sport; Travel; *Markets:* Adult

Editors: Georgie Corlett-Pitt

Magazine publishing articles on sailing techniques and lifestyle.

Yorkshire Ridings Magazine
Seasiders Way
Blackpool
Lancashire
FY1 6NZ
Tel: +44 (0) 1253 336588
Fax: +44 (0) 1253 336587
Website: http://www. yorkshireridingsmagazine.com

Publishes: Articles; News; *Areas:* Beauty and Fashion; Business; Cookery; Entertainment; Finance; Gardening; Historical; Leisure; Lifestyle; Sport; Travel; *Markets:* Adult

County magazine for Yorkshire. All material must be related to the people and places of Yorkshire.

Your Cat
1-6 Buckminster Yard
Main Street
Buckminster
Grantham
Lincs
NG33 5SB
Tel: +44 (0) 1476 859820
Email: editorial@yourcat.co.uk
Website: http://www.yourcat.co.uk

Publishes: Articles; Fiction; Nonfiction; *Areas:* How-to; Short Stories; *Markets:* Adult

Editors: Chloë Hukin

Practical magazine covering the care of cats and kittens. No poetry and no articles written from the cat's viewpoint. Fiction by commission only. Send query by email with outline by post or by email.

Your Dog Magazine
BPG Stamford Ltd
1-6 Buckminster Yard
Main Street
Buckminster
Grantham
Lincs
NG33 5SA
Tel: +44 (0) 1476 859830
Email: editorial@yourdog.co.uk
Website: http://www.yourdog.co.uk

Publishes: Articles; Features; News;
Nonfiction; *Areas:* Hobbies; How-to;
Leisure; Lifestyle; *Markets:* Adult

Editors: Sarah Wright

Publishes news articles (up to 400 words)
and feature articles (up to 2,500 words)
aimed at dog owners, offering practical
advice and some personal experience pieces.
No fiction. Approach by phone in first
instance.

Yours
Media House
Peterborough Business Park
Peterborough
PE2 6EA
Tel: +44 (0) 1733 468000
Email: yours@bauermedia.co.uk
Website: http://www.yours.co.uk

Publishes: Articles; Features; Fiction;
Nonfiction; *Areas:* Lifestyle; Short Stories;
Women's Interests; *Markets:* Adult;
Treatments: Positive

Editors: Sharon Red

Lifestyle magazine aimed at women over 55.
Welcomes nonfiction articles. Uses one or
two pieces of fiction each issue. Send
complete MS with SAE.

Canadian Magazines

For the most up-to-date listings of these and hundreds of other magazines, visit http://www.firstwriter.com/magazines

*To claim your **free** access to the site, please see the back of this book.*

Abilities

c/o Canadian Abilities Foundation
340 College Street, Suite 270
Toronto, Ontario M5T 3A9
Tel: +1 (416) 923-9829
Email: jennifer@abilities.ca
Website: http://abilities.ca

Publishes: Articles; Nonfiction; *Areas:*
Health; Lifestyle; Self-Help; Sport; Travel;
Markets: Adult

Editors: Jennifer Rivkin

Lifestyle magazine for the disabled. Covers
areas such as travel, health, careers,
education, relationships, parenting, new
products, social policy, organisations, events
and activities, sports, education, careers and
more. No fiction, poetry, cartoons/comics or
drama. Send query by email.

Alberta Views

208, 320 23rd Ave SW
Calgary AB, T2S 0J2
Tel: +1 (403) 243-5334
Fax: +1 (403) 243-8599
Email: queries@albertaviews.ab.ca
Website: https://albertaviews.ab.ca

Publishes: Articles; Features; Fiction;
Nonfiction; Poetry; Reviews; *Areas:* Arts;
Business; Culture; Finance; Politics; Short
Stories; Sociology; *Markets:* Adult

Regional magazine for Alberta, publishing
articles about the culture, politics and
economy of Alberta; book reviews of books
written or published in the province; poetry;
and fiction. Accepted unsolicited poetry
submissions. For nonfiction, query. Accepts
fiction only through annual fiction
competition. See website for full details.

Canadian Gardening

Transcontinental Media Inc.
25 Sheppard Avenue West, Suite 100
Toronto, ON M2N 6S7
Tel: +1 (416) 733-7600
Website: http://www.canadiangardening.com

Publishes: Articles; Nonfiction; *Areas:*
Gardening; How-to; *Markets:* Adult

Magazine on gardening, covering all of
Canada. Send query in first instance.

The Capilano Review

281 Industrial Avenue
Vancouver, BC V6A 2P2
Email: contact@thecapilanoreview.ca
Website: https://www.thecapilanoreview.ca

Publishes: Fiction; Interviews; Nonfiction;
Poetry; Reviews; *Markets:* Adult;
Treatments: Experimental; Literary

Publishes experimental writing and art.
Submit up to 8 pages of poetry; reviews up

to 600 words; fiction up to 5,000 words; or interviews up to 4,000 words, through online submission system. No submissions by post or email.

The Claremont Review

Suite 101
1581-H Hillside Avenue
Victoria, BC V8T 2C1
Email: claremontreview@gmail.com
Website: http://www.theclaremontreview.ca

Publishes: Fiction; Poetry; Scripts; *Areas:* Drama; Short Stories; *Markets:* Children's; Youth

Publishes poetry, short stories, and short plays by young writers aged 13-19 from anywhere in the English-speaking world. Send submissions from September 1 to April 30 annually. See website for submission guidelines.

Coast & Kayak Magazine

PO Box 24
Stn A Nanaimo, BC
Tel: +1 (866) 984-6437
Fax: +1 (866) 654-1937
Email: kayak@coastandkayak.com
Website: http://www.coastandkayak.com

Publishes: Articles; Nonfiction; *Areas:* Hobbies; Leisure; Sport; Travel; *Markets:* Adult

Magazine for kayak enthusiasts, focussing on the Pacific coast. Queries accepted by post or by email.

Common Ground

Common Ground Publishing Corp
3152 West 8th Avenue
Vancouver, BC V6K 2C3
Tel: +1 (604) 733-2215
Fax: +1 (604) 733-4415
Email: editor@commonground.ca
Website: http://commonground.ca

Publishes: Articles; Features; Nonfiction; *Areas:* Health; Lifestyle; Nature; Self-Help; Travel; *Markets:* Adult

Publishes articles and features on health, wellness, the environment, transformational travel and personal growth. Send query by email including description of the proposed article, title, approximate length, and optionally the first paragraph, along with author bio and details of qualifications for writing on the subject. No attachments. See website for full guidelines.

Flare

Rogers Communications
One Mt Pleasant Road, 8th Floor
Toronto
Ontario
M4Y 2Y5
Tel: +1 (416) 764-1829
Fax: +1 (416) 764-2866
Email: editors@flare.com
Website: http://www.flare.com/about/writers-guidelines/

Publishes: Articles; News; Nonfiction; *Areas:* Beauty and Fashion; Entertainment; Women's Interests; *Markets:* Adult

Canada's best-selling fashion magazine, celebrating "smart fashion, Canadian style". Publishes articles on the home, fashion, beauty, celebrity, and weddings. Welcomes pitches from experienced writers familiar with the magazine's tone and content. Send query by email with published writing samples.

subTerrain Magazine

PO Box 3008, MPO
Vancouver, BC V6B 3X5
Tel: +1 (604) 876-8710
Fax: +1 (604) 879-2667
Email: subter@portal.ca
Website: http://www.subterrain.ca

Publishes: Essays; Fiction; Nonfiction; Poetry; *Areas:* Short Stories; *Markets:* Adult; *Treatments:* Literary

Publishes fiction up to 3,000 words, creative nonfiction and commentary up to 4,000 words, and poetry. Each issue has a theme (see website for details of upcoming themes). Poetry only accepted if it relates directly to the theme, however prose may or may not

make use of the theme. See website for full
guidelines.

Irish Magazines

For the most up-to-date listings of these and hundreds of other magazines, visit http://www.firstwriter.com/magazines

*To claim your **free** access to the site, please see the back of this book.*

Books Ireland
Unit 9
78 Furze Road
Sandyford
Dublin 18
Tel: +353-1-2933568
Fax: +353-1-2939377
Email: office@wordwellbooks.com
Website: http://www.wordwellbooks.com

Publishes: Articles; Nonfiction; Reviews; *Areas:* Literature; *Markets:* Adult; Professional

Magazine publishing reviews of books by Irish authors or of Irish interest, plus articles aimed at booksellers, readers, and general readers.

The Caterpillar
Drummullen
Cavan
Co. Cavan
Tel: 353 49 4362677
Email: editor@thecaterpillarmagazine.com
Website: http://www.thecaterpillarmagazine.com

Publishes: Fiction; Poetry; *Areas:* Short Stories; *Markets:* Children's

Editors: Rebecca O'Connor

Magazine of stories and poems for children aged 7-11. Send up to six poems or short stories up to 1,000 words by email or by post. See website for full submission guidelines.

Cyphers
3 Selskar Terrace
Ranelagh
Dublin 6
Email: letters@cyphers.ie
Website: http://www.cyphers.ie

Publishes: Fiction; Poetry; *Areas:* Short Stories; Translations; *Markets:* Adult; *Treatments:* Literary

Publishes poetry and fiction in English and Irish, from Ireland and around the world. Translations are welcome. No unsolicited critical articles. Submissions by post only. Attachments sent by email will be deleted. See website for full guidelines.

The Dublin Review
PO Box 7948
Dublin 1
Email: enquiry@thedublinreview.com
Website: http://thedublinreview.com

Publishes: Essays; Fiction; Nonfiction; *Areas:* Criticism; Literature; Short Stories; *Markets:* Adult; *Treatments:* Literary

Publishes essays, criticism, reportage, and

fiction for a general, intelligent readership. No poetry. Send submissions by post only with email address for response. Material is not returned, so do not include return postage. No response without email address.

Into The Void Magazine

Email: intothevoidmag@gmail.com
Website: https://intothevoidmagazine.com

Publishes: Essays; Fiction; Nonfiction; Poetry; *Areas:* Adventure; Anthropology; Arts; Crime; Current Affairs; Drama; Fantasy; Film; Gothic; Historical; Horror; Humour; Literature; Mystery; Nature; Philosophy; Politics; Psychology; Romance; Science; Sci-Fi; Short Stories; Sociology; Suspense; Thrillers; Westerns; *Markets:* Adult; *Treatments:* Commercial; Contemporary; Cynical; Dark; Experimental; Light; Literary; Mainstream; Niche; Popular; Positive; Progressive; Satirical; Serious; Traditional

Editors: Philip Elliott, Gabriela McAdams

A non-profit print and digital literary magazine dedicated to providing a platform for fantastic fiction, nonfiction and poetry from all over the world. We accept writing of all genres and styles, striving to publish work that we feel is heartfelt, genuine and screaming to be read. We adore beautiful and unique styles of writing but clarity is most important. We are committed to giving writers of all experience levels an opportunity. Unpublished writers have just as good a chance of getting published as established ones – it's all about the writing.

Ireland's Own

Channing House
Rowe Street
Wexford
Tel: 053 9140140
Email: info@irelandsown.ie
Website: https://irelandsown.ie

Publishes: Articles; Features; Fiction; Nonfiction; *Areas:* Short Stories; *Markets:* Adult; Children's; Family; Youth; *Treatments:* Literary; Traditional

Editors: Sean Nolan

Magazine publishing stories and articles of Irish interest for the whole family, plus puzzles and games.

Irish Arts Review

15 Harcourt Terrace
Dublin 2
Tel: +353 1 676 6711
Fax: +353 1 676 6700
Email: editorial@irishartsreview.com
Website: http://www.irishartsreview.com

Publishes: Articles; Nonfiction; *Areas:* Architecture; Arts; Design; Photography; *Markets:* Adult

Quarterly review of Irish arts and design, from pre-history to contemporary.

Irish Printer

Tel: 01 432 2271
Email: maeve.martin@ ashvillemediagroup.com
Website: http://www.irishprinter.ie

Publishes: Articles; News; *Areas:* Business; Technology; *Markets:* Professional

Editors: Maev Martin

Magazine publishing news and articles for the printing industry.

The Moth

Ardan Grange
Milltown
Belturbet
Co. Cavan
Tel: 353 (0) 49 4362677
Email: editor@themothmagazine.com
Website: http://www.themothmagazine.com

Publishes: Fiction; Poetry; *Areas:* Short Stories; *Markets:* Adult; *Treatments:* Literary

Editors: Rebecca O'Connor

Submit up to six poems or up to two short

stories or novel extracts by post or by email. See website for full submission guidelines.

The Penny Dreadful
Email: The.P.Dreadful@Gmail.com
Website: http://thepennydreadful.org

Publishes: Fiction; Poetry; *Areas:* Short Stories; *Markets:* Adult; *Treatments:* Literary

Editors: John Keating; Marc O'Connell

Publishes short stories up to 3,000 words (submit up to two at a time) and poems (submit up to six of any length). Include bio up to 100 words. Query by email in first instance. No submissions by email.

Poetry Ireland Review
Poetry Ireland
32 Kildare Street
Dublin 2
Tel: +353 (0)1 6789815
Fax: +353 (0)1 6789782
Email: info@poetryireland.ie
Website: http://www.poetryireland.ie

Publishes: Articles; Nonfiction; Poetry; Reviews; *Areas:* Literature; *Markets:* Adult

Editors: Vona Groarke

Send up to 6 poems with SASE / IRCs or email address for response. Poetry is accepted from around the world, but must be previously unpublished. No sexism or racism. No submissions by email. Articles

and reviews are generally commissioned, however proposals are welcome. No unsolicited reviews or articles.

Reality Magazine
Redemptorist Communications
75 Orwell Road
Rathgar
Dublin 6
Tel: 353 1 492 2488
Email: sales@redcoms.org
Website: http://www.redcoms.org

Publishes: Articles; Nonfiction; *Areas:* Leisure; Religious; *Markets:* Adult; Youth

Catholic magazine, covering all aspects of modern life from a Christian perspective.

U Magazine
Harmonia Ltd
Rosemount House
Dundrum Road
Dundrum
Dublin 14
Tel: +353 1 240 5300
Fax: +353 1 661 9486
Email: webmaster@harmonia.ie
Website: http://umagazine.ie

Publishes: Articles; Features; Interviews; Nonfiction; *Areas:* Beauty and Fashion; Cookery; Design; Entertainment; Film; Health; Lifestyle; Music; Travel; Women's Interests; *Markets:* Adult

Magazine aimed at Irish women aged 18-25. Most material is commissioned.

Australian Magazines

For the most up-to-date listings of these and hundreds of other magazines, visit http://www.firstwriter.com/magazines

To claim your **free** access to the site, please see the back of this book.

Alternative Law Journal

c/- Law Faculty
Monash University
Victoria
3800
Tel: +61 (0) 3 9544 0974
Fax: +61 (0) 3 9905 5305
Email: altlj.org@monash.edu
Website: http://www.altlj.org

Publishes: Articles; Features; Nonfiction; *Areas:* Legal; *Markets:* Professional

Legal journal with the following goals:

-promotion of social justice, human rights and law reform issues

-critique of the legal system

-monitoring developments in alternative legal practice

-community legal education.

Meanjin

Melbourne University Publishing
Level 1, 11-15 Argyle Place South
Carlton Victoria 3053
Tel: +61 3 9342 0317
Email: meanjin@unimelb.edu.au
Website: http://meanjin.com.au

Publishes: Essays; Fiction; Nonfiction;
Poetry; *Areas:* Autobiography; *Markets:* Adult

Editors: Jonathan Green; Catherine McInnis (Deputy Editor); Judith Beveridge (Poetry Editor)

Publishes fiction, essays, memoir, creative nonfiction, and poetry. May be open to different types of material at different times. See website for current status and online form for submission. $2 submission fee.

Online Quilt Magazine

Email: jody@onlinequiltmagazine.com
Website: http://www.onlinequiltmagazine.com

Publishes: Articles; Features; Nonfiction; *Areas:* Crafts; Hobbies; *Markets:* Adult

Editors: Jody Anderson

Online magazine covering quilt-making.

Verandah Literary Journal

Deakin University
221 Burwood Highway
Burwood Victoria 3125
Email: verandah@deakin.edu.au
Website: http://verandahjournal.wordpress.com

Publishes: Fiction; Nonfiction; Poetry;

Scripts; *Areas:* Drama; Short Stories; *Markets:* Adult; *Treatments:* Literary

Submit fiction or nonfiction between 350 and 2,500 words; or poems / suites of poems up to 100 lines total. Also accepts scripts 5-7 minutes long. Submit by post or by email. Reading period each year runs from February 1 to June 10. Non students must pay an entry fee of $10 for one submission or $15 for up to three submissions. See website for full details.

Magazines Subject Index

This section lists magazines by their subject matter, with directions to the section of the book where the full listing can be found.

You can create your own customised lists of magazines using different combinations of these subject areas, plus over a dozen other criteria, instantly online at http://www.firstwriter.com.

To claim your *free* access to the site, please see the back of this book.

Bellevue Literary Review (*US*)
Berkeley Fiction Review (*US*)
Best New Writing (*US*)
Big Bridge (*US*)
Big Pulp (*US*)
Bilingual Review (*US*)
Black Static (*UK*)
Blackbird (*US*)
Blueline (*US*)
Bluestem (*US*)
Boys' Quest (*US*)
Bread for God's Children (*US*)
Brilliant Corners (*US*)
Bryant Literary Review (*US*)
Bugle (*US*)
Bunbury Magazine (*UK*)
Burnside Review (*US*)
Bust (*US*)
Cadet Quest (*US*)
The Cafe Irreal (*US*)
Callaloo (*US*)
Camas (*US*)
The Capilano Review (*Can*)
Carbon Culture Review (*US*)
The Carolina Quarterly (*US*)
Carve Magazine (*US*)
The Casket of Fictional Delights (*UK*)
The Caterpillar (*Ire*)
Caveat Lector (*US*)
Cemetery Moon (*US*)
The Chaffin Journal (*US*)
Chapman (*UK*)
The Chattahoochee Review (*US*)
Chicago Quarterly Review (*US*)
Chicago Review (*US*)
Cimarron Review (*US*)
The Claremont Review (*Can*)
Cloud Rodeo (*US*)
Cloudbank (*US*)
Coal City Review (*US*)
Cold Mountain Review (*US*)
The Collagist (*US*)
Colorado Review (*US*)
Columbia: A Journal of Literature and Art (*US*)
Commando (*UK*)
Common Ground Review (*US*)
Compose (*US*)
Confrontation Magazine (*US*)
Critical Quarterly (*UK*)
Crystal Magazine (*UK*)
Cura – A Literary Magazine of Art and Action (*US*)
Cyphers (*Ire*)
Dragon's Haul (*UK*)
Dream Catcher (*UK*)
Drunken Boat (*US*)
The Dublin Review (*Ire*)
The Edge (*UK*)
Epoch (*US*)
Erotic Review (*UK*)
Feminist Review (*UK*)
Fence (*US*)

Flash: The International Short-Short Story Magazine (*UK*)
Graffiti Magazine (*UK*)
Granta (*UK*)
Gutter Magazine (*UK*)
Interzone (*UK*)
Into The Void Magazine (*Ire*)
Ireland's Own (*Ire*)
Irish Pages (*UK*)
Iron Horse Literary Review (*US*)
Jewish Quarterly (*UK*)
Kalyna Review (*UK*)
Kids Alive! (*UK*)
Leopard Magazine (*UK*)
Litro Magazine (*UK*)
Little Patuxent Review (*US*)
Ms. Magazine (*US*)
The Maine Review (*US*)
Meanjin (*Aus*)
The Moth (*Ire*)
Mslexia (*UK*)
New Fairy Tales (*UK*)
New London Writers (*UK*)
New Welsh Review (*UK*)
Orson Scott Card's InterGalactic Medicine Show (*US*)
The Ottawa Object (*US*)
Painted Bride Quarterly (*US*)
Painted Cave (*US*)
The Penny Dreadful (*Ire*)
The People's Friend (*UK*)
People's Friend Pocket Novels (*UK*)
Planet (*UK*)
Postcard Poems and Prose (*US*)
Prole (*UK*)
Prospect (*UK*)
Rappahannock Review (*US*)
The Realm Beyond (*US*)
Sarasvati (*UK*)
Sequestrum (*US*)
Shooter Literary Magazine (*UK*)
Shoreline of Infinity (*UK*)
ShortStorySunday.com (*UK*)
Sixpenny Magazine (*US*)
Sling Magazine (*US*)
St Petersburg Review (*US*)
Stand Magazine (*UK*)
Star 82 Review (*US*)
Straylight (*US*)
Struggle (*US*)
subTerrain Magazine (*Can*)
The Summerset Review (*US*)
The Sun (*US*)
Suspense Magazine (*US*)
T. Gene Davis's Speculative Blog (*US*)
Tales of the Talisman (*US*)
Talking River (*US*)
Tattoo Highway (*US*)
The Teacher's Voice (*US*)
The Write Place at the Write Time (*US*)
34th Parallel (*US*)
Timber (*US*)
Toad Suck Review (*US*)

Historical

Akron Life (*US*)
Autograph Collector (*US*)
B'nai B'rith Magazine (*US*)
Barbaric Yawp (*US*)
Bugle (*US*)
Cape Cod Life (*US*)
Classic Boat (*UK*)
Classic Cars (*UK*)
The Dickensian (*UK*)
Early American Life (*US*)
Evansville Living (*US*)
Evergreen (*UK*)
Film Comment (*US*)
France (*UK*)
Girlfriendz Magazine (*US*)
GuestLife (*US*)
Hortus (*UK*)
Hyde Park Living (*US*)
Into The Void Magazine (*Ire*)
Irish Pages (*UK*)
Jewish Quarterly (*UK*)
Kent Life (*UK*)
Lakeland Boating (*US*)
Leopard Magazine (*UK*)
Main Line Today (*US*)
Military Vehicles Magazine (*US*)
Mobile Bay (*US*)
New Humanist (*UK*)
News Photographer (*US*)
Nob Hill Gazette (*US*)
Northwest Quarterly Magazine (*US*)
Nostalgia Magazine (*US*)
Oregon Coast (*US*)
Preservation in Print (*US*)
Scots Heritage Magazine (*UK*)
Scottish Memories (*UK*)
ShortStorySunday.com (*UK*)
Shropshire Magazine (*UK*)
The Times Literary Supplement (TLS) (*UK*)
Wine Press Northwest (*US*)
Writing Short Fiction (*UK*)
Yorkshire Ridings Magazine (*UK*)

Hobbies

Angler's Mail (*UK*)
Astronomy (*US*)
ATV Rider Magazine (*US*)
Autograph Collector (*US*)
Backpacker (*US*)
Bee Culture (*US*)
BirdWatching Magazine (*US*)
Boys' Quest (*US*)
Brew Your Own (*US*)
Bugle (*US*)
Cadet Quest (*US*)
Caravan Magazine (*UK*)
Carbon Culture Review (*US*)
Classic Boat (*UK*)
Coast & Kayak Magazine (*Can*)
Creating Keepsakes (*US*)
Dime (Designs in Machine Embroidery) (*US*)
Dogs Today (*UK*)
Field & Stream (*US*)

FineScale Modeler (*US*)
Interweave Knits (*US*)
Lost Treasure, Inc. (*US*)
Military Modelling Magazine (*UK*)
Model Engineer (*US*)
Online Quilt Magazine (*Aus*)
The People's Friend (*UK*)
Total Off-Road (*UK*)
Wine Spectator (*US*)
Yachting Magazine (*US*)
Yachts & Yachting (*UK*)
Your Dog Magazine (*UK*)

Horror

Allegory (*US*)
Artifact Nouveau (*US*)
Barbaric Yawp (*US*)
Big Pulp (*US*)
Black Static (*UK*)
Cemetery Moon (*US*)
The Edge (*UK*)
Into The Void Magazine (*Ire*)
The Realm Beyond (*US*)
Sequestrum (*US*)
ShortStorySunday.com (*UK*)
Suspense Magazine (*US*)
T. Gene Davis's Speculative Blog (*US*)
Tales of the Talisman (*US*)

How-to

Adventure Cyclist (*US*)
African-American Career World (*US*)
Akron Life (*US*)
American Careers (*US*)
Android Magazine (*UK*)
Angus Beef Bulletin (*US*)
Aquatics International (*US*)
Astronomy (*US*)
The Author (*UK*)
Autograph Collector (*US*)
Backpacker (*US*)
BirdWatching Magazine (*US*)
Brew Your Own (*US*)
Business NH Magazine (*US*)
Canadian Gardening (*Can*)
Cat Fancy (*US*)
Chef Magazine (*US*)
Compose (*US*)
Cruising Outpost Magazine (*US*)
Dance Teacher (*US*)
Digital Camera World (*UK*)
Dime (Designs in Machine Embroidery) (*US*)
The English Garden (*UK*)
Equal Opportunity (*US*)
The Fabricator (*US*)
Field & Stream (*US*)
FineScale Modeler (*US*)
Food Product Design (*US*)
Freelance Writer's Report (FWR) (*US*)
Girlfriendz Magazine (*US*)
Golf News Magazine (*US*)
Governance + Compliance (*UK*)
Grain Journal (*US*)
Grow Your Own (*UK*)
Guitarist Magazine (*UK*)

Homes and Gardens (*UK*)
InTents (*US*)
Interweave Knits (*US*)
Jamie Magazine (*UK*)
KNOWAtlanta (*US*)
Lakeland Boating (*US*)
Living France Magazine (*UK*)
Main Line Today (*US*)
Massage & Bodywork (*US*)
Military Modelling Magazine (*UK*)
Military Vehicles Magazine (*US*)
Model Engineer (*US*)
Mother & Baby Magazine (*UK*)
Nails Magazine (*US*)
The National Jurist (*US*)
News Photographer (*US*)
Overtones (*US*)
Play & Playground Magazine (*US*)
Police and Security News (*US*)
Practical Photography (*UK*)
SelfBuild & Design (*UK*)
Sky at Night Magazine (*UK*)
Style at Home (*UK*)
Today's Golfer (*UK*)
Woodshop News (*US*)
Yachts & Yachting (*UK*)
Your Cat (*UK*)
Your Dog Magazine (*UK*)

Humour
Aesthetica: A Review of Contemporary Artists (*UK*)
Akron Life (*US*)
Allegory (*US*)
Artifact Nouveau (*US*)
Asinine Poetry (*US*)
The Beano (*UK*)
Bugle (*US*)
Cadet Quest (*US*)
Carbon Culture Review (*US*)
The Christian Century (*US*)
Crystal Magazine (*UK*)
The Friend (*UK*)
Girlfriendz Magazine (*US*)
Hyde Park Living (*US*)
Into The Void Magazine (*Ire*)
Main Line Today (*US*)
Northwest Quarterly Magazine (*US*)
Private Eye (*UK*)
Resurgence & Ecologist (*UK*)
ShortStorySunday.com (*UK*)
10th Muse (*UK*)
Viz (*UK*)
Writing Short Fiction (*UK*)

Legal
Alternative Law Journal (*Aus*)
The Author (*UK*)
California Lawyer (*US*)
Dance Teacher (*US*)
Family Law Journal (*UK*)
Fishing News (*UK*)
Governance + Compliance (*UK*)
Legal Week (*UK*)
Ms. Magazine (*US*)

The National Jurist (*US*)
O'Dwyer's (*US*)
Police and Security News (*US*)
Taxation (*UK*)

Leisure
Akron Life (*US*)
Artifact Nouveau (*US*)
Caravan Magazine (*UK*)
Coast & Kayak Magazine (*Can*)
Field & Stream (*US*)
GuestLife (*US*)
Health Club Management (*UK*)
Kent Life (*UK*)
Lakeland Boating (*US*)
Living France Magazine (*UK*)
Northwest Quarterly Magazine (*US*)
Oregon Coast (*US*)
Play & Playground Magazine (*US*)
PN (Paraplegia News) (*US*)
Reality Magazine (*Ire*)
Shropshire Magazine (*UK*)
Vegan Life (*UK*)
Writing Short Fiction (*UK*)
Yorkshire Ridings Magazine (*UK*)
Your Dog Magazine (*UK*)

Lifestyle
Abilities (*Can*)
Akron Life (*US*)
Artifact Nouveau (*US*)
Attitude (*UK*)
B'nai B'rith Magazine (*US*)
Bible Advocate (*US*)
Cambridge Magazine (*UK*)
Cape Cod Life (*US*)
Cat Fancy (*US*)
Cincy (*US*)
Closer (*UK*)
Common Ground (*Can*)
Cosmopolitan (*US*)
Erotic Review (*UK*)
Escapees Magazine (*US*)
Esquire (*UK*)
Evansville Living (*US*)
Gay Times (GT Magazine) (*UK*)
Glamour (*UK*)
Indianapolis Monthly (*US*)
Kent Life (*UK*)
KNOWAtlanta (*US*)
Living France Magazine (*UK*)
Main Line Today (*US*)
Metro Parent (*US*)
Mobile Bay (*US*)
More (*US*)
Mother & Baby Magazine (*UK*)
Nob Hill Gazette (*US*)
Northwest Quarterly Magazine (*US*)
Organic Life (*US*)
Palm Springs Life (*US*)
Parents (*US*)
Phoenix Magazine (*US*)
PN (Paraplegia News) (*US*)
Shropshire Magazine (*UK*)
Stuff (*UK*)

Bee Culture (*US*)
BirdWatching Magazine (*US*)
Blueline (*US*)
Bow & Arrow Hunting (*US*)
Boys' Quest (*US*)
British Birds (*UK*)
Bugle (*US*)
Camas (*US*)
Cape Cod Life (*US*)
Cat Fancy (*US*)
Common Ground (*Can*)
Crystal Magazine (*UK*)
Dogs Today (*UK*)
Evergreen (*UK*)
Field & Stream (*US*)
Fishing News (*UK*)
The Friend (*UK*)
Fruit Growers News Magazine (*US*)
Into The Void Magazine (*Ire*)
Irish Pages (*UK*)
Ms. Magazine (*US*)
Northwest Quarterly Magazine (*US*)
Onion World (*US*)
Oregon Coast (*US*)
Organic Life (*US*)
The People's Friend (*UK*)
Pest Management Professional (*US*)
Poultry World (*UK*)
Resurgence & Ecologist (*UK*)
Shooting Times (*UK*)
ShortStorySunday.com (*UK*)
Smallholder (*UK*)
Toad Suck Review (*US*)
Whole Life Times (*US*)
Writing Short Fiction (*UK*)
New Age
Artifact Nouveau (*US*)
ShortStorySunday.com (*UK*)
Whole Life Times (*US*)
Nonfiction
A New Heart (*US*)
A&U (*US*)
American Indian Art Magazine (*US*)
Abilities (*Can*)
Able Muse (*US*)
Acumen (*UK*)
The Adirondack Review (*US*)
Adventure Cyclist (*US*)
Aesthetica: A Review of Contemporary Artists (*UK*)
Africa Confidential (*UK*)
Africa-Asia Confidential (*UK*)
African Business (*UK*)
African-American Career World (*US*)
Akron Life (*US*)
Alberta Views (*Can*)
Alebrijes (*US*)
Alimentum (*US*)
All Out Cricket (*UK*)
The Allegheny Review (*US*)
Allegory (*US*)
Alligator Juniper (*US*)
Alternative Law Journal (*Aus*)

American Careers (*US*)
American Turf Monthly (*US*)
Android Magazine (*UK*)
Angler's Mail (*UK*)
Angus Beef Bulletin (*US*)
Another Chicago Magazine (ACM) (*US*)
Apalachee Review (*US*)
Appalachian Heritage (*US*)
Apple Valley Review (*US*)
Aquatics International (*US*)
Aquila (*UK*)
Arc (*UK*)
Architecture Today (*UK*)
Aries (*US*)
Arms Control Today (*US*)
Artifact Nouveau (*US*)
ArtReview (*UK*)
Assent (*UK*)
Athletics Weekly (*UK*)
Attitude (*UK*)
ATV Rider Magazine (*US*)
The Author (*UK*)
Autograph Collector (*US*)
The Avalon Literary Review (*US*)
B'nai B'rith Magazine (*US*)
Backpacker (*US*)
Baltimore Magazine (*US*)
The Baltimore Review (*US*)
Bare Fiction Magazine (*UK*)
Bayou Magazine (*US*)
Bee Culture (*US*)
Bellevue Literary Review (*US*)
Best New Writing (*US*)
Bible Advocate (*US*)
Big Bridge (*US*)
Bilingual Review (*US*)
BirdWatching Magazine (*US*)
Bizarre (*UK*)
Blackbird (*US*)
Blueline (*US*)
Bluestem (*US*)
Books Ireland (*Ire*)
Bow & Arrow Hunting (*US*)
Boys' Quest (*US*)
Bread for God's Children (*US*)
Brew Your Own (*US*)
Brilliant Corners (*US*)
British Birds (*UK*)
British Journal of Photography (*UK*)
British Journalism Review (*UK*)
Bugle (*US*)
Building (*UK*)
Bunbury Magazine (*UK*)
Buses (*UK*)
Business NH Magazine (*US*)
Bust (*US*)
Cadet Quest (*US*)
California Lawyer (*US*)
Callaloo (*US*)
Camas (*US*)
Cambridge Magazine (*UK*)
Canadian Gardening (*Can*)
Cape Cod Life (*US*)

The Capilano Review (*Can*)
Caravan Magazine (*UK*)
Carbon Culture Review (*US*)
The Carolina Quarterly (*US*)
Carousel (*UK*)
Cat Fancy (*US*)
The Caterer (*UK*)
The Catholic Herald (*UK*)
Caveat Lector (*US*)
Central and Eastern European London Review (*UK*)
Ceramic Review (*UK*)
Chamber Music Magazine (*US*)
Chapman (*UK*)
The Chattahoochee Review (*US*)
Chef Magazine (*US*)
Chicago Quarterly Review (*US*)
Chicago Review (*US*)
The Christian Century (*US*)
Cincy (*US*)
Classic Boat (*UK*)
Classic Cars (*UK*)
Closer (*UK*)
Cloud Rodeo (*US*)
Coast & Kayak Magazine (*Can*)
Cold Mountain Review (*US*)
The Collagist (*US*)
Colorado Review (*US*)
Common Ground (*Can*)
Common Ground Review (*US*)
Compose (*US*)
Confrontation Magazine (*US*)
Consumer Goods Technology (*US*)
Cook Vegetarian (*UK*)
Cosmopolitan (*US*)
craft&design Magazine (*UK*)
Crafts (*UK*)
Creating Keepsakes (*US*)
Critical Quarterly (*UK*)
Cruising Outpost Magazine (*US*)
Crystal Magazine (*UK*)
Cura – A Literary Magazine of Art and Action (*US*)
Current Nursing in Geriatric Care (*US*)
Cycle Sport (*UK*)
Dance Teacher (*US*)
Dare (*UK*)
Decanter (*UK*)
The Dickensian (*UK*)
Digital Camera World (*UK*)
Dime (Designs in Machine Embroidery) (*US*)
Dogs Today (*UK*)
Dollars & Sense (*US*)
Drapers (*UK*)
Dream Catcher (*UK*)
Drunken Boat (*US*)
The Dublin Review (*Ire*)
Early American Life (*US*)
East Lothian Life (*UK*)
The Edge (*UK*)
Education Journal (*UK*)
El Restaurante (*US*)
Electrical Apparatus (*US*)

Energy Engineering (*UK*)
The English Garden (*UK*)
Envoi (*UK*)
Epoch (*US*)
Equal Opportunity (*US*)
Erotic Review (*UK*)
Escapees Magazine (*US*)
Esquire (*UK*)
Evansville Living (*US*)
The Fabricator (*US*)
Family Law Journal (*UK*)
Fast Company (*US*)
Feminist Review (*UK*)
Fence (*US*)
Field & Stream (*US*)
Film Comment (*US*)
FineScale Modeler (*US*)
Fire Magazine (*UK*)
Fishing News (*UK*)
Flare (*Can*)
Food Product Design (*US*)
Forage (*UK*)
France (*UK*)
Freelance Writer's Report (FWR) (*US*)
The Friend (*UK*)
Fruit Growers News Magazine (*US*)
Gay Times (GT Magazine) (*UK*)
Glamour (*UK*)
Golf News Magazine (*US*)
The Good Book Guide (*UK*)
Governance + Compliance (*UK*)
Grain Journal (*US*)
Granta (*UK*)
The Grocer (*UK*)
Grow Your Own (*UK*)
GuestLife (*US*)
Guitarist Magazine (*UK*)
Hard Hat News (*US*)
Health Club Management (*UK*)
Hill Country Sun (*US*)
Home Energy Magazine (*US*)
Homes and Gardens (*UK*)
The Horn Book Magazine (*US*)
Hortus (*UK*)
Housebuilder (*UK*)
Houston Press (*US*)
Hyde Park Living (*US*)
Index on Censorship (*UK*)
Indianapolis Monthly (*US*)
InTents (*US*)
International Affairs (*UK*)
Interweave Knits (*US*)
Into The Void Magazine (*Ire*)
Ireland's Own (*Ire*)
Irish Arts Review (*Ire*)
Irish Pages (*UK*)
Iron Horse Literary Review (*US*)
Jamie Magazine (*UK*)
Jewish Quarterly (*UK*)
The Journal of Adventist Education (*US*)
Kashrus Magazine (*US*)
Kent Life (*UK*)
Kids Alive! (*UK*)

Television (*UK*)
Tempo: A Quarterly Review of New Music (*UK*)
10th Muse (*UK*)
The Health Journal (*US*)
The Voice (*UK*)
The Write Place at the Write Time (*US*)
34th Parallel (*US*)
Timber (*US*)
The Times Literary Supplement (TLS) (*UK*)
Toad Suck Review (*US*)
Today's Golfer (*UK*)
Top Sante (*UK*)
Total Off-Road (*UK*)
Trajectory (*US*)
Transition Magazine (*US*)
TriQuarterly (*US*)
Truck & Driver (*UK*)
U Magazine (*Ire*)
Unthology (*UK*)
US Catholic (*US*)
Vegan Life (*UK*)
Verandah Literary Journal (*Aus*)
Verse (*US*)
Wanderlust Magazine (*UK*)
Wasafiri (*UK*)
The Week (*UK*)
Wesleyan Life (*US*)
What Car? (*UK*)
The White Review (*UK*)
Whole Life Times (*US*)
Willow Review (*US*)
Windhover (*US*)
Wine Press Northwest (*US*)
Wine Spectator (*US*)
Wisconsin Review (*US*)
Witches & Pagans (*US*)
Woman & Home Feel Good Food (*UK*)
Woman's Own (*UK*)
Woman's Weekly (*UK*)
Woodshop News (*US*)
The Worcester Review (*US*)
Word Riot (*US*)
Wordpeace (*US*)
The World Today (*UK*)
Writer's Bloc (*US*)
The Writing Disorder (*US*)
Writing Short Fiction (*UK*)
Written By (*US*)
Xavier Review (*US*)
Yachting Magazine (*US*)
Yachts & Yachting (*UK*)
Your Cat (*UK*)
Your Dog Magazine (*UK*)
Yours (*UK*)
Zeek (*US*)
Zink (*US*)
ZYZZYVA (*US*)
Philosophy
Artifact Nouveau (*US*)
Carbon Culture Review (*US*)
Into The Void Magazine (*Ire*)
Jewish Quarterly (*UK*)

New Humanist (*UK*)
New London Writers (*UK*)
Resurgence & Ecologist (*UK*)
Sequestrum (*US*)
ShortStorySunday.com (*UK*)
The Sun (*US*)
The Times Literary Supplement (TLS) (*UK*)
Photography
The Adirondack Review (*US*)
Artifact Nouveau (*US*)
BirdWatching Magazine (*US*)
British Journal of Photography (*UK*)
Carbon Culture Review (*US*)
Digital Camera World (*UK*)
Irish Arts Review (*Ire*)
News Photographer (*US*)
The Photographer (*UK*)
Practical Photography (*UK*)
Poetry
The Alembic (*US*)
A New Heart (*US*)
A&U (*US*)
Able Muse (*US*)
Acumen (*UK*)
The Adirondack Review (*US*)
Aesthetica: A Review of Contemporary Artists (*UK*)
Agenda (*UK*)
Alberta Views (*Can*)
Alebrijes (*US*)
Alimentum (*US*)
The Allegheny Review (*US*)
Alligator Juniper (*US*)
Ambit (*UK*)
Analog Science Fiction & Fact (*US*)
Ancient Paths (*US*)
Another Chicago Magazine (ACM) (*US*)
Apalachee Review (*US*)
Appalachian Heritage (*US*)
Apple Valley Review (*US*)
Aries (*US*)
Arsenic Lobster Poetry Journal (*US*)
Artifact Nouveau (*US*)
Artificium (*UK*)
Asinine Poetry (*US*)
Assent (*UK*)
The Avalon Literary Review (*US*)
The Baltimore Review (*US*)
Banipal (*UK*)
Bare Fiction Magazine (*UK*)
Bayou Magazine (*US*)
Bellevue Literary Review (*US*)
Bible Advocate (*US*)
Big Bridge (*US*)
Big Pulp (*US*)
Bilingual Review (*US*)
Blackbird (*US*)
Blueline (*US*)
Bluestem (*US*)
Boys' Quest (*US*)
Brilliant Corners (*US*)
Bryant Literary Review (*US*)
Bugle (*US*)

Verandah Literary Journal (*Aus*)
Writer's Bloc (*US*)
Self-Help
Abilities (*Can*)
African-American Career World (*US*)
American Careers (*US*)
Common Ground (*Can*)
Equal Opportunity (*US*)
Girlfriendz Magazine (*US*)
KNOWAtlanta (*US*)
Short Stories
The Alembic (*US*)
A&U (*US*)
Able Muse (*US*)
The Adirondack Review (*US*)
Aesthetica: A Review of Contemporary Artists (*UK*)
Alberta Views (*Can*)
Alimentum (*US*)
The Allegheny Review (*US*)
Allegory (*US*)
Alligator Juniper (*US*)
Ambit (*UK*)
Analog Science Fiction & Fact (*US*)
Ancient Paths (*US*)
Another Chicago Magazine (ACM) (*US*)
Apalachee Review (*US*)
Appalachian Heritage (*US*)
Apple Valley Review (*US*)
Aquila (*UK*)
Arc (*UK*)
Aries (*US*)
Artifact Nouveau (*US*)
Artificium (*UK*)
Asinine Poetry (*US*)
The Avalon Literary Review (*US*)
The Baltimore Review (*US*)
Banipal (*UK*)
Barbaric Yawp (*US*)
Bare Fiction Magazine (*UK*)
Bartleby Snopes (*US*)
Bayou Magazine (*US*)
The Beano (*UK*)
Bellevue Literary Review (*US*)
Berkeley Fiction Review (*US*)
Best New Writing (*US*)
Big Bridge (*US*)
Big Pulp (*US*)
Bilingual Review (*US*)
Black Static (*UK*)
Blackbird (*US*)
Blueline (*US*)
Bluestem (*US*)
Boys' Quest (*US*)
Bryant Literary Review (*US*)
Bunbury Magazine (*UK*)
Burnside Review (*US*)
Cadet Quest (*US*)
The Cafe Irreal (*US*)
Callaloo (*US*)
Carbon Culture Review (*US*)
The Carolina Quarterly (*US*)
Carve Magazine (*US*)

The Casket of Fictional Delights (*UK*)
The Caterpillar (*Ire*)
Caveat Lector (*US*)
Cemetery Moon (*US*)
The Chaffin Journal (*US*)
Chapman (*UK*)
The Chattahoochee Review (*US*)
Chicago Quarterly Review (*US*)
Chicago Review (*US*)
Cimarron Review (*US*)
The Claremont Review (*Can*)
Cloudbank (*US*)
Coal City Review (*US*)
Cold Mountain Review (*US*)
The Collagist (*US*)
Colorado Review (*US*)
Columbia: A Journal of Literature and Art (*US*)
Commando (*UK*)
Common Ground Review (*US*)
Compose (*US*)
Confrontation Magazine (*US*)
Critical Quarterly (*UK*)
Crystal Magazine (*UK*)
Cura – A Literary Magazine of Art and Action (*US*)
Cyphers (*Ire*)
Dream Catcher (*UK*)
Drunken Boat (*US*)
The Dublin Review (*Ire*)
Epoch (*US*)
Erotic Review (*UK*)
Fence (*US*)
Flash: The International Short-Short Story Magazine (*UK*)
Graffiti Magazine (*UK*)
Granta (*UK*)
Gutter Magazine (*UK*)
Interzone (*UK*)
Into The Void Magazine (*Ire*)
Ireland's Own (*Ire*)
Irish Pages (*UK*)
Iron Horse Literary Review (*US*)
Jewish Quarterly (*UK*)
Kalyna Review (*UK*)
Leopard Magazine (*UK*)
Litro Magazine (*UK*)
Little Patuxent Review (*US*)
Ms. Magazine (*US*)
The Maine Review (*US*)
The Moth (*Ire*)
Mslexia (*UK*)
New Fairy Tales (*UK*)
New London Writers (*UK*)
New Welsh Review (*UK*)
Orson Scott Card's InterGalactic Medicine Show (*US*)
The Ottawa Object (*US*)
Painted Bride Quarterly (*US*)
Painted Cave (*US*)
The Penny Dreadful (*Ire*)
The People's Friend (*UK*)
Planet (*UK*)
Postcard Poems and Prose (*US*)

Electrical Apparatus (*US*)
Energy Engineering (*UK*)
Esquire (*UK*)
The Fabricator (*US*)
Fast Company (*US*)
Gay Times (GT Magazine) (*UK*)
Grain Journal (*US*)
Housebuilder (*UK*)
InTents (*US*)
Irish Printer (*Ire*)
Lakeland Boating (*US*)
Military Vehicles Magazine (*US*)
Model Engineer (*US*)
News Photographer (*US*)
O'Dwyer's (*US*)
Photonics & Imaging Technology (*US*)
Play & Playground Magazine (*US*)
Popular Science (*US*)
Rail (*UK*)
Scientific Computing World (*UK*)
Sky at Night Magazine (*UK*)
Stuff (*UK*)
Television (*UK*)
Today's Golfer (*UK*)
Total Off-Road (*UK*)
What Car? (*UK*)
Theatre
Aesthetica: A Review of Contemporary Artists (*UK*)
Aquatics International (*US*)
Aries (*US*)
Artifact Nouveau (*US*)
Bare Fiction Magazine (*UK*)
Central and Eastern European London Review (*UK*)
Chapman (*UK*)
Planet (*UK*)
St Petersburg Review (*US*)
The Times Literary Supplement (TLS) (*UK*)
Thrillers
Artifact Nouveau (*US*)
Carbon Culture Review (*US*)
Crystal Magazine (*UK*)
Into The Void Magazine (*Ire*)
The People's Friend (*UK*)
ShortStorySunday.com (*UK*)
Suspense Magazine (*US*)
Translations
Able Muse (*US*)
The Adirondack Review (*US*)
Banipal (*UK*)
Carbon Culture Review (*US*)
The Chattahoochee Review (*US*)
Columbia: A Journal of Literature and Art (*US*)
Cyphers (*Ire*)
Dream Catcher (*UK*)
Drunken Boat (*US*)
Envoi (*UK*)
Irish Pages (*UK*)
Kalyna Review (*UK*)
PN Review (*UK*)
Poetry London (*UK*)
Stand Magazine (*UK*)

Washington Square Review (*US*)
Writer's Bloc (*US*)
ZYZZYVA (*US*)
Travel
Abilities (*Can*)
Adventure Cyclist (*US*)
Akron Life (*US*)
Attitude (*UK*)
ATV Rider Magazine (*US*)
B'nai B'rith Magazine (*US*)
Backpacker (*US*)
BirdWatching Magazine (*US*)
Buses (*UK*)
Bust (*US*)
Cape Cod Life (*US*)
Caravan Magazine (*UK*)
The Carolina Quarterly (*US*)
Central and Eastern European London Review (*UK*)
Cincy (*US*)
Classic Boat (*UK*)
Classic Cars (*UK*)
Coast & Kayak Magazine (*Can*)
Common Ground (*Can*)
Cruising Outpost Magazine (*US*)
Crystal Magazine (*UK*)
Decanter (*UK*)
Dogs Today (*UK*)
Escapees Magazine (*US*)
Evansville Living (*US*)
Evergreen (*UK*)
France (*UK*)
GuestLife (*US*)
Hill Country Sun (*US*)
Hyde Park Living (*US*)
Kashrus Magazine (*US*)
Kent Life (*UK*)
KNOWAtlanta (*US*)
Lakeland Boating (*US*)
Leisure Group Travel (*US*)
Litro Magazine (*UK*)
Living France Magazine (*UK*)
Main Line Today (*US*)
Nob Hill Gazette (*US*)
The People's Friend (*UK*)
Phoenix Magazine (*US*)
Prima (*UK*)
Rail (*UK*)
Truck & Driver (*UK*)
U Magazine (*Ire*)
Vegan Life (*UK*)
Wanderlust Magazine (*UK*)
What Car? (*UK*)
Wine Press Northwest (*US*)
Wine Spectator (*US*)
Woman's Weekly (*UK*)
Writing Short Fiction (*UK*)
Yachting Magazine (*US*)
Yachts & Yachting (*UK*)
Yorkshire Ridings Magazine (*UK*)
TV
Artifact Nouveau (*US*)
Epoch (*US*)

US Literary Agents

For the most up-to-date listings of these and hundreds of other literary agents, visit http://www.firstwriter.com/Agents

*To claim your **free** access to the site, please see the back of this book.*

Abbot Management

PO Box 430, S Pasadena, CA 91031
Tel: +1 (626) 441-4410
Email: a@abbotent.com
Website: http://www.abbotmanagement.com

Handles: Scripts; *Areas:* Adventure;
Anthropology; Antiques; Archaeology;
Architecture; Arts; Autobiography; Beauty
and Fashion; Biography; Business; Cookery;
Crafts; Crime; Criticism; Culture; Current
Affairs; Design; Drama; Entertainment;
Erotic; Fantasy; Film; Finance; Gardening;
Gothic; Health; Historical; Hobbies; Horror;
How-to; Humour; Legal; Leisure; Lifestyle;
Literature; Media; Medicine; Men's Interests;
Military; Music; Mystery; Nature; New Age;
Philosophy; Photography; Politics;
Psychology; Radio; Religious; Romance;
Science; Sci-Fi; Self-Help; Short Stories;
Sociology; Spiritual; Sport; Suspense;
Technology; Theatre; Thrillers; Translations;
Travel; TV; Westerns; Women's Interests;
Markets: Academic; Adult; Children's;
Family; Professional; Youth; *Treatments:*
Commercial; Contemporary; Cynical; Dark;
Experimental; In-depth; Light; Literary;
Mainstream; Niche; Popular; Positive;
Progressive; Satirical; Serious; Traditional

Our mission is simple: to provide a steady
flow of high quality film and television
screenplays to Producers and Production
Companies in the New York City and Los
Angeles areas. Scripts must be an industry
standard final draft (properly formatted;
grammatically correct; 88-125 pages; written
without camera angles) created on
screenwriting software. Approach via
screenplay submission form on website.

Above the Line Agency

468 N. Camden Drive, #200, Beverly Hills,
CA 90210
Tel: +1 (310) 859-6115
Fax: +1 (310) 859-6119
Website: http://www.
abovethelineagency.com

Handles: Scripts; *Areas:* Film; TV; *Markets:*
Adult; Children's

Send query via online web system only.
Represents writers and directors; feature
films, movies of the week, animation. Offers
consultations at a rate of $200 per hour.

Abrams Artists Agency

275 Seventh Ave, 26th Floor, New York,
NY 10001
Tel: +1 (646) 486-4600
Fax: +1 (646) 486-2358
Email: literary@abramsartny.com
Website: http://www.abramsartists.com

Handles: Scripts; *Areas:* Drama; Film;
Humour; Music; Mystery; Romance;
Suspense; TV; *Markets:* Adult

Send query with SASE via industry professional only. Specialises in film, TV, theatre, and publishing.

Bret Adams Ltd
448 West 44th Street, New York, NY 10036
Tel: +1 (212) 765-5630
Fax: +1 (212) 265-2212
Email: bretadamsltd@bretadamsltd.net
Website: http://www.bretadamsltd.net

Handles: Scripts; *Areas:* Film; Theatre; TV; *Markets:* Adult

Handles projects for theatre, film, and TV only. No books. No unsolicited submissions. Accepts approaches by referral only.

Adler & Robin Books, Inc
3000 Connecticut Avenue, NW, Suite 317, Washington DC, 20008
Tel: +1 (202) 986-9275
Fax: +1 (202) 986-9485
Email: submissions@adlerrobin.com
Website: http://www.adlerrobin.com

Handles: Nonfiction; Reference; *Areas:* Autobiography; Biography; Culture; Historical; How-to; Humour; Lifestyle; Self-Help; Technology; *Markets:* Adult; Children's

Send queries by email only.

The Ahearn Agency, Inc
2021 Pine St., New Orleans, LA 70118-5456
Tel: +1 (504) 861-8395
Fax: +1 (504) 866-6434
Email: pahearn@aol.com
Website: http://www.ahearnagency.com

Handles: Fiction; Nonfiction; *Areas:* Autobiography; Biography; Crime; Current Affairs; Health; Historical; Humour; Lifestyle; Mystery; Nature; Romance; Short Stories; Suspense; Thrillers; Women's Interests; *Markets:* Adult; *Treatments:* Literary

Send one page query with SASE, description, length, market info, and any writing credits. Accepts email queries

without attachments. Response in 2-3 months.

Specialises in women's fiction and suspense. No nonfiction, poetry, juvenile material or science fiction.

Alive Communications, Inc
7680 Goodard Street, Suite 200, Colorado Springs, CO 80920
Tel: +1 (719) 260-7080
Fax: +1 (719) 260-8223
Email: Submissions@aliveliterary.com
Website: http://aliveliterary.com

Handles: Fiction; Nonfiction; *Areas:* Adventure; Autobiography; Biography; Business; Crime; Historical; How-to; Humour; Lifestyle; Mystery; Religious; Self-Help; Short Stories; Spiritual; Sport; Suspense; Thrillers; Westerns; Women's Interests; *Markets:* Adult; Children's; *Treatments:* Commercial; Literary; Mainstream; Popular

Accepts queries from referred authors only. Works primarily with well-established, best-selling, and career authors. Referred authors may submit query by email with bio, name of the client referring you, synopsis, and first three chapters. See website for full details.

Miriam Altshuler Literary Agency
53 Old Post Road North, Red Hook, NY 12571
Tel: +1 (845) 758-9408
Fax: +1 (845) 758-3118
Email: query@maliterary.com
Website: http://www.miriamaltshulerliteraryagency.com

Handles: Fiction; Nonfiction; *Areas:* Autobiography; Culture; Fantasy; How-to; Psychology; Self-Help; Sociology; Spiritual; *Markets:* Adult; Children's; Youth; *Treatments:* Commercial; Literary

Send query by post or by email. If submitting by post, include email address for reply. Only include SASE if no email address available, but note that a response is not guaranteed, even with an SASE. Include brief author bio, synopsis, and the first chapter, pasted into the body of the email (no attachments). See website for full guidelines. No Mystery, Romance, Poetry, Fantasy, Science Fiction, Thrillers, Screenplays, Horror, or Westerns.

Betsy Amster Literary Enterprises

6312 SW Capitol Hwy. #503, Portland, OR 97239
Email: b.amster.assistant@gmail.com
Website: http://amsterlit.com

Handles: Fiction; Nonfiction; Poetry; *Areas:* Autobiography; Biography; Cookery; Culture; Fantasy; Gardening; Health; Historical; Humour; Lifestyle; Medicine; Mystery; Psychology; Self-Help; Sociology; Thrillers; Travel; Women's Interests; *Markets:* Adult; Children's; Youth; *Treatments:* Commercial; Contemporary; Literary

Send query by email only. For fiction and memoirs include the first three pages in the body of your email; for nonfiction include your proposal, again in the body of the email. See website for different email addresses for adult and children's/YA submissions. No unsolicited attachments or queries by phone or fax.

No romances, screenplays, adult poetry, westerns, adult fantasy, horror, science fiction, techno thrillers, spy capers, apocalyptic scenarios, or political or religious arguments.

Marcia Amsterdam Agency

41 W. 82nd St., New York, NY 10024-5613
Tel: +1 (212) 873-4945

Handles: Fiction; Scripts; *Areas:* Adventure; Crime; Film; Historical; Horror; Humour; Mystery; Romance; Science; Thrillers; TV; *Markets:* Adult; Youth; *Treatments:* Contemporary; Mainstream

Send query with SASE. No poetry, how-to, books for the 8-10 age-group, or unsolicited MSS. Response to queries usually in one month.

Arcadia

31 Lake Place North, Danbury, CT 06810
Email: arcadialit@sbcglobal.net

Handles: Nonfiction; *Areas:* Autobiography; Biography; Current Affairs; Health; Historical; Lifestyle; Music; Nature; Politics; Psychology; Science; Self-Help; Spiritual; Technology; Women's Interests; *Markets:* Adult; *Treatments:* Commercial; Literary

Send query with proposal or up to 50 sample pages by email (no attachments) or by post with SASE. No fiction.

Movable Type Management

244 Madison Avenue, Suite 334, New York, NY 10016
Tel: +1 (646) 431-6134
Email: AChromy@MovableTM.com
Website: http://www.mtmgmt.net

Handles: Fiction; Nonfiction; Culture; *Markets:* Adult; Family

Works with authors in a wide variety of categories and genres. Aims to develop properties for distribution across platforms, devices, and territories. Send queries by email only. For nonfiction send query describing topic, approach, and bio. For fiction send query with first 10 pages. Include "Query" in the subject line. No attachments or approaches by post.

Audrey A. Wolf Literary Agency

2510 Virginia Avenue NW, #702N, Washington, DC 20037
Email: audreyrwolf@gmail.com

Handles: Nonfiction; *Areas:* Autobiography; Biography; Business; Current Affairs; Finance; Health; Historical; Lifestyle; Politics; Self-Help; Sport; *Markets:* Adult

Send query by post or email, including synopsis up to two pages long showing the full structure of the book: beginning, middle, and end. Also include chapter outline.

The August Agency LLC
Email: submissions@augustagency.com
Website: http://www.augustagency.com

Handles: Fiction; Nonfiction; *Areas:* Arts;
Autobiography; Biography; Business;
Culture; Current Affairs; Entertainment;
Finance; Historical; Media; Politics;
Sociology; Technology; Women's Interests;
Markets: Adult; Family; Literary

Accepts queries by referral or by request at a
writers' conference only.

The Axelrod Agency
55 Main Street, P.O. Box 357, Chatham, NY
12037
Tel: +1 (518) 392-2100
Fax: +1 (518) 392-2944
Email: steve@axelrodagency.com
Website: http://axelrodagency.com

Handles: Fiction; *Areas:* Crime; Erotic;
Mystery; Romance; Thrillers; Women's
Interests; *Markets:* Adult

Send query by email only. No nonfiction,
African-American, Christian, comedy,
humour, comics, graphic novels, gay/lesbian,
historical, horror, literary, poetry, puzzles,
games, science fiction, fantasy, or westerns.

Ayesha Pande Literary
128 West 132 Street, New York, NY 10027
Email: queries@pandeliterary.com
Website: http://pandeliterary.com

Handles: Fiction; Nonfiction; *Areas:*
Autobiography; Biography; Culture;
Finance; Historical; Humour; Women's
Interests; *Markets:* Adult; Youth;
Treatments: Literary; Popular

Send query describing your project in a
paragraph, with brief author bio and any
publishing history. Prefers queries by email
with first five pages pasted into the body of
the email (no attachments). Also accepts
submissions by post with SASE and first five
pages. No fantasy, science fiction, romance,
poetry, screenplays or children's books
including middle grade fiction. Will consider

young adult and graphic novels. See website
for full guidelines.

Baldi Agency
233 West 99th Street, 19C, New York, NY
10025
Tel: +1 (212) 222-3213
Email: info@baldibooks.com
Website: http://www.baldibooks.com

Handles: Fiction; Nonfiction; Reference;
Areas: Autobiography; Biography; Business;
Cookery; Culture; Historical; Lifestyle;
Science; Spiritual; Technology; Travel;
Markets: Adult; *Treatments:* Literary

Send one page query by email, or by post
with SASE.

Barbara Hogenson Agency
165 West End Ave., Suite 19-C, New York,
NY 10023
Tel: +1 (212) 874-8084
Fax: +1 (212) 362-3011
Email: Bhogenson@aol.com

Handles: Fiction; Nonfiction; Scripts; *Areas:*
Theatre; *Markets:* Adult

Represents fiction, nonfiction, and stage
plays. Send query by email only. No
unsolicited MSS.

Belcastro Agency
721 Virginia Ave, Tarpon Springs, FL 34689
Tel: +1 (330) 766-4885
Email: queries@belcastroagency.com
Website: http://www.belcastroagency.com

Handles: Fiction; *Areas:* Adventure; Crime;
Erotic; Fantasy; Mystery; Romance; Sci-Fi;
Suspense; Thrillers; Women's Interests;
Markets: Adult; Children's; Youth;
Treatments: Commercial; Contemporary;
Literary; Mainstream

We are a passionate, hands-on, editorially-
focused boutique agency with a focus on
women's fiction and YA. We work closely
with our writers in developing manuscripts
and proposals for submission. Queries
welcome by email.

The Bent Agency

204 Park Place, Number Two, Brooklyn, NY
11238
Email: queries@thebentagency.com
Website: http://www.thebentagency.com

Handles: Fiction; Nonfiction; *Areas:*
Adventure; Autobiography; Cookery; Crime;
Culture; Fantasy; Historical; Horror;
Humour; Lifestyle; Mystery; Romance;
Science; Sci-Fi; Suspense; Thrillers;
Women's Interests; *Markets:* Adult;
Children's; Youth; *Treatments:* Commercial;
Contemporary; Literary; Popular

Accepts email queries only. See website for
agent bios and specific interests and email
addresses, then query one agent only. See
website for full submission guidelines.

Meredith Bernstein Literary Agency, Inc.

2095 Broadway, Suite 505, New York, NY
10023
Tel: +1 (212) 799-1007
Fax: +1 (212) 799-1145
Email: mgoodbern@aol.com
Website: http://www.
meredithbernsteinliteraryagency.com

Handles: Fiction; Nonfiction; *Areas:*
Mystery; Romance; Thrillers; *Markets:*
Adult; Youth; *Treatments:* Literary

Send query with SASE. An eclectic agency
which does not specialise in any one
particular area. Accepts queries by post, or
via form on website. No poetry or
screenplays. See website for full guidelines.

David Black Literary Agency

335 Adams Street, Suite 2707, Brooklyn, NY
11201
Tel: +1 (718) 852-5500
Fax: +1 (718) 852-5539
Email: dblack@dblackagency.com
Website: http://www.davidblackagency.com

Handles: Fiction; Nonfiction; *Areas:*
Autobiography; Biography; Business;
Cookery; Crafts; Current Affairs;
Entertainment; Finance; Health; Historical;
Humour; Legal; Lifestyle; Military; Mystery;
Politics; Psychology; Romance; Science;
Self-Help; Spiritual; Sport; Thrillers;
Women's Interests; *Markets:* Adult;
Children's; Youth; *Treatments:* Commercial;
Literary; Mainstream

See website for details of different agents,
and specific interests and submission
guidelines of each. Otherwise, query the
agency generally by post only and allow 8
weeks for a response. See website for full
details.

Bleecker Street Associates, Inc.

217 Thompson Street, #519, New York, NY
10012
Tel: +1 (212) 677-4492
Fax: +1 (212) 388-0001
Email: bleeckerst@hotmail.com

Handles: Fiction; Nonfiction; *Areas:*
Autobiography; Biography; Business;
Cookery; Crime; Culture; Current Affairs;
Entertainment; Erotic; Health; Historical;
Horror; How-to; Humour; Lifestyle;
Military; Mystery; Nature; New Age;
Politics; Psychology; Religious; Romance;
Science; Self-Help; Sociology; Spiritual;
Sport; Technology; Thrillers; Women's
Interests; *Markets:* Adult; Youth;
Treatments: Literary

Send query with SASE for response. No
poetry, plays, scripts, short stories, academic,
scholarly, professional, science fiction,
westerns, children's books, or phone calls,
faxes, or emails.

The Blumer Literary Agency, Inc.

809 West 181 Street, Suite 201, New York,
NY 10033
Tel: +1 (212) 947-3040
Email: livblumer@earthlink.net

Handles: Fiction; Nonfiction; *Areas:*
Anthropology; Archaeology; Architecture;
Arts; Autobiography; Biography; Business;
Cookery; Crafts; Crime; Criticism; Culture;
Design; Entertainment; Finance; Health;
Historical; Hobbies; How-to; Humour;
Literature; Medicine; Mystery; Nature; New

Age; Photography; Psychology; Religious; Self-Help; Suspense; Thrillers; Travel; Women's Interests; *Markets: Adult; Treatments:* Contemporary; Literary; Mainstream

Send query by email or by post with SASE. One page or two pages maximum. Include summary and bio. No sample chapters or attachments. Queries by post are more likely to be read and receive a response.

The Book Group
20 West 20th Street, Suite 601, New York, NY 10011
Tel: +1 (212) 803-3360
Email: submissions@thebookgroup.com
Website: http://www.thebookgroup.com

Handles: Fiction; Nonfiction; *Areas:* Autobiography; Biography; Cookery; Historical; Lifestyle; Psychology; *Markets:* Adult; Children's; Youth; *Treatments:* Commercial; Literary

Represents a broad range of fiction and nonfiction. No poetry or screenplays. Send query by email only with ten sample pages and the first and last name of the agent you are querying in the subject line (see website for individual agent interests). No attachments. Include all material in the body of the email. See website for full guidelines. Response only if interested.

BookEnds, LLC
Tel: +1 (908) 362-0090
Email: submissions@bookends-inc.com
Website: http://www.bookends-inc.com

Handles: Fiction; Nonfiction; Reference; *Areas:* Business; Culture; Current Affairs; Erotic; Fantasy; Historical; Lifestyle; Mystery; Romance; Sci-Fi; Suspense; Women's Interests; *Markets:* Adult; Youth; *Treatments:* Contemporary

Accepts queries from both published and unpublished authors by email only. No postal approaches. Send query directly to specific agent (see website for specific interests and email addresses). No children's picture

books, short fiction, poetry, screenplays, or techno-thrillers.

Books & Such Literary Agency
52 Mission Circle, Suite 122, PMB 170, Santa Rosa, CA 95409-5370
Email: representation@booksandsuch.com
Website: http://www.booksandsuch.biz

Handles: Fiction; Nonfiction; *Areas:* Historical; Humour; Lifestyle; Religious; Romance; Women's Interests; *Markets:* Adult; Children's; Youth

Send query by email only. No attachments. Query should be up to one page detailing your book, your market, your experience, etc., as well as why you chose to contact this agency and if you are contacting others. Particularly interested in material for the Christian market. No queries by post or phone. See website for full details.

Georges Borchardt, Inc.
136 East 57th Street, New York, NY 10022
Tel: +1 (212) 753-5785
Fax: +1 (212) 838-6518
Email: office@gbagency.com
Website: http://www.gbagency.com

Handles: Fiction; Nonfiction; *Areas:* Autobiography; Biography; Historical; *Markets:* Adult; Youth; *Treatments:* Commercial; Literary

New York based literary agency founded in 1967. No unsolicited MSS or screenplays.

Brandt & Hochman Literary Agents, Inc.
1501 Broadway, Suite 2310, New York, NY 10036
Tel: +1 (212) 840-5760
Fax: +1 (212) 840-5776
Email: ghochman@bromasite.com
Website: http://brandthochman.com

Handles: Fiction; Nonfiction; *Areas:* Arts; Autobiography; Culture; Current Affairs; Health; Historical; Lifestyle; Mystery; Science; Thrillers; *Markets:* Adult;

Children's; Youth; *Treatments:* Commercial; Literary; Popular

Send query by post with SASE or by email with query letter up to two pages long, including overview and author details and writing credits. See website for full submission guidelines and for details of individual agents' interests and direct contact details, then approach one agent specifically. No screenplays or textbooks. Response to email queries not guaranteed.

Barbara Braun Associates, Inc.

7 East 14th St #19F, New York, NY 10003
Email: bbasubmissions@gmail.com
Website: http://www.
barbarabraunagency.com

Handles: Fiction; Nonfiction; *Areas:* Architecture; Arts; Beauty and Fashion; Biography; Criticism; Culture; Design; Film; Historical; Mystery; Photography; Politics; Psychology; Sociology; Thrillers; Women's Interests; *Markets:* Adult; *Treatments:* Commercial; Literary; Serious

Send query by email only, with "Query" in the subject line, including brief summary, word count, genre, any relevant publishing experience, and the first five pages pasted into the body of the email. No attachments. No poetry, science fiction, fantasy, horror, or screenplays. Particularly interested in stories for women, art-related fiction, historical and multicultural stories, and to a lesser extent mysteries and thrillers. Also interested in narrative nonfiction and current affairs books by journalists.

Bresnick Weil Literary Agency, LLC

115 West 29th Street, 3rd Floor, New York, NY 10001
Tel: +1 (212) 239-3166
Fax: +1 (212) 239-3165
Email: query@bresnickagency.com
Website: http://bresnickagency.com

Handles: Fiction; Nonfiction; *Areas:* Autobiography; Biography; Crime; Culture; Health; Historical; Humour; Lifestyle;

Music; Politics; Psychology; Science; Sport; Travel; Women's Interests; *Markets:* Adult; *Treatments:* Commercial; Literary; Popular

Send query by email only, with two sample chapters (fiction) or proposal (nonfiction).

Marie Brown Associates, Inc.

412 W. 154th Street, New York, NY 10032
Tel: +1 (212) 939-9725
Fax: +1 (212) 939-9728
Email: mbrownlit@aol.com

Handles: Fiction; Nonfiction; *Areas:* Biography; Business; Culture; Historical; Music; Religious; Women's Interests; *Markets:* Adult; Youth; *Treatments:* Literary; Mainstream

Send query with SASE. Particularly interested in multicultural and African-American writers. MSS should preferably not be submitted elsewhere simultaneously.

Browne & Miller Literary Associates

410 S. Michigan Avenue, Suite 460, Chicago, IL 60605
Tel: +1 (312) 922-3063
Fax: +1 (312) 922-1905
Email: mail@browneandmiller.com
Website: http://www.browneandmiller.com

Handles: Fiction; Nonfiction; *Areas:* Anthropology; Archaeology; Autobiography; Biography; Business; Cookery; Crafts; Crime; Culture; Current Affairs; Finance; Health; Historical; Hobbies; How-to; Humour; Lifestyle; Medicine; Mystery; Nature; Psychology; Religious; Science; Self-Help; Sociology; Sport; Technology; Women's Interests; *Markets:* Adult; Youth; *Treatments:* Commercial; Literary; Satirical

Particularly interested in literary/commercial fiction/women's fiction, women's historical fiction, literary-leaning crime fiction, romance, Amish fiction, time travel stories, Christian/inspirational fiction by established authors, literary and commercial Young Adult fiction, nonfiction by nationally-recognised, platformed author/experts. No children's picture books, horror or sci-fi novels, short stories, poetry, original screenplays, articles, or software. Send query by email with synopsis and first five chapters for fiction, or proposal and three chapters for nonfiction, in the body of the email (attachments will not be opened). See website for full details.

Kelvin C. Bulger and Associates

4540 W. Washington Blvd , Suite 101, Chicago, IL 60624
Tel: +1 (312) 218-1943
Fax: +1 (773) 261-5950
Email: bulgerassociates@gmail.com
Website: http://bulgerandassociates.biz

Handles: Scripts; *Areas:* Adventure; Film; Humour; Religious; TV; *Markets:* Adult

Send query by post with SASE, or by fax or email. Include first ten pages of your screenplay, one-page plot synopsis and one-page logline.

Sheree Bykofsky Associates, Inc.

4326 Harbor Beach Boulevard, PO Box 706, Brigantine, NJ 08203
Email: submitbee@aol.com
Website: http://www.shereebee.com

Handles: Fiction; Nonfiction; Reference; *Areas:* Biography; Business; Cookery; Culture; Current Affairs; Film; Hobbies; Humour; Lifestyle; Mystery; Psychology; Self-Help; Spiritual; Women's Interests; *Markets:* Adult; *Treatments:* Commercial; Literary

Send query by email only. Include one page query, and for fiction a one page synopsis, and first page of manuscript, all in the body of the email. No attachments. Always looking for a bestseller in any category, but generally not interested in poetry, thrillers, westerns, romances, occult, science fiction, fantasy, children's or young adult.

Carnicelli Literary Management

7 Kipp Road, Rhinebeck, NY 12572

Email: queries@carnicellilit.com
Website: http://www.carnicellilit.com

Handles: Fiction; Nonfiction; *Areas:* Autobiography; Biography; Business; Culture; Current Affairs; Health; Historical; Psychology; Science; Spiritual; Sport; *Markets:* Adult; *Treatments:* Commercial; Literary; Popular; Serious

Handles mainly nonfiction. Send query by email, or using form on website. Restrict queries to one page. If approaching by email, include the word "Query" in the subject line and do not include attachments. See website for full guidelines. No poetry, plays, screenplays, or books for children.

Maria Carvainis Agency, Inc.

1270 Avenue of the Americas, Suite 2320, New York, NY 10020
Tel: +1 (212) 245-6365
Fax: +1 (212) 245-7196
Email: mca@mariacarvainisagency.com
Website: http://mariacarvainisagency.com

Handles: Fiction; Nonfiction; *Areas:* Autobiography; Biography; Business; Culture; Finance; Historical; Mystery; Psychology; Science; Suspense; Technology; Thrillers; Women's Interests; *Markets:* Adult; Children's; Youth; *Treatments:* Contemporary; Literary; Mainstream; Popular

Send query with synopsis, two sample chapters, and details of any previous writing credits, by post or by email. If sending by post and return of the material is required, include SASE; otherwise include email address for response, usually within 5-10 days. If submitting by email, all documents must be Word or PDF. No screenplays, children's picture books, science fiction, or poetry.

Castiglia Literary Agency

1155 Camino Del Mar, Suite 510, Del Mar, CA 92014
Tel: +1 (858) 755-8761
Fax: +1 (858) 755-7063
Email: CastigliaAgency-query@yahoo.com
Website: http://www.castigliaagency.com

Handles: Fiction; Nonfiction; *Areas:* Architecture; Biography; Business; Cookery; Crime; Culture; Current Affairs; Design; Finance; Health; Lifestyle; Mystery; Science; Sci-Fi; Thrillers; *Markets:* Adult; Youth; *Treatments:* Contemporary; Literary; Mainstream

Send one-page query by email, including brief description / synopsis and background / short bio of author. See website for full guidelines.

Chalberg & Sussman

115 West 29th St, Third Floor , New York, NY 10001
Email: rachel@chalbergsussman.com
Website: http://www.chalbergsussman.com

Handles: Fiction; Nonfiction; *Areas:* Autobiography; Culture; Historical; Psychology; Science; Self-Help; Suspense; Thrillers; Women's Interests; *Markets:* Adult; Children's; *Treatments:* Commercial; Dark; Literary; Popular

Send query by email. See website for specific agent interests and email addresses.

Jane Chelius Literary Agency, Inc.

548 Second Street, Brooklyn, NY 11215
Tel: +1 (718) 499-0236
Fax: +1 (718) 832-7335
Email: queries@janechelius.com
Website: http://www.janechelius.com

Handles: Fiction; Nonfiction; *Areas:* Biography; Culture; Humour; Lifestyle; Medicine; *Markets:* Adult; *Treatments:* Satirical

Note: Not currently accepting submissions as at February 2015

Send query by email with query letter, one-page synopsis, and first ten pages in the body of the email. No email attachments. Considers all genres except children's books, poetry, science fiction, fantasy, category romance, stage plays or screenplays. Response only if interested.

Elyse Cheney Literary Associates, LLC

78 Fifth Avenue, 3rd Floor, New York, NY 10011
Tel: +1 (212) 277-8007
Fax: +1 (212) 614-0728
Email: submissions@cheneyliterary.com
Website: http://www.cheneyliterary.com

Handles: Fiction; Nonfiction; *Areas:* Autobiography; Biography; Business; Culture; Current Affairs; Finance; Historical; Horror; Literature; Politics; Romance; Science; Sport; Suspense; Thrillers; Women's Interests; *Markets:* Adult; *Treatments:* Commercial; Contemporary; Literary

Send query with up to three chapters of sample material by post with SASE, or by email (no attachments). Response not guaranteed.

Linda Chester & Associates

630 Fifth Avenue, Suite 2000, Rockefeller Center, New York, NY 10111
Tel: +1 (212) 218-3350
Fax: +1 (212) 218-3343
Email: submissions@lindachester.com
Website: http://www.lindachester.com

Handles: Fiction; Nonfiction; *Markets:* Adult; *Treatments:* Commercial; Literary

Send query by email only with short bio and first five pages pasted directly into the body of the email. Response within 4 weeks if interested only. No submissions by post.

The Choate Agency, LLC

1320 Bolton Road, Pelham, NY 10803
Tel: +1 (917) 446-2694
Email: mickey@thechoateagency.com
Website: http://www.thechoateagency.com

Handles: Fiction; Nonfiction; *Areas:* Biography; Cookery; Current Affairs; Historical; Military; Mystery; Nature; Politics; Science; Thrillers; *Markets:* Adult; *Treatments:* Commercial

Handles commercial fiction and narrative nonfiction. Send query with brief synopsis/

outline by post with SASE, or by email.
Strongly prefers submissions by email. No
genre fiction, romance, self-help,
confessional memoirs, spirituality, pop
psychology, religion, how-to, New Age
titles, children's books poetry, self-published
works or screenplays. See website for full
details.

The Chudney Agency

72 North State Road, Suite 501, Briarcliff
Manor , NY 10510
Tel: +1 (201) 758-8739
Fax: +1 (201) 758-8739
Email: steven@thechudneyagency.com
Website: http://www.thechudneyagency.com

Handles: Fiction; *Areas:* Historical;
Humour; Mystery; Suspense; *Markets:*
Adult; Children's; Youth; *Treatments:*
Commercial; Literary; Mainstream

Handles children's and young adult books.
Send query only in first instance. Happy to
accept queries by email. Submit material
upon invitation only. No fantasy, science
fiction, early readers, or scripts. See website
for full guidelines.

Frances Collin Literary Agent

PO Box 33, Wayne, PA 19087-0033
Tel: +1 (610) 254-0555
Fax: +1 (610) 254-5029
Email: queries@francescollin.com
Website: http://www.francescollin.com

Handles: Fiction; Nonfiction; *Areas:*
Autobiography; Biography; Culture;
Fantasy; Historical; Nature; Sci-Fi; Travel;
Women's Interests; *Markets:* Adult;
Treatments: Literary

Send query by email (no attachments) or by
post with SASE or IRCs if outside the US.
No queries by phone or fax.

Don Congdon Associates, Inc.

110 William St. Suite 2202, New York, NY
10038
Tel: +1 (212) 645-1229
Fax: +1 (212) 727-2688
Email: dca@doncongdon.com

Website: http://doncongdon.com

Handles: Fiction; Nonfiction; *Areas:*
Adventure; Anthropology; Archaeology;
Autobiography; Biography; Cookery; Crime;
Culture; Current Affairs; Film; Health;
Historical; Humour; Legal; Lifestyle;
Literature; Medicine; Military; Music;
Mystery; Nature; Politics; Psychology;
Science; Technology; Theatre; Thrillers;
Travel; Women's Interests; *Markets:* Adult;
Treatments: Literary; Mainstream

Send query by email (no attachments) or by
post with SASE. Include one-page synopsis,
relevant background info, and first chapter,
all within the body of the email if submitting
by email. Include the word "Query" in the
subject line. See website for full guidelines.
No unsolicited MSS.

Connor Literary Agency

2911 West 71st Street, Minneapolis, MN
55423
Tel: +1 (612) 866-1486
Email: connoragency@aol.com
Website: http://www.connorliteraryagency.
webs.com

Handles: Fiction; Nonfiction; *Areas:*
Autobiography; Cookery; Crafts; Crime;
Criticism; Culture; Current Affairs; Design;
Finance; Health; Historical; Hobbies;
Horror; How-to; Humour; Legal; Lifestyle;
Literature; Medicine; Photography; Politics;
Self-Help; Women's Interests; *Markets:*
Adult; Children's;
*Treatments:*Contemporary; Literary;
Mainstream; Satirical

Send query by email or via contact form on
website. Seeking previously published
authors and talented new writers. Prefers
writers who have or have the potential to
gain national exposure through their own
efforts. No unsolicited MSS.

The Doe Coover Agency

PO Box 668, Winchester, MA 01890
Tel: +1 (781) 721-6000
Fax: +1 (781) 721-6727
Email: info@doecooveragency.com
Website: http://doecooveragency.com

Handles: Fiction; Nonfiction; Reference; *Areas:* Autobiography; Biography; Business; Cookery; Finance; Gardening; Health; Historical; Music; Politics; Psychology; Science; Sociology; Sport; Technology; *Markets:* Adult; *Treatments:* Commercial; Literary; Popular

Send query by email only with (for nonfiction) a detailed proposal, including overview, table of contents or detailed outline, author biography, and pertinent marketing information; or (for fiction) a detailed synopsis, the first 50 pages, and author bio. Specialises in cookery, general nonfiction (particularly interested in books on social issues), and journalism, as well as both commercial and literary fiction. No children's books, or queries by fax or by post.

Crawford Literary Agency
92 Evans Road, Barnstead, NH 03218
Tel: +1 (603) 269-5851
Fax: +1 (603) 269-2533
Email: crawfordlit@att.net

Handles: Fiction; Nonfiction; *Areas:* Adventure; Crime; Entertainment; How-to; Legal; Media; Medicine; Psychology; Romance; Self-Help; Suspense; Thrillers; Women's Interests; *Markets:* Adult; *Treatments:* Commercial

No poetry or short stories. Send query with SASE.

Crichton & Associates, Inc.
6940 Carroll Avenue, Takoma Park, MD 20912
Tel: +1 (301) 495-9663
Fax: +1 (202) 318-0050
Email: query@crichton-associates.com
Website: http://crichton-associates.com

Handles: Fiction; Nonfiction; *Areas:* Crime; Culture; Legal; Mystery; Politics; Religious; Romance; Suspense; Women's Interests; *Markets:* Adult; *Treatments:* Literary; Mainstream

Send query by email with description of project and author bio, and proposal for nonfiction or synopsis and first three chapters for fiction, all in the body of the email (no attachments). Indicate in subject line if fiction or nonfiction. Postal submissions also accepted, but include email address for response. No poetry, screenplays, children's, young adult, or science fiction.

The Croce Agency
1213 Anderson Avenue, Suite 3161, Fort Lee, NJ 07024
Tel: +1 (201) 248-3175
Email: submissions@thecroceagency.com
Website: http://www.thecroceagency.com

Handles: Fiction; Nonfiction; *Markets:* Adult; *Treatments:* Mainstream

Boutique literary agency, representing mainstream fiction and nonfiction. Send query via online form on website.

The Culinary Entertainment Agency (CEA)
53 W 36, #706, New York, NY 10018
Tel: +1 (212) 380-1264
Email: info@the-cea.com
Website: http://www.the-cea.com

Handles: Nonfiction; *Areas:* Cookery; Lifestyle; *Markets:* Adult

Literary agency focused on the cooking and lifestyle markets.

Curtis Brown Ltd
10 Astor Place, New York, NY 10003
Tel: +1 (212) 473-5400
Fax: +1 (212) 598-0917
Email: gc@cbltd.com
Website: http://www.curtisbrown.com

Handles: Fiction; Nonfiction; *Markets:* Adult; Children's; Youth

Handles material for adults and children in all genres. Send query with SASE, synopsis, CV and a sample chapter. No unsolicited MSS. No scripts.

Richard Curtis Associates, Inc.

171 East 74th Street, Floor 2, New York, NY 10021
Tel: +1 (212) 772-7363
Fax: +1 (212) 772-7393
Email: info@curtisagency.com
Website: http://www.curtisagency.com

Handles: Fiction; Nonfiction; *Areas:* Autobiography; Biography; Business; Fantasy; Finance; Health; Historical; Medicine; Mystery; Romance; Science; Sci-Fi; Technology; Thrillers; Westerns; *Markets:* Adult; Children's; Youth

Accepts approaches from authors previously published with national publishing houses only.

Laura Dail Literary Agency

350 Seventh Avenue, Suite 2003, New York, NY 10001
Tel: +1 (212) 239-7477
Fax: +1 (212) 947-0460
Email: queries@ldlainc.com
Website: http://www.ldlainc.com

Handles: Fiction; Nonfiction; *Areas:* Autobiography; Biography; Cookery; Crime; Fantasy; Historical; Humour; Mystery; Science; Sci-Fi; Technology; Thrillers; Women's Interests; *Markets:* Adult; Children's; Youth; *Treatments:* Commercial; Light; Literary; Serious

Send query by email (preferred) with the word "query" in the subject line, or by post with SASE. You may optionally include a synopsis and up to 10 pages. Particularly interested in historical and high-concept fiction, funny YA, humour, and serious nonfiction. Also considers graphical novels. No children's picture books, new age, screenplays, poetry, or unsolicited Spanish material.

Darhansoff & Verrill Literary Agents

133 West 72nd Street, Room 304, New York, NY 10023
Tel: +1 (917) 305-1300

Fax: +1 (917) 305-1400
Email: submissions@dvagency.com
Website: http://www.dvagency.com

Handles: Fiction; Nonfiction; *Areas:* Mystery; Suspense; *Markets:* Adult; Children's; Youth; *Treatments:* Literary

Particularly interested in literary fiction, narrative nonfiction, memoir, sophisticated suspense, and fiction and nonfiction for younger readers. No theatrical plays or film scripts. Send queries by post or email. See website for full submission guidelines.

Liza Dawson Associates

350 Seventh Avenue, Suite 2003, New York, NY 10001
Tel: +1 (212) 465-9071
Fax: +1 (212) 947-0460
Email: queryliza@LizaDawsonAssociates.com
Website: http://www.lizadawsonassociates.com

Handles: Fiction; Nonfiction; *Areas:* Autobiography; Business; Culture; Current Affairs; Fantasy; Historical; Humour; Lifestyle; Medicine; Military; Mystery; Politics; Psychology; Religious; Romance; Science; Sci-Fi; Self-Help; Sociology; Spiritual; Suspense; Theatre; Thrillers; Women's Interests; *Markets:* Academic; Adult; Children's; Youth; *Treatments:* Commercial; Literary; Mainstream; Popular

See website for specific agent interests and query appropriate agent directly. Specific agent submission guidelines and contact details are available on website.

Deal Points Ent.

Tel: +1 (424) 652-4411
Email: ak@dealpointsent.com
Website: http://www.dealpointsent.com

Handles: Fiction; Nonfiction; Scripts; *Areas:* Crime; *Markets:* Academic; Adult; Professional; *Treatments:* Commercial; Literary

A strictly literary focused agency for writers, producers, and directors.

The Jennifer DeChiara Literary Agency

31 East 32nd Street, Suite 300, New York, NY 10016
Tel: +1 (212) 481-8484
Fax: +1 (212) 481-9582
Email: jenndec@aol.com
Website: http://www.jdlit.com

Handles: Fiction; Nonfiction; *Areas:* Autobiography; Biography; Cookery; Culture; Fantasy; Film; Health; Historical; How-to; Humour; Lifestyle; Literature; Mystery; Science; Self-Help; Sociology; Sport; Suspense; Theatre; Thrillers; Travel; Women's Interests; *Markets:* Adult; Children's; Youth; *Treatments:* Commercial; Contemporary; Literary; Mainstream; Popular

Send query by email only. Posted submissions will be discarded. See website for full guidelines and for specific agent interests and email addresses.

DeFiore and Company

47 East 19th Street, 3rd Floor, New York, NY 10003
Tel: +1 (212) 925-7744
Fax: +1 (212) 925-9803
Email: submissions@defioreandco.com
Website: http://www.defioreandco.com

Handles: Fiction; Nonfiction; *Areas:* Arts; Biography; Culture; Current Affairs; Historical; Lifestyle; Literature; Medicine; Military; Music; Nature; Philosophy; Politics; Psychology; Romance; Science; Short Stories; Sociology; Technology; Thrillers; *Markets:* Adult; Children's; Youth; *Treatments:* Commercial; Literary; Mainstream

Always looking for exciting, fresh, new talent, and currently accepting queries for both fiction and nonfiction. Send query with summary, description of why you're writing the book, any specific credentials, and (for fiction) first five pages. Send by email (with all material in the body of the text; no attachments; and the word "Query" in the subject line) or post with SASE. See website

for specific agent interests and methods of approach. No scripts for film, TV, or theatre.

Joëlle Delbourgo Associates, Inc.

101 Park St., Montclair, Montclair, NJ 07042
Tel: +1 (973) 773-0836
Email: submissions@delbourgo.com
Website: http://www.delbourgo.com

Handles: Fiction; Nonfiction; Reference; *Areas:* Autobiography; Biography; Business; Culture; Current Affairs; Fantasy; Health; Historical; Lifestyle; Mystery; Psychology; Science; Sci-Fi; Thrillers; Women's Interests; *Markets:* Adult; Children's; Youth; *Treatments:* Commercial; Popular

We are a highly selective agency, broad in our interests. No category romance, Westerns, early readers, or picture books. Send query by email to specific agent (see website for interests and email addresses) or to generic submissions address. Submissions must include the word "QUERY" in the subject line. See website for full guidelines.

Sandra Dijkstra Literary Agency

PMB 515, 1155 Camino Del Mar, Del Mar, CA 92014
Tel: +1 (858) 755-3115
Fax: +1 (858) 794-2822
Email: queries@dijkstraagency.com
Website: http://www.dijkstraagency.com

Handles: Fiction; Nonfiction; *Areas:* Autobiography; Business; Cookery; Culture; Current Affairs; Design; Fantasy; Health; Historical; Humour; Lifestyle; Music; Mystery; Politics; Religious; Romance; Science; Sci-Fi; Self-Help; Short Stories; Sociology; Sport; Thrillers; Travel; Women's Interests; *Markets:* Adult; Children's; Youth; *Treatments:* Commercial; Contemporary; Literary

Check author bios on website and submit query by email to one agent only. For fiction, include a one-page synopsis, brief bio, and first 10-15 pages. For nonfiction, include overview, chapter outline, brief bio, and first 10-15 pages. All material must be in the body of the email. No attachments. See website for full submission guidelines.

Donadio & Olson, Inc.

40 West 27th Street, 5th Floor, New York, NY 10001
Tel: +1 (212) 691-8077
Fax: +1 (212) 633-2837
Email: mail@donadio.com
Website: http://donadio.com

Handles: Fiction; Nonfiction; *Areas:* Arts; Biography; Culture; Historical; Literature; Nature; Science; *Markets:* Adult; Children's; Youth; *Treatments:* Commercial; Literary; Mainstream

Send query by email with first three chapters or first 25 pages. Allow at least one month for reply.

Janis A. Donnaud & Associates, Inc.

525 Broadway, 2nd Floor, New York, NY 10012
Tel: +1 (212) 431-2664
Fax: +1 (212) 431-2667
Email: jdonnaud@aol.com

Handles: Nonfiction; *Areas:* Beauty and Fashion; Biography; Business; Cookery; Finance; Gardening; Health; Lifestyle; Science; Sport; Travel; Women's Interests; *Markets:* Adult

The agency represents, develops, and packages a wide range of commercially successful properties. It negotiates publishing agreements with the top trade houses in the U.S., licenses all subsidiary rights, arranges foreign editions and translation rights, and licenses film and performance rights. The agency has a working relationship with Artists Agency to handle television clients. The agency's varied list is concentrated mainly on nonfiction, with a special emphasis on the culinary.

Jim Donovan Literary

5635 SMU Boulevard, Suite 201, Dallas, TX 75206

Email: jdliterary@sbcglobal.net

Handles: Fiction; Nonfiction; Reference; *Areas:* Adventure; Autobiography; Biography; Business; Crime; Culture; Current Affairs; Finance; Health; Historical; How-to; Legal; Lifestyle; Medicine; Military; Music; Mystery; Nature; Politics; Science; Sport; Suspense; Thrillers; Westerns; Women's Interests; *Markets:* Adult; *Treatments:* Commercial; Contemporary; Literary; Mainstream; Popular

Send query with SASE or by email. For fiction, include first 30-50 pages and a 2-5 page outline. Handles mainly nonfiction, and specialises in commercial fiction and nonfiction. No poetry, children's, science fiction, fantasy short stories, autobiography, or inspirational.

Doyen Literary Services, Inc.

1931 660th Street, Newell, IA 50568-7613
Tel: +1 (712) 272-3300
Email: bestseller@barbaradoyen.com
Website: http://www.barbaradoyen.com

Handles: Nonfiction; *Areas:* Anthropology; Archaeology; Architecture; Arts; Autobiography; Biography; Business; Cookery; Crafts; Crime; Culture; Current Affairs; Design; Film; Finance; Gardening; Health; How-to; Leisure; Lifestyle; Politics; Psychology; Science; Self-Help; Sociology; Technology; Theatre; Women's Interests; *Markets:* Adult

Send query by email. Handles adult trade nonfiction only. No poetry, screenplays, children's books, or teen books.

The Dravis Agency, Inc.

4370 Tujunga AVE, Suite 145, Studio City, CA 91604
Tel: +1 (818) 501-1177
Fax: +1 (818) 501-1194
Email: monrose@monteiro-rose.com
Website: http://www.monteiro-rose.com

Handles: Scripts; *Areas:* Adventure; Crime; Drama; Film; Historical; Humour; Mystery; Romance; Sci-Fi; Suspense; Thrillers; TV;

Markets: Adult; Children's; Family; Youth;
Treatments: Contemporary; Mainstream

Handles for TV, film, and animation. No
unsolicited mss. Accepts new clients by
referral only.

Dunham Literary, Inc.

110 William Street, Suite 2202, New York,
NY 10038
Tel: +1 (212) 929-0994
Fax: +1 (212) 929-0904
Email: query@dunhamlit.com
Website: http://www.dunhamlit.com

Handles: Fiction; Nonfiction; *Areas:*
Autobiography; Biography; Culture; Current
Affairs; Fantasy; Historical; Lifestyle;
Music; Nature; Politics; Science; Sci-Fi;
Spiritual; Technology; Travel; Women's
Interests; *Markets:* Adult; Children's; Youth;
Treatments: Literary

Handles quality fiction and nonfiction for
adults and children. Send query by email or
by post with SASE. See website for full
guidelines. No genre romance, Westerns,
poetry, or approaches by phone or fax. No
email attachments.

Dunow, Carlson & Lerner Agency

27 West 20th Street, Suite 1107, New York,
NY 10011
Tel: +1 (212) 645-7606
Email: mail@dclagency.com
Website: http://www.dclagency.com

Handles: Fiction; Nonfiction; *Areas:* Arts;
Autobiography; Biography; Criticism;
Culture; Current Affairs; Health; Historical;
Humour; Music; Mystery; Science; Sport;
Suspense; Thrillers; Women's Interests;
Markets: Adult; Children's; Youth;
Treatments: Commercial; Literary

Send query by post with SASE or by email.
No attachments. Does not respond to all
email queries.

Dystel & Goderich Literary Management

One Union Square West, Suite 904, New
York, NY 10003
Tel: +1 (212) 627-9100
Fax: +1 (212) 627-9313
Email: miriam@dystel.com
Website: http://www.dystel.com

Handles: Fiction; Nonfiction; *Areas:*
Adventure; Anthropology; Archaeology;
Autobiography; Biography; Business;
Cookery; Crime; Culture; Current Affairs;
Fantasy; Finance; Health; Historical;
Humour; Lifestyle; Military; Mystery; New
Age; Politics; Psychology; Religious;
Romance; Science; Sci-Fi; Spiritual;
Suspense; Technology; Thrillers; Women's
Interests; *Markets:* Adult; Children's; Youth;
Treatments: Commercial; Contemporary;
Literary; Mainstream; Popular

Prefers email approaches, but will also still
accept queries by post with brief synopsis
and sample chapter with SASE. Email
queries should include the cover letter in the
body of the email, and synopsis and sample
material (a chapter or the first 25 pages)
either below the query letter or in an attached
document. Attachments to blank emails will
not be opened.. Queries should be brief,
devoid of gimmicks, and professionally
presented, including author details and any
writing credits. See website for more details.

East West Literary Agency LLC

1158 26th Street, Suite 462, Santa Monica,
CA 90403
Tel: +1 (310) 573-9303
Fax: +1 (310) 453-9008
Email: dwarren@
eastwestliteraryagency.com
Website: http://eastwestliteraryagency.com

Handles: Fiction; Nonfiction; *Markets:*
Children's; Youth; *Treatments:* Niche

Specialises in children's books of all genres:
from concept, novelty and picture books toh
young adult literature. Represents both
authors and illustrators.

Accepts queries via email only and by referral only. See website for current details.

Ebeling & Associates

PO Box 2529, Lyons, CO 80540
Tel: +1 (808) 579-6414
Fax: +1 (808) 579-9294
Email: michael@ebelingagency.com
Website: http://www.ebelingagency.com

Handles: Nonfiction; *Areas:* Business; Health; Self-Help; *Markets:* Adult; *Treatments:* Commercial

Accepts queries and proposals by email only. Write "Inquiry for Author Representation" in subject line and outline your book in up to 200 words in the body of the email. Attach proposal as Word or PDF document. See website for proposal requirements. Submissions by post are not accepted. No fiction, poetry, or children's.

Anne Edelstein Literary Agency

404 Riverside Drive, New York, NY 10025
Tel: +1 (212) 414-4923
Fax: +1 (212) 414-2930
Email: info@aeliterary.com
Website: http://www.aeliterary.com

Handles: Fiction; Nonfiction; *Areas:* Autobiography; Historical; Psychology; Religious; *Markets:* Adult; *Treatments:* Commercial; Literary

Note: Note accepting approaches as at August 2014

Send query letter with SASE and for fiction a summary of your novel plus the first 25 pages, or for nonfiction an outline of your book and one or two sample chapters. No queries by email.

Judith Ehrlich Literary Management

146 Central Park West, 20E, New York, NY 10023
Tel: +1 (646) 505-1570
Email: jehrlich@judithehrlichliterary.com
Website: http://www.

judithehrlichliterary.com

Handles: Fiction; Nonfiction; *Areas:* Arts; Autobiography; Biography; Business; Culture; Current Affairs; Fantasy; Health; Historical; How-to; Humour; Legal; Lifestyle; Medicine; Mystery; Politics; Psychology; Romance; Science; Self-Help; Sociology; Sport; Thrillers; Women's Interests; *Markets:* Adult; Children's; Youth; *Treatments:* Commercial; Literary; Mainstream

Send query by email only. No attachments. For nonfiction give details of your book, your qualifications for writing it, and any existing platform. For fiction include synopsis, writing credentials, and 7-10 sample pages, pasted into the body of the email. No poetry, textbooks, plays or screenplays. See website for full guidelines and individual agent details and email addresses. Response not guaranteed.

Einstein Literary Management

27 West 20th Street, Suite 1003, New York, NY 10011
Tel: +1 (212) 221-8797
Fax: +1 (212) 221-8722
Email: submissions@einsteinliterary.com
Website: http://einsteinliterary.com

Handles: Fiction; Nonfiction; *Areas:* Autobiography; Biography; Historical; Mystery; Romance; Thrillers; Women's Interests; *Markets:* Adult; Children's; Youth; *Treatments:* Literary

No picture books, poetry, textbooks, or screenplays. Accepts submissions by email only. See website for full submission guidelines. No queries by post or by phone.

Ethan Ellenberg Literary Agency

548 Broadway, #5E, New York, NY 10012
Tel: +1 (212) 431-4554
Fax: +1 (212) 941-4652
Email: agent@ethanellenberg.com
Website: http://www.ethanellenberg.com

Handles: Fiction; Nonfiction; *Areas:* Adventure; Autobiography; Biography;

Cookery; Crime; Culture; Current Affairs; Fantasy; Health; Historical; Mystery; New Age; Psychology; Romance; Science; Sci-Fi; Spiritual; Thrillers; Women's Interests; *Markets:* Adult; Children's; *Treatments:* Commercial; Literary

Actively looking for established and new writers in a wide range of genres. Send query by email (no attachments; paste material into the body of the email) or by post with SASE. For fiction send synopsis and first 50 pages. For nonfiction send proposal, author bio, and sample chapters. For picture books send complete MS. No poetry, short stories, scripts, or queries by fax.

We have been in business for over 17 years. We are a member of the AAR. We accept unsolicited submissions and, of course, do not charge reading fees.

Nicholas Ellison, Inc.

55 Fifth Avenue, 15th Floor, New York, NY 10003
Tel: +1 (212) 206-5600
Fax: +1 (212) 436-8718
Email: nellison@sjga.com
Website: http://www.greenburger.com

Handles: Fiction; Nonfiction; *Markets:* Adult; *Treatments:* Literary; Mainstream

Represents primarily fiction, along with a select list of nonfiction. Send queries by email including brief description and any relevant credentials in the body of the email, and attach at least 50 pages along with any other relevant material. Assume rejection if no response within 6 weeks.

Ann Elmo Agency, Inc.

305 Seventh Avenue, #1101, New York, NY 10001
Tel: +1 (212) 661-2880
Fax: +1 (212) 661-2883
Email: aalitagent@aol.com

Handles: Fiction; Nonfiction; *Areas:* Biography; Culture; Current Affairs; Gothic; Health; Historical; How-to; Romance; Science; Thrillers; Women's Interests; *Markets:* Adult; Family; *Treatments:*

Contemporary; Mainstream

No unsolicited mss.

Elaine P. English, Attorney & Literary Agent

4710 41st Street, NW, Suite D, Wahington, DC 20016
Tel: +1 (202) 362-5190
Fax: +1 (202) 362-5192
Email: queries@elaineenglish.com
Website: http://www.elaineenglish.com

Handles: Fiction; *Areas:* Erotic; Fantasy; Gothic; Historical; Humour; Mystery; Romance; Women's Interests; *Markets:* Adult; *Treatments:* Commercial; Contemporary; Dark; Light; Serious; Traditional

Closed to approaches as at September 2015. Check website for current status.

Handles women's fiction, mysteries, and thrillers. Handles romance ranging from historical to contemporary, funny to erotic, and paranormal. No memoirs, science fiction, fantasy (unless romance fantasy), children's, young adult, horror, thrillers, short stories, screenplays, or nonfiction. Send query by email in first instance – see website for full guidelines. No attachments or unsolicited materials.

Felicia Eth Literary Representation

555 Bryant Street, Suite 350, Palo Alto, CA 94301
Tel: +1 (650) 375-1276
Fax: +1 (650)401-8892
Email: feliciaeth.literary@gmail.com
Website: http://ethliterary.com

Handles: Fiction; Nonfiction; *Areas:* Anthropology; Autobiography; Biography; Business; Crime; Culture; Current Affairs; Finance; Health; Historical; Legal; Lifestyle; Medicine; Nature; Politics; Psychology; Science; Sociology; Spiritual; Technology; Travel; Women's Interests; *Markets:* Adult; *Treatments:* Commercial; Contemporary; Literary; Mainstream

Send query by email or by post with SASE, including details about yourself and your project. Send sample pages upon invitation only.

Mary Evans, Inc.

242 East Fifth Street, New York, NY 10003
Tel: +1 (212) 979-0880
Fax: +1 (212) 979-5344
Email: info@maryevansinc.com
Website: http://www.maryevansinc.com

Handles: Fiction; Nonfiction; *Areas:* Culture; Historical; Medicine; Politics; Science; Sociology; Technology; *Markets:* Adult; Children's; Youth; *Treatments:* Commercial; Literary

Send query by email or by with SASE. Does not represent scriptwriters, unless they also write books. See website for full submission guidelines.

Evatopia, Inc.

8447 Wilshire Boulevard, Suite 401, Beverly Hills, CA 90211
Email: submissions@evatopia.com
Website: http://www.evatopia.com

Handles: Fiction; Nonfiction; Scripts; *Areas:* Adventure; Autobiography; Biography; Crime; Drama; Fantasy; Film; Historical; Horror; Humour; Mystery; Romance; Sport; Suspense; Thrillers; Women's Interests; *Markets:* Adult; Children's; Youth; *Treatments:* Contemporary; Mainstream

Send query by email only. Handles scripts, TV/reality series; fiction graphic novels, nonfiction, and music, aimed at women, teens, and children. See website for full guidelines.

Fairbank Literary Representation

P.O. Box 6, Hudson, NY 12534-0006
Tel: +1 (617) 576-0030
Fax: +1 (617) 576-0030
Email: queries@fairbankliterary.com
Website: http://www.fairbankliterary.com

Handles: Fiction; Nonfiction; Reference;

Areas: Architecture; Biography; Cookery; Culture; Design; Humour; Lifestyle; Mystery; Science; Sport; Thrillers; *Markets:* Adult; *Treatments:* Literary; Mainstream

No romance, poetry, screenplays, science fiction or fantasy, paranormal, young adult, children's books, or novels set before 1900. Send one-page query outlining work by post or email. If sending by post a sample chapter may be included, plus SASE if return is required. If sending by email, do not include attachments, but you may include up to the first three pages pasted into the email. No queries by fax, or phone calls. Works over 120,000 by unpublished authors are probably too long to be accepted.

The Fielding Agency, LLC

269 South Beverly Drive, #341, Beverly Hills, CA 90212
Tel: +1 (323) 461-4791
Email: wlee@fieldingagency.com
Website: http://fieldingagency.com

Handles: Fiction; Nonfiction; *Areas:* Adventure; Anthropology; Archaeology; Architecture; Arts; Autobiography; Biography; Business; Cookery; Crafts; Crime; Culture; Current Affairs; Design; Fantasy; Finance; Health; Historical; Horror; How-to; Humour; Legal; Lifestyle; Literature; Medicine; Military; Mystery; Nature; Politics; Psychology; Romance; Science; Self-Help; Short Stories; Sociology; Sport; Technology; Thrillers; Translations; Women's Interests; *Markets:* Adult; Children's; Youth; *Treatments:* Literary; Mainstream; Satirical

Send query with SASE or by email (no attachments), including detailed outline / proposal of your book, and brief description of your writing background. Handles all genres of fiction and nonfiction, but need to feel passionately about a book to accept it. Handles film rights to books already represented only. No screenplays or queries by phone.

Diana Finch Literary Agency

116 West 23rd Street, Suite 500, New York, NY 10011

Tel: +1 (917) 544-4470
Email: diana.finch@verizon.net
Website: http://dianafinchliteraryagency.
blogspot.com

Handles: Fiction; Nonfiction; *Areas:*
Adventure; Autobiography; Biography;
Business; Crime; Culture; Current Affairs;
Film; Finance; Health; Historical; How-to;
Humour; Legal; Lifestyle; Medicine;
Military; Music; Nature; Photography;
Politics; Psychology; Science; Self-Help;
Sport; Technology; Theatre; Thrillers;
Translations; Women's Interests; *Markets:*
Academic; Adult; Youth; *Treatments:*
Literary; Mainstream; Satirical

Approach using online submission system –
see website for link. Particularly interested in
narrative nonfiction, health, and popular
science, however actively looking for new
fiction to balance the list. No children's
picture books, romance, or mysteries.

Fine Literary

1236 Comstock Avenue, Los Angeles, CA
90024
Email: asst@FineLiterary.com
Website: http://www.FineLiterary.com

Handles: Fiction; Nonfiction; *Areas:*
Adventure; Antiques; Architecture; Arts;
Autobiography; Beauty and Fashion;
Biography; Business; Cookery; Crafts;
Crime; Culture; Current Affairs; Design;
Drama; Entertainment; Gardening; Health;
Historical; How-to; Humour; Leisure;
Lifestyle; Literature; Men's Interests; Music;
Mystery; Psychology; Romance; Science;
Self-Help; Spiritual; Sport; Suspense;
Technology; Theatre; Thrillers; Travel;
Women's Interests; *Markets:* Adult; Youth;
Treatments: Commercial; Contemporary;
Cynical; Dark; Light; Literary; Mainstream;
Niche; Popular; Positive; Progressive;
Satirical; Serious; Traditional

Literary agency based in Los Angeles,
focused on the development of Literary
careers.

Interested in queries of all kinds: from
Romance and Thrillers to Literary Fiction
and Cookbooks. Our interests are vast but

our attention is micro-focused on selling
your work to the right publisher.

Accepts submissions by post or by email.
Send query with brief synopsis along with
first 20 pages for fiction, or details of why
you are writing the book and its place in the
market for nonfiction. See website for full
guidelines. Response to email queries not
guaranteed.

The James Fitzgerald Agency

118 Waverly Pl., #1B, New York, NY 10011
Tel: +1 (212) 308-1122
Email: submissions@jfitzagency.com
Website: http://www.jfitzagency.com

Handles: Fiction; Nonfiction; *Areas:*
Culture; *Markets:* Adult

Primarily represents books reflecting the
popular culture of the day, in fiction,
nonfiction, graphic and packaged books. No
poetry or screenplays. All information must
be submitted in English, even if the
manuscript is in another language. See
website for detailed submission guidelines.

Flannery Literary

1140 Wickfield Court, Naperville, IL 60563-
3300
Tel: +1 (630) 428-2682
Fax: +1 (630) 428-2683
Email: jennifer@flanneryliterary.com
Website: http://flanneryliterary.com

Handles: Fiction; Nonfiction; *Markets:*
Children's; Youth

Send query with SASE. Deals exclusively in
children's and young adults' fiction and
nonfiction, including picture books. No
queries by fax or email. See website for full
guidelines.

Peter Fleming Agency

PO Box 458, Pacific Palisades, CA 90272
Tel: +1 (310) 454-1373
Email: peterfleming@earthlink.net

Handles: Nonfiction; *Markets:* Adult;
Treatments: Commercial

Send query with SASE. Seeks one-of-a-kind nonfiction books that unearth innovative and uncomfortable truths, and which have bestseller potential. Must be backed up by author's expertise in given area.

Fletcher & Company

78 Fifth Avenue, Third Floor, New York, NY 10011
Tel: +1 (212) 614-0778
Fax: +1 (212) 614-0728
Email: info@fletcherandco.com
Website: http://www.fletcherandco.com

Handles: Fiction; Nonfiction; *Areas:* Autobiography; Biography; Business; Current Affairs; Health; Historical; Humour; Lifestyle; Science; Sport; Travel; *Markets:* Adult; Youth; *Treatments:* Commercial; Literary

Full-service literary agency representing writers of nonfiction and commercial and literary fiction. Send query with brief synopsis by post with SASE, or by email (no attachments). No genre fiction. Query only one agent at a time and allow 4-6 weeks before following up.

Folio Literary Management, LLC

630 9th Avenue, Suite 1101, New York, NY 10036
Email: jeff@foliolit.com
Website: http://www.foliolit.com

Handles: Fiction; Nonfiction; Reference; *Areas:* Autobiography; Business; Cookery; Crime; Culture; Entertainment; Fantasy; Health; Historical; Horror; How-to; Humour; Lifestyle; Media; Military; Music; Mystery; Politics; Psychology; Religious; Romance; Science; Sci-Fi; Self-Help; Spiritual; Sport; Suspense; Technology; Thrillers; Women's Interests; *Markets:* Adult; Children's; Youth; *Treatments:* Commercial; Contemporary; Dark; Literary; Popular; Serious

Read agent bios on website and decide which agent to approach. Do not submit to multiple agents simultaneously. Each agent has different submission requirements: consult

website for details. No unsolicited MSS or multiple submissions.

Jeanne Fredericks Literary Agency, Inc.

221 Benedict Hill Road, New Canaan, CT 06840
Tel: +1 (203) 972-3011
Fax: +1 (203) 972-3011
Email: jeanne.fredericks@gmail.com
Website: http://jeannefredericks.com

Handles: Nonfiction; Reference; *Areas:* Antiques; Arts; Biography; Business; Cookery; Crafts; Design; Finance; Gardening; Health; Historical; How-to; Legal; Leisure; Lifestyle; Medicine; Nature; Photography; Psychology; Science; Self-Help; Sport; Travel; Women's Interests; *Markets:* Adult

Send query by email (no attachments) or post with SASE. Specialises in adult nonfiction by authorities in their fields. No fiction, true crime, juvenile, textbooks, poetry, essays, screenplays, short stories, science fiction, pop culture, guides to computers and software, politics, horror, pornography, books on overly depressing or violent topics, romance, teacher's manuals, or memoirs. See website for full guidelines.

Grace Freedson's Publishing Network

375 North Broadway, Suite 102, Jericho, NY 11753
Tel: +1 (516) 931-7757
Fax: +1 (516) 931-7759
Email: gfreedson@worldnet.att.net

Handles: Nonfiction; *Areas:* Business; Cookery; Crafts; Culture; Current Affairs; Finance; Health; Historical; Hobbies; How-to; Humour; Lifestyle; Medicine; Nature; Psychology; Religious; Science; Self-Help; Sport; Technology; *Markets:* Adult; Children's; Youth

Handles nonfiction from qualified authors with credentials and platforms only. No fiction. Send query with synopsis and SASE.

Samuel French, Inc.
235 Park Avenue South, Fifth Floor, New York, NY 10003
Tel: +1 (212) 206-8990
Fax: +1 (212) 206-1429
Email: info@samuelfrench.com
Website: http://www.samuelfrench.com

Handles: Scripts; *Areas:* Crime; Fantasy; Horror; Humour; Mystery; Theatre; Thrillers; *Markets:* Adult

Note: Not accepting unsolicited submissions as at March 2015

Publishes plays and represents writers of plays. Deals in well-known plays from Broadway and London's West End.

Fresh Books Literary Agency
231 Diana Street, Placerville, CA 95667
Email: matt@fresh-books.com
Website: http://www.fresh-books.com

Handles: Nonfiction; Reference; *Areas:* Business; Design; Finance; Health; How-to; Humour; Lifestyle; Photography; Science; Self-Help; Technology; *Markets:* Adult; *Treatments:* Popular

Handles narrative non-fiction, lifestyle and reference titles on subjects such as popular science, technology, health, fitness, photography, design, computing, gadgets, social media, career development, education, business, leadership, personal finance, how-to, and humour. No fiction, children's books, screenplays, or poetry. Send query by email. No attachments. Send further material upon request only.

Sarah Jane Freymann Literary Agency
59 West 71st Street, New York, NY 10023
Tel: +1 (212) 362-9277
Fax: +1 (212) 501-8240
Email: Submissions@
SarahJaneFreymann.com
Website: http://www.sarahjanefreymann.com

Handles: Fiction; Nonfiction; *Areas:* Autobiography; Business; Cookery; Crime; Culture; Health; Historical; Humour;
Lifestyle; Men's Interests; Nature; Psychology; Science; Self-Help; Spiritual; Sport; Thrillers; Travel; Women's Interests; *Markets:* Adult; Youth; *Treatments:* Literary; Mainstream

Prefers to receive queries by email. Include pitch letter and first ten pages pasted into the body of the email (no attachments). See website for full details.

Fredrica S. Friedman and Co. Inc.
857 Fifth Avenue, New York, NY 10065
Tel: +1 (212) 829-9600
Fax: +1 (212) 829-9669
Email: submissions@fredricafriedman.com
Website: http://www.fredricafriedman.com

Handles: Fiction; Nonfiction; *Areas:* Arts; Autobiography; Biography; Business; Cookery; Crime; Culture; Current Affairs; Design; Film; Finance; Health; Historical; How-to; Humour; Lifestyle; Music; Photography; Politics; Psychology; Self-Help; Sociology; Women's Interests; *Markets:* Adult; *Treatments:* Literary

Send query with synopsis by email. For fiction, include ten-page sample. All material must be in the body of the email – no attachments. No poetry, plays, screenplays, children's books, sci-fi/fantasy, or horror.

The G Agency, LLC
PO Box 374, Bronx, NY 10471
Tel: +1 (718) 664-4505
Email: gagencyquery@gmail.com

Handles: Fiction; Nonfiction; *Areas:* Biography; Business; Culture; Finance; Historical; Military; Mystery; Sport; Technology; *Markets:* Adult; *Treatments:* Commercial; Literary; Mainstream; Serious

Send queries by post or by email (prefers email submissions) with sample chapters or proposal. Write "QUERY" in the subject line or on the envelope of postal queries. Email submissions get priority. No screenplays, sci-fi, or romance.

Nancy Gallt Literary Agency

273 Charlton Avenue, South Orange , NJ
07079
Tel: +1 (973) 761-6358
Fax: +1 (973) 761-6318
Email: nancy@nancygallt.com
Website: http://www.nancygallt.com

Handles: Fiction; *Markets:* Children's;
Youth

Handles children's books only. Use
submission form on website or submit by
post with SASE and appropriate postage if
return of material required. All online
submissions must go through the submission
form on the website.

Gelfman Schneider Literary Agents, Inc.

850 Seventh Avenue, Suite 903, New York,
NY 10019
Tel: +1 (212) 245-1993
Email: mail@gelfmanschneider.com
Website: http://www.gelfmanschneider.com

Handles: Fiction; Nonfiction; *Areas:*
Autobiography; Culture; Current Affairs;
Historical; Mystery; Politics; Science;
Suspense; Thrillers; Women's Interests;
Markets: Adult; *Treatments:* Commercial;
Literary; Mainstream; Popular

Different agents within the agency have
different submission guidelines. See website
for full details. No screenplays, or poetry.

The Gernert Company

136 East 57th Street, New York, NY 10022
Tel: +1 (212) 838-7777
Fax: +1 (212) 838-6020
Email: info@thegernertco.com
Website: http://www.thegernertco.com

Handles: Fiction; Nonfiction; *Areas:*
Adventure; Arts; Autobiography; Biography;
Crafts; Crime; Current Affairs; Fantasy;
Historical; Politics; Science; Sci-Fi;
Sociology; Sport; Thrillers; Women's
Interests; *Markets:* Academic; Adult;
Children's; Youth; *Treatments:* Commercial;
Literary; Popular

Send query describing work by post with
SASE or email with author info and sample
chapter. If querying by email, send to generic
email and indicate which agent you would
like to query. No queries by fax. Response
only if interested.

Global Lion Intellectual Property Management, Inc.

PO BOX 669238, Pompano Beach, FL
33066
Email: queriesgloballionmgt@gmail.com
Website: http://www.
globallionmanagement.com

Handles: Fiction; Nonfiction; *Markets:*
Adult

Looks for cutting-edge authors of both
fiction and nonfiction with global marketing
and motion picture/television production
potential. Authors must not only have a great
book and future, but also a specific game-
plan of how to use social media to grow their
fan base. Send query by email only with
synopsis, up to 20 pages if available
(otherwise, chapter synopsis), author bio,
and any social media outlets. See website for
full details.

Barry Goldblatt Literary Agency, Inc.

320 7th Avenue, #266, Brooklyn, NY 11215
Email: query@bgliterary.com
Website: http://www.bgliterary.com

Handles: Fiction; *Areas:* Fantasy; Sci-Fi;
Markets: Children's; Youth

Handles books for young people; from
picture books to middle grade and young
adult. Send query by email including the
word "Query" in the subject line and
synopsis and first five pages in the body of
the email. No attachments. Emails with
attachments will be ignored. See website for
full details.

Frances Goldin Literary Agency, Inc.

57 E. 11th Street, Suite 5B, New York, NY
10003

Tel: +1 (212) 777-0047
Fax: +1 (212) 228-1660
Email: agency@goldinlit.com
Website: http://www.goldinlit.com

Handles: Fiction; Nonfiction; *Areas:* Arts;
Autobiography; Culture; Current Affairs;
Entertainment; Film; Historical; Nature;
Philosophy; Science; Sociology; Sport;
Technology; *Markets:* Adult; Children's;
Youth; *Treatments:* Commercial; Literary;
Progressive

Submit through online system available at
website. No screenplays, illustrated books,
genre fiction, romance, science fiction,
cookery, business, diet, racism, sexism,
ageism, homophobia, or pornography.

Goodman Associates

500 West End Avenue, New York, NY
10024
Tel: +1 (212) 873-4806

Handles: Fiction; Nonfiction; *Areas:*
Adventure; Anthropology; Archaeology;
Autobiography; Biography; Business;
Cookery; Crime; Criticism; Culture; Current
Affairs; Erotic; Film; Finance; Health;
Historical; Legal; Leisure; Literature;
Medicine; Military; Music; Mystery; Nature;
Philosophy; Politics; Psychology; Science;
Sociology; Sport; Suspense; Technology;
Theatre; Thrillers; Translations; Travel;
Women's Interests; *Markets:* Adult;
Treatments: Contemporary; Literary;
Mainstream

Send query with SASE. Accepting new
clients by recommendation only. No poetry,
articles, children's, young adult, or individual
stories.

Irene Goodman Literary Agency

27 W. 24 Street, Suite 700B, New York, NY
10010
Tel: +1 (212) 604-0330
Fax: +1 (212) 675-1381
Email: irene.queries@irenegoodman.com
Website: http://www.irenegoodman.com

Handles: Fiction; Nonfiction; *Areas:*

Autobiography; Cookery; Culture; Fantasy;
Historical; Lifestyle; Mystery; Romance;
Science; Sociology; Suspense; Thrillers;
Women's Interests; *Markets:* Adult;
Children's; Youth; *Treatments:* Commercial;
Literary; Popular

Select specific agent to approach based on
details given on website (specific agent
email addresses on website). Send query by
email only with synopsis, bio, and first ten
pages in the body of the email. No poetry,
inspirational fiction, screenplays, or
children's picture books. Response only if
interested. See website for further details.

Kathryn Green Literary Agency, LLC

250 West 57th Street, Suite 2302, New York,
NY 10107
Tel: +1 (212) 245-4225
Fax: +1 (212) 245-4042
Email: query@kgreenagency.com

Handles: Fiction; Nonfiction; *Areas:*
Autobiography; Biography; Business;
Cookery; Crime; Culture; Current Affairs;
Design; Finance; Health; Historical; How-to;
Humour; Lifestyle; Psychology; Romance;
Self-Help; Sport; Suspense; Thrillers;
Women's Interests; *Markets:* Adult;
Children's; Youth;
*Treatments:*Contemporary; Literary;
Mainstream; Satirical

Send query by email. Do not send samples
unless requested. No science fiction, fantasy,
or queries by fax.

Sanford J. Greenburger Associates, Inc

15th Floor, 55 Fifth Avenue, New York, NY
10003
Tel: +1 (212) 206-5600
Fax: +1 (212) 463-8718
Email: queryHL@sjga.com
Website: http://www.greenburger.com

Handles: Fiction; Nonfiction; Reference;
Areas: Arts; Autobiography; Biography;
Business; Entertainment; Fantasy; Health;
Historical; Humour; Lifestyle; Music;
Mystery; Nature; Politics; Psychology;

Romance; Science; Sci-Fi; Self-Help;
Sociology; Sport; Thrillers; Women's
Interests; *Markets:* Adult; Children's;
Youth;*Treatments:* Commercial; Literary;
Popular

Check website for specific agent interests,
guidelines, and contact details. Most will not
accept submissions by post. Aims to respond
to queries within 6-8 weeks.

Blanche C. Gregory Inc.
2 Tudor City Place, New York, NY 10017
Tel: +1 (212) 697-0828
Email: info@bcgliteraryagency.com
Website: http://www.bcgliteraryagency.com

Handles: Fiction; Nonfiction; *Markets:*
Adult; Children's

Specialises in adult fiction and nonfiction,
but will also consider children's literature.
Send query describing your background with
SASE and synopsis. No stage, film or TV
scripts, or queries by fax or email.

Greyhaus Literary Agency
3021 20th St. Pl. SW, Puyallup, WA 98373
Email: submissions@greyhausagency.com
Website: http://www.greyhausagency.com

Handles: Fiction; *Areas:* Romance;
Women's Interests; *Markets:* Adult;
Treatments: Contemporary; Traditional

Small agency focussing only on romance and
women's fiction. To query, send query by
email (no attachments); complete online
form on website; or send query by post with
3-5 page synopsis, first three pages, and
SASE.

Laura Gross Literary Agency
PO Box 610326, Newton Highlands, MA
02461
Tel: +1 (617) 964-2977
Fax: +1 (617) 964-3023
Email: query@lg-la.com
Website: http://lauragrossliteraryagency.com

Handles: Fiction; Nonfiction; *Areas:*
Autobiography; Biography; Culture; Current

Affairs; Health; Historical; Legal; Lifestyle;
Medicine; Mystery; Politics; Psychology;
Sport; Suspense; Thrillers; Women's
Interests; *Markets:* Adult; *Treatments:*
Literary; Mainstream

Submit query using online web form,
including your book's genre and a synopsis
or plot summary. No sample chapters in first
instance.

The Mitchell J. Hamilburg Agency
149 South Barrington Avenue #732, Los
Angeles, CA 90049-2930
Tel: +1 (310) 471-4024
Fax: +1 (310) 471-9588

Handles: Fiction; Nonfiction; Poetry; *Areas:*
Adventure; Anthropology; Architecture;
Autobiography; Biography; Business;
Cookery; Crime; Current Affairs; Fantasy;
Finance; Gardening; Health; Historical;
Horror; Humour; Leisure; Lifestyle;
Military; Mystery; Nature; New Age;
Politics; Psychology; Religious; Romance;
Science; Sci-Fi; Self-Help; Short Stories;
Sociology; Spiritual; Sport; Suspense;
Thrillers; Travel; Women's Interests;
Markets: Adult; Children's; *Treatments:*
Experimental; Literary; Mainstream

Send query with SASE, outline, and 2
sample chapters.

Hannigan Salky Getzler (HSG) Agency
37 West 28th St, 8th floor, New York, NY
10001
Tel: +1 (646) 442-5770
Email: channigan@hsgagency.com
Website: http://hsgagency.com

Handles: Fiction; Nonfiction; *Areas:*
Adventure; Business; Cookery; Current
Affairs; Finance; Historical; Lifestyle;
Mystery; Photography; Politics; Psychology;
Science; Sociology; Thrillers; Travel;
Women's Interests; *Markets:* Adult;
Children's; Youth; *Treatments:* Commercial;
Literary

Send query by email only with first five

pages pasted into the body of the email (no attachments), or the full ms for picture books. See website for agent interests and individual email addresses, and contact one agent only. No screenplays, romance fiction, science fiction, or religious fiction.

Joy Harris Literary Agency, Inc.

381 Park Avenue South, Suite 428, New York, NY 10016
Tel: +1 (212) 924-6269
Fax: +1 (212) 725-5275
Email: submissions@joyharrisliterary.com
Website: http://www.joyharrisliterary.com

Handles: Fiction; Nonfiction; *Areas:* Autobiography; Biography; Culture; Historical; Humour; Media; Mystery; Short Stories; Spiritual; Suspense; Translations; Women's Interests; *Markets:* Adult; Youth; *Treatments:* Experimental; Literary; Mainstream; Satirical

Send query by post with SASE or by email, including sample chapter or outline. Prefers submissions by email. No poetry, screenplays, genre fiction, self-help, or unsolicited mss.

John Hawkins & Associates, Inc.

80 Maiden Lane, STE 1503, New York, NY 10038
Tel: +1 (212) 807-7040
Fax: +1 (212) 807-9555
Email: jha@jhalit.com
Website: http://www.jhalit.com

Handles: Fiction; Nonfiction; *Areas:* Autobiography; Biography; Business; Crime; Current Affairs; Fantasy; Gardening; Health; Historical; Lifestyle; Mystery; Nature; Politics; Psychology; Science; Sci-Fi; Short Stories; Technology; Thrillers; Travel; Women's Interests; *Markets:* Adult

Send query by email with details about you and your writing, and for fiction the first three chapters as a single Word attachment, or for nonfiction include proposal as a single attachment. Include the word "Query" in the subject line. See website for full guidelines.

The Helen Brann Agency, Inc.

94 Curtis Road, Bridgewater, CT 06752
Fax: +1 (860) 355-2572
Email: helenbrannagency@earthlink.net

Handles: Fiction; Nonfiction; *Markets:* Adult

Works mostly with established writers and referrals.

The Jeff Herman Agency, LLC

PO Box 1522, Stockbridge, MA 01262
Tel: +1 (413) 298-0077
Fax: +1 (413) 298-8188
Email: submissions@jeffherman.com
Website: http://www.jeffherman.com

Handles: Nonfiction; Reference; *Areas:* Autobiography; Business; Crime; Culture; Health; Historical; How-to; Lifestyle; Psychology; Self-Help; Spiritual; *Markets:* Academic; Adult

Send query by post with SASE, or by email. With few exceptions, handles nonfiction only, with particular interest in the genres given above. No scripts or unsolicited MSS.

Hidden Value Group

27758 Santa Margarita Pkwy #361, Mission Viejo, CA 92691
Tel: +1 (951) 549-8891
Fax: +1 (951) 549-8891
Email: bookquery@hiddenvaluegroup.com
Website: http://www.hiddenvaluegroup.com

Handles: Fiction; Nonfiction; *Areas:* Business; Lifestyle; Men's Interests; Religious; Self-Help; Women's Interests; *Markets:* Adult; Youth; *Treatments:* Literary

Represents previously published Christian authors (not including self-published authors). Send one-page summary, marketing information, author bio, and two or three sample chapters by email or by post with SASE. Cannot guarantee a response to all email queries. No poetry or short stories, or queries by phone.

Hill Nadell Literary Agency

8899 Beverly Bl., Suite 805, Los Angeles,
CA 90040
Tel: +1 (310) 860-9605
Fax: +1 (310) 860-9672
Email: queries@hillnadell.com
Website: http://www.hillnadell.com

Handles: Fiction; Nonfiction; *Areas:*
Autobiography; Biography; Cookery;
Culture; Current Affairs; Health; Historical;
Legal; Nature; Politics; Science; Thrillers;
Women's Interests; *Markets:* Adult; Youth;
Treatments: Literary; Mainstream

Handles current affairs, food, memoirs and
other narrative nonfiction, fiction, thrillers,
upmarket women's fiction, literary fiction,
genre fiction, graphic novels, and occasional
young adult novels. No scripts or
screenplays. Accepts queries both by post
and by email. See website for full
submission guidelines.

Hopkins Literary Associates

2117 Buffalo Road, Ste. 327, Rochester, NY
14624
Tel: +1 (585) 352-6268
Email: hlasubmissions@rochester.rr.com

Handles: Fiction; *Areas:* Historical;
Romance; Women's Interests; *Markets:*
Adult; Youth; *Treatments:* Contemporary;
Mainstream

Send query by email only. Specialises in
women's fiction, particularly historical and
contemporary romance. No queries by fax or
email.

Hornfischer Literary Management, L.P.

PO Box 50544, Austin, Texas 78763
Email: queries@hornfischerlit.com
Website: http://www.hornfischerlit.com

Handles: Nonfiction; *Areas:* Anthropology;
Archaeology; Autobiography; Biography;
Business; Crime; Culture; Current Affairs;
Finance; Health; Historical; How-to;
Humour; Legal; Lifestyle; Medicine;
Military; Nature; Politics; Psychology;
Religious; Science; Self-Help; Sociology;
Sport; Technology; *Markets:*
Adult;*Treatments:* Commercial; Satirical;
Serious

Send query by email, or by post with SASE.
Response to email queries only if interested.

Andrea Hurst Literary Management

PO Box 1467, Coupeville, WA 98239
Email: info@andreahurst.com
Website: http://www.andreahurst.com

Handles: Fiction; Nonfiction; *Areas:*
Adventure; Autobiography; Business;
Cookery; Crime; Current Affairs; Fantasy;
Historical; How-to; Humour; Politics;
Psychology; Religious; Romance; Science;
Sci-Fi; Self-Help; Thrillers; Westerns;
Women's Interests; *Markets:* Adult; Youth;
Treatments: Commercial; Contemporary

Agent has semi-retired from the agent
division of her business and is now accepting
queries by referral through an existing client,
agent, or publisher only.

InkWell Management

521 Fifth Avenue, 26th Floor, New York,
NY 10175
Tel: +1 (212) 922-3500
Fax: +1 (212) 922-0535
Email: submissions@
inkwellmanagement.com
Website: http://www.
inkwellmanagement.com

Handles: Fiction; Nonfiction; Business;
Crime; Current Affairs; Finance; Health;
Historical; Medicine; Mystery; Psychology;
Self-Help; Thrillers; *Markets:* Adult;
Treatments: Contemporary; Literary;
Mainstream

Send query by email with up to two sample
chapters. No large attachments. Response not
guaranteed. Response within two months if
interested. See website for full guidelines.

International Transactions, Inc.

PO Box 97, Gila, NM 88038-0097

Tel: +1 (845) 373-9696
Fax: +1 (480) 393-5162
Email: info@intltrans.com
Website: http://www.intltrans.com

Handles: Fiction; Nonfiction; *Areas:*
Adventure; Arts; Biography; Crime;
Historical; Medicine; Mystery; Short Stories;
Thrillers; Women's Interests; *Markets:*
Academic; Adult; Youth; *Treatments:*
Contemporary; Literary; Mainstream

Send query with outline or synopsis by
email. No nonfiction enquiries from
unpublished authors. No queries by fax, or
material which is too influenced by TV or
other successful novels. See website for full
submission guidelines.

J de S Associates Inc

9 Shagbark Road, Wilson Point, South
Norwalk, CT 06854
Tel: +1 (203) 838-7571
Fax: +1 (203) 866-2713
Email: jdespoel@aol.com
Website: http://www.jdesassociates.com

Handles: Fiction; *Areas:* Autobiography;
Biography; Business; Crime; Culture;
Current Affairs; Finance; Health; Historical;
How-to; Legal; Lifestyle; Medicine;
Military; Mystery; New Age; Politics; Self-
Help; Sociology; Sport; Suspense; Thrillers;
Translations; Westerns; *Markets:* Adult;
Children's; Youth; *Treatments:*Literary;
Mainstream

Welcomes brief queries by post and by
email, but no samples or other material
unless requested.

Jabberwocky Literary Agency

49 West 45th Street, 12th Floor North, New
York, NY 10036
Tel: +1 (917) 388-3010
Fax: +1 (917) 388-2998
Email: queryeddie@awfulagent.com
Website: http://awfulagent.com

Handles: Fiction; Nonfiction; *Areas:*
Fantasy; Historical; Science; Sci-Fi;
Markets: Adult; Children's; Youth;
Treatments: Literary

Handles a broad range of fiction and
nonfiction intended for general audiences,
but no series romance or poetry. Book-length
material only. Also considers graphic novels
and comics. Send query by post with SASE
or IRC, or by email. No queries by phone or
by fax. See website for full guidelines.

The Jean V. Naggar Literary Agency

216 East 75th Street, New York, NY 10021
Tel: +1 (212) 794-1082
Email: jvnla@jvnla.com
Website: http://www.jvnla.com

Handles: Fiction; Nonfiction; *Areas:*
Adventure; Autobiography; Biography;
Culture; Current Affairs; Fantasy; Gothic;
Health; Historical; Horror; Humour;
Lifestyle; Music; Mystery; Psychology;
Romance; Science; Suspense; Thrillers;
Markets: Adult; Children's; Youth;
Treatments: Commercial; Dark; Literary;
Mainstream; Popular

Accepts queries via online submission
system only. See website for more details.

Jill Grinberg Literary Management LLC

392 Vanderbilt Avenue, Brooklyn, NY
11238
Tel: +1 (212) 620-5883
Email: info@jillgrinbergliterary.com
Website: http://www.jillgrinbergliterary.com

Handles: Fiction; Nonfiction; *Areas:*
Autobiography; Biography; Business;
Culture; Current Affairs; Entertainment;
Fantasy; Finance; Health; Historical;
Humour; Legal; Lifestyle; Medicine; Nature;
Politics; Psychology; Romance; Science;
Sci-Fi; Spiritual; Sport; Technology; Travel;
Women's Interests; *Markets:* Adult;
Children's; Youth; *Treatments:* Commercial;
Literary

Send query with synopsis and first 50 pages
for fiction, or proposal and author bio for
nonfiction.

The Joan Brandt Agency
788 Wesley Drive, Atlanta, GA 30305-3933
Tel: +1 (404) 351-0077

Handles: Fiction; Nonfiction; *Areas:* How-to; Mystery; Suspense; Women's Interests; *Markets:* Adult; *Treatments:* Literary; Mainstream

Send query with SASE. Simultaneous submissions are accepted.

Ken Sherman & Associates
1275 N. Hayworth, Suite 103, Los Angeles, CA 90046
Tel: +1 (310) 273-8840
Fax: +1 (310) 271-2875
Email: ken@kenshermanassociates.com
Website: http://www.kenshermanassociates.com

Handles: Fiction; Nonfiction; Scripts; *Areas:* Film; TV; *Markets:* Adult

Handles fiction, nonfiction, and writers for film and TV. Query by referral only.

Virginia Kidd Agency, Inc
PO Box 278, Milford, PA 18337
Tel: +1 (570) 296-6205
Fax: +1 (570) 296-7266
Email: subs@vk-agency.com
Website: http://www.vk-agency.com

Handles: Fiction; *Areas:* Fantasy; Historical; Mystery; Sci-Fi; Suspense; Women's Interests; *Markets:* Adult; *Treatments:* Mainstream

Specialises in science fiction and fantasy. Send query by post or email with brief synopsis and a few sample pages (not necessarily the opening). See website for full details.

Harvey Klinger, Inc
300 West 55th Street, Suite 11V, New York, NY 10019
Tel: +1 (212) 581-7068
Fax: +1 (212) 315-3823
Email: david@harveyklinger.com
Website: http://www.harveyklinger.com

Handles: Fiction; Nonfiction; *Areas:* Adventure; Autobiography; Biography; Cookery; Crime; Culture; Fantasy; Health; How-to; Humour; Medicine; Music; Mystery; Psychology; Romance; Science; Sci-Fi; Self-Help; Spiritual; Sport; Suspense; Technology; Thrillers; Women's Interests; *Markets:* Adult; Children's; Youth;*Treatments:* Literary; Mainstream; Popular

Send query by email or through submission form on website. No submissions by post. Include short synopsis, author bio, and first five pages, pasted into the body of your email. No attachments. Do not query more than one agent at the agency at a time. See website for individual agent interests and email addresses. No screenplays, or queries by phone or fax. See website for full submission guidelines.

Kneerim & Williams
90 Canal Street, Boston, MA 02114
Tel: +1 (617) 303-1650
Fax: +1 (617) 542-1660
Email: jill@kwlit.com
Website: http://www.kwlit.com

Handles: Fiction; Nonfiction; *Areas:* Adventure; Anthropology; Archaeology; Autobiography; Biography; Business; Crime; Culture; Current Affairs; Finance; Health; Historical; Legal; Lifestyle; Literature; Medicine; Nature; Politics; Psychology; Religious; Science; Sociology; Sport; Technology; Women's Interests;*Markets:* Adult; *Treatments:* Commercial; Literary; Mainstream; Serious

Send query by email to individual agent. See website for specific agent interests and email addresses.

The Knight Agency
Email: submissions@knightagency.net
Website: http://www.knightagency.net

Handles: Fiction; *Areas:* Autobiography; Beauty and Fashion; Business; Cookery; Crime; Culture; Entertainment; Fantasy; Finance; Health; Historical; How-to; Lifestyle; Media; Mystery; Psychology;

Religious; Romance; Sci-Fi; Self-Help; Suspense; Thrillers; Women's Interests; *Markets:* Adult; Children's; Youth;*Treatments:* Commercial; Contemporary; Literary; Popular

Send one-page query by email, with the first five pages of your manuscript in the body of the email. No attachments or paper or phone queries. Paper queries will not be returned.

Not accepting Screen Plays, Short Story Collections, Poetry Collections, Essay Collections, Photography, Film Treatments, Picture Books (excluding graphic novels), Children's Books (excluding young adult and middle grade), Biographies, Nonfiction Historical Treatments.

Linda Konner Literary Agency

10 West 15 Street, Suite 1918, New York, NY 10011
Tel: +1 (212) 691-3419
Email: ldkonner@cs.com
Website: http://www.
lindakonnerliteraryagency.com

Handles: Nonfiction; Reference; *Areas:* Biography; Business; Cookery; Culture; Entertainment; Finance; Health; How-to; Lifestyle; Psychology; Science; Self-Help; Women's Interests; *Markets:* Adult; *Treatments:* Popular

Send one-two page query by email or by post with SASE, synopsis, and author bio. Attachments from unknown senders will be deleted unread. Nonfiction only. Books must be written by or with established experts in their field. No Fiction, Memoir, Religion, Spiritual/Christian, Children's/young adult, Games/puzzles, Humour, History, Politics, or unsolicited MSS. See website for full guidelines.

Elaine Koster Literary Agency LLC

55 Central Park West Suite 6, New York, NY 10023
Tel: +1 (212) 362-9488
Fax: +1 (212) 712-0164
Email: ElaineKost@aol.com

Handles: Fiction; Nonfiction; *Areas:* Biography; Business; Cookery; Culture; Current Affairs; Finance; Health; Historical; How-to; Mystery; Nature; Psychology; Self-Help; Spiritual; Thrillers; Women's Interests; *Markets:* Adult; *Treatments:* Literary; Mainstream

Send query with SASE. No science fiction, children's, screenplays, simultaneous submissions, or queries by fax or email.

Barbara S. Kouts, Literary Agent

PO Box 560, Bellport, NY 11713
Tel: +1 (631) 286-1278
Fax: +1 (631) 286-1538
Email: bkouts@aol.com

Handles: Fiction; *Areas:* Autobiography; Biography; Crime; Current Affairs; Health; Historical; Lifestyle; Mystery; Nature; Psychology; Suspense; Thrillers; Women's Interests; *Markets:* Adult; Children's; *Treatments:* Literary

Send query with SASE. Postal queries only. Particularly interested in adult fiction and nonfiction and children's books.

Bert P. Krages

6665 S.W. Hampton Street, Suite 200, Portland, Oregon 97223
Tel: +1 (503) 597-2525
Fax: +1 (503) 597-2549
Email: krages@onemain.com
Website: http://www.krages.com/lvaserv.htm

Handles: Nonfiction; *Areas:* Health; Historical; Psychology; Science; *Markets:* Adult

Send query by email, with outline, similar books and how yours will compete with them, and your relevant qualifications and writing experience. Query letters should not exceed one page. Particularly interested in science, health, psychology, and history. Not currently accepting fiction. Do not call or send MS instead of query.

Edite Kroll Literary Agency, Inc.

20 Cross Street, Saco, ME 04072
Tel: +1 (207) 283-8797
Fax: +1 (207) 283-8799
Email: ekroll@maine.rr.com

Handles: Fiction; Nonfiction; *Areas:*
Autobiography; Biography; Culture; Current
Affairs; Health; Humour; Legal; Medicine;
Politics; Psychology; Religious; Self-Help;
Women's Interests; *Markets:* Academic;
Adult; Children's; Youth; *Treatments:*
Literary

Handles mainly nonfiction so very selective
about fiction. Particularly interested in
international feminists and women writers
and artists. No genre books such as
mysteries, romance, or thrillers; no diet,
cookery, etc.; no photography books, coffee
table books, or commercial fiction. Send
query by email, fax, or by post with SASE,
including synopsis, author bio, and one or
two sample chapters. For picture books, send
complete MS. No queries by phone.

Kuhn Projects

19 West 21st Street., Suite 501, New York,
NY 10010
Tel: +1 (212) 929-2227
Fax: +1 (212) 929-2583
Email: submissions@kuhnprojects.com
Website: http://www.kuhnprojects.com

Handles: Fiction; Nonfiction; *Areas:* Arts;
Autobiography; Beauty and Fashion;
Business; Cookery; Culture; Current Affairs;
Design; Health; Historical; Humour; Politics;
Psychology; Science; Spiritual; Technology;
Markets: Adult; Children's; Youth

Handles mainly adult nonfiction. Send query
by email with description of the project,
author bio, and sample pages up to one
chapter, if included in the body of the email.
See website for full details.

The LA Literary Agency

PO Box 46370, Los Angeles, CA 90046
Tel: +1 (323) 654-5288
Email: ann@laliteraryagency.com
Website: http://www.laliteraryagency.com

Handles: Fiction; Nonfiction; *Areas:*
Autobiography; Biography; Business;
Cookery; Health; Historical; Lifestyle;
Psychology; Science; Sport; *Markets:* Adult;
Treatments: Commercial; Contemporary;
Literary; Mainstream

Send query with proposal (nonfiction) or full
ms (fiction) by email. Response only if
interested. Sister company offers editorial
services.

Peter Lampack Agency, Inc

The Empire State Building, 350 Fifth
Avenue, Suite 5300, New York, NY 10118
Tel: +1 (212) 687-9106
Fax: +1 (212) 687-9109
Email: andrew@peterlampackagency.com
Website: http://www.
peterlampackagency.com

Handles: Fiction; Nonfiction; *Markets:*
Adult; *Treatments:* Commercial; Literary;
Mainstream

Specialises in commercial and literary fiction
as well as nonfiction by recognised experts
in a given field. Send query by email only,
with cover letter, author bio, sample chapter,
and 1-2 page synopsis. No children's books,
horror, romance, westerns, science fiction or
screenplays.

Laura Langlie, Literary Agent

147-149 Green Street, Hudson, NY 12534
Tel: +1 (518) 828-4708
Fax: +1 (518) 828-4787
Email: laura@lauralanglie.com

Handles: Fiction; Nonfiction; *Areas:*
Autobiography; Biography; Crime; Culture;
Current Affairs; Film; Historical; Humour;
Legal; Literature; Mystery; Nature; Politics;
Psychology; Suspense; Theatre; Thrillers;
Women's Interests; *Markets:* Adult;
Children's; Youth; *Treatments:* Literary;
Mainstream

Send query by post with SASE, or by fax.
No poetry, children's picture books, hardcore
science fiction, men's adventure, how-to, or
erotica. Simultaneous submissions accepted.

Larsen Pomada Literary Agents

1029 Jones Street, San Francisco, CA 94109-5023
Tel: +1 (415) 673-0939
Fax: +1 (415) 673-0367
Email: larsenpoma@aol.com
Website: http://www.Larsen-Pomada.com

Handles: Fiction; Nonfiction; *Areas:* Anthropology; Architecture; Arts; Autobiography; Biography; Business; Cookery; Crime; Culture; Current Affairs; Design; Fantasy; Film; Finance; Health; Historical; How-to; Humour; Legal; Lifestyle; Medicine; Music; Mystery; Nature; New Age; Politics; Psychology; Religious; Romance; Science; Self-Help; Sociology; Sport; Suspense; Thrillers; Travel; Women's Interests; *Markets:* Adult; Children's; *Treatments:* Commercial; Literary; Mainstream; Satirical

See website for detailed submission guidelines.

The Steve Laube Agency

5025 N. Central Ave., #635, Phoenix, AZ 85012-1502
Email: krichards@stevelaube.com
Website: http://www.stevelaube.com

Handles: Fiction; Nonfiction; *Areas:* Religious; *Markets:* Adult; Youth

Handles quality Christian fiction and nonfiction in all genres, except poetry, personal biographies, personal stories, end-times literature (either fiction or nonfiction), and children's picture books. Accepts submissions by post or by email. See website for extensive information on making submissions.

LaunchBooks Literary Agency

Tel: +1 (760) 944-9909
Email: david@launchbooks.com
Website: http://www.launchbooks.com

Handles: Fiction; Nonfiction; *Areas:* Adventure; Business; Culture; Current Affairs; Humour; Politics; Science; Sci-Fi; Sociology; Sport; Technology; Thrillers;

Markets: Adult; *Treatments:* Contemporary; Mainstream; Popular

Handles nonfiction and fiction. Send query or proposal with one sample chapter and author bio by email.

Sarah Lazin Books

19 West 21st Street, Suite 501, New York, NY 10001
Tel: +1 (212) 989-5757
Fax: +1 (212) 989-1393
Email: slazin@lazinbooks.com
Website: http://lazinbooks.com

Handles: Fiction; Nonfiction; *Areas:* Autobiography; Biography; Culture; Current Affairs; Historical; Music; Politics; *Markets:* Adult

Accepting queries via referral only. No queries by email.

Levine Greenberg Literary Agency, Inc.

307 Seventh Ave., Suite 2407, New York, NY 10001
Tel: +1 (212) 337-0934
Fax: +1 (212) 337-0948
Email: submit@levinegreenberg.com
Website: http://www.levinegreenberg.com

Handles: Fiction; Nonfiction; *Areas:* Arts; Autobiography; Biography; Business; Cookery; Crafts; Crime; Culture; Finance; Gardening; Health; Historical; Hobbies; Humour; Leisure; Lifestyle; Mystery; Nature; New Age; Politics; Psychology; Religious; Romance; Science; Self-Help; Sociology; Spiritual; Sport; Suspense; Technology; Thrillers; Travel; Women's Interests; *Markets:* Adult; Children's; Youth; *Treatments:* Literary; Mainstream; Popular

No queries by mail. Send query using online form at website, or send email attaching no more than 50 pages. See website for detailed submission guidelines. No response to submissions by post.

Lippincott Massie McQuilkin

27 West 20th Street, Suite 305, New York,

NY 10011
Tel: +1 (212) 352-2055
Fax: +1 (212) 352-2059
Email: info@lmqlit.com
Website: http://www.lmqlit.com

Handles: Fiction; Nonfiction; *Areas:*
Autobiography; Biography; Crime; Culture;
Current Affairs; Fantasy; Health; Historical;
Humour; Politics; Psychology; Science;
Sociology; Sport; Suspense; Thrillers;
Women's Interests; *Markets:* Adult;
Children's; Youth; *Treatments:* Commercial;
Literary

See website for specific agent interests and
contact details. Query only one agent at a
time.

The Lisa Ekus Group, LLC

57 North Street, Hatfield, MA 01038
Tel: +1 (413) 247-9325
Email: info@lisaekus.com
Website: http://www.lisaekus.com

Handles: Nonfiction; *Areas:* Cookery;
Markets: Adult

Send query with table of contents, summary
of chapters, one complete sample chapter,
author bio, explanation of concept, potential
market, and potential competition. Handles
cookery books only. See website for full
submission guidelines.

Literary & Creative Artists Inc.

3543 Albemarle Street NW, Washington, DC
20008-4213
Tel: +1 (202) 362-4688
Fax: +1 (202) 362-8875
Email: lca9643@lcadc.com
Website: http://www.lcadc.com

Handles: Fiction; Nonfiction; *Areas:* Arts;
Autobiography; Biography; Business;
Cookery; Crime; Current Affairs; Drama;
Health; Historical; How-to; Legal; Lifestyle;
Medicine; Nature; Philosophy; Politics;
Religious; Spiritual; *Markets:* Adult

Send query by post with SASE, or by email
without attachments. No poetry, academic /
educational textbooks, or unsolicited MSS.

Currently only accepts projects from
established authors.

Literary Management Group, Inc.

16970 San Carlos Boulevard, Suite 160-100,
Ft Myers, FL 33908
Tel: +1 (615) 812-4445
Email: BruceBarbour@
LiteraryManagementGroup.com
Website: http://
literarymanagementgroup.com

Handles: Nonfiction; *Areas:* Biography;
Business; Lifestyle; Religious; Spiritual;
Markets: Adult

Handles Christian books (defined as books
which are consistent with the historical,
orthodox teachings of the Christian fathers).
Handles adult nonfiction only. No children's
or illustrated books, poetry, memoirs, YA
Fiction or text/academic books. Download
proposal from website then complete and
send with sample chapters.

The Literary Group International

1357 Broadway, Suite 316, New York, NY
10018
Tel: +1 (212) 400-1494
Email: fweimann@theliterarygroup.com
Website: http://www.theliterarygroup.com

Handles: Fiction; Nonfiction; *Areas:*
Adventure; Anthropology; Autobiography;
Biography; Business; Crime; Culture;
Fantasy; Historical; How-to; Humour;
Lifestyle; Military; Music; Mystery;
Psychology; Religious; Romance; Science;
Self-Help; Sociology; Sport; Thrillers;
Travel; Women's Interests; *Markets:* Adult;
Youth; *Treatments:* Contemporary;
Experimental; Literary

Send query by email only, with writing
credentials, 2 page synopsis, and 50-page
writing sample. Response only if interested.
Asks for a 30-day exclusivity period,
beginning from the date the material is
received.

Sterling Lord Literistic, Inc.
65 Bleecker Street, New York, NY 10012
Tel: +1 (212) 780-6050
Fax: +1 (212) 780-6095
Email: sterling@sll.com
Website: http://www.sll.com

Handles: Fiction; Nonfiction; *Areas:*
Autobiography; Biography; Business;
Culture; Current Affairs; Health; Historical;
Lifestyle; Science; Self-Help; Women's
Interests; *Markets:* Adult; Children's; Youth;
Treatments: Commercial; Literary

Send query with SASE, synopsis, brief
author bio, and first three chapters. Literary
value considered above all else. No response
to unsolicited email queries.

Julia Lord Literary Management
38 W. Ninth Street, New York, NY 10011
Tel: +1 (212) 995-2333
Fax: +1 (212) 995-2332
Email: query@julialordliterary.com
Website: http://julialordliterary.com

Handles: Fiction; Nonfiction; Reference;
Areas: Adventure; Autobiography;
Biography; Crafts; Crime; Current Affairs;
Entertainment; Health; Historical; Hobbies;
Humour; Lifestyle; Music; Mystery; Politics;
Science; Self-Help; Sport; Technology;
Thrillers; Women's Interests; *Markets:*
Adult; Youth

Send query by post or by email. If sending
by email, include synopsis and first five
pages in the body of the email. Responds
only if interested and does not open or
respond to emails with attachments.

If sending by post include synopsis, first five
pages, and SASE for response. Responds to
all postal submissions.

Lowenstein Associates, Inc.
115 East 23rd Street, 4th Floor, New York,
NY 10010
Tel: +1 (212) 206-1630
Email: assistant@bookhaven.com
Website: http://www.
lowensteinassociates.com

Handles: Fiction; Nonfiction; *Areas:*
Autobiography; Business; Crime; Fantasy;
Health; Lifestyle; Literature; Psychology;
Science; Sci-Fi; Sociology; Spiritual;
Thrillers; Women's Interests; *Markets:*
Adult; *Treatments:* Commercial; Literary

Send query by email with one-page query
letter and first ten pages pasted into the body
of the email (fiction) or table of contents and
(if available) proposal. See website for full
guidelines. No Westerns, textbooks,
children's picture books, or books in need of
translation.

The Jennifer Lyons Literary Agency, LLC
151 West 19th Street 3rd floor, New York,
NY 10011
Tel: +1 (212) 368-2812
Email: jenniferlyonsagency@gmail.com
Website: http://www.
jenniferlyonsliteraryagency.com

Handles: Fiction; Nonfiction; *Areas:*
Autobiography; Biography; Current Affairs;
Finance; Historical; Science; Sport;
Thrillers; *Markets:* Adult; Children's; Youth

See website for agent preferences and
submission policies, plus specific email
addresses.

Donald Maass Literary Agency
Suite 801, 121 West 27th Street, New York,
NY 10001
Tel: +1 (212) 727-8383
Fax: +1 (212) 727-3271
Email: info@maassagency.com
Website: http://www.maassagency.com

Handles: Fiction; *Areas:* Crime; Fantasy;
Historical; Horror; Humour; Mystery;
Romance; Sci-Fi; Suspense; Westerns;
Women's Interests; *Markets:* Adult; Youth;
Treatments: Dark; Literary; Mainstream

Welcomes all genres, in particular science
fiction, fantasy, mystery, suspense, horror,
romance, historical, literary and mainstream
novels. Send query to a specific agent, by
email, with "query" in the subject line, or by

post with SASE, with synopsis and first five pages. Prefers electronic approaches, but no attachments (include all material within the body of the email). No screenplays, poetry or picture books. See website for individual agent interests and email addresses.

Gina Maccoby Agency

PO Box 60, Chappaqua, NY 10514
Tel: +1 (914) 238-5630
Email: query@maccobylit.com

Handles: Fiction; Nonfiction; *Areas:* Autobiography; Biography; Culture; Current Affairs; Entertainment; Health; Historical; Lifestyle; Mystery; Nature; Politics; Self-Help; Thrillers; Women's Interests; *Markets:* Adult; Children's; Youth; *Treatments:* Literary; Mainstream

Send query by post with SASE, or by email with "Query" in the subject line. No attachments. Response not guaranteed.

MacGregor Literary

PO Box 1316, Manzanita, OR 97130
Tel: +1 (503) 389-4803
Email: chip@macgregorliterary.com
Website: http://www.macgregorliterary.com

Handles: Fiction; Nonfiction; *Areas:* Autobiography; Biography; Business; Crime; Culture; Current Affairs; Finance; Historical; How-to; Humour; Lifestyle; Mystery; Religious; Romance; Self-Help; Short Stories; Sport; Suspense; Thrillers; Women's Interests; *Markets:* Academic; Adult; *Treatments:* Contemporary; Mainstream

Handles work in a variety of genres, but all from a Christian perspective. Not accepting unpublished authors, except through conferences and referrals from current clients. Unsolicited MSS will not be returned, even if an SASE is provided.

Ricia Mainhardt Agency (RMA)

85 Lincoln Street, First Floor, Meriden, CT 06451
Email: ricia@ricia.com
Website: http://www.ricia.com

Handles: Fiction; Nonfiction; *Areas:* Adventure; Autobiography; Biography; Crime; Culture; Current Affairs; Erotic; Fantasy; Gothic; Historical; Horror; Humour; Leisure; Mystery; New Age; Romance; Sci-Fi; Self-Help; Spiritual; Sport; Suspense; Thrillers; Westerns; Women's Interests; *Markets:* Adult; Children's; Family; Youth; *Treatments:* Commercial; Contemporary; Cynical; Dark; Light; Literary; Mainstream; Niche; Popular; Progressive; Serious; Traditional

Send complete MS as an attachment by email. In the body of the email, include a brief one-paragraph pitch. No poetry, shildren's picture books, or screenplays (except from existing clients). See website for full guidelines.

Kirsten Manges Literary Agency, LLC

115 West 29th Street, 3rd Floor, New York, NY 10001
Email: kirsten@mangeslit.com
Website: http://www.mangeslit.com

Handles: Fiction; Nonfiction; *Areas:* Autobiography; Cookery; Culture; Health; Historical; Psychology; Science; Spiritual; Sport; Technology; Travel; Women's Interests; *Markets:* Adult; Youth; *Treatments:* Commercial; Literary

Particularly interested in women's issues. Most new clients by recommendation.

Carol Mann Agency

55 Fifth Avenue, New York, NY 10003
Tel: +1 (212) 206-5635
Fax: +1 (212) 674-4809
Email: submissions@carolmannagency.com
Website: http://www.carolmannagency.com

Handles: Fiction; Nonfiction; *Areas:* Anthropology; Archaeology; Architecture; Arts; Autobiography; Biography; Business; Culture; Current Affairs; Design; Finance; Health; Historical; Humour; Legal; Lifestyle; Medicine; Music; Nature; Politics; Psychology; Religious; Self-Help; Sociology; Spiritual; Sport; Women's Interests; *Markets:* Adult; Youth;

Treatments: Commercial; Literary

Send query by email only, including synopsis, brief bio, and (in the case of fiction and memoir) first 25 pages. No submissions by post, or phone calls. Allow 3-4 weeks for response.

Manus & Associates Literary Agency, Inc.

425 Sherman Avenue, Suite 200, Palo Alto, CA 94306
Tel: +1 (650) 470-5151
Fax: +1 (650) 470-5159
Email: ManusLit@ManusLit.com
Website: http://www.ManusLit.com

Handles: Fiction; Nonfiction; *Areas:* Autobiography; Biography; Business; Culture; Current Affairs; Finance; Health; How-to; Lifestyle; Mystery; Nature; Psychology; Romance; Science; Self-Help; Suspense; Thrillers; Women's Interests; *Markets:* Adult; *Treatments:* Literary; Mainstream

Send query letter describing your project and giving pertinent biographical info only by fax or email, or send query letter by post with SASE and include complete proposal (nonfiction), or first 30 pages (fiction). When querying by email use one of the direct personal emails of a specific agent as given on the website, not the generic inbox shown on this page. Approach only one agent. No horror, romance, science fiction, fantasy, western, young adult, children's, poetry, cookbooks, or magazine articles. See website for full guidelines.

March Tenth, Inc.

24 Hillside Terrace, Montvale, NJ 07645
Tel: +1 (201) 387-6551
Fax: +1 (201) 387-6552
Email: schoron@aol.com
Website: http://www.marchtenthinc.com

Handles: Fiction; Nonfiction; Reference; *Areas:* Autobiography; Biography; Culture; Current Affairs; Film; Health; Historical; Humour; Literature; Medicine; Music; Theatre; *Markets:* Adult; *Treatments:* Literary; Satirical

Send query by email or by post with SASE. In your query, include the genre of your work, a brief description of the project, and the approximate word count; your qualifications and previous writing or publishing experience or some basic information about your background; all your contact information; a one to two page synopsis if you are submitting a novel as well as the first three chapters; and state whether or not your work has been previously shown to publishers.

No poetry, scripts, children's or young adult novels.

Elaine Markson Literary Agency

450 Seventh Ave, Suite 1408, New York, NY 10123
Tel: +1 (212) 243-8480
Fax: +1 (212) 691-9014
Email: gary@marksonagency.com
Website: http://www.marksonagency.com

Handles: Fiction; Nonfiction; *Markets:* Adult; *Treatments:* Literary

Most new clients obtained through recommendation.

Marly Russoff & Associates

PO Box 524, Bronxville, NY 10708
Tel: +1 (914) 961-7939
Website: http://www.rusoffagency.com

Handles: Fiction; Nonfiction; *Markets:* Adult

Note: Note accepting submissions as at August 2015. Check website for current status.

Send 1-2 page query by post or email, with synopsis and relevant author info, plus word or page count and email address for response. All email queries must have the word "query" in the subject line.

Material is never returned so do not send return postage.

The Martell Agency

1350 Avenue of the Americas, Suite 1205,
New York, NY 10019
Tel: +1 (212) 317-2672
Email: submissions@themartellagency.com
Website: http://www.themartellagency.com

Handles: Fiction; Nonfiction; *Areas:*
Autobiography; Business; Finance; Health;
Historical; Medicine; Mystery; Psychology;
Self-Help; Suspense; Thrillers; Women's
Interests; *Markets:* Adult; *Treatments:*
Commercial

Send query by post or by email, including
summary, short bio, any information, if
appropriate, as to why you are qualified to
write on the subject of your book, any
publishing credits, the year of publication
and the publisher. No original screenplays or
poetry.

Martin Literary Management

7683 SE 27th Street, #307, Mercer Island,
WA 98040
Tel: +1 (206) 466-1773
Fax: +1 (206) 466-1774
Email: Sharlene@
martinliterarymanagement.com
Website: http://www.
martinliterarymanagement.com

Handles: Fiction; Nonfiction; *Areas:*
Autobiography; Biography; Business; Crime;
Current Affairs; Entertainment; Health;
How-to; Lifestyle; Media; Self-Help;
Women's Interests; *Markets:* Adult;
Children's; Youth; *Treatments:* Commercial;
Literary; Mainstream; Popular; Positive;
Traditional

This agency has strong ties to film/TV.
Actively seeking nonfiction that is highly
commercial and that can be adapted to film.
Please review our website carefully to make
sure we're a good match for your work. How
to contact: Completely electronic: emails and
MS Word only. No attachments on queries.
Place letter in body of email. See submission
requirements on website. Do not send
materials unless requested. We give very
serious consideration to the material

requested. We are actively seeing new
submissions. We only ask to see materials
that we intend to offer representation for – IF
the work is saleable. Therefore, in exchange
for that close evaluation, we require a two
week exclusive consideration period,
whereby your agree if we offer
representation, you are already certain you
are willing to accept pending our contract.

No adult fiction. Principal agent handles
adult nonfiction only. See website for
submission guidelines and separate email
address for submissions of picture books,
middle grade, and young adult fiction and
nonfiction.

Mendel Media Group, LLC

115 West 30th Street, Suite 800, New York,
NY 10001
Tel: +1 (646) 239-9896
Fax: +1 (212) 685-4717
Email: scott@mendelmedia.com
Website: http://www.mendelmedia.com

Handles: Fiction; Nonfiction; *Areas:*
Autobiography; Biography; Culture; Current
Affairs; Entertainment; Finance; Historical;
How-to; Humour; Literature; Media;
Mystery; Politics; Religious; Science; Self-
Help; Spiritual; Thrillers; Women's Interests;
Markets: Adult; Children's; Youth;
Treatments: Contemporary; Literary;
Mainstream

Send query by regular mail. Works mainly
with established authors, but accepts queries
from unpublished authors who have
researched the publishing industry and have
a polished proposal or manuscript ready for
consideration.

Represents a wide range of fiction and
nonfiction. In fiction, particularly interested
in historical and contemporary multicultural
fiction, contemporary thrillers and
mainstream women's fiction. In nonfiction,
represents both individual authors and
institutions. Also accepts young adult fiction
and nonfiction, Chapter Books and Picture
Books. No poetry, screenplays, or queries by
fax or email. See website for full guidelines.

Martha Millard Literary Agency

50 West 67th Street #1G, New York, NY 10023
Tel: +1 (212) 662-1030
Email: marmillink@aol.com

Handles: Fiction; Nonfiction; *Areas:* Architecture; Arts; Autobiography; Biography; Business; Cookery; Crime; Culture; Current Affairs; Design; Fantasy; Film; Finance; Health; Historical; Horror; How-to; Lifestyle; Music; Mystery; New Age; Photography; Psychology; Romance; Sci-Fi; Self-Help; Short Stories; Suspense; Theatre; Thrillers; Women's Interests; *Markets:* Adult; Children's; Youth

No unsolicited queries or queries by fax or email. Authors wishing to approach this agency will need to be recommended to the agent by someone else in the profession.

The Miller Agency

630 Ninth Ave., Suite 1102, New York, NY 10036
Tel: +1 (212) 206-0913
Email: info@milleragency.net
Website: http://www.milleragency.net

Handles: Nonfiction; *Areas:* Arts; Autobiography; Biography; Cookery; Culture; Psychology; Self-Help; Sport; Travel; *Markets:* Adult

No unsolicited MSS. Any unsolicited MSS submitted will not be responded to or returned.

Patricia Moosbrugger Literary Agency

Email: pm@pmagency.net
Website: http://www.pmagency.net

Handles: Fiction; Nonfiction; *Areas:* Literature; *Markets:* Adult; Youth

Accepts submissions of adult fiction and nonfiction and young adult literature. No science fiction, fantasy or category romance. Send query by email with brief synopsis.

Howard Morhaim Literary Agency

30 Pierrepont Street, Brooklyn, NY 11201
Tel: +1 (718) 222-8400
Fax: +1 (718) 222-5056
Email: kmckean@morhaimliterary.com
Website: http://morhaimliterary.com

Handles: Fiction; Nonfiction; *Areas:* Autobiography; Biography; Business; Cookery; Crafts; Culture; Design; Fantasy; Finance; Health; Historical; Horror; Humour; Romance; Sci-Fi; Sport; Thrillers; Women's Interests; *Markets:* Adult; Children's; Youth; *Treatments:* Contemporary; Literary

Enthusiastically accept unsolicited submissions. Send query by email only with outline / proposal for nonfiction, or three sample chapters for fiction. Attachments are accepted. See website for specific agent interests and contact details.

Nappaland Literary Agency

PO Box 1674, Loveland, CO 80539-1674
Fax: +1 (970) 635-9869
Email: Literary@nappaland.com
Website: http://www.nappaland.com/literary

Handles: Fiction; Nonfiction; *Areas:* Culture; Historical; Humour; Lifestyle; Religious; Suspense; Women's Interests; *Markets:* Adult; Youth; *Treatments:* Literary; Popular

Deliberately small boutique-sized agency. Send query letter only by email during specific submission windows (see website). No children's books, memoirs, screenplays, poetry, or anything about cats.

Nelson Literary Agency, LLC

1732 Wazee Street, Suite 207, Denver, CO 80202
Tel: +1 (303) 292-2805
Email: querykristin@nelsonagency.com
Website: http://www.nelsonagency.com

Handles: Fiction; *Areas:* Fantasy; Historical; Romance; Sci-Fi; Women's Interests;

Markets: Adult; Children's; Youth; *Treatments:* Commercial; Literary; Mainstream

Handles young adult, upper-level middle grade, "big crossover novels with one foot squarely in genre", literary commercial novels, upmarket women's fiction, single-title romances (especially historicals), and lead title or hardcover science fiction and fantasy. No nonfiction, screenplays, short story collections, poetry, children's picture books or chapter books, or material for the Christian/inspirational market. No queries by post, phone, in person, or through Facebook. No email attachments. See website for full submission guidelines.

New Leaf Literary & Media, Inc.

110 West 40th Street, Suite 410, New York, NY 10018
Tel: +1 (646) 248-7989
Fax: +1 (646) 861-4654
Email: query@newleafliterary.com
Website: http://www.newleafliterary.com

Handles: Fiction; Nonfiction; *Areas:* Culture; Entertainment; Erotic; Fantasy; Historical; Romance; Sci-Fi; Technology; Thrillers; Women's Interests; *Markets:* Adult; Children's; Youth; *Treatments:* Mainstream

Send query by email only, with the word "Query" along with the specific agent's name in the subject line. Do not query more than one agent. Include up to five double-spaced sample pages in the body of the email -- no attachments. Response only if interested.

Niad Management

15021 Ventura Blvd. #860, Sherman Oaks, CA 91403
Tel: +1 (818) 774-0051
Fax: +1 (818) 774-1740
Email: queries@niadmanagement.com
Website: http://www.niadmanagement.com

Handles: Fiction; Nonfiction; Scripts; *Areas:* Adventure; Autobiography; Biography; Crime; Culture; Drama; Film; Humour; Mystery; Romance; Sport; Suspense;

Theatre; Thrillers; TV; *Markets:* Adult; Youth; *Treatments:* Contemporary; Literary; Mainstream

Manages mainly Hollywood writers, actors, and directors, although does also handle a very small number of books. Send query by email or by post with SASE. Responds only if interested.

Northern Lights Literary Services

762 State Road 458, Bedford, IN 47421
Email: queries@northernlightsls.com
Website: http://www.northernlightsls.com

Handles: Fiction; Nonfiction; *Areas:* Biography; Business; Health; Historical; How-to; Lifestyle; Medicine; Mystery; New Age; Psychology; Romance; Self-Help; Suspense; Women's Interests; *Markets:* Adult

Our goal is to provide personalized service to clients and create a bond that will endure throughout your career. We seriously consider each query we receive and will accept hardworking new authors who are willing to develop their talents and skills.

Encourages email queries but responds only if interested (within 5 working days). No horror or books for children.

Harold Ober Associates

425 Madison Avenue, New York, NY 10017
Tel: +1 (212) 759-8600
Fax: +1 (212) 759-9428
Email: phyllis@haroldober.com
Website: http://www.haroldober.com

Handles: Fiction; Nonfiction; *Markets:* Adult; Children's

Send query addressed to a specific agent by post only, including first five pages and SASE for reply. No plays, screenplays, or queries by fax.

Fifi Oscard Agency, Inc.

110 West 40th Street, 16th Floor, New York, NY 10018

Tel: +1 (212) 764-1100
Fax: +1 (212)840-5019
Email: agency@fifioscard.com
Website: http://www.fifioscard.com

Handles: Fiction; Nonfiction; Scripts; *Areas:* Biography; Business; Cookery; Finance; Health; Historical; Lifestyle; Religious; Science; Spiritual; Sport; Technology; Theatre; Women's Interests; *Markets:* Adult

Send query via online submission form. No unsolicited MSS. Due to volume of queries, unable to acknowledge each one.

Paradigm Talent and Literary Agency

360 Park Avenue South, 16th Floor, New York, NY 10010
Tel: +1 (212) 897-6400
Fax: +1 (212) 764-8941
Email: books@paradigmagency.com
Website: http://www.paradigmagency.com

Handles: Scripts; *Areas:* Film; Theatre; TV; *Markets:* Adult

Talent agency with offices in Los Angeles, New York City, Monterey, California and Nashville, Tennessee, representing actors, musical artists, directors, writers and producers. No unsolicited approaches unless by referral or through meeting an agent at an event.

The Park Literary Group LLC

270 Lafayette Street, Suite 1504, New York, NY 10012
Tel: +1 (212) 691-3500
Fax: +1 (212) 691-3540
Email: queries@parkliterary.com
Website: http://www.parkliterary.com

Handles: Fiction; Nonfiction; *Areas:* Adventure; Arts; Autobiography; Culture; Current Affairs; Historical; Politics; Science; Women's Interests; *Markets:* Adult; *Treatments:* Commercial; Literary

Send query by email only, with all materials in the body of the email (no attachments). See website for individual agent details and

query one specific agent with their first and last name in the subject line of your email. See website for full guidelines. No poetry or screenplays.

Kathi J. Paton Literary Agency

PO Box 2236, Radio City Station, New York, NY 10101-2236
Tel: +1 (212) 265-6586
Email: kjplitbiz@optonline.net

Handles: Fiction; Nonfiction; *Areas:* Biography; Business; Culture; Current Affairs; Finance; Health; Historical; Humour; Lifestyle; Politics; Religious; Science; Sport; Technology; *Markets:* Adult; *Treatments:* Literary; Mainstream; Popular

Send query with brief description by email only. No attachments or referrals to websites. Specialises in adult nonfiction. No science fiction, fantasy, horror, category romance, juvenile, young adult or self-published books. Response only if interested.

Pavilion Literary Management

660 Massachusetts Avenue, Suite 4, Boston, MA 02118
Tel: +1 (617) 792-5218
Email: jeff@pavilionliterary.com
Website: http://www.pavilionliterary.com

Handles: Fiction; Nonfiction; *Areas:* Adventure; Autobiography; Fantasy; Historical; Mystery; Science; Thrillers; *Markets:* Adult; Children's; Youth; *Treatments:* Popular

Only accepting approaches for fiction work by previously published authors or client referral. Send query by email specifying fiction or nonfiction and title of work in the subject line. No attachments. See website for full details.

Peregrine Whittlesey Agency

279 Central Park West, New York, NY 10024
Tel: +1 (212) 787-1802
Fax: +1 (212) 787-4985
Email: pwwagy@aol.com

Handles: Scripts; *Areas:* Film; Theatre; TV; *Markets:* Adult

Handles mainly theatre scripts, plus a small number of film/TV scripts by playwrights who also write for screen. Send query with SASE. No simultaneous submissions.

Pinder Lane & Garon-Brooke Associates Ltd

159 West 53rd Street, Suite 14-E, New York, NY 10019
Tel: +1 (212) 489-0880
Fax: +1 (212) 489-7104
Email: pinderlanegaronbrooke@gmail.com
Website: http://www.pinderlane.com

Handles: Fiction; Nonfiction; *Areas:* Arts; Autobiography; Biography; Business; Cookery; Crime; Culture; Current Affairs; Entertainment; Erotic; Fantasy; Film; Health; Historical; Horror; Humour; Music; Mystery; Photography; Politics; Romance; Sci-Fi; Self Help; Spiritual; Sport; Theatre; Thrillers; Travel; Westerns; Women's Interests; *Markets:* Adult; Children's; Youth; *Treatments:* Mainstream

Send query by email or by post with SASE, including brief synopsis and first three chapters only. No film, TV, or theatre scripts, or unsolicited MSS.

Pippin Properties, Inc

110 West 40th Street, Suite 1704, New York, NY 10016
Tel: +1 (212) 338-9310
Fax: +1 (212) 338-9579
Email: info@pippinproperties.com
Website: http://www.pippinproperties.com

Handles: Fiction; *Markets:* Adult; Children's; Youth

Devoted primarily to picture books, middle-grade, and young adult novels, but also represents adult projects on occasion. Send query by email with synopsis, first chapter, or entire picture book manuscript in the body of your email. No attachments. See website for full guidelines.

Rebecca Pratt Literary Group

Seven Mile House, PO Box 77, Lititz, PA 17543
Tel: +1 (717) 625-2186
Fax: +1 (717) 625-3754
Email: Query@agentR.com
Website: http://www.agentr.com

Handles: Fiction; Nonfiction; *Areas:* Adventure; Autobiography; Biography; Fantasy; Historical; Horror; How-to; Mystery; Sci-Fi; Self-Help; Thrillers; *Markets:* Adult; *Treatments:* Literary; Mainstream

Send query in first instance by email only. No attachments (unsolicited email attachments will not be opened). No previously published works; juvenile, young adult, or children's; scripts; poetry, graphic novels; short stories; anything not between 70,000 and 120,000 words. See website for full guidelines.

Linn Prentis Literary

c/o Trodayne Northern, Acquisitions Director, for: Amy Hayden, Acquisitions, Linn Prentis Literary, PO Box 674, New York, NY 10035
Tel: +1 (212) 875-8557
Fax: +1 (425) 489-2809
Email: ahayden@linnprentis.com
Website: http://www.linnprentis.com

Handles: Fiction; Nonfiction; *Areas:* Autobiography; Fantasy; Mystery; Sci-Fi; Women's Interests; *Markets:* Adult; Youth; *Treatments:* Contemporary; Literary; Mainstream

Particularly interested in science fiction and fantasy, but willing to consider any fiction of interest. Send query by email or by post with SASE, including synopsis and first ten pages. No books for small children, or queries by fax or phone.

Aaron M. Priest Literary Agency

708 Third Avenue, 23rd Floor, New York, NY 10017-4201
Tel: +1 (212) 818-0344
Fax: +1 (212) 573-9417

Email: querypriest@aaronpriest.com
Website: http://www.aaronpriest.com

Handles: Fiction; Nonfiction; *Areas:*
Autobiography; Biography; Crime; Culture;
Fantasy; Gothic; Historical; How-to;
Mystery; Politics; Suspense; Thrillers;
Translations; Women's Interests; *Markets:*
Adult; Youth; *Treatments:* Commercial;
Contemporary; Literary

Send one-page query by email, describing
your work and your background. No
attachments, but you may paste the first
chapter into the body of the email. Query one
agent only. See website for specific agent
interests and email addresses. No poetry,
screenplays, sci-fi, or horror.

Prospect Agency

551 Valley Rd., PMB 377, Upper Montclair,
NJ 07043
Tel: +1 (718) 788-3217
Fax: +1 (718) 360-9582
Email: esk@prospectagency.com
Website: http://www.prospectagency.com

Handles: Fiction; Nonfiction; *Areas:*
Adventure; Autobiography; Crime; Erotic;
Fantasy; Mystery; Romance; Science; Sci-Fi;
Suspense; Thrillers; Westerns; Women's
Interests; *Markets:* Adult; Children's; Youth;
Treatments: Contemporary; Literary;
Mainstream

Handles very little nonfiction. Specialises in
romance, women's fiction, literary fiction,
young adult/children's literature, and science
fiction. Send submissions via website
submission **only** (no email queries –
**email queries are not accepted or
responded to** – or queries by post (these will
be recycled). No poetry, short stories, text
books, screenplays, or most nonfiction.

Queen Literary Agency, Inc.

30 East 60th Street, Suite 1004, New York,
NY 10024
Tel: +1 (212) 974-8333
Fax: +1 (212) 974-8347
Email: submissions@queenliterary.com
Website: http://www.queenliterary.com

Handles: Fiction; Nonfiction; *Areas:*
Business; Cookery; Historical; Mystery;
Psychology; Science; Sport; Thrillers;
Markets: Adult; *Treatments:* Commercial;
Literary

Founded by a former publishing executive,
most recently head of IMG
WORLDWIDE'S literary division. Handles
a wide range of nonfiction titles, with a
particular interest in business books, food
writing, science and popular psychology, as
well as books by well-known chefs, radio
and television personalities and sports
figures. Also handles commercial and
literary fiction, including historical fiction,
mysteries, and thrillers.

Lynne Rabinoff Agency

72-11 Austin Street, No. 201, Forest Hills,
NY 11375
Tel: +1 (718) 459-6894
Email: lynne@lynnerabinoff.com

Handles: Nonfiction; *Areas:* Anthropology;
Archaeology; Autobiography; Biography;
Business; Culture; Current Affairs; Finance;
Historical; Legal; Military; Politics;
Psychology; Religious; Science;
Technology; Women's Interests; *Markets:*
Adult

Particularly interested in politics, history,
current affairs, and religion. Send query by
email or by post with SASE, including
proposal, sample chapter, and author bio. No
queries by fax.

Raines & Raines

103 Kenyon Road, Medusa, NY 12120
Tel: +1 (518) 239-8311
Fax: +1 (518) 239-6029

Handles: Fiction; Nonfiction; *Areas:*
Adventure; Autobiography; Biography;
Crime; Fantasy; Finance; Historical;
Military; Mystery; Psychology; Sci-Fi;
Suspense; Thrillers; Westerns; *Markets:*
Adult

Handles nonfiction in all areas, and fiction in
the areas specified above. Send query with
SASE.

Rebecca Friedman Literary Agency

Email: brandie@rfliterary.com
Website: http://rfliterary.com

Handles: Fiction; Nonfiction; *Areas:*
Autobiography; Fantasy; Mystery; Romance;
Sci-Fi; Suspense; Thrillers; Women's
Interests; *Markets:* Adult; Youth;
Treatments: Commercial; Contemporary;
Literary

See website for full submission guidelines
and specific agent interests and contact
details. Aims to respond in 6-8 weeks, but
may take longer.

Rees Literary Agency

14 Beacon St., Suite 710, Boston, MA 02108
Tel: +1 (617) 227-9014
Fax: +1 (617) 227-8762
Email: reesagency@reesagency.com
Website: http://www.reesagency.com

Handles: Fiction; *Areas:* Autobiography;
Biography; Business; Historical; Military;
Mystery; Psychology; Romance; Science;
Self-Help; Suspense; Thrillers; Women's
Interests; *Markets:* Adult; Children's; Youth;
Treatments: Commercial; Literary

See website for specific agents' interests and
submission requirements.

Regina Ryan Publishing Enterprises

251 Central Park West, #7D, New York, NY
10024
Tel: +1 (212) 787-5589
Email: queries@reginaryanbooks.com
Website: http://www.reginaryanbooks.com

Handles: Nonfiction; Reference; *Areas:*
Adventure; Architecture; Autobiography;
Business; Cookery; Gardening; Health;
Historical; Legal; Leisure; Lifestyle; Nature;
Politics; Psychology; Science; Spiritual;
Sport; Travel; Women's Interests; *Markets:*
Adult; *Treatments:* Popular

Send query by email, stating what your
books is about, why you are qualified to
write it, your plans for promotion, and
analysis of competing books. See website for
full guidelines.

Renee Zuckerbrot Literary Agency

115 West 29th Street, 10th floor, New York,
NY 10001
Tel: +1 (212) 967-0072
Fax: +1 (212) 967-0073
Email: Submissions@rzagency.com
Website: http://rzagency.com

Handles: Fiction; Nonfiction; *Areas:*
Culture; Historical; Literature; Mystery;
Science; Short Stories; Thrillers; Women's
Interests; *Markets:* Adult; *Treatments:*
Commercial; Literary; Popular

Send query by email only, with synopsis,
publication history, brief bio, contact
information, and excerpt (up to three sample
chapters) as a Word document attachment
(for novels, should be the first three
chapters). See website for full details. No
screenplays.

The Amy Rennert Agency, Inc.

1550 Tiburon Boulevard #302, Tiburon, CA
94920
Email: queries@amyrennert.com
Website: http://www.amyrennert.com

Handles: Fiction; Nonfiction; *Areas:*
Autobiography; Biography; Business;
Finance; Health; Historical; Lifestyle;
Literature; Mystery; Spiritual; Sport;
Markets: Adult; *Treatments:* Literary

Not accepting unsolicited mss, but referrals
still welcome. Send query by email, with
cover letter in body of email and a Word file
attachment containing proposal and first
chapter (nonfiction) or first 10-20 pages
(fiction). For picture books, send cover letter
in the body of the email and attach file with
the text. Include phone number. Response
only if interested.

Riverside Literary Agency

41 Simon Keets Road, Leyden, MA 01337
Tel: +1 (413) 772-0067

Fax: +1 (413) 772-0969
Email: rivlit@sover.net

Handles: Fiction; Nonfiction; *Markets:* Adult

Send query with outline by email. Usually obtains new clients by referral.

B.J. Robbins Literary Agency

5130 Bellaire Avenue, North Hollywood, CA 91607
Tel: +1 (818) 760-6602
Fax: +1 (818) 760-6616
Email: Robbinsliterary@gmail.com

Handles: Fiction; Nonfiction; *Areas:* Autobiography; Biography; Crime; Culture; Current Affairs; Film; Health; Humour; Medicine; Music; Mystery; Psychology; Self-Help; Sociology; Sport; Suspense; Theatre; Thrillers; Travel; Women's Interests; *Markets:* Adult; *Treatments:* Literary; Mainstream

Send query with outline / proposal and three sample chapters by post with SASE or by email (no attachments).

Rita Rosenkranz Literary Agency

440 West End Ave, Suite 15D, New York, NY 10024
Tel: +1 (212) 873-6333
Email: rrosenkranz@mindspring.com
Website: http://www.
ritarosenkranzliteraryagency.com

Handles: Nonfiction; *Areas:* Anthropology; Arts; Autobiography; Biography; Business; Cookery; Crafts; Culture; Current Affairs; Design; Finance; Health; Historical; Hobbies; How-to; Humour; Legal; Lifestyle; Literature; Medicine; Military; Music; Nature; Photography; Politics; Psychology; Religious; Science; Self-Help; Sport; Technology; Theatre; Women's Interests; *Markets:* Adult

Send query only by post or email. Submit proposal on request only. Deals specifically in adult nonfiction. No screenplays, poetry,

fiction, children's or YA books. No queries by fax.

Ross Yoon Agency

1666 Connecticut Avenue, NW, Suite 500, Washington, DC 20009
Tel: +1 (202) 328-3282
Fax: +1 (202) 328-9162
Email: submissions@rossyoon.com
Website: http://www.rossyoon.com

Handles: Nonfiction; *Areas:* Autobiography; Biography; Business; Culture; Current Affairs; Historical; Psychology; Science; *Markets:* Adult; *Treatments:* Commercial; Popular; Serious

Handles nonfiction only. Send query by email only with proposal in body of email or as .doc or .docx attachment. No unsolicited MSS or approaches by post or phone.

Andy Ross Agency

767 Santa Ray Avenue, Oakland, CA 94610
Tel: +1 (510) 238-8965
Email: andyrossagency@hotmail.com
Website: http://www.andyrossagency.com

Handles: Fiction; Nonfiction; *Areas:* Culture; Current Affairs; Historical; Religious; Science; *Markets:* Adult; Children's; Youth; *Treatments:* Commercial; Contemporary; Literary

We encourage queries for material in our fields of interest. No poetry, short stories, adult romance, science fiction and fantasy, adult and teen paranormal, or film scripts.

The agent has worked in the book business for 36 years, all of his working life. He was owner and general manager of Cody's Books in Berkeley, California from 1977-2006. Cody's has been recognised as one of America's great independent book stores.

During this period, the agent was the primary trade book buyer. This experience has given him a unique understanding of the retail book market, of publishing trends and, most importantly and uniquely, the hand selling of books to book buyers.

The agent is past president of the Northern California Booksellers Association, a board member and officer of the American Booksellers Association and a national spokesperson for issues concerning independent businesses. He has had significant profiles in the Wall Street Journal, Time Magazine, and the San Francisco Chronicle.

Queries by email only. See website for full guidelines.

The Damaris Rowland Agency

420 East 23rd Street, Suite 6F, New York, NY 10010-5040

Handles: Fiction; Nonfiction; *Areas:* Women's Interests; *Markets:* Adult; *Treatments:* Literary; Popular

Closed to queries as at August 2014.

The Rudy Agency

825 Wildlife Lane, Estes Park, CO 80517
Tel: +1 (970) 577-8500
Fax: +1 (970) 577-8600
Email: mak@rudyagency.com
Website: http://www.rudyagency.com

Handles: Fiction; Nonfiction; *Areas:* Autobiography; Biography; Business; Culture; Current Affairs; Health; Historical; Lifestyle; Medicine; Military; Politics; Science; Technology; Thrillers; *Markets:* Adult; Children's

Concentrates on adult nonfiction in the areas listed above. In fiction, accepts only historical fiction and thrillers. See website for full guidelines, and appropriate email addresses for different types of submissions.

Marly Rusoff & Associates, Inc.

PO Box 524, Bronxville, NY 10708
Tel: +1 (914) 961-7939
Email: mra_queries3@rusoffagency.com
Website: http://www.rusoffagency.com

Handles: Fiction; Nonfiction; *Areas:* Architecture; Arts; Autobiography;

Biography; Business; Culture; Design; Finance; Health; Historical; Medicine; Psychology; *Markets:* Adult; *Treatments:* Commercial; Literary

Note: Not accepting new clients as at January 2016. See website for current status

Send 1-2 page query by post or email, including synopsis and relevant author info and page or word count. Queries sent by email should include the word "query" in the subject line. Changes email address regularly to avoid spam, so check website before querying and notify firstwriter.com via the "Report an Error" button if address has changed from that displayed. May not respond if not interested. No PDFs, CDs, or directions to view material on websites.

Salkind Literary Agency

62 Nassau Drive, Great Neck, NY 11021
Tel: +1 (785) 371-0101
Fax: +1 (516) 706-2369
Email: neil@studiob.com
Website: http://www.salkindagency.com

Handles: Fiction; Nonfiction; *Areas:* Adventure; Arts; Autobiography; Biography; Business; Cookery; Crafts; Crime; Culture; Current Affairs; Design; Fantasy; Finance; Health; Historical; How-to; Humour; Lifestyle; Mystery; Photography; Politics; Psychology; Religious; Science; Sci-Fi; Self-Help; Spiritual; Suspense; Technology; Thrillers; Travel; Women's Interests; *Markets:* Academic; Adult; *Treatments:* Commercial

Handles general nonfiction trade, fiction, and textbook authors. Query by email or telephone.

Victoria Sanders & Associates LLC

241 Avenue of the Americas, Suite 11H, New York, NY 10014
Tel: +1 (212) 633-8811
Fax: +1 (212) 633-0525
Email: queriesvsa@gmail.com
Website: http://www.victoriasanders.com

Handles: Fiction; Nonfiction; *Areas:*

Adventure; Arts; Autobiography; Biography; Crime; Culture; Current Affairs; Fantasy; Film; Historical; Humour; Legal; Literature; Music; Mystery; Politics; Psychology; Sociology; Suspense; Theatre; Thrillers; Translations; Women's Interests; *Markets:* Adult; Children's; Youth;*Treatments:* Commercial; Contemporary; Light; Literary; Mainstream; Satirical

Send one-page query describing the work and the author by email only, with the first 25 pages pasted into the body of the email. No attachments.

Susan Schulman, A Literary Agency

454 West 44th Street, New York, NY 10036
Tel: +1 (212) 713-1633
Fax: +1 (212) 581-8830
Email: queries@schulmanagency.com
Website: http://schulmanagency.com

Handles: Fiction; Nonfiction; Scripts; *Areas:* Adventure; Anthropology; Archaeology; Arts; Autobiography; Biography; Business; Cookery; Crafts; Crime; Culture; Current Affairs; Entertainment; Film; Finance; Health; Historical; Hobbies; How-to; Humour; Legal; Lifestyle; Literature; Medicine; Music; Mystery; Nature; Photography; Politics; Psychology; Religious; Science; Self-Help; Sociology; Spiritual; Sport; Suspense; Technology; Theatre; Thrillers; Travel; Women's Interests; *Markets:* Adult; Children's; Youth; *Treatments:* Commercial; Literary; Mainstream

Send query with synopsis by email in the body of the email or by post with SASE. Include author resume and outline. For fiction, include three sample chapters. For nonfiction, include at least one. No poetry, TV scripts, concepts for TV, email attachments, submissions via UPS or FedEx, or unsolicited MSS.

Scribe Agency LLC

5508 Joylynne Drive, Madison, WI 53716
Tel: +1 (608) 259-0491
Email: submissions@scribeagency.com
Website: http://www.scribeagency.com

Handles: Fiction; *Areas:* Fantasy; Literature; Sci-Fi; Short Stories; *Markets:* Adult; *Treatments:* Commercial; Literary; Mainstream

Handles science fiction, fantasy, and literary fiction. No nonfiction, humour, cozy mysteries, faith-based fiction, screenplays, poetry, or works based on another's ideas. Send query in body of email, with synopsis and first three chapters as Word docs, RTFs, or PDFs. No hard copy approaches. If unable to submit material electronically, send email query in first instance.

Secret Agent Man

PO Box 1078, Lake Forest, CA 92609-1078
Tel: +1 (949) 698-6987
Email: query@secretagentman.net
Website: http://www.secretagentman.net

Handles: Fiction; Nonfiction; *Areas:* Crime; Mystery; Religious; Suspense; Thrillers; Westerns; *Markets:* Adult

Send query by email only (no postal submissions) with the word "Query" in the subject line, sample consecutive chapter(s), synopsis and/or outline. No first contact by phone. Not interested in vampire; sci-fi; fantasy; horror; cold war, military or political thrillers; children's or young adult; short stories; screenplays; poetry collections; romance; or historical. Christian nonfiction should be based on Biblical theology, not speculative. No self-published works.

Lynn Seligman, Literary Agent

400 Highland Avenue, Upper Montclair, NJ 07043
Tel: +1 (973) 783-3631

Handles: Fiction; Nonfiction; *Areas:* Anthropology; Arts; Biography; Business; Cookery; Crime; Culture; Current Affairs; Design; Fantasy; Film; Finance; Health; Historical; Horror; How-to; Humour; Lifestyle; Music; Mystery; Nature; Photography; Politics; Psychology; Romance; Science; Sci-Fi; Self-Help; Sociology; Women's Interests; *Markets:* Adult; *Treatments:* Contemporary; Literary; Mainstream

Send query with SASE.

The Seymour Agency
475 Miner Street Road, Canton, NY 13617
Tel: +1 (315) 386-1831
Email: marysue@theseymouragency.com
Website: http://www.theseymouragency.com

Handles: Fiction; Nonfiction; *Areas:*
Adventure; Fantasy; Historical; Mystery;
Religious; Romance; Sci-Fi; Suspense;
Thrillers; Women's Interests; *Markets:*
Adult; Children's; Youth

Brief email queries accepted (no
attachments), including first five pages
pasted into the bottom of your email. No
poetry or erotica. All agents prefer queries
by email and one accepts email queries only.
See website for full submission guidelines
and specific interests of each agent.

Denise Shannon Literary Agency, Inc.
20 West 22nd Street, Suite 1603, New York,
NY 10010
Tel: +1 (212) 414-2911
Fax: +1 (212) 414-2930
Email: submissions@
deniseshannonagency.com
Website: http://deniseshannonagency.com

Handles: Fiction; Nonfiction; *Areas:*
Autobiography; Biography; Business;
Current Affairs; Health; Historical; Politics;
Sociology; *Markets:* Adult; *Treatments:*
Literary

Send query by email, or by post with SASE,
including outline and bio listing any previous
publishing credits. Notify if simultaneous
submission. No unsolicited MSS, or queries
for incomplete fiction MSS.

Wendy Sherman Associates, Inc.
27 West 24th Street, Suite 700B, New York,
NY 10010
Tel: +1 (212) 279-9027
Email: submissions@wsherman.com
Website: http://www.wsherman.com

Handles: Fiction; Nonfiction; *Areas:*
Autobiography; Biography; Cookery;
Culture; Entertainment; Health; Historical;
Lifestyle; Nature; Psychology; Self-Help;
Spiritual; Sport; Suspense; Women's
Interests; *Markets:* Adult; Youth;
Treatments: Literary

Send queries by email only, including query
letter and (for fiction) first ten pages pasted
into the body of the email, or (for nonfiction)
author bio. No unsolicited attachments. Do
not send emails to personal agent addresses
(these are deleted unread). Response only if
interested.

Rosalie Siegel, International Literary Agency, Inc.
1 Abbey Drive, Pennington, NJ 08534
Tel: +1 (609) 737-1007
Fax: +1 (609) 737-3708
Email: rosalie@rosaliesiegel.com
Website: http://www.rosaliesiegel.com

Handles: Fiction; Nonfiction; *Areas:*
Biography; Current Affairs; Historical;
Nature; Psychology; Science; Short Stories;
Markets: Adult

Not currently accepting unsolicited MSS or
queries. Any unsolicited material will not be
returned. Accepts new authors by referral
only.

SLW Literary Agency
4100 Ridgeland Avenue, Northbrook, IL
60062
Tel: +1 (847) 207-2075
Email: shariwenk@swenkagency.com

Handles: Nonfiction; *Areas:* Sport; *Markets:*
Adult

Handles sports celebrities and sports writers
only.

Solow Literary Enterprises, Inc.
769 Center Blvd., #148, Fairfax, CA 94930
Email: info@solowliterary.com
Website: http://www.solowliterary.com

Handles: Nonfiction; *Areas:* Autobiography; Business; Culture; Finance; Health; Historical; Nature; Psychology; Science; *Markets:* Adult

Handles nonfiction in the stated areas only. Send single-page query by email or by post with SASE, providing information on what your book is about; why you think it has to be written; and why you are the best person to write it.

Spectrum Literary Agency

320 Central Park West, Suite 1-D, New York, NY 10025
Tel: +1 (212) 362-4323
Fax: +1 (212) 362-4562
Email: ruddigore1@aol.com
Website: http://www.spectrumliteraryagency.com

Handles: Fiction; Nonfiction; *Areas:* Fantasy; Historical; Mystery; Romance; Sci-Fi; Suspense; *Markets:* Adult; *Treatments:* Contemporary; Mainstream

Send query with SASE describing your book and providing background information, publishing credits, and relevant qualifications. The first 10 pages of the work may also be included. Response within three months. No unsolicited MSS or queries by fax, email, or phone.

Spencerhill Associates

8131 Lakewood Main Street, #205, Lakewood Ranch, FL 34202
Tel: +1 (941) 907-3700
Email: submission@spencerhillassociates.com
Website: http://spencerhillassociates.com

Handles: Fiction; Nonfiction; *Areas:* Erotic; Fantasy; Historical; Mystery; Romance; Thrillers; *Markets:* Adult; Youth; *Treatments:* Commercial; Literary

Handles commercial, general-interest fiction, romance including historical romance, paranormal romance, urban fantasy, erotic fiction, category romance, literary fiction, thrillers and mysteries, young adult, and nonfiction. No children's. Send query by email with synopsis and first three chapters attached in .doc / .rtf / .txt format. See website for full details.

The Spieler Agency

27 West 20th Street, Suite 305, New York, NY 10011
Tel: +1 (212) 757-4439, ext.1
Fax: +1 (212) 333.2019
Email: thespieleragency@gmail.com
Website: http://thespieleragency.com

Handles: Fiction; Nonfiction; Poetry; *Areas:* Autobiography; Biography; Business; Cookery; Crime; Culture; Current Affairs; Film; Finance; Health; Historical; Humour; Legal; Lifestyle; Music; Mystery; Nature; Photography; Politics; Science; Sociology; Spiritual; Theatre; Thrillers; Travel; Women's Interests; *Markets:* Adult; Children's; Youth; *Treatments:* Literary; Popular

Consult website for details of specific agents' interests and contact details. Send query by email or by post with SASE. Response not guaranteed if not interested. No response to postal submissions without SASE.

Nancy Stauffer Associates

PO Box 1203, Darien, CT 06820
Tel: +1 (203) 202-2500
Fax: +1 (203) 655-3704
Email: nancy@staufferliterary.com

Handles: Fiction; Nonfiction; *Areas:* Culture; Current Affairs; *Markets:* Adult; Youth; *Treatments:* Contemporary; Literary

Specialises in literary fiction, young adult, and narrative nonfiction. Send query by email only including first 10 pages. Most new clients taken on via referral by existing clients. No genre fiction (mysteries, science fiction/fantasy, romance), historical fiction, thrillers, or action/adventure. Does not respond to all queries.

Sternig & Byrne Literary Agency

2370 S. 107th Street, Apt 4, Milwaukee, Wisconsin 53227-2036

Tel: +1 (414) 328-8034
Fax: +1 (414) 328-8034
Email: jackbyrne@hotmail.com
Website: http://sff.net/people/jackbyrne

Handles: Fiction; Nonfiction; *Areas:*
Fantasy; Horror; Mystery; Sci-Fi; Suspense;
Markets: Adult; Youth

Send brief query by post or email in first
instance (if sending by email send in the
body of the mail, do not send attachments).
Will request further materials if interested.
Currently only considering science fiction,
fantasy, and mysteries. Preference given to
writers with a publishing history.

Stone Manners Salners Agency

6100 Wilshire Boulevard, Suite 1400, Los
Angeles, CA 90048
Tel: +1 (323) 655-1313 / +1 (212) 505-1400
Email: info@smsagency.com
Website: http://www.smsagency.com

Handles: Scripts; *Areas:* Film; TV; *Markets:*
Adult

Handles movie and TV scripts. Send query
by email or post with SASE. No queries by
fax.

Stonesong

270 West 39th Street #201, New York, NY
10018
Tel: +1 (212) 929-4600
Email: submissions@stonesong.com
Website: http://stonesong.com

Handles: Fiction; Nonfiction; *Areas:*
Autobiography; Beauty and Fashion;
Business; Cookery; Crafts; Culture; Current
Affairs; Design; Finance; Health; Lifestyle;
Psychology; Science; Self-Help; *Markets:*
Adult; Children's; Youth; *Treatments:*
Commercial; Literary

Send query by email with the word "Query"
in the subject line, and the first chapter or 10
pages pasted into the body of the email. See
website for specific agent interests and
approach one agent only. No plays,

screenplays, or poetry. Also offers self-
publishing services.

The Strothman Agency

63 East 9th Street, 10X, New York, NY
10003
Email: strothmanagency@gmail.com
Website: http://www.strothmanagency.com

Handles: Fiction; Nonfiction; *Areas:*
Business; Current Affairs; Finance;
Historical; Nature; Science; *Markets:* Adult;
Children's; Youth

Send query by email only. Postal approaches
will be recycled or returned unread. Include
query, details about yourself, a synopsis, and
(for fiction) 2-10 sample pages. All material
must be in the body of the email – no
attachments. No romance, science fiction,
picture books, or poetry.

Stuart Krichevsky Literary Agency, Inc.

381 Park Avenue South, Suite 428, New
York, NY 10016
Tel: +1 (212) 725-5288
Fax: +1 (212) 725-5275
Email: query@skagency.com
Website: http://www.skagency.com

Handles: Fiction; Nonfiction; *Areas:*
Adventure; Autobiography; Biography;
Business; Culture; Current Affairs; Fantasy;
Historical; Nature; Politics; Science; Sci-Fi;
Technology; *Markets:* Adult; Youth;
Treatments: Commercial; Literary

Send query by email with first few pages of
your manuscript (up to 10) pasted into body
of the email (no attachments). See website
for complete submission guidelines and
appropriate submission addresses for each
agent.

The Stuart Agency

260 West 52 Street, Suite #25C, New York,
NY 10019
Tel: +1 (212) 586-2711
Email: andrew@stuartagency.com
Website: http://www.stuartagency.com

Handles: Fiction; Nonfiction; *Areas:* Arts; Autobiography; Business; Culture; Current Affairs; Design; Health; Historical; Horror; Humour; Lifestyle; Music; Psychology; Religious; Science; Sport; Thrillers; *Markets:* Adult; *Treatments:* Commercial; Literary

Send query using submission form on website.

Susanna Lea Associates
331 West 20th Street, New York, NY 10011
Tel: +1 (646) 638-1435
Fax: +1 (646) 638 1436
Email: us-submission@susannalea.com
Website: http://www.
susannaleaassociates.com

Handles: Fiction; Nonfiction; *Markets:* Adult

Agency based in France with US office in New York and UK office in London. No poetry, plays, screenplays, science fiction, educational text books, short stories, illustrated works, or queries by fax or post. Submit by email. See website for specific email addresses for US, UK, and French submissions. Include query letter, brief synopsis, first three chapters and/or proposal. Response not guaranteed.

The Swetky Agency and Associates
Trininad, CO 81082
Tel: +1 (435) 313-8006
Email: fayeswetky@amsaw.org
Website: http://www.amsaw.org/
swetkyagency/

Handles: Fiction; Nonfiction; Scripts; *Areas:* Adventure; Anthropology; Archaeology; Architecture; Arts; Autobiography; Business; Cookery; Crime; Criticism; Culture; Current Affairs; Design; Erotic; Fantasy; Film; Finance; Gardening; Gothic; Health; Historical; How-to; Humour; Legal; Leisure; Literature; Medicine; Military; Mystery; Nature; Philosophy; Photography; Politics; Psychology; Religious; Romance; Science; Sci-Fi; Self-Help; Short Stories; Sociology;

Sport; Suspense; Technology; Theatre; Thrillers; Translations; Travel; TV; Westerns; Women's Interests; *Markets:* Adult; Children's; Youth; *Treatments:* Contemporary; Experimental; Literary; Mainstream

Submit query using submission form on website only. Do not send any portion of your work until requested to do so. Follow guidelines on website precisely. Failure to so results in automatic rejection. Willing to consider anything marketable, except short stories, poetry and children's picture books (but accepts children's fiction and nonfiction).

Talcott Notch Literary
31 Cherry Street, Suite 104, Milford, CT 06460
Fax: +1 (203) 876-9517
Email: editorial@talcottnotch.net
Website: http://www.talcottnotch.net

Handles: Fiction; Nonfiction; *Areas:* Autobiography; Business; Cookery; Crafts; Crime; Fantasy; Gardening; Historical; Horror; Lifestyle; Mystery; Nature; Science; Sci-Fi; Suspense; Technology; Thrillers; Women's Interests; *Markets:* Adult; Children's; Family; Youth; *Treatments:* Mainstream

Currently closed to unsolicited queries and submissions. Will continue to consider works requested as a result of meeting writers through conferences, pitch slams, writing workshops, bootcamps, and client referrals.

Talent Source
1711 Dean Forest Road, Suite H, Savannah, Georgia 31408
Tel: +1 (912) 232-9390
Fax: +1 (912) 232-8213
Email: michael@talentsource.com
Website: http://www.talentsource.com

Handles: Scripts; *Areas:* Drama; Humour; Religious; *Markets:* Adult

Send query with synopsis covering Exposition, Conflict and Resolution, by email. It should not tease the reader, but be an outline of the complete story.

Interested only in character-driven comedies and dramas, e.g.: Something about Mary, Sex, Lies and Videotape, SlingBlade, The Spitfire Grill, The Apostle, Chasing Amy, Pulp Fiction, Monster's Ball, Clerks, Reservoir Dogs, My Big Fat Greek Wedding, etc. Also handles TV movies, series, and one-off specials.

No unsolicited MSS, books, poetry, science fiction, horror, period/costume, road pictures, or big budget special effects/CGI feature films.

Tessler Literary Agency

27 West 20th Street, Suite 1003, New York, NY 10011
Tel: +1 (212) 242-0466
Fax: +1 (212) 242-2366
Website: http://www.tesslieragency.com

Handles: Fiction; Nonfiction; *Areas:* Autobiography; Biography; Business; Cookery; Culture; Health; Historical; Psychology; Science; Travel; Women's Interests; *Markets:* Adult; *Treatments:* Commercial; Literary; Popular

Welcomes appropriate queries. Handles quality nonfiction and literary and commercial fiction. No genre fiction or children's fiction. Send query via form on website only.

Thompson Literary Agency

115 West 29th St, Third Floor, New York, NY 10001
Tel: +1 (347) 281-7685
Email: submissions@thompsonliterary.com
Website: http://thompsonliterary.com

Handles: Fiction; Nonfiction; *Areas:* Arts; Autobiography; Beauty and Fashion; Biography; Cookery; Culture; Health; Historical; Music; Politics; Science; Spiritual; Sport; *Markets:* Adult; Children's; Youth; *Treatments:* Commercial; Literary; Popular

Always on the lookout for commercial and

literary fiction, but specialises in nonfiction. See website for list of agent interests and address submission by email to specific agent.

Tracy Brown Literary Agency

PO Box 772, Nyack, NY 10960
Tel: +1 (914) 400-4147
Fax: +1 (914) 931-1746
Email: tracy@brownlit.com

Handles: Fiction; Nonfiction; *Areas:* Biography; Current Affairs; Health; Historical; Psychology; Travel; Women's Interests; *Markets:* Adult; *Treatments:* Literary; Popular; Serious

Particularly interested in serious nonfiction and fiction. Send query with author bio, outline/proposal, and synopsis. Queries accepted by email but not by fax. No Young Adult, Science Fiction, or Romance.

TriadaUS Literary Agency, Inc.

P.O.Box 561, Sewickley, PA 15143
Tel: +1 (412) 401-3376
Email: uwe@triadaus.com
Website: http://www.triadaus.com

Handles: Fiction; Nonfiction; *Areas:* Adventure; Autobiography; Biography; Business; Cookery; Crafts; Crime; Culture; Current Affairs; Fantasy; Finance; Gardening; Health; Historical; How-to; Humour; Lifestyle; Music; Mystery; Politics; Psychology; Romance; Science; Sci-Fi; Self-Help; Sport; Suspense; Thrillers; Travel; Women's Interests; *Markets:* Adult; Children's; Youth; *Treatments:* Commercial; Literary; Mainstream

Prefers email queries. No attachments, unless requested. Accepts submissions by post, but no response without SASE. No response to queries that do not follow the guidelines.

2M Literary Agency Ltd

19 West 21 Street Suite 501, New York, NY 10010
Tel: +1 (212) 741-1509
Fax: +1 (212) 691-4460
Email: morel@2mcommunications.com

Website: http://www.
2mcommunications.com

Handles: Nonfiction; *Areas:* Autobiography;
Beauty and Fashion; Business; Cookery;
Crime; Culture; Film; Health; Lifestyle;
Medicine; Music; Politics; Psychology;
Science; Sport; *Markets:* Adult; Family;
Treatments: Contemporary; Mainstream;
Niche; Popular; Progressive; Traditional

Only accepts queries from established
ghostwriters, collaborators, and editors with
experience in the fields of business; film,
music and television; health and fitness;
medicine and psychology; parenting;
politics; science; sport; true crime; or the
world of food.

United Talent Agency
142 West 57th Street, Sixth Floor, New
York, NY 10019
Tel: +1 (212) 581-3100
Fax: +1 (212) 581-0015
Email: Sasha.Raskin@Unitedtalent.com
Website: http://www.theagencygroup.com

Handles: Fiction; Nonfiction; *Areas:*
Business; Historical; Science; Sci-Fi;
Markets: Adult; *Treatments:* Literary

Multimedia agency representing recording
artists, celebrities, and with a literary agency
operating out of the New York and London
offices. Send query letter with synopsis and
first 100 pages.

Venture Literary
2683 Via de la Valle, G-714, Del Mar, CA
92014
Tel: +1 (619) 807-1887
Fax: +1 (772) 365-8321
Email: submissions@ventureliterary.com
Website: http://www.ventureliterary.com

Handles: Fiction; Nonfiction; *Areas:*
Adventure; Anthropology; Antiques;
Archaeology; Architecture; Arts;
Autobiography; Beauty and Fashion;
Biography; Business; Cookery; Crafts;
Crime; Criticism; Culture; Current Affairs;
Design; Drama; Entertainment; Erotic; Film;
Finance; Gardening; Gothic; Health;

Historical; Hobbies; Horror; How-to;
Humour; Legal; Leisure; Lifestyle;
Literature; Media; Medicine; Men's Interests;
Military; Music; Mystery; Nature; New Age;
Philosophy; Photography; Politics;
Psychology; Radio; Religious; Science; Self-
Help; Short Stories; Sociology; Spiritual;
Sport; Suspense; Technology; Theatre;
Thrillers; Translations; Travel; TV; Women's
Interests; *Markets:* Adult

Willing to consider queries in all genres
except fantasy, sci-fi, romance, children's
picture books, and westerns. Send query
letter by email only. First 50 pages will be
requested by email if interested in proposal.
Unsolicited queries, proposals, or
manuscripts via snail mail, and all snail mail
submissions will be discarded unopened.

Waterside Productions, Inc
2055 Oxford Avenue, Cardiff, CA 92007
Tel: +1 (760) 632-9190
Fax: +1 (760) 632-9295
Email: admin@waterside.com
Website: http://www.waterside.com

Handles: Nonfiction; *Areas:* Business;
Cookery; Health; Hobbies; How-to;
Lifestyle; Sociology; Spiritual; Sport;
Technology; *Markets:* Adult

Described itself as the world's premiere
literary agency for computer and technology
authors. Send query by post or fill in online
form. You are expected to show knowledge
of your market, established titles you will be
competing with, and to have researched the
niche for your book thoroughly. See website
for full proposal guidelines. No unsolicited
MSS.

The Weingel-Fidel Agency
310 East 46th Street, Suite 21-E, New York,
NY 10017
Tel: +1 (212) 599-2959

Handles: Fiction; Nonfiction; *Areas:* Arts;
Autobiography; Biography; Music;
Psychology; Science; Sociology;
Technology; Women's Interests; *Markets:*
Adult; *Treatments:* Commercial; Literary;
Mainstream

Accepts new clients by referral only –
approach only via an existing client or
industry contact. Specialises in commercial
and literary fiction and nonfiction.
Particularly interested in investigative
journalism. No children's books, science
fiction, fantasy, or self-help.

Wernick & Pratt Agency

1207 North Avenue , Beacon, NY 12508
Email: submissions@wernickpratt.com
Website: http://www.wernickpratt.com

Handles: Fiction; Nonfiction; *Markets:*
Children's; Youth; *Treatments:* Commercial;
Literary

Handles children's books of all genres, from
picture books to young adult literature.
Particularly interested in authors who also
illustrate their picture books; humorous
young chapter books; literary and
commercial middle grade / young adult
books.

Not interested in picture book manuscripts of
more than 750 words, mood pieces, work
specifically targeted to the educational
market, or fiction about the American
Revolution, Civil War, or World War II
(unless told from a very unique perspective).
Accepts queries by email only. See website
for full guidelines. Response only if
interested.

Wm Clark Associates

186 Fifth Avenue, 2nd Floor, New York, NY
10010
Tel: +1 (212) 675-2784
Fax: +1 (347) 649-9262
Email: general@wmclark.com
Website: http://www.wmclark.com

Handles: Fiction; Nonfiction; *Areas:*
Architecture; Arts; Autobiography;
Biography; Culture; Current Affairs; Design;
Film; Historical; Music; Philosophy;
Religious; Science; Sociology; Technology;
Theatre; Translations; *Markets:* Adult;
Treatments: Contemporary; Literary;
Mainstream

Query through online form on website only.
No simultaneous submissions or screenplays.

Wolfson Literary Agency

Email: query@wolfsonliterary.com
Website: http://www.wolfsonliterary.com

Handles: Fiction; Nonfiction; *Areas:*
Culture; Health; How-to; Humour; Lifestyle;
Medicine; Mystery; Romance; Suspense;
Thrillers; Women's Interests; *Markets:*
Adult; Youth; *Treatments:* Mainstream;
Popular

Accepts queries by email only. Response
only if interested. See website for full
submission guidelines.

Writers' Representatives, LLC

116 W. 14th St., 11th Fl., New York, NY
10011-7305
Tel: +1 (212) 620-0023
Fax: +1 (212) 620-0023
Email: transom@writersreps.com
Website: http://www.writersreps.com

Handles: Fiction; Nonfiction; Poetry;
Reference; *Areas:* Autobiography;
Biography; Business; Cookery; Criticism;
Current Affairs; Finance; Historical;
Humour; Legal; Literature; Mystery;
Philosophy; Politics; Science; Self-Help;
Thrillers; *Markets:* Adult; *Treatments:*
Literary; Serious

Send email describing your project and
yourself, or send proposal, outline, CV, and
sample chapters, or complete unsolicited
MS, with SASE. See website for submission
requirements in FAQ section. Specialises in
serious and literary fiction and nonfiction.
No screenplays. No science fiction or
children's or young adult fiction unless it
aspires to serious literature.

The Zack Company, Inc

PMB 525, 4653 Carmel Mountain Rd, Ste
308, San Diego, CA 92130-6650
Website: http://www.zackcompany.com

Handles: Fiction; Nonfiction; Reference;
Areas: Adventure; Autobiography;

Biography; Cookery; Crime; Culture; Current Affairs; Erotic; Fantasy; Film; Finance; Gardening; Health; Historical; Horror; How-to; Humour; Medicine; Military; Music; Mystery; Nature; Politics; Religious; Romance; Science; Sci-Fi; Self-Help; Spiritual; Sport; Suspense; Technology; Thrillers; TV; Women's Interests; *Markets:* Adult; *Treatments:* Popular

Requirements change frequently, so check the agency website before approaching. Please note that approaches are not accepted to the former submissions email address (submissions@zackcompany.com). Electronic approaches must be made via the form on the website. Also accepts approaches by post.

Karen Gantz Zahler Literary Agency

860 Fifth Ave Suite 7J, New York, NY 10021
Tel: +1 (212) 734-3619
Email: karen@karengantzlit.com
Website: http://www.karengantzlit.com

Handles: Fiction; Nonfiction; *Areas:* Autobiography; Cookery; Design; Entertainment; Historical; Lifestyle; Politics; Psychology; Religious; Sociology; Spiritual; *Markets:* Adult

Considers all genres but specialises in nonfiction. Send query and summary by email only.

Helen Zimmermann Literary Agency

58 South Manheim Boulevard, Suite 25,

New Paltz, NY 12561
Tel: +1 (845) 256-0977
Fax: +1 (845) 256-0979
Email: Submit@ZimmAgency.com
Website: http://www.zimmagency.com

Handles: Fiction; Nonfiction; *Areas:* Autobiography; Biography; Cookery; Culture; Health; Historical; How-to; Humour; Lifestyle; Music; Mystery; Nature; Science; Spiritual; Sport; Suspense; Technology; Thrillers; Women's Interests; *Markets:* Adult; *Treatments:* Literary

Particularly interested in health and wellness, relationships, popular culture, women's issues, lifestyle, sports, and music. No poetry, science fiction, horror, or romance. Prefers email queries, but no attachments unless requested. Send pitch letter – for fiction include summary, bio, and first chapter in the body of the email.

Zoë Pagnamenta Agency, LLC

20 West 22nd Street, Suite 1603, New York, NY 10010
Tel: +1 (212) 253-1074
Fax: +1 (212) 253-1075
Email: mail@zpagency.com
Website: http://www.zpagency.com

Handles: Fiction; Nonfiction; *Areas:* Autobiography; Biography; Business; Historical; Science; Short Stories; *Markets:* Adult; *Treatments:* Commercial; Literary; Popular

No screenplays, poetry, self-help, or genre fiction, including mystery, romance or science fiction. Send queries by post only, with SASE (or return email address) and up to 25 pages of sample material.

UK Literary Agents

For the most up-to-date listings of these and hundreds of other literary agents, visit http://www.firstwriter.com/Agents

*To claim your **free** access to the site, please see the back of this book.*

A & B Personal Management Ltd
PO Box 64671, London, NW3 9LH
Tel: +44 (0) 20 7794 3255
Email: b.ellmain@aandb.co.uk

Handles: Fiction; Nonfiction; Scripts; *Areas:* Film; Theatre; TV; *Markets:* Adult

Handles full-length mss and scripts for film, TV, and theatre. No unsolicited mss. Query by email or by phone in first instance.

A for Authors
73 Hurlingham Road, Bexleyheath, Kent DA7 5PE
Email: enquiries@aforauthors.co.uk
Website: http://aforauthors.co.uk

Handles: Fiction; Nonfiction; *Markets:* Adult; Children's; *Treatments:* Commercial; Literary

Query by email only. Include synopsis and first three chapters (or up to 50 pages) and short author bio. All attachments must be Word format documents. No scripts, poetry, fantasy, SF, horror, short stories, adult illustrated books on art, architecture, design, visual culture, or submissions by post, hand delivery, or on discs, memory sticks, or other electronic devices. See website for full details.

Sheila Ableman Literary Agency
36 Duncan House, Fellows Road, London, NW3 3LZ
Tel: +44 (0) 20 7586 2339
Email: sheila@sheilaableman.co.uk
Website: http://www.sheilaableman.com

Handles: Nonfiction; *Areas:* Autobiography; Biography; Historical; Science; TV; *Markets:* Adult; *Treatments:* Commercial; Popular

Send query with SAE, brief bio, one-page synopsis, and two sample chapters. Specialises in popular history, science, biography, autobiography, general narrative and 'quirky' nonfiction with strong commercial appeal, TV tie-ins and celebrity ghost writing. No poetry, children's books, gardening, or sport.

The Agency (London) Ltd
24 Pottery Lane, Holland Park, London, W11 4LZ
Tel: +44 (0) 20 7727 1346
Fax: +44 (0) 20 7727 9037
Email: info@theagency.co.uk
Website: http://www.theagency.co.uk

Handles: Fiction; Nonfiction; Scripts; *Areas:* Film; Radio; Theatre; TV; *Markets:* Adult; Children's

Represents writers and authors for film, television, radio and the theatre. Also represents directors, producers, composers, and film and television rights in books, as well as authors of children's books from picture books to teen fiction. **Handles adult fiction and nonfiction for existing clients only.** Does not consider adult fiction or nonfiction from writers who are not already clients. For script writers, only considers unsolicited material if it has been recommended by a producer, development executive or course tutor. If this is the case send CV, covering letter and details of your referee to the relevant agent, or to the email address below. Do not email more than one agent at a time. For directors, send CV, showreel and cover letter by email. For children's authors, send query by email with synopsis and first three chapters (middle grade and teen) or complete ms (picture books) to address given on website.

Aitken Alexander Associates

18–21 Cavaye Place, London, SW10 9PT
Tel: +44 (0) 20 7373 8672
Fax: +44 (0) 20 7373 6002
Email: submissions@aitkenalexander.co.uk
Website: http://www.aitkenalexander.co.uk

Handles: Fiction; Nonfiction; *Markets:* Adult

Send query by email, with short synopsis, and first 30 pages as a Word document. No illustrated children's books, poetry or screenplays. No submissions or queries by post.

The Ampersand Agency Ltd

Ryman's Cottages, Little Tew, Chipping Norton, Oxfordshire OX7 4JJ
Tel: +44 (0) 1608 683677 / 683898
Fax: +44 (0) 1608 683449
Email: amd@theampersandagency.co.uk
Website: http://www.theampersandagency.co.uk

Handles: Fiction; Nonfiction; *Areas:* Autobiography; Biography; Crime; Current Affairs; Fantasy; Historical; Horror; Sci-Fi; Thrillers; Women's Interests; *Markets:* Adult; Youth; *Treatments:* Commercial;

Contemporary; Literary

We handle literary and commercial fiction and nonfiction, including contemporary and historical novels, crime, thrillers, biography, women's fiction, history, current affairs, and memoirs. Send query by post or email with brief bio, outline, and first two chapters. Also accepts science fiction, fantasy, horror, and Young Adult material to separate email address listed on website. No scripts except those by existing clients, no poetry, self-help or illustrated children's books. No unpublished American writers, because in our experience British and European publishers aren't interested unless there is an American publisher on board. And we'd like to make it clear that American stamps are no use outside America!

Andlyn

Tel: +44 (0) 20 3290 5638
Email: submissions@andlyn.co.uk
Website: http://www.andlyn.co.uk

Handles: Fiction; *Markets:* Children's

Specialises in children's fiction and content. Handles picture books, middle-grade, young adult, and cross-over. Send query by email with one-page synopsis and first three chapters.

Andrew Lownie Literary Agency Ltd

36 Great Smith Street, London, SW1P 3BU
Tel: +44 (0) 20 7222 7574
Fax: +44 (0) 20 7222 7576
Email: mail@andrewlownie.co.uk
Website: http://www.andrewlownie.co.uk

Handles: Fiction; Nonfiction; *Areas:* Autobiography; Biography; Crime; Culture; Current Affairs; Fantasy; Finance; Health; Historical; Horror; How-to; Lifestyle; Literature; Media; Medicine; Men's Interests; Military; Music; Mystery; Politics; Psychology; Romance; Science; Sci-Fi; Self-Help; Sport; Suspense; Technology; Thrillers; Translations; Westerns; *Markets:* Academic; Adult; Family; Professional; *Treatments:* Commercial; Mainstream; Popular; Serious; Traditional

This agency, founded in 1988, is now one of the UK's leading boutique literary agencies with some two hundred nonfiction and fiction authors and is actively building its fiction list through its new agent (see website for specific contact address for fiction submissions). It prides itself on its personal attention to its clients and specialises both in launching new writers and taking established writers to a new level of recognition.

Anne Clark Literary Agency

PO Box 1221 , Harlton, Cambridge , CB23 1WW
Tel: +44 (0) 1223 262160
Email: submissions@ anneclarkliteraryagency.co.uk
Website: http://www. anneclarkliteraryagency.co.uk

Handles: Fiction; *Markets:* Children's; Youth

Handles fiction and picture books for children and young adults. Focusses on clients based in the UK and Ireland. Send query by email only with first 20 pages, or complete ms for picture books. No submissions by post. See website for full guidelines.

Anthony Sheil in Association with Aitken Alexander Associates

18-21 Cavaye Place, London, SW10 9PT
Tel: +44 (0) 20 7373 8672
Fax: +44 (0) 20 7373 6002
Website: http://www.aitkenalexander.co.uk/agents/anthony-sheil/

Handles: Fiction; Nonfiction; *Markets:* Adult

Handles fiction and nonfiction. No scripts, poetry, short stories, or children's fiction. Send query by post with SAE, synopsis up to half a page, and first 30 pages.

Anubis Literary Agency

6 Birdhaven Close, Lighthorne Heath, CV35 0BE
Tel: +44 (0) 1926 642588
Fax: +44 (0) 1926 642588
Email: writerstuff2@btopenworld.com

Handles: Fiction; *Areas:* Fantasy; Horror; Sci-Fi; *Markets:* Adult

No children's books, poetry, short stories, journalism, TV or film scripts, academic or nonfiction. Only considers genre fiction as listed above. Send a covering letter with one-page synopsis and 50-page sample. SAE essential. No telephone calls, or email / fax queries. Simultaneous queries accepted, but no material returned without SAE. Usually responds in six weeks to queries and three months to MSS. Runs regular writers' workshops/seminars to help writers. Email for details.

Author Literary Agents

53 Talbot Road, Highgate, London, N6 4QX
Tel: +44 (0) 20 8341 0442
Fax: +44 (0) 20 8341 0442
Email: a@authors.co.uk

Handles: Fiction; Nonfiction; Scripts; *Areas:* Thrillers; *Markets:* Adult; Children's

Send query with SAE, one-page outline and first chapter, scene, or writing sample. Handles fiction, nonfiction, novels, thrillers, graphic novels, children's books, and media entertainment concepts. Handles material for book publishers, screen producers, and graphic media ideas.

AVAnti Productions & Management

Units 2-8, 31 St. Aubyns, Brighton, BN3 2TH
Tel: +44 (0) 07999 193311
Email: avantiproductions@live.co.uk
Website: http://www.avantiproductions.co.uk

Handles: Fiction; Nonfiction; Poetry; Scripts; *Areas:* Film; Theatre; *Markets:* Adult; *Treatments:* Contemporary

Talent and literary representation – also, a film and theatre production company. Open to screenplay submissions, but no unsolicited theatre scripts.

Bath Literary Agency
5 Gloucester Road, Bath, BA1 7BH
Email: gill.mclay@bathliteraryagency.com
Website: http://bathliteraryagency.com

Handles: Fiction; Nonfiction; *Markets:*
Children's; Youth

Handles fiction and nonfiction for children,
from picture books to Young Adult. Send
query by post with SAE for reply and return
of materials if required, along with the first
three chapters (fiction) or the full manuscript
(picture books). See website for full details.

Bell Lomax Moreton Agency
Suite C, 131 Queensway, Petts Wood, Kent
BR5 1DG
Tel: +44 (0) 20 7930 4447
Fax: +44 (0) 1689 820061
Email: agency@bell-lomax.co.uk
Website: http://www.
belllomaxmoreton.co.uk

Handles: Fiction; Nonfiction; *Areas:*
Biography; Business; Sport; *Markets:* Adult;
Children's

Considers most fiction, nonfiction, and
children's book proposals. No poetry, short
stories, novellas, textbooks, film scripts,
stage plays, or science fiction. Send query by
email with details of any previous work,
short synopsis, and first three chapters (up to
50 pages). For children's picture books send
complete ms. Also accepts postal
submissions. See website for full guidelines.

Lorella Belli Literary Agency (LBLA)
54 Hartford House, 35 Tavistock Crescent,
Notting Hill, London, W11 1AY
Tel: +44 (0) 20 7727 8547
Fax: +44 (0) 870 787 4194
Email: info@lorellabelliagency.com
Website: http://www.lorellabelliagency.com

Handles: Fiction; Nonfiction; *Markets:*
Adult; *Treatments:* Literary

Send query by post or by email in first
instance. No attachments. Particularly
interested in multicultural / international

writing, and books relating to Italy, or
written in Italian; first novelists, and
journalists; successful sel-published authors.
Welcomes queries from new authors and will
suggest revisions where appropriate. No
poetry, children's, original scripts, academic,
SF, or fantasy.

Berlin Associates
7 Tyers Gate, London , SE1 3HX
Tel: +44 (0) 20 7836 1112
Fax: +44 (0) 20 7632 5296
Email: submissions@berlinassociates.com
Website: http://www.berlinassociates.com

Handles: Scripts; *Areas:* Film; Radio;
Theatre; TV; *Markets:* Adult

Most clients through recommendation or
invitation, but accepts queries by email with
CV, experience, and outline of work you
would like to submit.

The Blair Partnership
PO Box, 7828, London, W1A 4GE
Tel: +44 (0) 20 7504 2520
Fax: +44 (0) 20 7504 2521
Email: submissions@
theblairpartnership.com
Website: http://www.theblairpartnership.com

Handles: Fiction; Nonfiction; *Markets:*
Adult; Children's; Family; Youth

Open to all genres of fiction and nonfiction.
Send query by email with one-page synopsis
and first ten pages, including some detail
about yourself. Will also accept submissions
by post with SAE, but prefers digital
approaches.

Blake Friedmann Literary Agency Ltd
First Floor, Selous House, 5-12 Mandela
Street, London, NW1 0DU
Tel: +44 (0) 20 7387 0842
Fax: +44 (0) 20 7691 9626
Email: info@blakefriedmann.co.uk
Website: http://www.blakefriedmann.co.uk

Handles: Fiction; Nonfiction; Scripts; *Areas:*
Autobiography; Biography; Cookery; Crime;

Culture; Current Affairs; Film; Historical; Military; Mystery; Politics; Psychology; Radio; Science; Sociology; Suspense; Technology; Thrillers; Travel; TV; Women's Interests; *Markets:* Adult; Children's; Youth; *Treatments:*Commercial; Contemporary; Literary; Popular

Send query by email to a specific agent best suited to your work. See website for full submission guidelines, details of agents, and individual agent contact details.

No poetry or plays. Short stories and journalism for existing clients only.

Media department currently only accepting submissions from writers with produced credits.

Reply not guaranteed. If no response within 8 weeks, assume rejection.

Luigi Bonomi Associates Ltd

91 Great Russell Street, London, WC1 3PS
Tel: +44 (0) 20 7637 1234
Fax: +44 (0) 20 7637 2111
Email: info@lbabooks.com
Website: http://www.lbabooks.com

Handles: Fiction; Nonfiction; *Areas:* Adventure; Cookery; Crime; Fantasy; Health; Historical; Lifestyle; Romance; Science; Sci-Fi; Thrillers; TV; Women's Interests; *Markets:* Adult; Children's; Youth; *Treatments:* Commercial; Literary

Send query with synopsis and first three chapters by post with SAE (if return of material required) or email address for response, or by email (Word or PDF attachments only). See website for specific agents' interests and email addresses. No scripts or poetry.

BookBlast Ltd.

PO Box 20184, London, W10 5AU
Tel: +44 (0) 20 8968 3089
Fax: +44 (0) 20 8932 4087
Email: gen@bookblast.com
Website: http://www.bookblast.com

Handles: Fiction; Nonfiction; *Areas:*

Autobiography; Culture; Travel; *Markets:* Adult

Handles adult fiction and nonfiction. Currently reading very selectively. Send query with one-page synopsis for fiction, or full outline for nonfiction, with first three chapters and SAE. No scripts or children's books. Film, TV, and radio rights normally sold for works by existing clients. Also offers translation consultancy service. No submissions on fax, email, or disc. Notification must be given of any other agencies previously or currently submitted to.

The Bright Literary Academy

Studio 102, 250 York Road, London, SW11 1RJ
Tel: +44 (0) 20 7326 9140
Email: literarysubmissions@ brightgroupinternational.com
Website: http://brightliteraryagency.com

Handles: Fiction; *Areas:* Autobiography; Entertainment; Literature; Mystery; Sci-Fi; Self-Help; Short Stories; Thrillers; TV; Women's Interests; *Markets:* Children's; Youth; *Treatments:* Commercial; Contemporary; Mainstream; Positive

A boutique literary agency representing the most fabulous new talent to grace the publishing industry in recent years. Born out of the success of a leading illustration agency with an outstanding global client list this agency aims to produce sensational material across all genres of children's publishing, including novelty, picture books, fiction and adult autobiographies, in order to become a one-stop-shop for publishers looking for something extra special to fit into their lists.

Prides itself on nurturing the creativity of its authors and illustrators so that they can concentrate on their craft rather than negotiate their contracts. As a creative agency we develop seeds of ideas into something extraordinary, before searching for the right publisher with which to develop them further to create incredible and unforgettable books.

We are fortunate enough to have a never-ending source of remarkable material at our fingertips and a stable of exceptional creators who are all united by one common goal – a deep passion and dedication to children's books and literature in all its shapes and forms.

Alan Brodie Representation Ltd

Paddock Suite, The Courtyard, 55 Charterhouse Street, London, EC1M 6HA
Tel: +44 (0) 20 7253 6226
Fax: +44 (0) 20 7183 7999
Email: ABR@alanbrodie.com
Website: http://www.alanbrodie.com

Handles: Scripts; *Areas:* Film; Radio; Theatre; TV; *Markets:* Adult

Handles scripts only. No books. Approach with preliminary letter, recommendation from industry professional, CV, and SAE. Do not send a sample of work unless requested. No fiction, nonfiction, or poetry.

Jenny Brown Associates

33 Argyle Place, Edinburgh, Scotland EH9 1JT
Tel: +44 (0) 1312 295334
Email: info@jennybrownassociates.com
Website: http://www. jennybrownassociates.com

Handles: Fiction; Nonfiction; *Areas:* Biography; Crime; Culture; Finance; Historical; Humour; Music; Romance; Science; Sport; Thrillers; Women's Interests; *Markets:* Adult; Children's; *Treatments:* Commercial; Literary; Popular

Strongly prefers queries by email. Approach by post only if not possible to do so by email. Send query with market information, bio, synopsis and first 50 pages in one document (fiction) or sample chapter and info on market and your background (nonfiction). No academic, poetry, short stories, science fiction, or fantasy. Responds only if interested. If no response in 8 weeks assume rejection. See website for individual agent interests and email addresses.

Felicity Bryan

2a North Parade Avenue, Danbury Road, Oxford, OX2 6LX
Tel: +44 (0) 1865 513816
Fax: +44 (0) 1865 310055
Email: submissions@felicitybryan.com
Website: http://www.felicitybryan.com

Handles: Fiction; Nonfiction; *Areas:* Biography; Current Affairs; Historical; Science; *Markets:* Adult; Children's; Youth; *Treatments:* Commercial; Literary

Particularly interested in commercial and literary fiction and nonfiction for the adult market, children's fiction for 8+, and Young Adult. Send query by post with sufficient return postage, or by email with Word or PDF attachments. See website for detailed submission guidelines. No science fiction, horror, adult fantasy, light romance, self-help, memoir, film and TV scripts, plays, poetry or picture/illustrated books.

Juliet Burton Literary Agency

2 Clifton Avenue, London, W12 9DR
Tel: +44 (0) 20 8762 0148
Email: juliet.burton@btinternet.com

Handles: Fiction; Nonfiction; *Areas:* Crime; Women's Interests; *Markets:* Adult

Particularly interested in crime and women's fiction. Send query with SAE, synopsis, and two sample chapters. No poetry, plays, film scripts, children's, articles, academic material, science fiction, fantasy, unsolicited MSS, or email submissions.

CardenWright Literary Agency

27 Khyber Road, London, SW11 2PZ
Tel: +44 (0) 20 7771 0012
Email: gen@cardenwright.com
Website: http://www.cardenwright.com

Handles: Fiction; Nonfiction; Scripts; *Areas:* Theatre; *Markets:* Adult; Youth; *Treatments:* Commercial; Literary

Handles commercial and literary fiction and nonfiction, plus theatre scripts. Will consider teenage / young adult. No poetry, screenplays, or children's books. See website for submission guidelines.

The Catchpole Agency

56 Gilpin Avenue, London, SW14 8QY
Tel: +44 (0) 20 8878 0594
Email: catchpolesubmissions@
googlemail.com
Website: http://www.celiacatchpole.co.uk

Handles: Fiction; *Markets:* Children's

Works on children's books with both artists and writers. Send query by email with sample pasted directly into the body of the email (no attachments). See website for full guidelines.

Catherine Pellegrino & Associates

148 Russell Court, Woburn Place, London, WC1H 0LR
Email: catherine@catherinepellegrino.co.uk
Website: http://catherinepellegrino.co.uk

Handles: Fiction; *Markets:* Children's; Youth; *Treatments:* Commercial; Literary

Handles children's books, from picture books to young adult. Send query by email with some background on you and the book, plus synopsis and first three chapters or approximately 50 pages, up to a natural break. See website for full details.

Teresa Chris Literary Agency Ltd

43 Musard Road, London, W6 8NR
Tel: +44 (0) 20 7386 0633
Email: teresachris@litagency.co.uk
Website: http://www.
teresachrisliteraryagency.co.uk

Handles: Fiction; Nonfiction; *Areas:* Biography; Cookery; Crafts; Crime; Gardening; Historical; Lifestyle; Women's Interests; *Markets:* Adult; *Treatments:* Commercial; Literary

Welcomes submissions. Overseas authors may approach by email, otherwise hard copy submissions preferred. For fiction, send

query with SAE, first three chapters, and one-page synopsis. For nonfiction, send overview with two sample chapters. Specialises in crime fiction and commercial women's fiction. No poetry, short stories, fantasy, science fiction, horror, children's fiction or young adult.

The Christopher Little Literary Agency

48 Walham Grove, London, SW6 1QR
Tel: +44 (0) 20 7736 4455
Fax: +44 (0) 20 7736 4490
Email: submissions@christopherlittle.net
Website: http://www.christopherlittle.net

Handles: Fiction; Nonfiction; *Markets:* Adult; *Treatments:* Commercial; Literary

Closed to submissions as at June 2016

Handles commercial and literary full-length fiction and nonfiction. Film scripts handled for existing clients only (no submissions of film scripts). Send query by email (preferred) or by post with SAE or IRCs. Attach one-page synopsis and three consecutive chapters (fiction) or proposal (nonfiction). No poetry, plays, textbooks, short stories, illustrated children's books, science fiction, fantasy, or submissions by email.

Clare Hulton Literary Agency

Email: info@clarehulton.co.uk
Website: http://www.clarehulton.com

Handles: Fiction; Nonfiction; *Areas:* Autobiography; Cookery; Culture; Historical; Humour; Lifestyle; Music; Philosophy; Self-Help; TV; *Markets:* Adult; Children's; *Treatments:* Commercial; Popular

Specialises in nonfiction, but also has a small commercial fiction and children's list. Finds most authors through recommendation, but open to brief queries by email, explaining what your book is about. No attachments.

Mary Clemmey Literary Agency

6 Dunollie Road, London, NW5 2XP

Tel: +44 (0) 20 7267 1290
Fax: +44 (0) 20 7813 9757
Email: mcwords@googlemail.com

Handles: Fiction; Nonfiction; Scripts; *Areas:* Film; Radio; Theatre; TV; *Markets:* Adult

Send query with SAE and description of work only. Handles high-quality work with an international market. No children's books, science fiction, fantasy, or unsolicited MSS or submissions by email. Scripts handled for existing clients only. Do not submit a script or idea for a script unless you are already a client.

Jonathan Clowes Ltd

10 Iron Bridge House, Bridge Approach, London, NW1 8BD
Tel: +44 (0) 20 7722 7674
Fax: +44 (0) 20 7722 7677
Email: olivia@jonathanclowes.co.uk
Website: http://www.jonathanclowes.co.uk

Handles: Fiction; Nonfiction; Scripts; *Areas:* Film; Radio; Theatre; TV; *Markets:* Adult; *Treatments:* Commercial; Literary

Send query with synopsis and three chapters (or equivalent sample) by email. No science fiction, poetry, short stories, academic. Only considers film/TV clients with previous success in TV/film/theatre. If no response within six weeks, assume rejection.

Rosica Colin Ltd

1 Clareville Grove Mews, London, SW7 5AH
Tel: +44 (0) 20 7370 1080
Fax: +44 (0) 20 7244 6441

Handles: Fiction; Nonfiction; Scripts; *Areas:* Autobiography; Beauty and Fashion; Biography; Cookery; Crime; Current Affairs; Erotic; Fantasy; Film; Gardening; Health; Historical; Horror; Humour; Leisure; Lifestyle; Men's Interests; Military; Mystery; Nature; Psychology; Radio; Religious; Romance; Science; Sport; Suspense; Theatre; Thrillers; Travel; TV; Women's Interests; *Markets:* Academic; Adult; Children's; *Treatments:* Literary

Send query with SAE, CV, synopsis, and list of other agents and publishers where MSS has already been sent. Considers any full-length mss (except science fiction and poetry), plus scripts, but few new writers taken on. Responds in 3-4 months to full mss – synopsis preferred in first instance.

Conville & Walsh Ltd

5th Floor, Haymarket House, 28-29 Haymarket, London, SW1Y 4SP
Tel: +44 (0) 20 7393 4200
Email: submissions@convilleandwalsh.com
Website: http://www.convilleandwalsh.com

Handles: Fiction; Nonfiction; *Areas:* Autobiography; Biography; Crime; Current Affairs; Historical; Humour; Leisure; Lifestyle; Men's Interests; Military; Mystery; Psychology; Science; Sport; Suspense; Thrillers; Travel; Women's Interests; *Markets:* Adult; Children's; Youth; *Treatments:* Commercial; Literary

See website for agent profiles and submit to one particular agent only. Send submissions by email as Word .doc files, or by post. For fiction, please submit the first three sample chapters of the completed manuscript (or about 50 pages) with a one to two page synopsis. For nonfiction, send 30-page proposal. No poetry or scripts, or picture books. See website for full guidelines.

Jane Conway-Gordon Ltd

38 Cromwell Grove, London, W6 7RG
Tel: +44 (0) 20 7371 6939
Email: jane@conway-gordon.co.uk
Website: http://www.janeconwaygordon.com

Handles: Fiction; Nonfiction; *Markets:* Adult

Handles fiction and general nonfiction. Send query by post with SASE, synopsis, and first 3 chapters or 40 pages; or short email describing the book (no attachments). No poetry, children's or science fiction.

Coombs Moylett & Maclean Literary Agency

120 New Kings Road, London, SW6 4LZ

Email: lisa@coombsmoylett.com
Website: http://www.coombsmoylett.com

Handles: Fiction; Nonfiction; *Areas:*
Biography; Cookery; Crime; Current Affairs;
Historical; Mystery; Suspense; Thrillers;
Women's Interests; *Markets:* Adult;
Children's; Youth; *Treatments:* Commercial;
Contemporary; Literary

Handles historical fiction, crime/ mystery/
suspense and thrillers, women's fiction from
chick-lit to sagas to contemporary and
literary fiction. Also looking to build a
children's list concentrating on Young Adult
fiction. In nonfiction, considers history,
biography, current affairs and cookery.

Send query with synopsis and first three
chapters by post. No submissions by fax, but
accepts email queries. No poetry, plays or
scripts for film and TV.

The Creative Rights Agency
17 Prior Street, London, SE10 8SF
Tel: +44 (0) 20 3371 7673
Email: info@creativerightsagency.co.uk
Website: http://www.
creativerightsagency.co.uk

Handles: Fiction; Nonfiction; *Areas:*
Autobiography; Culture; Men's Interests;
Sport; Thrillers; *Markets:* Adult; *Treatments:*
Contemporary

Specialises in men's interests. Send query by
email with sample chapters, synopsis, and
author bio.

Creative Authors Ltd
11A Woodlawn Street, Whitstable, Kent
CT5 1HQ
Tel: +44 (0) 01227 770947
Email: write@creativeauthors.co.uk
Website: http://www.creativeauthors.co.uk

Handles: Fiction; Nonfiction; *Areas:* Arts;
Autobiography; Biography; Business;
Cookery; Crafts; Crime; Culture; Health;
Historical; Humour; Nature; Women's
Interests; *Markets:* Adult; Children's;
Treatments: Commercial; Literary

**As at November 2015, not accepting new
fiction clients. See website for current
situation.**

We are a dynamic literary agency –
established to provide an attentive and
unique platform for writers and scriptwriters
and representing a growing list of clients.
We're on the lookout for fresh talent and
books with strong commercial potential. No
unsolicited MSS, but considers queries by
email. No paper submissions. Do not
telephone regarding submissions.

Rupert Crew Ltd
6 Windsor Road, London, N3 3SS
Tel: +44 (0) 20 8346 3000
Fax: +44 (0) 20 8346 3009
Email: info@rupertcrew.co.uk
Website: http://www.rupertcrew.co.uk

Handles: Fiction; Nonfiction; *Markets:*
Adult

Send query with SAE, synopsis, and first
two or three consecutive chapters.
International representation, handling
volume and subsidiary rights in fiction and
nonfiction properties. No Short Stories,
Science Fiction, Fantasy, Horror, Poetry or
original scripts for Theatre, Television and
Film. Email address for correspondence
only. No response by post and no return of
material with insufficient return postage.

Curtis Brown Group Ltd
Haymarket House, 28/29 Haymarket,
London, SW1Y 4SP
Tel: +44 (0) 20 7393 4400
Fax: +44 (0) 20 7393 4401
Email: cbcsubmissions@curtisbrown.co.uk
Website: http://www.
curtisbrowncreative.co.uk

Handles: Fiction; Nonfiction; Scripts; *Areas:*
Biography; Crime; Fantasy; Film; Historical;
Radio; Science; Suspense; Theatre; Thrillers;
TV; *Markets:* Adult; Children's; Youth;
Treatments: Literary; Mainstream; Popular

Renowned and long established London
agency. Handles general fiction and

nonfiction, and scripts. Also represents directors, designers, and presenters. No longer accepts submissions by post or email – all submissions must be made using online submissions manager. Also offers services such as writing courses for which authors are charged.

The Darley Anderson Agency

Estelle House, 11 Eustace Road, London, SW6 1JB
Tel: +44 (0) 20 7385 6652
Email: enquiries@darleyanderson.com
Website: http://www.darleyanderson.com

Handles: Fiction; Nonfiction; *Areas:* Adventure; Arts; Autobiography; Beauty and Fashion; Biography; Business; Cookery; Crafts; Crime; Criticism; Culture; Current Affairs; Design; Drama; Entertainment; Erotic; Fantasy; Film; Finance; Gardening; Gothic; Health; Historical; Hobbies; Horror; How-to; Humour; Legal; Leisure; Lifestyle; Literature; Media; Medicine; Men's Interests; Military; Music; Mystery; Nature; New Age; Philosophy; Photography; Politics; Psychology; Radio; Religious; Romance; Science; Sci-Fi; Self-Help; Sociology; Spiritual; Sport; Suspense; Technology; Theatre; Thrillers; Translations; Travel; TV; Westerns; Women's Interests; *Markets:* Adult; Children's; Family; Youth; *Treatments:* Commercial; Contemporary; Dark; Light; Mainstream; Popular; Positive; Serious; Traditional

We do not accept Scripts, Screenplays, TV programme ideas, short stories or poetry.

Accepts submissions by email and by post. See website for individual agent requirements, submission guidelines, and contact details.

David Luxton Associates

23 Hillcourt Avenue, London, N12 8EY
Tel: +44 (0) 20 8922 3942
Email: nick@davidluxtonassociates.co.uk
Website: http://www.
davidluxtonassociates.co.uk

Handles: Nonfiction; Reference; *Areas:* Autobiography; Biography; Culture;

Historical; Politics; Sport; *Markets:* Adult; *Treatments:* Popular

Specialises in nonfiction, including sports, memoir, history, popular reference and politics. No scripts or screenplays. Most clients by recommendation, but will consider email queries. See website for correct email addresses for different subjects. No submissions by post.

Caroline Davidson Literary Agency

5 Queen Anne's Gardens, London, W4 1TU
Tel: +44 (0) 20 8995 5768
Fax: +44 (0) 20 8994 2770
Email: enquiries@cdla.co.uk
Website: http://www.cdla.co.uk

Handles: Fiction; Nonfiction; Reference; *Areas:* Archaeology; Architecture; Arts; Biography; Cookery; Culture; Design; Gardening; Health; Historical; Lifestyle; Medicine; Nature; Politics; Psychology; Science; *Markets:* Adult

Send query with CV, SAE, outline and history of work, and (for fiction) the first 50 pages and last 10 pages of novel. For nonfiction, include table of contents, detailed chapter-by-chapter synopsis, description of sources and / or research for the book, market and competition analysis, and (if possible) one or two sample chapters.

Submissions without adequate return postage are neither returned or considered. No Chick lit, romance, erotica, Crime and thrillers, Science fiction, fantasy, Poetry, Individual short stories, Children's, Young Adult, Misery memoirs or fictionalised autobiography. Completed and polished first novels positively welcomed. See website for more details. No submissions by fax and only in exceptional circumstances accepts submissions by email.

See website for full details.

Felix de Wolfe

20 Old Compton Street, London, W1D 4TW
Tel: +44 (0) 20 7242 5066
Fax: +44 (0) 20 7242 8119

Email: info@felixdewolfe.com
Website: http://www.felixdewolfe.com

Handles: Fiction; Scripts; *Areas:* Film;
Radio; Theatre; TV; *Markets:* Adult

Send query letter with SAE, short synopsis,
and CV by post only, unless alternative
arrangements have been made with the
agency in advance. Quality fiction and
scripts only. No nonfiction, children's books,
or unsolicited MSS.

DHH Literary Agency Ltd

23-25 Cecil Court, London, WC2N 4EZ
Tel: +44 (0) 20 7836 7376
Email: submission@dhhliteraryagency.com
Website: http://www.dhhliteraryagency.com

Handles: Fiction; Nonfiction; Scripts; *Areas:*
Adventure; Archaeology; Autobiography;
Biography; Crime; Fantasy; Film; Historical;
Sci-Fi; Theatre; Thrillers; TV; Women's
Interests; *Markets:* Adult; Children's; Youth;
Treatments: Literary

Accepts submissions by email only. No
postal submissions. See website for specific
agent interests and email addresses and
approach one agent only.

Diamond Kahn and Woods (DKW) Literary Agency Ltd

Top Floor, 66 Onslow Gardens, London,
N10 3JX
Tel: +44 (0) 20 3514 6544
Email: submissions.bryony@
dkwlitagency.co.uk
Website: http://dkwlitagency.co.uk

Handles: Fiction; Nonfiction; *Areas:*
Adventure; Archaeology; Biography; Crime;
Culture; Fantasy; Gothic; Historical;
Humour; Politics; Sci-Fi; Sociology;
Suspense; Thrillers; *Markets:* Adult;
Children's; Youth; *Treatments:* Commercial;
Contemporary; Literary

Send submissions by email. See website for
specific agent interests and contact details.

Diane Banks Associates Literary Agency

Email: submissions@dianebanks.co.uk
Website: http://www.dianebanks.co.uk

Handles: Fiction; Nonfiction; *Areas:*
Autobiography; Beauty and Fashion;
Business; Crime; Culture; Current Affairs;
Entertainment; Health; Historical; Lifestyle;
Psychology; Science; Self-Help; Thrillers;
Women's Interests; *Markets:* Adult; Youth;
Treatments: Commercial; Literary; Popular

Send query with author bio, synopsis, and
the first three chapters by email as Word or
Open Document attachments. No poetry,
plays, scripts, academic books, short stories
or children's books, with the exception of
young adult fiction. Hard copy submissions
are not accepted will not be read or returned.

Dorian Literary Agency (DLA)

32 Western Road, St Marychurch, Torquay,
Devon TQ1 4RL
Tel: +44 (0) 1803 320934
Email: doriandot@compuserve.com

Handles: Fiction; *Areas:* Crime; Fantasy;
Historical; Horror; Romance; Sci-Fi;
Thrillers; Women's Interests; *Markets:*
Adult; *Treatments:* Popular

**Principal agent passed away in October,
2013 – continues to be listed as a member
of the AAA, but a user reports
submissions being returned by solicitors
advising that no new submissions are
being accepted.**

Concentrates on popular genre fiction. Send
query by post with SAE or email address for
response, including outline and up to three
sample chapters. No queries or submissions
by fax, telephone, or email. No poetry,
scripts, short stories, nonfiction, children's,
young adult, or comic material.

Toby Eady Associates Ltd

Third Floor, 9 Orme Court, London, W2
4RL
Tel: +44 (0) 20 7792 0092
Fax: +44 (0) 20 7792 0879

Claim your free access to www.firstwriter.com: See p.423

Email: submissions@
tobyeadyassociates.co.uk
Website: http://www.
tobyeadyassociates.co.uk

Handles: Fiction; Nonfiction; *Markets:*
Adult

Send first 50 pages of your fiction or
nonfiction work by email, with a synopsis,
and a letter including biographical
information. If submitting by post, include
SAE for return of material, if required. No
film / TV scripts or poetry. Particular interest
in China, Middle East, India, and Africa.

Eddison Pearson Ltd
West Hill House, 6 Swains Lane, London,
N6 6QS
Tel: +44 (0) 20 7700 7763
Fax: +44 (0) 20 7700 7866
Email: enquiries@eddisonpearson.com
Website: http://www.eddisonpearson.com

Handles: Fiction; Nonfiction; Poetry;
Markets: Children's; Youth; *Treatments:*
Literary

Send query by email only (or even blank
email) for auto-response containing up-to-
date submission guidelines and email address
for submissions. No unsolicited MSS. No
longer accepts submissions or enquiries by
post. Send query with first two chapters by
email only to address provided in auto-
response. Response in 6-10 weeks. If no
response after 10 weeks send email query.

Edwards Fuglewicz
49 Great Ormond Street, London, WC1N
3HZ
Tel: +44 (0) 20 7405 6725
Fax: +44 (0) 20 7405 6726
Email: info@efla.co.uk

Handles: Fiction; Nonfiction; *Areas:*
Biography; Crime; Culture; Historical;
Humour; Mystery; Romance; Thrillers;
Markets: Adult; *Treatments:* Commercial;
Literary

Handles literary and commercial fiction, and

nonfiction. No children's, science fiction,
horror, or email submissions.

Elise Dillsworth Agency (EDA)
9 Grosvenor Road, London, N10 2DR
Email: submissions@
elisedillsworthagency.com
Website: http://elisedillsworthagency.com

Handles: Fiction; Nonfiction;
Autobiography; Biography; *Markets:* Adult;
Treatments: Commercial; Literary

Represents writers from around the world.
Looking for literary and commercial fiction,
and nonfiction (especially memoir and
autobiography). No science fiction, fantasy,
young adult, or children's. Send query by
email or by post with SAE or email address
for response. Include synopsis up to two
pages and first three chapters, up to about 50
pages, as Word or PDF attachments. See
website for full guidelines. Response in 6-8
weeks

Elizabeth Roy Literary Agency
White Cottage, Greatford, Stamford,
Lincolnshire PE9 4PR
Tel: +44 (0) 1778 560672
Website: http://www.elizabethroy.co.uk

Handles: Fiction; Nonfiction; *Markets:*
Children's

Handles fiction and nonfiction for children.
Particularly interested in funny fiction,
gentle romance for young teens, picture book
texts for pre-school children, and books with
international market appeal. Send query by
post with return postage, synopsis, and
sample chapters. No science fiction, poetry,
plays or adult books.

Emily Sweet Associates
Website: http://www.
emilysweetassociates.com

Handles: Fiction; Nonfiction; *Areas:*
Biography; Cookery; Current Affairs;
Historical; *Markets:* Adult; *Treatments:*
Commercial; Literary

No Young Adult or children's. Query through form on website in first instance.

Faith Evans Associates

27 Park Avenue North, London, N8 7RU
Tel: +44 (0) 20 8340 9920
Fax: +44 (0) 20 8340 9410
Email: faith@faith-evans.co.uk

Handles: Fiction; Nonfiction; *Markets:* Adult

Small agency with full list. Not accepting new clients as at January 2016. No phone calls, or unsolicited MSS.

Film Rights Ltd in association with Laurence Fitch Ltd

11 Pandora Road, London, NW6 1TS
Tel: +44 (0) 20 8001 3040
Fax: +44 (0) 20 8711 3171
Email: information@filmrights.ltd.uk
Website: http://filmrights.ltd.uk

Handles: Fiction; Scripts; *Areas:* Film; Horror; Radio; Theatre; TV; *Markets:* Adult; Children's

Represents films, plays, and novels, for adults and children.

Jill Foster Ltd (JFL)

48 Charlotte Street, London, W1T 2NS
Tel: +44 (0) 20 3137 8182
Email: agents@jflagency.com
Website: http://www.jflagency.com

Handles: Scripts; *Areas:* Drama; Film; Humour; Radio; Theatre; TV; *Markets:* Adult

Handles scripts only (for television, film, theatre and radio). Considers approaches from established writers with broadcast experience, but only accepts submissions from new writers during specific periods – consult website for details.

Fox & Howard Literary Agency

39 Eland Road, London, SW11 5JX

Tel: +44 (0) 20 7352 8691
Email: enquiries@foxandhoward.co.uk
Website: http://www.foxandhoward.co.uk

Handles: Nonfiction; Reference; *Areas:* Biography; Business; Culture; Health; Historical; Lifestyle; Psychology; Self-Help; Spiritual; *Markets:* Adult

Closed to submissions as at February 2016. Please check website for current status.

Send query with synopsis and SAE for response. Small agency specialising in nonfiction that works closely with its authors. No unsolicited MSS.

Fraser Ross Associates

6/2 Wellington Place, Edinburgh, Scotland EH6 7EQ
Tel: +44 (0) 01315 532759
Email: fraserrossassociates@gmail.com
Website: http://www.fraserross.co.uk

Handles: Fiction; *Markets:* Adult; Children's; *Treatments:* Commercial; Literary; Mainstream

Send query by email or by post with SAE, including CV, the first three chapters and synopsis for fiction, or a one page proposal and the opening and a further two chapters for nonfiction. For picture books, send complete MS, without illustrations. Rarely accept poetry, playscripts or short stories.

Furniss Lawton

James Grant Group Ltd, 94 Strand on the Green, Chiswick, London, W4 3NN
Tel: +44 (0) 20 8987 6804
Email: info@furnisslawton.co.uk
Website: http://furnisslawton.co.uk

Handles: Fiction; Nonfiction; *Areas:* Autobiography; Biography; Business; Cookery; Crime; Fantasy; Historical; Politics; Psychology; Science; Sociology; Suspense; Thrillers; Women's Interests; *Markets:* Adult; Children's; Youth; *Treatments:* Commercial; Literary

Send query with synopsis and first 10,000

words / three chapters as a Word or PDF document by email. Include the word "Submission" in the subject line, and your name and the title of the work in any attachments. No submissions by post. Does not handle screenwriters for film or TV. See website for full details.

Georgina Capel Associates Ltd
29 Wardour Street, London, W1D 6PS
Tel: +44 (0) 20 7734 2414
Fax: +44 (0) 20 7734 8101
Email: georgina@georginacapel.com
Website: http://www.georginacapel.com

Handles: Fiction; Nonfiction; *Areas:* Biography; Film; Historical; Radio; TV; *Markets:* Adult; *Treatments:* Commercial; Literary

Handles general fiction and nonfiction. Send query outlining writing history (for nonfiction, what qualifies you to write your book), with synopsis around 500 words and first three chapters, plus SAE or email address for reply. Submissions are not returned. Mark envelope for the attention of the Submissions Department. Accepts submissions by email, but prefers them by post. Response only if interested, normally within 6 weeks.

Eric Glass Ltd
25 Ladbroke Crescent, London, W11 1PS
Tel: +44 (0) 20 7229 9500
Fax: +44 (0) 20 7229 6220
Email: eglassltd@aol.com

Handles: Fiction; Nonfiction; Scripts; *Areas:* Film; Theatre; TV; *Markets:* Adult

Handles full-length mss and scripts for film, TV, and theatre. Send query with SAE. No children's books, short stories, poetry, or unsolicited MSS.

David Godwin Associates
55 Monmouth Street, London, WC2H 9DG
Tel: +44 (0) 20 7240 9992
Fax: +44 (0) 20 7395 6110
Email: assistant@

davidgodwinassociates.co.uk
Website: http://www.
davidgodwinassociates.co.uk

Handles: Fiction; Nonfiction; *Areas:* Biography; *Markets:* Adult; Children's; Youth; *Treatments:* Literary

Handles nonfiction (including biography) and fiction (general and literary). Send query by email with synopsis and first 30 pages. Accepts submissions for children's (9+) and young adult books by email to address specified on website (see submissions page). No reference, science fiction, fantasy, self-help, poetry or collections of short stories. No picture books, except for existing clients.

Graham Maw Christie Literary Agency
37 Highbury Place, London, N5 1QP
Tel: +44 (0) 7971 268342
Email: submissions@
grahammawchristie.com
Website: http://www.
grahammawchristie.com

Handles: Nonfiction; Reference; *Areas:* Autobiography; Business; Cookery; Crafts; Gardening; Health; Historical; Humour; Lifestyle; Philosophy; Science; Self-Help; *Markets:* Adult; Children's

No fiction, poetry, or scripts. Send query with one-page summary, a paragraph on the contents of each chapter, your qualifications for writing it, details of your online presence, market analysis, what you could do to help promote your book, and a sample chapter. Accepts approaches by email.

Christine Green Authors' Agent
LSBU Technopark, 90 London Road, London, SE1 6LN
Tel: +44 (0) 20 7401 8844
Email: info@christinegreen.co.uk
Website: http://www.christinegreen.co.uk

Handles: Fiction; Nonfiction; *Markets:* Adult; Youth; *Treatments:* Commercial; Literary

Focusses on fiction for adult and young adult, and also considers narrative nonfiction. No children's books, genre science-fiction/fantasy, poetry or scripts. Send query by email (preferred) or by post with SAE. No submissions by fax or CD. See website for full submission guidelines.

Louise Greenberg Books Ltd

The End House, Church Crescent, London, N3 1BG
Tel: +44 (0) 20 8349 1179
Email: louisegreenberg@msn.com

Handles: Fiction; Nonfiction; *Markets:* Adult; *Treatments:* Literary; Serious

Handles full-length literary fiction and serious nonfiction only. All approaches must be accompanied by SAE. No approaches by telephone.

Greene & Heaton Ltd

37 Goldhawk Road, London, W12 8QQ
Tel: +44 (0) 20 8749 0315
Fax: +44 (0) 20 8749 0318
Email: submissions@greeneheaton.co.uk
Website: http://www.greeneheaton.co.uk

Handles: Fiction; Nonfiction; *Areas:* Arts; Autobiography; Biography; Cookery; Crime; Culture; Current Affairs; Gardening; Health; Historical; Humour; Philosophy; Politics; Romance; Science; Sci-Fi; Thrillers; Travel; *Markets:* Adult; Children's; *Treatments:* Commercial; Contemporary; Literary; Traditional

Send query by email or by post with SAE, including synopsis and three chapters or approximately 50 pages. No response to unsolicited MSS with no SAE or inadequate means of return postage provided. No response to email submissions unless interested. Handles all types of fiction and nonfiction, but no scripts.

The Greenhouse Literary Agency

Tel: +44 (0) 20 7841 3959
Email: submissions@
greenhouseliterary.com

Website: http://www.greenhouseliterary.com

Handles: Fiction; *Markets:* Children's; Youth

Transatlantic agency with offices in the US and London. Handles children's and young adult fiction only. For novels, send query by email with first five pages pasted into the body of the email. For picture books (maximum 1,000 words) paste full text into the boxy of the email. No illustrations required at this stage, unless you are an author/illustrator. No attachments or hard copy submissions.

Gregory & Company, Authors' Agents

3 Barb Mews, London, W6 7PA
Tel: +44 (0) 20 7610 4676
Fax: +44 (0) 20 7610 4686
Email: maryjones@
gregoryandcompany.co.uk
Website: http://www.
gregoryandcompany.co.uk

Handles: Fiction; *Areas:* Crime; Historical; Thrillers; *Markets:* Adult; *Treatments:* Commercial

Particularly interested in Crime, Family Sagas, Historical Fiction, Thrillers and Upmarket Commercial Fiction.
Send query with CV, one-page synopsis, future writing plans, and first ten pages, by post with SAE, or by email. No unsolicited MSS, Business Books, Children's, Young Adult Fiction, Plays, Screenplays, Poetry, Science Fiction, Future Fiction, Fantasy, Self Help, Lifestyle books, Short Stories, Spiritual, New Age, Philosophy, Supernatural, Paranormal, Horror, Travel, or True Crime.

David Grossman Literary Agency Ltd

118b Holland Park Avenue, London, W11 4UA
Tel: +44 (0) 20 7221 2770
Email: david@dglal.co.uk

Handles: Fiction; Nonfiction; *Markets:* Adult

Send preliminary letter before making a submission. No approaches or submissions by fax or email. Usually works with published fiction writers, but well-written and original work from beginners considered. No poetry, scripts, technical books for students, or unsolicited MSS.

Gunn Media Associates

50 Albemarle Street, London, W1S 4BD
Tel: +44 (0) 20 7529 3745
Email: ali@gunnmedia.co.uk
Website: http://www.gunnmedia.co.uk

Handles: Fiction; Nonfiction; *Areas:*
Autobiography; Entertainment; Thrillers;
Markets: Adult; *Treatments:* Commercial;
Literary

Handles commercial fiction and nonfiction, including literary, thrillers, and celebrity autobiographies.

Hardman & Swainson

4 Kelmscott Road, London, SW11 6QY
Tel: +44 (0) 20 7223 5176
Email: submissions@hardmanswainson.com
Website: http://www.hardmanswainson.com

Handles: Fiction; Nonfiction; *Areas:*
Autobiography; Crime; Historical; Horror;
Philosophy; Science; Thrillers; Women's
Interests; *Markets:* Adult; Children's; Youth;
Treatments: Literary; Popular

Agency launched June 2012 by former colleagues at an established agency. Welcomes submissions of fiction and nonfiction. No poetry, plays / screenplays / scripts, or very young children's / picture books. No submissions by post. See website for full submission guidelines.

Antony Harwood Limited

103 Walton Street, Oxford, OX2 6EB
Tel: +44 (0) 1865 559615
Fax: +44 (0) 1865 310660
Email: mail@antonyharwood.com
Website: http://www.antonyharwood.com

Handles: Fiction; Nonfiction; *Areas:*
Adventure; Anthropology; Antiques;
Archaeology; Architecture; Arts;
Autobiography; Beauty and Fashion;
Biography; Business; Cookery; Crafts;
Crime; Criticism; Culture; Current Affairs;
Design; Drama; Entertainment; Erotic;
Fantasy; Film; Finance; Gardening; Gothic;
Health; Historical; Hobbies; Horror; How-to;
Humour; Legal; Leisure; Lifestyle;
Literature; Media; Medicine; Men's Interests;
Military; Music; Mystery; Nature; New Age;
Philosophy; Photography; Politics;
Psychology; Radio; Religious; Romance;
Science; Sci-Fi; Self-Help; Short Stories;
Sociology; Spiritual; Sport; Suspense;
Technology; Theatre; Thrillers; Translations;
Travel; TV; Westerns; Women's Interests;
Markets: Adult; Children's; Youth

Handles fiction and nonfiction in every genre and category, except for screenwriting and poetry. Send brief outline and first 50 pages by email, or by post with SASE.

A M Heath & Company Limited, Author's Agents

6 Warwick Court, Holborn, London, WC1R 5DJ
Tel: +44 (0) 20 7242 2811
Fax: +44 (0) 20 7242 2711
Email: enquiries@amheath.com
Website: http://www.amheath.com

Handles: Fiction; Nonfiction; *Areas:*
Biography; Cookery; Crime; Historical;
Nature; Psychology; Sport; Suspense;
Thrillers; Women's Interests; *Markets:*
Adult; Children's; Youth; *Treatments:*
Commercial; Literary

Handles general commercial and literary fiction and nonfiction. Submit work with cover letter and synopsis via online submission system only. No paper submissions. Aims to respond within six weeks.

Rupert Heath Literary Agency

50 Albemarle Street, London, W1S 4BD
Tel: +44 (0) 20 7060 3385
Email: emailagency@rupertheath.com
Website: http://www.rupertheath.com

Handles: Fiction; Nonfiction; *Areas:* Arts;

Autobiography; Biography; Crime; Culture; Current Affairs; Historical; Humour; Nature; Politics; Science; Sci-Fi; Thrillers; *Markets:* Adult; *Treatments:* Commercial; Literary; Popular

Send query giving some information about yourself and the work you would like to submit. Prefers queries by email. Response only if interested.

hhb agency ltd

6 Warwick Court, London, WC1R 5DJ
Tel: +44 (0) 20 7405 5525
Email: jack@hhbagency.com
Website: http://www.hhbagency.com

Handles: Fiction; Nonfiction; *Areas:* Adventure; Autobiography; Biography; Business; Cookery; Crime; Culture; Entertainment; Historical; Humour; Politics; Travel; TV; Women's Interests; *Markets:* Adult; *Treatments:* Commercial; Contemporary; Literary; Popular

Represents nonfiction writers, particularly in the areas of journalism, history and politics, travel and adventure, contemporary autobiography and biography, books about words and numbers, popular culture and quirky humour, entertainment and television, business, family memoir, food and cookery. Also handles commercial fiction. Send query by email with cover letter, synopsis, and first three chapters. If unable to submit by email, send by post with SAE. No international postal vouchers. Does not represent writers outside Europe.

David Higham Associates Ltd

7th Floor, Waverley House, 7–12 Noel Street, London, W1F 8GQ
Tel: +44 (0) 20 7434 5900
Fax: +44 (0) 20 7437 1072
Email: dha@davidhigham.co.uk
Website: http://www.davidhigham.co.uk

Handles: Fiction; Nonfiction; Scripts; *Areas:* Autobiography; Biography; Cookery; Crime; Current Affairs; Drama; Film; Historical; Humour; Nature; Theatre; Thrillers; TV;

Markets: Adult; Children's; *Treatments:* Commercial; Literary; Serious

For adult fiction and nonfiction contact "Adult Submissions Department" by post only with SASE, covering letter, CV, and synopsis (fiction)/proposal (nonfiction) and first two or three chapters. For children's fiction submit by email to the specific children's submission address given on the website, with covering letter, synopsis, CV, and first two or three chapters (or complete MS if a picture book). See website for complete guidelines. Scripts by referral only.

Vanessa Holt Ltd

59 Crescent Road, Leigh-on-Sea, Essex SS9 2PF
Tel: +44 (0) 1702 473787
Email: v.holt791@btinternet.com

Handles: Fiction; Nonfiction; *Markets:* Adult

General fiction and nonfiction. No unsolicited mss or overseas approaches.

Kate Hordern Literary Agency

18 Mortimer Road, Clifton, Bristol, BS8 4EY
Tel: +44 (0) 117 923 9368
Email: katehordern@blueyonder.co.uk
Website: http://www.katehordern.co.uk

Handles: Fiction; Nonfiction; Reference; *Areas:* Autobiography; Business; Crime; Culture; Current Affairs; Historical; Sociology; Thrillers; Women's Interests; *Markets:* Adult; Children's; Youth; *Treatments:* Commercial; Contemporary; Literary; Popular

Send query by email only with pitch, outline or synopsis, and first three chapters. No submissions by post, or from authors not resident in the UK.

Valerie Hoskins Associates

20 Charlotte Street, London, W1T 2NA
Tel: +44 (0) 20 7637 4490

Fax: +44 (0) 20 7637 4493
Email: info@vhassociates.co.uk
Website: http://www.vhassociates.co.uk

Handles: Scripts; *Areas:* Film; Radio; TV; *Markets:* Adult

Always on the lookout for screenwriters with an original voice and creatives with big ideas. Query by email or by phone. Allow up to eight weeks for response to submissions.

Hunter Profiles
London,
Email: info@hunterprofiles.com
Website: http://www.hunterprofiles.com

Handles: Fiction; Nonfiction; *Markets:* Adult; *Treatments:* Commercial

We specialise in commercial and narrative fiction and nonfiction. We only accept proposals by email. See website for submission guidelines.

Independent Talent Group Ltd
40 Whitfield Street, London, W1T 2RH
Tel: +44 (0) 20 7636 6565
Fax: +44 (0) 20 7323 0101
Email: laurarourke@independenttalent.com
Website: http://www.independenttalent.com

Handles: Scripts; *Areas:* Film; Radio; Theatre; TV; *Markets:* Adult

Specialises in scripts and works in association with agencies in Los Angeles and New York. No unsolicited MSS. Materials submitted will not be returned.

Intercontinental Literary Agency
5 New Concordia Wharf, Mill Street, London, SE1 2BB
Tel: +44 (0) 20 7379 6611
Fax: +44 (0) 20 7240 4724
Email: ila@ila-agency.co.uk
Website: http://www.ila-agency.co.uk

Handles: Fiction; Nonfiction; *Areas:* Translations; *Markets:* Adult; Children's

Handles translation rights only for, among others, the authors of LAW Ltd, London; Harold Matson Co. Inc., New York; PFD, London. Submissions accepted via client agencies and publishers only – no submissions from writers seeking agents.

Isabel White Literary Agent
Tel: +44 (0) 20 3070 1602
Email: query.isabelwhite@googlemail.com

Handles: Fiction; Nonfiction; *Markets:* Adult

Selective one-woman agency, not taking on new clients as at June 2015.

Janet Fillingham Associates
52 Lowther Road , London, SW13 9NU
Tel: +44 (0) 20 8748 5594
Fax: +44 (0) 20 8748 7374
Email: info@janetfillingham.com
Website: http://www.janetfillingham.com

Handles: Scripts; *Areas:* Film; Theatre; TV; *Markets:* Adult; Children's; Youth

Represents writers and directors for stage, film and TV, as well as librettists, lyricists and composers in musical theatre. Does not represent books. Prospective clients may register via website.

Jo Unwin Literary Agency
RCW, 20 Powis Mews, London, W11 1JN
Tel: +44 (0) 20 7221 3717
Email: jo@jounwin.co.uk
Website: http://www.jounwin.co.uk

Handles: Fiction; Nonfiction; *Areas:* Humour; Women's Interests; *Markets:* Adult; Children's; Youth; *Treatments:* Commercial; Literary

Handles literary fiction, commercial women's fiction, comic writing, narrative nonfiction, Young Adult fiction and fiction for children aged 9+. No poetry, picture books, or screenplays, except for existing clients. Accepts submissions by email but prefers submissions by post. Mainly represents authors from the UK and Ireland,

and sometimes Australia and New Zealand. Only represents US authors in very exceptional circumstances. See website for full guidelines.

Johnson & Alcock

Clerkenwell House, 45/47 Clerkenwell Green, London, EC1R 0HT
Tel: +44 (0) 20 7251 0125
Fax: +44 (0) 20 7251 2172
Email: info@johnsonandalcock.co.uk
Website: http://www.johnsonandalcock.co.uk

Handles: Fiction; Nonfiction; Poetry; *Areas:* Arts; Autobiography; Biography; Crime; Culture; Current Affairs; Design; Film; Health; Historical; Lifestyle; Music; Nature; Psychology; Science; Sci-Fi; Self-Help; Sport; Suspense; Thrillers; Women's Interests; *Markets:* Adult; Children's; Youth; *Treatments:* Commercial; Literary; Popular

Send query by email (response only if interested), or by post with SASE. Include synopsis and first three chapters (approximately 50 pages). Email submissions should go to specific agents. See website for list of agents and full submission guidelines. No poetry, screenplays, children's books 0-7, or board or picture books.

Michelle Kass Associates

85 Charing Cross Road, London, WC2H 0AA
Tel: +44 (0) 20 7439 1624
Fax: +44 (0) 20 7734 3394
Email: office@michellekass.co.uk
Website: http://www.michellekass.co.uk

Handles: Fiction; Scripts; *Areas:* Film; Literature; TV; *Markets:* Adult; *Treatments:* Literary

No email submissions. Approach by telephone in first instance.

Keane Kataria Literary Agency

1 Queen Square, Bath, BA1 2HA
Email: info@keanekataria.co.uk
Website: http://www.keanekataria.co.uk

Handles: Fiction; Nonfiction; *Areas:* Biography; Crime; Historical; Romance; Women's Interests; *Markets:* Adult; *Treatments:* Commercial

Actively seeking commercial fiction and nonfiction. In fiction, handles crime, romance, women's, sagas, historical and general. In nonfiction, handles narrative nonfiction, biography, and subjects with wide general appeal. No science fiction, fantasy or children's books. Send query by email only with synopsis and first three chapters. Attachments in PDF format only.

Frances Kelly

111 Clifton Road, Kingston upon Thames, Surrey KT2 6PL
Tel: +44 (0) 20 8549 7830
Fax: +44 (0) 20 8547 0051

Handles: Nonfiction; Reference; *Areas:* Arts; Biography; Business; Cookery; Finance; Health; Historical; Lifestyle; Medicine; Self-Help; *Markets:* Academic; Adult; Professional

Send query with SAE, CV, and synopsis or brief description of work. Scripts handled for existing clients only. No unsolicited MSS.

Ki Agency Ltd

Studio 315, Screenworks, 22 Highbury Grove, London, N5 2ER
Tel: +44 (0) 20 3214 8287
Email: meg@ki-agency.co.uk
Website: http://www.ki-agency.co.uk

Handles: Fiction; Nonfiction; Scripts; *Areas:* Culture; Film; Historical; Politics; Science; Self-Help; Sport; Theatre; TV; *Markets:* Adult; *Treatments:* Popular

Represents novelists and scriptwriters in all media. No children's or YA novels, humorous science fiction or commercial women's fiction. Send synopsis and first three chapters by email. See website for individual agent interests.

Knight Hall Agency

Lower Ground Floor, 7 Mallow Street,

London, EC1Y 8RQ
Tel: +44 (0) 20 3397 2901
Fax: +44 (0) 871 918 6068
Email: office@knighthallagency.com
Website: http://www.knighthallagency.com

Handles: Scripts; *Areas:* Drama; Film;
Theatre; TV; *Markets:* Adult

Note: Closed to submissions on February 19, 2014. Check website for current status.

Send query by post or email (no attachments). Only send sample if requested. Represents playwrights, screenwriters and writer-directors. Handles adaptation rights for novels, but does not handle books directly.

Barbara Levy Literary Agency
64 Greenhill, Hampstead High Street, London, NW3 5TZ
Tel: +44 (0) 20 7435 9046
Fax: +44 (0) 20 7431 2063
Email: blevysubmissions@gmail.com

Handles: Fiction; Nonfiction; *Markets:* Adult

Send query with synopsis by email or by post with SAE.

Limelight Management
10 Filmer Mews, 75 Filmer Road , London, SW6 7JF
Tel: +44 (0) 20 7384 9950
Fax: +44 (0) 20 7384 9955
Email: mail@limelightmanagement.com
Website: http://www.limelightmanagement.com

Handles: Fiction; Nonfiction; *Areas:* Arts; Autobiography; Biography; Business; Cookery; Crafts; Crime; Health; Historical; Lifestyle; Mystery; Nature; Science; Sport; Suspense; Thrillers; Travel; Women's Interests; *Markets:* Adult; *Treatments:* Commercial; Literary

Always looking for exciting new authors. Send query by email with the word "Submission" in the subject line and synopsis and first three chapters as Word or

Open Document attachments. Also include market info. and details of your professional life and writing ambitions. Film and TV scripts for existing clients only. See website for full guidelines.

Lindsay Literary Agency
East Worldham House, East Worldham, Alton GU34 3AT
Tel: +44 (0) 0142 083143
Email: info@lindsayliteraryagency.co.uk
Website: http://www.lindsayliteraryagency.co.uk

Handles: Fiction; Nonfiction; *Markets:* Adult; Children's; *Treatments:* Literary; Serious

Send query by post with SASE or by email, including single-page synopsis and first three chapters. For picture books send complete ms.

London Independent Books
26 Chalcot Crescent, London, NW1 8YD
Tel: +44 (0) 20 7722 7160

Handles: Fiction; Nonfiction; *Areas:* Fantasy; *Markets:* Adult; Youth; *Treatments:* Commercial

Send query with synopsis, SASE, and first two chapters. All fiction and nonfiction subjects considered if treatment is strong and saleable, but no computer books, young children's, or unsolicited MSS. Particularly interested in commercial fiction, fantasy, and teen fiction. Scripts handled for existing clients only.

Lutyens and Rubinstein
21 Kensington Park Road, London, W11 2EU
Tel: +44 (0) 20 7792 4855
Email: submissions@lutyensrubinstein.co.uk
Website: http://www.lutyensrubinstein.co.uk

Handles: Fiction; Nonfiction; *Areas:* Cookery; *Markets:* Adult; Children's; Youth; *Treatments:* Commercial; Literary

Send up to 5,000 words or first three

chapters by email with covering letter and short synopsis. No film or TV scripts, or unsolicited submissions by hand or by post.

Macnaughton Lord Representation

44 South Molton Street, London, W1K 5RT
Tel: +44 (0) 20 7499 1411
Email: info@mlrep.com
Website: http://www.mlrep.com

Handles: Scripts; *Areas:* Arts; Film; Theatre; TV; *Markets:* Adult

Theatrical and literary agency representing established names and emerging talent in theatre, film, tv and the performing arts. Send query by email with CV and a sample of your work.

Marjacq Scripts Ltd

Box 412, 19/21 Crawford St, London, W1H 1PJ
Tel: +44 (0) 20 7935 9499
Fax: +44 (0) 20 7935 9115
Email: subs@marjacq.com
Website: http://www.marjacq.com

Handles: Fiction; Nonfiction; Scripts; *Areas:* Biography; Crime; Film; Health; Historical; Radio; Sci-Fi; Sport; Thrillers; Travel; TV; Women's Interests; *Markets:* Adult; Children's; *Treatments:* Commercial; Literary

For books, send query with synopsis and three sample chapters. For scripts, send short treatment and entire screenplay. All queries must include an SAE for response, if sent by post. If sent by email send only Word or PDF documents less than 2MB. Do not paste work into the body of the email. See website for full details. No poetry, short stories, or stage plays. Do not send queries without including samples of the actual work.

The Marsh Agency

50 Albemarle Street, London, W1S 4BD
Tel: +44 (0) 20 7493 4361
Fax: +44 (0) 20 7495 8961
Email: english.language@marsh-agency.co.uk

Website: http://www.marsh-agency.co.uk

Handles: Fiction; Nonfiction; *Markets:* Adult; Youth; *Treatments:* Literary

Use online submission system to send brief query letter with contact details, relevant information, details of any previously published work, and any experience which relates to the book's subject matter; an outline of the plot and main characters for fiction, or a summary of the work and chapter outlines for nonfiction. Include three consecutive chapters up to 100 pages, and your CV. See website for full guidelines and online submission system. No TV, film, radio or theatre scripts, poetry, or children's/picture books. Does not handle US authors as a primary English Language Agent. Do not call or email until at least 8 weeks have elapsed from submission date.

MBA Literary Agents Ltd

62 Grafton Way, London, W1T 5DW
Tel: +44 (0) 20 7387 2076
Fax: +44 (0) 20 7387 2042
Email: submissions@mbalit.co.uk
Website: http://www.mbalit.co.uk

Handles: Fiction; Nonfiction; Scripts; *Areas:* Arts; Biography; Crafts; Film; Health; Historical; Lifestyle; Radio; Self-Help; Theatre; TV; *Markets:* Adult; Children's; Youth; *Treatments:* Commercial; Literary

For books, send query with synopsis and first three chapters. For scripts, send query with synopsis, CV, and finished script. Submissions by email only. No submissions by post. See website for full submission guidelines. Works in conjunction with agents in most countries.

Duncan McAra

28 Beresford Gardens, Edinburgh, Scotland EH5 3ES
Tel: +44 (0) 131 552 1558
Email: duncanmcara@mac.com

Handles: Fiction; Nonfiction; *Areas:* Archaeology; Architecture; Arts; Biography; Historical; Military; Travel; *Markets:* Adult; *Treatments:* Literary

Also interested in books of Scottish interest. Send query letter with SAE in first instance.

Miles Stott Children's Literary Agency

East Hook Farm, Lower Quay Road, Hook, Haverfordwest, Pembrokeshire SA62 4LR
Tel: +44 (0) 1437 890570
Email: submissions@milesstottagency.co.uk
Website: http://www.milesstottagency.co.uk

Handles: Fiction; *Markets:* Children's

Handles picture books, novelty books, and children's fiction. No poetry or nonfiction. Not accepting new fiction submissions as at July 2015, however this is due to be reviewed in late 2015. Check website for current status. For picture book submissions, send query by email only, with short covering letter, details about you and your background, and up to three stories a Word or PDF attachments. See website for full guidelines.

Mulcahy Associates

First Floor, 7 Meard Street, London, W1F 0EW
Email: submissions@ma-agency.com
Website: http://www.ma-agency.com

Handles: Fiction; Nonfiction; *Areas:* Biography; Crime; Finance; Historical; Lifestyle; Sport; Thrillers; Women's Interests; *Markets:* Adult; Children's; Youth; *Treatments:* Commercial; Literary

Send query with synopsis and first three chapters by email only. See website for full guidelines.

Judith Murdoch Literary Agency

19 Chalcot Square, London, NW1 8YA
Tel: +44 (0) 20 7722 4197
Email: jmlitag@btinternet.com
Website: http://www.judithmurdoch.co.uk

Handles: Fiction; *Areas:* Crime; Women's Interests; *Markets:* Adult; *Treatments:* Commercial; Literary; Popular

Send query by post with SAE or email address for response, brief synopsis, and and first three chapters. Provides editorial advice. No short stories, children's books, science fiction, email submissions, or unsolicited MSS.

Andrew Nurnberg Associates, Ltd

20-23 Greville Street, London, EC1N 8SS
Tel: +44 (0) 20 3327 0400
Fax: +44 (0) 20 7430 0801
Email: submissions@andrewnurnberg.com
Website: http://www.andrewnurnberg.com

Handles: Fiction; Nonfiction; *Markets:* Adult; Children's

Handles adult fiction and nonfiction, and children's fiction. No poetry, or scripts for film, TV, radio or theatre. Send query with one-page synopsis and first three chapters by post with SAE (if return required) or by email as attachments.

Deborah Owen Ltd

78 Narrow Street, Limehouse, London, E14 8BP
Tel: +44 (0) 20 7987 5119 / 5441

Handles: Fiction; Nonfiction

Represents only two authors worldwide. Not accepting any new authors.

John Pawsey

8 Snowshill Court, Giffard Park, Milton Keynes, MK14 5QG
Tel: +44 (0) 1908 611841
Email: john.pawsey@virgin.net

Handles: Nonfiction; *Areas:* Biography; Sport; *Markets:* Adult

No fiction, poetry, scripts, journalism, academic, or children's books. Particularly interested in sport and biography. Send query by email only, with synopsis and opening chapter.

PBJ and JBJ Management

22 Rathbone Street, London, W1T 1LA
Tel: +44 (0) 20 7287 1112
Fax: +44 (0) 20 7637 0899
Email: general@pbjmanagement.co.uk
Website: http://www.pbjmgt.co.uk

Handles: Scripts; *Areas:* Drama; Film;
Humour; Radio; Theatre; TV; *Markets:*
Adult

Handles scripts for film, TV, theatre, and
radio. Send complete MS with cover letter
and CV, if you have one. Send one script
only. No submissions by email. Particularly
interested in comedy and comedy drama.

Maggie Pearlstine Associates Ltd

31 Ashley Gardens, Ambrosden Avenue,
London, SW1P 1QE
Tel: +44 (0) 20 7828 4212
Fax: +44 (0) 20 7834 5546
Email: maggie@pearlstine.co.uk

Handles: Fiction; Nonfiction; *Areas:*
Biography; Current Affairs; Health;
Historical; *Markets:* Adult

Small, selective agency, not currently taking
on new clients.

Jonathan Pegg Literary Agency

32 Batoum Gardens, London, W6 7QD
Tel: +44 (0) 20 7603 6830
Fax: +44 (0) 20 7348 0629
Email: submissions@jonathanpegg.com
Website: http://www.jonathanpegg.com

Handles: Fiction; Nonfiction; *Areas:* Arts;
Autobiography; Biography; Culture; Current
Affairs; Historical; Lifestyle; Nature;
Psychology; Science; Thrillers; *Markets:*
Adult; *Treatments:* Commercial; Literary;
Popular

Established by the agent after twelve years at
Curtis Brown. The agency's main areas of
interest are:
Fiction: literary fiction, thrillers and quality
commercial in general

Non-Fiction: current affairs, memoir and
biography, history, popular science, nature,
arts and culture, lifestyle, popular
psychology

Rights:
Aside from the UK market, the agency will
work in association with translation, US, TV
& film agents according to each client's best
interests.

If you're looking for an agent:
I accept submissions by email. Please
include a 1-page mini-synopsis, a half-page
cv, a longer synopsis (for non-fiction) and
the first three chapters, or around 50 pages to
a natural break. Please ensure it is via 'word
document' attachments, 1.5 line spacing.

See website for full submission guidelines.

Shelley Power Literary Agency Ltd

20 Powell Gardens, South Heighton,
Newhaven, BN9 0PS
Tel: +44 (0) 1273 512347
Email: sp@shelleypower.co.uk

Handles: Fiction; Nonfiction; *Markets:*
Adult

Send query by post with return postage. No
attachments. No poetry, scripts, or children's
books.

Redhammer

186 Bickenhall Mansions, Bickenhall Street,
London, W1U 6BX
Tel: +44 (0) 20 7486 3465
Fax: +44 (0) 20 7000 1249
Email: admin@redhammer.info
Website: http://redhammer.info

Handles: Fiction; Nonfiction; *Areas:*
Autobiography; Crime; Entertainment;
Mystery; Thrillers; *Markets:* Adult

Handles fiction and nonfiction. Would love
to discover a big, sprawling crime / mystery /
thriller with international blockbuster
potential. Also keen on autobiographies,
whistleblowers, and celebrity tales. Submit

first ten pages of manuscript using online
form on website only.

Richford Becklow Literary Agency

Tel: +44 (0)7510 023823
Email: enquiries@richfordbecklow.co.uk
Website: http://www.richfordbecklow.com

Handles: Fiction; Nonfiction; *Areas:* Arts;
Autobiography; Biography; Cookery; Crime;
Fantasy; Gardening; Gothic; Historical;
Horror; Lifestyle; Literature; Romance; Sci-
Fi; Self-Help; Women's Interests; *Markets:*
Adult; Youth; *Treatments:* Commercial;
Contemporary; Literary; Satirical; Serious

Company founded in 2011 by an
experienced agent, previously at the longest
established literary agency in the world.
Interested in fiction and nonfiction. Email
submissions only. Does not accept postal
submissions and cannot currently offer to
represent American or Australian authors.
No picture book texts for babies and
toddlers, or erotica. No submissions in April
or October. See website for full submission
guidelines.

Robert Dudley Agency

135A Bridge Street, Ashford, Kent TN25
5DP
Email: info@robertdudleyagency.co.uk
Website: http://www.
robertdudleyagency.co.uk

Handles: Nonfiction; *Areas:* Adventure;
Biography; Business; Current Affairs;
Historical; Medicine; Military; Sport;
Technology; Travel; *Markets:* Adult;
Treatments: Popular

Specialises in nonfiction. No fiction
submissions. Send query outlining your idea
by post or by email in first instance. See
website for full guidelines.

Robin Jones Literary Agency

6b Marmora Road, London, SE22 0RX
Tel: +44 (0) 20 8693 6062
Email: robijones@gmail.com

Handles: Fiction; Nonfiction; *Markets:*
Adult; *Treatments:* Commercial; Literary

London-based literary agency founded in
2007 by an agent who has previously worked
at four other agencies, and was the UK scout
for international publishers in 11 countries.
Handles commercial and literary fiction and
nonfiction for adults, and occasional
children's for ages 8 and over. Welcomes
Russian language fiction and nonfiction. No
poetry, young adult, academic, religious, or
original scripts. Accepts full mss or query
with synopsis and 50-page sample.

Rochelle Stevens & Co.

2 Terretts Place, Upper Street, London, N1
1QZ
Tel: +44 (0) 20 7359 3900
Email: info@rochellestevens.com
Website: http://www.rochellestevens.com

Handles: Scripts; *Areas:* Film; Radio;
Theatre; TV; *Markets:* Adult

Handles script writers for film, television,
theatre, and radio. No longer handles writers
of fiction, nonfiction, or children's books.
Submit by post only. See website for full
submission guidelines.

Rocking Chair Books

2 Rudgwick Terrace, St Stephens Close,
London, NW8 6BR
Tel: +44 (0) 7809 461342
Email: representme@rockingchairbooks.com
Website: http://www.rockingchairbooks.com

Handles: Fiction; Nonfiction; *Areas:*
Adventure; Arts; Crime; Culture; Current
Affairs; Entertainment; Historical; Horror;
Lifestyle; Literature; Mystery; Nature;
Romance; Thrillers; Translations; Travel;
Women's Interests; *Markets:* Adult;
Treatments: Commercial; Contemporary;
Cynical; Dark; Experimental; In-depth;
Light; Literary; Mainstream; Popular;
Positive; Progressive; Satirical; Serious;
Traditional

Founded in 2011 after the founder worked
for five years as a Director at an established
London literary agency. Send complete ms

or a few chapters by email only. No Children's, YA or Science Fiction / Fantasy.

Roger Hancock Ltd
44 South Grove House, London, N6 6LR
Tel: +44 (0) 20 8341 7243
Email: enquiries@rogerhancock.com
Website: http://www.rogerhancock.com

Handles: Scripts; *Areas:* Drama; Entertainment; Humour; *Markets:* Adult; *Treatments:* Light

Enquire by phone in first instance. Handles scripts only. Interested in comedy dramas and light entertainment. No books or unsolicited MSS.

Uli Rushby-Smith Literary Agency
72 Plimsoll Road, London, N4 2EE
Tel: +44 (0) 20 7354 2718
Fax: +44 (0) 20 7354 2718
Email: uli.rushby-smith@btconnect.com

Handles: Fiction; Nonfiction; *Markets:* Adult; Children's; *Treatments:* Commercial; Literary

Send query with SAE, outline, and two or three sample chapters. Film and TV rights handled in conjunction with a sub-agent. No disks, poetry, picture books, films, or plays.

The Sayle Literary Agency
1 Petersfield, Cambridge, CB1 1BB
Tel: +44 (0) 1223 303035
Fax: +44 (0) 1223 301638
Email: info@sayleliteraryagency.com
Website: http://www.
sayleliteraryagency.com

Handles: Fiction; Nonfiction; *Areas:* Biography; Crime; Current Affairs; Historical; Music; Science; Travel; *Markets:* Adult; *Treatments:* Literary

Note: Not accepting new manuscripts as at August 2015. See website for current status.

Send query with CV, synopsis, and three

sample chapters. No text books, technical, legal, medical, children's, plays, poetry, unsolicited MSS, or approaches by email. Do not include SAE as all material submitted is recycled. If no response after three months assume rejection.

Sayle Screen Ltd
11 Jubilee Place, London, SW3 3TD
Tel: +44 (0) 20 7823 3883
Fax: +44 (0) 20 7823 3363
Email: info@saylescreen.com
Website: http://www.saylescreen.com

Handles: Scripts; *Areas:* Film; Radio; Theatre; TV; *Markets:* Adult

Only considers material which has been recommended by a producer, development executive or course tutor. In this case send query by email with cover letter and details of your referee to the relevant agent. Query only one agent at a time.

The Science Factory
Scheideweg 34C, Hamburg, Germany 20253
Tel: +44 (0) 20 7193 7296 (Skype)
Email: info@sciencefactory.co.uk
Website: http://www.sciencefactory.co.uk

Handles: Fiction; Nonfiction; *Areas:* Autobiography; Biography; Current Affairs; Historical; Medicine; Politics; Science; Technology; Travel; *Markets:* Adult

Specialises in science, technology, medicine, and natural history, but will also consider other areas of nonfiction. Novelists handled only occasionally, and if there is some special relevance to the agency (e.g. a thriller about scientists, or a novel of ideas). See website for full submission guidelines.

Please note that the agency address is in Germany, but the country is listed as United Kingdom, as the company is registered in the United Kingdom.

Linda Seifert Management
Screenworks Room 315, 22 Highbury Grove, Islington, London, N5 2ER
Tel: +44 (0) 20 3214 8293

Email: contact@lindaseifert.com
Website: http://www.lindaseifert.com

Handles: Scripts; *Areas:* Film; TV; *Markets:* Adult; Children's

A London-based management company representing screenwriters and directors for film and television. Our outstanding client list ranges from the highly established to the new and exciting emerging talent of tomorrow. Represents UK-based writers and directors only. Accepts submissions by post only. No novels or short stories. See website for full submission guidelines.

Sheil Land Associates Ltd

52 Doughty Street, London, WC1N 2LS
Tel: +44 (0) 20 7405 9351
Fax: +44 (0) 20 7831 2127
Email: info@sheilland.co.uk
Website: http://www.sheilland.co.uk

Handles: Fiction; Nonfiction; Scripts; *Areas:* Autobiography; Biography; Cookery; Crime; Drama; Fantasy; Film; Gardening; Historical; Humour; Lifestyle; Military; Mystery; Politics; Psychology; Radio; Romance; Science; Sci-Fi; Self-Help; Theatre; Thrillers; Travel; TV; Women's Interests; *Markets:* Adult; Children's; Youth; *Treatments:* Commercial; Contemporary; Literary

Send query with synopsis, CV, and first three chapters (or around 50 pages), by post addressed to "The Submissions Dept", or by email. Do not include SAE or return postage with postal submissions as all submissions are recycled.

Caroline Sheldon Literary Agency

71 Hillgate Place, London, W8 7SS
Tel: +44 (0) 20 7727 9102
Email: carolinesheldon@
carolinesheldon.co.uk
Website: http://www.carolinesheldon.co.uk

Handles: Fiction; Nonfiction; *Areas:* Autobiography; Historical; Humour; Women's Interests; *Markets:* Adult; Children's; Youth; *Treatments:* Commercial;

Contemporary; Literary

Send query by email only. Do not query both agents. See website for both email addresses and appropriate subject line to include. Handles fiction and human-interest nonfiction for adults, and fiction for children, including full-length and picture books.

Dorie Simmonds Agency

Riverbank House, 1 Putney Bridge Approach, London, SW6 3JD
Tel: +44 (0) 20 7736 0002
Fax: +44 (0) 20 7736 0010
Email: info@doriesimmonds.com
Website: http://doriesimmonds.com

Handles: Fiction; Nonfiction; *Areas:* Biography; Historical; Women's Interests; *Markets:* Adult; Children's; *Treatments:* Commercial; Contemporary

Send query by email as Word or PDF attachments or by post with SAE. Include details on your background and relevant writing experience, and first three chapters or fifty pages. See website for full details.

Jeffrey Simmons

15 Penn House, Mallory Street, London, NW8 8SX
Tel: +44 (0) 20 7224 8917
Email: jasimmons@unicombox.co.uk

Handles: Fiction; Nonfiction; *Areas:* Autobiography; Biography; Crime; Current Affairs; Entertainment; Film; Historical; Legal; Politics; Psychology; Sport; Theatre; *Markets:* Adult; *Treatments:* Commercial; Literary

Send query with brief bio, synopsis, history of any prior publication, and list of any publishers or agents to have already seen the MSS. Particularly interested in personality books of all kinds and fiction from young writers (under 40) with a future. No children's books, science fiction, fantasy, cookery, crafts, gardening, or hobbies. Film scripts handled for existing book clients only.

Sinclair-Stevenson

3 South Terrace, London, SW7 2TB
Tel: +44 (0) 20 7581 2550
Fax: +44 (0) 20 7581 2550

Handles: Fiction; Nonfiction; *Areas:* Arts;
Biography; Current Affairs; Historical;
Travel; *Markets:* Adult

Send query with synopsis and SAE. No
children's books, scripts, academic, science
fiction, or fantasy.

Robert Smith Literary Agency Ltd

12 Bridge Wharf, 156 Caledonian Road,
London, N1 9UU
Tel: +44 (0) 20 7278 2444
Fax: +44 (0) 20 7833 5680
Email: robertsmith.literaryagency@
virgin.net
Website: http://www.
robertsmithliteraryagency.com

Handles: Nonfiction; *Areas:* Autobiography;
Biography; Crime; Culture; Current Affairs;
Health; Historical; Humour; Lifestyle;
Military; Self-Help; *Markets:* Adult;
Treatments: Mainstream; Popular

Send query with synopsis initially and
sample chapter if available, by post or by
email. No poetry, fiction, scripts, children's
books, academic, or unsolicited MSS. Will
suggest revision. See website for full
guidelines.

Sophie Hicks Agency

60 Gray's Inn Road, London, WC1X 8AQ
Email: submissions@
sophiehicksagency.com
Website: http://www.sophiehicksagency.com

Handles: Fiction; Nonfiction; *Markets:*
Adult; Children's; Youth

Welcomes submissions for fiction and
nonfiction for adults, young adults, teens,
and children 9+. Send query by email only
with sample pages attached as Word or PDF
documents. See website for full guidelines.

Elaine Steel

49 Greek Street, London, W1D 4EG
Tel: +44 (0) 1273 739022
Email: info@elainesteel.com
Website: http://www.elainesteel.com

Handles: Fiction; Nonfiction; Scripts; *Areas:*
Film; Radio; TV; *Markets:* Adult

Send query by email with CV and outline,
along with details of experience. No
unsolicited mss.

Abner Stein

10 Roland Gardens, London, SW7 3PH
Tel: +44 (0) 20 7373 0456
Fax: +44 (0) 20 7370 6316
Email: caspian@abnerstein.co.uk
Website: http://www.abnerstein.co.uk

Handles: Fiction; Nonfiction; *Markets:*
Adult; Children's

Agency based in London. Handles fiction,
general nonfiction, and children's.

Steph Roundsmith Agent and Editor

3 Bowes Road, Billingham, Stockton-on-
Tees TS23 2BU
Email: agent@stephroundsmith.co.uk
Website: http://www.stephroundsmith.co.uk

Handles: Fiction; *Areas:* Adventure;
Fantasy; Historical; Humour; Literature;
Mystery; Sci-Fi; *Markets:* Children's;
Treatments: Commercial; Literary;
Mainstream

I only represent children's authors and I am
currently looking for new clients. If you
would like to submit your work for
consideration then please send me a one page
synopsis (including age range and word
count), a paragraph or two about yourself,
and your first three chapters. Please send
everything by email and I will endeavour to
get back to you within two weeks.

Ideally, I'm looking for writers who write for
children (up to 12 years) in any genre.
Whether it's a picture book or a full-length
novel, I'd love to see your work. If you'd like

to ask any questions then please don't hesitate to contact me.

Sarah Such Literary Agency

81 Arabella Drive, London, SW15 5LL
Tel: +44 (0) 20 8876 4228
Fax: +44 (0) 20 8878 8705
Email: info@sarah-such.com
Website: http://www.sarahsuch.com

Handles: Fiction; Nonfiction; *Areas:*
Autobiography; Biography; Culture;
Historical; Humour; *Markets:* Adult;
Children's; Youth; *Treatments:* Commercial;
Literary; Popular

Handles literary and commercial nonfiction and fiction for adults, young adults and children. Particularly interested in debut novels, biography, memoir, history, popular culture and humour. Works mainly by recommendation, but does also accept unsolicited approaches, by email only. Send synopsis, author bio, and sample chapter as Word attachment. No unsolicited mss or queries by phone. Handles TV and film scripts for existing clients, but no radio or theatre scripts. No poetry, fantasy, self-help or short stories.

Susanna Lea Associates (UK)

55 Monmouth Street, London, WC2H 9DG
Tel: +44 (0) 20 7287 7757
Fax: +44 (0) 20 7287 7775
Email: uk-submission@susannalea.com
Website: http://www.susannalea.com

Handles: Fiction; Nonfiction; *Markets:*
Adult

Literary agency with offices in Paris, London, and New York. Always on the lookout for exciting new talent. No poetry, plays, screen plays, science fiction, educational text books, short stories or illustrated works. No queries by fax or post. Accepts queries by email only. Include cover letter, synopsis, and first three chapters or proposal. Response not guaranteed.

The Susijn Agency

820 Harrow Road, London, NW10 5JU

Tel: +44 (0) 20 8968 7435
Fax: +44 (0) 20 7580 8626
Email: submissions@thesusijnagency.com
Website: http://www.thesusijnagency.com

Handles: Fiction; Nonfiction; *Markets:*
Adult; *Treatments:* Literary

Send query with synopsis and three sample chapters only by post or by email. Include SASE if return of material required. Response in 8-10 weeks. Specialises in selling rights worldwide and also represents non-English language authors and publishers for US, UK, and translation rights worldwide. No self-help, science-fiction, fantasy, romance, children's, illustrated, business, screenplays, or theatre plays.

SYLA – Susan Yearwood Literary Agency

2 Knebworth House, Londesborough Road, Stoke Newington, London N16 8RL
Tel: +44 (0) 20 7503 0954
Email: fiction@susanyearwood.com
Website: http://www.susanyearwood.com

Handles: Fiction; Nonfiction; *Areas:*
Autobiography; Biography; Business; Crime;
Lifestyle; Psychology; Thrillers; Women's
Interests; *Markets:* Adult; Children's; Youth;
Treatments: Commercial; Literary; Popular

Send query by email, including synopsis and first thirty pages in one Word file attachment. No poetry or screenwriting, or submissions by post. Check website for specific email address to query, as this differs by genre.

The Tennyson Agency

10 Cleveland Avenue, Wimbledon Chase, London, SW20 9EW
Tel: +44 (0) 20 8543 5939
Email: enquiries@tenagy.co.uk
Website: http://www.tenagy.co.uk

Handles: Scripts; *Areas:* Drama; Film;
Radio; Theatre; TV; *Markets:* Adult

Mainly deals in scripts for film, TV, theatre, and radio, along with related material on an ad-hoc basis. Handles writers in the

European Union only. Send query with CV and outline of work. Prefers queries by email. No nonfiction, poetry, short stories, science fiction and fantasy or children's writing, or unsolicited MSS.

Toby Mundy Associates Ltd
6 Bayley Street, Bedford Square, London, WC1B 3HE
Tel: +44 (0) 20 3713 0067
Email: submissions@tma-agency.com
Website: http://tma-agency.com

Handles: Fiction; Nonfiction; *Areas:* Autobiography; Biography; Crime; Current Affairs; Historical; Politics; Science; Thrillers; *Markets:* Adult; *Treatments:* Literary

Send query by email with brief synopsis, first chapter, and a note about yourself, all pasted into the body of the email. No poetry, plays, short stories, science fiction, horror, attachments or hard copy submissions.

Jane Turnbull
Barn Cottage, Veryan, Truro TR2 5QA
Tel: +44 (0) 20 7727 9409 / +44 (0) 1872 501317
Email: jane@janeturnbull.co.uk
Website: http://www.janeturnbull.co.uk

Handles: Fiction; Nonfiction; *Areas:* Biography; Current Affairs; Entertainment; Gardening; Historical; Humour; Lifestyle; Nature; TV; *Markets:* Adult; *Treatments:* Commercial; Literary; Mainstream

Agency with offices in London and Cornwall. New clients always welcome and a few taken on every year. Send query by post to Cornwall office with short description of your book or idea. No unsolicited MSS.

United Agents
12–26 Lexington Street, London, W1F 0LE
Tel: +44 (0) 20 3214 0800
Fax: +44 (0) 20 3214 0802
Email: info@unitedagents.co.uk
Website: http://unitedagents.co.uk

Handles: Fiction; Nonfiction; Scripts; *Areas:* Biography; Film; Radio; Theatre; TV; *Markets:* Adult; Children's; Youth

Do not approach the book department generally. Consult website and view details of each agent before selecting a specific agent to approach personally. Accepts submissions by email only. Submissions by post will not be returned or responded to.

Ed Victor Ltd
6 Bayley Street, Bedford Square, London, WC1B 3HE
Tel: +44 (0) 20 7304 4100
Fax: +44 (0) 20 7304 4111
Email: info@edvictor.com
Website: http://www.edvictor.com

Handles: Fiction; Nonfiction; *Areas:* Autobiography; Biography; Cookery; Historical; Politics; Travel; *Markets:* Adult; Children's; *Treatments:* Commercial; Literary

Handles authors of both literary and commercial fiction, as well as children's books and nonfiction in areas including biography, memoir, politics, travel, food and history. Send query by email with synopsis/outline and first five chapters as an attachment – do not include in the body of the email. Response not guaranteed unless interested.

Wade & Co Literary Agency
33 Cormorant Lodge, Thomas More Street, London, E1W 1AU
Tel: +44 (0) 20 7488 4171
Fax: +44 (0) 20 7488 4172
Email: rw@rwla.com
Website: http://www.rwla.com

Handles: Fiction; Nonfiction; *Markets:* Adult; Youth

New full-length proposals for adult and young adult fiction and nonfiction always welcome. Send query with detailed 1–6 page synopsis, brief biography, and first 10,000 words via email as Word documents (.doc) or PDF; or by post with SAE if return required. We much prefer to correspond by email. Actively seeking new writers across the literary spectrum. No poetry, children's, short stories, scripts or plays.

Cecily Ware Literary Agents

19C John Spencer Square, London, N1 2LZ
Tel: +44 (0) 20 7359 3787
Fax: +44 (0) 20 7226 9828
Email: info@cecilyware.com
Website: http://www.cecilyware.com

Handles: Scripts; *Areas:* Drama; Film; Humour; TV; *Markets:* Adult; Children's

Handles film and TV scripts only. No books or theatre scripts. Submit complete script with covering letter, CV, and SAE. No email submissions or return of material without SAE and correct postage.

Watson, Little Ltd

Suite 315, ScreenWorks, 22 Highbury Grove, London, N5 2ER
Tel: +44 (0) 20 7388 7529
Fax: +44 (0) 20 7388 8501
Email: submissions@watsonlittle.com
Website: http://www.watsonlittle.com

Handles: Fiction; Nonfiction; *Areas:* Business; Crime; Film; Historical; Humour; Leisure; Music; Psychology; Science; Self-Help; Sport; Technology; Women's Interests; *Markets:* Adult; Children's; Youth; *Treatments:* Commercial; Literary; Popular

Send query by post with SAE (if return required) or email (preferred) with synopsis and sample material, addressed to a specific agent. See website for full guidelines and details of specific agents. No scripts, poetry, or unsolicited MSS.

Whispering Buffalo Literary Agency Ltd

97 Chesson Road, London, W14 9QS
Tel: +44 (0) 20 7565 4737
Email: info@whisperingbuffalo.com
Website: http://www.whisperingbuffalo.com

Handles: Fiction; Nonfiction; *Areas:* Adventure; Anthropology; Arts; Autobiography; Beauty and Fashion; Design; Entertainment; Film; Health; Humour; Lifestyle; Music; Nature; Politics; Romance; Sci-Fi; Self-Help; Thrillers; *Markets:* Adult; Children's; Youth; *Treatments:* Commercial; Literary

Handles commercial/literary fiction/nonfiction and children's/YA fiction with special interest in book to film adaptations. No TV, film, radio or theatre scripts, or poetry or academic. Accepts submissions by email only. For fiction, send query with CV, synopsis, and first three chapters. For nonfiction, send proposal and sample chapter. Response only if interested.

Eve White: Literary Agent

54 Gloucester Street, London, SW1V 4EG
Tel: +44 (0) 20 7630 1155
Email: eve@evewhite.co.uk
Website: http://www.evewhite.co.uk

Handles: Fiction; Nonfiction; *Markets:* Adult; Children's; *Treatments:* Commercial; Literary

Important! Check and follow website submission guidelines before contacting!

DO NOT send submissions to email address listed on this page – see website for specific submission email addresses for different areas.

QUERIES ONLY to the email address on this page.

This agency requests that you go to their website for up-to-date submission procedure.

Commercial and literary fiction, nonfiction, children's fiction and picture books ages 7+ (home 15%, overseas 20%). No reading fee. No poetry, short stories, novellas, screenplays, or science fiction/fantasy for adults. Does not consider approaches from US writers. See website for detailed submission guidelines. Submission by email only.

Dinah Wiener Ltd
12 Cornwall Grove, Chiswick, London, W4
2LB
Tel: +44 (0) 20 8994 6011
Fax: +44 (0) 20 8994 6044
Email: dinah@dwla.co.uk

Handles: Fiction; Nonfiction; *Areas:*
Autobiography; Biography; Cookery;
Science; *Markets:* Adult

Send preliminary query letter with SAE. No
poetry, scripts, or children's books.

William Morris Endeavor (WME) London
100 New Oxford Street, London, WC1A
1HB
Tel: +44 (0) 20 7534 6800
Fax: +44 (0) 20 7534 6900
Email: ldnsubmissions@
wmeentertainment.com
Website: http://www.wmeauthors.co.uk

Handles: Fiction; Nonfiction; *Areas:*
Autobiography; Biography; Crime; Culture;
Historical; Thrillers; *Markets:* Adult; Youth;
Treatments: Commercial; Literary

London office of a worldwide theatrical and
literary agency, with offices in New York,
Beverly Hills, Nashville, Miami, and
Shanghai, as well as associates in Sydney.
No unsolicited scripts for film, TV, or
theatre. No self-help, poetry or picture
books. Send query by email, using link on
website. See website for full guidelines.

Writers House UK
7th Floor, Waverley House, 7-12 Noel
Street, London, W1F 8GQ
Email: akowal@writershouse.com
Website: http://www.writershouse.com

Handles: Fiction; Nonfiction; *Areas:*
Autobiography; Biography; Business;
Cookery; Fantasy; Finance; Historical; How-
to; Lifestyle; Psychology; Science; Sci-Fi;
Self-Help; Women's Interests; *Markets:*
Adult; Children's; Youth; *Treatments:*
Commercial; Literary

UK branch of established US agency with
offices in New York and California. Actively
seeking new material.

The Writers' Practice
28 Denmark Street, London, WC2H 8NJ
Tel: +44 (0) 845 680 6578
Email: jemima@thewriterspractice.com
Website: http://www.thewriterspractice.com

Handles: Fiction; Nonfiction; *Markets:*
Adult; *Treatments:* Commercial; Literary

Send query by email with for fiction a
synopsis, brief bio, and first three chapters;
and for nonfiction a pitch, brief bio, chapter
outline, and at least one sample chapter. Also
offers consultancy services to writers.

The Wylie Agency (UK) Ltd
17 Bedford Square, London, WC2B 3JA
Tel: +44 (0) 20 7908 5900
Fax: +44 (0) 20 7908 5901
Email: mail@wylieagency.co.uk
Website: http://www.wylieagency.co.uk

Handles: Fiction; Nonfiction; *Markets:*
Adult

**Note: Not accepting unsolicited mss as at
June 2015**

Send query by post or email before
submitting. All submissions must include
adequate return postage. No scripts,
children's books, or unsolicited MSS.

Zeno Agency Ltd
Primrose Hill Business Centre, 110
Gloucester Avenue, London, NW1 3LH
Tel: +44 (0) 20 7096 0927
Email: info@zenoagency.com
Website: http://zenoagency.com

Handles: Fiction; *Areas:* Crime; Fantasy;
Historical; Horror; Sci-Fi; Thrillers;
Markets: Adult; Youth; *Treatments:*
Commercial

London-based literary agency specialising in
Science Fiction, Fantasy, and Horror.

Temporarily closed to submissions of science fiction and fantasy as at June 2013 (check website for current status), but accepting approaches regarding completed horror, crime, or thriller fiction of over 75,000 words. No crossover fiction Submissions by email only. See website for full guidelines.

Canadian Literary Agents

For the most up-to-date listings of these and hundreds of other literary agents, visit http://www.firstwriter.com/Agents

To claim your free access to the site, please see the back of this book.

Rick Broadhead & Associates Literary Agency

47 St. Clair Avenue West, Suite 501, Toronto, Ontario M4V 3A5
Tel: +1 (416) 929-0516
Fax: +1 (416) 927-8732
Email: submissions@rbaliterary.com
Website: http://www.rbaliterary.com

Handles: Nonfiction; *Areas:* Biography; Business; Culture; Current Affairs; Health; Historical; Humour; Lifestyle; Medicine; Military; Nature; Politics; Science; Self-Help; *Markets:* Adult; *Treatments:* Popular

Prefers queries by email. Send brief query outlining your project and your credentials. Responds only if interested. No screenplays, poetry, children's books, or fiction.

The Characters Talent Agency

8 Elm Street, Toronto, Ontario M3H 1Y9
Tel: +1 (416) 964-8522
Fax: +1 (416) 964-8206
Email: litsubmissionsto@thecharacters.com
Website: http://www.thecharacters.com

Handles: Scripts; *Areas:* Biography; Drama; Erotic; Fantasy; Film; Historical; Horror; Humour; Mystery; Romance; Science; Sport; Thrillers; TV; Westerns; Women's Interests; *Markets:* Adult; Children's; Youth; *Treatments:* Contemporary; Mainstream

Approach by email. Response only if interested.

The Cooke Agency

75 Sherbourne Street., Suite 501, Toronto, Ontario M5A 2P9
Tel: +1 (647) 788-4010
Email: egriffin@cookeagency.ca
Website: http://www.cookeagency.ca

Handles: Fiction; Nonfiction; *Areas:* Crime; Culture; Fantasy; Historical; Nature; Politics; Romance; Science; Sci-Fi; Spiritual; *Markets:* Adult; Children's; Youth; *Treatments:* Commercial; Literary

Send query by email only with "Author Query" in the subject line (no attachments). No illustrated, photographic or children's picture books, US political thrillers, or poetry. No queries or submissions by post. Consult website before making contact.

The Helen Heller Agency

4-216 Heath Street West, Toronto, ON M5P 1N7
Tel: +1 (416) 489-0396
Email: info@helenhelleragency.com
Website: http://www.helenhelleragency.com

Handles: Fiction; Nonfiction; *Areas:* Historical; Thrillers; *Markets:* Adult; Youth; *Treatments:* Commercial

Handles adult and young adult nonfiction and fiction. No children's, screenplays, or genre fiction (sci-fi / fantasy etc.). Send query by email including synopsis, bio, and recent writing sample, pasted into the body of the email. No attachments or postal submission.

Robert Lecker Agency

4055 Melrose Avenue, Montréal, Québec H4A 2S5
Tel: +1 (514) 830-4818
Fax: +1 (514) 483-1644
Email: robert.lecker@gmail.com
Website: http://www.leckeragency.com

Handles: Fiction; Nonfiction; *Areas:* Adventure; Autobiography; Biography; Cookery; Crime; Culture; Entertainment; Erotic; Film; Historical; How-to; Literature; Music; Mystery; Science; Suspense; Theatre; Thrillers; Travel; *Markets:* Academic; Adult; *Treatments:* Contemporary, Literary; Mainstream

Specialises in books about entertainment, music, popular culture, popular science, intellectual and cultural history, food, and travel, but willing to consider any original and well presented material. No children's literature, screenplays, poetry, self-help books, or spiritual guides. Send query by email in first instance with brief description of your project. No proposals or attachments unless requested. No response unless interested.

Anne McDermid & Associates Ltd

64 Bloem Avenue, Toronto, Ontario M6E 1S1
Tel: +1 (416) 324-8845
Fax: +1 (416) 324-8870
Email: info@mcdermidagency.com
Website: http://www.mcdermidagency.com

Handles: Fiction; Nonfiction; *Areas:* Autobiography; Biography; Fantasy; Historical; Science; Sci-Fi; Travel; *Markets:* Adult; Children's; Youth; *Treatments:* Commercial; Literary

Send query by post or email, describing you and your project. You may also include the first 5 pages of your mss only. No unsolicited mss or queries by telephone.

Seventh Avenue Literary Agency

2052 – 124th Street , South Surrey, BC V4A 9K3
Tel: +1 (604) 538-7252
Fax: +1 (604) 538-7252
Email: info@seventhavenuelit.com
Website: http://www.seventhavenuelit.com

Handles: Nonfiction; *Markets:* Adult

Handles nonfiction only and takes on few new clients. Send query by email with 2-3 paragraph description of your project and one paragraph about you; or by post with description of your book and its category, its potential market, table of contents with short description of each chapter, one sample chapter, and author bio, including previously published material and your qualifications on the subject you have written on.

Transatlantic Literary Agency, Inc.

2 Bloor Street East, Suite 3500, Toronto, Ontario M4W 1A8
Tel: +1 (416) 488-9214
Fax: +1 (416) 929-3174
Email: info@transatlanticagency.com
Website: http://transatlanticagency.com

Handles: Fiction; Nonfiction; *Areas:* Autobiography; Biography; Crime; Historical; Humour; Mystery; Nature; Politics; Travel; Women's Interests; *Markets:* Adult; Children's; Youth; *Treatments:* Commercial; Contemporary; Literary

Canadian branch of international agency with agents in Canada, the US, and the UK, founded in Canada in 1993. The different agents have different interests and different submission requirements, so essential to consult website before submitting.

Irish Literary Agents

For the most up-to-date listings of these and hundreds of other literary agents, visit http://www.firstwriter.com/Agents

*To claim your **free** access to the site, please see the back of this book.*

Frank Fahy

129 Delwood Close, Castleknock, Dublin 15
Tel: +353 (0) 86 226 9330
Email: submissions@frank-fahy.com
Website: http://www.frank-fahy.com

Handles: Fiction; *Markets:* Adult; Youth

Handles adult and young adult fiction. No picture books, poetry, or nonfiction. Send query by email with author profile, synopsis, and first three chapters by email. No hard copy submissions.

Marianne Gunn O'Connor Literary Agency

Morrison Chambers, Suite 17, 32 Nassau Street, Dublin, 2
Tel: 353 1 677 9100
Fax: 353 1 677 9101
Email: mgoclitagency@eircom.net

Handles: Fiction; Nonfiction; *Areas:* Biography; Health; *Markets:* Adult; Children's; *Treatments:* Commercial; Literary

Send query with half-page synopsis by email.

The Lisa Richards Agency

108 Upper Leeson Street, Dublin, 4
Tel: +353 1 637 5000
Fax: +353 1 667 1256
Email: info@lisarichards.ie
Website: http://www.lisarichards.ie

Handles: Fiction; Nonfiction; Scripts; *Areas:* Autobiography; Biography; Culture; Historical; Humour; Lifestyle; Self-Help; Sport; Theatre; *Markets:* Adult; Children's; *Treatments:* Commercial; Literary; Popular

Send query by email or by post with SASE, including three or four sample chapters in the case of fiction, or proposal and sample chapter for nonfiction. No horror, science fiction, screenplays, or children's picture books.

Literary Agents Subject Index

This section lists literary agents by their subject matter, with directions to the section of the book where the full listing can be found.

You can create your own customised lists of literary agents using different combinations of these subject areas, plus over a dozen other criteria, instantly online at http://www.firstwriter.com.

*To claim your **free** access to the site, please see the back of this book.*

The Mitchell J. Hamilburg Agency (*US*)
Antony Harwood Limited (*UK*)
Hornfischer Literary Management, L.P. (*US*)
Kneerim & Williams (*US*)
Larsen Pomada Literary Agents (*US*)
The Literary Group International (*US*)
Carol Mann Agency (*US*)
Lynne Rabinoff Agency (*US*)
Rita Rosenkranz Literary Agency (*US*)
Susan Schulman, A Literary Agency (*US*)
Lynn Seligman, Literary Agent (*US*)
The Swetky Agency and Associates (*US*)
Venture Literary (*US*)
Whispering Buffalo Literary Agency Ltd (*UK*)

Antiques
Abbot Management (*US*)
Fine Literary (*US*)
Jeanne Fredericks Literary Agency, Inc. (*US*)
Antony Harwood Limited (*UK*)
Venture Literary (*US*)

Archaeology
Abbot Management (*US*)
The Blumer Literary Agency, Inc. (*US*)
Browne & Miller Literary Associates (*US*)
Don Congdon Associates, Inc. (*US*)
Caroline Davidson Literary Agency (*UK*)
DHH Literary Agency Ltd (*UK*)
Diamond Kahn and Woods (DKW) Literary
Agency Ltd (*UK*)
Doyen Literary Services, Inc. (*US*)
Dystel & Goderich Literary Management (*US*)
The Fielding Agency, LLC (*US*)
Goodman Associates (*US*)
Antony Harwood Limited (*UK*)
Hornfischer Literary Management, L.P. (*US*)
Kneerim & Williams (*US*)
Carol Mann Agency (*US*)
Duncan McAra (*UK*)
Lynne Rabinoff Agency (*US*)
Susan Schulman, A Literary Agency (*US*)
The Swetky Agency and Associates (*US*)
Venture Literary (*US*)

Architecture
Abbot Management (*US*)
The Blumer Literary Agency, Inc. (*US*)
Barbara Braun Associates, Inc. (*US*)
Castiglia Literary Agency (*US*)
Caroline Davidson Literary Agency (*UK*)
Doyen Literary Services, Inc. (*US*)
Fairbank Literary Representation (*US*)
The Fielding Agency, LLC (*US*)
Fine Literary (*US*)
The Mitchell J. Hamilburg Agency (*US*)
Antony Harwood Limited (*UK*)
Larsen Pomada Literary Agents (*US*)
Carol Mann Agency (*US*)
Duncan McAra (*UK*)
Martha Millard Literary Agency (*US*)
Regina Ryan Publishing Enterprises (*US*)
Marly Rusoff & Associates, Inc. (*US*)
The Swetky Agency and Associates (*US*)
Venture Literary (*US*)
Wm Clark Associates (*US*)

Arts
Abbot Management (*US*)
The August Agency LLC (*US*)
The Blumer Literary Agency, Inc. (*US*)
Brandt & Hochman Literary Agents, Inc. (*US*)
Barbara Braun Associates, Inc. (*US*)
Creative Authors Ltd (*UK*)
The Darley Anderson Agency (*UK*)
Caroline Davidson Literary Agency (*UK*)
DeFiore and Company (*US*)
Donadio & Olson, Inc. (*US*)
Doyen Literary Services, Inc. (*US*)
Dunow, Carlson & Lerner Agency (*US*)
Judith Ehrlich Literary Management (*US*)
The Fielding Agency, LLC (*US*)
Fine Literary (*US*)
Jeanne Fredericks Literary Agency, Inc. (*US*)
Fredrica S. Friedman and Co. Inc. (*US*)
The Gernert Company (*US*)
Frances Goldin Literary Agency, Inc. (*US*)
Sanford J. Greenburger Associates, Inc (*US*)
Greene & Heaton Ltd (*UK*)
Antony Harwood Limited (*UK*)
Rupert Heath Literary Agency (*UK*)
International Transactions, Inc. (*US*)
Johnson & Alcock (*UK*)
Frances Kelly (*UK*)
Kuhn Projects (*US*)
Larsen Pomada Literary Agents (*US*)
Levine Greenberg Literary Agency, Inc. (*US*)
Limelight Management (*UK*)
Literary & Creative Artists Inc. (*US*)
Macnaughton Lord Representation (*UK*)
Carol Mann Agency (*US*)
MBA Literary Agents Ltd (*UK*)
Duncan McAra (*UK*)
Martha Millard Literary Agency (*US*)
The Miller Agency (*US*)
The Park Literary Group LLC (*US*)
Jonathan Pegg Literary Agency (*UK*)
Pinder Lane & Garon-Brooke Associates Ltd
(*US*)
Richford Becklow Literary Agency (*UK*)
Rocking Chair Books (*UK*)
Rita Rosenkranz Literary Agency (*US*)
Marly Rusoff & Associates, Inc. (*US*)
Salkind Literary Agency (*US*)
Victoria Sanders & Associates LLC (*US*)
Susan Schulman, A Literary Agency (*US*)
Lynn Seligman, Literary Agent (*US*)
Sinclair-Stevenson (*UK*)
The Stuart Agency (*US*)
The Swetky Agency and Associates (*US*)
Thompson Literary Agency (*US*)
Venture Literary (*US*)
The Weingel-Fidel Agency (*US*)
Whispering Buffalo Literary Agency Ltd (*UK*)
Wm Clark Associates (*US*)

Autobiography
Abbot Management (*US*)
Sheila Ableman Literary Agency (*UK*)
Adler & Robin Books, Inc (*US*)
The Ahearn Agency, Inc (*US*)

The Miller Agency (*US*)
Howard Morhaim Literary Agency (*US*)
Niad Management (*US*)
The Park Literary Group LLC (*US*)
Pavilion Literary Management (*US*)
Jonathan Pegg Literary Agency (*UK*)
Pinder Lane & Garon-Brooke Associates Ltd (*US*)
Rebecca Pratt Literary Group (*US*)
Linn Prentis Literary (*US*)
Aaron M. Priest Literary Agency (*US*)
Prospect Agency (*US*)
Lynne Rabinoff Agency (*US*)
Raines & Raines (*US*)
Rebecca Friedman Literary Agency (*US*)
Redhammer (*UK*)
Rees Literary Agency (*US*)
Regina Ryan Publishing Enterprises (*US*)
The Amy Rennert Agency, Inc. (*US*)
The Lisa Richards Agency (*Ire*)
Richford Becklow Literary Agency (*UK*)
B.J. Robbins Literary Agency (*US*)
Rita Rosenkranz Literary Agency (*US*)
Ross Yoon Agency (*US*)
The Rudy Agency (*US*)
Marly Rusoff & Associates, Inc. (*US*)
Salkind Literary Agency (*US*)
Victoria Sanders & Associates LLC (*US*)
Susan Schulman, A Literary Agency (*US*)
The Science Factory (*UK*)
Denise Shannon Literary Agency, Inc. (*US*)
Sheil Land Associates Ltd (*UK*)
Caroline Sheldon Literary Agency (*UK*)
Wendy Sherman Associates, Inc. (*US*)
Jeffrey Simmons (*UK*)
Robert Smith Literary Agency Ltd (*UK*)
Solow Literary Enterprises, Inc. (*US*)
The Spieler Agency (*US*)
Stonesong (*US*)
Stuart Krichevsky Literary Agency, Inc. (*US*)
The Stuart Agency (*US*)
Sarah Such Literary Agency (*UK*)
The Swetky Agency and Associates (*US*)
SYLA – Susan Yearwood Literary Agency (*UK*)
Talcott Notch Literary (*US*)
Tessler Literary Agency (*US*)
Thompson Literary Agency (*US*)
Toby Mundy Associates Ltd (*UK*)
Transatlantic Literary Agency, Inc. (*Can*)
TriadaUS Literary Agency, Inc. (*US*)
2M Literary Agency Ltd (*US*)
Venture Literary (*US*)
Ed Victor Ltd (*UK*)
The Weingel-Fidel Agency (*US*)
Whispering Buffalo Literary Agency Ltd (*UK*)
Dinah Wiener Ltd (*UK*)
William Morris Endeavor (WME) London (*UK*)
Wm Clark Associates (*US*)
Writers House UK (*UK*)
Writers' Representatives, LLC (*US*)
The Zack Company, Inc (*US*)

Karen Gantz Zahler Literary Agency (*US*)
Helen Zimmermann Literary Agency (*US*)
Zoë Pagnamenta Agency, LLC (*US*)

Beauty and Fashion
Abbot Management (*US*)
Barbara Braun Associates, Inc. (*US*)
Rosica Colin Ltd (*UK*)
The Darley Anderson Agency (*UK*)
Diane Banks Associates Literary Agency (*UK*)
Janis A. Donnaud & Associates, Inc. (*US*)
Fine Literary (*US*)
Antony Harwood Limited (*UK*)
The Knight Agency (*US*)
Kuhn Projects (*US*)
Stonesong (*US*)
Thompson Literary Agency (*US*)
2M Literary Agency Ltd (*US*)
Venture Literary (*US*)
Whispering Buffalo Literary Agency Ltd (*UK*)

Biography
Abbot Management (*US*)
Sheila Ableman Literary Agency (*UK*)
Adler & Robin Books, Inc (*US*)
The Ahearn Agency, Inc (*US*)
Alive Communications, Inc (*US*)
The Ampersand Agency Ltd (*UK*)
Betsy Amster Literary Enterprises (*US*)
Andrew Lownie Literary Agency Ltd (*UK*)
Arcadia (*US*)
Audrey A. Wolf Literary Agency (*US*)
The August Agency LLC (*US*)
Ayesha Pande Literary (*US*)
Baldi Agency (*US*)
Bell Lomax Moreton Agency (*UK*)
David Black Literary Agency (*US*)
Blake Friedmann Literary Agency Ltd (*UK*)
Bleecker Street Associates, Inc. (*US*)
The Blumer Literary Agency, Inc. (*US*)
The Book Group (*US*)
Georges Borchardt, Inc. (*US*)
Barbara Braun Associates, Inc. (*US*)
Bresnick Weil Literary Agency, LLC (*US*)
Rick Broadhead & Associates Literary Agency (*Can*)
Jenny Brown Associates (*UK*)
Marie Brown Associates, Inc. (*US*)
Browne & Miller Literary Associates (*US*)
Felicity Bryan (*UK*)
Sheree Bykofsky Associates, Inc. (*US*)
Carnicelli Literary Management (*US*)
Maria Carvainis Agency, Inc. (*US*)
Castiglia Literary Agency (*US*)
The Characters Talent Agency (*Can*)
Jane Chelius Literary Agency, Inc. (*US*)
Elyse Cheney Literary Associates, LLC (*US*)
The Choate Agency, LLC (*US*)
Teresa Chris Literary Agency Ltd (*UK*)
Rosica Colin Ltd (*UK*)
Frances Collin Literary Agent (*US*)
Don Congdon Associates, Inc. (*US*)
Conville & Walsh Ltd (*UK*)
Coombs Moylett & Maclean Literary Agency (*UK*)

The Doe Coover Agency (*US*)
Creative Authors Ltd (*UK*)
Curtis Brown Group Ltd (*UK*)
Richard Curtis Associates, Inc. (*US*)
Laura Dail Literary Agency (*US*)
The Darley Anderson Agency (*UK*)
David Luxton Associates (*UK*)
Caroline Davidson Literary Agency (*UK*)
The Jennifer DeChiara Literary Agency (*US*)
DeFiore and Company (*US*)
Joëlle Delbourgo Associates, Inc. (*US*)
DHH Literary Agency Ltd (*UK*)
Diamond Kahn and Woods (DKW) Literary
Agency Ltd (*UK*)
Donadio & Olson, Inc. (*US*)
Janis A. Donnaud & Associates, Inc. (*US*)
Jim Donovan Literary (*US*)
Doyen Literary Services, Inc. (*US*)
Dunham Literary, Inc. (*US*)
Dunow, Carlson & Lerner Agency (*US*)
Dystel & Goderich Literary Management (*US*)
Edwards Fuglewicz (*UK*)
Judith Ehrlich Literary Management (*US*)
Einstein Literary Management (*US*)
Elise Dillsworth Agency (EDA) (*UK*)
Ethan Ellenberg Literary Agency (*US*)
Ann Elmo Agency, Inc. (*US*)
Emily Sweet Associates (*UK*)
Felicia Eth Literary Representation (*US*)
Evatopia, Inc. (*US*)
Fairbank Literary Representation (*US*)
The Fielding Agency, LLC (*US*)
Diana Finch Literary Agency (*US*)
Fine Literary (*US*)
Fletcher & Company (*US*)
Fox & Howard Literary Agency (*UK*)
Jeanne Fredericks Literary Agency, Inc. (*US*)
Fredrica S. Friedman and Co. Inc. (*US*)
Furniss Lawton (*UK*)
The G Agency, LLC (*US*)
Georgina Capel Associates Ltd (*UK*)
The Gernert Company (*US*)
David Godwin Associates (*UK*)
Goodman Associates (*US*)
Kathryn Green Literary Agency, LLC (*US*)
Sanford J. Greenburger Associates, Inc (*US*)
Greene & Heaton Ltd (*UK*)
Laura Gross Literary Agency (*US*)
Marianne Gunn O'Connor Literary Agency
(*Ire*)
The Mitchell J. Hamilburg Agency (*US*)
Joy Harris Literary Agency, Inc. (*US*)
Antony Harwood Limited (*UK*)
John Hawkins & Associates, Inc. (*US*)
A M Heath & Company Limited, Author's
Agents (*UK*)
Rupert Heath Literary Agency (*UK*)
hhb agency ltd (*UK*)
David Higham Associates Ltd (*UK*)
Hill Nadell Literary Agency (*US*)
Hornfischer Literary Management, L.P. (*US*)
International Transactions, Inc. (*US*)
J de S Associates Inc (*US*)

The Jean V. Naggar Literary Agency (*US*)
Jill Grinberg Literary Management LLC (*US*)
Johnson & Alcock (*UK*)
Keane Kataria Literary Agency (*UK*)
Frances Kelly (*UK*)
Harvey Klinger, Inc (*US*)
Kneerim & Williams (*US*)
Linda Konner Literary Agency (*US*)
Elaine Koster Literary Agency LLC (*US*)
Barbara S. Kouts, Literary Agent (*US*)
Edite Kroll Literary Agency, Inc. (*US*)
The LA Literary Agency (*US*)
Laura Langlie, Literary Agent (*US*)
Larsen Pomada Literary Agents (*US*)
Sarah Lazin Books (*US*)
Robert Lecker Agency (*Can*)
Levine Greenberg Literary Agency, Inc. (*US*)
Limelight Management (*UK*)
Lippincott Massie McQuilkin (*US*)
Literary & Creative Artists Inc. (*US*)
Literary Management Group, Inc. (*US*)
The Literary Group International (*US*)
Sterling Lord Literistic, Inc. (*US*)
Julia Lord Literary Management (*US*)
The Jennifer Lyons Literary Agency, LLC (*US*)
Gina Maccoby Agency (*US*)
MacGregor Literary (*US*)
Ricia Mainhardt Agency (RMA) (*US*)
Carol Mann Agency (*US*)
Manus & Associates Literary Agency, Inc.
(*US*)
March Tenth, Inc. (*US*)
Marjacq Scripts Ltd (*UK*)
Martin Literary Management (*US*)
MBA Literary Agents Ltd (*UK*)
Duncan McAra (*UK*)
Anne McDermid & Associates Ltd (*Can*)
Mendel Media Group, LLC (*US*)
Martha Millard Literary Agency (*US*)
The Miller Agency (*US*)
Howard Morhaim Literary Agency (*US*)
Mulcahy Associates (*UK*)
Niad Management (*US*)
Northern Lights Literary Services (*US*)
Fifi Oscard Agency, Inc. (*US*)
Kathi J. Paton Literary Agency (*US*)
John Pawsey (*UK*)
Maggie Pearlstine Associates Ltd (*UK*)
Jonathan Pegg Literary Agency (*UK*)
Pinder Lane & Garon-Brooke Associates Ltd
(*US*)
Rebecca Pratt Literary Group (*US*)
Aaron M. Priest Literary Agency (*US*)
Lynne Rabinoff Agency (*US*)
Raines & Raines (*US*)
Rees Literary Agency (*US*)
The Amy Rennert Agency, Inc. (*US*)
The Lisa Richards Agency (*Ire*)
Richford Becklow Literary Agency (*UK*)
B.J. Robbins Literary Agency (*US*)
Robert Dudley Agency (*UK*)
Rita Rosenkranz Literary Agency (*US*)
Ross Yoon Agency (*US*)

The Rudy Agency (*US*)
Marly Rusoff & Associates, Inc. (*US*)
Salkind Literary Agency (*US*)
Victoria Sanders & Associates LLC (*US*)
The Sayle Literary Agency (*UK*)
Susan Schulman, A Literary Agency (*US*)
The Science Factory (*UK*)
Lynn Seligman, Literary Agent (*US*)
Denise Shannon Literary Agency, Inc. (*US*)
Sheil Land Associates Ltd (*UK*)
Wendy Sherman Associates, Inc. (*US*)
Rosalie Siegel, International Literary Agency, Inc. (*US*)
Dorie Simmonds Agency (*UK*)
Jeffrey Simmons (*UK*)
Sinclair-Stevenson (*UK*)
Robert Smith Literary Agency Ltd (*UK*)
The Spieler Agency (*US*)
Stuart Krichevsky Literary Agency, Inc. (*US*)
Sarah Such Literary Agency (*UK*)
SYLA – Susan Yearwood Literary Agency (*UK*)
Tessler Literary Agency (*US*)
Thompson Literary Agency (*US*)
Toby Mundy Associates Ltd (*UK*)
Tracy Brown Literary Agency (*US*)
Transatlantic Literary Agency, Inc. (*Can*)
TriadaUS Literary Agency, Inc. (*US*)
Jane Turnbull (*UK*)
United Agents (*UK*)
Venture Literary (*US*)
Ed Victor Ltd (*UK*)
The Weingel-Fidel Agency (*US*)
Dinah Wiener Ltd (*UK*)
William Morris Endeavor (WME) London (*UK*)
Wm Clark Associates (*US*)
Writers House UK (*UK*)
Writers' Representatives, LLC (*US*)
The Zack Company, Inc (*US*)
Helen Zimmermann Literary Agency (*US*)
Zoë Pagnamenta Agency, LLC (*US*)

Business
Abbot Management (*US*)
Alive Communications, Inc (*US*)
Audrey A. Wolf Literary Agency (*US*)
The August Agency LLC (*US*)
Baldi Agency (*US*)
Bell Lomax Moreton Agency (*UK*)
David Black Literary Agency (*US*)
Bleecker Street Associates, Inc. (*US*)
The Blumer Literary Agency, Inc. (*US*)
BookEnds, LLC (*US*)
Rick Broadhead & Associates Literary Agency (*Can*)
Marie Brown Associates, Inc. (*US*)
Browne & Miller Literary Associates (*US*)
Sheree Bykofsky Associates, Inc. (*US*)
Carnicelli Literary Management (*US*)
Maria Carvainis Agency, Inc. (*US*)
Castiglia Literary Agency (*US*)
Elyse Cheney Literary Associates, LLC (*US*)
The Doe Coover Agency (*US*)

Creative Authors Ltd (*UK*)
Richard Curtis Associates, Inc. (*US*)
The Darley Anderson Agency (*UK*)
Liza Dawson Associates (*US*)
Joëlle Delbourgo Associates, Inc. (*US*)
Diane Banks Associates Literary Agency (*UK*)
Sandra Dijkstra Literary Agency (*US*)
Janis A. Donnaud & Associates, Inc. (*US*)
Jim Donovan Literary (*US*)
Doyen Literary Services, Inc. (*US*)
Dystel & Goderich Literary Management (*US*)
Ebeling & Associates (*US*)
Judith Ehrlich Literary Management (*US*)
Felicia Eth Literary Representation (*US*)
The Fielding Agency, LLC (*US*)
Diana Finch Literary Agency (*US*)
Fine Literary (*US*)
Fletcher & Company (*US*)
Folio Literary Management, LLC (*US*)
Fox & Howard Literary Agency (*UK*)
Jeanne Fredericks Literary Agency, Inc. (*US*)
Grace Freedson's Publishing Network (*US*)
Fresh Books Literary Agency (*US*)
Sarah Jane Freymann Literary Agency (*US*)
Fredrica S. Friedman and Co. Inc. (*US*)
Furniss Lawton (*UK*)
The G Agency, LLC (*US*)
Goodman Associates (*US*)
Graham Maw Christie Literary Agency (*UK*)
Kathryn Green Literary Agency, LLC (*US*)
Sanford J. Greenburger Associates, Inc (*US*)
The Mitchell J. Hamilburg Agency (*US*)
Hannigan Salky Getzler (HSG) Agency (*US*)
Antony Harwood Limited (*UK*)
John Hawkins & Associates, Inc. (*US*)
The Jeff Herman Agency, LLC (*US*)
hhb agency ltd (*UK*)
Hidden Value Group (*US*)
Kate Hordern Literary Agency (*UK*)
Hornfischer Literary Management, L.P. (*US*)
Andrea Hurst Literary Management (*US*)
InkWell Management (*US*)
J de S Associates Inc (*US*)
Jill Grinberg Literary Management LLC (*US*)
Frances Kelly (*UK*)
Kneerim & Williams (*US*)
The Knight Agency (*US*)
Linda Konner Literary Agency (*US*)
Elaine Koster Literary Agency LLC (*US*)
Kuhn Projects (*US*)
The LA Literary Agency (*US*)
Larsen Pomada Literary Agents (*US*)
LaunchBooks Literary Agency (*US*)
Levine Greenberg Literary Agency, Inc. (*US*)
Limelight Management (*UK*)
Literary & Creative Artists Inc. (*US*)
Literary Management Group, Inc. (*US*)
The Literary Group International (*US*)
Sterling Lord Literistic, Inc. (*US*)
Lowenstein Associates, Inc. (*US*)
MacGregor Literary (*US*)
Carol Mann Agency (*US*)

Manus & Associates Literary Agency, Inc.
(*US*)
The Martell Agency (*US*)
Martin Literary Management (*US*)
Martha Millard Literary Agency (*US*)
Howard Morhaim Literary Agency (*US*)
Northern Lights Literary Services (*US*)
Fifi Oscard Agency, Inc. (*US*)
Kathi J. Paton Literary Agency (*US*)
Pinder Lane & Garon-Brooke Associates Ltd
(*US*)
Queen Literary Agency, Inc. (*US*)
Lynne Rabinoff Agency (*US*)
Rees Literary Agency (*US*)
Regina Ryan Publishing Enterprises (*US*)
The Amy Rennert Agency, Inc. (*US*)
Robert Dudley Agency (*UK*)
Rita Rosenkranz Literary Agency (*US*)
Ross Yoon Agency (*US*)
The Rudy Agency (*US*)
Marly Rusoff & Associates, Inc. (*US*)
Salkind Literary Agency (*US*)
Susan Schulman, A Literary Agency (*US*)
Lynn Seligman, Literary Agent (*US*)
Denise Shannon Literary Agency, Inc. (*US*)
Solow Literary Enterprises, Inc. (*US*)
The Spieler Agency (*US*)
Stonesong (*US*)
The Strothman Agency (*US*)
Stuart Krichevsky Literary Agency, Inc. (*US*)
The Stuart Agency (*US*)
The Swetky Agency and Associates (*US*)
SYLA – Susan Yearwood Literary Agency
(*UK*)
Talcott Notch Literary (*US*)
Tessler Literary Agency (*US*)
TriadaUS Literary Agency, Inc. (*US*)
2M Literary Agency Ltd (*US*)
United Talent Agency (*US*)
Venture Literary (*US*)
Waterside Productions, Inc (*US*)
Watson, Little Ltd (*UK*)
Writers House UK (*UK*)
Writers' Representatives, LLC (*US*)
Zoë Pagnamenta Agency, LLC (*US*)

Cookery
Abbot Management (*US*)
Betsy Amster Literary Enterprises (*US*)
Baldi Agency (*US*)
The Bent Agency (*US*)
David Black Literary Agency (*US*)
Blake Friedmann Literary Agency Ltd (*UK*)
Bleecker Street Associates, Inc. (*US*)
The Blumer Literary Agency, Inc. (*US*)
Luigi Bonomi Associates Ltd (*UK*)
The Book Group (*US*)
Browne & Miller Literary Associates (*US*)
Sheree Bykofsky Associates, Inc. (*US*)
Castiglia Literary Agency (*US*)
The Choate Agency, LLC (*US*)
Teresa Chris Literary Agency Ltd (*UK*)
Clare Hulton Literary Agency (*UK*)
Rosica Colin Ltd (*UK*)

Don Congdon Associates, Inc. (*US*)
Connor Literary Agency (*US*)
Coombs Moylett & Maclean Literary Agency
(*UK*)
The Doe Coover Agency (*US*)
Creative Authors Ltd (*UK*)
The Culinary Entertainment Agency (CEA)
(*US*)
Laura Dail Literary Agency (*US*)
The Darley Anderson Agency (*UK*)
Caroline Davidson Literary Agency (*UK*)
The Jennifer DeChiara Literary Agency (*US*)
Sandra Dijkstra Literary Agency (*US*)
Janis A. Donnaud & Associates, Inc. (*US*)
Doyen Literary Services, Inc. (*US*)
Dystel & Goderich Literary Management (*US*)
Ethan Ellenberg Literary Agency (*US*)
Emily Sweet Associates (*UK*)
Fairbank Literary Representation (*US*)
The Fielding Agency, LLC (*US*)
Fine Literary (*US*)
Folio Literary Management, LLC (*US*)
Jeanne Fredericks Literary Agency, Inc. (*US*)
Grace Freedson's Publishing Network (*US*)
Sarah Jane Freymann Literary Agency (*US*)
Fredrica S. Friedman and Co. Inc. (*US*)
Furniss Lawton (*UK*)
Goodman Associates (*US*)
Irene Goodman Literary Agency (*US*)
Graham Maw Christie Literary Agency (*UK*)
Kathryn Green Literary Agency, LLC (*US*)
Greene & Heaton Ltd (*UK*)
The Mitchell J. Hamilburg Agency (*US*)
Hannigan Salky Getzler (HSG) Agency (*US*)
Antony Harwood Limited (*UK*)
A M Heath & Company Limited, Author's
Agents (*UK*)
hhb agency ltd (*UK*)
David Higham Associates Ltd (*UK*)
Hill Nadell Literary Agency (*US*)
Andrea Hurst Literary Management (*US*)
Frances Kelly (*UK*)
Harvey Klinger, Inc (*US*)
The Knight Agency (*US*)
Linda Konner Literary Agency (*US*)
Elaine Koster Literary Agency LLC (*US*)
Kuhn Projects (*US*)
The LA Literary Agency (*US*)
Larsen Pomada Literary Agents (*US*)
Robert Lecker Agency (*Can*)
Levine Greenberg Literary Agency, Inc. (*US*)
Limelight Management (*UK*)
The Lisa Ekus Group, LLC (*US*)
Literary & Creative Artists Inc. (*US*)
Lutyens and Rubinstein (*UK*)
Kirsten Manges Literary Agency, LLC (*US*)
Martha Millard Literary Agency (*US*)
The Miller Agency (*US*)
Howard Morhaim Literary Agency (*US*)
Fifi Oscard Agency, Inc. (*US*)
Pinder Lane & Garon-Brooke Associates Ltd
(*US*)
Queen Literary Agency, Inc. (*US*)

Design
Abbot Management (*US*)
The Blumer Literary Agency, Inc. (*US*)
Barbara Braun Associates, Inc. (*US*)
Castiglia Literary Agency (*US*)
Connor Literary Agency (*US*)
The Darley Anderson Agency (*UK*)
Caroline Davidson Literary Agency (*UK*)
Sandra Dijkstra Literary Agency (*US*)
Doyen Literary Services, Inc. (*US*)
Fairbank Literary Representation (*US*)
The Fielding Agency, LLC (*US*)
Fine Literary (*US*)
Jeanne Fredericks Literary Agency, Inc. (*US*)
Fresh Books Literary Agency (*US*)
Fredrica S. Friedman and Co. Inc. (*US*)
Kathryn Green Literary Agency, LLC (*US*)
Antony Harwood Limited (*UK*)
Johnson & Alcock (*UK*)
Kuhn Projects (*US*)
Larsen Pomada Literary Agents (*US*)
Carol Mann Agency (*US*)
Martha Millard Literary Agency (*US*)
Howard Morhaim Literary Agency (*US*)
Rita Rosenkranz Literary Agency (*US*)
Marly Rusoff & Associates, Inc. (*US*)
Salkind Literary Agency (*US*)
Lynn Seligman, Literary Agent (*US*)
Stonesong (*US*)
The Stuart Agency (*US*)
The Swetky Agency and Associates (*US*)
Venture Literary (*US*)
Whispering Buffalo Literary Agency Ltd (*UK*)
Wm Clark Associates (*US*)
Karen Gantz Zahler Literary Agency (*US*)

Drama
Abbot Management (*US*)
Abrams Artists Agency (*US*)
The Characters Talent Agency (*Can*)
The Darley Anderson Agency (*UK*)
The Dravis Agency, Inc. (*US*)
Evatopia, Inc. (*US*)
Fine Literary (*US*)
Jill Foster Ltd (JFL) (*UK*)
Antony Harwood Limited (*UK*)
David Higham Associates Ltd (*UK*)
Knight Hall Agency (*UK*)
Literary & Creative Artists Inc. (*US*)
Niad Management (*US*)
PBJ and JBJ Management (*UK*)
Roger Hancock Ltd (*UK*)
Sheil Land Associates Ltd (*UK*)
Talent Source (*US*)
The Tennyson Agency (*UK*)
Venture Literary (*US*)
Cecily Ware Literary Agents (*UK*)

Entertainment
Abbot Management (*US*)
The August Agency LLC (*US*)
David Black Literary Agency (*US*)
Bleecker Street Associates, Inc. (*US*)
The Blumer Literary Agency, Inc. (*US*)
The Bright Literary Academy (*UK*)

Crawford Literary Agency (*US*)
The Darley Anderson Agency (*UK*)
Diane Banks Associates Literary Agency (*UK*)
Fine Literary (*US*)
Folio Literary Management, LLC (*US*)
Frances Goldin Literary Agency, Inc. (*US*)
Sanford J. Greenburger Associates, Inc (*US*)
Gunn Media Associates (*UK*)
Antony Harwood Limited (*UK*)
hhb agency ltd (*UK*)
Jill Grinberg Literary Management LLC (*US*)
The Knight Agency (*US*)
Linda Konner Literary Agency (*US*)
Robert Lecker Agency (*Can*)
Julia Lord Literary Management (*US*)
Gina Maccoby Agency (*US*)
Martin Literary Management (*US*)
Mendel Media Group, LLC (*US*)
New Leaf Literary & Media, Inc. (*US*)
Pinder Lane & Garon-Brooke Associates Ltd (*US*)
Redhammer (*UK*)
Rocking Chair Books (*UK*)
Roger Hancock Ltd (*UK*)
Susan Schulman, A Literary Agency (*US*)
Wendy Sherman Associates, Inc. (*US*)
Jeffrey Simmons (*UK*)
Jane Turnbull (*UK*)
Venture Literary (*US*)
Whispering Buffalo Literary Agency Ltd (*UK*)
Karen Gantz Zahler Literary Agency (*US*)

Erotic
Abbot Management (*US*)
The Axelrod Agency (*US*)
Belcastro Agency (*US*)
Bleecker Street Associates, Inc. (*US*)
BookEnds, LLC (*US*)
The Characters Talent Agency (*Can*)
Rosica Colin Ltd (*UK*)
The Darley Anderson Agency (*UK*)
Elaine P. English, Attorney & Literary Agent (*US*)
Goodman Associates (*US*)
Antony Harwood Limited (*UK*)
Robert Lecker Agency (*Can*)
Ricia Mainhardt Agency (RMA) (*US*)
New Leaf Literary & Media, Inc. (*US*)
Pinder Lane & Garon-Brooke Associates Ltd (*US*)
Prospect Agency (*US*)
Spencerhill Associates (*US*)
The Swetky Agency and Associates (*US*)
Venture Literary (*US*)
The Zack Company, Inc (*US*)

Fantasy
Abbot Management (*US*)
Miriam Altshuler Literary Agency (*US*)
The Ampersand Agency Ltd (*UK*)
Betsy Amster Literary Enterprises (*US*)
Andrew Lownie Literary Agency Ltd (*UK*)
Anubis Literary Agency (*UK*)
Belcastro Agency (*US*)
The Bent Agency (*US*)

The Mitchell J. Hamilburg Agency (*US*)
Hannigan Salky Getzler (HSG) Agency (*US*)
Hardman & Swainson (*UK*)
Joy Harris Literary Agency, Inc. (*US*)
Antony Harwood Limited (*UK*)
John Hawkins & Associates, Inc. (*US*)
A M Heath & Company Limited, Author's Agents (*UK*)
Rupert Heath Literary Agency (*UK*)
The Helen Brann Agency, Inc. (*US*)
The Helen Heller Agency (*Can*)
hhb agency ltd (*UK*)
Hidden Value Group (*US*)
David Higham Associates Ltd (*UK*)
Hill Nadell Literary Agency (*US*)
Vanessa Holt Ltd (*UK*)
Hopkins Literary Associates (*US*)
Kate Hordern Literary Agency (*UK*)
Hunter Profiles (*UK*)
Andrea Hurst Literary Management (*US*)
InkWell Management (*US*)
Intercontinental Literary Agency (*UK*)
International Transactions, Inc. (*US*)
Isabel White Literary Agent (*UK*)
J de S Associates Inc (*US*)
Jabberwocky Literary Agency (*US*)
The Jean V. Naggar Literary Agency (*US*)
Jill Grinberg Literary Management LLC (*US*)
Jo Unwin Literary Agency (*UK*)
The Joan Brandt Agency (*US*)
Johnson & Alcock (*UK*)
Michelle Kass Associates (*UK*)
Keane Kataria Literary Agency (*UK*)
Ken Sherman & Associates (*US*)
Ki Agency Ltd (*UK*)
Virginia Kidd Agency, Inc (*US*)
Harvey Klinger, Inc (*US*)
Kneerim & Williams (*US*)
The Knight Agency (*US*)
Elaine Koster Literary Agency LLC (*US*)
Barbara S. Kouts, Literary Agent (*US*)
Edite Kroll Literary Agency, Inc. (*US*)
Kuhn Projects (*US*)
The LA Literary Agency (*US*)
Peter Lampack Agency, Inc (*US*)
Laura Langlie, Literary Agent (*US*)
Larsen Pomada Literary Agents (*US*)
The Steve Laube Agency (*US*)
LaunchBooks Literary Agency (*US*)
Sarah Lazin Books (*US*)
Robert Lecker Agency (*Can*)
Levine Greenberg Literary Agency, Inc. (*US*)
Barbara Levy Literary Agency (*UK*)
Limelight Management (*UK*)
Lindsay Literary Agency (*UK*)
Lippincott Massie McQuilkin (*US*)
Literary & Creative Artists Inc. (*US*)
The Literary Group International (*US*)
London Independent Books (*UK*)
Sterling Lord Literistic, Inc. (*US*)
Julia Lord Literary Management (*US*)
Lowenstein Associates, Inc. (*US*)
Lutyens and Rubinstein (*UK*)

The Jennifer Lyons Literary Agency, LLC (*US*)
Donald Maass Literary Agency (*US*)
Gina Maccoby Agency (*US*)
MacGregor Literary (*US*)
Ricia Mainhardt Agency (RMA) (*US*)
Kirsten Manges Literary Agency, LLC (*US*)
Carol Mann Agency (*US*)
Manus & Associates Literary Agency, Inc. (*US*)
March Tenth, Inc. (*US*)
Marjacq Scripts Ltd (*UK*)
Elaine Markson Literary Agency (*US*)
Marly Russoff & Associates (*US*)
The Marsh Agency (*UK*)
The Martell Agency (*US*)
Martin Literary Management (*US*)
MBA Literary Agents Ltd (*UK*)
Duncan McAra (*UK*)
Anne McDermid & Associates Ltd (*Can*)
Mendel Media Group, LLC (*US*)
Miles Stott Children's Literary Agency (*UK*)
Martha Millard Literary Agency (*US*)
Patricia Moosbrugger Literary Agency (*US*)
Howard Morhaim Literary Agency (*US*)
Mulcahy Associates (*UK*)
Judith Murdoch Literary Agency (*UK*)
Nappaland Literary Agency (*US*)
Nelson Literary Agency, LLC (*US*)
New Leaf Literary & Media, Inc. (*US*)
Niad Management (*US*)
Northern Lights Literary Services (*US*)
Andrew Nurnberg Associates, Ltd (*UK*)
Harold Ober Associates (*US*)
Fifi Oscard Agency, Inc. (*US*)
Deborah Owen Ltd (*UK*)
The Park Literary Group LLC (*US*)
Kathi J. Paton Literary Agency (*US*)
Pavilion Literary Management (*US*)
Maggie Pearlstine Associates Ltd (*UK*)
Jonathan Pegg Literary Agency (*UK*)
Pinder Lane & Garon-Brooke Associates Ltd (*US*)
Pippin Properties, Inc (*US*)
Shelley Power Literary Agency Ltd (*UK*)
Rebecca Pratt Literary Group (*US*)
Linn Prentis Literary (*US*)
Aaron M. Priest Literary Agency (*US*)
Prospect Agency (*US*)
Queen Literary Agency, Inc. (*US*)
Raines & Raines (*US*)
Rebecca Friedman Literary Agency (*US*)
Redhammer (*UK*)
Rees Literary Agency (*US*)
Renee Zuckerbrot Literary Agency (*US*)
The Amy Rennert Agency, Inc. (*US*)
The Lisa Richards Agency (*Ire*)
Richford Becklow Literary Agency (*UK*)
Riverside Literary Agency (*US*)
B.J. Robbins Literary Agency (*US*)
Robin Jones Literary Agency (*UK*)
Rocking Chair Books (*UK*)
Andy Ross Agency (*US*)
The Damaris Rowland Agency (*US*)

Film

MBA Literary Agents Ltd (*UK*)
Martha Millard Literary Agency (*US*)
Niad Management (*US*)
Paradigm Talent and Literary Agency (*US*)
PBJ and JBJ Management (*UK*)
Peregrine Whittlesey Agency (*US*)
Pinder Lane & Garon-Brooke Associates Ltd (*US*)
B.J. Robbins Literary Agency (*US*)
Rochelle Stevens & Co. (*UK*)
Victoria Sanders & Associates LLC (*US*)
Sayle Screen Ltd (*UK*)
Susan Schulman, A Literary Agency (*US*)
Linda Seifert Management (*UK*)
Lynn Seligman, Literary Agent (*US*)
Sheil Land Associates Ltd (*UK*)
Jeffrey Simmons (*UK*)
The Spieler Agency (*US*)
Elaine Steel (*UK*)
Stone Manners Salners Agency (*US*)
The Swetky Agency and Associates (*US*)
The Tennyson Agency (*UK*)
2M Literary Agency Ltd (*US*)
United Agents (*UK*)
Venture Literary (*US*)
Cecily Ware Literary Agents (*UK*)
Watson, Little Ltd (*UK*)
Whispering Buffalo Literary Agency Ltd (*UK*)
Wm Clark Associates (*US*)
The Zack Company, Inc (*US*)

Finance
Abbot Management (*US*)
Andrew Lownie Literary Agency Ltd (*UK*)
Audrey A. Wolf Literary Agency (*US*)
The August Agency LLC (*US*)
Ayesha Pande Literary (*US*)
David Black Literary Agency (*US*)
The Blumer Literary Agency, Inc. (*US*)
Jenny Brown Associates (*UK*)
Browne & Miller Literary Associates (*US*)
Maria Carvainis Agency, Inc. (*US*)
Castiglia Literary Agency (*US*)
Elyse Cheney Literary Associates, LLC (*US*)
Connor Literary Agency (*US*)
The Doe Coover Agency (*US*)
Richard Curtis Associates, Inc. (*US*)
The Darley Anderson Agency (*UK*)
Janis A. Donnaud & Associates, Inc. (*US*)
Jim Donovan Literary (*US*)
Doyen Literary Services, Inc. (*US*)
Dystel & Goderich Literary Management (*US*)
Felicia Eth Literary Representation (*US*)
The Fielding Agency, LLC (*US*)
Diana Finch Literary Agency (*US*)
Jeanne Fredericks Literary Agency, Inc. (*US*)
Grace Freedson's Publishing Network (*US*)
Fresh Books Literary Agency (*US*)
Fredrica S. Friedman and Co. Inc. (*US*)
The G Agency, LLC (*US*)
Goodman Associates (*US*)
Kathryn Green Literary Agency, LLC (*US*)
The Mitchell J. Hamilburg Agency (*US*)
Hannigan Salky Getzler (HSG) Agency (*US*)

Antony Harwood Limited (*UK*)
Hornfischer Literary Management, L.P. (*US*)
InkWell Management (*US*)
J de S Associates Inc (*US*)
Jill Grinberg Literary Management LLC (*US*)
Frances Kelly (*UK*)
Kneerim & Williams (*US*)
The Knight Agency (*US*)
Linda Konner Literary Agency (*US*)
Elaine Koster Literary Agency LLC (*US*)
Larsen Pomada Literary Agents (*US*)
Levine Greenberg Literary Agency, Inc. (*US*)
The Jennifer Lyons Literary Agency, LLC (*US*)
MacGregor Literary (*US*)
Carol Mann Agency (*US*)
Manus & Associates Literary Agency, Inc. (*US*)
The Martell Agency (*US*)
Mendel Media Group, LLC (*US*)
Martha Millard Literary Agency (*US*)
Howard Morhaim Literary Agency (*US*)
Mulcahy Associates (*UK*)
Fifi Oscard Agency, Inc. (*US*)
Kathi J. Paton Literary Agency (*US*)
Lynne Rabinoff Agency (*US*)
Raines & Raines (*US*)
The Amy Rennert Agency, Inc. (*US*)
Rita Rosenkranz Literary Agency (*US*)
Marly Rusoff & Associates, Inc. (*US*)
Salkind Literary Agency (*US*)
Susan Schulman, A Literary Agency (*US*)
Lynn Seligman, Literary Agent (*US*)
Solow Literary Enterprises, Inc. (*US*)
The Spieler Agency (*US*)
Stonesong (*US*)
The Strothman Agency (*US*)
The Swetky Agency and Associates (*US*)
TriadaUS Literary Agency, Inc. (*US*)
Venture Literary (*US*)
Writers House UK (*UK*)
Writers' Representatives, LLC (*US*)
The Zack Company, Inc (*US*)

Gardening
Abbot Management (*US*)
Betsy Amster Literary Enterprises (*US*)
Teresa Chris Literary Agency Ltd (*UK*)
Rosica Colin Ltd (*UK*)
The Doe Coover Agency (*US*)
The Darley Anderson Agency (*UK*)
Caroline Davidson Literary Agency (*UK*)
Janis A. Donnaud & Associates, Inc. (*US*)
Doyen Literary Services, Inc. (*US*)
Fine Literary (*US*)
Jeanne Fredericks Literary Agency, Inc. (*US*)
Graham Maw Christie Literary Agency (*UK*)
Greene & Heaton Ltd (*UK*)
The Mitchell J. Hamilburg Agency (*US*)
Antony Harwood Limited (*UK*)
John Hawkins & Associates, Inc. (*US*)
Levine Greenberg Literary Agency, Inc. (*US*)
Regina Ryan Publishing Enterprises (*US*)
Richford Becklow Literary Agency (*UK*)
Sheil Land Associates Ltd (*UK*)

The Swetky Agency and Associates (*US*)
Falcott Hotch Literary (*UK*)
TriadaUS Literary Agency, Inc. (*US*)
Jane Turnbull (*UK*)
Venture Literary (*US*)
The Zack Company, Inc (*US*)

Gothic

Abbot Management (*US*)
The Darley Anderson Agency (*UK*)
Diamond Kahn and Woods (DKW) Literary Agency Ltd (*UK*)
Ann Elmo Agency, Inc. (*US*)
Elaine P. English, Attorney & Literary Agent (*US*)
Antony Harwood Limited (*UK*)
The Jean V. Naggar Literary Agency (*US*)
Ricia Mainhardt Agency (RMA) (*US*)
Aaron M. Priest Literary Agency (*US*)
Richford Becklow Literary Agency (*UK*)
The Swetky Agency and Associates (*US*)
Venture Literary (*US*)

Health

Abbot Management (*US*)
The Ahearn Agency, Inc (*US*)
Betsy Amster Literary Enterprises (*US*)
Andrew Lownie Literary Agency Ltd (*UK*)
Arcadia (*US*)
Audrey A. Wolf Literary Agency (*US*)
David Black Literary Agency (*US*)
Bleecker Street Associates, Inc. (*US*)
The Blumer Literary Agency, Inc. (*US*)
Luigi Bonomi Associates Ltd (*UK*)
Brandt & Hochman Literary Agents, Inc. (*US*)
Bresnick Weil Literary Agency, LLC (*US*)
Rick Broadhead & Associates Literary Agency (*Can*)
Browne & Miller Literary Associates (*US*)
Carnicelli Literary Management (*US*)
Castiglia Literary Agency (*US*)
Rosica Colin Ltd (*UK*)
Don Congdon Associates, Inc. (*US*)
Connor Literary Agency (*US*)
The Doe Coover Agency (*US*)
Creative Authors Ltd (*UK*)
Richard Curtis Associates, Inc. (*US*)
The Darley Anderson Agency (*UK*)
Caroline Davidson Literary Agency (*UK*)
The Jennifer DeChiara Literary Agency (*US*)
Joëlle Delbourgo Associates, Inc. (*US*)
Diane Banks Associates Literary Agency (*UK*)
Sandra Dijkstra Literary Agency (*US*)
Janis A. Donnaud & Associates, Inc. (*US*)
Jim Donovan Literary (*US*)
Doyen Literary Services, Inc. (*US*)
Dunow, Carlson & Lerner Agency (*US*)
Dystel & Goderich Literary Management (*US*)
Ebeling & Associates (*US*)
Judith Ehrlich Literary Management (*US*)
Ethan Ellenberg Literary Agency (*US*)
Ann Elmo Agency, Inc. (*US*)
Felicia Eth Literary Representation (*US*)
The Fielding Agency, LLC (*US*)
Diana Finch Literary Agency (*US*)

Fine Literary (*US*)
Fletcher & Company (*US*)
Folio Literary Management, LLC (*US*)
Fox & Howard Literary Agency (*UK*)
Jeanne Fredericks Literary Agency, Inc. (*US*)
Grace Freedson's Publishing Network (*US*)
Fresh Books Literary Agency (*US*)
Sarah Jane Freymann Literary Agency (*US*)
Fredrica S. Friedman and Co. Inc. (*US*)
Goodman Associates (*US*)
Graham Maw Christie Literary Agency (*UK*)
Kathryn Green Literary Agency, LLC (*US*)
Sanford J. Greenburger Associates, Inc (*US*)
Greene & Heaton Ltd (*UK*)
Laura Gross Literary Agency (*US*)
Marianne Gunn O'Connor Literary Agency (*Ire*)
The Mitchell J. Hamilburg Agency (*US*)
Antony Harwood Limited (*UK*)
John Hawkins & Associates, Inc. (*US*)
The Jeff Herman Agency, LLC (*US*)
Hill Nadell Literary Agency (*US*)
Hornfischer Literary Management, L.P. (*US*)
InkWell Management (*US*)
J de S Associates Inc (*US*)
The Jean V. Naggar Literary Agency (*US*)
Jill Grinberg Literary Management LLC (*US*)
Johnson & Alcock (*UK*)
Frances Kelly (*UK*)
Harvey Klinger, Inc (*US*)
Kneerim & Williams (*US*)
The Knight Agency (*US*)
Linda Konner Literary Agency (*US*)
Elaine Koster Literary Agency LLC (*US*)
Barbara S. Kouts, Literary Agent (*US*)
Bert P. Krages (*US*)
Edite Kroll Literary Agency, Inc. (*US*)
Kuhn Projects (*US*)
The LA Literary Agency (*US*)
Larsen Pomada Literary Agents (*US*)
Levine Greenberg Literary Agency, Inc. (*US*)
Limelight Management (*UK*)
Lippincott Massie McQuilkin (*US*)
Literary & Creative Artists Inc. (*US*)
Sterling Lord Literistic, Inc. (*US*)
Julia Lord Literary Management (*US*)
Lowenstein Associates, Inc. (*US*)
Gina Maccoby Agency (*US*)
Kirsten Manges Literary Agency, LLC (*US*)
Carol Mann Agency (*US*)
Manus & Associates Literary Agency, Inc. (*US*)
March Tenth, Inc. (*US*)
Marjacq Scripts Ltd (*UK*)
The Martell Agency (*US*)
Martin Literary Management (*US*)
MBA Literary Agents Ltd (*UK*)
Martha Millard Literary Agency (*US*)
Howard Morhaim Literary Agency (*US*)
Northern Lights Literary Services (*US*)
Fifi Oscard Agency, Inc. (*US*)
Kathi J. Paton Literary Agency (*US*)
Maggie Pearlstine Associates Ltd (*UK*)

Pinder Lane & Garon-Brooke Associates Ltd (*US*)
Regina Ryan Publishing Enterprises (*US*)
The Amy Rennert Agency, Inc. (*US*)
B.J. Robbins Literary Agency (*US*)
Rita Rosenkranz Literary Agency (*US*)
The Rudy Agency (*US*)
Marly Rusoff & Associates, Inc. (*US*)
Salkind Literary Agency (*US*)
Susan Schulman, A Literary Agency (*US*)
Lynn Seligman, Literary Agent (*US*)
Denise Shannon Literary Agency, Inc. (*US*)
Wendy Sherman Associates, Inc. (*US*)
Robert Smith Literary Agency Ltd (*UK*)
Solow Literary Enterprises, Inc. (*US*)
The Spieler Agency (*US*)
Stonesong (*US*)
The Stuart Agency (*US*)
The Swetky Agency and Associates (*US*)
Tessler Literary Agency (*US*)
Thompson Literary Agency (*US*)
Tracy Brown Literary Agency (*US*)
TriadaUS Literary Agency, Inc. (*US*)
2M Literary Agency Ltd (*US*)
Venture Literary (*US*)
Waterside Productions, Inc (*US*)
Whispering Buffalo Literary Agency Ltd (*UK*)
Wolfson Literary Agency (*US*)
The Zack Company, Inc (*US*)
Helen Zimmermann Literary Agency (*US*)

Historical
Abbot Management (*US*)
Sheila Ableman Literary Agency (*UK*)
Adler & Robin Books, Inc (*US*)
The Ahearn Agency, Inc (*US*)
Alive Communications, Inc (*US*)
The Ampersand Agency Ltd (*UK*)
Betsy Amster Literary Enterprises (*US*)
Marcia Amsterdam Agency (*US*)
Andrew Lownie Literary Agency Ltd (*UK*)
Arcadia (*US*)
Audrey A. Wolf Literary Agency (*US*)
The August Agency LLC (*US*)
Ayesha Pande Literary (*US*)
Baldi Agency (*US*)
The Bent Agency (*US*)
David Black Literary Agency (*US*)
Blake Friedmann Literary Agency Ltd (*UK*)
Bleecker Street Associates, Inc. (*US*)
The Blumer Literary Agency, Inc. (*US*)
Luigi Bonomi Associates Ltd (*UK*)
The Book Group (*US*)
BookEnds, LLC (*US*)
Books & Such Literary Agency (*US*)
Georges Borchardt, Inc. (*US*)
Brandt & Hochman Literary Agents, Inc. (*US*)
Barbara Braun Associates, Inc. (*US*)
Bresnick Weil Literary Agency, LLC (*US*)
Rick Broadhead & Associates Literary Agency (*Can*)
Jenny Brown Associates (*UK*)
Marie Brown Associates, Inc. (*US*)
Browne & Miller Literary Associates (*US*)

Felicity Bryan (*UK*)
Carnicelli Literary Management (*US*)
Maria Carvainis Agency, Inc. (*US*)
Chalberg & Sussman (*US*)
The Characters Talent Agency (*Can*)
Elyse Cheney Literary Associates, LLC (*US*)
The Choate Agency, LLC (*US*)
Teresa Chris Literary Agency Ltd (*UK*)
The Chudney Agency (*US*)
Clare Hulton Literary Agency (*UK*)
Rosica Colin Ltd (*UK*)
Frances Collin Literary Agent (*US*)
Don Congdon Associates, Inc. (*US*)
Connor Literary Agency (*US*)
Conville & Walsh Ltd (*UK*)
The Cooke Agency (*Can*)
Coombs Moylett & Maclean Literary Agency (*UK*)
The Doe Coover Agency (*US*)
Creative Authors Ltd (*UK*)
Curtis Brown Group Ltd (*UK*)
Richard Curtis Associates, Inc. (*US*)
Laura Dail Literary Agency (*US*)
The Darley Anderson Agency (*UK*)
David Luxton Associates (*UK*)
Caroline Davidson Literary Agency (*UK*)
Liza Dawson Associates (*US*)
The Jennifer DeChiara Literary Agency (*US*)
DeFiore and Company (*US*)
Joëlle Delbourgo Associates, Inc. (*US*)
DHH Literary Agency Ltd (*UK*)
Diamond Kahn and Woods (DKW) Literary Agency Ltd (*UK*)
Diane Banks Associates Literary Agency (*UK*)
Sandra Dijkstra Literary Agency (*US*)
Donadio & Olson, Inc. (*US*)
Jim Donovan Literary (*US*)
Dorian Literary Agency (DLA) (*UK*)
The Dravis Agency, Inc. (*US*)
Dunham Literary, Inc. (*US*)
Dunow, Carlson & Lerner Agency (*US*)
Dystel & Goderich Literary Management (*US*)
Anne Edelstein Literary Agency (*US*)
Edwards Fuglewicz (*UK*)
Judith Ehrlich Literary Management (*US*)
Einstein Literary Management (*US*)
Ethan Ellenberg Literary Agency (*US*)
Ann Elmo Agency, Inc. (*US*)
Emily Sweet Associates (*UK*)
Elaine P. English, Attorney & Literary Agent (*US*)
Felicia Eth Literary Representation (*US*)
Mary Evans, Inc. (*US*)
Evatopia, Inc. (*US*)
The Fielding Agency, LLC (*US*)
Diana Finch Literary Agency (*US*)
Fine Literary (*US*)
Fletcher & Company (*US*)
Folio Literary Management, LLC (*US*)
Fox & Howard Literary Agency (*UK*)
Jeanne Fredericks Literary Agency, Inc. (*US*)
Grace Freedson's Publishing Network (*US*)
Sarah Jane Freymann Literary Agency (*US*)

Fredrica S. Friedman and Co. Inc. (*US*)
Furniss Lawton (*UK*)
The G Agency, LLC (*US*)
Gelfman Schneider Literary Agents, Inc. (*US*)
Georgina Capel Associates Ltd (*UK*)
The Gernert Company (*US*)
Frances Goldin Literary Agency, Inc. (*US*)
Goodman Associates (*US*)
Irene Goodman Literary Agency (*US*)
Graham Maw Christie Literary Agency (*UK*)
Kathryn Green Literary Agency, LLC (*US*)
Sanford J. Greenburger Associates, Inc (*US*)
Greene & Heaton Ltd (*UK*)
Gregory & Company, Authors' Agents (*UK*)
Laura Gross Literary Agency (*US*)
The Mitchell J. Hamilburg Agency (*US*)
Hannigan Salky Getzler (HSG) Agency (*US*)
Hardman & Swainson (*UK*)
Joy Harris Literary Agency, Inc. (*US*)
Antony Harwood Limited (*UK*)
John Hawkins & Associates, Inc. (*US*)
A M Heath & Company Limited, Author's
Agents (*UK*)
Rupert Heath Literary Agency (*UK*)
The Helen Heller Agency (*Can*)
The Jeff Herman Agency, LLC (*US*)
hhb agency ltd (*UK*)
David Higham Associates Ltd (*UK*)
Hill Nadell Literary Agency (*US*)
Hopkins Literary Associates (*US*)
Kate Hordern Literary Agency (*UK*)
Hornfischer Literary Management, L.P. (*US*)
Andrea Hurst Literary Management (*US*)
InkWell Management (*US*)
International Transactions, Inc. (*US*)
J de S Associates Inc (*US*)
Jabberwocky Literary Agency (*US*)
The Jean V. Naggar Literary Agency (*US*)
Jill Grinberg Literary Management LLC (*US*)
Johnson & Alcock (*UK*)
Keane Kataria Literary Agency (*UK*)
Frances Kelly (*UK*)
Ki Agency Ltd (*UK*)
Virginia Kidd Agency, Inc (*US*)
Kneerim & Williams (*US*)
The Knight Agency (*US*)
Elaine Koster Literary Agency LLC (*US*)
Barbara S. Kouts, Literary Agent (*US*)
Bert P. Krages (*US*)
Kuhn Projects (*US*)
The LA Literary Agency (*US*)
Laura Langlie, Literary Agent (*US*)
Larsen Pomada Literary Agents (*US*)
Sarah Lazin Books (*US*)
Robert Lecker Agency (*Can*)
Levine Greenberg Literary Agency, Inc. (*US*)
Limelight Management (*UK*)
Lippincott Massie McQuilkin (*US*)
Literary & Creative Artists Inc. (*US*)
The Literary Group International (*US*)
Sterling Lord Literistic, Inc. (*US*)
Julia Lord Literary Management (*US*)
The Jennifer Lyons Literary Agency, LLC (*US*)

Donald Maass Literary Agency (*US*)
Gina Maccoby Agency (*US*)
MacGregor Literary (*US*)
Ricia Mainhardt Agency (RMA) (*US*)
Kirsten Manges Literary Agency, LLC (*US*)
Carol Mann Agency (*US*)
March Tenth, Inc. (*US*)
Marjacq Scripts Ltd (*UK*)
The Martell Agency (*US*)
MBA Literary Agents Ltd (*UK*)
Duncan McAra (*UK*)
Anne McDermid & Associates Ltd (*Can*)
Mendel Media Group, LLC (*US*)
Martha Millard Literary Agency (*US*)
Howard Morhaim Literary Agency (*US*)
Mulcahy Associates (*UK*)
Nappaland Literary Agency (*US*)
Nelson Literary Agency, LLC (*US*)
New Leaf Literary & Media, Inc. (*US*)
Northern Lights Literary Services (*US*)
Fifi Oscard Agency, Inc. (*US*)
The Park Literary Group LLC (*US*)
Kathi J. Paton Literary Agency (*US*)
Pavilion Literary Management (*US*)
Maggie Pearlstine Associates Ltd (*UK*)
Jonathan Pegg Literary Agency (*UK*)
Pinder Lane & Garon-Brooke Associates Ltd
(*US*)
Rebecca Pratt Literary Group (*US*)
Aaron M. Priest Literary Agency (*US*)
Queen Literary Agency, Inc. (*US*)
Lynne Rabinoff Agency (*US*)
Raines & Raines (*US*)
Rees Literary Agency (*US*)
Regina Ryan Publishing Enterprises (*US*)
Renee Zuckerbrot Literary Agency (*US*)
The Amy Rennert Agency, Inc. (*US*)
The Lisa Richards Agency (*Ire*)
Richford Becklow Literary Agency (*UK*)
Robert Dudley Agency (*UK*)
Rocking Chair Books (*UK*)
Rita Rosenkranz Literary Agency (*US*)
Ross Yoon Agency (*US*)
Andy Ross Agency (*US*)
The Rudy Agency (*US*)
Marly Rusoff & Associates, Inc. (*US*)
Salkind Literary Agency (*US*)
Victoria Sanders & Associates LLC (*US*)
The Sayle Literary Agency (*UK*)
Susan Schulman, A Literary Agency (*US*)
The Science Factory (*UK*)
Lynn Seligman, Literary Agent (*US*)
The Seymour Agency (*US*)
Denise Shannon Literary Agency, Inc. (*US*)
Sheil Land Associates Ltd (*UK*)
Caroline Sheldon Literary Agency (*UK*)
Wendy Sherman Associates, Inc. (*US*)
Rosalie Siegel, International Literary Agency,
Inc. (*US*)
Dorie Simmonds Agency (*UK*)
Jeffrey Simmons (*UK*)
Sinclair-Stevenson (*UK*)
Robert Smith Literary Agency Ltd (*UK*)

Solow Literary Enterprises, Inc. (*US*)
Spectrum Literary Agency (*US*)
Spencerhill Associates (*US*)
The Spieler Agency (*US*)
Steph Roundsmith Agent and Editor (*UK*)
The Strothman Agency (*US*)
Stuart Krichevsky Literary Agency, Inc. (*US*)
The Stuart Agency (*US*)
Sarah Such Literary Agency (*UK*)
The Swetky Agency and Associates (*US*)
Talcott Notch Literary (*US*)
Tessler Literary Agency (*US*)
Thompson Literary Agency (*US*)
Toby Mundy Associates Ltd (*UK*)
Tracy Brown Literary Agency (*US*)
Transatlantic Literary Agency, Inc. (*Can*)
TriadaUS Literary Agency, Inc. (*US*)
Jane Turnbull (*UK*)
United Talent Agency (*US*)
Venture Literary (*US*)
Ed Victor Ltd (*UK*)
Watson, Little Ltd (*UK*)
William Morris Endeavor (WME) London (*UK*)
Wm Clark Associates (*US*)
Writers House UK (*UK*)
Writers' Representatives, LLC (*US*)
The Zack Company, Inc (*US*)
Karen Gantz Zahler Literary Agency (*US*)
Zeno Agency Ltd (*UK*)
Helen Zimmermann Literary Agency (*US*)
Zoë Pagnamenta Agency, LLC (*US*)

Hobbies
Abbot Management (*US*)
The Blumer Literary Agency, Inc. (*US*)
Browne & Miller Literary Associates (*US*)
Sheree Bykofsky Associates, Inc. (*US*)
Connor Literary Agency (*US*)
The Darley Anderson Agency (*UK*)
Grace Freedson's Publishing Network (*US*)
Antony Harwood Limited (*UK*)
Levine Greenberg Literary Agency, Inc. (*US*)
Julia Lord Literary Management (*US*)
Rita Rosenkranz Literary Agency (*US*)
Susan Schulman, A Literary Agency (*US*)
Venture Literary (*US*)
Waterside Productions, Inc (*US*)

Horror
Abbot Management (*US*)
The Ampersand Agency Ltd (*UK*)
Marcia Amsterdam Agency (*US*)
Andrew Lownie Literary Agency Ltd (*UK*)
Anubis Literary Agency (*UK*)
The Bent Agency (*US*)
Bleecker Street Associates, Inc. (*US*)
The Characters Talent Agency (*Can*)
Elyse Cheney Literary Associates, LLC (*US*)
Rosica Colin Ltd (*UK*)
Connor Literary Agency (*US*)
The Darley Anderson Agency (*UK*)
Dorian Literary Agency (DLA) (*UK*)
Evatopia, Inc. (*US*)
The Fielding Agency, LLC (*US*)

Film Rights Ltd in association with Laurence Fitch Ltd (*UK*)
Folio Literary Management, LLC (*US*)
Samuel French, Inc. (*US*)
The Mitchell J. Hamilburg Agency (*US*)
Hardman & Swainson (*UK*)
Antony Harwood Limited (*UK*)
The Jean V. Naggar Literary Agency (*US*)
Donald Maass Literary Agency (*US*)
Ricia Mainhardt Agency (RMA) (*US*)
Martha Millard Literary Agency (*US*)
Howard Morhaim Literary Agency (*US*)
Pinder Lane & Garon-Brooke Associates Ltd (*US*)
Rebecca Pratt Literary Group (*US*)
Richford Becklow Literary Agency (*UK*)
Rocking Chair Books (*UK*)
Lynn Seligman, Literary Agent (*US*)
Sternig & Byrne Literary Agency (*US*)
The Stuart Agency (*US*)
Talcott Notch Literary (*US*)
Venture Literary (*US*)
The Zack Company, Inc (*US*)
Zeno Agency Ltd (*UK*)

How-to
Abbot Management (*US*)
Adler & Robin Books, Inc (*US*)
Alive Communications, Inc (*US*)
Miriam Altshuler Literary Agency (*US*)
Andrew Lownie Literary Agency Ltd (*UK*)
Bleecker Street Associates, Inc. (*US*)
The Blumer Literary Agency, Inc. (*US*)
Browne & Miller Literary Associates (*US*)
Connor Literary Agency (*US*)
Crawford Literary Agency (*US*)
The Darley Anderson Agency (*UK*)
The Jennifer DeChiara Literary Agency (*US*)
Jim Donovan Literary (*US*)
Doyen Literary Services, Inc. (*US*)
Judith Ehrlich Literary Management (*US*)
Ann Elmo Agency, Inc. (*US*)
The Fielding Agency, LLC (*US*)
Diana Finch Literary Agency (*US*)
Fine Literary (*US*)
Folio Literary Management, LLC (*US*)
Jeanne Fredericks Literary Agency, Inc. (*US*)
Grace Freedson's Publishing Network (*US*)
Fresh Books Literary Agency (*US*)
Fredrica S. Friedman and Co. Inc. (*US*)
Kathryn Green Literary Agency, LLC (*US*)
Antony Harwood Limited (*UK*)
The Jeff Herman Agency, LLC (*US*)
Hornfischer Literary Management, L.P. (*US*)
Andrea Hurst Literary Management (*US*)
J de S Associates Inc (*US*)
The Joan Brandt Agency (*US*)
Harvey Klinger, Inc (*US*)
The Knight Agency (*US*)
Linda Konner Literary Agency (*US*)
Elaine Koster Literary Agency LLC (*US*)
Larsen Pomada Literary Agents (*US*)
Robert Lecker Agency (*Can*)
Literary & Creative Artists Inc. (*US*)

Dunow, Carlson & Lerner Agency (*US*)
Diana Finch Literary Agency (*US*)
Fine Literary (*US*)
Folio Literary Management, LLC (*US*)
Fredrica S. Friedman and Co. Inc. (*US*)
Goodman Associates (*US*)
Sanford J. Greenburger Associates, Inc (*US*)
Antony Harwood Limited (*UK*)
The Jean V. Naggar Literary Agency (*US*)
Johnson & Alcock (*UK*)
Harvey Klinger, Inc (*US*)
Larsen Pomada Literary Agents (*US*)
Sarah Lazin Books (*US*)
Robert Lecker Agency (*Can*)
The Literary Group International (*US*)
Julia Lord Literary Management (*US*)
Carol Mann Agency (*US*)
March Tenth, Inc. (*US*)
Martha Millard Literary Agency (*US*)
Pinder Lane & Garon-Brooke Associates Ltd (*US*)
B.J. Robbins Literary Agency (*US*)
Rita Rosenkranz Literary Agency (*US*)
Victoria Sanders & Associates LLC (*US*)
The Sayle Literary Agency (*UK*)
Susan Schulman, A Literary Agency (*US*)
Lynn Seligman, Literary Agent (*US*)
The Spieler Agency (*US*)
The Stuart Agency (*US*)
Thompson Literary Agency (*US*)
TriadaUS Literary Agency, Inc. (*US*)
2M Literary Agency Ltd (*US*)
Venture Literary (*US*)
Watson, Little Ltd (*UK*)
The Weingel-Fidel Agency (*US*)
Whispering Buffalo Literary Agency Ltd (*UK*)
Wm Clark Associates (*US*)
The Zack Company, Inc (*US*)
Helen Zimmermann Literary Agency (*US*)

Mystery
Abbot Management (*US*)
Abrams Artists Agency (*US*)
The Ahearn Agency, Inc (*US*)
Alive Communications, Inc (*US*)
Betsy Amster Literary Enterprises (*US*)
Marcia Amsterdam Agency (*US*)
Andrew Lownie Literary Agency Ltd (*UK*)
The Axelrod Agency (*US*)
Belcastro Agency (*US*)
The Bent Agency (*US*)
Meredith Bernstein Literary Agency, Inc. (*US*)
David Black Literary Agency (*US*)
Blake Friedmann Literary Agency Ltd (*UK*)
Bleecker Street Associates, Inc. (*US*)
The Blumer Literary Agency, Inc. (*US*)
BookEnds, LLC (*US*)
Brandt & Hochman Literary Agents, Inc. (*US*)
Barbara Braun Associates, Inc. (*US*)
The Bright Literary Academy (*UK*)
Browne & Miller Literary Associates (*US*)
Sheree Bykofsky Associates, Inc. (*US*)
Maria Carvainis Agency, Inc. (*US*)
Castiglia Literary Agency (*US*)

The Characters Talent Agency (*Can*)
The Choate Agency, LLC (*US*)
The Chudney Agency (*US*)
Rosica Colin Ltd (*UK*)
Don Congdon Associates, Inc. (*US*)
Conville & Walsh Ltd (*UK*)
Coombs Moylett & Maclean Literary Agency (*UK*)
Crichton & Associates, Inc. (*US*)
Richard Curtis Associates, Inc. (*US*)
Laura Dail Literary Agency (*US*)
Darhansoff & Verrill Literary Agents (*US*)
The Darley Anderson Agency (*UK*)
Liza Dawson Associates (*US*)
The Jennifer DeChiara Literary Agency (*US*)
Joëlle Delbourgo Associates, Inc. (*US*)
Sandra Dijkstra Literary Agency (*US*)
Jim Donovan Literary (*US*)
The Dravis Agency, Inc. (*US*)
Dunow, Carlson & Lerner Agency (*US*)
Dystel & Goderich Literary Management (*US*)
Edwards Fuglewicz (*UK*)
Judith Ehrlich Literary Management (*US*)
Einstein Literary Management (*US*)
Ethan Ellenberg Literary Agency (*US*)
Elaine P. English, Attorney & Literary Agent (*US*)
Evatopia, Inc. (*US*)
Fairbank Literary Representation (*US*)
The Fielding Agency, LLC (*US*)
Fine Literary (*US*)
Folio Literary Management, LLC (*US*)
Samuel French, Inc. (*US*)
The G Agency, LLC (*US*)
Gelfman Schneider Literary Agents, Inc. (*US*)
Goodman Associates (*US*)
Irene Goodman Literary Agency (*US*)
Sanford J. Greenburger Associates, Inc (*US*)
Laura Gross Literary Agency (*US*)
The Mitchell J. Hamilburg Agency (*US*)
Hannigan Salky Getzler (HSG) Agency (*US*)
Joy Harris Literary Agency, Inc. (*US*)
Antony Harwood Limited (*UK*)
John Hawkins & Associates, Inc. (*US*)
InkWell Management (*US*)
International Transactions, Inc. (*US*)
J de S Associates Inc (*US*)
The Jean V. Naggar Literary Agency (*US*)
The Joan Brandt Agency (*US*)
Virginia Kidd Agency, Inc (*US*)
Harvey Klinger, Inc (*US*)
The Knight Agency (*US*)
Elaine Koster Literary Agency LLC (*US*)
Barbara S. Kouts, Literary Agent (*US*)
Laura Langlie, Literary Agent (*US*)
Larsen Pomada Literary Agents (*US*)
Robert Lecker Agency (*Can*)
Levine Greenberg Literary Agency, Inc. (*US*)
Limelight Management (*UK*)
The Literary Group International (*US*)
Julia Lord Literary Management (*US*)
Donald Maass Literary Agency (*US*)
Gina Maccoby Agency (*US*)

Ethan Ellenberg Literary Agency (*US*)
The Mitchell J. Hamilburg Agency (*US*)
Antony Harwood Limited (*UK*)
J de S Associates Inc (*US*)
Larsen Pomada Literary Agents (*US*)
Levine Greenberg Literary Agency, Inc. (*US*)
Ricia Mainhardt Agency (RMA) (*US*)
Martha Millard Literary Agency (*US*)
Northern Lights Literary Services (*US*)
Venture Literary (*US*)

Nonfiction
A & B Personal Management Ltd (*UK*)
A for Authors (*UK*)
Sheila Ableman Literary Agency (*UK*)
Adler & Robin Books, Inc (*US*)
The Agency (London) Ltd (*UK*)
The Ahearn Agency, Inc (*US*)
Aitken Alexander Associates (*UK*)
Alive Communications, Inc (*US*)
Miriam Altshuler Literary Agency (*US*)
The Ampersand Agency Ltd (*UK*)
Betsy Amster Literary Enterprises (*US*)
Andrew Lownie Literary Agency Ltd (*UK*)
Anthony Sheil in Association with Aitken
Alexander Associates (*UK*)
Arcadia (*US*)
Movable Type Management (*US*)
Audrey A. Wolf Literary Agency (*US*)
The August Agency LLC (*US*)
Author Literary Agents (*UK*)
AVAnti Productions & Management (*UK*)
Ayesha Pande Literary (*US*)
Baldi Agency (*US*)
Barbara Hogenson Agency (*US*)
Bath Literary Agency (*UK*)
Bell Lomax Moreton Agency (*UK*)
Lorella Belli Literary Agency (LBLA) (*UK*)
The Bent Agency (*US*)
Meredith Bernstein Literary Agency, Inc. (*US*)
David Black Literary Agency (*US*)
The Blair Partnership (*UK*)
Blake Friedmann Literary Agency Ltd (*UK*)
Bleecker Street Associates, Inc. (*US*)
The Blumer Literary Agency, Inc. (*US*)
Luigi Bonomi Associates Ltd (*UK*)
The Book Group (*US*)
BookBlast Ltd. (*UK*)
BookEnds, LLC (*US*)
Books & Such Literary Agency (*US*)
Georges Borchardt, Inc. (*US*)
Brandt & Hochman Literary Agents, Inc. (*US*)
Barbara Braun Associates, Inc. (*US*)
Bresnick Weil Literary Agency, LLC (*US*)
Rick Broadhead & Associates Literary Agency
(*Can*)
Jenny Brown Associates (*UK*)
Marie Brown Associates, Inc. (*US*)
Browne & Miller Literary Associates (*US*)
Felicity Bryan (*UK*)
Juliet Burton Literary Agency (*UK*)
Sheree Bykofsky Associates, Inc. (*US*)
CardenWright Literary Agency (*UK*)
Carnicelli Literary Management (*US*)

Maria Carvainis Agency, Inc. (*US*)
Castiglia Literary Agency (*US*)
Chalberg & Sussman (*US*)
Jane Chelius Literary Agency, Inc. (*US*)
Elyse Cheney Literary Associates, LLC (*US*)
Linda Chester & Associates (*US*)
The Choate Agency, LLC (*US*)
Teresa Chris Literary Agency Ltd (*UK*)
The Christopher Little Literary Agency (*UK*)
Clare Hulton Literary Agency (*UK*)
Mary Clemmey Literary Agency (*UK*)
Jonathan Clowes Ltd (*UK*)
Rosica Colin Ltd (*UK*)
Frances Collin Literary Agent (*US*)
Don Congdon Associates, Inc. (*US*)
Connor Literary Agency (*US*)
Conville & Walsh Ltd (*UK*)
Jane Conway-Gordon Ltd (*UK*)
The Cooke Agency (*Can*)
Coombs Moylett & Maclean Literary Agency
(*UK*)
The Doe Coover Agency (*US*)
Crawford Literary Agency (*US*)
The Creative Rights Agency (*UK*)
Creative Authors Ltd (*UK*)
Rupert Crew Ltd (*UK*)
Crichton & Associates, Inc. (*US*)
The Croce Agency (*US*)
The Culinary Entertainment Agency (CEA)
(*US*)
Curtis Brown Ltd (*US*)
Curtis Brown Group Ltd (*UK*)
Richard Curtis Associates, Inc. (*US*)
Laura Dail Literary Agency (*US*)
Darhansoff & Verrill Literary Agents (*US*)
The Darley Anderson Agency (*UK*)
David Luxton Associates (*UK*)
Caroline Davidson Literary Agency (*UK*)
Liza Dawson Associates (*US*)
Deal Points Ent. (*US*)
The Jennifer DeChiara Literary Agency (*US*)
DeFiore and Company (*US*)
Joëlle Delbourgo Associates, Inc. (*US*)
DHH Literary Agency Ltd (*UK*)
Diamond Kahn and Woods (DKW) Literary
Agency Ltd (*UK*)
Diane Banks Associates Literary Agency (*UK*)
Sandra Dijkstra Literary Agency (*US*)
Donadio & Olson, Inc. (*US*)
Janis A. Donnaud & Associates, Inc. (*US*)
Jim Donovan Literary (*US*)
Doyen Literary Services, Inc. (*US*)
Dunham Literary, Inc. (*US*)
Dunow, Carlson & Lerner Agency (*US*)
Dystel & Goderich Literary Management (*US*)
Toby Eady Associates Ltd (*UK*)
East West Literary Agency LLC (*US*)
Ebeling & Associates (*US*)
Eddison Pearson Ltd (*UK*)
Anne Edelstein Literary Agency (*US*)
Edwards Fuglewicz (*UK*)
Judith Ehrlich Literary Management (*US*)
Einstein Literary Management (*US*)

The Martell Agency (*US*)
Martin Literary Management (*US*)
MBA Literary Agents Ltd (*UK*)
Duncan McAra (*UK*)
Anne McDermid & Associates Ltd (*Can*)
Mendel Media Group, LLC (*US*)
Martha Millard Literary Agency (*US*)
The Miller Agency (*US*)
Patricia Moosbrugger Literary Agency (*US*)
Howard Morhaim Literary Agency (*US*)
Mulcahy Associates (*UK*)
Nappaland Literary Agency (*US*)
New Leaf Literary & Media, Inc. (*US*)
Niad Management (*US*)
Northern Lights Literary Services (*US*)
Andrew Nurnberg Associates, Ltd (*UK*)
Harold Ober Associates (*US*)
Fifi Oscard Agency, Inc. (*US*)
Deborah Owen Ltd (*UK*)
The Park Literary Group LLC (*US*)
Kathi J. Paton Literary Agency (*US*)
Pavilion Literary Management (*US*)
John Pawsey (*UK*)
Maggie Pearlstine Associates Ltd (*UK*)
Jonathan Pegg Literary Agency (*UK*)
Pinder Lane & Garon-Brooke Associates Ltd (*US*)
Shelley Power Literary Agency Ltd (*UK*)
Rebecca Pratt Literary Group (*US*)
Linn Prentis Literary (*US*)
Aaron M. Priest Literary Agency (*US*)
Prospect Agency (*US*)
Queen Literary Agency, Inc. (*US*)
Lynne Rabinoff Agency (*US*)
Raines & Raines (*US*)
Rebecca Friedman Literary Agency (*US*)
Redhammer (*UK*)
Regina Ryan Publishing Enterprises (*US*)
Renee Zuckerbrot Literary Agency (*US*)
The Amy Rennert Agency, Inc. (*US*)
The Lisa Richards Agency (*Ire*)
Richford Becklow Literary Agency (*UK*)
Riverside Literary Agency (*US*)
B.J. Robbins Literary Agency (*US*)
Robert Dudley Agency (*UK*)
Robin Jones Literary Agency (*UK*)
Rocking Chair Books (*UK*)
Rita Rosenkranz Literary Agency (*US*)
Ross Yoon Agency (*US*)
Andy Ross Agency (*US*)
The Damaris Rowland Agency (*US*)
The Rudy Agency (*US*)
Uli Rushby-Smith Literary Agency (*UK*)
Marly Rusoff & Associates, Inc. (*US*)
Salkind Literary Agency (*US*)
Victoria Sanders & Associates LLC (*US*)
The Sayle Literary Agency (*UK*)
Susan Schulman, A Literary Agency (*US*)
The Science Factory (*UK*)
Secret Agent Man (*US*)
Lynn Seligman, Literary Agent (*US*)
Seventh Avenue Literary Agency (*Can*)
The Seymour Agency (*US*)

Denise Shannon Literary Agency, Inc. (*US*)
Sheil Land Associates Ltd (*UK*)
Caroline Sheldon Literary Agency (*UK*)
Wendy Sherman Associates, Inc. (*US*)
Rosalie Siegel, International Literary Agency, Inc. (*US*)
Dorie Simmonds Agency (*UK*)
Jeffrey Simmons (*UK*)
Sinclair-Stevenson (*UK*)
SLW Literary Agency (*US*)
Robert Smith Literary Agency Ltd (*UK*)
Solow Literary Enterprises, Inc. (*US*)
Sophie Hicks Agency (*UK*)
Spectrum Literary Agency (*US*)
Spencerhill Associates (*US*)
The Spieler Agency (*US*)
Nancy Stauffer Associates (*US*)
Elaine Steel (*UK*)
Abner Stein (*UK*)
Sternig & Byrne Literary Agency (*US*)
Stonesong (*US*)
The Strothman Agency (*US*)
Stuart Krichevsky Literary Agency, Inc. (*US*)
The Stuart Agency (*US*)
Sarah Such Literary Agency (*UK*)
Susanna Lea Associates (*US*)
Susanna Lea Associates (UK) (*UK*)
The Susijn Agency (*UK*)
The Swetky Agency and Associates (*US*)
SYLA – Susan Yearwood Literary Agency (*UK*)
Talcott Notch Literary (*US*)
Tessler Literary Agency (*US*)
Thompson Literary Agency (*US*)
Toby Mundy Associates Ltd (*UK*)
Tracy Brown Literary Agency (*US*)
Transatlantic Literary Agency, Inc. (*Can*)
TriadaUS Literary Agency, Inc. (*US*)
Jane Turnbull (*UK*)
2M Literary Agency Ltd (*US*)
United Talent Agency (*US*)
United Agents (*UK*)
Venture Literary (*US*)
Ed Victor Ltd (*UK*)
Wade & Co Literary Agency (*UK*)
Waterside Productions, Inc (*US*)
Watson, Little Ltd (*UK*)
The Weingel-Fidel Agency (*US*)
Wernick & Pratt Agency (*US*)
Whispering Buffalo Literary Agency Ltd (*UK*)
Eve White: Literary Agent (*UK*)
Dinah Wiener Ltd (*UK*)
William Morris Endeavor (WME) London (*UK*)
Wm Clark Associates (*US*)
Wolfson Literary Agency (*US*)
Writers House UK (*UK*)
The Writers' Practice (*UK*)
Writers' Representatives, LLC (*US*)
The Wylie Agency (UK) Ltd (*UK*)
The Zack Company, Inc (*US*)
Karen Gantz Zahler Literary Agency (*US*)
Helen Zimmermann Literary Agency (*US*)

Rita Rosenkranz Literary Agency (*US*)
The Rudy Agency (*US*)
Salkind Literary Agency (*US*)
Victoria Sanders & Associates LLC (*US*)
Susan Schulman, A Literary Agency (*US*)
The Science Factory (*UK*)
Lynn Seligman, Literary Agent (*US*)
Denise Shannon Literary Agency, Inc. (*US*)
Sheil Land Associates Ltd (*UK*)
Jeffrey Simmons (*UK*)
The Spieler Agency (*US*)
Stuart Krichevsky Literary Agency, Inc. (*US*)
The Swetky Agency and Associates (*US*)
Thompson Literary Agency (*US*)
Toby Mundy Associates Ltd (*UK*)
Transatlantic Literary Agency, Inc. (*Can*)
TriadaUS Literary Agency, Inc. (*US*)
2M Literary Agency Ltd (*US*)
Venture Literary (*US*)
Ed Victor Ltd (*UK*)
Whispering Buffalo Literary Agency Ltd (*UK*)
Writers' Representatives, LLC (*US*)
The Zack Company, Inc (*US*)
Karen Gantz Zahler Literary Agency (*US*)
Psychology
Abbot Management (*US*)
Miriam Altshuler Literary Agency (*US*)
Betsy Amster Literary Enterprises (*US*)
Andrew Lownie Literary Agency Ltd (*UK*)
Arcadia (*US*)
David Black Literary Agency (*US*)
Blake Friedmann Literary Agency Ltd (*UK*)
Bleecker Street Associates, Inc. (*US*)
The Blumer Literary Agency, Inc. (*US*)
The Book Group (*US*)
Barbara Braun Associates, Inc. (*US*)
Bresnick Weil Literary Agency, LLC (*US*)
Browne & Miller Literary Associates (*US*)
Sheree Bykofsky Associates, Inc. (*US*)
Carnicelli Literary Management (*US*)
Maria Carvainis Agency, Inc. (*US*)
Chalberg & Sussman (*US*)
Rosica Colin Ltd (*UK*)
Don Congdon Associates, Inc. (*US*)
Conville & Walsh Ltd (*UK*)
The Doe Coover Agency (*US*)
Crawford Literary Agency (*US*)
The Darley Anderson Agency (*UK*)
Caroline Davidson Literary Agency (*UK*)
Liza Dawson Associates (*US*)
DeFiore and Company (*US*)
Joëlle Delbourgo Associates, Inc. (*US*)
Diane Banks Associates Literary Agency (*UK*)
Doyen Literary Services, Inc. (*US*)
Dystel & Goderich Literary Management (*US*)
Anne Edelstein Literary Agency (*US*)
Judith Ehrlich Literary Management (*US*)
Ethan Ellenberg Literary Agency (*US*)
Felicia Eth Literary Representation (*US*)
The Fielding Agency, LLC (*US*)
Diana Finch Literary Agency (*US*)
Fine Literary (*US*)
Folio Literary Management, LLC (*US*)

Fox & Howard Literary Agency (*UK*)
Jeanne Fredericks Literary Agency, Inc. (*US*)
Grace Freedson's Publishing Network (*US*)
Sarah Jane Freymann Literary Agency (*US*)
Fredrica S. Friedman and Co. Inc. (*US*)
Furniss Lawton (*UK*)
Goodman Associates (*US*)
Kathryn Green Literary Agency, LLC (*US*)
Sanford J. Greenburger Associates, Inc (*US*)
Laura Gross Literary Agency (*US*)
The Mitchell J. Hamilburg Agency (*US*)
Hannigan Salky Getzler (HSG) Agency (*US*)
Antony Harwood Limited (*UK*)
John Hawkins & Associates, Inc. (*US*)
A M Heath & Company Limited, Author's
Agents (*UK*)
The Jeff Herman Agency, LLC (*US*)
Hornfischer Literary Management, L.P. (*US*)
Andrea Hurst Literary Management (*US*)
InkWell Management (*US*)
The Jean V. Naggar Literary Agency (*US*)
Jill Grinberg Literary Management LLC (*US*)
Johnson & Alcock (*UK*)
Harvey Klinger, Inc (*US*)
Kneerim & Williams (*US*)
The Knight Agency (*US*)
Linda Konner Literary Agency (*US*)
Elaine Koster Literary Agency LLC (*US*)
Barbara S. Kouts, Literary Agent (*US*)
Bert P. Krages (*US*)
Edite Kroll Literary Agency, Inc. (*US*)
Kuhn Projects (*US*)
The LA Literary Agency (*US*)
Laura Langlie, Literary Agent (*US*)
Larsen Pomada Literary Agents (*US*)
Levine Greenberg Literary Agency, Inc. (*US*)
Lippincott Massie McQuilkin (*US*)
The Literary Group International (*US*)
Lowenstein Associates, Inc. (*US*)
Kirsten Manges Literary Agency, LLC (*US*)
Carol Mann Agency (*US*)
Manus & Associates Literary Agency, Inc.
(*US*)
The Martell Agency (*US*)
Martha Millard Literary Agency (*US*)
The Miller Agency (*US*)
Northern Lights Literary Services (*US*)
Jonathan Pegg Literary Agency (*UK*)
Queen Literary Agency, Inc. (*US*)
Lynne Rabinoff Agency (*US*)
Raines & Raines (*US*)
Rees Literary Agency (*US*)
Regina Ryan Publishing Enterprises (*US*)
B.J. Robbins Literary Agency (*US*)
Rita Rosenkranz Literary Agency (*US*)
Ross Yoon Agency (*US*)
Marly Rusoff & Associates, Inc. (*US*)
Salkind Literary Agency (*US*)
Victoria Sanders & Associates LLC (*US*)
Susan Schulman, A Literary Agency (*US*)
Lynn Seligman, Literary Agent (*US*)
Sheil Land Associates Ltd (*UK*)
Wendy Sherman Associates, Inc. (*US*)

Rosalie Siegel, International Literary Agency, Inc. (*US*)
Jeffrey Simmons (*UK*)
Solow Literary Enterprises, Inc. (*US*)
Stonesong (*US*)
The Stuart Agency (*US*)
The Swetky Agency and Associates (*US*)
SYLA – Susan Yearwood Literary Agency (*UK*)
Tessler Literary Agency (*US*)
Tracy Brown Literary Agency (*US*)
TriadaUS Literary Agency, Inc. (*US*)
2M Literary Agency Ltd (*US*)
Venture Literary (*US*)
Watson, Little Ltd (*UK*)
The Weingel-Fidel Agency (*US*)
Writers House UK (*UK*)
Karen Gantz Zahler Literary Agency (*US*)

Radio
Abbot Management (*US*)
The Agency (London) Ltd (*UK*)
Berlin Associates (*UK*)
Blake Friedmann Literary Agency Ltd (*UK*)
Alan Brodie Representation Ltd (*UK*)
Mary Clemmey Literary Agency (*UK*)
Jonathan Clowes Ltd (*UK*)
Rosica Colin Ltd (*UK*)
Curtis Brown Group Ltd (*UK*)
The Darley Anderson Agency (*UK*)
Felix de Wolfe (*UK*)
Film Rights Ltd in association with Laurence Fitch Ltd (*UK*)
Jill Foster Ltd (JFL) (*UK*)
Georgina Capel Associates Ltd (*UK*)
Antony Harwood Limited (*UK*)
Valerie Hoskins Associates (*UK*)
Independent Talent Group Ltd (*UK*)
Marjacq Scripts Ltd (*UK*)
MBA Literary Agents Ltd (*UK*)
PBJ and JBJ Management (*UK*)
Rochelle Stevens & Co. (*UK*)
Sayle Screen Ltd (*UK*)
Sheil Land Associates Ltd (*UK*)
Elaine Steel (*UK*)
The Tennyson Agency (*UK*)
United Agents (*UK*)
Venture Literary (*US*)

Reference
Adler & Robin Books, Inc (*US*)
Baldi Agency (*US*)
BookEnds, LLC (*US*)
Sheree Bykofsky Associates, Inc. (*US*)
The Doe Coover Agency (*US*)
David Luxton Associates (*UK*)
Caroline Davidson Literary Agency (*UK*)
Joëlle Delbourgo Associates, Inc. (*US*)
Jim Donovan Literary (*US*)
Fairbank Literary Representation (*US*)
Folio Literary Management, LLC (*US*)
Fox & Howard Literary Agency (*UK*)
Jeanne Fredericks Literary Agency, Inc. (*US*)
Fresh Books Literary Agency (*US*)
Graham Maw Christie Literary Agency (*UK*)

Sanford J. Greenburger Associates, Inc (*US*)
The Jeff Herman Agency, LLC (*US*)
Kate Hordern Literary Agency (*UK*)
Frances Kelly (*UK*)
Linda Konner Literary Agency (*US*)
Julia Lord Literary Management (*US*)
March Tenth, Inc. (*US*)
Regina Ryan Publishing Enterprises (*US*)
Writers' Representatives, LLC (*US*)
The Zack Company, Inc (*US*)

Religious
Abbot Management (*US*)
Alive Communications, Inc (*US*)
Bleecker Street Associates, Inc. (*US*)
The Blumer Literary Agency, Inc. (*US*)
Books & Such Literary Agency (*US*)
Marie Brown Associates, Inc. (*US*)
Browne & Miller Literary Associates (*US*)
Kelvin C. Bulger and Associates (*US*)
Rosica Colin Ltd (*UK*)
Crichton & Associates, Inc. (*US*)
The Darley Anderson Agency (*UK*)
Liza Dawson Associates (*US*)
Sandra Dijkstra Literary Agency (*US*)
Dystel & Goderich Literary Management (*US*)
Anne Edelstein Literary Agency (*US*)
Folio Literary Management, LLC (*US*)
Grace Freedson's Publishing Network (*US*)
The Mitchell J. Hamilburg Agency (*US*)
Antony Harwood Limited (*UK*)
Hidden Value Group (*US*)
Hornfischer Literary Management, L.P. (*US*)
Andrea Hurst Literary Management (*US*)
Kneerim & Williams (*US*)
The Knight Agency (*US*)
Edite Kroll Literary Agency, Inc. (*US*)
Larsen Pomada Literary Agents (*US*)
The Steve Laube Agency (*US*)
Levine Greenberg Literary Agency, Inc. (*US*)
Literary & Creative Artists Inc. (*US*)
Literary Management Group, Inc. (*US*)
The Literary Group International (*US*)
MacGregor Literary (*US*)
Carol Mann Agency (*US*)
Mendel Media Group, LLC (*US*)
Nappaland Literary Agency (*US*)
Fifi Oscard Agency, Inc. (*US*)
Kathi J. Paton Literary Agency (*US*)
Lynne Rabinoff Agency (*US*)
Rita Rosenkranz Literary Agency (*US*)
Andy Ross Agency (*US*)
Salkind Literary Agency (*US*)
Susan Schulman, A Literary Agency (*US*)
Secret Agent Man (*US*)
The Seymour Agency (*US*)
The Stuart Agency (*US*)
The Swetky Agency and Associates (*US*)
Talent Source (*US*)
Venture Literary (*US*)
Wm Clark Associates (*US*)
The Zack Company, Inc (*US*)
Karen Gantz Zahler Literary Agency (*US*)

Romance
Abbot Management (*US*)
Abrams Artists Agency (*US*)
The Ahearn Agency, Inc (*US*)
Marcia Amsterdam Agency (*US*)
Andrew Lownie Literary Agency Ltd (*UK*)
The Axelrod Agency (*US*)
Belcastro Agency (*US*)
The Bent Agency (*US*)
Meredith Bernstein Literary Agency, Inc. (*US*)
David Black Literary Agency (*US*)
Bleecker Street Associates, Inc. (*US*)
Luigi Bonomi Associates Ltd (*UK*)
BookEnds, LLC (*US*)
Books & Such Literary Agency (*US*)
Jenny Brown Associates (*UK*)
The Characters Talent Agency (*Can*)
Elyse Cheney Literary Associates, LLC (*US*)
Rosica Colin Ltd (*UK*)
The Cooke Agency (*Can*)
Crawford Literary Agency (*US*)
Crichton & Associates, Inc. (*US*)
Richard Curtis Associates, Inc. (*US*)
The Darley Anderson Agency (*UK*)
Liza Dawson Associates (*US*)
DeFiore and Company (*US*)
Sandra Dijkstra Literary Agency (*US*)
Dorian Literary Agency (DLA) (*UK*)
The Dravis Agency, Inc. (*US*)
Dystel & Goderich Literary Management (*US*)
Edwards Fuglewicz (*UK*)
Judith Ehrlich Literary Management (*US*)
Einstein Literary Management (*US*)
Ethan Ellenberg Literary Agency (*US*)
Ann Elmo Agency, Inc. (*US*)
Elaine P. English, Attorney & Literary Agent (*US*)
Evatopia, Inc. (*US*)
The Fielding Agency, LLC (*US*)
Fine Literary (*US*)
Folio Literary Management, LLC (*US*)
Irene Goodman Literary Agency (*US*)
Kathryn Green Literary Agency, LLC (*US*)
Sanford J. Greenburger Associates, Inc (*US*)
Greene & Heaton Ltd (*UK*)
Greyhaus Literary Agency (*US*)
The Mitchell J. Hamilburg Agency (*US*)
Antony Harwood Limited (*UK*)
Hopkins Literary Associates (*US*)
Andrea Hurst Literary Management (*US*)
The Jean V. Naggar Literary Agency (*US*)
Jill Grinberg Literary Management LLC (*US*)
Keane Kataria Literary Agency (*UK*)
Harvey Klinger, Inc (*US*)
The Knight Agency (*US*)
Larsen Pomada Literary Agents (*US*)
Levine Greenberg Literary Agency, Inc. (*US*)
The Literary Group International (*US*)
Donald Maass Literary Agency (*US*)
MacGregor Literary (*US*)
Ricia Mainhardt Agency (RMA) (*US*)
Manus & Associates Literary Agency, Inc. (*US*)

Martha Millard Literary Agency (*US*)
Howard Morhaim Literary Agency (*US*)
Nelson Literary Agency, LLC (*US*)
New Leaf Literary & Media, Inc. (*US*)
Niad Management (*US*)
Northern Lights Literary Services (*US*)
Pinder Lane & Garon-Brooke Associates Ltd (*US*)
Prospect Agency (*US*)
Rebecca Friedman Literary Agency (*US*)
Rees Literary Agency (*US*)
Richford Becklow Literary Agency (*UK*)
Rocking Chair Books (*UK*)
Lynn Seligman, Literary Agent (*US*)
The Seymour Agency (*US*)
Sheil Land Associates Ltd (*UK*)
Spectrum Literary Agency (*US*)
Spencerhill Associates (*US*)
The Swetky Agency and Associates (*US*)
TriadaUS Literary Agency, Inc. (*US*)
Whispering Buffalo Literary Agency Ltd (*UK*)
Wolfson Literary Agency (*US*)
The Zack Company, Inc (*US*)

Science
Abbot Management (*US*)
Sheila Ableman Literary Agency (*UK*)
Marcia Amsterdam Agency (*US*)
Andrew Lownie Literary Agency Ltd (*UK*)
Arcadia (*US*)
Baldi Agency (*US*)
The Bent Agency (*US*)
David Black Literary Agency (*US*)
Blake Friedmann Literary Agency Ltd (*UK*)
Bleecker Street Associates, Inc. (*US*)
Luigi Bonomi Associates Ltd (*UK*)
Brandt & Hochman Literary Agents, Inc. (*US*)
Bresnick Weil Literary Agency, LLC (*US*)
Rick Broadhead & Associates Literary Agency (*Can*)
Jenny Brown Associates (*UK*)
Browne & Miller Literary Associates (*US*)
Felicity Bryan (*UK*)
Carnicelli Literary Management (*US*)
Maria Carvainis Agency, Inc. (*US*)
Castiglia Literary Agency (*US*)
Chalberg & Sussman (*US*)
The Characters Talent Agency (*Can*)
Elyse Cheney Literary Associates, LLC (*US*)
The Choate Agency, LLC (*US*)
Rosica Colin Ltd (*UK*)
Don Congdon Associates, Inc. (*US*)
Conville & Walsh Ltd (*UK*)
The Cooke Agency (*Can*)
The Doe Coover Agency (*US*)
Curtis Brown Group Ltd (*UK*)
Richard Curtis Associates, Inc. (*US*)
Laura Dail Literary Agency (*US*)
The Darley Anderson Agency (*UK*)
Caroline Davidson Literary Agency (*UK*)
Liza Dawson Associates (*US*)
The Jennifer DeChiara Literary Agency (*US*)
DeFiore and Company (*US*)
Joëlle Delbourgo Associates, Inc. (*US*)

Diane Banks Associates Literary Agency (*UK*)
Sandra Dijkstra Literary Agency (*US*)
Donadio & Olson, Inc. (*US*)
Janis A. Donnaud & Associates, Inc. (*US*)
Jim Donovan Literary (*US*)
Doyen Literary Services, Inc. (*US*)
Dunham Literary, Inc. (*US*)
Dunow, Carlson & Lerner Agency (*US*)
Dystel & Goderich Literary Management (*US*)
Judith Ehrlich Literary Management (*US*)
Ethan Ellenberg Literary Agency (*US*)
Ann Elmo Agency, Inc. (*US*)
Felicia Eth Literary Representation (*US*)
Mary Evans, Inc. (*US*)
Fairbank Literary Representation (*US*)
The Fielding Agency, LLC (*US*)
Diana Finch Literary Agency (*US*)
Fine Literary (*US*)
Fletcher & Company (*US*)
Folio Literary Management, LLC (*US*)
Jeanne Fredericks Literary Agency, Inc. (*US*)
Grace Freedson's Publishing Network (*US*)
Fresh Books Literary Agency (*US*)
Sarah Jane Freymann Literary Agency (*US*)
Furniss Lawton (*UK*)
Gelfman Schneider Literary Agents, Inc. (*US*)
The Gernert Company (*US*)
Frances Goldin Literary Agency, Inc. (*US*)
Goodman Associates (*US*)
Irene Goodman Literary Agency (*US*)
Graham Maw Christie Literary Agency (*UK*)
Sanford J. Greenburger Associates, Inc (*US*)
Greene & Heaton Ltd (*UK*)
The Mitchell J. Hamilburg Agency (*US*)
Hannigan Salky Getzler (HSG) Agency (*US*)
Hardman & Swainson (*UK*)
Antony Harwood Limited (*UK*)
John Hawkins & Associates, Inc. (*US*)
Rupert Heath Literary Agency (*UK*)
Hill Nadell Literary Agency (*US*)
Hornfischer Literary Management, L.P. (*US*)
Andrea Hurst Literary Management (*US*)
Jabberwocky Literary Agency (*US*)
The Jean V. Naggar Literary Agency (*US*)
Jill Grinberg Literary Management LLC (*US*)
Johnson & Alcock (*UK*)
Ki Agency Ltd (*UK*)
Harvey Klinger, Inc (*US*)
Kneerim & Williams (*US*)
Linda Konner Literary Agency (*US*)
Bert P. Krages (*US*)
Kuhn Projects (*US*)
The LA Literary Agency (*US*)
Larsen Pomada Literary Agents (*US*)
LaunchBooks Literary Agency (*US*)
Robert Lecker Agency (*Can*)
Levine Greenberg Literary Agency, Inc. (*US*)
Limelight Management (*UK*)
Lippincott Massie McQuilkin (*US*)
The Literary Group International (*US*)
Sterling Lord Literistic, Inc. (*US*)
Julia Lord Literary Management (*US*)
Lowenstein Associates, Inc. (*US*)

The Jennifer Lyons Literary Agency, LLC (*US*)
Kirsten Manges Literary Agency, LLC (*US*)
Manus & Associates Literary Agency, Inc. (*US*)
Anne McDermid & Associates Ltd (*Can*)
Mendel Media Group, LLC (*US*)
Fifi Oscard Agency, Inc. (*US*)
The Park Literary Group LLC (*US*)
Kathi J. Paton Literary Agency (*US*)
Pavilion Literary Management (*US*)
Jonathan Pegg Literary Agency (*UK*)
Prospect Agency (*US*)
Queen Literary Agency, Inc. (*US*)
Lynne Rabinoff Agency (*US*)
Rees Literary Agency (*US*)
Regina Ryan Publishing Enterprises (*US*)
Renee Zuckerbrot Literary Agency (*US*)
Rita Rosenkranz Literary Agency (*US*)
Ross Yoon Agency (*US*)
Andy Ross Agency (*US*)
The Rudy Agency (*US*)
Salkind Literary Agency (*US*)
The Sayle Literary Agency (*UK*)
Susan Schulman, A Literary Agency (*US*)
The Science Factory (*UK*)
Lynn Seligman, Literary Agent (*US*)
Sheil Land Associates Ltd (*UK*)
Rosalie Siegel, International Literary Agency, Inc. (*US*)
Solow Literary Enterprises, Inc. (*US*)
The Spieler Agency (*US*)
Stonesong (*US*)
The Strothman Agency (*US*)
Stuart Krichevsky Literary Agency, Inc. (*US*)
The Stuart Agency (*US*)
The Swetky Agency and Associates (*US*)
Talcott Notch Literary (*US*)
Tessler Literary Agency (*US*)
Thompson Literary Agency (*US*)
Toby Mundy Associates Ltd (*UK*)
TriadaUS Literary Agency, Inc. (*US*)
2M Literary Agency Ltd (*US*)
United Talent Agency (*US*)
Venture Literary (*US*)
Watson, Little Ltd (*UK*)
The Weingel-Fidel Agency (*US*)
Dinah Wiener Ltd (*UK*)
Wm Clark Associates (*US*)
Writers House UK (*UK*)
Writers' Representatives, LLC (*US*)
The Zack Company, Inc (*US*)
Helen Zimmermann Literary Agency (*US*)
Zoë Pagnamenta Agency, LLC (*US*)

Sci-Fi
Abbot Management (*US*)
The Ampersand Agency Ltd (*UK*)
Andrew Lownie Literary Agency Ltd (*UK*)
Anubis Literary Agency (*UK*)
Belcastro Agency (*US*)
The Bent Agency (*US*)
Luigi Bonomi Associates Ltd (*UK*)
BookEnds, LLC (*US*)
The Bright Literary Academy (*UK*)

Castiglia Literary Agency (*US*)
Frances Collin Literary Agent (*US*)
The Cooke Agency (*Can*)
Richard Curtis Associates, Inc. (*US*)
Laura Dail Literary Agency (*US*)
The Darley Anderson Agency (*UK*)
Liza Dawson Associates (*US*)
Joëlle Delbourgo Associates, Inc. (*US*)
DHH Literary Agency Ltd (*UK*)
Diamond Kahn and Woods (DKW) Literary
Agency Ltd (*UK*)
Sandra Dijkstra Literary Agency (*US*)
Dorian Literary Agency (DLA) (*UK*)
The Dravis Agency, Inc. (*US*)
Dunham Literary, Inc. (*US*)
Dystel & Goderich Literary Management (*US*)
Ethan Ellenberg Literary Agency (*US*)
Folio Literary Management, LLC (*US*)
The Gernert Company (*US*)
Barry Goldblatt Literary Agency, Inc. (*US*)
Sanford J. Greenburger Associates, Inc (*US*)
Greene & Heaton Ltd (*UK*)
The Mitchell J. Hamilburg Agency (*US*)
Antony Harwood Limited (*UK*)
John Hawkins & Associates, Inc. (*US*)
Rupert Heath Literary Agency (*UK*)
Andrea Hurst Literary Management (*US*)
Jabberwocky Literary Agency (*US*)
Jill Grinberg Literary Management LLC (*US*)
Johnson & Alcock (*UK*)
Virginia Kidd Agency, Inc (*US*)
Harvey Klinger, Inc (*US*)
The Knight Agency (*US*)
LaunchBooks Literary Agency (*US*)
Lowenstein Associates, Inc. (*US*)
Donald Maass Literary Agency (*US*)
Ricia Mainhardt Agency (RMA) (*US*)
Marjacq Scripts Ltd (*UK*)
Anne McDermid & Associates Ltd (*Can*)
Martha Millard Literary Agency (*US*)
Howard Morhaim Literary Agency (*US*)
Nelson Literary Agency, LLC (*US*)
New Leaf Literary & Media, Inc. (*US*)
Pinder Lane & Garon-Brooke Associates Ltd
(*US*)
Rebecca Pratt Literary Group (*US*)
Linn Prentis Literary (*US*)
Prospect Agency (*US*)
Raines & Raines (*US*)
Rebecca Friedman Literary Agency (*US*)
Richford Becklow Literary Agency (*UK*)
Salkind Literary Agency (*US*)
Scribe Agency LLC (*US*)
Lynn Seligman, Literary Agent (*US*)
The Seymour Agency (*US*)
Sheil Land Associates Ltd (*UK*)
Spectrum Literary Agency (*US*)
Steph Roundsmith Agent and Editor (*UK*)
Sternig & Byrne Literary Agency (*US*)
Stuart Krichevsky Literary Agency, Inc. (*US*)
The Swetky Agency and Associates (*US*)
Talcott Notch Literary (*US*)
TriadaUS Literary Agency, Inc. (*US*)

United Talent Agency (*US*)
Whispering Buffalo Literary Agency Ltd (*UK*)
Writers House UK (*UK*)
The Zack Company, Inc (*US*)
Zeno Agency Ltd (*UK*)
Scripts
A & B Personal Management Ltd (*UK*)
Abbot Management (*US*)
Above the Line Agency (*US*)
Abrams Artists Agency (*US*)
Bret Adams Ltd (*US*)
The Agency (London) Ltd (*UK*)
Marcia Amsterdam Agency (*US*)
Author Literary Agents (*UK*)
AVAnti Productions & Management (*UK*)
Barbara Hogenson Agency (*US*)
Berlin Associates (*UK*)
Blake Friedmann Literary Agency Ltd (*UK*)
Alan Brodie Representation Ltd (*UK*)
Kelvin C. Bulger and Associates (*US*)
CardenWright Literary Agency (*UK*)
The Characters Talent Agency (*Can*)
Mary Clemmey Literary Agency (*UK*)
Jonathan Clowes Ltd (*UK*)
Rosica Colin Ltd (*UK*)
Curtis Brown Group Ltd (*UK*)
Deal Points Ent. (*US*)
Felix de Wolfe (*UK*)
DHH Literary Agency Ltd (*UK*)
The Dravis Agency, Inc. (*US*)
Evatopia, Inc. (*US*)
Film Rights Ltd in association with Laurence
Fitch Ltd (*UK*)
Jill Foster Ltd (JFL) (*UK*)
Samuel French, Inc. (*US*)
Eric Glass Ltd (*UK*)
David Higham Associates Ltd (*UK*)
Valerie Hoskins Associates (*UK*)
Independent Talent Group Ltd (*UK*)
Janet Fillingham Associates (*UK*)
Michelle Kass Associates (*UK*)
Ken Sherman & Associates (*US*)
Ki Agency Ltd (*UK*)
Knight Hall Agency (*UK*)
Macnaughton Lord Representation (*UK*)
Marjacq Scripts Ltd (*UK*)
MBA Literary Agents Ltd (*UK*)
Niad Management (*US*)
Fifi Oscard Agency, Inc. (*US*)
Paradigm Talent and Literary Agency (*US*)
PBJ and JBJ Management (*UK*)
Peregrine Whittlesey Agency (*US*)
The Lisa Richards Agency (*Ire*)
Rochelle Stevens & Co. (*UK*)
Roger Hancock Ltd (*UK*)
Sayle Screen Ltd (*UK*)
Susan Schulman, A Literary Agency (*US*)
Linda Seifert Management (*UK*)
Sheil Land Associates Ltd (*UK*)
Elaine Steel (*UK*)
Stone Manners Salners Agency (*US*)
The Swetky Agency and Associates (*US*)
Talent Source (*US*)

The Tennyson Agency (*UK*)
United Agents (*UK*)
Cecily Ware Literary Agents (*UK*)
Self-Help
Abbot Management (*US*)
Adler & Robin Books, Inc (*US*)
Alive Communications, Inc (*US*)
Miriam Altshuler Literary Agency (*US*)
Betsy Amster Literary Enterprises (*US*)
Andrew Lownie Literary Agency Ltd (*UK*)
Arcadia (*US*)
Audrey A. Wolf Literary Agency (*US*)
David Black Literary Agency (*US*)
Bleecker Street Associates, Inc. (*US*)
The Blumer Literary Agency, Inc. (*US*)
The Bright Literary Academy (*UK*)
Rick Broadhead & Associates Literary Agency (*Can*)
Browne & Miller Literary Associates (*US*)
Sheree Bykofsky Associates, Inc. (*US*)
Chalberg & Sussman (*US*)
Clare Hulton Literary Agency (*UK*)
Connor Literary Agency (*US*)
Crawford Literary Agency (*US*)
The Darley Anderson Agency (*UK*)
Liza Dawson Associates (*US*)
The Jennifer DeChiara Literary Agency (*US*)
Diane Banks Associates Literary Agency (*UK*)
Sandra Dijkstra Literary Agency (*US*)
Doyen Literary Services, Inc. (*US*)
Ebeling & Associates (*US*)
Judith Ehrlich Literary Management (*US*)
The Fielding Agency, LLC (*US*)
Diana Finch Literary Agency (*US*)
Fine Literary (*US*)
Folio Literary Management, LLC (*US*)
Fox & Howard Literary Agency (*UK*)
Jeanne Fredericks Literary Agency, Inc. (*US*)
Grace Freedson's Publishing Network (*US*)
Fresh Books Literary Agency (*US*)
Sarah Jane Freymann Literary Agency (*US*)
Fredrica S. Friedman and Co. Inc. (*US*)
Graham Maw Christie Literary Agency (*UK*)
Kathryn Green Literary Agency, LLC (*US*)
Sanford J. Greenburger Associates, Inc (*US*)
The Mitchell J. Hamilburg Agency (*US*)
Antony Harwood Limited (*UK*)
The Jeff Herman Agency, LLC (*US*)
Hidden Value Group (*US*)
Hornfischer Literary Management, L.P. (*US*)
Andrea Hurst Literary Management (*US*)
InkWell Management (*US*)
J de S Associates Inc (*US*)
Johnson & Alcock (*UK*)
Frances Kelly (*UK*)
Ki Agency Ltd (*UK*)
Harvey Klinger, Inc (*US*)
The Knight Agency (*US*)
Linda Konner Literary Agency (*US*)
Elaine Koster Literary Agency LLC (*US*)
Edite Kroll Literary Agency, Inc. (*US*)
Larsen Pomada Literary Agents (*US*)
Levine Greenberg Literary Agency, Inc. (*US*)

The Literary Group International (*US*)
Sterling Lord Literistic, Inc. (*US*)
Julia Lord Literary Management (*US*)
Gina Maccoby Agency (*US*)
MacGregor Literary (*US*)
Ricia Mainhardt Agency (RMA) (*US*)
Carol Mann Agency (*US*)
Manus & Associates Literary Agency, Inc. (*US*)
The Martell Agency (*US*)
Martin Literary Management (*US*)
MBA Literary Agents Ltd (*UK*)
Mendel Media Group, LLC (*US*)
Martha Millard Literary Agency (*US*)
The Miller Agency (*US*)
Northern Lights Literary Services (*US*)
Pinder Lane & Garon-Brooke Associates Ltd (*US*)
Rebecca Pratt Literary Group (*US*)
Rees Literary Agency (*US*)
The Lisa Richards Agency (*Ire*)
Richford Becklow Literary Agency (*UK*)
B.J. Robbins Literary Agency (*US*)
Rita Rosenkranz Literary Agency (*US*)
Salkind Literary Agency (*US*)
Susan Schulman, A Literary Agency (*US*)
Lynn Seligman, Literary Agent (*US*)
Sheil Land Associates Ltd (*UK*)
Wendy Sherman Associates, Inc. (*US*)
Robert Smith Literary Agency Ltd (*UK*)
Stonesong (*US*)
The Swetky Agency and Associates (*US*)
TriadaUS Literary Agency, Inc. (*US*)
Venture Literary (*US*)
Watson, Little Ltd (*UK*)
Whispering Buffalo Literary Agency Ltd (*UK*)
Writers House UK (*UK*)
Writers' Representatives, LLC (*US*)
The Zack Company, Inc (*US*)
Short Stories
Abbot Management (*US*)
The Ahearn Agency, Inc (*US*)
Alive Communications, Inc (*US*)
The Bright Literary Academy (*UK*)
DeFiore and Company (*US*)
Sandra Dijkstra Literary Agency (*US*)
The Fielding Agency, LLC (*US*)
The Mitchell J. Hamilburg Agency (*US*)
Joy Harris Literary Agency, Inc. (*US*)
Antony Harwood Limited (*UK*)
John Hawkins & Associates, Inc. (*US*)
International Transactions, Inc. (*US*)
MacGregor Literary (*US*)
Martha Millard Literary Agency (*US*)
Renee Zuckerbrot Literary Agency (*US*)
Scribe Agency LLC (*US*)
Rosalie Siegel, International Literary Agency, Inc. (*US*)
The Swetky Agency and Associates (*US*)
Venture Literary (*US*)
Zoë Pagnamenta Agency, LLC (*US*)
Sociology
Abbot Management (*US*)

Miriam Altshuler Literary Agency (*US*)
Betsy Amster Literary Enterprises (*US*)
The August Agency LLC (*US*)
Blake Friedmann Literary Agency Ltd (*UK*)
Bleecker Street Associates, Inc. (*US*)
Barbara Braun Associates, Inc. (*US*)
Browne & Miller Literary Associates (*US*)
The Doe Coover Agency (*US*)
The Darley Anderson Agency (*UK*)
Liza Dawson Associates (*US*)
The Jennifer DeChiara Literary Agency (*US*)
DeFiore and Company (*US*)
Diamond Kahn and Woods (DKW) Literary
Agency Ltd (*UK*)
Sandra Dijkstra Literary Agency (*US*)
Doyen Literary Services, Inc. (*US*)
Judith Ehrlich Literary Management (*US*)
Felicia Eth Literary Representation (*US*)
Mary Evans, Inc. (*US*)
The Fielding Agency, LLC (*US*)
Fredrica S. Friedman and Co. Inc. (*US*)
Furniss Lawton (*UK*)
The Gernert Company (*US*)
Frances Goldin Literary Agency, Inc. (*US*)
Goodman Associates (*US*)
Irene Goodman Literary Agency (*US*)
Sanford J. Greenburger Associates, Inc (*US*)
The Mitchell J. Hamilburg Agency (*US*)
Hannigan Salky Getzler (HSG) Agency (*US*)
Antony Harwood Limited (*UK*)
Kate Hordern Literary Agency (*UK*)
Hornfischer Literary Management, L.P. (*US*)
J de S Associates Inc (*US*)
Kneerim & Williams (*US*)
Larsen Pomada Literary Agents (*US*)
LaunchBooks Literary Agency (*US*)
Levine Greenberg Literary Agency, Inc. (*US*)
Lippincott Massie McQuilkin (*US*)
The Literary Group International (*US*)
Lowenstein Associates, Inc. (*US*)
Carol Mann Agency (*US*)
B.J. Robbins Literary Agency (*US*)
Victoria Sanders & Associates LLC (*US*)
Susan Schulman, A Literary Agency (*US*)
Lynn Seligman, Literary Agent (*US*)
Denise Shannon Literary Agency, Inc. (*US*)
The Spieler Agency (*US*)
The Swetky Agency and Associates (*US*)
Venture Literary (*US*)
Waterside Productions, Inc (*US*)
The Weingel-Fidel Agency (*US*)
Wm Clark Associates (*US*)
Karen Gantz Zahler Literary Agency (*US*)
Spiritual
Abbot Management (*US*)
Alive Communications, Inc (*US*)
Miriam Altshuler Literary Agency (*US*)
Arcadia (*US*)
Baldi Agency (*US*)
David Black Literary Agency (*US*)
Bleecker Street Associates, Inc. (*US*)
Sheree Bykofsky Associates, Inc. (*US*)
Carnicelli Literary Management (*US*)

The Cooke Agency (*Can*)
The Darley Anderson Agency (*UK*)
Liza Dawson Associates (*US*)
Dunham Literary, Inc. (*US*)
Dystel & Goderich Literary Management (*US*)
Ethan Ellenberg Literary Agency (*US*)
Felicia Eth Literary Representation (*US*)
Fine Literary (*US*)
Folio Literary Management, LLC (*US*)
Fox & Howard Literary Agency (*UK*)
Sarah Jane Freymann Literary Agency (*US*)
The Mitchell J. Hamilburg Agency (*US*)
Joy Harris Literary Agency, Inc. (*US*)
Antony Harwood Limited (*UK*)
The Jeff Herman Agency, LLC (*US*)
Jill Grinberg Literary Management LLC (*US*)
Harvey Klinger, Inc (*US*)
Elaine Koster Literary Agency LLC (*US*)
Kuhn Projects (*US*)
Levine Greenberg Literary Agency, Inc. (*US*)
Literary & Creative Artists Inc. (*US*)
Literary Management Group, Inc. (*US*)
Lowenstein Associates, Inc. (*US*)
Ricia Mainhardt Agency (RMA) (*US*)
Kirsten Manges Literary Agency, LLC (*US*)
Carol Mann Agency (*US*)
Mendel Media Group, LLC (*US*)
Fifi Oscard Agency, Inc. (*US*)
Pinder Lane & Garon-Brooke Associates Ltd
(*US*)
Regina Ryan Publishing Enterprises (*US*)
The Amy Rennert Agency, Inc. (*US*)
Salkind Literary Agency (*US*)
Susan Schulman, A Literary Agency (*US*)
Wendy Sherman Associates, Inc. (*US*)
The Spieler Agency (*US*)
Thompson Literary Agency (*US*)
Venture Literary (*US*)
Waterside Productions, Inc (*US*)
The Zack Company, Inc (*US*)
Karen Gantz Zahler Literary Agency (*US*)
Helen Zimmermann Literary Agency (*US*)
Sport
Abbot Management (*US*)
Alive Communications, Inc (*US*)
Andrew Lownie Literary Agency Ltd (*UK*)
Audrey A. Wolf Literary Agency (*US*)
Bell Lomax Moreton Agency (*UK*)
David Black Literary Agency (*US*)
Bleecker Street Associates, Inc. (*US*)
Bresnick Weil Literary Agency, LLC (*US*)
Jenny Brown Associates (*UK*)
Browne & Miller Literary Associates (*US*)
Carnicelli Literary Management (*US*)
The Characters Talent Agency (*Can*)
Elyse Cheney Literary Associates, LLC (*US*)
Rosica Colin Ltd (*UK*)
Conville & Walsh Ltd (*UK*)
The Doe Coover Agency (*US*)
The Creative Rights Agency (*UK*)
The Darley Anderson Agency (*UK*)
David Luxton Associates (*UK*)
The Jennifer DeChiara Literary Agency (*US*)

Johnson & Alcock (*UK*)
Virginia Kidd Agency, Inc (*US*)
Harvey Klinger, Inc (*US*)
The Knight Agency (*US*)
Barbara S. Kouts, Literary Agent (*US*)
Laura Langlie, Literary Agent (*US*)
Larsen Pomada Literary Agents (*US*)
Robert Lecker Agency (*Can*)
Levine Greenberg Literary Agency, Inc. (*US*)
Limelight Management (*UK*)
Lippincott Massie McQuilkin (*US*)
Donald Maass Literary Agency (*US*)
MacGregor Literary (*US*)
Ricia Mainhardt Agency (RMA) (*US*)
Manus & Associates Literary Agency, Inc.
(*US*)
The Martell Agency (*US*)
Martha Millard Literary Agency (*US*)
Nappaland Literary Agency (*US*)
Niad Management (*US*)
Northern Lights Literary Services (*US*)
Aaron M. Priest Literary Agency (*US*)
Prospect Agency (*US*)
Raines & Raines (*US*)
Rebecca Friedman Literary Agency (*US*)
Rees Literary Agency (*US*)
B.J. Robbins Literary Agency (*US*)
Salkind Literary Agency (*US*)
Victoria Sanders & Associates LLC (*US*)
Susan Schulman, A Literary Agency (*US*)
Secret Agent Man (*US*)
The Seymour Agency (*US*)
Wendy Sherman Associates, Inc. (*US*)
Spectrum Literary Agency (*US*)
Sternig & Byrne Literary Agency (*US*)
The Swetky Agency and Associates (*US*)
Talcott Notch Literary (*US*)
TriadaUS Literary Agency, Inc. (*US*)
Venture Literary (*US*)
Wolfson Literary Agency (*US*)
The Zack Company, Inc (*US*)
Helen Zimmermann Literary Agency (*US*)

Technology
Abbot Management (*US*)
Adler & Robin Books, Inc (*US*)
Andrew Lownie Literary Agency Ltd (*UK*)
Arcadia (*US*)
The August Agency LLC (*US*)
Baldi Agency (*US*)
Blake Friedmann Literary Agency Ltd (*UK*)
Bleecker Street Associates, Inc. (*US*)
Browne & Miller Literary Associates (*US*)
Maria Carvainis Agency, Inc. (*US*)
Don Congdon Associates, Inc. (*US*)
The Doe Coover Agency (*US*)
Richard Curtis Associates, Inc. (*US*)
Laura Dail Literary Agency (*US*)
The Darley Anderson Agency (*UK*)
DeFiore and Company (*US*)
Doyen Literary Services, Inc. (*US*)
Dunham Literary, Inc. (*US*)
Dystel & Goderich Literary Management (*US*)
Felicia Eth Literary Representation (*US*)

Mary Evans, Inc. (*US*)
The Fielding Agency, LLC (*US*)
Diana Finch Literary Agency (*US*)
Fine Literary (*US*)
Folio Literary Management, LLC (*US*)
Grace Freedson's Publishing Network (*US*)
Fresh Books Literary Agency (*US*)
The G Agency, LLC (*US*)
Frances Goldin Literary Agency, Inc. (*US*)
Goodman Associates (*US*)
Antony Harwood Limited (*UK*)
John Hawkins & Associates, Inc. (*US*)
Hornfischer Literary Management, L.P. (*US*)
Jill Grinberg Literary Management LLC (*US*)
Harvey Klinger, Inc (*US*)
Kneerim & Williams (*US*)
Kuhn Projects (*US*)
LaunchBooks Literary Agency (*US*)
Levine Greenberg Literary Agency, Inc. (*US*)
Julia Lord Literary Management (*US*)
Kirsten Manges Literary Agency, LLC (*US*)
New Leaf Literary & Media, Inc. (*US*)
Fifi Oscard Agency, Inc. (*US*)
Kathi J. Paton Literary Agency (*US*)
Lynne Rabinoff Agency (*US*)
Robert Dudley Agency (*UK*)
Rita Rosenkranz Literary Agency (*US*)
The Rudy Agency (*US*)
Salkind Literary Agency (*US*)
Susan Schulman, A Literary Agency (*US*)
The Science Factory (*UK*)
Stuart Krichevsky Literary Agency, Inc. (*US*)
The Swetky Agency and Associates (*US*)
Talcott Notch Literary (*US*)
Venture Literary (*US*)
Waterside Productions, Inc (*US*)
Watson, Little Ltd (*UK*)
The Weingel-Fidel Agency (*US*)
Wm Clark Associates (*US*)
The Zack Company, Inc (*US*)
Helen Zimmermann Literary Agency (*US*)

Theatre
A & B Personal Management Ltd (*UK*)
Abbot Management (*US*)
Bret Adams Ltd (*US*)
The Agency (London) Ltd (*UK*)
AVAnti Productions & Management (*UK*)
Barbara Hogenson Agency (*US*)
Berlin Associates (*UK*)
Alan Brodie Representation Ltd (*UK*)
CardenWright Literary Agency (*UK*)
Mary Clemmey Literary Agency (*UK*)
Jonathan Clowes Ltd (*UK*)
Rosica Colin Ltd (*UK*)
Don Congdon Associates, Inc. (*US*)
Curtis Brown Group Ltd (*UK*)
The Darley Anderson Agency (*UK*)
Liza Dawson Associates (*US*)
The Jennifer DeChiara Literary Agency (*US*)
Felix de Wolfe (*UK*)
DHH Literary Agency Ltd (*UK*)
Doyen Literary Services, Inc. (*US*)

Rupert Heath Literary Agency (*UK*)
The Helen Heller Agency (*Can*)
David Higham Associates Ltd (*UK*)
Hill Nadell Literary Agency (*US*)
Kate Hordern Literary Agency (*UK*)
Andrea Hurst Literary Management (*US*)
InkWell Management (*US*)
International Transactions, Inc. (*US*)
J de S Associates Inc (*US*)
The Jean V. Naggar Literary Agency (*US*)
Johnson & Alcock (*UK*)
Harvey Klinger, Inc (*US*)
The Knight Agency (*US*)
Elaine Koster Literary Agency LLC (*US*)
Barbara S. Kouts, Literary Agent (*US*)
Laura Langlie, Literary Agent (*US*)
Larsen Pomada Literary Agents (*US*)
LaunchBooks Literary Agency (*US*)
Robert Lecker Agency (*Can*)
Levine Greenberg Literary Agency, Inc. (*US*)
Limelight Management (*UK*)
Lippincott Massie McQuilkin (*US*)
The Literary Group International (*US*)
Julia Lord Literary Management (*US*)
Lowenstein Associates, Inc. (*US*)
The Jennifer Lyons Literary Agency, LLC (*US*)
Gina Maccoby Agency (*US*)
MacGregor Literary (*US*)
Ricia Mainhardt Agency (RMA) (*US*)
Manus & Associates Literary Agency, Inc. (*US*)
Marjacq Scripts Ltd (*UK*)
The Martell Agency (*US*)
Mendel Media Group, LLC (*US*)
Martha Millard Literary Agency (*US*)
Howard Morhaim Literary Agency (*US*)
Mulcahy Associates (*UK*)
New Leaf Literary & Media, Inc. (*US*)
Niad Management (*US*)
Pavilion Literary Management (*US*)
Jonathan Pegg Literary Agency (*UK*)
Pinder Lane & Garon-Brooke Associates Ltd (*US*)
Rebecca Pratt Literary Group (*US*)
Aaron M. Priest Literary Agency (*US*)
Prospect Agency (*US*)
Queen Literary Agency, Inc. (*US*)
Raines & Raines (*US*)
Rebecca Friedman Literary Agency (*US*)
Redhammer (*UK*)
Rees Literary Agency (*US*)
Renee Zuckerbrot Literary Agency (*US*)
B.J. Robbins Literary Agency (*US*)
Rocking Chair Books (*UK*)
The Rudy Agency (*US*)
Salkind Literary Agency (*US*)
Victoria Sanders & Associates LLC (*US*)
Susan Schulman, A Literary Agency (*US*)
Secret Agent Man (*US*)
The Seymour Agency (*US*)
Sheil Land Associates Ltd (*UK*)
Spencerhill Associates (*US*)
The Spieler Agency (*US*)

The Stuart Agency (*US*)
The Swetky Agency and Associates (*US*)
SYLA – Susan Yearwood Literary Agency (*UK*)
Talcott Notch Literary (*US*)
Toby Mundy Associates Ltd (*UK*)
TriadaUS Literary Agency, Inc. (*US*)
Venture Literary (*US*)
Whispering Buffalo Literary Agency Ltd (*UK*)
William Morris Endeavor (WME) London (*UK*)
Wolfson Literary Agency (*US*)
Writers' Representatives, LLC (*US*)
The Zack Company, Inc (*US*)
Zeno Agency Ltd (*UK*)
Helen Zimmermann Literary Agency (*US*)

Translations
Abbot Management (*US*)
Andrew Lownie Literary Agency Ltd (*UK*)
The Darley Anderson Agency (*UK*)
The Fielding Agency, LLC (*US*)
Diana Finch Literary Agency (*US*)
Goodman Associates (*US*)
Joy Harris Literary Agency, Inc. (*US*)
Antony Harwood Limited (*UK*)
Intercontinental Literary Agency (*UK*)
J de S Associates Inc (*US*)
Aaron M. Priest Literary Agency (*US*)
Rocking Chair Books (*UK*)
Victoria Sanders & Associates LLC (*US*)
The Swetky Agency and Associates (*US*)
Venture Literary (*US*)
Wm Clark Associates (*US*)

Travel
Abbot Management (*US*)
Betsy Amster Literary Enterprises (*US*)
Baldi Agency (*US*)
Blake Friedmann Literary Agency Ltd (*UK*)
The Blumer Literary Agency, Inc. (*US*)
BookBlast Ltd. (*UK*)
Bresnick Weil Literary Agency, LLC (*US*)
Rosica Colin Ltd (*UK*)
Frances Collin Literary Agent (*US*)
Don Congdon Associates, Inc. (*US*)
Conville & Walsh Ltd (*UK*)
The Darley Anderson Agency (*UK*)
The Jennifer DeChiara Literary Agency (*US*)
Sandra Dijkstra Literary Agency (*US*)
Janis A. Donnaud & Associates, Inc. (*US*)
Dunham Literary, Inc. (*US*)
Felicia Eth Literary Representation (*US*)
Fine Literary (*US*)
Fletcher & Company (*US*)
Jeanne Fredericks Literary Agency, Inc. (*US*)
Sarah Jane Freymann Literary Agency (*US*)
Goodman Associates (*US*)
Greene & Heaton Ltd (*UK*)
The Mitchell J. Hamilburg Agency (*US*)
Hannigan Salky Getzler (HSG) Agency (*US*)
Antony Harwood Limited (*UK*)
John Hawkins & Associates, Inc. (*US*)
hhb agency ltd (*UK*)
Jill Grinberg Literary Management LLC (*US*)

Larsen Pomada Literary Agents (*US*)
Robert Lecker Agency (*Can*)
Levine Greenberg Literary Agency, Inc. (*US*)
Limelight Management (*UK*)
The Literary Group International (*US*)
Kirsten Manges Literary Agency, LLC (*US*)
Marjacq Scripts Ltd (*UK*)
Duncan McAra (*UK*)
Anne McDermid & Associates Ltd (*Can*)
The Miller Agency (*US*)
Pinder Lane & Garon-Brooke Associates Ltd (*US*)
Regina Ryan Publishing Enterprises (*US*)
B.J. Robbins Literary Agency (*US*)
Robert Dudley Agency (*UK*)
Rocking Chair Books (*UK*)
Salkind Literary Agency (*US*)
The Sayle Literary Agency (*UK*)
Susan Schulman, A Literary Agency (*US*)
The Science Factory (*UK*)
Sheil Land Associates Ltd (*UK*)
Sinclair-Stevenson (*UK*)
The Spieler Agency (*US*)
The Swetky Agency and Associates (*US*)
Tessler Literary Agency (*US*)
Tracy Brown Literary Agency (*US*)
Transatlantic Literary Agency, Inc. (*Can*)
TriadaUS Literary Agency, Inc. (*US*)
Venture Literary (*US*)
Ed Victor Ltd (*UK*)

TV
A & B Personal Management Ltd (*UK*)
Abbot Management (*US*)
Sheila Ableman Literary Agency (*UK*)
Above the Line Agency (*US*)
Abrams Artists Agency (*US*)
Bret Adams Ltd (*US*)
The Agency (London) Ltd (*UK*)
Marcia Amsterdam Agency (*UK*)
Berlin Associates (*UK*)
Blake Friedmann Literary Agency Ltd (*UK*)
Luigi Bonomi Associates Ltd (*UK*)
The Bright Literary Academy (*UK*)
Alan Brodie Representation Ltd (*UK*)
Kelvin C. Bulger and Associates (*US*)
The Characters Talent Agency (*Can*)
Clare Hulton Literary Agency (*UK*)
Mary Clemmey Literary Agency (*UK*)
Jonathan Clowes Ltd (*UK*)
Rosica Colin Ltd (*UK*)
Curtis Brown Group Ltd (*UK*)
The Darley Anderson Agency (*UK*)
Felix de Wolfe (*UK*)
DHH Literary Agency Ltd (*UK*)
The Dravis Agency, Inc. (*US*)
Film Rights Ltd in association with Laurence Fitch Ltd (*UK*)
Jill Foster Ltd (JFL) (*UK*)
Georgina Capel Associates Ltd (*UK*)
Eric Glass Ltd (*UK*)
Antony Harwood Limited (*UK*)
hhb agency ltd (*UK*)
David Higham Associates Ltd (*UK*)

Valerie Hoskins Associates (*UK*)
Independent Talent Group Ltd (*UK*)
Janet Fillingham Associates (*UK*)
Michelle Kass Associates (*UK*)
Ken Sherman & Associates (*US*)
Ki Agency Ltd (*UK*)
Knight Hall Agency (*UK*)
Macnaughton Lord Representation (*UK*)
Marjacq Scripts Ltd (*UK*)
MBA Literary Agents Ltd (*UK*)
Niad Management (*US*)
Paradigm Talent and Literary Agency (*US*)
PBJ and JBJ Management (*UK*)
Peregrine Whittlesey Agency (*US*)
Rochelle Stevens & Co. (*UK*)
Sayle Screen Ltd (*UK*)
Linda Seifert Management (*UK*)
Sheil Land Associates Ltd (*UK*)
Elaine Steel (*UK*)
Stone Manners Salners Agency (*US*)
The Swetky Agency and Associates (*US*)
The Tennyson Agency (*UK*)
Jane Turnbull (*UK*)
United Agents (*UK*)
Venture Literary (*US*)
Cecily Ware Literary Agents (*UK*)
The Zack Company, Inc (*US*)

Westerns
Abbot Management (*US*)
Alive Communications, Inc (*US*)
Andrew Lownie Literary Agency Ltd (*UK*)
The Characters Talent Agency (*Can*)
Richard Curtis Associates, Inc. (*US*)
The Darley Anderson Agency (*UK*)
Jim Donovan Literary (*US*)
Antony Harwood Limited (*UK*)
Andrea Hurst Literary Management (*US*)
J de S Associates Inc (*US*)
Donald Maass Literary Agency (*US*)
Ricia Mainhardt Agency (RMA) (*US*)
Pinder Lane & Garon-Brooke Associates Ltd (*US*)
Prospect Agency (*US*)
Raines & Raines (*US*)
Secret Agent Man (*US*)
The Swetky Agency and Associates (*US*)

Women's Interests
Abbot Management (*US*)
The Ahearn Agency, Inc (*US*)
Alive Communications, Inc (*US*)
The Ampersand Agency Ltd (*UK*)
Betsy Amster Literary Enterprises (*US*)
Arcadia (*US*)
The August Agency LLC (*US*)
The Axelrod Agency (*US*)
Ayesha Pande Literary (*US*)
Belcastro Agency (*US*)
The Bent Agency (*US*)
David Black Literary Agency (*US*)
Blake Friedmann Literary Agency Ltd (*UK*)
Bleecker Street Associates, Inc. (*US*)
The Blumer Literary Agency, Inc. (*US*)
Luigi Bonomi Associates Ltd (*UK*)

US Publishers

For the most up-to-date listings of these and hundreds of other publishers, visit http://www.firstwriter.com/publishers

*To claim your **free** access to the site, please see the back of this book.*

Abrams ComicArts

115 West 18th Street, 6th Floor
New York, NY 10011
Tel: +1 (212) 206-7715
Fax: +1 (212) 519-1210
Email: abrams@abramsbooks.com
Website: http://www.abramsbooks.com

Publishes: Fiction; Nonfiction; *Markets:* Adult; Children's

Contact: Abrams ComicArts Editorial

Publishes graphic novels, illustrated books, and nonfiction books about comics and comic history. Send submissions by post with SASE.

ACTA Publications

4848 N. Clark Street
Chicago, IL 60640
Tel: +1 (800) 397-2282
Fax: +1 (800) 397-0079
Email: acta@actapublications.com
Website: http://www.actapublications.com

Publishes: Nonfiction; *Areas:* Religious; Self-Help; Spiritual; *Markets:* Adult

Send query with SASE, outline, table of contents, and one sample chapter. Publishes religious books, particularly Catholic, for a mainstream nonacademic audience. Do not submit unless you have read catalog or one of the books published by this company.

Ahsahta Press

Department of English
Boise State University
1910 University Drive
Boise, ID 83725-1525
Tel: +1 (208) 426-3134
Email: ahsahta@boisestate.edu
Website: http://ahsahtapress.org

Publishes: Poetry; *Markets:* Adult; *Treatments:* Literary

Contact: Janet Holmes

Submit poetry manuscripts between 50 and 100 pages long via online submissions system. Accepts open submissions during March each year only. Charges $5 per submission. Also runs poetry competitions at other times of the year.

Alondra Press

4119 Wildacres Drive
Houston, TX 77072
Email: lark@alondrapress.com
Website: http://www.alondrapress.com

Publishes: Fiction; Nonfiction; *Areas:* Anthropology; Archaeology; Historical; Philosophy; Psychology; Translations; *Markets:* Adult; *Treatments:* Literary

Contact: Fiction: "Editor"; Nonfiction: Armando Benitez Solomon Tager, or Henry Hollenbaugh

Send query by email, with synopsis up to 300 words and sample or full manuscript. See website for full guidelines.

Alpine Publications, Inc.
38262 Linman Road
Crawford, CO 81415
Email: editorialdept@alpinepub.com
Website: http://www.alpinepub.com

Publishes: Nonfiction; *Areas:* Biography; Hobbies; Nature; *Markets:* Adult

Publishes books on dogs and horses. Welcomes submissions. Send query by post or by email with synopsis, chapter outline, author bio, market analysis, and 1-3 sample chapters.

Amadeus Press
33 Plymouth Street, Suite 302
Montclair, NJ 07042
Email: jcerullo@halleonard.com
Website: http://www.amadeuspress.com

Publishes: Nonfiction; *Areas:* Music; *Markets:* Adult

Contact: John Cerullo

Publishes books on classical music and opera. Send query with outline or table of contents, one or two sample chapters, sample illustrations, and your schedule for completion. Prefers contact early in the project, but cannot guarantee a response. See website for full details.

Amakella Publishing
Arlington, VA
Email: info@amakella.com
Website: http://www.amakella.com

Publishes: Fiction; Nonfiction; *Areas:* Adventure; Anthropology; Biography; Business; Culture; Current Affairs; Historical; Hobbies; How-to; Leisure; Lifestyle; Literature; Media; Men's Interests;

Nature; Psychology; Romance; Self-Help; Short Stories; Sociology; Spiritual; Travel; Women's Interests; *Markets:* Academic; Family; Professional; *Treatments:* Commercial; Contemporary; Literary; Mainstream; Niche; Popular; Positive; Progressive; Serious

An independent publisher currently particularly interested in publishing books in areas such as social sciences, international development, environmental conservation, and current affairs.

American Counseling Association
6101 Stevenson Avenue
Alexandria, VA 22304
Tel: +1 (703) 823-9800
Fax: +1 (703) 823-0252
Email: cbaker@counseling.org
Website: https://www.counseling.org

Publishes: Nonfiction; *Areas:* Health; *Markets:* Academic; Professional

Publishes books on mental health for the professional and academic markets.

American Press
60 State Street #700
Boston, MA 02109
Tel: +1 (617) 247- 0022
Email: americanpress@flash.net
Website: http://www.
americanpresspublishers.com

Publishes: Nonfiction; *Areas:* Anthropology; Architecture; Arts; Business; Drama; Finance; Health; Historical; Legal; Music; Philosophy; Politics; Psychology; Religious; Science; Sociology; Sport; Technology; Theatre; *Markets:* Academic; Professional

Welcomes proposals for academic and professional titles in all subject areas. Accepts textbooks, handbooks, laboratory manuals, workbooks, study guides, journal research, reference books, DVDs, CDs and software programs and materials for college level courses. See website for more details.

American Quilter's Society

5801 Kentucky Dam Road
Paducah, KY 42003-9323
Tel: +1 (270) 898-7903
Fax: +1 (270) 898-1173
Email: editor@aqsquilt.com
Website: http://www.americanquilter.com

Publishes: Fiction; Nonfiction; *Areas:*
Crafts; Hobbies; How-to; Humour; Mystery;
Romance; *Markets:* Adult

Publishes nonfiction and fiction related to
quilts. Send proposal by post. See website
for complete guidelines.

AMG Publishers

6815 Shallowford Road
Chattanooga, TN 37421
Tel: +1 (423) 894-6060 (ext. 275)
Fax: +1 (423) 894-9511
Email: ricks@amgpublishers.com
Website: http://www.amgpublishers.com

Publishes: Fiction; Nonfiction; Reference;
Areas: Fantasy; Lifestyle; Politics;
Religious; Spiritual; *Markets:* Adult

Contact: Rick Steele

Publishes biblically oriented books
including: Biblical Reference, Applied
Theology and Apologetics, Christian
Ministry, Bible Study Books in the
Following God series format, Christian
Living, Women/Men/Family Issues, Single/
Divorce Issues, Contemporary Issues,
(unique) Devotionals, Inspirational, Prayer,
and Gift books. Introducing young adult
fiction titles. Send query letter by email or by
post, including proposed page count, brief
description of the proposed book, market
info, and author details. See website for full
guidelines.

Amira Press

Email: submissions@amirapress.com
Website: http://www.amirapress.com

Publishes: Fiction; *Areas:* Erotic; Fantasy;
Historical; Horror; Romance; Sci-Fi;
Suspense; Travel; Westerns; *Markets:* Adult;
Treatments: Contemporary

Contact: Y. Lynn; Dahlia Rose

Small ebook publisher of erotic romance.
Send complete ms by email. See website for
more details.

Ankerwycke

American Bar Association
321 North Clark Street
Chicago, IL 60654
Tel: +1 (312) 988-5000
Website: http://www.ababooks.org

Publishes: Fiction; Nonfiction; *Areas:*
Crime; Legal; *Markets:* Adult; *Treatments:*
Popular

Publishes books that bring law to the general
public, including legal fiction, true crime,
popular legal histories, handbooks, and
guides.

Arbordale Publishing

612 Johnnie Dodds., Suite A2
Mount Pleasant, SC 29464
Email: katie@arbordalepublishing.com
Website: http://www.
arbordalepublishing.com

Publishes: Fiction; Nonfiction; *Areas:*
Science; *Markets:* Children's

Contact: Katie Hall, Associate Editor

Publishes picture books that aim to get
children excited about science and maths.
Publishes mainly fiction with nonfiction
facts woven into the story, but will also
consider nonfiction stories. Submit by email
only. See website for full submission
guidelines.

Arcade Publishing

307 West 36th Street, 11th Floor
New York, NY 10018
Tel: +1 (212) 643-6816
Fax: +1 (212) 643-6819
Email: arcadesubmissions@
skyhorsepublishing.com
Website: http://www.arcadepub.com

Publishes: Fiction; Nonfiction; *Areas:*

Adventure; Arts; Autobiography; Business;
Cookery, Current Affairs; Historical;
Military; Nature; Science; Travel; *Markets:*
Adult; *Treatments:* Literary

Send query by email with a brief cover letter;
one-to-two page synopsis; annotated chapter
outline; market analysis, including
competitive research; 1-2 sample chapters;
author bio, including list of all previous
publishing credits.

Arch Street Press

1429 South 9th Street
Philadelphia, PA 19147
Tel: +1 (877) 732-ARCH
Email: contact@archstreetpress.org
Website: http://archstreetpress.org

Publishes: Fiction; Nonfiction; *Areas:* Arts;
Autobiography; Biography; Business;
Criticism; Culture; Finance; Historical;
Legal; Literature; Music; Nature;
Philosophy; Politics; Sociology; Spiritual;
Translations; Women's Interests; *Markets:*
Adult; *Treatments:* Contemporary; Literary

Independent nonprofit publisher dedicated to
the collaborative work of creative
visionaries, social entrepreneurs and leading
scholars worldwide. Send query with SASE,
outline, and three sample chapters.

Arrow Publications, LLC

20411 Sawgrass Drive
Montgomery Village, MD 20886
Tel: +1 (301) 299-9422
Fax: +1 (301) 632-8477
Email: arrow_info@arrowpub.com
Website: http://www.arrowpub.com

Publishes: Fiction; *Areas:* Adventure;
Crime; Fantasy; Humour; Mystery;
Romance; Suspense; Women's Interests;
Markets: Adult

Contact: Tom King; Maryan Gibson

Publishes romance fiction and selective
nonfiction, including women's interests. Also
considers supernatural, mystery, crime and
other genres if the story has a strong
romance element. Send query by email with

outline, word count, brief description, one
chapter (usually the first), and promotional
plan. See website for full guidelines.

ASCE Press

1801 Alexander Bell Drive
Reston, VA 20191
Tel: +1 (703) 295-6300
Email: ascepress@asce.org
Website: http://www.asce.org

Publishes: Nonfiction; *Areas:* Architecture;
Design; Science; Technology; *Markets:*
Professional

Publishes books for professional civil
engineers. Send proposal by email or by
post. See website for full submission
guidelines.

Astragal Press

3993 149th Street West, Suite 105
Apple Valley, MN 55124
Tel: +1 (866) 543-3045
Fax: +1 (800) 330-6232
Email: info@finneyco.com
Website: http://www.astragalpress.com

Publishes: Nonfiction; *Areas:* Antiques;
Crafts; Historical; Science; Technology;
Markets: Adult; *Treatments:* Niche

Send query with SASE, one-page overview,
table of contents, introduction, at least three
chapters, market info, and details of your
background and qualifications. Publishes
books for a niche market on subjects such as
antique tools, early sciences, the history of
the railroad, etc. See website for more
details.

The Backwater Press

3502 North 52nd Street
Omaha, NE 68104-3506
Tel: +1 (402) 451-4052
Email: thebackwaterspress@gmail.com
Website: http://thebackwaterspress.com

Publishes: Poetry; *Markets:* Adult;
Treatments: Literary

Publishes poetry. Currently closed to general

submissions, and is accepting work only through its poetry competition, for which there is a reading fee of $25. Submit online via website.

Bailiwick Press
309 East Mulberry Street
Fort Collins, Colorado 80524
Tel: +1 (970) 672-4878
Fax: +1 (970) 672-4731
Email: aldozelnick@gmail.com
Website: http://www.bailiwickpress.com

Publishes: Fiction; *Areas:* Humour; *Markets:* Children's; Youth

Publishes smart, funny, and layered writing for children and young adult. Looking for hysterically funny. Illustrated fiction is desired but not required. Approach through online form, where you will be required to submit the funniest part of your book, and display a knowledge of the publisher's existing work.

Baker Publishing Group
6030 East Fulton Road
Ada, MI 49301
Tel: +1 (616) 676-9185
Fax: +1 (616) 676-9573
Email: submissions@bakeracademic.com
Website: http://bakerpublishinggroup.com

Publishes: Nonfiction; *Areas:* Religious; *Markets:* Academic; Adult; Professional

Publishes Christian books. No unsolicited mss. Accepts approaches only through literary agent, writers' conferences, or third part manuscript submission services (see website for details).

Ball Publishing
622 Town Road
PO Box 1660
West Chicago, IL 60186
Tel: +1 (630) 231-3675
Fax: +1 (630) 231-5254
Email: cbeytes@ballpublishing.com
Website: http://www.ballpublishing.com

Publishes: Nonfiction; *Areas:* Gardening;

Markets: Adult; Professional

Contact: Chris Beytes (Editor)

Send query describing book and its "hook" with SASE. Include your qualifications to write the book (possibly in the form of a CV), market overview (including details of competing books, and how your book is different and superior), details of contents (table of contents, word count, illustrations), estimated completion time, and two or three sample chapters. See website for full guidelines. Publishes books on gardening and horticulture for both professionals and home gardeners.

Barron's Educational Series, Inc.
250 Wireless Blvd
Hauppauge, NY 11788
Tel: +1 (800) 645-3476
Email: waynebarr@barronseduc.com
Website: http://www.barronseduc.com

Publishes: Fiction; Nonfiction; *Areas:* Arts; Beauty and Fashion; Business; Cookery; Crafts; Finance; Health; Hobbies; Legal; Lifestyle; New Age; Photography; Sport; Travel; *Markets:* Adult; Children's; Youth

Contact: Wayne Barr, Acquisitions Editor

Particularly interested in children and young adult fiction and nonfiction books, foreign language learning books, New Age books, cookbooks, business and financial advice books, parenting advice books, art instruction books, sports, fashion, crafts, and study guides. No poetry. Send query by email or by post with SASE (if return of materials required). Only queries accepted by email. See website for full guidelines.

Beacon Press
24 Farnsworth Street
Boston, MA 02210
Tel: +1 (617) 742-2110
Fax: +1 (617) 723-3097
Email: editorial@beacon.org
Website: http://www.beacon.org

Publishes: Nonfiction; *Areas:* Arts;

Autobiography; Biography; Current Affairs; Historical, Lifestyle, Literature, Medicine, Nature; Politics; Religious; Science; Sociology; Women's Interests; *Markets:* Adult

Contact: Editorial Department

Publishes general trade nonfiction, in particular religion, history, current affairs, political science, gay/lesbian/gender studies, education, African-American studies, women's studies, child and family issues and nature and the environment. No poetry, fiction, or self-help books. Send query by email with 250-word description of your proposal. If interested, a full proposal will be requested within three weeks. Response not guaranteed.

BelleBooks
PO Box 300921
Memphis, TN 38130
Tel: +1 (901) 344-9024
Fax: +1 (901) 344-9068
Email: query@BelleBooks.com
Website: http://www.bellebooks.com

Publishes: Fiction; *Areas:* Fantasy; Historical; Horror; Mystery; Romance; Sci-Fi; Short Stories; Suspense; Thrillers; Women's Interests; *Markets:* Adult; Children's; Youth

Publishes women's fiction, cozy mysteries, well-researched civil war fiction, young adult fiction, urban fantasy and horror, young adult fantasy fiction, and fantasy. Send query by email with brief synopsis and credentials/credits. See website for full guidelines.

Bellevue Literary Press
Department of Medicine
NYU School of Medicine
550 First Avenue, OBV A612
New York, NY 10016
Tel: +1 (212) 263-7802
Email: blpsubmissions@gmail.com
Website: http://blpress.org

Publishes: Fiction; Nonfiction; *Markets:* Adult; *Treatments:* Literary

Contact: Erika Goldman, Publisher and Editorial Director

Publisher of literary fiction and narrative nonfiction. No poetry, single short stories, plays, screenplays, or self-help/instructional books. Send submissions by email. For fiction submissions, attach complete ms. For nonfiction, send complete ms or proposal. See website for full guidelines.

BenBella Books
10300 North Central Expy, Suite 530 Dallas, TX 75231
Tel: +1 (214) 750-3600
Email: glenn@benbellabooks.com
Website: http://www.benbellabooks.com

Publishes: Nonfiction; *Areas:* Autobiography; Biography; Business; Cookery; Culture; Health; Lifestyle; Politics; Science; Self-Help; Sociology; Sport; *Markets:* Adult; *Treatments:* Popular

Contact: Glenn Yeffeth

Marketing-focussed publishing house, publishing 30-40 titles a year. Actively acquiring strong nonfiction manuscripts. Send pitch of no more than a few pages describing your book, how it differs from others, your qualifications to write it, and explaining why you think the book will sell.

Bethany House Publishers
Baker Publishing Group
6030 East Fulton Road
Ada, MI 49301
Tel: +1 (616) 676-9185
Fax: +1 (616) 676-9573
Website: http://bakerpublishinggroup.com/bethanyhouse

Publishes: Fiction; Nonfiction; *Areas:* Fantasy; Historical; Mystery; Religious; Romance; Suspense; Women's Interests; *Markets:* Adult; Children's; Youth; *Treatments:* Contemporary; Literary

Publishes Christian fiction and nonfiction. No poetry, memoirs, picture books, Western, End-Times, Spiritual Warfare, or Chick-Lit. No unsolicited manuscripts, proposals or queries by mail, telephone, email, or fax. Approach through a literary agent, at a conference, or through an online manuscript service (see website for more details).

Bick Publishing House
16 Marion Road
Branford, CT 06405
Tel: +1 (203) 208-5253
Fax: +1 (203) 208-5253
Email: bickpubhse@aol.com
Website: http://www.bickpubhouse.com

Publishes: Fiction; Nonfiction; *Areas:* Arts; Health; Philosophy; Psychology; Science; Sci-Fi; Self-Help; *Markets:* Adult; Youth

Publishes Life Sciences and Self-Help Books for Teens; Young Adult: Psychology, Science and Philosophy; Science Fiction for Teens; Adult Health and Recovery; Meditation; Living with Disabilities; Wildlife Rehabilitation. See website for submission guidelines. No submissions by email.

Bilingual Review Press
Hispanic Research Center
Arizona State University
PO Box 875303
Tempe, AZ 85287-5303
Email: brp@asu.edu
Website: http://bilingualpress.clas.asu.edu/

Publishes: Fiction; Nonfiction; Poetry; Scripts; *Areas:* Short Stories; Translations; *Markets:* Academic; Adult; *Treatments:* Literary; Serious

Contact: Gary Francisco Keller

Publishes hardcover and paperback originals and reprints on US Hispanic themes, including creative literature (novels, short story collections, poetry, drama, translations), scholarly monographs and edited compilations, and other nonfiction. Particularly interested in Chicano, Puerto Rican, Cuban American, and other US Hispanic themes with strong and serious literary qualities and distinctive and intellectually important topics. Send query by post with SASE and sample chapter or

sample poems, plot summary / TOC, marketing info and brief bio. Accepts simultaneous submissions, but no electronic submissions. See website for full guidelines.

Black Lyon Publishing, LLC
PO Box 567
Baker City, OR 97814
Email: Queries@BlackLyonPublishing.com
Website: http://www.
blacklyonpublishing.com

Publishes: Fiction; Nonfiction; *Areas:* Adventure; Historical; Romance; Self-Help; Women's Interests; *Markets:* Adult; *Treatments:* Contemporary; Literary

Small, independent publishing house, publishing mainly romance (contemporary, paranormal, historical, inspirational, adventure, literary, and novellas), as well as self-help. Send query by email. See website for full submission guidelines.

Black Ocean
Email: carrie@blackocean.org
Website: http://www.blackocean.org

Publishes: Poetry; Translations; *Markets:* Adult; *Treatments:* Literary

Contact: Carrie O. Adams (Poetry Editor)

Publishes new poetry, and out-of-print or translated texts. Reading period runs from June 1 to June 30 each year. During reading period, submit via link on website.

Black Rose Writing
PO Box 1540
Castroville, TX 78009
Email: creator@blackrosewriting.com
Website: http://www.blackrosewriting.com

Publishes: Fiction; Nonfiction; *Markets:* Adult; Children's

Accepts all fiction and nonfiction for adults. Accepts children's books with full illustrations only. No poetry or short story collections. Submit via online submission system.

BlazeVOX [books]

Email: editor@blazevox.org
Website: http://www.blazevox.org

Publishes: Fiction; Nonfiction; Poetry; *Areas:* Criticism; Literature; Short Stories; *Markets:* Adult; *Treatments:* Experimental; Literary

Contact: Geoffrey Gatza

Publishes poetry, short stories, experimental fiction, literary criticism (including companions, studies and histories).

Blue Light Press

1563 – 45th Avenue
San Francisco, CA 94122
Email: bluelightpress@aol.com
Website: http://www.bluelightpress.com

Publishes: Poetry; *Markets:* Adult; *Treatments:* Literary

Contact: Diane Frank

Co-operative press run by a collective of poets and artists. Publishes chapbooks with print runs of 50-200 and full-length books that are printed on demand. Committed to the publication of poetry which is "imagistic, inventive, emotionally honest, and pushes the language to a deeper level of insight". Relies on poets to actively promote their books.

Blue River Press

2402 N. Shadeland Ave., Ste. A
Indianapolis, IN 46219
Tel: +1 (317) 352-8200
Fax: +1 (317) 352-8200
Email: proposals@brpressbooks.com
Website: http://www.brpressbooks.com

Publishes: Nonfiction; *Areas:* Culture; Health; Sport; Travel; *Markets:* Adult; *Treatments:* Popular

Publishes nonfiction for a general or specialised audience. Interested in both series products and stand-alone books. Seeks knowledgeable authors with a passion for their subject and a willingness to promote

their ideas and books. Send proposals by email.

Bold Strokes Books

PO Box 249
Valley Falls, NY 12185
Tel: +1 (518) 677-5127
Fax: +1 (518) 677-5291
Email: submissions@boldstrokesbooks.com
Website: http://www.boldstrokesbooks.com

Publishes: Fiction; Nonfiction; *Areas:* Adventure; Crime; Erotic; Fantasy; Historical; Horror; Mystery; Romance; Sci-Fi; *Markets:* Adult; Youth

Contact: Len Barot, Selections Director

Publishes LesbianGayBiTransQueer general and genre fiction, and nonfiction. Accepts unsolicited mss by email with one-page synopsis. See website for full guidelines.

BookFish Books

Email: bookfishbooks@gmail.com
Website: http://www.bookfishbooks.com

Publishes: Fiction; *Markets:* Adult; Children's; Youth

Publishes novels and novellas for middle grade, young adult, and new adult, in all subgenres. Novels should be between 40,000 and 80,000 words, and novellas between 20,000 and 35,000 words. Send query by email with synopsis up to two pages and first three chapters as Word attachment. See website for full guidelines.

Boyds Mills Press

815 Church Street
Honesdale, Pennsylvania 18431
Tel: +1 (570) 253-1164
Email: marketing@boydsmillspress.com
Website: http://www.boydsmillspress.com

Publishes: Fiction; Nonfiction; Poetry; *Markets:* Children's

Publishes a range of books for children, from pre-school to young adult, including fiction, nonfiction, and poetry. Send query with

SASE, synopsis, and three sample chapters for middle grade fiction, or complete ms for picture books and collections of poetry.

Bronze Man Books
Millikin University
1184 W. Main St.
Decatur, Illinois 62522
Tel: +1 (217) 424-6264
Email: rbrooks@millikin.edu
Website: http://www.bronzemanbooks.com

Publishes: Fiction; Poetry; Scripts; *Areas:* Drama; Short Stories; *Markets:* Adult; *Treatments:* Literary

Contact: Dr. Randy Brooks

Publishes 1-2 chapbooks per year of various genres (poetry, prose, drama, etc.). Always open to proposals. Poetry chapbooks should consist of 18-30 poems with a connecting theme or notion; fiction chapbooks should be 32-72 pages and may be short story collections or one or two longer works. Send proposal by email or by post with SASE in first instance. See website for more details.

Bucknell University Press
Bucknell University, One Dent Drive, Lewisburg, PA 17837
Tel: +1 (570) 577-3674
Email: clingham@bucknell.edu
Website: http://www.bucknell.edu/universitypress

Publishes: Nonfiction; *Areas:* Anthropology; Architecture; Arts; Criticism; Culture; Historical; Legal; Literature; Medicine; Philosophy; Politics; Psychology; Religious; Science; Sociology; *Markets:* Academic

Contact: Greg Clingham

Publishes scholarship in the humanities and social sciences, particularly literary criticism, Modern Languages, Classics, theory, cultural studies, historiography (including the history of law, of medicine, and of science), philosophy, psychology and psychoanalysis, religion, political science, cultural and political geography, and interdisciplinary

combinations of the above. Send proposal by post or by email.

Bullitt Publishing
Email: submissions@bullittpublishing.com
Website: http://bullittpublishing.com

Publishes: Fiction; *Areas:* Romance; *Markets:* Adult; *Treatments:* Contemporary

Publishes contemporary romance. Submissions by email only – see website for full guidelines.

Butte Publications, Inc.
PO Box 1328
Hillsboro, OR 97123-1328
Tel: +1 (503) 648-9791
Email: service@buttepublications.com
Website: http://www.buttepublications.com

Publishes: Nonfiction; *Markets:* Academic; Professional

Publishes special educational resources. All titles must be useful to Deaf and Hard of Hearing, Speech and Hearing, Special Education, English as a Second Language, or Early Intervention and Early Childhood. See website for submission guidelines.

By Light Unseen Media
PO Box 1233
Pepperell, MA 01463-3233
Email: vyrdolak@bylightunseenmedia.com
Website: http://www.bylightunseenmedia.com

Publishes: Fiction; Nonfiction; Culture; Fantasy; Historical; Horror; Sci-Fi; *Markets:* Adult; Youth

Publishes vampire fiction and nonfiction.

Fiction should be full-length novels 75,000 to 150,000 words in length. No short story collections. Interested in dramatic fiction with a realistic tone. All work must be entirely the author's work (not using any elements of other, established worlds). No slayers, hunters, etc.

Nonfiction of 50,000 words to 150,000 words exploring vampires in folklore, cultural tradition, occult theory and as a modern social subgroup or counter-culture are also sought.

Accepts approaches by post or email. See website for full guidelines.

Canterbury House Publishing, Ltd

7350 S. Tamiami Trail
Sarasota, FL 34231
Tel: +1 (941) 312-6912
Website: http://www.
canterburyhousepublishing.com

Publishes: Fiction; Nonfiction; *Areas:*
Autobiography; Mystery; Romance;
Suspense; *Markets:* Adult

Publishes manuscripts that have a strong Southeastern US regional setting. Gives preference to stories along the southern Appalachian trail. Seeks fiction with an unusual protagonist that could be part of a romance/suspense or mystery series. Will consider memoirs or inspirational novels with strong regional appeal. No spy thrillers, explicit material, or books for children or young adults. Make contact via web form in first instance, requesting editorial email address. See website for full guidelines. Also provides ebook formatting services.

Capstone

1710 Roe Crest Drive
North Mankato, MN 56003
Email: author.sub@capstonepub.com
Website: http://www.capstonepub.com

Publishes: Fiction; Nonfiction; Poetry;
Areas: Adventure; Autobiography;
Biography; Drama; Fantasy; Historical;
Humour; Military; Mystery; Sci-Fi; Sport;
Markets: Children's; Youth

Publishes fiction and nonfiction for children and young adults. Send query by email with CV, sample chapters, and list of any previous publishing credits. Response only if interested. See website for full submission guidelines.

Capstone Professional

Capstone Nonfiction
1710 Roe Crest Drive
North Mankato, MN 56003
Tel: +1 (312) 324-5200
Fax: +1 (312) 324-5201
Email: info@maupinhouse.com
Website: http://www.capstonepub.com/
classroom/professional-development/

Publishes: Nonfiction; *Markets:* Academic;
Professional

Publishes books for teaching professionals, written by classroom practitioners with vast experiences. Send query by US mail only, with cover letter, CV, and up to three writing samples.

The Catholic University of America Press

240 Leahy Hall
620 Michigan Avenue NE
Washington, DC 20064
Email: Lipscombe@cua.edu
Website: http://cuapress.cua.edu

Publishes: Nonfiction; *Areas:* Historical;
Literature; Philosophy; Politics; Religious;
Sociology; *Markets:* Academic; Professional

Contact: Trevor Lipscombe, Director

Publishes books disseminating scholarship in the areas of theology, philosophy, church history, and medieval studies. Send query with outline, CV, sample chapter, and publishing history.

CATO Institute

1000 Massachusetts Ave, NW
Washington, DC 20001-5403
Tel: +1 (202) 842 0200
Website: http://www.cato.org

Publishes: Nonfiction; *Areas:* Philosophy;
Politics; Sociology; *Markets:* Adult

Public policy think tank promoting individual liberty, limited government, free markets and peace. Send query by post with SASE.

Cave Books

277 Clamer Road
Trenton, NJ 08628
Tel: +1 (609) 530-9743
Email: editor@cavebooks.com
Website: http://www.cavebooks.com

Publishes: Fiction; Nonfiction; *Areas:*
Adventure; Anthropology; Archaeology;
Biography; Historical; Leisure; Nature;
Photography; Science; Sport; Travel;
Markets: Treatments: Literary; Serious

Contact: Elizabeth Winkler

!! Books about caves ONLY!!

Small press devoted to books on caves, karst,
and speleology.

Fiction: novels about cave exploration only.
Publishes hardcover and trade paperback
originals and reprints.

Books: acid-free paper, offset printing.

Published two debut authors within the last
year.

Needs: Adventure, historical, literary, caves,
karst, speleology.

How to Contact: Accepts unsolicited mss.
Query with SASE or submit complete ms.
Accepts queries by email. Send SASE for
return of ms or send a disposable ms and
SASE for reply only. Responds in 2 weeks to
queries; 3 months to mss. Accepts
simultaneous submissions, electronic
submissions.

Sometimes comments on rejected mss.

Terms: Pays 10% royalty on retail price.

Publishes ms 18 months after acceptance.

Advice: "In the last three years we have
received only three novels about caves, and
we have published one of them. We get
dozens of inappropriate submissions."

Cave Hollow Press

PO Drawer J

Warrensburg, MO 64093
Email: gbcrump@cavehollowpress.com
Website: http://www.cavehollowpress.com

Publishes: Fiction; *Markets:* Adult;
Treatments: Mainstream

Contact: Georgia R. Nagel; R.M. Kinder

**Note: Not accepting new material as at
April 2016**

Actively seeking mainstream novels between
60,000 and 80,000 words by authors from
Missouri, the Midwest, and surrounding
regions. Send query with SASE, 1-3 page
synopsis, and first three chapters or 30-40
pages of the completed MS.

Centerstream Publishing

Email: Centerstrm@aol.com
Website: http://www.centerstream-usa.com

Publishes: Nonfiction; Reference; *Areas:*
Biography; How-to; Music; *Markets:* Adult

Publishes music books on instruments,
instructional, reference, and biographies.

Chelsea Green Publishing, Inc.

85 North Main Street, Suite 120
White River Junction, VT 05001
Tel: +1 (802) 295-6300
Fax: +1 (802) 295-6444
Email: web@chelseagreen.com
Website: http://www.chelseagreen.com

Publishes: Nonfiction; *Areas:* Cookery;
Finance; Gardening; How-to; Lifestyle;
Nature; New Age; Politics; Science;
Spiritual; *Markets:* Academic; Adult;
Professional

Publishes books on organic gardening and
market farming, from home to professional
scale, and related topics, including renewable
energy, food politics, and alternative
economic models. Will only occasionally
publish academic, new age, or spiritual, and
does not publish fiction, poetry, or books for
children. See website for submission
guidelines.

Chicago Review Press
814 North Franklin Street
Chicago, Illinois 60610
Tel: +1 (312) 337-0747
Fax: +1 (312) 337-5110
Email: frontdesk@chicagoreviewpress.com
Website: http://www.
chicagoreviewpress.com

Publishes: Fiction; Nonfiction; *Areas:*
Autobiography; Biography; Crafts; Culture;
Film; Gardening; Historical; Lifestyle;
Music; Politics; Science; Sport; Travel;
Women's Interests; *Markets:* Adult;
Children's; Youth

Publishes nonfiction through all imprints,
and fiction through specific imprint listed
above. Also publishes children's and young
adult titles, but no picture books. See website
for full submission guidelines.

Children's Brains are Yummy (CBAY) Books
PO Box 670296
Dallas, TX 75367
Email: madeline@cbaybooks.com
Website: http://cbaybooks.com

Publishes: Fiction; *Areas:* Adventure;
Fantasy; Mystery; Sci-Fi; Short Stories;
Suspense; *Markets:* Children's; Youth

Contact: Madeline Smoot

Publishes fiction for children. Closed to
approaches for chapter books, midgrade or
YA novels as at September 2015, but open to
anthology submissions of short fiction. See
website for details.

Church Publishing Incorporated
445 Fifth Avenue
New York, NY 10016
Email: nabryan@cpg.org
Website: https://www.churchpublishing.org

Publishes: Nonfiction; *Areas:* Religious;
Markets: Adult; Professional

Contact: Nancy Bryan, Editorial Director

Publishes worship materials and resources
for The Episcopal Church, including works
on church leadership, pastoral care and
Christian formation.

Cinco Puntos Press
701 Texas Avenue
El Paso, Texas 79901
Tel: +1 (915) 838-1625
Fax: +1 (915) 838-1635
Email: info@cincopuntos.com
Website: http://www.cincopuntos.com

Publishes: Fiction; Nonfiction; Poetry;
Markets: Adult; Children's; Youth

Contact: Lee Byrd, Acquisitions Editor,

Small independent publishing company,
publishing fiction, poetry, nonfiction and
graphic novels for adults, young adults, and
children. Review books on website to see if
yours is a fit, and if so query Acquisitions
Editor by phone. See website for more
details.

Cleveland State University Poetry Center
2121 Euclid Avenue
Rhodes Tower, Room 1841
Cleveland, OH 44115
Email: poetrycenter@csuohio.edu
Website: http://www.csupoetrycenter.com

Publishes: Poetry; *Markets:* Adult

Most books published are received through
competitions run by the press, for which
there is an entry fee. Also publishes books
solicited from authors, but no unsolicited
mss, other than via the competitions or for
occasional anthologies (see website).

Conari Press
665 Third Street, Suite 400
San Francisco, CA 94107
Email: submissions@rwwbooks.com
Website: http://redwheelweiser.com

Publishes: Nonfiction; *Areas:* Cookery;
Health; Humour; Lifestyle; Self-Help;
Spiritual; Women's Interests; *Markets:* Adult

Contact: Pat Bryce

Publishes inspirational books: mind, body, spirit; health; food; wellness; women's; spirituality; parenting; social issues. Send query post or by email with proposal and sample illustrations or photographs is appropriate. See website for full guidelines.

Concordia Publishing House
3558 S. Jefferson
St. Louis, MO 63118-3968
Tel: +1 (314) 268-1000
Fax: +1 (800) 490 9889
Email: ideas@cph.org
Website: http://www.cph.org

Publishes: Nonfiction; *Areas:* Culture; Lifestyle; Religious; Spiritual; *Markets:* Adult; Children's; Family; Youth

No Christian fiction, autobiographies, poetry, or children's picture books. Send query by email.

Continental
520 East Bainbridge Street
Elizabethtown, PA 17022
Tel: +1 (800) 233-0759
Fax: +1 (888) 834-1303
Email: bspencer@continentalpress.com
Website: https://www.continentalpress.com

Publishes: Fiction; Nonfiction; *Areas:* Arts; Science; Sociology; Technology; *Markets:* Academic; Children's

Publishes educational materials for grades K–12, specialising in reading, mathematics, and test preparation materials. Also publishes fiction and nonfiction leveled readers and other materials that support early literacy in kindergarten through to second grade. See website for full submission guidelines.

Covenant Communications Inc.
920 E State Road
American Fork, UT 84003
Tel: +1 (801) 756-1041
Fax: +1 (801) 756-1049

Email: submissionsdesk@covenant-lds.com
Website: http://www.covenant-lds.com

Publishes: Fiction; Nonfiction; Reference; *Areas:* Adventure; Biography; Historical; Humour; Mystery; Religious; Romance; Spiritual; Suspense; *Markets:* Academic; Adult; Children's; Family; Youth; *Treatments:* Contemporary; Literary; Mainstream

Only publishes work that supports the doctrines and / or values of The Church of Jesus Christ of Latter-day Saints. Books should be original and well written, appeal to a broad readership, be consistent with the standards and principles of the restored gospel of Jesus Christ, and promote the faith of members of the Church and inspire them to lead better lives. Not generally interested in poetry, family histories, or personal journals. Send complete MS by email or by post. See website for full submission guidelines.

CQ Press
2455 Teller Road
Thousand Oaks, CA 91320
Tel: +1 (800) 818-7243
Fax: +1 (800) 583-2665
Email: michael.kerns@sagepub.com
Website: http://www.cqpress.com

Publishes: Nonfiction; Reference; *Areas:* Historical; Politics; *Markets:* Academic; Adult; Professional

Contact: Michael Kerns

Publishes books on American and international politics and people, including academic text books on political science, directories on governments, elections, etc. See website for full submission guidelines and individual Acquisition Editor contact details.

Craigmore Creations
Attn: Submissions
2900 SE Stark St, Suite 1A
Portland, OR 97214
Tel: +1 (503) 477-9562
Email: info@craigmorecreations.com

Website: http://www.craigmorecreations.com

Publishes: Fiction; Nonfiction; *Areas:*
Nature; Science; *Markets:* Children's

Graphic novel and children's book publisher,
publishing books focussed on science and
natural history. For picture books submit
complete ms; otherwise send query with one
or two sample chapters. Include SASE for
reply. No submissions by fax or email. No
approaches by phone. See website for full
submission guidelines.

Creative With Words (CWW)
PO Box 223226
Carmel, CA 93922
Fax: +1 (831) 655-8627
Email: geltrich@mbay.net
Website: http://creativewithwords.tripod.com

Publishes: Fiction; Poetry; *Areas:* Short
Stories; *Markets:* Adult; Children's; Family;
Youth

Contact: Brigitta Geltrich

Publishes themed anthologies of fiction and
prose by adults and children. See website for
details.

Creston Books
PO Box 9369
Berkeley, CA 94709
Email: submissions@crestonbooks.co
Website: http://crestonbooks.co

Publishes: Fiction; *Markets:* Children's

Publishes novels and picture books for
children. Send query by email with full text
(for picture books) or first chapters (novels)
pasted into the body of the email. Accepts
multiple submissions, but no more than one
project per month from the same author.

Cricket Books
70 East Lake Street, Suite 300
Chicago, IL 60601
Tel: +1 (603) 924-7209
Fax: +1 (603) 924-7380
Website: http://www.cricketmag.com

Publishes: Fiction; *Areas:* Adventure;
Fantasy; Historical; Horror; Mystery; Sci-Fi;
Sport; Suspense; Westerns; *Markets:*
Children's; Youth

Publishes books for children from 6 months
to teenagers 14+.

Crimson Romance
Email: editorcrimson@gmail.com
Website: http://www.crimsonromance.com

Publishes: Fiction; *Areas:* Historical;
Romance; Suspense; *Markets:* Adult;
Treatments: Contemporary

Digital-first romance publisher open to
submissions in five sub-genres: romantic
suspense, contemporary, paranormal,
historical, and spicy romance. Willing to
consider novels between 55,000 words and
90,000 words, and novellas between 20,000
and 50,000 words. See website for full
submission guidelines and specific
submission calls.

Crystal Spirit Publishing, Inc.
PO Box 12506
Durham, NC 27709
Email: submissions@crystalspiritinc.com
Website: http://www.crystalspiritinc.com

Publishes: Fiction; Nonfiction; Poetry;
Adventure; Business; Erotic; Religious;
Romance; Self-Help; Short Stories; *Markets:*
Adult; Children's

Send query by post with SASE or by email,
with synopsis and 30-page sample. Will not
consider one-page proposals or full mss. No
historical novels, science fiction, fantasy,
westerns, horror, plays, scientific or
technical reference, or books intended as
textbooks. See website for full details.

Cup of Tea Books
Email: weditor@pagespringpublishing.com
Website: http://cupofteabooks.com

Publishes: Fiction; *Areas:* Mystery;
Romance; Women's Interests; *Markets:*
Adult; *Treatments:* Commercial

Publishes fiction for women, including cozy mysteries, upmarket commercial fiction, and romance. Send query by email with synopsis and the first thirty pages in the body of the email. Include title and the word "Submission" in the subject line. Aims to respond within four weeks – follow up if no response in that time. No submissions or queries by post.

Curiosity Quills Press

PO Box 2160
Reston, VA 20195
Tel: +1 (800) 998-2509
Email: info@curiosityquills.com
Website: https://curiosityquills.com

Publishes: Fiction; *Areas:* Crime; Fantasy; Horror; Mystery; Romance; Thrillers; Women's Interests; *Markets:* Adult; Children's; Youth; *Treatments:* Contemporary; Dark

Publishes hard-hitting dark sci-fi, speculative fiction, and paranormal works aimed at adults, young adults, and new adults. Send query with first three chapters using online submission form.

Cyclotour Guide Books

PO Box 10585
Rochester, NY 14610
Tel: +1 (585) 244-6157
Email: cyclotour@cyclotour.com
Website: http://www.cyclotour.com

Publishes: Nonfiction; *Areas:* Sport; Travel; *Markets:* Adult

Publishes bicycle touring guide books.

Dark Horse Comics

10956 SE Main Street
Milwaukie, OR 97222
Email: prose@darkhorse.com
Website: http://www.darkhorse.com

Publishes: Fiction; *Areas:* Fantasy; Horror; *Markets:* Adult; Youth; *Treatments:* Dark

Publishes comics and prose books in the genres of horror, dark fantasy, and other

genres tangential to or overlapping those. Targets adult and young adult markets. Send query by post with CV, synopsis, and up to three sample chapters (up to about 10,000 words). See website for full submission guidelines.

Darkhouse Books

Email: submissions@darkhousebooks.com
Website: http://darkhousebooks.com

Publishes: Fiction; *Areas:* Crime; Mystery; Short Stories; *Markets:* Adult

Publishes crime and mystery novels and anthologies. See website for current calls for submissions.

David R. Godine, Publisher

Fifteen Court Square, Suite 320
Boston, MA 02108-2536
Tel: +1 (617) 451-9600
Fax: +1 (617) 350-0250
Email: info@godine.com
Website: http://www.godine.com

Publishes: Fiction; Nonfiction; Poetry; *Areas:* Architecture; Arts; Biography; Criticism; Gardening; Historical; Humour; Literature; Nature; Photography; Translations; *Markets:* Adult; *Treatments:* Literary

Recommends writers make approaches via agents. Any unsolicited material received without return postage will be disposed of. No telephone calls or email submissions.

Dawn Publications

12402 Bitney Springs Road
Nevada City, CA 95959
Tel: +1 (530) 274-7775
Fax: +1 (530) 274-7778
Email: submission@dawnpub.com
Website: http://www.dawnpub.com

Publishes: Nonfiction; *Areas:* Nature; *Markets:* Adult; Children's

Contact: Glenn Hovemann, Editor & Co-Publisher

Publisher of nature awareness titles for adults and children. Send complete MS by email or by post with SASE, with description of your work, including: audience age; previous publications (if any); your motivation; relevant background. No response to postal submissions without SASE.

Divertir Publishing LLC

PO Box 232
North Salem, NH 03073
Email: query@divertirpublishing.com
Website: http://divertirpublishing.com

Publishes: Fiction; Nonfiction; Poetry; *Areas:* Crafts; Current Affairs; Fantasy; Historical; Hobbies; Humour; Mystery; Politics; Religious; Romance; Sci-Fi; Self-Help; Short Stories; Spiritual; Suspense; *Markets:* Adult; Youth; *Treatments:* Contemporary; Satirical

Publishes full-length fiction, short fiction, poetry, and nonfiction. No erotica or material which is disrespectful to the opinions of others. Accepts queries and submissions by email only. See website for full guidelines.

Dog-Eared Publications

PO Box 620863
Middleton, WI 53562-0863
Tel: +1 (608) 831-1410
Fax: +1 (608) 831-1410
Email: field@dog-eared.com
Website: http://www.dog-eared.com

Publishes: Nonfiction; *Areas:* Nature; *Markets:* Children's

Publishes nature books for children.

Dufour Editions

PO Box 7
124 Byers Road
Chester Springs, PA 19425
Tel: +1 (610) 458-5005
Fax: +1 (610) 458-7103
Email: info@dufoureditions.com
Website: http://www.dufoureditions.com

Publishes: Fiction; Nonfiction; Poetry;

Areas: Biography; Historical; Short Stories; Translations; Markets. Adult; *Treatments:* Literary

Contact: Christopher May

Publishes fiction, poetry, and nonfiction for a sophisticated, literate audience. Particularly focuses on distributing the output of British and Irish publishers across the US and Canada, and translating foreign literature, as well as publishing American writers. Strong Irish-Celtic focus. Check website to see if you're material is suitable, and, if so, send query with SASE.

Duquesne University Press

600 Forbes Avenue
Pittsburgh, PA 15282
Tel: +1 (800) 666-2211
Email: wadsworth@duq.edu
Website: http://www.dupress.duq.edu

Publishes: Nonfiction; *Areas:* Literature; Philosophy; Psychology; Religious; Sociology; Spiritual; *Markets:* Academic

Contact: Susan Wadsworth-Booth, Director

Publishes monographs and collections in the humanities and social sciences, particularly literature studies (Medieval and Renaissance), philosophy, psychology, religious studies and theology, plus spirituality. No fiction, poetry, children's books, technical or "hard" science works, or unrevised theses or dissertations. Send query with outline, table of contents, sample chapter or introduction, author CV, and details of any previous publications. Submit by post (with SASE if return of material required) or by email (in the body of the email only – no attachments).

Eagle's View Publishing

6756 North Fork Road
Liberty, UT 84310
Tel: +1 (801) 393-4555
Email: sales@eaglefeathertrading.com
Website: http://www.eaglesviewpub.com

Publishes: Nonfiction; *Areas:* Anthropology; Archaeology; Crafts; Culture; Historical;

Hobbies; How-to; *Markets:* Adult

Contact: Denise Knight

Publishes books on Native American crafts, history, and culture. Send outline with one or two sample chapters.

Eakin Press
PO Box 331779
Fort Worth, Texas 76163
Tel: +1 (817) 344-7036
Fax: +1 (817) 344-7036
Website: http://www.eakinpress.com

Publishes: Fiction; Nonfiction; *Areas:*
Biography; Business; Cookery; Culture;
Finance; Historical; Military; Sport;
Markets: Adult; Children's; Youth

Publishes books on the history and culture of the Southwest, especially Texas and Oklahoma. Publishes nonfiction for adults, and books for children. Send query with outline/synopsis, or use author inquiry form on website.

Edward Elgar Publishing Inc.
The William Pratt House
9 Dewey Court
Northampton, MA 01060-3815
Tel: +1 (413) 584-5551
Fax: +1 (413) 584-9933
Email: elgarinfo@e-elgar.com
Website: http://www.e-elgar.com

Publishes: Nonfiction; *Areas:* Business;
Finance; Legal; Sociology; Travel; *Markets:*
Academic; Professional

Contact: Alan Sturmer; Stephen Gutierrez

International academic and professional publisher with a strong focus on the social sciences and legal fields. Actively commissioning new titles and happy to consider and advise on ideas for monograph books, textbooks, professional law books and academic journals at any stage. See website for more details and proposal forms.

William B. Eerdmans Publishing Co.
2140 Oak Industrial Dr. NE
Grand Rapids, MI 49505
Tel: +1 (616) 459-4591
Fax: +1 (616) 459-6540
Email: info@eerdmans.com
Website: http://www.eerdmans.com

Publishes: Nonfiction; Reference; *Areas:*
Historical; Philosophy; Religious; Spiritual;
Markets: Adult; Children's

Contact: Jon Pott, Editor-in-Chief

Publishes some regional books and other nonreligious titles, but essentially a religious publisher whose titles range from the academic to the semi-popular. It is now publishing a growing number of books in the areas of spirituality and the Christian life. It has long specialised, however, in biblical studies and Religious and in religious approaches to philosophy, history, art, literature, ethics, and contemporary social and cultural issues. See website for full submission guidelines.

Ellysian Press
Email: submissions@ellysianpress.com
Website: http://www.ellysianpress.com

Publishes: Fiction; *Areas:* Fantasy; Horror;
Romance; Sci-Fi; *Markets:* Adult; Youth

Publishes novels between 60,000 and 120,000 words. Send query by email with synopsis and first ten pages in the body of the email. See website for full guidelines.

Enete Enterprises
Tel: +1 (619) 618-0224
Email: EneteEnterprises@gmail.com
Website: http://www.eneteenterprises.com

Publishes: Nonfiction; *Areas:*
Autobiography; Travel; *Markets:* Adult

Publishes travel, guide books, and memoir genres. Send query by email with the subject line "Query", with marketing plan and sample chapters as a PDF attachment. Accepts simultaneous submissions and unagented authors. See website for full details

Entangled Teen

Website: http://www.entangledteen.com

Publishes: Fiction; *Areas:* Fantasy; Historical; Romance; Sci-Fi; Thrillers; *Markets:* Youth; *Treatments:* Contemporary

Publishes young adult romances between 50,000 and 100,000 words, aimed at ages 16-19. Submit via website using online submission system.

Facts on File, Inc.

Infobase Publishing
132 West 31st Street, 17th Floor
New York, NY 10001
Tel: +1 (800) 322-8755
Fax: +1 (800) 678-3633
Email: editorial@factsonfile.com
Website: http://www.factsonfile.com

Publishes: Nonfiction; Reference; *Markets:* Academic; Adult; Youth

Publishes print, eBooks, and online reference materials for the school and library market. Send query or manuscript proposal by post or by email. Publishes reference books, general trade, young adult trade, and academic, for the school and library markets; atlases, encyclopedias, biographical dictionaries, etc. No fiction, popular nonfiction, or cookery.

FalconGuides

246 Goose Lane
Guilford, CT 06357
Tel: +1 (203) 458-4500
Email: info@rowman.com
Website: http://www.falcon.com

Publishes: Nonfiction; *Areas:* Adventure; Nature; Travel; *Markets:* Adult

Publishes outdoor guidebooks covering hiking, climbing, paddling, and outdoor adventure.

Familius

1254 Commerce Way
Sanger, CA 93657
Tel: +1 (559) 876-2170
Fax: +1 (559) 876-2180
Email: bookideas@familius.com
Website: http://familius.com

Publishes: Fiction; Nonfiction; *Areas:* Autobiography; Cookery; Finance; Health; Hobbies; Humour; Lifestyle; Medicine; Self-Help; *Markets:* Adult; Children's; Youth

Publishes fiction and nonfiction for adults, young adults, and children, focussed on family as the fundamental unit of society. Submit by post or using online submission system. See website for full details.

Fantagraphics

7563 Lake City Way NE
Seattle, WA 98115
Tel: +1 (206) 524-1967
Fax: +1 (206) 524-2104
Email: FBIComix@fantagraphics.com
Website: http://www.fantagraphics.com

Publishes: Fiction; *Areas:* Arts; Autobiography; Culture; Humour; *Markets:* Adult; *Treatments:* Literary

Publishes comics for thinking readers. Previous work has covered autobiographical journalism, surrealism, arts, culture, etc. No mainstream comic genres or material aimed at children. Submit by post only. No response unless interested. See website for full guidelines.

Farrar, Straus & Giroux, Inc.

18 West 18th Street
New York, NY 10011
Tel: +1 (646)307-5151
Email: fsg.editorial@fsgbooks.com
Website: http://www.fsgbooks.com

Publishes: Fiction; Nonfiction; Poetry; *Markets:* Adult; Children's; Youth

Send query describing submission with first 50 pages (fiction and nonfiction), complete ms (picture books), or 3-4 poems.

Submissions by mail only – no queries or mss by email.

Farrar, Straus and Giroux Books for Younger Readers

175 Fifth Avenue
New York, NY 10010
Email: childrens.editorial@fsgbooks.com
Website: http://us.macmillan.com/publishers/
farrar-straus-giroux#FYR

Publishes: Fiction; Nonfiction; *Markets:*
Children's; Youth

Publishes fiction, nonfiction, and picture books for children and teenagers. Send query by post only with first 50 pages.

Ferguson Publishing

132 West 31st Street, 17th Floor
New York, NY 10001
Tel: +1 (800) 322-8755
Fax: +1 (800) 678-3633
Email: editorial@factsonfile.com
Website: http://ferguson.
infobasepublishing.com

Publishes: Nonfiction; Reference; *Areas:*
How-to; Lifestyle; Self-Help; *Markets:*
Academic; Adult; Children's; Professional;
Youth

Publishes career education books aimed at the middle school, high school, and public library markets. Send query or outline with one sample chapter. See website for full submission guidelines.

Fiction Collective Two (FC2)

University of Alabama Press
Box 870380
Tuscaloosa, AL 35487-0380
Tel: +1 (773) 702-7000
Email: fc2.cmu@gmail.com
Website: http://www.fc2.org

Publishes: Fiction; *Markets:* Adult;
Treatments: Experimental

An author-run, not-for-profit publisher of artistically adventurous, non-traditional fiction. Publishes the work of the members

of the Collective, and is committed to finding new and innovative work and continuously expanding the membership of the Collective. New members are acquired through contests (see website) and through member-sponsored submissions.

Filbert Publishing

140 3rd Street North
Kandiyohi, MN 56251-0326
Tel: +1 (320) 444-5080
Email: FilbertPublishing@
FilbertPublishing.com
Website: http://filbertpublishing.com

Publishes: Fiction; Nonfiction; *Areas:*
Cookery; Health; How-to; Lifestyle; Self-
Help; *Markets:* Adult

Publishes mainly nonfiction and a small amount of fiction every year. Particularly interested in books that help creative people make a living following their dream; healthy living; plant based cooking; but will also consider other topics. Considers manuscripts from 25,000 to 85,000 words (minimum for cookbooks is 5,000 words). Prefers conversational writing. Send query by email with synopsis and information about your ms. See website for full details.

Finney Company

5995 149th Street West, Suite 105
Apple Valley, MN 55124
Tel: +1 (952) 469-6699
Fax: +1 (952) 469-1968
Email: info@finneyco.com
Website: http://www.finneyco.com

Publishes: Nonfiction; *Areas:* Arts; Crafts;
Culture; Gardening; Historical; Leisure;
Nature; Science; Sport; Technology; Travel;
Markets: Adult; Children's

Independent publisher, distributor, and manufacturer of educational materials. No mysteries, romances, science fiction, poems, collections of short stories, religious material, or recipe/cookbooks. Send query outlining your MS and background with SASE, one-page outline, table of contents, at least the first three chapters, and market info.

No submissions by email. See website for full guidelines.

Floating Bridge Press

909 NE 43rd Street, #205
Seattle, WA 98105
Email: floatingbridgepress@yahoo.com
Website: http://www.floatingbridgepress.org

Publishes: Poetry; *Markets:* Adult

Publishes books of poetry by Washington State poets. All submissions must be made through the annual competition, entry fee: $12. Submit online.

Fodor's Travel Publications

1745 Broadway, 15th floor
New York, NY 10019
Email: editors@fodors.com
Website: http://www.fodors.com

Publishes: Nonfiction; *Areas:* Travel; *Markets:* Adult

Publishes travel books. Send query by email or by post with resume and writing clips. Writers generally live in the area they are covering. No unsolicited mss.

Folded Word LLC

Attn: Barbara Flaherty, Submissions Editor
79 Tracy Way
Meredith, NH 03253
Website: https://folded.wordpress.com

Publishes: Fiction; Nonfiction; Poetry; *Areas:* Humour; Literature; Nature; Translations; Travel; *Markets:* Adult; *Treatments:* Literary

Publishes fiction, poetry, literary essays, travel narratives, translation, and novels in verse / flash. Only accepting queries for chapbook-length manuscripts as at March 2016. Check website for current status. Send query by post only, with cover letter, three sample pages, and SASE (writers outside the US may omit the stamp). See website for full guidelines.

Fonthill Media LLC

60 Thoreau Street #204
Concord, MA 01742

UK OFFICE:
Millview House
Toadsmoor Road
Stroud
Gloucestershire
GL5 2TB
Email: submissions@fonthillmedia.com
Website: http://fonthillmedia.com

Publishes: Nonfiction; *Areas:* Archaeology; Biography; Historical; Military; Sociology; Sport; Travel; *Markets:* Adult

Independent publisher with offices in the UK and US. Publishes nonfiction only. Send query through website submissions form or by email, providing your project's title, description up to 200 words, description of yourself up to 100 words, proposed word count, and nature and number of illustrations.

Fordham University Press

2546 Belmont Avenue
University Box L
Bronx, NY 10458
Tel: +1 (718) 817-4795
Fax: +1 (718) 817-4785
Email: tlay@fordham.edu
Website: http://fordhampress.com

Publishes: Nonfiction; *Areas:* Anthropology; Architecture; Arts; Biography; Business; Culture; Finance; Historical; Legal; Literature; Media; Medicine; Music; Philosophy; Photography; Politics; Religious; Science; Sociology; Women's Interests; *Markets:* Academic; Adult

Contact: Tom Lay, Acquisitions Editor

Publishes scholarly books in the humanities and social sciences, as well as trade books of interest to the general public. Particularly interested in philosophy, religion, theology, literature, history, media studies, and books of both scholarly and general appeal about New York City and the Hudson Valley. Send proposal by post only (see website for list of appropriate contacts for different subjects). No fiction, or submissions by email.

Foreign Policy Association
470 Park Avenue South
New York, NY 10016
Email: info@fpa.org
Website: http://www.fpa.org

Publishes: Nonfiction; *Areas:* Historical; Legal; Politics; *Markets:* Adult

Publishes books that develop awareness, understanding, and informed opinion on US foreign policy and global issues.

4th Level Indie
Email: 4thlevelindie@gmail.com
Website: http://www.4thlevelindie.com

Publishes: Nonfiction; *Areas:* Crafts; Hobbies; *Markets:* Adult

Small publisher publishing 1-2 books a year on alternative crafts and hobbies.

Frederic C. Beil, Publisher
609 Whitaker Street
Savannah, GA 31401
Tel: +1 (912) 233-2446
Email: editor@beil.com
Website: http://www.beil.com

Publishes: Fiction; Nonfiction; *Areas:* Biography; Historical; *Markets:* Adult

Publishes general trade books in the fields of history, biography, and fiction. Will respond to email queries, but prefers queries by post with SASE. No unsolicited mss.

Free Spirit Publishing
217 Fifth Avenue North, Suite 200
Minneapolis, MN 55401-1299
Tel: +1 (800) 735-7323
Fax: +1 (866) 419-5199
Email: acquisitions@freespirit.com
Website: http://www.freespirit.com

Publishes: Fiction; Nonfiction; *Areas:* How-to; Lifestyle; Self-Help; Sociology; *Markets:* Academic; Adult; Children's; Youth

Publishes nonfiction books and learning materials for children and teens, parents, educators, counselors, and others who live and work with young people. Also publishes fiction relevant to the mission of providing children and teens with the tools they need to succeed in life, e.g.: self-esteem; conflict resolution, etc. No general fiction or storybooks; books with animal or mythical characters; books with religious or New Age content; or single biographies, autobiographies, or memoirs. No submissions by fax or email. See website for full submission guidelines.

FutureCycle Press
Email: dkistner@gmail.com
Website: http://www.futurecycle.org

Publishes: Poetry; *Markets:* Adult

Publishes contemporary English language poetry books and chapbooks. Submit via website through online submission system. $15 reading fee.

Geostar Publishing & Services LLC
6423 Woodbine Court
St. Louis, MO 63109
Tel: +1 (314) 260-9978
Email: opportunities@geostarpublishing.com
Website: http://www.geostarpublishing.com/opportunities.htm

Publishes: Nonfiction; Reference; *Areas:* Adventure; Anthropology; Antiques; Archaeology; Architecture; Arts; Autobiography; Beauty and Fashion; Biography; Business; Cookery; Crafts; Crime; Criticism; Culture; Current Affairs; Design; Drama; Entertainment; Erotic; Fantasy; Film; Finance; Gardening; Gothic; Health; Historical; Hobbies; Horror; How-to; Humour; Legal; Leisure; Lifestyle; Literature; Media; Medicine; Men's Interests; Military; Music; Mystery; Nature; New Age; Philosophy; Photography; Politics; Psychology; Radio; Religious; Romance; Science; Sci-Fi; Self-Help; Short Stories; Sociology; Spiritual; Sport; Suspense; Technology; Theatre; Thrillers; Translations;

Travel; TV; Westerns; Women's Interests;
Markets: Academic; Adult; Children's;
Family; Professional; Youth; *Treatments:*
Commercial; Contemporary; Cynical; Dark;
Experimental; In-depth; Light; Mainstream;
Niche; Popular; Positive; Progressive;
Satirical; Serious; Traditional

Contact: Richard J. Runion

We invite SMEs (Subject Matter Experts),
Small Businesspersons and Niche Service
Providers to visit our site.

We market your services, worldwide!
Absolutely Free!!
…And Pay You Too!!!

How Can Anyone Do That?
Sounds Too Good To Be True?
Is Geostar A Charity?
Is There A Catch?
…Read On!

We are a UNIQUE Publisher. Unlike Any
Other! We're like Venture Capital Investor
of the Publishing Industry. We publish
eBooks on topics people are desperately
looking for. We don't publish on a topic just
because we can find writers. We do
extensive & intensive research, secondary &
primary, on every topic we publish on. Our
customers for eBooks (like the ones on
Waste Water Treatment and Content
Management Systems) are more than eBook
buyers; many of them are actively looking
for a product/ service/ help from experts:
some are looking for Consultancy, some for
services, even on a long term basis.

We have evolved business models that will
work like a charm for you, fetching you pre-
qualified business leads, at no cost to you,
from across the globe. (Or locally if you so
prefer.)

If you want to work with us, please fill in the
form on our site, or contact us thru email/
phone.

Gibbs Smith, Publisher
PO Box 667
Layton, Utah, 84041
Tel: +1 (801) 544-9800

Fax: +1 (801) 544 5502
Email: DUribe@gibbs-smith.com
Website: http://www.gibbs-smith.com

Publishes: Nonfiction; *Areas:* Architecture;
Arts; Cookery; Crafts; Design; Humour;
Markets: Adult; Children's

Send query by email only. Main emphasis is
on interior design, architecture, children's
activities, and cookbooks. Will also accept
submissions of: Arts & Crafts, western
humour with general appeal,
general humour, gift books, and children's
activity books and board books. See website
for full submission guidelines. At this time
not accepting fiction, poetry, or picture
books.

Gival Press, LLC
PO Box 3812
Arlington, VA 22203
Tel: +1 (703) 351-0079
Email: givalpress@yahoo.com
Website: http://www.givalpress.com

Publishes: Fiction; Nonfiction; Poetry;
Areas: Culture; Philosophy; Sociology;
Translations; Women's Interests; *Markets:*
Adult; *Treatments:* Literary

Publishes fiction, nonfiction (including
essays and educational texts) and poetry by
poets and writers from many walks of life
whose work has a philosophical or social
message. See website for full submission
guidelines.

Goosebottom Books LLC
543 Trinidad Lane
Foster City, CA 94404
Tel: +1 (800) 788-3123
Fax: +1 (888) 407-5286
Email: submissions@
goosebottombooks.com
Website: http://goosebottombooks.com

Publishes: Fiction; Nonfiction; *Areas:*
Adventure; Historical; *Markets:* Children's;
Youth

Publishes books for children and young
adults, including fiction and nonfiction,

particularly historical. All work is commissioned. Send writing samples if you would like to be considered as a writer for future projects.

Grayson Books

Email: gconnors@graysonbooks.com
Website: http://www.graysonbooks.com

Publishes: Poetry; *Markets:* Adult

Small poetry publisher, publishing a few books each year. Send query by email with Word document attachment with a sample of 6-10 poems.

Great Potential Press, Inc.

1325 N. Wilmot Ave., #300
Tucson, AZ 85712
Tel: +1 (520) 777-6161
Fax: +1 (520) 777-6217
Email: info@greatpotentialpress.com
Website: http://www.greatpotentialpress.com

Publishes: Nonfiction; *Markets:* Academic;
Adult; Children's

Publishes books that support the academic, social, or emotional needs of gifted children and adults. No fiction, poetry, or K-12 classroom materials. Approach via proposal submission form on website.

Gun Digest Books

F+W Media
700 East State Street
Iola, WI 54990
Website: http://www.gundigest.com

Publishes: Nonfiction; Reference; *Areas:*
Historical; Hobbies; How-to; Technology;
Markets: Adult; *Treatments:* Mainstream

Publishes firearms books with mainstream appeal. Send complete ms or query with outline, author bio and two sample chapters.

Hachai Publishing

527 Empire Boulevard
Brooklyn, NY 11225
Tel: +1 (718) 633-0100
Fax: +1 (718) 633-0103

Email: editor@hachai.com
Website: http://hachai.com

Publishes: Fiction; Nonfiction; *Areas:*
Historical; Religious; *Markets:* Children's

Publishes children's fiction and nonfiction relating to the Jewish experience. No animal stories, romance, violence, preachy sermonising, or elements that violate Jewish Law. See website for full submission guidelines.

Harken Media

Seattle, WA
Email: hmeditors@gmail.com
Website: http://www.harkenmedia.com

Publishes: Fiction; *Areas:* Fantasy;
Historical; Humour; Mystery; Sci-Fi;
Markets: Adult; Youth; *Treatments:* Literary

Publishes books with unique insights or compelling themes for young adult, new adult, and adult audiences. Send query by email only. See website for full guidelines.

Harlequin American Romance

PO Box 5190
Buffalo, NY 14240-5190
Email: submisssions@harlequin.com
Website: http://www.harlequin.com

Publishes: Fiction; *Areas:* Romance;
Westerns; *Markets:* *Treatments:*
Contemporary

Contact: Kathleen Scheibling

Publishes heart-warming contemporary romances featuring small town America and cowboys, up to 55,000 words. See website for more details and to submit.

Harmony Ink Press

5032 Capital Circle SW, Ste 2 PMB 279
Tallahassee, FL 32305-7886
Tel: +1 (800) 970-3759
Fax: +1 (888) 308-3739
Email: submissions@harmonyinkpress.com
Website: https://www.harmonyinkpress.com

Publishes: Fiction; *Areas:* Fantasy; Mystery; Romance; Sci-Fi; *Markets:* Youth

Publishes Teen and New Adult fiction featuring significant personal growth of unforgettable characters across the LGBTQ+ spectrum. Closed to general submissions as at May 2016.

Harry N. Abrams, Inc.
115 West 18th Street
New York, NY 10011
Tel: +1 (212) 206-7715
Fax: +1 (212) 519-1210
Email: abrams@abramsbooks.com
Website: http://www.abramsbooks.com

Publishes: Fiction; Nonfiction; Reference; *Areas:* Architecture; Arts; Beauty and Fashion; Crafts; Culture; Design; Entertainment; Film; Gardening; Hobbies; Humour; Leisure; Lifestyle; Music; Nature; Photography; Religious; Science; Sport; *Markets:* Adult; Children's; Youth

In general, does not accept unsolicited manuscripts or book proposals without a literary agent, except for two imprints: one of comic art and one of crafts. Email approaches accepted only by crafts imprint. See website for full details.

Harvest House Publishers
990 Owen Loop North
Eugene, OR 97402-9173
Tel: +1 (800) 547-8979
Fax: +1 (888) 501-6012
Email: ContactRep@
harvesthousepublishers.com
Website: http://harvesthousepublishers.com

Publishes: Fiction; Nonfiction; *Areas:* Health; Historical; Humour; Lifestyle; Men's Interests; Mystery; Religious; Romance; Suspense; Westerns; Women's Interests; *Markets:* Adult; Children's; Youth

Publisher of Christian literature. Does not accept submissions directly, but is a member of an association which accepts proposals to share with their members. See website for full details.

Hearts 'N Tummies Cookbook Co. / Quixote Press
3544 Blakslee Street
Wever, IA 52658
Tel: +1 (800) 571 2665
Website: http://www.heartsntummies.com

Publishes: Fiction; Nonfiction; *Areas:* Cookery; Humour; Short Stories; Markets

Publishes books on cookery, ghosts, humour, and folklore. Send query with SASE. Also offers services for which writers are charged.

Helicon Nine Editions
PO Box 22412
Kansas City, MO 64113
Tel: +1 (816) 753-1095
Fax: +1 (816) 753-1016
Email: helicon9@aol.com
Website: http://www.heliconnine.com

Publishes: Fiction; Poetry; *Areas:* Short Stories; *Markets:* Adult; *Treatments:* Literary

Independent small, literary publisher, publishing books, chapbooks, and magazines of poetry and fiction.

Heyday Books
PO Box 9145
Berkeley, CA 94709
Tel: +1 (510) 549-3564
Fax: +1 (510) 549-1889
Email: heyday@heydaybooks.com
Website: http://www.heydaybooks.com

Publishes: Fiction; Nonfiction; Poetry; *Areas:* Arts; Culture; Historical; Literature; Nature; *Markets:* Adult; Children's; *Treatments:* Literary

Small publisher of natural and cultural history, literature, and arts, concentrating on California and the West. Consult website to see if your book is appropriate, then send query by post with author details, outline, table of contents and list of illustrations, market details, sample chapter, and SASE. Submissions for children's books may be sent by email. See website for full details.

Hill and Wang

Farrar Straus & Giroux, Inc.
19 Union Square West
New York, NY 10003
Email: fsg.editorial@fsgbooks.com
Website: http://us.macmillan.com/fsg

Publishes: Nonfiction; Historical; Politics;
Science; Sociology; *Markets:* Adult;
Treatments: Serious

Publisher of serious nonfiction covering
history, maths, science, and the social
sciences. No fiction, poetry, or drama. Send
query with SASE, outline, and sample
chapters.

Hipso Media

8151 East 29th Avenue
Denver, CO 80238
Email: rob@hipsomedia.com
Website: http://www.hipsomedia.com

Publishes: Fiction; Nonfiction; *Areas:*
Cookery; Culture; Erotic; Health; How-to;
Humour; Lifestyle; Medicine; Mystery; Self-
Help; Short Stories; Travel; *Markets:* Adult;
Youth

Contact: Rob Simon, Publisher

Digital-first publisher. Particularly keen on
work that lends itself to media enhancements
such as illustrations, videos, music, sound
effects, animations, hyperlinks, etc. Send
query by email with synopsis and author bio.
See website for full guidelines.

Holiday House, Inc.

425 Madison Ave
New York, NY 10017
Tel: +1 (212) 688-0085
Fax: +1 (212) 421-6134
Email: info@holidayhouse.com
Website: http://www.holidayhouse.com

Publishes: Fiction; Nonfiction; *Markets:*
Children's; Youth

Contact: Editorial Department

Independent publisher of children's books,
from picture books to young adult fiction and

nonfiction. Send complete ms by post only.
No need to include SASE. No submissions
by fax or email.

HOW Books

10151 Carver Road, Ste. #200
Blue Ash, OH 45242
Tel: +1 (513) 531-2690
Email: editorial@howdesign.com
Website: http://www.howdesign.com

Publishes: Nonfiction; *Areas:* Arts; Culture;
Design; Technology; *Markets:* Adult

Contact: Scott Francis

Publishes books on graphic design, web
design, and pop culture. Send query by email
with proposal, sample chapter, and sample
image(s) as PDFs.

IBEX Publishers, Inc.

Post Office Box 30087
Bethesda, MD 20824
Tel: +1 (301) 718-8188
Fax: +1 (301) 907-8707
Email: info@ibexpub.com
Website: http://ibexpub.com

Publishes: Nonfiction; Poetry; Reference;
Areas: Arts; Autobiography; Cookery;
Criticism; Historical; Humour; Literature;
Music; Philosophy; Politics; Religious;
Translations; *Markets:* Adult; Children's

Publishes books which introduce the best of
the Persian language, literature, culture and
history to the world. Accepts initial queries
by email but the actual submission must be
sent by post. See "Authors" section of
website for full guidelines. May consider
translations of Persian poetry, but generally
does not publish original poetry or fiction by
unknown authors.

Ig Publishing

392 Clinton Ave
Brooklyn, NY 11238
Tel: +1 (718) 797-0676
Email: robert@igpub.com
Website: http://igpub.com

Publishes: Fiction; Nonfiction; *Areas:* Culture; *Markets:* Adult; Youth; *Treatments:* Literary

Contact: Robert Lasner, Editor-in-Chief

Publishes original literary fiction from writers who are perceived to have been overlooked by the mainstream publishing establishment, plus political and cultural nonfiction. Young adult imprint is devoted to bringing back young adult literature from as far back as the '30s and '40s and as recently as the '70s and '80s. No unsolicited mss. Send query by email only.

Illusio & Baqer

Email: submissions@zharmae.com
Website: https://illusiobaqer.com

Publishes: Fiction; *Markets:* Children's; Youth

Contact: T Denise Clary, Emily Stanford; Cynthia Kumancik

Publishes Young Adult, New Adult, and Middle Grade. Always on the lookout for new, dynamic, and fresh voices. Send query by email with word count, brief author bio (100-200 words), one-page synopsis, and first 3-5 chapters. See website for full guidelines.

Image Comics

Submissions
c/o Image Comics
2001 Center Street, Sixth Floor
Berkeley, CA 94704
Email: submissions@imagecomics.com
Website: http://www.imagecomics.com

Publishes: Fiction; *Markets:* Adult; Youth

Third largest comic book publisher in the United States. Publishes comics and graphic novels. Only interested in creator-owned comics. Does not acquire any rights. Looking for comics that are well written and well drawn, by people who are dedicated and can meet deadlines, not any specific genre or type of comic book. See website for full submission guidelines.

Impact Publishers

PO Box 6016
Atascadero, CA 93423-6016
Tel: +1 (805) 466-5917
Email: submissions@impactpublishers.com
Website: http://impactpublishers.com

Publishes: Nonfiction; *Areas:* Psychology; Self-Help; *Markets:* Adult; *Treatments:* Popular

Publishes popular psychology and self-help written by professionals. Send query by post or email. See website for detailed submission guidelines.

Interlink Publishing Group, Inc.

46 Crosby Street
Northampton, MA 01060
Tel: +1 (413) 582 7054
Fax: +1 (413) 582 7057
Email: info@interlinkbooks.com
Website: http://www.interlinkbooks.com

Publishes: Fiction; Nonfiction; Reference; *Areas:* Arts; Cookery; Film; Historical; Leisure; Literature; Music; Photography; Politics; Sport; Translations; Travel; *Markets:* Adult; Children's

Research the types of books published by reading examples first. If you think your work is suitable, send query by email. In fiction, only publishes work by authors born outside the US, bringing it to the American audience. All children's books are aimed at ages between three and eight, and are illustrated. Manuscripts that do not have illustrations already included are not considered.

Publishes fiction, travel, Children's, politics, cookbooks, and specialises in Middle East titles and ethnicity. No poetry, plays, unsolicited MSS, or queries by fax or email. See website for full guidelines.

International Foundation of Employee Benefit Plans

18700 West Bluemound Road
Brookfield, WI 53045

Tel: +1 (888) 334-3327
Email: bookstore@ifebp.org
Website: http://www.ifebp.org

Publishes: Nonfiction; *Areas:* Business;
Health; *Markets:* Adult; Professional

Nonprofit organisation publishing material
relating to employee benefits, health care,
pensions, etc. Send query with outline.

JIST Publishing
875 Montreal Way
St Paul, MN 55102
Email: educate@emcp.com
Website: http://jist.emcp.com

Publishes: Nonfiction; Reference; *Areas:*
Business; How-to; Self-Help; *Markets:*
Adult

Published books to assist job finding and
career development. Send query with
proposal, one sample chapter, author CV,
competitive analysis, and marketing ideas.

Kansas City Star Books
The Kansas City Star
1729 Grand Boulevard
Kansas City, MO 64108
Email: dweaver@kcstar.com
Website: http://kansascitystarquilts.com

Publishes: Nonfiction; *Areas:* Crafts;
Design; Hobbies; Markets

Contact: Doug Weaver

Publishes books on quilting. See website for
full submission guidelines and downloadable
author form and book proposal form.

Kathy Dawson Books
Penguin Group
375 Hudson Street
New York, NY 10014
Website: http://kathydawsonbooks.
tumblr.com

Publishes: Fiction; *Markets:* Children's;
Youth

Publishes middle grade and young adult
fiction. Submit query by post only, with first
10 pages and details of any relevant
publishing history. Do not include SASE –
all submissions are recycled. Response only
if interested.

Kind of a Hurricane Press
Email: kindofahurricanepress@yahoo.com
Website: http://www.
kindofahurricanepress.com

Publishes: Fiction; Poetry; *Areas:* Short
Stories; *Markets:* Adult

Eclectic small press publishing anthologies
of poetry and flash fiction. See website for
calls for current anthologies and submission
guidelines.

Kirkbride Bible Company
1102 Deloss Street
Indianapolis, IN 46203
Tel: +1 (800) 428-4385
Fax: +1 (317) 633-1444
Email: info@kirkbride.com
Website: http://www.kirkbride.com

Publishes: Nonfiction; Reference; *Areas:*
Religious; *Markets:* Adult

Publisher of bible reference titles.

Leisure Arts, Inc.
104 Champs Boulevard, Suite 100
Maumelle, AR 72113
Tel: +1 (800) 643-8030
Email: submissions@leisurearts.com
Website: http://www.leisurearts.com

Publishes: Nonfiction; *Areas:* Crafts;
Hobbies; How-to; Lifestyle; *Markets:* Adult

Publisher of lifestyle and instructional craft
publications. Publishes books and leaflets in
virtually all craft categories. Send
photographs, swatches, sketches, outlines,
charts, artwork by post or by email, but do
not send actual designs or instructions unless
requested. See website for full details.

LexisNexis

230 Park Avenue, Suite 7
New York, NY 10169
Tel: +1 (212) 309-8100
Fax: +1 (800) 437-8674
Website: http://www.lexisnexis.com

Publishes: Nonfiction; Reference; *Areas:*
Legal; *Markets:* Professional

Publishes books and online materials for the
professional legal market.

Limitless Publishing

Email: submissions@
limitlesspublishing.com
Website: http://www.limitlesspublishing.net

Publishes: Fiction; Nonfiction; *Areas:*
Military; Mystery; Romance; Suspense;
Thrillers; *Markets:* Adult; Youth

Send submissions by email with brief bio,
writing background and publishing history,
social networks used, decsription of your
book, and the first four chapters as a
Microsoft Word attachment.

Lonely Planet Publications

150 Linden Street
Oakland, CA 94607
Tel: +1 (510) 250-6400
Fax: +1 (510) 893-8572
Email: info@lonelyplanet.com
Website: http://www.lonelyplanet.com

Publishes: Nonfiction; Reference; *Areas:*
Travel; *Markets:* Adult

Publisher of travel guides and other travel-
related material.

The Lyons Press Inc.

The Globe Pequot Press, Inc.
Box 480
246 Goose Lane
Guilford, CT 06437
Tel: +1 (203) 458-4500
Fax: +1 (203) 458-4668
Email: info@globepequot.com
Website: http://www.lyonspress.com

Publishes: Nonfiction; Reference; *Areas:*
Autobiography; Cookery; Culture; Current
Affairs; Historical; Nature; Sport; *Markets:*
Adult; *Treatments:* Popular

Publishes history, current affairs, popular
culture, memoir, sports, cooking, nature,
pets, fishing, hunting, reference and
equestrian books. Not accepting submissions
or proposals as at January 2015. Check
website for current situation.

M P Publishing USA

Email: mark@mpassociates.co.uk
Website: http://mppublishingusa.com

Publishes: Fiction; Nonfiction; *Areas:*
Adventure; Crime; Fantasy; Gothic;
Literature; Mystery; Romance; Sci-Fi; Short
Stories; Suspense; Thrillers; Women's
Interests; *Markets:* Adult; Youth;
Treatments: Commercial; Contemporary;
Dark; Experimental; In-depth; Light;
Literary; Mainstream; Niche; Popular;
Progressive; Satirical; Serious; Traditional

Contact: Mark Pearce

Publishes fiction and nonfiction. Not
accepting submissions for print publication
or American distribution as at March 2015.
Submitters should have bought or borrowed
one of the publisher's books prior to
submitting. Accepts submissions by post, but
prefers electronic submissions via form on
website.

McBooks Press

ID Booth Building
520 North Meadow Street
Ithaca NY 14850
Tel: +1 (607) 272-2114
Fax: +1 (607) 273-6068
Email: jackie@mcbooks.com
Website: http://www.mcbooks.com

Publishes: Fiction; Nonfiction; *Areas:*
Cookery; Historical; Military; Sport;
Markets: Adult

Contact: Jackie Swift, Editorial Director

Publishes historical and military / nautical /

naval historical fiction, plus historical, sports, and vegetarian nonfiction. Closed to submissions as at August 2014. Check website for current status.

McFarland & Company, Inc.
Box 611
Jefferson, NC 28640
Tel: +1 (336) 246-4460
Fax: +1 (336) 246-5018
Email: info@mcfarlandpub.com
Website: http://www.mcfarlandpub.com

Publishes: Nonfiction; Reference; *Areas:* Architecture; Arts; Culture; Current Affairs; Film; Health; Historical; Leisure; Literature; Medicine; Military; Music; Sport; Women's Interests; *Markets:* Adult

Publishes Pop Culture, Sports, Military History, Transportation, Body & Mind, History, Literature, Medieval Studies, and Graphic Novels. Send query with SASE, outline, and sample chapters. No fiction, poetry, or children's.

Metal Powder Industries Federation (MPIF)
105 College Road East
Princeton, NJ 08540
Tel: +1 (609) 452-7700
Fax: +1 (609) 987-8523
Email: info@mpif.org
Website: http://www.mpif.org

Publishes: Nonfiction; *Areas:* Technology; *Markets:* Professional

Publishes books on powder metallurgy and particulate materials.

Mitchell Lane Publishers, Inc.
PO Box 196
Hockessin, DE 19707
Tel: +1 (302) 234-9426
Fax: +1 (302) 234-4742
Email: customerservice@mitchelllane.com
Website: http://www.mitchelllane.com

Publishes: Nonfiction; *Areas:* Arts; Biography; Crafts; Health; Historical; Literature; Music; Politics; Science;

Technology; *Markets:* Children's

Publishes nonfiction for children. No unsolicited mss. Send query by post with SASE.

Museum of Northern Arizona
3101 North Fort Valley Road
Flagstaff, AZ 86001
Tel: +1 (928) 774-5213
Email: publications@mna.mus.az.us
Website: http://musnaz.org

Publishes: Nonfiction; *Areas:* Historical; Nature; *Markets:* Adult

Publishes natural history relating to Northern Arizona.

New York University (NYU) Press
838 Broadway, 3rd Floor
New York, NY 10003-4812
Email: information@nyupress.org
Website: http://nyupress.org

Publishes: Nonfiction; *Areas:* Anthropology; Crime; Culture; Historical; Legal; Literature; Media; Politics; Psychology; Religious; Sociology; Women's Interests; *Markets:* Academic

Publishes mainly for the academic market. Send proposals by post only. See website for full guidelines.

Nolo
950 Parker Street
Berkeley, CA 94710
Tel: +1 (510) 549-1976
Fax: +1 (510) 859-0025
Email: mantha@nolo.com
Website: http://www.nolo.com

Publishes: Nonfiction; Reference; *Areas:* Business; Finance; How-to; Legal; Self-Help; *Markets:* Adult; Professional

Publishes books that help individuals, small businesses, and other organisations handle their own legal matters.Send query with SASE, outline, and sample chapter.

NursesBooks

American Nurses Association
8515 Georgia Avenue, Suite 400
Silver Spring, MD 20910-3492
Tel: +1 (800) 637-0323
Email: joseph.vallina@ana.org
Website: http://www.nursesbooks.org

Publishes: Nonfiction; *Areas:* Health;
Markets: Professional

Publishes books for nurses. Send proposal,
saved as a Word file, by email.

The Overmountain Press

PO Box 1261
Johnson City, TN 37605
Tel: +1 (423) 926-2691
Fax: +1 (423) 232-1252
Email: submissions@overmtn.com
Website: http://overmtn.com

Publishes: Fiction; Nonfiction; *Areas:*
Cookery; Historical; Travel; *Markets:* Adult;
Children's; Youth

Contact: Beth Wright (Publisher); Daniel
Lewis (Managing Editor)

Primarily a publisher of Southern
Appalachian nonfiction. Publishes fiction in
the form of picture books for children only.
Publishes nonfiction for children and adults,
including histories, cookery, guidebooks,
ghost lore and folk lore. No email
submissions.

Papercutz

160 Broadway, Suite 700E
New York, NY 10038
Tel: +1 (646) 559-4681
Email: nantier@papercutz.com
Website: http://www.papercutz.com

Publishes: Fiction; *Areas:* Adventure;
Horror; Humour; Mystery; *Markets:*
Children's; Youth

Publisher dedicated to graphic novels for
children, tweens, and teens. Publishes a wide
range of genres, including humour, action
adventure, mystery, horror, and favourite
characters.

Paragon House

1600 Labore Road, Suite 1
St Paul, Minnesota 55110-4144
Tel: +1 (651) 644-3087
Fax: +1 (651) 644-0997
Email: submissions@paragonhouse.com
Website: http://www.paragonhouse.com

Publishes: Nonfiction; Reference; *Areas:*
Biography; Current Affairs; Finance;
Historical; Philosophy; Politics; Psychology;
Religious; Spiritual; *Markets:* Academic;
Adult

Submit by email only, as an attachment.
Include abstract of your project (summary of
your premise, main arguments, and
conclusions); table of contents; sample
chapter; CV; estimated number of diagrams,
figures, pictures or drawings; estimated
number of double-spaced manuscript pages,
in your completed project; tentative schedule
for completion; copies of any endorsements
or reviews; list of competing books, and a
brief note on how your book compares to
each; and SASE for entire MS.

Parallax Press

PO Box 7355
Berkeley, CA 94707
Tel: +1 (510) 540-6411
Email: rachel.neumann@parallax.org
Website: http://www.parallax.org

Publishes: Nonfiction; Markets

Buddhist publisher of books on mindfulness
in daily life. Committed to making these
teachings accessible to everyone and
preserving them for future generations.
Proposals accepted by post or by email. See
website for full guidelines.

Paul Dry Books, Inc.

1700 Sansom Street, Suite 700
Philadelphia, PA 19103
Tel: +1 (215) 231-9939
Fax: +1 (215) 231-9942
Email: editor@pauldrybooks.com
Website: http://pauldrybooks.com

Publishes: Fiction; Nonfiction; Poetry;
Areas: Architecture; Autobiography;

Biography; Criticism; Culture; Historical;
Philosophy; Science; Short Stories;
Translations; Travel; *Markets:* Adult; Youth;
Treatments: Contemporary; Literary

Publisher with the aim to publish lively
books "to awaken, delight, and educate"—
and to spark conversation. Publishes fiction,
including both novels and short stories; and
nonfiction, including biography, memoirs,
history, and essays.

Pauline Books and Media

50 St Paul's Avenue
Boston, MA 02130
Tel: +1 (617) 522-8911
Email: editorial@paulinemedia.com
Website: http://www.pauline.org

Publishes: Fiction; Nonfiction; *Areas:*
Biography; Religious; Self-Help; Spiritual;
Markets: Adult; Children's; Family; Youth

Catholic publisher, publishing nonfiction for
children and adults of all ages, as well as
fiction for children and teens only. Send
complete manuscript or table of contents
with sample chapter by email or by post. See
website for full guidelines.

Pen Books

Email: info@open-bks.com
Website: http://www.open-bks.com

Publishes: Fiction; Nonfiction; *Areas:*
Adventure; Anthropology; Autobiography;
Biography; Crime; Culture; Current Affairs;
Drama; Entertainment; Fantasy; Film;
Finance; Health; Historical; Horror;
Humour; Legal; Leisure; Lifestyle;
Literature; Media; Mystery; Philosophy;
Politics; Psychology; Sci-Fi; Sociology;
Sport; Suspense; Technology; Theatre;
Thrillers; Translations; Travel; Women's
Interests; *Markets:* Adult; *Treatments:*
Contemporary; Literary; Mainstream; Niche;
Popular; Progressive; Satirical; Serious;
Traditional

Contact: D. Ross, K. Huddleston

Publishes high quality fiction, nonfiction and
poetry in paperback and all eBook formats

Our focus is on high quality literary and
contemporary fiction, timely and entertaining
nonfiction and avant-garde poetry. It is our
aim to present the very best of a new
generation of authors to readers who are
looking for fresh voices.

A fully integrated royalty publisher. All our
publications are published in trade paperback
and eBook editions. Paperback editions are
available from the publisher and at many
high quality booksellers around the world.
eBook editions are multi-format and
available to read on all popular eReaders
including Amazon Kindle, Barnes & Noble
Nook, Sony Reader, Kobo Reader, Apple
iPad and others, as well as in PDF for your
PC.

Where to find and purchase our books

All titles can be purchased from our online
store. All transactions at are secure. Delivery
for paperback editions is within 7 -10 days.
Delivery is immediate for eBooks. All
relevant file formats are offered, so simply
choose the format that corresponds to the
device on which you will be reading. All
downloads are DRM free so you can share
your book with family and friends. And
remember, authors earn higher royalties
when you buy direct from the publisher.

Titles are also available from most of your
favorite online retailers including
Amazon.com, Amazon.co.uk, Barnes &
Noble, Books-A-Million, Waterstones, WH
Smith, Kobo, Diesel eBooks, Sony ebooks,
Apple iBookstore, Apple iPad, Google
eBooks, Angus & Robertson and
Smashwords, as well as many others. You
may also find titles at your local library. If
you do not find the title of your choice listed
there, please request that your library acquire
the book you want.

Persea Books

277 Broadway, Suite 708
New York, NY 10007
Tel: +1 (212) 260-9256
Fax: +1 (212) 267-3165
Email: info@perseabooks.com
Website: http://www.perseabooks.com

Publishes: Fiction; Nonfiction; Poetry; *Areas:* Autobiography; Biography; Criticism; Short Stories; Translations; *Markets:* Adult; Youth; *Treatments:* Literary

Publishes literary fiction and nonfiction manuscripts, including novels, novellas, short story collections, biography, essays, literary criticism, literature in translation, memoir. Encourages submissions to growing YA list in nonfiction, fiction, and poetry, aimed at the literary reader. No social science, psychology, self-help, textbooks, or children's books. Accepts submissions by post or by email. See website for full guidelines. For poetry, query by email in first instance.

Pflaum Publishing Group
2621 Dryden Road
Dayton, OH 45439
Tel: +1 (800) 543-4383
Email: Service@Pflaum.com
Website: http://www.pflaum.com

Publishes: Nonfiction; *Areas:* Religious; *Markets:* Academic

Publisher of religious education material, mainly catholic. Send query with SASE.

Piano Press
P.O. Box 85
Del Mar, CA 92014-0085
Tel: +1 (619) 884-1401
Fax: +1 (858) 755-1104
Email: pianopress@pianopress.com

Publishes: Fiction; Nonfiction; Poetry; *Areas:* Music; *Markets:* Children's; Youth

Publishes books related to music for young readers, middle readers and young adults. Includes fiction, nonfiction, poetry, colouring books, and songbooks. Send query by email only.

Picador USA
175 Fifth Avenue
New York, NY 10010
Tel: +1 (646) 307-5421
Fax: +1 (212) 388-9065

Email: publicity@picadorusa.com
Website: http://www.picadorusa.com

Publishes: Fiction; Nonfiction; *Markets:* Adult; *Treatments:* Literary

Publishes literary fiction and nonfiction. Submissions via a literary agent only.

Picton Press
814 East Elkcam Circle
Marco Island, FL 34145
Email: sales@pictonpress.com
Website: http://www.pictonpress.com

Publishes: Nonfiction; Reference; *Areas:* Historical; Hobbies; *Markets:* Adult

Publishes genealogical and historical books, specialising in research tools for the 17th-19th centuries. Send query with SASE and outline.

Plan B Press
PO Box 4067
Alexandria, VA 22303
Tel: +1 (215) 732-2663
Email: planbpress@gmail.com
Website: http://www.planbpress.com

Publishes: Poetry; *Markets:* Adult; *Treatments:* Literary

Small, independent publishing company primarily producing limited-run poetry chapbooks. Send 20-30 poems between June 1 and November 30, only, by post or by email. See website for full guidelines.

Possibility Press
One Oakglade circle
Hummelstown, PA 17036
Tel: +1 (717) 566-0468
Fax: +1 (717) 566-6423
Email: info@possibilitypress.com
Website: http://www.possibilitypress.com

Publishes: Fiction; Nonfiction; *Areas:* Business; Finance; Health; How-to; Lifestyle; Psychology; Religious; Self-Help; Spiritual; Technology; *Markets:* Adult

Contact: Mike Markowski; Marjie Markowski

Publishes mainly nonfiction books on personal improvement, covering finances, religion, relationships, self-esteem, public speaking, leadership, etc. Also considers fiction that teaches lessons about life and success. See website for detailed guide on preparing a submission.

Presa Press
PO Box 792
Rockford, MI 49341
Email: presapress@aol.com
Website: http://www.presapress.com

Publishes: Nonfiction; Poetry; *Areas:* Criticism; Literature; *Markets:* Adult; *Treatments:* Literary

Publishes poetry paperbacks and literary magazine, including poetry, reviews, essays, and criticism. Query for guidelines.

Press 53
411 West Fourth Street, Suite 101A
Winston-Salem, NC 27101
Tel: +1 (336) 770-5353
Email: kevin@press53.com
Website: http://www.press53.com

Publishes: Fiction; Poetry; *Areas:* Short Stories; *Markets:* Adult; *Treatments:* Literary

Contact: Kevin Morgan Watson

Publishes collections of poetry and short stories. No novels or book length fiction. Finds authors through its competitions, and through writers being active in the literary community and literary magazines.

Professional Publications, Inc. (PPI)
1250 Fifth Ave
Belmont, CA 94002
Tel: +1 (650) 593-9119
Fax: +1 (650) 592-4519
Email: acquisitions@ppi2pass.com

Website: http://ppi2pass.com
Publishes: Nonfiction; Reference; *Areas:* Architecture; Design; Science; *Markets:* Professional

Publishes books relating to architecture, engineering, design, matematics, science etc. and provides products and information for FE/EIT, PE, FS/PS, ARE, NCIDQ and LARE exam preparation. Send proposal with MS and market analysis, etc. Seeks technical, detailed material.

Prometheus Books
59 John Glenn Drive
Amherst, New York 14228-2197
Tel: +1 (716) 691-0133
Fax: +1 (716) 691-0137
Email: editorial@prometheusbooks.com
Website: http://www.prometheusbooks.com

Publishes: Nonfiction; *Areas:* Business; Current Affairs; Health; Philosophy; Science; Sociology; *Markets:* Adult

Send query by email in first instance. Do not send full proposal or complete MS unless requested, and then only by post. See website for full details.

Quarto Publishing Group USA
400 First Avenue North, Suite 400
Minneapolis, MN 55401
Tel: +1 (612) 344-8100
Fax: +1 (612) 344-8691
Website: http://www.quartous.com

Publishes: Nonfiction; Reference; *Areas:* Arts; Cookery; Crafts; Current Affairs; Design; Health; Historical; Hobbies; How-to; Military; Music; Politics; Science; Self-Help; Sport; Technology; Travel; *Markets:* Adult

Nonfiction publisher with offices in the US and UK. See website for specific interests and guidelines for different imprints.

Quill Driver Books
2006 South Mary Street
Fresno, CA 93721

Email: kent@lindenpub.com
Website: http://quilldriverbooks.com

Publishes: Nonfiction; *Areas:* Architecture; Arts; Biography; Business; Crime; Health; Hobbies; Humour; Lifestyle; Self-Help; Spiritual; Technology; Travel; *Markets:* Adult

Contact: Kent Sorsky

Publishes nonfiction only. Send a book proposal including synopsis; commercial info; author platform; and sample chapters or supporting materials. See website for full guidelines.

Ragged Sky Press

PO Box 312
Annandale, NJ 08801
Email: info@raggedsky.com
Website: http://www.raggedsky.com

Publishes: Poetry; *Areas:* Women's Interests; *Markets:* Adult; *Treatments:* Literary

Small and selective co-operative press publishing collections of poetry. Has historically focused on mature voices, overlooked poets, and women's perspectives. Does no accept unsolicited mss. Poets are encouraged to join the community. Submissions by invitation.

Rainbow Publishers

PO Box 261129
San Diego, CA 92196
Email: info@rainbowpublishers.com
Website: http://www.rainbowpublishers.com

Publishes: Nonfiction; *Areas:* Religious; *Markets:* Children's

Publishes reproducible classroom resource books for Sunday School. See website for submission guidelines. No academics, poetry, picture books, or fiction.

RainTown Press

1111 E. Burnside St. #309
Portland, OR 97214
Email: submissions@raintownpress.com

Website: http://raintownpress.com

Publishes: Fiction; *Markets:* Children's; Youth

Independent press dedicated to publishing literature for middle grade and young adults in any genre. No short stories or novellas – young adult novels should be at least 60,000 words and Middle Grade novels should be at least 45,000 words. No poems or poetry chapbooks; picture books; memoirs; nonfiction; or incomplete manuscripts. See website for full submission guidelines.

Reading Harbor

Lansdale, PA
Email: ReadingHarborCo@gmail.com
Website: http://www.readingharbor.com

Publishes: Fiction; Nonfiction; *Areas:* Autobiography; Culture; Current Affairs; Entertainment; Literature; Philosophy; Psychology; Self-Help; Short Stories; Women's Interests; *Markets:* Adult; Family; Youth; *Treatments:* Commercial; Literary; Mainstream; Niche; Popular; Positive

Contact: Grace C

An American-based Publication Company, founded in 2014. Our goal is to bring quality literature to the public. Reading should be a passtime that not only informs the mind but stirs the spirit and inspires the heart. A good book is a treasured find. We want to provide you memories you will share.

Red Empress Publishing

Email: submissions@redempresspublishing.com
Website: http://redempresspublishing.com

Publishes: Fiction; *Areas:* Adventure; Culture; Fantasy; Gothic; Historical; Mystery; Romance; Translations; Women's Interests; *Markets:* Adult; *Treatments:* Commercial; Light; Literary; Mainstream; Niche; Popular; Positive; Progressive; Traditional

A full-service publisher offering traditional and new services for our authors to help them succeed and stand out in an ever-changing market. Here are some of the benefits our authors enjoy.

Professional preparation – editing, cover design, layout, etc.
Digital book distribution through all major outlets – Amazon, Barns and Noble, iBooks, Kobo and more.
Physical book distribution at higher returns than CreateSpace or any other POD publisher because we invest in large print runs of our authors' books.
Audiobook creation and distribution.
Negotiate foreign rights with our partner publishers around the world.
Book launch tours with hundreds of book bloggers to get your book in front of as many readers as possible.

Redleaf Press

10 Yorkton Court
St. Paul, MN 55117-1065
Tel: +1 (800) 423-8309
Fax: +1 (800) 641-0115
Email: acquisitions@redleafpress.org
Website: http://www.redleafpress.org

Publishes: Nonfiction; *Markets:* Professional

Publishes resources for early childhood professionals. Send proposals by post or by email. See website for guidelines.

Reference Service Press

2310 Homestead Road, Suite C1 #219
Los Altos, CA 94024
Tel: +1 (650) 861-3170
Fax: +1 (650) 861-3171
Email: info@rspfunding.com
Website: http://www.rspfunding.com

Publishes: Nonfiction; Reference; *Areas:* Architecture; Arts; Business; Culture; Health; Historical; Medicine; Religious; Science; Sociology; Women's Interests; *Markets:* Professional

Contact: Stuart Hauser, Acquisitions Editor

Publishes financial aid publications for librarians, counselors, researchers, students,

re-entry women, scholars, and other fundseekers. Send outline with sample chapters.

Ripple Grove Press

PO Box 491
Hubbardston, MA 01452
Email: submit@ripplegrovepress.com
Website: http://www.ripplegrovepress.com

Publishes: Fiction; *Markets:* Children's

Publishes picture-driven stories for children aged 2-6. No early readers, middle grade, young adult, religious, or holiday-themed stories. Send submissions by post with SASE or by email, including cover letter with summary; age range of audience; brief bio; contact info; and full ms (as a PDF attachment if submitting by email). See website for full guidelines.

Roberts Press

685 Spring Street, PMB 161
Friday Harbor, WA 98250
Email: submit-robertspress@falsebaybooks.com
Website: https://robertsbookpressdotcom.wordpress.com

Publishes: Fiction; *Areas:* Fantasy; Mystery; Short Stories; Suspense; Women's Interests; *Markets:* Adult; Children's; Youth; *Treatments:* Literary; Mainstream

Small indie book publisher, publishing works of fiction only. Publishes novels between 45,000 and 80,000 words. Also has specific calls for anthologies. Send complete ms by email. See website for full guidelines.

The Rosen Publishing Group, Inc.

29 East 21st Street
New York, NY 10010
Tel: +1 (800) 237-9932
Fax: +1 (888) 436-4643
Website: http://www.rosenpublishing.com

Publishes: Nonfiction; *Areas:* Arts; Biography; Crafts; Culture; Health;

Historical; Religious; Science; Self-Help; Sociology; Sport; *Markets:* Academic; Children's; Youth

Independent educational publishing house serving the needs of students in grades Pre-K -12 with high interest, curriculum-correlated materials.

Running Press
2300 Chestnut Street
Philadelphia, PA 19103
Tel: +1 (215) 567-5080
Fax: +1 (215) 568-2919
Email: perseus.promos@perseusbooks.com
Website: http://www.runningpress.com

Publishes: Fiction; Nonfiction; *Areas:* Arts; Beauty and Fashion; Cookery; Crafts; Culture; Health; Hobbies; Humour; Leisure; Lifestyle; Self-Help; Sport; *Markets:* Adult

Publisher of nonfiction and fiction. No unsolicited submissions.

Saddleback Educational Publishing
Submissions
3120-A Pullman Street
Costa Mesa, CA 92626
Email: contact@sdlback.com
Website: http://www.sdlback.com

Publishes: Fiction; *Markets:* Children's; Youth

Publishes books in all genres and subjects for children aged 12-18, but focusses on original fiction. No K-3 elementary submissions. Submit by post or email. See website for full guidelines.

Sakura Publishing & Technologies
PO BOX 1681
Hermitage,PA 16148
Tel: +1 (330) 360-5131
Email: skpublishing124@gmail.com
Website: http://sakura-publishing.com

Publishes: Fiction; Nonfiction; Poetry; *Markets:* Adult

Publishes fiction, nonfiction, and poetry, but shies away from YA novels, vampires or zombies, and poorly written science-fiction and fantasy. Accepts queries by post or via online form. See website for details.

Saturnalia Books
105 Woodside Road
Ardmore, PA 19003
Tel: +1 (267) 278-9541
Email: info@saturnaliabooks.com
Website: http://www.saturnaliabooks.org

Publishes: Poetry; *Markets:* Adult

Poetry publisher and non-profit organisation. Accepts submissions only via annual poetry competition running Feb 1 to April 15; entry fee: $30; first prize: $2,000 and publication. No other unsolicited mss accepted.

Scarecrow Press Inc.
4501 Forbes Blvd, Suite 200
Lanham, MD 20706
Tel: +1 (717) 794-3800 ext. 3557
Email: asnider@scarecrowpress.com
Website: http://www.scarecrowpress.com

Publishes: Nonfiction; Reference; *Areas:* Culture; Film; Historical; Literature; Music; Philosophy; Religious; Sport; Theatre; *Markets:* Academic

Contact: April Snider, Acquisitions Editor

Publishes historical dictionaries; reference and general interest in history, philosophy, religion and related areas.

School Guide Publications
606 Halstead Avenue
Mamaroneck, NY 10543
Tel: +1 (800) 433-7771
Email: mridder@schoolguides.com
Website: http://www.schoolguides.com

Publishes: Nonfiction; Reference; *Markets:* Adult

Publishes directories and guides on 4 & 2-year colleges, Nursing Schools, Business Schools and Military Programs.

Seriously Good Books

999 Vanderbilt Beach Road
Naples, FL 34119
Tel: +1 (800) 431-1579
Email: seriouslygoodbks@aol.com
Website: http://www.seriouslygoodbooks.net

Publishes: Fiction; *Areas:* Historical;
Markets: Adult

Publishes historical fiction only. Send query
up to one and a half pages in the body of an
email, plus one-page synopsis and/or first ten
pages and/or bibliography of sources
consulted. No attachments. See website for
full submission guidelines. Response in 30-
60 days if interested. Mss must be
professionally edited prior to submission.

Shape & Nature Press

76 Hastings Street
Greenfield, MA 01301
Email: submission@shapeandnature.com
Website: http://www.shapeandnature.com

Publishes: Fiction; Poetry; *Areas:* Short
Stories; *Markets:* Adult; *Treatments:*
Literary

Publishes manuscripts of poetry, cross-genre
work, and fiction (including novels, novellas,
long stories, and short story collections).
Open to submissions September to
December. See website for full submission
guidelines.

Sidestreet Cookie Publishing

357 Hillandale rd Apt 82
Greenville, SC 39609
Tel: +1 (864) 990- 6502
Email: sscpsubmissions@Gmail.com
Website: http://www.
sidestreetcookiepublishing.com

Publishes: Fiction; *Areas:* Adventure;
Anthropology; Drama; Entertainment;
Erotic; Fantasy; Gothic; Historical; Horror;
Humour; Literature; Military; Mystery;
Romance; Sci-Fi; Suspense; Thrillers;
Women's Interests; *Markets:* Adult; Youth

Contact: Brenda Mcleod

Founded in September of 2012 to help new
independent authors navigate the muddy
waters of publishing. Intends to make
independent publishing equal in quality and
ease as traditional publishing by coaching
authors through the process and finding the
right and affordable services to make sure
their work is the best it can be. We provide
authors with a consulting service to help
them through the process of publishing and
we even do project management for those
who want us to take the work out of
publishing.

Sierra Club Books

85 Second Street, 2nd Floor
San Francisco, CA 94105
Tel: +1 (415) 977-5500
Fax: +1 (415) 977-5797
Email: books.publishing@sierraclub.org
Website: http://www.sierraclub.org

Publishes: Nonfiction; Nature; Travel;
Markets: Adult

Publishes books on the natural world,
exploring nature, and environmental issues.
Send query with SASE.

Silverfish Review Press

PO Box 3541
Eugene, OR 97403
Tel: +1 (541) 344-5060
Email: sfrpress@earthlink.net
Website: http://www.
silverfishreviewpress.com

Publishes: Poetry; *Markets:* Adult;
Treatments: Literary

Non-profit independent literary press,
publishing poetry and sponsoring an annual
poetry competition.

Small Beer Press

150 Pleasant Street, #306
Easthampton, MA 01027
Email: info@smallbeerpress.com
Website: http://smallbeerpress.com

Publishes: Fiction; *Areas:* Humour; Sci-Fi;
Short Stories; *Markets:* Adult; *Treatments:*

Experimental; Literary

Publishes literary and experimental fiction and short story collections. Does not publish poetry collections or chapbooks. No email queries or unsolicited mss. Familiarise yourself with books already published before approaching. Send query with SASE and first 10-20 pages. See website for full guidelines.

Soft Skull Press

1919 Fifth Street
Berkeley, CA 94710
Email: info@softskull.com
Website: http://softskull.com

Publishes: Fiction; Nonfiction; *Areas:* Arts; Autobiography; Biography; Cookery; Crime; Culture; Current Affairs; Fantasy; Film; Health; Historical; Humour; Lifestyle; Literature; Media; Mystery; Philosophy; Politics; Religious; Sociology; Thrillers; Travel; TV; Women's Interests; *Markets:* Adult; *Treatments:* Literary; Popular

Seeks books that are "new, fun, smart, revelatory, quirky, groundbreaking, cage-rattling and/or otherwise unusual." Send query describing your project with proposal and two sample chapters (nonfiction), or complete manuscript (fiction). Material will not be returned, and response only if interested. No electronic submissions, and no follow-ups by phone or email.

St. Johann Press

PO Box 241
Haworth, NJ 07641
Email: d.biesel@verizon.net
Website: http://stjohannpress.com

Publishes: Fiction; Nonfiction; Poetry; *Areas:* Autobiography; Biography; Hobbies; Religious; Short Stories; Sport; *Markets:* Adult

Contact: David Biesel

Small, independent press located in Northern New Jersey specialising in niche publishing of nonfiction titles, though also some poetry and fiction collections. Send query with SASE.

Standard Publishing

8805 Governor's Hill Drive, Suite 400
Cincinnati, OH 45249
Tel: +1 (800) 543-1353
Email: customerservice@standardpub.com
Website: http://standardpub.com

Publishes: Nonfiction; *Areas:* Religious; *Markets:* Adult; Children's; Youth

Publisher serving Christian churches worldwide. Most widely known as a publisher of Children's and Adult resources. See website for submission guidelines.

STC Craft

115 West 18th Street, 6th Floor
New York, NY 10011
Tel: +1 (212) 206-7715
Fax: +1 (212) 519-1210
Email: stccraft@abramsbooks.com
Website: http://www.abramsbooks.com

Publishes: Nonfiction; *Areas:* Crafts; Hobbies; *Markets:* Adult

Publishes books on crafts, such as knitting, sewing, felting, quilting, etc.

Steel Toe Books

Department of English
Western Kentucky University
1906 College Heights Blvd. #11086
Bowling Green, KY 42101-1086
Email: tom.hunley@wku.edu
Website: http://www.steeltoebooks.com

Publishes: Poetry; *Markets:* Adult; *Treatments:* Literary

Contact: Tom C. Hunley

Publishes single-author poetry collections. No reading fee, but asks those who submit to purchase one of their titles directly from them. See website for full submission guidelines and details of reading periods, etc.

Stone Bridge Press

PO Box 8208
Berkeley, CA 94707

STREET ADDRESS:
1393 Solano Avenue, Suite C
Albany, CA 94706
Tel: +1 (510) 524-8732
Fax: +1 (888) 411-8527
Email: sbpedit@stonebridge.com
Website: http://www.stonebridge.com

Publishes: Fiction; Nonfiction; Reference;
Areas: Business; Crafts; Culture; Design;
Film; Lifestyle; Literature; Spiritual;
Translations; Travel; *Markets:* Adult;
Children's

Publishes books about Asia and in particular
Japan. Publishes mainly nonfiction and
fiction in translation, but will in rare cases
consider original fiction if appropriate. No
poetry. Prefers submissions by email, but
will accept submissions by post (use street
address if sending by express mail or
delivery service such as UPS). See website
for full guidelines.

Stoneslide Books

Email: editors@stoneslidecorrective.com
Website: http://stoneslidecorrective.com

Publishes: Fiction; *Markets:* Adult

Publishes novels "with strong character
development and narrative thrust, brought
out with writing that's clear and expressive".
Pays modest advance and offers competitive
revenue sharing arrangement after
publication. Submit using submission form
on website.

Storey Publishing

210 MASS MoCA Way
North Adams, MA 01247
Tel: +1 (413) 346-2100
Fax: +1 (413) 346-2199
Email: feedback@storey.com
Website: http://www.storey.com

Publishes: Nonfiction; *Areas:* Business;
Cookery; Crafts; Gardening; Health; Nature;
Spiritual; *Markets:* Adult

Contact: Deborah Balmuth: Building and
mind/body/spirit; Deborah Burns: Equine,
animals, nature; Gwen Steege: Crafts;
Carleen Madigan: Gardening; Margaret
Sutherland: Cooking, wine, and beer.

Send query by post with description, market
info, author details, table of contents, details
of final length and any photos/illustrations,
writing sample from previous books or
magazines, and sample chapter. Address
material to appropriate Acquiring Editor. See
website for more details.

Strategic Media Books

782 Wofford Street
Rock Hill, SC 29730
Email: contact@strategicmediabooks.com
Website: http://strategicmediabooks.com

Publishes: Fiction; Nonfiction; *Areas:*
Crime; Current Affairs; Politics; *Markets:*
Adult

Publishes true crime, crime and mystery
fiction, southern interest, international
politics, and "books that have a compelling
story line and a riveting narrative". Send
query by post or email with cover letter
outlining the story or theme, how long it will
take to complete, brief bio, one or two
chapters, and marketing plan. See website
for full guidelines.

Sunscribe

1735 Heckle Blvd
Suite 103
Rock Hill, SC 29732
Tel: +1 (704) 467-4067
Email: sunscribepublishers@gmail.com
Website: http://sunscribe.net

Publishes: Fiction; Nonfiction; Poetry;
Reference; Scripts; *Areas:* Adventure;
Anthropology; Antiques; Archaeology;
Architecture; Arts; Autobiography; Beauty
and Fashion; Biography; Business; Cookery;
Crafts; Crime; Criticism; Culture; Current
Affairs; Design; Drama; Entertainment;
Fantasy; Film; Finance; Gardening; Gothic;
Health; Historical; Hobbies; How-to;
Humour; Legal; Leisure; Lifestyle;
Literature; Media; Medicine; Men's Interests;

Military; Music; Mystery; Nature; New Age; Philosophy; Photography; Politics; Psychology; Radio; Religious; Romance; Science; Sci-Fi; Self-Help; Short Stories; Sociology; Spiritual; Sport; Suspense; Technology; Theatre; Thrillers; Translations; Travel; TV; Westerns; Women's Interests; *Markets:* Academic; Adult; Children's; Family; Professional; Youth; *Treatments:* Commercial; Contemporary; Experimental; In-depth; Light; Literary; Mainstream; Niche; Popular; Positive; Progressive; Serious; Traditional

Contact: Roxanne Hanna

Traditional publishing company with three imprints, partnering with writers: we are proud members of AAP and IBPA. Our works adhere to our philosophy of pairing our expertise with excellent writing by establishing a culture of collaboration, focusing on talent and text. Our mission is to offer writers an opportunity to write: we handle editing, marketing, and distribution. Our standard is excellence, and we strive to team with writers passionate about their craft.

Swan Isle Press

PO Box 408790
Chicago, IL 60640-8790
Email: info@swanislepress.com
Website: http://www.swanislepress.com

Publishes: Fiction; Nonfiction; Poetry; *Areas:* Arts; Culture; Literature; Translations; *Markets:* Adult; *Treatments:* Literary

Independent, not-for-profit, literary publisher publishing works of poetry, fiction and nonfiction intended to inspire and educate while advancing the knowledge and appreciation of literature, art, and culture. Particularly interested in books related to Spanish and Latin American literature, art, and culture. Welcomes queries, but no unsolicited submissions. No queries by email.

Swan Scythe Press

1468 Mallard Way

Sunnyvale, CA 94087
Email: robert.pesich@gmail.com
Website: http://www.swanscythe.com

Publishes: Poetry; *Areas:* Translations; *Markets:* Adult

Contact: Robert Pesich

Publishes poetry collections and anthologies, including translations from Spanish and indigenous languages of the Americas into English. Send query before submitting ms.

Swedenborg Foundation

320 North Church Street
West Chester, PA 19380
Tel: +1 (610) 430-3222
Fax: +1 (610) 430-7982
Email: info@swedenborg.com
Website: http://www.swedenborg.com

Publishes: Nonfiction; *Areas:* Philosophy; Psychology; Religious; Science; *Markets:* Adult

Publishes books by and about Emanuel Swedenborg, and/or related to his ideas. Send query by post with SASE or by email, including synopsis, sample chapters, and outline.

SynergEbooks

948 New Highway 7
Columbia, TN 38401
Tel: +1 (931) 223-5990
Email: synergebooks@aol.com
Website: http://www.synergebooks.com

Publishes: Fiction; Nonfiction; Poetry; Reference; *Areas:* Business; Cookery; Crime; Fantasy; Horror; Humour; Music; Mystery; New Age; Religious; Romance; Sci-Fi; Self-Help; Spiritual; Suspense; Thrillers; Travel; Westerns; *Markets:* Adult; Children's; Youth

A non-subsidy digital publishing house. See website for full guidelines and current status regarding submissions.

Tarpaulin Sky Press
PO Box 189
Grafton, VT 05146
Email: editors@tarpaulinsky.com
Website: http://tarpaulinsky.com

Publishes: Fiction; Poetry; *Markets:* Adult;
Treatments: Literary

Contact: Resh Daily

Accepts works of full-length prose and
poetry during specific reading periods only.
See website for details and join mailing list
to be notified when these occur. Describes
itself as "cross-genre, trans-genre, anti-
genre".

Tate Publishing and Enterprises, LLC
127 East Trade Center Terrace
Mustang, OK 73064
Tel: +1 (405) 376-4900
Fax: +1 (405) 376-4401
Website: https://www.tatepublishing.com

Publishes: Fiction; Nonfiction; Poetry;
Areas: Adventure; Arts; Biography;
Business; Cookery; Entertainment; Fantasy;
Health; Historical; Humour; Lifestyle;
Military; Mystery; Philosophy; Politics;
Religious; Romance; Sci-Fi; Self-Help;
Short Stories; Spiritual; Sport; Suspense;
Thrillers; Westerns; *Markets:* Adult;
Children's

Describes itself as "a Christian-based,
family-owned, mainline publishing
organization with a mission to discover
unknown authors." Aims to combine high
royalties with good author relations, but
accepts less than 10% of submissions.
Submit proposals or manuscripts online
using web form, or by post. See website for
full details.

Teachers College Press
1234 Amsterdam Avenue
New York, NY 10027
Tel: +1 (212) 678-3929
Fax: +1 (212) 678-4149
Email: tcpress@tc.columbia.edu
Website: http://www.

teacherscollegepress.com

Publishes: Nonfiction; *Areas:* Film;
Historical; Philosophy; Politics; Sociology;
Technology; Theatre; Women's Interests;
Markets: Academic

Publishes educational titles for all levels of
students.

Tebot Bach
PO Box 7887
Huntington Beach, CA 92615-7887
Email: info@tebotbach.org
Website: http://www.tebotbach.org

Publishes: Poetry; *Markets:* Adult;
Treatments: Literary

Poetry publisher. Send query by email with
sample poems and brief bio.

The Poisoned Pencil
6962 E. First Avenue, Suite 103
Scottsdale, AZ 85251
Tel: +1 (480) 945-3375
Email: ellen@thepoisonedpencil.com
Website: http://thepoisonedpencil.com

Publishes: Fiction; *Areas:* Mystery;
Markets: Youth

Publishes young adult mystery by authors
from the US and Canada. Avoid serial
killers, excessive gore or horror, or heavy
SF, supernatural, or fantasy content. No short
story collections or middle grade fiction.
Submit online via submission manager on
website.

Tia Chucha Press
PO Box 328
San Fernando, CA 91341
Tel: +1 (818) 528-4511
Fax: +1 (818) 367-5600
Email: tcpress@tiachucha.org
Website: http://www.tiachucha.com

Publishes: Poetry; *Areas: Markets:* Adult

Contact: Luis J. Rodriguez, Editor

Publishes all types of poetic expression and are not bound by poetic style, form, school, or era. Cross-cultural – published poets have included Chicano, African American, Jamaican American, Native American, Irish American, Italian American, Korean American, Japanese American, Puerto Rican, Cuban American, and more. All ages, genders, sexual orientations, disabilities, and spiritual persuasions are welcome, but publishes only two books per year (1% of submissions). Send complete poetry ms between 60 and 120 pages by hard copy only. See website for full guidelines.

Top Cow Productions, Inc
Email: betsy@topcow.com
Website: http://www.topcow.com

Publishes: Fiction; *Areas:* Adventure; Fantasy; Sci-Fi; *Markets:* Adult; Youth

Contact: Betsy Gonia

Publishes comic books.

Torquere Press
1380 Rio Rancho Blvd #1319
Rio Rancho, NM 87124
Email: submissions@torquerepress.com
Website: http://www.torquerepress.com

Publishes: Fiction; *Areas:* Romance; Short Stories; *Markets:* Adult

Publisher of GLBT romance and all its sub-genres. Publishes works from 3,000 words up, including short stories, novelettes, novellas, and novels. A happy ending is required. See website for full submission guidelines.

Tower Publishing
588 Saco Road
Standish, ME 04084
Tel: +1 (800) 969-8693
Fax: +1 (800) 264-3870
Email: info@towerpub.com
Website: http://www.towerpub.com

Publishes: Nonfiction; Reference; *Areas:* Business; Legal; *Markets:* Professional

Contact: Michael Lyons (michaell@ towerpub.com)

Independent publisher of legal publications, business directories, and data lists. Send query by email or by post with SASE, with sample chapters, proposed chapter outline, marketing plan, details of competing books, and ideas for business development. See website for full details.

Triumph Books
814 North Franklin Street
Chicago, IL 60610
Tel: +1 (312) 337-0747
Fax: +1 (312) 337-5985
Email: orders@ipgbook.com
Website: http://www.triumphbooks.com

Publishes: Nonfiction; *Areas:* Autobiography; Biography; Sport; *Markets:* Adult

Describes itself as the nation's leading sports book publisher. Send query with SASE.

Tsaba House
2252 12th Street
Reedley, CA 93654
Tel: +1 (559) 643-8575
Fax: +1 (559) 638-2640
Website: http://www.TsabaHouse.com

Publishes: Fiction; Nonfiction; *Areas:* Adventure; Autobiography; Beauty and Fashion; Biography; Current Affairs; Fantasy; Finance; How-to; Leisure; Lifestyle; Literature; Men's Interests; Mystery; Nature; Psychology; Religious; Romance; Science; Self-Help; Spiritual; Suspense; Thrillers; Women's Interests; *Markets:* Adult; Family; Youth; *Treatments:* Contemporary; Mainstream; Positive

Contact: Corrie Schwagerl

Dedicated to promoting the Gospel through the written word by producing quality, family friendly literature that covers a myriad of topics ranging from educational nonfiction to entertaining fiction and providing Christian based reading entertainment for all ages.

We accept unsolicited submissions once a year during the month of January ONLY. Full Submission guidelines are on our website. We are not a subsidy publisher and take full financial responsibility for publishing and marketing but we do require that our authors be willing to do a book tour and be actively involved in our Marketing Plan.

Tu Books

95 Madison Avenue, Suite #1205
New York, NY 10016
Tel: +1 (212) 779-4400
Fax: +1 (212) 683-1894
Email: tu@leeandlow.com
Website: https://www.leeandlow.com/writers-illustrators/writing-guidelines-tu-books

Publishes: Fiction; *Areas:* Culture; Fantasy; Mystery; Sci-Fi; *Markets:* Children's; Youth

Publishes speculative fiction for children and young adults featuring diverse characters and settings. Focusses on well-told, exciting, adventurous fantasy, science fiction, and mystery novels featuring people of colour set in worlds inspired by non-Western folklore or culture. Publishes books for ages 8-12 and 12-18. No picture books, chapter books, or short stories. Send submissions by post only, with synopsis and first three chapters. Response only if interested, so do not include SASE. See website for full guidelines.

Turn the Page Publishing LLC

PO Box 3179
Upper Montclair, NJ 07043
Email: inquiry@turnthepagepublishing.com
Website: http://turnthepagepublishing.com

Publishes: Fiction; Nonfiction; *Areas:* Autobiography; Cookery; Finance; Humour; Lifestyle; Military; New Age; Spiritual; Suspense; Women's Interests; *Markets:* Adult; Youth; *Treatments:* Contemporary; Literary; Mainstream

Describes itself as "an independent press staffed by professional editors and artists dedicated to offering quality fiction and non-

fiction to discerning readers". Publishes hardcover, softcover, and digital formats. May not be open to submissions at all times. See website for details.

Twilight Times Books

P O Box 3340
Kingsport, TN 37664
Fax: +1 (423) 323-0183
Email: publisher@twilighttimes.com
Website: http://www.twilighttimesbooks.com

Publishes: Fiction; *Areas:* Fantasy; Historical; Mystery; New Age; Romance; Sci-Fi; Suspense; Women's Interests; *Markets:* Adult; Children's; Youth; *Treatments:* Dark; Literary; Mainstream

Contact: Lida E. Quillen, Publisher

Send query by email only, including author bio, publishing credits, estimated word count, and marketing plan. Do not send complete ms.

Tyrus Books

1213 N. Sherman Ave. #306
Madison, WI 53704
Tel: +1 (508) 427-7100
Email: submissions@tyrusbooks.com
Website: http://www.tyrusbooks.com

Publishes: Fiction; *Areas:* Crime; *Markets:* Adult; *Treatments:* Literary

Publishes crime and literary fiction. Not interested in books that are heavy on explosions, violence, or cliched plots or characters. Stories should be approximately 60,000 to 100,000 words. See website for full guidelines. Send query by email with synopsis and optionally up to 20 pages in the body of the email. No attachments. If no response after a few months, assume rejection.

University of Alabama Press

Box 870380
Tuscaloosa, AL 35487-0380
Tel: +1 (205) 348-5180
Fax: +1 (205) 348-9201

Publishes: Nonfiction; Anthropology; Archaeology; Biography; Criticism; Historical; Literature; Military; Politics; Religious; Technology; Theatre; *Markets:* Academic

Publishes American history and religious history, Latin American history, as well as African-American, Judaic, Native-American, and theatre studies. No poetry, fiction, or drama.

University of Chicago Press

Editorial Department
The University of Chicago Press
1427 East 60th Street
Chicago, IL 60637
Tel: +1 (773) 702-7700
Fax: +1 (773) 702-9756
Email: chenry@uchicago.edu
Website: http://www.press.uchicago.edu

Publishes: Nonfiction; Reference; *Areas:* Anthropology; Archaeology; Architecture; Arts; Biography; Film; Gardening; Historical; Legal; Medicine; Music; Philosophy; Politics; Psychology; Religious; Science; Sociology; Technology; Translations; Travel; *Markets:* Academic

Contact: See website for appropriate editorial contact.

Send query by post or email, with CV, table of contents, brief prospectus including a description of the work and intended audience, expected length and number of illustrations, and information on the schedule for completion of the manuscript. A sample chapter may be included. Consult website for appropriate editorial contact. No fiction, poetry, or unsolicited MSS.

University of South Carolina Press

1600 Hampton Street, 5th Floor
Columbia, SC 29208
Email: lfogle@mailbox.sc.edu
Website: http://www.sc.edu/uscpress

Publishes: Fiction; Nonfiction; Poetry; *Areas:* Architecture; Arts; Cookery; Culture; Gardening; Historical; Literature; Military;

Nature; Religious; Women's Interests; *Markets:* Academic; Adult

Publishes works of original scholarship and regional general interest, as well as poetry and original fiction, focussed on the American South. See website for full details.

University of Tampa Press

401 W. Kennedy Blvd
Tampa, FL 33606
Tel: +1 (813) 253-6266
Fax: +1 (813) 258-7593
Email: utpress@ut.edu
Website: http://www.ut.edu/tampapress/
pressmain.aspx

Publishes: Fiction; Nonfiction; Poetry; *Areas:* Arts; Historical; *Markets:* Academic; Adult; *Treatments:* Literary

Has been dedicated to the publication of books and periodicals featuring poetry, fiction and nonfiction from Florida and around the globe for more than 50 years. Publishes poetry, Florida history, supernatural literature, book arts, and other titles. Also publishes literary journal and runs annual poetry and fiction competitions.

Urban Ministries, Inc.

PO Box 87618
Chicago, IL 60680-0618
Tel: +1 (800) 860-8642
Website: http://urbanministries.com

Publishes: Nonfiction; *Areas:* Religious; *Markets:* Academic; Adult; Children's

Publishes Christian education resources, including Bible studies, Sunday School and Vacation Bible School curriculum books, movies, and websites designed for African American churches and individuals.

Utah State University Press

3078 Old Main Hill
Logan, UT 84322-3078
Tel: +1 (720) 406-8849
Fax: +1 (720) 406-8849
Email: jessica@upcolorado.com
Website: http://www.usu.edu/usupress

Publishes: Nonfiction; *Areas:* Anthropology; Archaeology; Culture; Historical; Nature; Science; *Markets:* Academic

Contact: Jessica d'Arbonne, Acquisitions Editor

Academic publisher. Prefers to receive submissions through online submission system. See website for details.

Vanderbilt University Press

Vanderbilt University
PMB 351813 2301 Vanderbilt Place
Nashville, TN 37235-1813
Tel: +1 (615) 322-3585
Email: vupress@vanderbilt.edu
Website: http://www.vanderbilt.edu/
university-press/

Publishes: Nonfiction; *Areas:* Anthropology; Archaeology; Culture; Health; Historical; Literature; Medicine; Music; Nature; Philosophy; Politics; Women's Interests; *Markets:* Academic; Adult

Contact: Michael Ames, Director

Publishes books in most areas of the humanities and social sciences, as well as health care and education. See website for full submission guidelines.

Veritas Publications

7-8 Lower Abbey Street
Dublin 1
Email: donna.doherty@veritas.ie
Website: http://www.veritasbooksonline.com

Publishes: Nonfiction; *Areas:* Psychology; Religious; Self-Help; Sociology; Spiritual; *Markets:* Adult

Contact: Donna Doherty, Commissioning Editor

Publishes theology, philosophy, spirituality, psychology, self-help, family, social issues, parish and church resources, bible study, etc. Send proposal or complete ms by post or by email. See website for full guidelines.

Vernon Press (an imprint of Vernon Art and Science Inc.)

Vernon Art and Science Inc.
1000 N West Street, Suite 1200
Wilmington, Delaware 19801
Tel: +1 (302) 250-4440
Email: info@vernonpress.com
Website: http://www.vernonpress.com

Publishes: Nonfiction; Reference; *Areas:* Arts; Biography; Business; Criticism; Culture; Current Affairs; Finance; Historical; Literature; Music; Philosophy; Politics; Psychology; Science; Sociology; Technology; *Markets:* Academic; Professional; *Treatments:* Experimental; Niche; Progressive

Contact: Rosario Batana

An independent publisher of scholarly books in the social sciences and humanities.

Our mission is to serve the community of academic and professional scholars by providing a visible, quality platform for the dissemination of emergent ideas.

We welcome academic book proposals from both experienced and first time authors.

Our acquisition process has as its central criterion the contribution of a work to knowledge. It is necessary for such a contribution to be scientifically rigorous and of current interest to the academic communities to which it belongs, but saleability is not as central to our commitment to scholarship as has widely become the case over the last few years. Peer-review and close collaboration with academic associations and other research communities ensure our titles are meaningful and relevant.

We have a particular interest in the following subjects:

- Economics (including economic history)
- Sociology and social psychology
- Politics and public policy
- Finance, Business and Management
- Philosophy
- Fine art (including the history of art)

- Statistics and mathematics
  Education and pedagogy
- Linguistics

Please send a short book proposal (5 pages maximum) or abstract by email. To speed up initial screening, you may include a brief overview of competing titles and the names of two possible reviewers who are (academically/professionally) qualified to comment on the originality, rigor and potential impact of your work.

We commit to reply to all complete proposals and endeavor to offer constructive feedback whenever possible.

Verso

Editorial Dept.
20 Jay Street, Suite 1010
Brooklyn, NY 11201
Tel: +1 (718) 246-8160
Fax: +1 (718) 246-8165
Email: submissions@versobooks.com
Website: http://www.versobooks.com

Publishes: Nonfiction; *Areas:* Business; Finance; Historical; Philosophy; Politics; Sociology; Women's Interests; *Markets:* Adult

Queries from North America should be directed to the US address. Queries from elswhere in the world should be directed to the UK address (see separate listing). Send query with overview, list of contents, author info, market info, and timetable. 15 pages maximum. See website for full guidelines.

Voyageur Press

Book Proposals—Voyageur Press
Quayside Publishing Group
400 First Avenue North, Suite 300
Minneapolis, MN 55401
Tel: +1 (800) 458-0454
Fax: +1 (612) 344-8691
Email: customerservice@quaysidepub.com
Website: http://www.voyageurpress.com

Publishes: Nonfiction; *Areas:* Culture; Historical; Lifestyle; Music; Nature; Photography; Travel; *Markets:* Adult

Publishes books on nature and the environment; country living and farming heritage; regional and cultural history; music; travel and photography. See website for full submission guidelines.

Wannabee Books

750 Pinehurst Drive
Rio Vista, CA 94571
Tel: +1 (707) 398-6430
Email: Books@WannabeeBooks.com
Website: http://www.wannabeebooks.com

Publishes: Nonfiction; *Areas:* Anthropology; Archaeology; Architecture; Arts; Criticism; Gardening; Health; Legal; Literature; Medicine; Music; Nature; Photography; Psychology; Science; Sport; Technology; *Markets:* Children's

Publishes nonfiction for children, organised around what they might want to be when they grow up.

Waveland Press, Inc.

4180 IL Route 83, Suite 101
Long Grove, Illinois 60047
Tel: +1 (847) 634-0081
Fax: +1 (847) 634-9501
Email: info@waveland.com
Website: http://www.waveland.com

Publishes: Nonfiction; *Areas:* Anthropology; Archaeology; Architecture; Arts; Business; Design; Finance; Health; Historical; Legal; Literature; Music; Nature; Philosophy; Politics; Psychology; Religious; Science; Sociology; Technology; Theatre; Women's Interests; *Markets:* Academic

Publisher of college textbooks and supplements, providing reasonably priced teaching materials for the classroom. See website for submission guidelines.

Wesleyan Publishing House

PO Box 50434
Indianapolis, IN 46250
Tel: +1 (800) 493-7539
Email: submissions@wesleyan.org
Website: https://www.wesleyan.org

Publishes: Nonfiction; *Areas:* Religious; Spiritual; *Markets:* Adult

Publishes topical, adult, Christian nonfiction titles on Discipleship Group Study; Deeper Devotion; Christian Living; Spiritual Growth; Social Issues; and Ministry Leadership. No fiction, children's books, Bible studies, biographies, autobiographies, poetry, academic works, or textbooks. Send all proposals by email. No queries.

Western Psychological Services

625 Alaska Avenue
Torrance, CA 90503-5124
Tel: +1 (800) 648-8857
Email: review@wpspublish.com
Website: http://www.wpspublish.com

Publishes: Fiction; Nonfiction; Reference; *Areas:* Psychology; Sociology; *Markets:* Children's; Professional

Publishes books for professionals in the areas of psychology and education, and children's fiction dealing with feelings, anger, social skills, autism, family problems, etc. for use by professionals when dealing with children. Send complete ms.

Westminster John Knox Press (WJK)

100 Witherspoon Street
Louisville, KY 40202-1396
Tel: +1 (800) 523-1631
Fax: +1 (800) 541-5113
Email: submissions@wjkbooks.com
Website: http://www.wjkbooks.com

Publishes: Nonfiction; *Areas:* Culture; Religious; Spiritual; *Markets:* Academic; Adult; Professional

Publishes books specifically related to the Presbyterian Church (USA), including theology, biblical studies, preaching, worship, ethics, religion and culture, and other related fields. Serves four main Markets: scholars and students in colleges, universities, seminaries, and divinity schools; preachers, educators, and counselors working in churches; members of mainline Protestant congregations; and general readers. See website for detailed submission guidelines.

Whitaker House

1030 Hunt Valley Circle
New Kensington, PA 15068
Tel: +1 (724) 334-7000
Fax: +1 (724) 334-1200
Email: publisher@whitakerhouse.com
Website: http://www.whitakerhouse.com

Publishes: Fiction; Nonfiction; *Areas:* Autobiography; Biography; Historical; How-to; Lifestyle; Men's Interests; Religious; Self-Help; Spiritual; Women's Interests; *Markets:* Adult

Publisher of inspiring and uplifting Christian fiction and nonfiction. Establish contact with a representative prior to submitting a manuscript or proposal.

John Wiley & Sons, Inc.

111 River Street
Hoboken, NJ 07030
Tel: +1 (212) 850-6000
Fax: +1 (212) 850-6088
Email: info@wiley.com
Website: http://www.wiley.com

Publishes: Nonfiction; Reference; *Areas:* Architecture; Business; Cookery; Design; Finance; Medicine; Psychology; Religious; Science; Sociology; Technology; *Markets:* Academic; Adult; Professional

Publishes professional, trade, and educational material as print books, journals, and in electronic format.

William S. Hein & Co., Inc.

2350 North Forest Road
Getzville, NY 14068
Tel: +1 (716) 882-2600
Fax: +1 (716) 883-8100
Email: mail@wshein.com
Website: https://www.wshein.com

Publishes: Nonfiction; Reference; *Areas:* Legal; *Markets:* Professional

Publishes reference books for the law library community,

Williamson Books
2630 Elm Hill Pike, Suite 100
Nashville, TN 37214
Tel: +1 (615) 781-1451
Email: kwest@guideposts.org

Publishes: Nonfiction; Arts; Cookery;
Crafts; Historical; Hobbies; Science;
Markets: Children's

Publishes nonfiction titles for children aged
3 to 12 that emphasise hands-on learning
through crafts and activities. Subject matter
ranges from maths and science to geography,
history, art, and cooking. Send query with
SASE for guidelines.

Wilshire Book Company
9731 Variel Avenue
Chatsworth, CA 91311-4315
Tel: +1 (818) 700-1522
Fax: +1 (818) 700-1527
Email: mpowers@mpowers.com
Website: http://www.mpowers.com

Publishes: Fiction; Nonfiction; *Areas:* How-
to; Humour; Psychology; Self-Help;
Spiritual; *Markets:* Adult; *Treatments:*
Commercial

Publishes psychology and self help
nonfiction, plus adult allegories that teach
principles of psychological and spiritual
growth. Advises writers to read the
bestsellers listed on their website and
duplicate their winning elements in your own
style with a creative new approach and fresh
material. Submissions should be conceived
and developed with market potential
uppermost in your mind. Send synopsis for
fiction or detailed chapter outline for
nonfiction with three sample chapters,
SASE, and contact email address (however
no email submissions). Queries accepted by
telephone for instant feedback on ideas.

WordSong
815 Church Street
Honesdale, PA 18431

Tel: +1 (570) 253-1164
Email: submissions@boydsmillspress.com
Website: https://www.boydsmillspress.com

Publishes: Poetry; *Markets:* Children's

Describes itself as "the only children's
imprint in the United States specifically
dedicated to poetry". Send book-length
collection of poetry by post with SASE. Do
not make initial query prior to submission.

World Book, Inc.
233 North Michigan Avenue, Suite 2000
Chicago, IL 60601
Tel: +1 (312) 729-5800
Fax: +1 (312) 729-5600
Email: service@worldbook.com
Website: http://www.worldbook.com

Publishes: Nonfiction; Reference; *Areas:*
Health; Historical; Science; Sociology;
Markets: Children's

Publishes nonfiction and reference for
children aged 3-14. No poetry or fiction.

Yale University Press
PO Box 209040
New Haven, CT 06520-9040
Tel: +1 (203) 432-0960
Fax: +1 (203) 432-0948
Email: Sarah.Miller@yale.edu
Website: http://yalepress.yale.edu/yupbooks

Publishes: Nonfiction; Poetry; *Areas:*
Architecture; Arts; Current Affairs;
Historical; Legal; Literature; Medicine;
Nature; Philosophy; Politics; Psychology;
Religious; Science; *Markets:* Academic;
Adult

Publishes nonfiction and one book of poetry
a year. Poetry must be submitted through
annual contest. For nonfiction, see website
for list of editors and submit to one editor
only, by post or by email. See website for
full guidelines.

Zebra
Kensington Publishing Corp.
119 West 40th Street

New York, New York, 10018
Tel: +1 (800) 221-2647
Email: esogah@kensingtonbooks.com
Website: http://www.kensingtonbooks.com

Publishes: Fiction; *Areas:* Romance;
Women's Interests; *Markets:* Adult

Contact: Esi Sogah, Senior Editor

Publishes women's fiction, including
romance. Send query only by email. No
attachments or proposals. Response only if
interested. See website for full guidelines.

Zenith Press
400 First Avenue North, Suite 400

Minneapolis, MN 55401
Tel: +1 (612) 344-8100
Fax: +1 (612) 344-8691
Email: erik.gilg@quartous.com
Website: http://www.zenithpress.com

Publishes: Nonfiction; *Areas:* Culture;
Historical; Military; Science; Sociology;
Technology; Travel; *Markets:* Adult

Contact: Erik Gilg, Editorial Director

Publishes engaging American stories with a
firm historical foundation; particularly in the
areas of military history and aviation.
Accepts submissions by post, but prefers
them by email. See website for full
guidelines.

UK Publishers

For the most up-to-date listings of these and hundreds of other publishers, visit http://www.firstwriter.com/publishers

*To claim your **free** access to the site, please see the back of this book.*

A Swift Exit

Email: aswiftexit@gmail.com
Website: http://aswiftexit.co.uk

Publishes: Fiction; Nonfiction; Poetry; *Areas:* Short Stories; *Markets:* Adult; *Treatments:* Literary

Contact: Jim Ladd and Will Vigar

Publishes new collections of poetry and prose from the finest new writers as ebooks and in print. Currently working on a strict back end profit share basis. See website for current calls for submissions and guidelines.

AA Publishing

The Automobile Association
Fanum House
Basingstoke
RG21 4EA
Tel: +44 (0) 1256 491524
Fax: +44 (0) 1614 887544
Email: AAPublish@TheAA.com
Website: http://www.theAA.com

Publishes: Nonfiction; Reference; *Areas:* Leisure; Lifestyle; Travel; *Markets:* Adult

Contact: David Watchus

Publishes motoring and travel books including atlases, maps, travel and leisure guides for the UK and the rest of the world.

Also walking, cycling, lifestyle and driving test guides.

Akasha Publishing Ltd

145-157 St John Street
London
EC1V 4PW
Tel: +44 (0) 7436 849371
Email: info@akashapublishing.co.uk
Website: http://www.akashapublishing.co.uk

Publishes: Fiction; Nonfiction; *Areas:* Autobiography; Biography; Culture; Fantasy; Finance; Historical; Sci-Fi; Spiritual; *Markets:* Adult; Children's

Independent publishing company located in the South London and Surrey area, publishing trade fiction and nonfiction and children's books in the areas of African and Caribbean interest, fantasy, science fiction, spirituality, metaphysical, Mind, Body and Spirit, ancient and classical history, alternative history, economics, Nuwaupian books, biographies and autobiographies. Send submissions by email. See website for guidelines.

J.A. Allen

Clerkenwell House
45–47 Clerkenwell Green
London
EC1R 0HT
Tel: +44 (0) 20 7251 2661

Claim your free access to www.firstwriter.com: See p.423

Fax: +44 (0) 20 7490 4958
Email: allen@halebooks.com
Website: http://halebooks.com/jaallen/

Publishes: Nonfiction; *Areas:* How-to;
Markets: Adult

Contact: Lesley Gowers

Publishes books on horses and
horsemanship. Send proposal with SASE,
outline, aim, background and market,
detailed synopsis, and three sample chapters.

Alma Books Ltd
Hogarth House
32-34 Paradise Road
Richmond
TW9 1SE
Tel: +44 (0) 20 8940 6917
Fax: +44 (0) 20 8948 5599
Email: info@almabooks.com
Website: http://www.almabooks.co.uk

Publishes: Fiction; Nonfiction; *Areas:*
Historical; Literature; *Markets:* Adult;
Treatments: Contemporary; Literary

Publishes literary fiction and a small number
of nonfiction titles with a strong literary or
historical connotation. No novellas, short
stories, children's books, poetry, academic
works, science fiction, horror, or fantasy.
Accepts unsolicited MSS by post with
synopsis, two sample chapters, and SAE if
return of material required. No submissions
by email, or submissions from outside the
UK. Submissions received from outside the
UK will not receive a response.

Alma Classics
Hogarth House
32-34 Paradise Road
Richmond
TW9 1SE
Tel: +44 (0) 20 8940 6917
Fax: +44 (0) 20 8948 5599
Email: info@almabooks.com
Website: http://www.almaclassics.com

Publishes: Fiction; Poetry; Scripts; *Areas:*
Arts; Autobiography; Biography; Literature;
Sociology; Translations; *Markets:* Adult;

Treatments: Literary

Publishes classic European literature.
Welcomes suggestions and ideas for the list,
as well as proposals from translators. Send
proposals by post with SAE, CV, and sample
from the original text.

Anness Publishing Ltd
108 Great Russell Street
London
WC1B 3NA
Email: info@anness.com
Website: http://www.aquamarinebooks.com

Publishes: Nonfiction; Reference; *Areas:*
Arts; Cookery; Crafts; Design; Gardening;
Health; Historical; Hobbies; Leisure;
Lifestyle; Military; Music; New Age;
Photography; Spiritual; Sport; Travel;
Markets: Adult; Children's

Publishes co-edition books in the above-
listed areas; usually heavily illustrated

Appletree Press Ltd
Roycroft House
164 Malone Road
Belfast
BT9 5LL
Tel: +44 (0) 28 90 243074
Fax: +44 (0) 28 90 246756
Email: editorial@appletree.ie
Website: http://www.appletree.ie

Publishes: Nonfiction; *Markets:* Adult

Send query with synopsis, descriptive
chapter list, and two or three chapters by
email. Publishes small-format gift books and
general nonfiction books of Irish and
Scottish interest. No unsolicited MSS.

Arc Publications
Nanholme Mill
Shaw Wood Road
Todmorden
Lancs
OL14 6DA
Tel: +44 (0) 1706 812338
Fax: +44 (0) 1706 818948
Email: info@arcpublications.co.uk

Website: http://www.arcpublications.co.uk/ submissions

Publishes: Poetry; *Areas:* Music; Translations; *Markets:* Adult; *Treatments:* Contemporary

Send 16-24 poems by email as a Word / PDF attachment, maximum one poem per page. Submissions from outside the UK and Ireland should be sent to specific address for international submissions, available on website. Cover letter should include short bio and details of the contemporary poets you read.

The Armchair Traveller at the bookHaus
Haus Publishing Ltd
70 Cadogan Place
London
SW1X 9AH
Tel: +44 (0) 20 7838 9055
Email: emma@hauspublishing.com
Website: http://www.
thearmchairtraveller.com

Publishes: Nonfiction; *Areas:* Travel; *Markets:* Adult

Contact: Emma Henderson

Publishes travel writing. Send query by email only with book proposal, and sample three chapters if book has already been written.

Arrowhead Press
70 Clifton Road
Darlington
Co. Durham
DL1 5DX
Email: editor@arrowheadpress.co.uk
Website: http://www.arrowheadpress.co.uk

Publishes: Poetry; *Markets:* Adult

Contact: Joanna Boulter, Poetry Editor

Publishes poetry books and pamphlets. Not accepting unsolicited submissions as at February 2016.

Atlantic Europe Publishing
The Barn
Bottom Farm
Bottom Lane
Henley-on-Thames
Oxon
RG8 0NR
Tel: +44 (0) 1491 684028
Email: info@atlanticeurope.com
Website: http://www.atlanticeurope.com

Publishes: Nonfiction; *Areas:* Historical; Science; Sociology; Technology; *Markets:* Academic; Children's

Publisher of illustrated nonfiction books for children, mainly National Curriculum titles. Accepts approaches by email only – no postal approaches and no attachments.

Authentic Media
PO Box 6326
Bletchley
Milton Keynes
MK1 9GG
Tel: +44 (0) 1908 268500
Email: submissions@authenticmedia.co.uk
Website: http://www.authenticmedia.co.uk

Publishes: Nonfiction; *Areas:* Biography; Religious; Spiritual; *Markets:* Academic; Adult

Publisher of Christian books, journals, and other media. Particularly interested in biographies and church and personal spiritual growth. No fiction, poetry, Phds, or children's books. Download and complete pitch form from website and return it by email.

Barefoot Books Ltd
294 Banbury Road
Oxford
OX2 7ED
Tel: +44 (0) 1865 311100
Fax: +44 (0) 1865 514965
Email: help@barefootbooks.com
Website: http://www.barefootbooks.com

Publishes: Fiction; *Markets:* Children's

Publishing program currently full as at

June 2015. Check website for current status

Publishes high-quality picture-books for children. Particularly interested in both new and traditional stories from a variety of cultures. Submit material via submission form on website.

Bennion Kearny

6 Woodside
Churnet View Road
Oakamoor
ST10 3AE
Tel: +44 (0) 1538 703 591
Email: editorial@BennionKearny.com
Website: http://www.bennionkearny.com

Publishes: Nonfiction; *Areas:* Business;
Sport; Travel; Markets

Nonfiction publisher. Particularly interested in sport, business, and travel.

Berlitz Publishing

1st Floor West
Magdalen House
136-148 Tooley Street
London
SE1 2TU
Tel: +44 (0) 20 7403 0284
Email: london@berlitzpublishing.com
Website: http://www.berlitzpublishing.com

Publishes: Nonfiction; Reference; *Areas:*
Travel; *Markets:* Adult

Publishes books on travel and language.

Bernard Babani (publishing) Ltd

The Grampians
Shepherds Bush Road
London
W6 7NF
Email: enquiries@babanibooks.com
Website: http://www.babanibooks.com

Publishes: Nonfiction; *Areas:* Technology;
Markets: Adult

Publishes books on robotics, computing, and

electronics. Always interested in hearing from potential authors. Send query by email with synopsis and details of your qualifications for writing on hte topic.

John Blake Publishing

3 Bramber Court
2 Bramber Road
London
W14 9PB
Tel: +44 (0) 20 7381 0666
Fax: +44 (0) 20 7381 6868
Email: submissions@johnblakebooks.com
Website: https://johnblakebooks.com

Publishes: Fiction; Nonfiction; *Areas:*
Autobiography; Biography; Business;
Cookery; Crime; Entertainment; Film;
Health; Historical; Humour; Legal; Military;
Music; Nature; Politics; Science; Self-Help;
Sport; Travel; TV; *Markets:* Adult;
Treatments: Commercial; Mainstream;
Popular

Welcomes synopses and ideas for nonfiction. Send query with chapter-by-chapter synopsis, personal details, publishing history, sample chapters, and SAE for response. Always looking for inspiring/ shocking real life stories from ordinary people. Not currently accepting fiction. No unsolicited MSS. If submitting by email, attachments should be no larger than 1MB and be saved in .rtf format. See website for full submission guidelines.

Blink Publishing

Deepdene Lodge
Deepdene Avenue
Dorking
RH5 4AT
Tel: +44 (0) 1306 876361
Email: info@blinkpublishing.co.uk
Website: http://www.blinkpublishing.co.uk

Publishes: Nonfiction; *Areas:*
Autobiography; Cookery; Culture;
Historical; Humour; Lifestyle; Military;
Music; Sport; *Markets:* Adult; *Treatments:*
Popular

Publishes illustrated and non-illustrated adult

nonfiction. No fiction. Send queries with ideas or synopses. No unsolicited mss.

Bloomsbury Publishing Plc

50 Bedford Square
London
WC1B 3DP
Tel: +44 (0) 20 7631 5600
Fax: +44 (0) 20 7631 5800
Email: contact@bloomsbury.com
Website: http://www.bloomsbury.com

Publishes: Fiction; Nonfiction; Reference; *Areas:* Arts; Historical; Hobbies; Music; Nature; Sport; *Markets:* Academic; Adult; Children's; Professional

No longer accepting submissions of fiction, or nonfiction other than in the following Areas: Education, Music, Military History, Natural History, Nautical and Sport. See website for full submission guidelines.

Blue Guides Limited

27 John Street
London
WC1N 2BX
Email: editorial@blueguides.com
Website: http://blueguides.com

Publishes: Nonfiction; *Areas:* Culture; Travel; *Markets:* Adult

Publishes travel guides. Always on the lookout for new authors. Contact by email in first instance, giving an indication of your areas of interest.

Bodleian Library

Commissioning Editor
Communications & Publishing Office
Broad Street
Oxford
OX1 3BG
Tel: +44 (0) 1865 277108
Fax: +44 (0) 1865 277218
Email: publishing@bodleian.ox.ac.uk
Website: http://www.bodleianbookshop.co.uk

Publishes: Nonfiction; *Areas:* Arts; Historical; Literature; *Markets:* Academic;

Adult

Publishes books relating to the library collections only. Send synopses and ideas by post. No unsolicited MSS.

Bowker (UK) Ltd

5th Floor
3 Dorset Rise
London
EC4Y 8EN
Tel: +44 (0) 20 7832 1770
Fax: +44 (0) 20 7832 1710
Email: sales@bowker.co.uk
Website: http://www.bowker.co.uk

Publishes: Reference; *Areas:* Biography; Business; *Markets:* Academic; Professional

Publishes reference books; professional and business directories; bibliographies and biographies.

Boydell & Brewer Ltd

Bridge Farm Business Park
Top Street
Martlesham
Suffolk
IP12 4RB
Tel: +44 (0) 1394 411320
Email: cpalmer@boydell.co.uk
Website: http://www.boydellandbrewer.com

Publishes: Nonfiction; *Areas:* Archaeology; Arts; Historical; Literature; Military; Music; Religious; *Markets:* Academic; Adult

Contact: Caroline Palmer (Medieval Studies); Michael Middeke (Modern History and Music); Peter Sowden (Maritime History)

Publishes nonfiction in the areas of medieval studies; music; early modern and modern history. Specialist areas include Arthurian studies; the history of religion; military history; and local history. Send proposals by post or by email. See website for specific contacts and individual email addresses.

Brilliant Publications

Unit 10, Sparrow Hall Farm

Edlesborough
Dunstable
Bedfordshire
LU6 2ES
Tel: +44 (0) 1525 222292
Fax: +44 (0) 1525 222720
Email: info@brilliantpublications.co.uk
Website: https://www.
brilliantpublications.co.uk

Publishes: Nonfiction; *Markets:* Professional

Contact: Priscilla Hannaford

Independent educational publisher
specialising in books for teachers. See FAQ
section of website for instructions on
submitting a new book proposal.

Bryntirion Press

Waterton Cross Business Park
South Road
Bridgend
CF31 3UL
Tel: +44 (0) 1656 655886
Fax: +44 (0) 1656 665919
Email: office@emw.org.uk
Website: http://www.emw.org.uk

Publishes: Nonfiction; *Areas:* Religious;
Markets: Adult

Welcomes synopses and ideas, but no
unsolicited MSS. Publishes Christian books
both in English and in Welsh.

Canongate Books

14 High Street
Edinburgh
EH1 1TE
Tel: +44 (0) 1315 575111
Fax: +44 (0) 1315 575211
Email: support@canongate.co.uk
Website: http://www.canongate.net

Publishes: Fiction; Nonfiction; *Areas:*
Autobiography; Biography; Culture;
Historical; Humour; Politics; Science;
Translations; Travel; *Markets:* Adult;
Treatments: Literary

Contact: Jamie Byng, Publisher

Publisher of a wide range of literary fiction
and nonfiction, with a traditionally Scottish
slant but becoming increasingly
international. Publishes fiction in translation
under its international imprint. No children's
books, poetry, or drama. Send synopsis with
three sample chapters and info about
yourself. No submissions by fax, email or on
disk.

Carina UK

Harlequin
1 London Bridge Street
London
SE1 9GF
Email: CarinaUKSubs@hqnuk.co.uk
Website: https://www.millsandboon.co.uk

Publishes: Fiction; *Areas:* Adventure;
Crime; Erotic; Fantasy; Gothic; Historical;
Horror; Humour; Literature; Men's Interests;
Mystery; Romance; Sci-Fi; Short Stories;
Suspense; Thrillers; Westerns; Women's
Interests; *Markets:* Adult; Children's;
Family; Youth

Digital imprint from a major publisher,
considering all genres of writing, whether
novels, novellas, serials, or a series.
Particularly interested in authors from the
UK, Ireland, South Africa and India. Send
submissions by email with any type of
attachment.

Carlton Publishing Group

20 Mortimer Street
London
W1T 3JW
Tel: +44 (0) 20 7612 0400
Fax: +44 (0) 20 7612 0401
Email: pmurrayhill@carltonbooks.co.uk
Website: http://www.carltonbooks.co.uk

Publishes: Nonfiction; Reference; *Areas:*
Architecture; Arts; Beauty and Fashion;
Biography; Culture; Design; Entertainment;
Film; Historical; Humour; Music; Sport;
Markets: Adult; Children's; *Treatments:*
Commercial; Mainstream; Popular

Publishes illustrated reference, sport,
entertainment and children's books.
Synopses and ideas for suitable books are

welcomed, but no unsolicited MSS, academic, fiction, or poetry. Send query by email only with short synopsis, author bio, market info, and up to two chapters up to a maximum of 20 pages. See website for full guidelines.

Chapman Publishing
4 Broughton Place
Edinburgh
EH1 3RX
Tel: +44 (0) 131 557 2207
Fax: +44 (0) 131 556 9565
Email: chapman-pub@blueyonder.co.uk
Website: http://www.chapman-pub.co.uk

Publishes: Fiction; Poetry; Scripts; *Areas:* Drama; Short Stories; *Markets:* Adult; *Treatments:* Literary

Contact: Joy Hendry

Note: No new books being undertaken as at January 2014. Check website for current status.

Publishes one or two books of short stories, drama, and (mainly) poetry by established and rising Scottish writers per year. No novels. Only considers writers who have previously been published in the press's magazine (see entry in magazines database). Only publishes plays that have been previously performed. No unsolicited MSS.

Chipping Norton Publishers
12 Edward Stone Rise
Chipping Norton
Tel: +44 (0) 1608 430229
Email: cnwriters@gmx.co.uk
Website: http://www.cnwriters.webs.com

Publishes: Fiction; *Areas:* Fantasy; Gothic; Horror; Mystery; Short Stories; Thrillers; *Markets:* Adult; Youth; *Treatments:* Commercial; Experimental; Mainstream

Contact: Andy Hesford

Publisher based in Oxfordshire. Actively looking for authors of short stories to be included in another compendium. We are also looking for fantasy novels.

Christian Education
1020 Bristol Road
Selly Oak
Birmingham
B29 6LB
Email: sales@christianeducation.org.uk
Website: http://shop.christianeducation.org.uk

Publishes: Nonfiction; *Areas:* Religious; *Markets:* Adult; Family; Professional

Publishes Christian resources for use by individuals, families and churches.

Churchwarden Publications Ltd
PO Box 420
WARMINSTER
BA12 9XB
Tel: +44 (0) 1985 840189
Fax: +44 (0) 1985 840243
Email: enquiries@churchwardenbooks.co.uk
Website: http://www.churchwardenbooks.co.uk

Publishes: Nonfiction; Reference; *Areas:* Religious; *Markets:* Professional

Contact: John Stidolph

Publisher of books and stationery for churchwardens and church administrators.

Classical Comics Limited
PO Box 16310
Birmingham
B30 9EL
Tel: +44 (0) 845 812 3000
Fax: +44 (0) 845 812 3005
Email: info@classicalcomics.com
Website: http://www.classicalcomics.com

Publishes: Fiction; *Areas:* Literature; *Markets:* Children's

Contact: Gary Bryant (Managing Director); Jo Wheeler (Creative Director)

Publishes graphic novel adaptations of classical literature.

Connections Book Publishing Ltd

St. Chad's House
148 King's Cross Road
London
WC1X 9DH
Tel: +44 (0) 20 7837 1968
Fax: +44 (0) 20 7837 2025
Email: info@connections-publishing.com
Website: http://www.connections-publishing.com

Publishes: Nonfiction; Reference; *Areas:* Health; Leisure; Lifestyle; Men's Interests; New Age; Philosophy; Psychology; Religious; Self-Help; Spiritual; Women's Interests; *Markets:* Adult; Family; Youth; *Treatments:* Light; Mainstream; Positive

Contact: Ian Jackson – Editorial Director

Specialises in New Age and spiritual. Emphasis on oracles and self help approach. Interest in martial arts and yoga as well as new healing and physical well being techniques. No academic. Most authors are well known from previous success and widely published books.

Corazon Books

Wyndham Media Ltd
27 Old Gloucester Street
London
WC1N 3AX
Email: editor@greatstorieswithheart.com
Website: http://www.greatstorieswithheart.com

Publishes: Fiction; *Areas:* Gothic; Historical; Romance; Thrillers; Women's Interests; *Markets:* Adult; *Treatments:* Contemporary

Publishes contemporary romance, historical romance (including family sagas), chick lit, gothic romance and romantic thrillers. Historical imprint launching autumn 2014 will welcome all historical fiction submissions, but will be particularly interested in historical novels and novellas with a romantic element.

In early 2014 will be considering submissions from published authors only, but in later 2014 will consider submissions from unpublished authors.

Crescent Moon Publishing

PO Box 393
Maidstone
Kent
ME14 5XU
Tel: +44 (0) 1622 729593
Email: cresmopub@yahoo.co.uk
Website: http://www.crescentmoon.org.uk

Publishes: Fiction; Nonfiction; Poetry; *Areas:* Arts; Criticism; Culture; Film; Literature; Media; Music; Philosophy; Politics; Women's Interests; *Markets:* Adult; *Treatments:* Contemporary; Literary

Contact: Jeremy Robinson

Publishes nonfiction on literature, culture, media, and the arts; as well as poetry and some fiction. Non-rhyming poetry is preferred. Send query with one or two sample chapters or up to six poems, with author bio and appropriate return postage for response. Material is only returned if requested and if adequate postage is provided.

Cressrelles Publishing Co. Ltd

10 Station Road Industrial Estate
Colwall
Malvern
WR13 6RN
Tel: +44 (0) 1684 540154
Fax: +44 (0) 1684 540154
Email: simon@cressrelles.co.uk
Website: http://www.cressrelles.co.uk

Publishes: Nonfiction; Scripts; *Areas:* Drama; *Markets:* Academic; Adult

Contact: Simon Smith

Welcomes submissions. Publishes plays, theatre and drama textbooks, and local interest books.

CTS (Catholic Truth Society)

40 Harleyford Road

Vauxhall
London
SE11 5AY
Tel: +44 (0) 20 7640 0042
Fax: +44 (0) 20 7640 0046
Email: f.martin@cts-online.org.uk
Website: http://www.cts-online.org.uk

Publishes: Nonfiction; *Areas:* Religious;
Markets: Adult

Contact: Fergal Martin (Publisher)

Publisher of Roman Catholic religious
books. Publishes a range of books in this
area, including Vatican documents and
sources, as well as moral, doctrinal,
liturgical, and biographical books. Welcomes
appropriate ideas, synopses, and unsolicited
MSS. Send query with 1-2 page synopsis or
a sample text.

Curious Fox

Brunel Road
Handmills
Basingstoke Hants
RG21 6XS
Tel: +44 (0) 845 070 5656
Fax: +44 (0) 1256 812558
Email: submissions@curious-fox.com
Website: http://www.curious-fox.com

Publishes: Fiction; *Areas:* Adventure;
Crime; Fantasy; Historical; Humour; Nature;
Romance; Sci-Fi; Thrillers; *Markets:*
Children's

Publishes fiction for children. Send query by
email with CV, sample chapters, and list of
any previous writing credits in the body of
the email.

DC Thomson

2 Albert Square
Dundee
DD1 9QJ
Tel: +44 (0) 1382 223131
Email: innovation@dcthomson.co.uk
Website: http://www.dcthomson.co.uk

Publishes: Fiction; Nonfiction; *Markets:*
Adult; Children's

Publisher of newspapers, magazines, comics,
and books, with offices in Dundee,
Aberdeen, Glasgow, and London. For fiction
guidelines send large SAE marked for the
attention of the Central Fiction Department.

Dedalus Ltd

Langford Lodge
St Judith's Lane
Sawtry
PE28 5XE
Tel: +44 (0) 1487 832382
Fax: +44 (0) 1487 832382
Email: info@dedalusbooks.com
Website: http://www.dedalusbooks.com

Publishes: Fiction; *Areas:* Literature;
Translations; *Markets:* Adult; *Treatments:*
Contemporary; Literary

Send query letter describing yourself along
with SAE, synopsis, three sample chapters,
and explanation of why you think this
publisher in particular is right for you –
essential to be familiar with and have read
other books on this publisher's list before
submitting, as most material received is
entirely inappropriate. Welcomes
submissions of suitable original fiction and is
particularly interested in intellectually clever
and unusual fiction. No email or disk
submissions, or collections of short stories
by unknown authors. Novels should be over
40,000 words – ideally over 50,000. Most
books are translations.

Dino Books

3 Bramber Court
2 Bramber Road
London
W14 9PB
Tel: +44 (0) 20 7381 0666
Email: help@dinobooks.co.uk
Website: https://dinobooks.co.uk

Publishes: Nonfiction; *Areas:* Humour;
Sport; *Markets:* Children's

Publishes nonfiction for children aged 9-12,
that aim to entertain, educate, and "turn your
way of thinking upside down".

Dynasty Press

36 Ravensdon Street
Kennington
London
SE11 4AR
Tel: +44 (0) 7970 066894
Email: admin@dynastypress.co.uk
Website: http://www.dynastypress.co.uk

Publishes: Nonfiction; *Areas:* Biography;
Historical; *Markets:* Adult

Publishes books connected to royalty,
dynasties and people of influence.

Edward Elgar Publishing Ltd

The Lypiatts
15 Lansdown Road
Cheltenham
Glos
GL50 2JA
Tel: +44 (0) 1242 226934
Fax: +44 (0) 1242 262111
Email: info@e-elgar.com
Website: http://www.e-elgar.co.uk

Publishes: Nonfiction; *Areas:* Business;
Culture; Finance; Legal; Nature; Politics;
Sociology; *Markets:* Academic; Professional

Contact: [See website for contact details for
different areas]

Academic and professional publisher of
books and journals, with a strong focus on
the social sciences and legal fields. Actively
commissioning new titles. See website for
contact details and proposal forms.

Egmont UK Ltd

First Floor
The Yellow Building
1 Nicholas Road
London
W11 4AN
Tel: +44 (0) 20 3220 0400
Fax: +44 (0) 20 3220 0401
Email: service@egmont.co.uk
Website: http://www.egmont.co.uk

Publishes: Fiction; *Markets:* Children's

Publishes picture books and children's
fiction. Agented submissions only.

Eland Publishing Ltd

61 Exmouth Market
Clerkenwell
London
EC1R 4QL
Tel: +44 (0) 20 7833 0762
Fax: +44 (0) 20 7833 4434
Email: info@travelbooks.co.uk
Website: http://www.travelbooks.co.uk

Publishes: Nonfiction; Poetry; *Areas:*
Travel; *Markets:* Adult

Contact: Rose Baring; John Hatt; Barnaby
Rogerson; Stephanie Allen

Specialises in keeping the classics of travel
literature in print. Also publishes books of
poetry relating to particular places.

The Emma Press Ltd

Email: queries@theemmapress.com
Website: http://theemmapress.com

Publishes: Fiction; Nonfiction; Poetry;
Markets: Adult; Children's

Contact: Emma Wright

Publishes themed anthologies of poetry,
stories, and essays. See website for themes of
current calls for submissions. In order to
submit, must have been previously accepted
by or purchased from the press.

Enitharmon Press

10 Bury Place
London
WC1A 2JL
Tel: +44 (0) 20 7430 0844
Email: info@enitharmon.co.uk
Website: http://www.enitharmon.co.uk

Publishes: Fiction; Poetry; *Areas:* Arts;
Criticism; Photography; *Markets:* Adult;
Treatments: Literary

One of Britain's leading literary publishers,
specialising in poetry and in high-quality

artists' books and original prints. It is divided into two companies: the press, which publishes poetry and general literature in small-format volumes and anthologies, and the editions, which produces de luxe artists' books in the tradition of the livre d'artiste. Send a preliminary enquiry to the editor before submitting material.

Euromonitor

60-61 Britton Street
London
EC1M 5UX
Tel: +44 (0) 20 7251 8024
Fax: +44 (0) 20 7608 3149
Email: info@euromonitor.com
Website: http://www.euromonitor.com

Publishes: Nonfiction; Reference; *Areas:* Business; *Markets:* Professional

International publisher of business reference and nonfiction, including market reports, directories, etc. for the professional market.

Ex-L-Ence Publishing

Deepfurrow Bungalow
Main Road
Minsterworth
Gloucestershire
GL2 8JH
Tel: +44 (0) 1452 751 276
Email: robert@winghigh.co.uk
Website: http://www.kindlebook.me

Publishes: Fiction; Nonfiction; Poetry; Reference; *Areas:* Adventure; Anthropology; Antiques; Archaeology; Architecture; Arts; Autobiography; Beauty and Fashion; Biography; Business; Cookery; Crafts; Crime; Criticism; Culture; Current Affairs; Design; Drama; Entertainment; Fantasy; Film; Finance; Gardening; Gothic; Health; Historical; Hobbies; How-to; Humour; Leisure; Lifestyle; Literature; Media; Medicine; Men's Interests; Military; Music; Mystery; Nature; New Age; Philosophy; Photography; Politics; Psychology; Religious; Romance; Science; Sci-Fi; Self-Help; Short Stories; Sociology; Spiritual; Sport; Suspense; Technology; Theatre; Thrillers; Travel; TV; Westerns; Women's Interests; *Markets:* Family; Professional;

Treatments: Commercial; Contemporary; Experimental; In-depth; Light; Literary; Mainstream; Niche; Popular; Positive; Progressive; Satirical; Serious; Traditional

Contact: Robert Agar-Hutton

We get your manuscript ready for publication without it costing you any money, and then we pay you 50% of net royalties. Please visit our website then call or email to discuss how we can work together.

Eye Books

Tel: +44 (0) 7973 861869
Email: dan@eye-books.com
Website: http://eye-books.com

Publishes: Nonfiction; *Areas:* Travel; *Markets:* Adult

Contact: Dan Hiscocks

Small independent publisher, publishing books about ordinary people doing extraordinary things. Often includes strong travel element. See website for detailed submission guidelines and online submission system.

Faber & Faber Ltd

Bloomsbury House
74-77 Great Russell Street
London
WC1B 3DA
Tel: +44 (0) 20 7927 3800
Fax: +44 (0) 20 7927 3801
Website: http://www.faber.co.uk

Publishes: Fiction; Nonfiction; Poetry; Scripts; *Areas:* Biography; Drama; Film; Music; Politics; Theatre; *Markets:* Adult; Children's

Originally published poetry and plays but has expanded into other areas. Has published some of the most prominent writers of the twentieth century, including several poet laureates. No longer accepting unsolicited MSS in any areas other than poetry. Submit 6 poems in first instance, with adequate return postage. Submissions of material other than poetry will neither be read nor returned. No submissions by email, fax, or on disk.

Fabian Society
61 Petty France
Westminster
London
SW1H 9EU
Tel: +44 (0) 20 7227 4900
Email: info@fabians.org.uk
Website: http://www.fabians.org.uk

Publishes: Nonfiction; *Areas:* Current Affairs; Finance; Nature; Politics; Sociology; *Markets:* Adult

Left-leaning political think tank publishing books on current affairs, politics, economics, environment, social policy, etc.

Fingerpress UK
Email: firstwriter@fingerpress.co.uk
Website: http://www.fingerpress.co.uk

Publishes: Fiction; *Areas:* Historical; Sci-Fi; Thrillers; *Markets:* Adult; *Treatments:* Commercial

Note: Not accepting submissions as at May 2016 – check website for current status.

*** Please read the submissions page on our website before submitting anything... ***

Only open to submissions at certain times. Check website for current status. When open to submissions, this will be announced on our Facebook and Twitter pages.

We're an independent publisher based in London; we publish high quality Historical Fiction and Science Fiction. We're building a range of savvy, entertaining titles that are both thought-provoking and a good read. The ideal novel will have memorable characters with good plot development and pacing.

If your book isn't either Historical Fiction or Science Fiction, please don't submit it to us - - many thanks for your understanding.

We look for:

* submissions of completed, professionally edited, commercial-grade novels

Please check out our sister website – a virtual reality Facebook for authors, publishers and readers.

Fisherton Press
Email: general@fishertonpress.co.uk
Website: http://fishertonpress.co.uk

Publishes: Fiction; *Markets:* Children's

Contact: Eleanor Levenson

Aims to publish books for children that adults will also enjoy reading, whether for the first time or the hundredth. Send query with ideas or fully written or illustrated texts with short bio, by email.

Fitzrovia Press Limited
10 Grafton Mews
London
W1T 5JG
Tel: +44 (0) 20 7380 0749
Email: info@fitzroviapress.co.uk
Website: http://www.fitzroviapress.com

Publishes: Fiction; Nonfiction; *Areas:* Philosophy; Spiritual; *Markets:* Adult

Contact: Ranchor Prime

Publishes fiction and nonfiction on Hinduism, spirituality, and Eastern philosophy. No unsolicited mss. Send query with outline and sample chapter.

Fleming Publications
134 Renfrew Street
Glasgow
G3 6ST
Email: info@ettadunn.com
Website: http://www. flemingpublications.com

Publishes: Fiction; Nonfiction; Poetry; *Areas:* Biography; Historical; Photography; Self-Help; *Markets:* Adult

Contact: Etta Dunn

Publishes nonfiction, fiction, and poetry for "mindful individuals".

Floris Books

15 Harrison Gardens
Edinburgh
EH11 1SH
Tel: +44 (0) 1313 372372
Fax: +44 (0) 1313 479919
Email: floris@florisbooks.co.uk
Website: http://www.florisbooks.co.uk

Publishes: Fiction; Nonfiction; *Areas:* Architecture; Arts; Biography; Crafts; Health; Historical; Literature; Philosophy; Religious; Science; Self-Help; Sociology; Spiritual; *Markets:* Adult; Children's; Youth

Publishes a wide range of books including adult nonfiction, picture books and children's novels. No poetry or verse, fiction for people over the age of 15, or autobiography, unless it specifically relates to a relevant nonfiction subject area. No submissions by email. See website for full details of areas covered and submission guidelines.

Fonthill Media Ltd

Millview House
Toadsmoor Road
Stroud
Gloucestershire
GL5 2TB

US OFFICE:
60 Thoreau Street #204
Concord, MA 01742
Email: submissions@fonthillmedia.com
Website: http://fonthillmedia.com

Publishes: Nonfiction; *Areas:* Archaeology; Biography; Historical; Military; Sociology; Sport; Travel; *Markets:* Adult

Independent publisher with offices in the UK and US. Publishes nonfiction only. Send query through website submissions form or by email, providing your project's title, description up to 200 words, description of yourself up to 100 words, proposed word count, and nature and number of illustrations.

Frances Lincoln Children's Books

74-77 White Lion Street
London
N1 9PF
Tel: +44 (0) 20 7284 9300
Fax: +44 (0) 20 7485 0490
Email: QuartoKidsSubmissions@ Quarto.com
Website: http://www.quartoknows.com/ Frances-Lincoln-Childrens-Books

Publishes: Fiction; Nonfiction; Poetry; *Areas:* Culture; *Markets:* Children's

Contact: Rachel Williams, Publisher; Janetta Otter-Barry, Publisher; Katie Cotton, Editor

Publishes picture books, multicultural books, poetry, picture books and information books. Submit by email. See website for full guidelines.

Frontinus

4 The Links
Cambridge Road
Newmarket
Suffolk
CB8 0TG
Tel: +44 (0) 1638 663456
Email: info@frontinus.org.uk
Website: http://www.frontinus.org.uk

Publishes: Nonfiction; *Areas:* Design; Technology; *Markets:* Academic; Professional

Publishes academic and professional nonfiction for engineers.

Galley Beggar Press

37 Dover Street
Norwich
NR2 3LG
Email: info@galleybeggar.co.uk
Website: http://galleybeggar.co.uk

Publishes: Fiction; Nonfiction; *Areas:* Literature; Sci-Fi; Short Stories; *Markets:* Adult; *Treatments:* Literary

Publishing company specifically set up to act as a sponsor to writers who have struggled to either find or retain a publisher, and whose writing shows great ambition and literary merit. Publishes a wide range of nonfiction and fiction, including quality SF, but no poetry, children's, young adult, or specialist nonfiction. When submitting, authors must be able to prove that they have read something published by the press. Closed to submissions as at November 2015, but due to re-open soon. See website for current status and full submission guidelines.

GEY Books
Email: geybooks@gmail.com

Publishes: Fiction; Nonfiction; Poetry; *Areas:* Culture; Drama; Entertainment; Erotic; Fantasy; Men's Interests; Romance; Short Stories; Thrillers; Travel; *Markets:* Adult; *Treatments:* Contemporary; Experimental; Literary

Contact: Thomas Moore

We are interested in publishing writers who identify on the LGBTQIA spectrum. The work we publish represents the many complexities of human relationships within the crazy, brilliant and beautiful LGBTQIA community.

We are interested in publishing: Fiction, Non-fiction, Poetry, Photography, Art and Comics. We are open to all types of media so long as we can create a product out of the work.

We will only publish original and previously unpublished works.

As a standard we pay our authors 50% of profits made from all sales.

We will not accept a full submission in the first instance. Please send over a brief outline of the project attaching a small sample of the work no more then 2 sides of A4 in PDF form. We will not accept any submissions via any other form besides email or any attachments other then PDFs.

Ghostwoods Books
Email: ghostwoodsbooks@gmail.com

Website: http://www.gwdbooks.com

Publishes: Fiction; *Areas:* Crime; Fantasy; Gothic; Historical; Horror; Romance; Sci-Fi; Short Stories; Thrillers; Women's Interests; *Markets:* Adult; *Treatments:* Dark

Contact: Tim Dedopulos; Salome Jones

In the process of expanding. In order to do that we need to publish good books that attract readers. Providing information about your target market is helpful in your approach.

From personal interest, we like smart, funny, or dark fiction. Answering one of our specific calls for submissions, especially for an anthology, is a good way to get in.

Gibson Square Books Ltd
47 Lonsdale Square
London
N1 1EW
Tel: +44 (0) 20 7096 1100
Fax: +44 (0) 20 7993 2214
Email: info@gibsonsquare.com
Website: http://www.gibsonsquare.com

Publishes: Fiction; Nonfiction; *Areas:* Arts; Biography; Criticism; Culture; Current Affairs; Historical; Philosophy; Politics; Psychology; Travel; Women's Interests; *Markets:* Adult

Synopses and ideas welcomed. Send query by email only. Publishes books which contribute to a general debate. Almost exclusively nonfiction, but does publish a small amount of fiction. See website for full guidelines.

Gingko Library
70 Cadogan Place
London
SW1X 9AH
Tel: +44 (0) 20 7838 9055
Email: aran@thegingkolibrary.com
Website: http://www.gingkolibrary.com

Publishes: Nonfiction; *Areas:* Architecture; Arts; Biography; Finance; Historical; Literature; Music; Philosophy; Politics;

Religious; Science; Technology; *Markets:* Academic; Adult

Publisher promoting dialogue between the West and the Middle East and North Africa. Publishes collected articles and academic monographs, peer-reviewed by scholars and academic advisors. See website for submission guidelines.

Gomer Press

Llandysul Enterprise Park
Llandysul
Ceredigion
SA44 4JL
Tel: +44 (0) 1559 362371
Fax: +44 (0) 1559 363758
Email: gwasg@gomer.co.uk
Website: http://www.gomer.co.uk

Publishes: Fiction; Nonfiction; Poetry; Reference; Scripts; *Areas:* Arts; Autobiography; Biography; Culture; Drama; Historical; Leisure; Literature; Music; Nature; Religious; Sport; Theatre; Travel; *Markets:* Academic; Adult; Children's

Publishes fiction, nonfiction, plays, poetry, language books, and educational material, for adults and children, in English and in Welsh. See website for contact details of editors and query appropriate editor with sample chapter, synopsis, CV, and sales strengths of your proposal. Do not send complete MS in first instance.

Goss & Crested China Club

62 Murray Road
Horndean
Waterlooville
PO8 9JL
Tel: +44 (0) 23 9259 7440
Fax: +44 (0) 23 9259 7440
Email: info@gosschinaclub.co.uk
Website: http://www.gosschinaclub.co.uk

Publishes: Nonfiction; Reference; *Areas:* Antiques; *Markets:* Adult; Professional

Publishes books on crested heraldic china and antique porcelain.

Granta Books

12 Addison Avenue
London
W11 4QR
Tel: +44 (0) 20 7605 1360
Fax: +44 (0) 20 7605 1361
Email: info@grantabooks.com
Website: http://www.grantabooks.com

Publishes: Fiction; Nonfiction; *Areas:* Autobiography; Biography; Criticism; Culture; Historical; Nature; Politics; Sociology; Travel; *Markets:* Adult; *Treatments:* Literary; Serious

Publishes around 70% nonfiction / 30% fiction. In nonfiction publishes serious cultural, political and social history, narrative history, or memoir. Rarely publishes straightforward biographies. No genre fiction. Accepts submissions via literary agent only.

Green Bottle Press

83 Grove Avenue
London
N10 2AL
Website: http://greenbottlepress.com

Publishes: Poetry; *Markets:* Adult; *Treatments:* Literary

Publishes poetry by poets writing in English who have not yet published a pamphlet or full collection. Will also consider new work by more established poets. Do not submit unless already published by several poetry journals. See website for full submission guidelines and online submission form, or send submission by post.

Grub Street Publishing

4 Rainham Close
London
SW11 6SS
Tel: +44 (0) 20 7924 3966 / 20 7738 1008
Fax: +44 (0) 20 7738 1009
Email: post@grubstreet.co.uk
Website: http://www.grubstreet.co.uk

Publishes: Nonfiction; Reference; *Areas:* Cookery; Health; Historical; Military; *Markets:* Adult

Contact: John Davies (Military); Anne Dolamore (Cookery)

Publishes books on cookery and military aviation history only. No fiction or poetry. Accepts synopses and unsolicited MSS by post only with SASE. No email queries or submissions. See website for full submission guidelines.

Guild of Master Craftsman (GMC) Publications Ltd
166 High Street
Lewes
BN7 1XU
Tel: +44 (0) 1273 477374
Fax: +44 (0) 1273 402866
Email: pubs@thegmcgroup.com
Website: http://www.gmcbooks.com

Publishes: Nonfiction; Reference; *Areas:* Architecture; Arts; Cookery; Crafts; Film; Gardening; Hobbies; How-to; Humour; Photography; TV; *Markets:* Adult; Children's

Publishes books on the above topics, plus woodworking, dolls houses, and miniatures. Also publishes magazines and videos. No fiction.

Halban Publishers
22 Golden Square
London
W1F 9JW
Tel: +44 (0) 20 7437 9300
Fax: +44 (0) 20 7437 9512
Email: books@halbanpublishers.com
Website: http://www.halbanpublishers.com

Publishes: Fiction; Nonfiction; *Areas:* Autobiography; Biography; Criticism; Historical; Literature; Philosophy; Politics; Religious; *Markets:* Adult

Contact: Peter Halban; Martine Halban

Independent publisher of fiction, memoirs, history, biography, and books of Jewish interest. Send query by post or by email. No unsolicited MSS. Unsolicited emails deleted unread.

Haldane Mason Ltd
PO Box 34196
London
NW10 3YB
Tel: +44 (0) 20 8459 2131
Fax: +44 (0) 20 8728 1216
Email: sfrancis@haldanemason.com
Website: http://haldanemason.com

Publishes: Nonfiction; *Areas:* Crafts; Health; Historical; Lifestyle; Science; *Markets:* Adult; Children's; Youth

Publishes books and box-sets – mainly for children through children's imprint, but also for adults, covering such topics as alternative health, yoga, henna body art, Feng Shui, etc. Children's books include crafts, puzzles, history, science, maths, etc. Send query by email in first instance.

Halsgrove
Halsgrove House
Ryelands Business Park
Bagley Road
Wellington
Somerset
TA21 9PZ
Tel: +44 (0) 1823 653777
Fax: +44 (0) 1823 216796
Email: sales@halsgrove.com
Website: http://www.halsgrove.com

Publishes: Nonfiction; *Areas:* Arts; Biography; Historical; Photography; *Markets:* Adult

Publishes regional material covering various regions in the areas of history, biography, photography, and art. No fiction or poetry. Send query by email with brief synopsis in first instance.

Harlequin Mills & Boon Ltd
Harlequin
1 London Bridge Street
London
SE1 9GF
Email: submissions@harlequin.com
Website: http://www.millsandboon.co.uk

Publishes: Fiction; *Areas:* Crime; Historical; Romance; *Markets:* Adult; *Treatments:*

Commercial; Contemporary

Major publisher with extensive romance list and various romance imprints. Submit via online submission system.

Also includes digital imprint accepting submissions in any genre, and particularly interested in authors from rapidly expanding digital markets in the UK, Ireland, South Africa and India. See website for separate submission guidelines and specific email address for this imprint. Commercial fiction and crime imprint accepts submissions via literary agents only.

HarperCollins Publishers Ltd
The News Building
1 London Bridge Street
London
SE1 9GF
Tel: +44 (0) 20 8741 7070
Fax: +44 (0) 20 8307 4440
Email: enquiries@harpercollins.co.uk
Website: http://www.harpercollins.co.uk

Publishes: Fiction; Nonfiction; Reference; *Areas:* Autobiography; Biography; Cookery; Crafts; Crime; Entertainment; Fantasy; Film; Gardening; Health; Historical; Leisure; Lifestyle; Media; Military; Science; Sci-Fi; Sport; Thrillers; *Markets:* Adult; Children's; *Treatments:* Literary

One of the UK's three largest publishers, with one of the broadest ranges of material published. Authors include many award-winning bestsellers, and significant figures of literary history. Accepts approaches through agents and from published authors only, or if accompanied by a positive assessment from a manuscript assessment agency. No unsolicited MSS.

HarperImpulse
Email: romance@harpercollins.co.uk
Website: http://www.harperimpulseromance.com

Publishes: Fiction; *Areas:* Erotic; Historical; Romance; Short Stories; *Markets:* Adult; *Treatments:* Contemporary; Experimental; Mainstream

Contact: Kimberley Young, Publishing Director

Digital-first romance publisher publishing fun and fast Adult and New Adult genre fiction to more mainstream novels; particularly contemporary, historical, paranormal and erotic fiction. Will consider work of any length (including short form fiction targetted at mobile devices), and is keen to see work that experiments with length, genre, and form, etc. Submit complete ms with covering letter and synopsis by email. See website for full guidelines.

Hart Publishing Ltd
16c Worcester Place
Oxford
OX1 2JW
Tel: +44 (0) 1865 517530
Fax: +44 (0) 1865 510710
Email: sinead@hartpub.co.uk
Website: http://www.hartpub.co.uk

Publishes: Nonfiction; *Areas:* Legal; *Markets:* Academic; Professional

Contact: Sinead Moloney; Bill Asquith; Rachel Turner

Publisher or legal books and journals for the professional and academic markets. See website for submission guidelines and specific editor subject areas and contact details.

Haus Publishing
70 Cadogan Place
London
SW1X 9AH
Tel: +44 (0) 20 7838 9055
Fax: +44 (0) 20 7584 9501
Email: emma@hauspublishing.com
Website: http://www.hauspublishing.com

Publishes: Fiction; Nonfiction; *Areas:* Arts; Biography; Film; Historical; Music; Photography; Politics; Theatre; Travel; *Markets:* Adult; *Treatments:* Literary

Contact: Emma Henderson

Publishes non-academic biographies of historical figures, and literary travel accounts (not guides). No autobiographies, fiction for children or young adults, or biographies of living people. Send query by email only, with synopsis, author bio, sample chapter headings, and the first three chapters. If the book is not yet written, send a proposal and sample chapter of your writing. Allow 6-8 weeks for response.

Hawthorn Press

1 Lansdown Lane
Stroud
Gloucestershire
GL5 1BJ
Tel: +44 (0) 1453 757040
Fax: +44 (0) 1453 751138
Email: info@hawthornpress.com
Website: http://www.hawthornpress.com

Publishes: Nonfiction; *Areas:* Lifestyle; Self-Help; *Markets:* Adult

Publisher aiming to contribute to a more creative, peaceful and sustainable world through its publishing. Publishes mainly commissioned work, but will consider approaches. Send first two chapters with introduction, full table of contents/book plan, brief author biography and/or CV, and SAE. Allow at least 2–4 months for response. Accepts email enquiries, but full submissions should be made by post.

Hay House Publishers

33 Notting Hill Gate
London
W11 3JQ
Tel: +44 (0) 20 3675 2450
Fax: +44 (0) 20 3675 2451
Email: submissions@hayhouse.co.uk
Website: http://www.hayhouse.co.uk

Publishes: Nonfiction; *Areas:* Biography; Business; Current Affairs; Finance; Health; Lifestyle; Medicine; Men's Interests; Nature; Philosophy; Psychology; Religious; Self-Help; Sociology; Spiritual; Women's Interests; *Markets:* Adult; *Treatments:* Positive

Describes itself as the world's leading mind body and spirit publisher. Open to submissions from April 4 2016. Accepts proposals as hard copy by post or by email, but prefers email approaches. See website for full submission guidelines.

Haynes Publishing

Sparkford
Near Yeovil
Somerset
BA22 7JJ
Tel: +44 (0) 1963 440635
Fax: +44 (0) 1963 440023
Email: bookseditorial@haynes.co.uk
Website: http://www.haynes.co.uk

Publishes: Nonfiction; Reference; *Areas:* How-to; Leisure; Sport; Technology; *Markets:* Adult

Contact: John H. Haynes OBE (Chairman)

Mostly publishes motoring and transport titles, including DIY service and repair manuals for cars and motorbikes, motoring in general (including Motor Sports), but also home, DIY, and leisure titles. Unsolicited MSS welcome, if on one of the above areas of interest.

Head of Zeus

Clerkenwell House
45-47 Clerkenwell Green
London
EC1R 0HT
Email: info@headofzeus.com
Website: http://www.headofzeus.com

Publishes: Fiction; Nonfiction; *Areas:* Biography; Crime; Fantasy; Historical; Mystery; Philosophy; Romance; Sci-Fi; Short Stories; Sociology; Sport; Suspense; Thrillers; *Markets:* Adult; Youth; *Treatments:* Commercial; Literary

Publishes general and literary fiction, genre fiction, and nonfiction. Submit via online submission system.

Headland Publications

38 York Avenue
West Kirby

Wirral
CH48 3JF
Tel: +44 (0) 01516 259128
Email: headlandpublications@hotmail.co.uk
Website: http://www.
headlandpublications.co.uk

Publishes: Fiction; Nonfiction; Poetry;
Areas: Biography; Short Stories; *Markets:*
Adult

Specialises in poetry, but has expanded
scope to include short stories and biography.

Headline Publishing Group
Carmelite House
50 Victoria Embankment
London
EC4Y 0DZ
Tel: +44 (0) 20 3122 7222
Email: enquiries@headline.co.uk
Website: https://www.headline.co.uk

Publishes: Fiction; Nonfiction; *Areas:*
Autobiography; Biography; Cookery;
Gardening; Historical; Science; Sport; TV;
Markets: Adult; *Treatments:* Commercial;
Literary; Popular

Publishes hardback and paperback
commercial and literary fiction, as well as
popular nonfiction.

Hesperus Press Limited
28 Mortimer Street
London
W1W 7RD
Tel: +44 (0) 20 7436 0869
Email: info@hesperuspress.com
Website: http://www.hesperuspress.com

Publishes: Fiction; Nonfiction; Poetry;
Reference; *Areas:* Autobiography;
Biography; Crime; Culture; Erotic; Fantasy;
Historical; Literature; Romance; Sci-Fi;
Thrillers; Translations; Travel; *Markets:*
Adult; Children's; *Treatments:*
Contemporary; Literary; Traditional

Publishes the lesser known works of
classical authors, both in English and in
translation. No unsolicited MSS and no
submissions.

Hippopotamus Press
22 Whitewell Road
Frome
Somerset BA11 4EL
Tel: +44 (0) 1373 466653
Email: rjhippopress@aol.com

Publishes: Poetry; *Markets:* Adult;
Treatments: Literary

Contact: Roland John

Publishes first collections of poetry by poets
who have an established track-record of
publication in poetry magazines.

The History Press
The Mill,
Brimscombe Port
Stroud
Gloucestershire
GL5 2QG
Email: web@thehistorypress.co.uk
Website: http://www.thehistorypress.co.uk

Publishes: Nonfiction; *Areas:* Archaeology;
Biography; Crime; Historical; Military;
Sport; *Markets:* Adult

Publishes books on history, from local to
international. Send query by email. No
unsolicited mss. See website for full
guidelines.

Hodder Education
338 Euston Road
London
NW1 3BH
Tel: +44 (0) 20 7873 6000
Fax: +44 (0) 20 7873 6299
Email: educationenquiries@hodder.co.uk
Website: http://www.hoddereducation.co.uk

Publishes: Nonfiction; Reference; *Areas:*
Health; Medicine; Science; Self-Help;
Markets: Academic; Adult

Publishes educational and reference books
including home learning and school
textbooks. See website for more details and
for specific submission addresses for
different types of books.

Honno Welsh Women's Press
Honno
Unit 14, Creative Units
Aberystwyth Arts Centre
Aberystwyth
Ceredigion
SY23 3GL
Tel: +44 (0) 1970 623150
Fax: +44 (0) 1970 623150
Email: post@honno.co.uk
Website: http://www.honno.co.uk

Publishes: Fiction; Nonfiction; Poetry;
Areas: Autobiography; Crime; Fantasy;
Short Stories; Women's Interests; *Markets:*
Adult; Children's; Youth; *Treatments:*
Literary

Contact: Caroline Oakley

Welcomes MSS and ideas for books from
women born in, living in, or significantly
connected to Wales, only. Publishes fiction,
autobiographical writing and reprints of
classic titles in English and Welsh, as well as
anthologies of poetry and short stories.
Particularly looking for more literary, crime,
and fantasy titles, among others. All
submissions must be sent as hard copy; no
email submissions. Send query with synopsis
and first 50 pages. Not currently accepting
children/teenage novels or poetry or short
story collections by a single author.

Hopscotch
Jesses Farm
Snow Hill
Dinton
Salisbury
Wiltshire
SP3 5HN
Tel: +44 (0) 1722 716 935
Email: info@hopscotchbooks.com
Website: http://www.hopscotchbooks.com

Publishes: Nonfiction; *Markets:* Professional

Publishes teaching resources for primary
school teachers. Happy to hear from authors
both new and established, with completed
mss or just ideas. Contact editorial
department by phone or submit complete ms.

House of Lochar
Isle of Colonsay
PA61 7YR
Tel: +44 (0) 1951 200232
Fax: +44 (0) 1951 200232
Email: sales@houseoflochar.com
Website: http://www.houseoflochar.com

Publishes: Fiction; Nonfiction; *Areas:*
Biography; Historical; Literature; Travel;
Markets: Adult; Children's

Publishes fiction and nonfiction related to
Scotland and / or Celtic themes, including
history, fiction, transport, maritime,
genealogy, Gaelic, and books for children.
No poetry or books unrelated to Scottish or
Celtic themes.

Hymns Ancient & Modern Ltd
3rd Floor, Invicta House
108-114 Golden Lane
London
EC1Y 0TG
Tel: +44 (0) 20 7776 7548
Fax: +44 (0) 20 7776 7556
Email: mary@hymnsam.co.uk
Website: http://www.hymnsam.co.uk

Publishes: Nonfiction; Reference; *Areas:*
Biography; Humour; Music; Religious;
Spiritual; *Markets:* Academic; Adult

Contact: Mary Matthews, Editorial Manager

Publishes religious books including hymn
books, liturgical material, and schoolbooks.
No proposals for dissertations, fiction,
poetry, drama, children's books, books of
specialist local interest, or (generally) multi-
authored collections of essays or symposium
papers. Send query with contents page,
synopsis, and first chapter with SAE.

Icon Books Ltd
Omnibus Business Centre
39-41 North Road
London
N7 9DP
Tel: +44 (0) 20 7697 9695
Fax: +44 (0) 20 7697 9501
Email: submissions@iconbooks.net
Website: http://www.iconbooks.co.uk

Publishes: Nonfiction; *Areas:* Arts;
Historical; Humour; Philosophy; Politics;
Psychology; Religious; Science; Sport;
Markets: Adult; *Treatments:* Popular

Submit by email only. See website for full
guidelines. Has in the past tended to publish
series of books, including an ongoing series
of graphic introductions to key figure and
ideas in history, science, psychology,
philosophy, religion, and the arts, but
increasingly publishing individual nonfiction
titles in such areas as politics, popular
philosophy and psychology, history, sport,
humour and, especially, popular science.

Igloo Books Limited

Cottage Farm
Mears Ashby Road
Sywell
Northants
NN6 0BJ
Tel: +44 (0) 1604 741116
Fax: +44 (0) 1604 670495
Email: customerservice@igloobooks.com
Website: http://igloobooks.com

Publishes: Fiction; Nonfiction; Reference;
Areas: Cookery; Hobbies; Lifestyle;
Markets: Adult; Children's

Publishes nonfiction and gift and puzzle
books for adults, and fiction, nonfiction, and
novelty books for children.

The Ilex Press

Tel: +44 (0) 1273 403124
Email: jones@ilex-press.com
Website: http://www.ilex-press.com

Publishes: Nonfiction; Reference; *Areas:*
Arts; Culture; Photography; *Markets:* Adult

Contact: Nick Jones

Publishes high quality illustrated reference
books which cover all aspects of creativity
and popular culture. Send query by email in
first instance.

Imprint Academic

PO Box 200

Exeter
EX5 5YX
Tel: +44 (0) 1392 851550
Fax: +44 (0) 1392 851178
Email: keith@imprint.co.uk
Website: http://www.imprint-academic.com

Publishes: Nonfiction; *Areas:* Criticism;
Philosophy; Politics; Psychology; *Markets:*
Academic; Adult

Contact: Keith Sutherland

Publisher of books on politics, psychology,
and philosophy for both academic and
general readership. Welcomes ideas and
unsolicited MSS by email or by post,
provided return postage is included.

Independent Music Press

PO Box 69
Church Stretton
Shropshire
SY6 6WZ
Email: info@impbooks.com
Website: http://www.impbooks.com

Publishes: Nonfiction; *Areas:* Biography;
Culture; Music; *Markets:* Adult; Youth

Contact: Martin Roach

Publishes biographies of music stars, and
books on youth culture.

Indigo Dreams Publishing

24 Forest Houses
Halwill
Beaworthy
Devon
EX21 5UU
Email: publishing@indigodreams.co.uk
Website: http://www.indigodreams.co.uk

Publishes: Poetry; *Markets:* Adult;
Treatments: Literary

Contact: Ronnie Goodyer

Publishes poetry collections up to 60/70
pages and poetry pamphlets up to 36 pages.
See website for submission guidelines.

Influx Press

Unit 25
Heartspace Hackney Downs Studios 17
Amhurst Terrace
London
E8 2BT
Email: submissions@influxpress.com
Website: http://www.influxpress.com

Publishes: Fiction; Nonfiction; Poetry;
Areas: Literature; Short Stories; *Markets:*
Adult; *Treatments:* Literary

Publishes novels, novellas, creative
nonfiction, and themed collections of poetry
and short stories. Accepts submissions only
during specific submission windows – see
website for details.

Iron Press

5 Marden Terrace
Cullercoats
North Shields
Northumberland
NE30 4PD
Tel: +44 (0) 191 253 1901
Fax: +44 (0) 191 253 1901
Email: contact@ironpress.co.uk
Website: http://www.ironpress.co.uk

Publishes: Fiction; Poetry; *Areas:* Short
Stories; *Markets:* Adult; *Treatments:*
Literary

Contact: Peter Mortimer

Poetry and fiction publisher championing
quality new writing since 1973. Publishes
poetry, (including haiku), collections of short
stories, and anthologies of verse and prose.
No novels or unsolicited mss. Send query by
email in first instance.

IWM (Imperial War Museums)

IWM London
Lambeth Road
London
SE1 6HZ
Tel: +44 (0) 20 7416 5000
Email: publishing@iwm.org.uk
Website: http://www.iwm.org.uk/
commercial/publishing

Publishes: Nonfiction; *Areas:* Historical;
Military; *Markets:* Adult

Publishes books linked to its exhibitions and
archives. Send query by email with brief
outline and sample material.

Jacaranda Books Art Music Ltd

Unit 304 Metal Box Factory
30 Great Guildford Street
London
SE1 0HS
Email: office@
jacarandabooksartmusic.co.uk
Website: http://www.
jacarandabooksartmusic.co.uk

Publishes: Fiction; Nonfiction; *Areas:* Arts;
Autobiography; Beauty and Fashion;
Biography; Crime; Photography; Romance;
Markets: Adult; *Treatments:* Contemporary

Contact: Valerie Brandes, Founder &
Publisher

Publishes adult fiction and nonfiction,
including crime, romance, illustrated books,
biography, memoir, and autobiography.
Particularly interested in books where the
central character or theme relates to minority
groups and/or has strong female
protagonists. Also interested in original
works from or about African, African-
American, Caribbean and black British
artists working in the fields of photography,
fine art, fashion, and contemporary and
modern art, and artists of calibre from the
soul, blues, R&B and reggae traditions. Send
query by email with writer CV, detailed
synopsis, and two sample chapters. See
website for full submission guidelines.

Joffe Books Ltd

Unit 3, 7a Plough Yard
London
EC2A 3LP
Email: submissions@joffebooks.com
Website: http://www.joffebooks.com

Publishes: Fiction; *Areas:* Crime; Mystery;
Romance; Suspense; *Markets:* Adult

Contact: Jasper Joffe

Publishes full-length mysteries, romances, thrillers, detective stories, and suspense. No kids books, sci-fi, nonfiction, conspiracy theories, or erotic. Send query by email with complete ms as an attachment, a synopsis in the body of the email, and 100 words about yourself. Include "submission" in the subject line. See website for full guidelines.

Jordan Publishing
21 St Thomas Street
Bristol
BS1 6JS

20-22 Bedford Row
London
WC1R 4JS
Tel: +44 (0) 1179 230600
Fax: +44 (0) 1179 250486
Email: editor@jordanpublishing.co.uk
Website: http://www.jordanpublishing.co.uk

Publishes: Nonfiction; *Areas:* Legal; *Markets:* Professional

Legal publisher specialising in family law, company and commercial, insolvency, private client, civil litigation and personal injury. Welcomes proposals in these and other areas of legal practice. Submit query via website.

Josef Weinberger Ltd
12-14 Mortimer Street
London
W1T 3JJ
Tel: +44 (0) 20 7580 2827
Fax: +44 (0) 20 7436 9616
Email: general.info@jwmail.co.uk
Website: http://www.josef-weinberger.com

Publishes: Scripts; *Areas:* Theatre; *Markets:* Adult

Publishes theatre scripts for musicals, plays, pantomimes, operas, and operettas.

Kube Publishing
MCC, Ratby Lane
Markfield

Leicestershire
LE67 9SY
Tel: +44 (0) 1530 249230
Fax: +44 (0) 1530 249656
Email: info@kubepublishing.com
Website: http://www.kubepublishing.com

Publishes: Fiction; Nonfiction; Poetry; *Areas:* Biography; Culture; Historical; Lifestyle; Politics; Religious; Sociology; Spiritual; *Markets:* Academic; Adult; Children's; Youth

Independent publisher of general interest, academic, and children's books on Islam and the Muslim experience. Publishes nonfiction for children, young people, and adults, but fiction and poetry for children and teens only. See website for full guidelines.

Kyle Books
192-198 Vauxhall Bridge Road
London
SW1V 1DX
Tel: +44 (0) 20 7692 7215
Fax: +44 (0) 20 7692 7260
Email: general.enquiries@kylebooks.com
Website: http://www.kylebooks.com

Publishes: Nonfiction; Reference; *Areas:* Beauty and Fashion; Cookery; Gardening; Health; Lifestyle; *Markets:* Adult

Describes itself as "one of the UK's leading publishers in the areas of cookery, health, lifestyle and gardening."

Legend Business
175-185 Gray's Inn Road
London
WC1X 8UE
Tel: +44 (0) 20 7812 0641
Email: submissions@legend-paperbooks.co.uk
Website: http://www.legendtimesgroup.co.uk/legend-business

Publishes: Nonfiction; *Areas:* Business; *Markets:* Professional

Publishes a wide-ranging list of business titles. Welcomes proposals and finished manuscripts. Submit synopsis and first three chapters through online submission system. See website for more details.

Legend Press

175-185 Gray's Inn Road
London
WC1X 8UE
Tel: +44 (0) 20 7812 0641
Email: info@legend-paperbooks.co.uk
Website: http://www.legendpress.co.uk

Publishes: Fiction; *Markets:* Adult; *Treatments:* Commercial; Contemporary; Mainstream

Contact: Tom Chalmers

Publishes a diverse list of contemporary adult novels. No historical fiction, children's books, poetry or travel writing. See website for full submission guidelines and online submission system.

Frances Lincoln Ltd

74-77 White Lion Street
Islington
London
N1 9PF
Tel: +44 (0) 20 7284 9300
Fax: +44 (0) 20 7485 0490
Email: fl@frances-lincoln.com
Website: http://www.franceslincoln.com

Publishes: Fiction; Nonfiction; Poetry; *Areas:* Architecture; Arts; Design; Gardening; Leisure; Lifestyle; Nature; Travel; *Markets:* Adult; Children's

Publishers of illustrated nonfiction books for adults, particularly on gardening, walking and the outdoors, art, architecture, design and landscape. In the area of children's books, publishes picture books, multicultural books, poetry, and information books. No poetry or novel submissions for adults. See website for full submission guidelines.

Lion Hudson Plc

Wilkinson House
Jordan Hill Road
Oxford
OX2 8DR

Tel: +44 (0) 1865 302750
Fax: +44 (0) 1865 302757
Email: SubmissionstoLionBooksMonarchLionFiction@LionHudson.com
Website: http://www.lionhudson.com

Publishes: Fiction; Nonfiction; Reference; *Areas:* Autobiography; Biography; Health; Religious; Spiritual; *Markets:* Adult; Children's; *Treatments:* Positive

Publishes books that reflect Christian values or are inspired by a Christian world view, including adult nonfiction / reference, and children's fiction and nonfiction. See website for specific submission guidelines for different imprints.

Liverpool University Press

4 Cambridge Street
Liverpool
L69 7ZU
Tel: +44 (0) 1317 942233
Fax: +44 (0) 1517 942235
Email: lup@liv.ac.uk
Website: http://www.liverpooluniversitypress.co.uk

Publishes: Nonfiction; *Areas:* Archaeology; Architecture; Arts; Culture; Historical; Literature; Politics; Sci-Fi; Sociology; *Markets:* Academic

Contact: Alison Welsby; Anthony Cond

Publishes books and journals, specialising in Modern Languages, Postcolonial, Slavery and Migration Studies, Irish History, Labour History, Science Fiction Studies and Art History. Download proposal submission form from website.

Logaston Press

Little Logaston
Woonton
Almeley
Herefordshire
HR3 6QH
Tel: +44 (0) 1544 327344
Email: logastonpress@phonecoop.coop
Website: http://www.logastonpress.co.uk

Publishes: Nonfiction; *Areas:* Archaeology; Biography; Historical; Sociology; Travel; *Markets:* Adult

Contact: Andy and Karen Johnson

Publishes biographies and books on the rural West Midlands and mid and South Wales. Welcomes ideas: submit synopsis in first instance.

Lost Tower Publications

Email: losttowerpublications@yahoo.com
Website: http://losttowerpublications.
jigsy.com

Publishes: Fiction; Poetry; *Areas:* Adventure; Autobiography; Crime; Fantasy; Gothic; Horror; Leisure; Lifestyle; Mystery; Sci-Fi; Spiritual; Suspense; Thrillers; Women's Interests; *Markets:* Adult; Children's; Family; Youth; *Treatments:* Contemporary; Dark; Experimental; Niche; Positive; Progressive

Contact: Harry Yang

Formed in 2011 as part of a poetry book publishing campaign to promote poetry world wide as an attractive and entertaining art form for the twenty first century. We print 3-4 books a year collecting the best photographs and poetry from around the world, to produce high quality books for people to enjoy. Our books are available to buy worldwide either from Amazon or to order through your local bookshop.

In March 2013 we published a journey of hope through poems and photographs which have been collected from around the world. The work in this anthology has been collected from every continent of our planet and illustrates ideas of hope from many of the world religions; looks at the different forms hope can take and how hope can always be found if you look carefully into the world which surrounds you.

Luath Press Ltd

543/2 Castlehill
The Royal Mile
Edinburgh

EH1 2ND
Tel: +44 (0) 131 225 4326
Fax: +44 (0) 131 225 4324
Email: sales@luath.co.uk
Website: http://www.luath.co.uk

Publishes: Fiction; Nonfiction; Poetry; *Areas:* Arts; Beauty and Fashion; Biography; Crime; Current Affairs; Drama; Historical; Leisure; Lifestyle; Nature; Photography; Politics; Sociology; Sport; Thrillers; Travel; *Markets:* Adult; Children's; Youth

Contact: G.H. MacDougall, Managing Editor

Publishes a range of books, usually with a Scottish connection. Check upcoming publishing schedule on website, and – if you think your book fits – send query with SAE, synopsis up to 250 words, manuscript or sample chapters, author bio, and any other relevant material. See website for full submission guidelines. Approaches by email will not be considered.

Luna Press Publishing

149/4 Morrison Street
Edinburgh
EH3 8AG
Email: lunapress@outlook.com
Website: http://www.
lunapresspublishing.com

Publishes: Fiction; *Areas:* Fantasy; Sci-Fi; Short Stories; *Markets:* Academic; Adult; *Treatments:* Dark

Publishes Science Fiction, Fantasy, and Dark Fantasy (including their sub-genres). Will consider short stories, novelettes, novellas, novels, graphic novels, academic material. See website for submission guidelines.

Note: not accepting novel submissions as at May 2016 – check website for current status.

Macmillan

The Macmillan Building
4 Crinan Street
London
N1 9XW

Tel: +44 (0) 20 7833 4000
Fax: +44 (0) 20 7843 4640
Website: http://www.macmillan.com

Publishes: Fiction; Nonfiction; Poetry; Reference; *Areas:* Autobiography; Biography; Business; Cookery; Crime; Culture; Current Affairs; Fantasy; Film; Finance; Gardening; Health; Historical; Horror; Humour; Military; Music; Nature; Philosophy; Politics; Psychology; Romance; Science; Sci-Fi; Sport; Theatre; Thrillers; Travel; TV; *Markets:* Academic; Adult; Children's; Family; Professional; Youth; *Treatments:* Commercial; Literary; Popular

Large publishing company publishing a wide range of titles through its various divisions and imprints. Policies towards submissions and material published varies across these divisions and imprints (as does the address to contact), so further research essential.

Mainstream Publishing Co. (Edinburgh) Ltd

7 Albany Street
Edinburgh
EH1 3UG
Tel: +44 (0) 131 557 2959
Fax: +44 (0) 131 556 8720
Email: admin@mainstreampublishing.com
Website: http://www.
mainstreampublishing.com

Publishes: Nonfiction; *Areas:* Arts; Autobiography; Biography; Culture; Current Affairs; Health; Historical; Politics; Sport; *Markets:* Adult

Nonfiction publisher based in Scotland, with particular emphasis on biography, history, politics, art, popular culture, sport, health and current affairs.

Management Books 2000 Ltd

36 Western Road
Oxford
OX1 4LG
Tel: +44 (0) 1865 600738
Email: info@mb2000.com
Website: http://www.mb2000.com

Publishes: Nonfiction; *Areas:* Business;

Finance; Lifestyle; Self-Help; *Markets:* Adult

Send outline of book, including why it was written, where it would be sold and read, etc. synopsis or detailed contents page, and a couple of sample chapters. Publishes books on management, business, finance, and related topics. Welcomes new ideas.

Manchester University Press

Floor J, Renold Building
Altrincham Street
Manchester
M1 7JA
Tel: +44 (0) 1612 752310
Fax: +44 (0) 1612 757711
Email: mup@manchester.ac.uk
Website: http://www.
manchesteruniversitypress.co.uk

Publishes: Nonfiction; Reference; *Areas:* Arts; Business; Criticism; Culture; Design; Film; Finance; Historical; Legal; Literature; Media; Politics; Theatre; TV; *Markets:* Academic

Publishes mainly textbooks for undergraduates and A-level students, plus research monographs.

Mandrake of Oxford

PO Box 250
Oxford
OX1 1AP
Email: mandrake@mandrake.uk.net
Website: http://mandrake.uk.net

Publishes: Fiction; Nonfiction; *Areas:* Arts; Crime; Culture; Erotic; Health; Horror; Lifestyle; Mystery; Philosophy; Sci-Fi; Self-Help; Spiritual; *Markets:* Adult

Send query by post or by email. May also include synopsis. See website for full guidelines, and for examples of the kind of material published.

Marion Boyars Publishers

26 Parke Road
London
SW13 9NG

Tel: +44 (0) 20 8788 9522
Fax: +44 (0) 20 8789 8122
Email: catheryn@marionboyars.com
Website: http://www.marionboyars.co.uk

Publishes: Fiction; Nonfiction; *Areas:*
Anthropology; Autobiography; Biography;
Criticism; Culture; Drama; Film; Literature;
Music; Philosophy; Psychology; Sociology;
Theatre; Women's Interests; *Markets:* Adult

Contact: Catheryn Kilgarriff (Director),
catheryn@marionboyars.com; Rebecca
Gillieron (Fiction Editor), rebecca@
marionboyars.com; Amy Christian
(Nonfiction Editor), amy@
marionboyars.com

**Note: Not accepting new submissions as at
June 2015. Check website for current
status.**

For nonfiction, send synopses and ideas with
SAE. Particularly interested in music, film,
and contemporary culture. Fiction
submissions via a literary agent only. No
poetry submissions or approaches by email.

Maverick Reads

124 Cromwell Road
Kensington
London
SW7 4ET
Email: Editor@maverick-reads.com
Website: http://www.maverick-reads.com

Publishes: Fiction; Nonfiction; Poetry;
Reference; *Areas:* Adventure; Criticism;
Culture; Fantasy; Gothic; Historical;
Literature; Media; Music; Mystery; Nature;
New Age; Philosophy; Psychology;
Religious; Romance; Science; Sci-Fi; Self-
Help; Short Stories; Spiritual; Suspense;
Theatre; Thrillers; Women's Interests;
Markets: Academic; Adult; Children's;
Family; Professional; Youth; *Treatments:*
Contemporary; Dark; Experimental; In-
depth; Literary; Niche; Positive; Progressive;
Satirical; Serious

Contact: The Editor, Adriano Bulla

Please submit:
A bio and description of book.

- 6-10 short poems or a long one of about 10
pages for Poetry
- 2-4 chapters for prose (max 15 pages)
- A sample, a plan and qualifications for
nonfiction.

The Merlin Press

99b Wallis Road
London
E9 5LN
Tel: +44 (0) 20 8533 5800
Email: info@merlinpress.co.uk
Website: http://www.merlinpress.co.uk

Publishes: Nonfiction; *Areas:* Historical;
Philosophy; Politics; *Markets:* Adult

Publisher based in London specialising in
history, philosophy, and politics.

Merlin Unwin Books

Palmers House
7 Corve Street
Ludlow
Shropshire
SY8 1DB
Tel: +44 (0) 1584 877456
Fax: +44 (0) 1584 877457
Email: books@merlinunwin.co.uk
Website: http://www.merlinunwin.co.uk

Publishes: Nonfiction; *Areas:*
Autobiography; Cookery; Humour; Leisure;
Nature; Sport; *Markets:* Adult

Publishes books on the countryside and
countryside pursuits, covering such topics as
nature, fishing, shooting, etc.

Merrell Publishers Limited

70 Cowcross Street
London
EC1M 6EJ
Tel: +44 (0) 20 7928 8880
Fax: +44 (0) 20 7928 1199
Email: hm@merrellpublishers.com
Website: http://www.merrellpublishers.com

Publishes: Nonfiction; *Areas:* Architecture;
Arts; Beauty and Fashion; Culture; Design;
Photography; *Markets:* Adult

Contact: Hugh Merrell, Publisher

Send query, preferably by email, with one-page synopsis of the project, highlighting its subject-matter, scope, approach and purpose, and indicating why you believe it to be commercially viable; an annotated table of contents to indicate how the book will be structured and what each chapter will contain in terms of subject-matter, numbers of words and numbers of illustrations; a single chapter of sample text, if already written; photocopies or printouts of sample images from the book, if available; a brief (one-paragraph) biography of each author, which should highlight, in particular, why they are qualified to write on the subject of the proposed book and provide details of any previous publications; an annotated list of related or competing works currently in print, highlighting how the proposed book differs from anything already available.

Methodist Publishing

Methodist Church House
25 Marylebone Road
London
NW1 5JR
Tel: +44 (0) 20 7486 5502
Email: helpdesk@methodistchurch.org.uk
Website: http://www.mph.org.uk

Publishes: Nonfiction; *Areas:* Philosophy; Religious; *Markets:* Adult

Publishes resources for the Methodist Church in Britain. No unsolicited mss.

Michelin Maps and Guides

Hannay House
39 Clarendon Road
Watford
Hertfordshire
WD17 1JA
Tel: +44 (0) 1923 205247
Email: themichelinguide-gbirl@uk.michelin.com
Website: http://travel.michelin.co.uk

Publishes: Nonfiction; Reference; *Areas:* Travel; *Markets:* Adult

Publishes travel guides; maps; atlases; and hotel and restaurant guides.

Milo Books Ltd

The Old Weighbridge
Station Road
Wrea Green
Lancashire
PR4 2PH
Email: publish@milobooks.com
Website: http://www.milobooks.com

Publishes: Nonfiction; *Areas:* Autobiography; Biography; Crime; Culture; Current Affairs; Sport; *Markets:* Adult; Youth

Will consider books in any nonfiction genre, but specialises in true crime, autobiography/biography, sports, current affairs and youth culture. Send query by post (with return postage if return required) or by email, with first couple of chapters.

Monarch Books

Lion Hudson Plc.
Wilkinson House
Jordan Hill Road
Oxford
OX2 8DR
Tel: +44 (0) 1865 302750
Fax: +44 (0) 1865 302757
Email: SubmissionstoLionBooksMonarchLionFiction@LionHudson.com
Website: http://www.lionhudson.com/page.asp?pid=monarch_books

Publishes: Fiction; Nonfiction; *Areas:* Politics; Psychology; Religious; Spiritual; *Markets:* Adult

Publishes a wide range of Christian books. Accepts unsolicited MSS, synopses, and ideas. Accepts submissions by email. See website for full guidelines. Response not guaranteed unless interested. If no response after three months assume rejection.

Mudfog Press

C/o Arts and Events
Culture and Tourism

P.O Box 99A
Civic Centre
Middlesbrough
TS1 2QQ
Email: contact@mudfog.co.uk
Website: http://www.mudfog.co.uk

Publishes: Fiction; Poetry; *Areas:* Short
Stories; *Markets:* Adult

Publishes poetry and short fiction by writers
in the Tees Valley area. Send query with 15-
20 poems or 2-3 stories. See website for full
details. No email submissions.

National Museum Wales
Cathays Park
Cardiff
CF10 3NP
Email: books@museumwales.ac.uk
Website: http://www.museumwales.ac.uk

Publishes: Nonfiction; *Areas:* Archaeology;
Arts; Historical; Nature; Sociology; *Markets:*
Academic; Adult; Children's

Publishes books based on the collections and
research of the museum, aimed at adults,
children, and schools. Publishes in both
Welsh and English.

Natural History Museum Publishing
The Natural History Museum
Cromwell Road
London
SW7 5BD
Tel: +44 (0) 20 7942 5336
Email: publishing@nhm.ac.uk
Website: http://www.nhm.ac.uk/business-
services/publishing.html

Publishes: Nonfiction; *Areas:* Arts; Nature;
Science; *Markets:* Adult; *Treatments:*
Popular

Publishes accessible, fully illustrated books
about the natural world.

Neil Wilson Publishing Ltd
226 King Street
Castle Douglas

DG7 1DS
Tel: +44 (0) 1556 504119
Fax: +44 (0) 1556 504065
Email: submissions@nwp.co.uk
Website: http://www.nwp.co.uk

Publishes: Nonfiction; Reference; *Areas:*
Biography; Cookery; Crime; Culture;
Historical; Humour; Music; Nature; Travel;
Markets: Adult

Welcomes approaches by email only.
Publishes books of Scottish interest through
a variety of imprints, including history, hill-
walking, humour, food and drink (including
whisky), biography, true crime, and
reference. Has published fiction in the past,
but longer does so. No academic, political,
fiction, or technical. See website for full
guidelines.

Neon
Email: info@neonmagazine.co.uk
Website: http://neonmagazine.co.uk

Publishes: Fiction; Poetry; *Areas:* Short
Stories; *Markets:* Adult; *Treatments:*
Literary

Publishes chapbooks and pamphlets of
poetry and fiction. Chapbooks and pamphlets
contain the work of a single author and may
be a collection of poetry, a single long story,
or a collection of short stories, but the
material should be thematically linked.
Authors will receive payment for chapbooks
but not for pamphlets, as these are given
away free and distributed as widely as
possible. Send query via form on website.

New Cavendish Books
3 Denbigh Road
London
W11 2SJ
Tel: +44 (0) 20 7229 6765
Fax: +44 (0) 20 7792 0027
Email: sales@newcavendishbooks.co.uk
Website: http://www.
newcavendishbooks.co.uk

Publishes: Nonfiction; Reference; *Areas:*
Antiques; Arts; Hobbies; *Markets:* Adult

Independent publisher publishing books on collectable items.

New Holland Publishers (UK) Ltd

The Chandlery Unit 009
50 Westminster Road
London
SE1 7QY
Tel: +44 (0) 20 7953 7565
Email: enquiries@nhpub.co.uk
Website: http://www.newhollandpublishers.com

Publishes: Nonfiction; Reference; *Areas:* Arts; Biography; Cookery; Crafts; Design; Gardening; Health; Historical; How-to; Humour; Lifestyle; Nature; Photography; Self-Help; Spiritual; Sport; Travel; *Markets:* Adult

International publisher of nonfiction and reference. Send query with SAE, synopsis, CV, and sample chapters.

New Playwrights' Network (NPN)

10 Station Road Industrial Estate
Colwall
Herefordshire
WR13 6RN
Tel: +44 (0) 1684 540154
Email: simon@cressrelles.co.uk
Website: http://www.cressrelles.co.uk

Publishes: Scripts; *Areas:* Drama; Theatre; *Markets:* Adult

Contact: Simon Smith

Established in the 1970s to promote scripts by new writers. Send scripts by email or by post.

Nick Hern Books Ltd

The Glasshouse
49a Goldhawk Road
London
W12 8QP
Tel: +44 (0) 20 8749 4953
Fax: +44 (0) 20 8735 0250
Email: matt@nickhernbooks.co.uk

Website: http://www.nickhernbooks.co.uk

Publishes: Nonfiction; Scripts; *Areas:* Film; Theatre; *Markets:* Adult; Professional

Contact: Matt Applewhite, Commissioning Editor

Publishes plays attached to significant professional productions in major theatres only. No unsolicited scripts. Also publishes books by theatre practitioners and for theatre practitioners. No critical, analytical or historical studies.

Nightingale Press

Manning Partnership
7 Green Park Station
Green Park Road
Bath
BA1 1JB
Tel: +44 (0) 1225 478444
Fax: +44 (0) 1225 478440
Email: karen@manning-partnership.co.uk
Website: http://www.manning-partnership.co.uk

Publishes: Nonfiction; *Areas:* Humour; Lifestyle; *Markets:* Adult

Contact: Karen Twissell

Publishes health, lifestyle, humour, gift, and language and learning.

Michael O'Mara Books Ltd

9 Lion Yard
Tremadoc Road
London
SW4 7NQ
Tel: +44 (0) 20 7720 8643
Fax: +44 (0) 20 7627 4900
Email: enquiries@mombooks.com
Website: http://www.mombooks.com

Publishes: Nonfiction; *Areas:* Biography; Historical; Humour; *Markets:* Adult; Children's

Independent publisher dealing in general nonfiction, royal and celebrity biographies, humour, and anthologies, and books for children through its imprint (including quirky nonfiction, humour, novelty, picture, and board books). Welcomes ideas, and prefers synopses and sample text to unsolicited mss. No fiction. See website for full details.

Oberon Books
521 Caledonian Road
London
N7 9RH
Tel: +44 (0) 20 7607 3637
Fax: +44 (0) 20 7607 3629
Email: andrew@oberonbooks.com
Website: http://www.oberonbooks.com

Publishes: Nonfiction; Scripts; *Areas:* Drama; Theatre; *Markets:* Adult; Professional

Contact: Andrew Walby, Senior Editor

Publishes play texts, and books on dance and theatre. Specialises in translations of European classics and contemporary plays, though also publishes edited performance versions of classics including Shakespeare. Play texts are usually published in conjunction with a production. Play scripts may be submitted by post or by email. Book proposals for trade and professional titles should include summary, table of contents, estimate word count, and sample chapter.

Octopus Publishing Group Limited
Carmelite House
50 Victoria Embankment
London
EC4Y 0DZ
Tel: +44 (0) 20 3122 6400
Email: info@octopusbooks.co.uk
Website: https://www.octopusbooks.co.uk

Publishes: Nonfiction; Reference; *Areas:* Antiques; Architecture; Arts; Beauty and Fashion; Cookery; Crafts; Culture; Design; Film; Gardening; Health; Historical; Humour; Lifestyle; Music; Psychology; Spiritual; Sport; Travel; *Markets:* Adult; Children's

Publisher with wide range of imprints dealing with a variety of nonfiction and reference subjects. See website for specific email addresses dedicated to each individual imprint.

Omnibus Press
14/15 Berners Street
London
W1T 3LJ
Tel: +44 (0) 20 7612 7400
Fax: +44 (0) 20 7612 7545
Email: info@omnibuspress.com
Website: http://www.omnibuspress.com

Publishes: Nonfiction; *Areas:* Biography; Music; *Markets:* Adult

Contact: Chris Charlesworth

Publisher of music books, including song sheets and rock and pop biographies. Welcomes ideas, synopses, and unsolicited MSS for appropriate books.

Oneworld Publications
10 Bloomsbury Street
London
WC1B 3SR
Tel: +44 (0) 20 7307 8900
Email: submissions@oneworld-publications.com
Website: http://www.oneworld-publications.com

Publishes: Fiction; Nonfiction; *Areas:* Biography; Business; Current Affairs; Historical; Nature; Philosophy; Politics; Psychology; Religious; Science; Self-Help; *Markets:* Adult; *Treatments:* Commercial; Literary; Popular

Nonfiction authors must be academics and/or experts in their field. Approaches for fiction must provide a clear and concise synopsis, outlining the novel's main themes. See website for full submission guidelines, and forms for fiction and nonfiction, which may be submitted by email.

Osprey Publishing Ltd
Commissioning Editor
Editorial Department
Osprey Publishing

Kemp House
Chawley Park
Cumnor Hill
Oxford
OX2 9PH
Tel: +44 (0) 1865 757022
Fax: +44 (0) 1865 242009
Email: editorial@ospreypublishing.com
Website: http://www.ospreypublishing.com

Publishes: Nonfiction; *Areas:* Historical;
Military; *Markets:* Adult

Publishes illustrated books on military
history and aviation. Welcomes synopses
and ideas for books by post or by email, but
no unsolicited MSS. See website for full
guidelines.

Ouen Press

Email: submissions@ouenpress.com
Website: http://www.ouenpress.com

Publishes: Fiction; Nonfiction; *Areas:*
Biography; Short Stories; Travel; *Markets:*
Adult; *Treatments:* Contemporary

Publishes contemporary fiction, travel
literature, short story collections and
biography, if edgy. No genre, children's
books, poetry, single short stories, guide
books or recipe books. Send query by email
only with outline, brief resume of your
writing experience, and first 4,000 words, all
in the body of the email. Do not include a
cover letter. No attachments, or submissions
by post. If no reponse within 60 days,
assume rejection.

Oversteps Books

6 Halwell House
South Pool
Nr Kingsbridge
Devon
TQ7 2RX
Email: alwynmarriage@overstepsbooks.com
Website: http://www.overstepsbooks.com

Publishes: Poetry; *Markets:* Adult

Poetry publisher. Send email with copies of
six poems that have been published in
magazines or won competitions, along with

details of dates or issue numbers and email
addresses of the editors. Include poems and
information in the body of your email. No
submissions by post.

Peter Owen Publishers

81 Ridge Road
London
N8 9NP
Tel: +44 (0) 20 8350 1775
Fax: +44 (0) 20 8340 9488
Email: info@peterowen.com
Website: http://www.peterowen.com

Publishes: Fiction; Nonfiction; *Areas:* Arts;
Biography; Criticism; Historical; Literature;
Translations; *Markets:* Adult; *Treatments:*
Literary

Contact: Antonia Owen (Editorial Director)

Publishes general nonfiction and
international literary fiction. No first novels,
short stories, poetry, plays, sport, spirituality,
self-help, or children's or genre fiction.
Prefers query by email or alternatively by
post with return postage, including cover
letter, synopsis, and one or two sample
chapters. Prefers fiction to come from an
agent or translator as appropriate.

PaperBooks

The Old Fire Station
140 Tabernacle Street
London
EC2A 4SD
Tel: +44 (0) 20 7300 7370
Email: submissions@legend-
paperbooks.co.uk
Website: http://www.
legendtimesgroup.co.uk/paperbooks

Publishes: Nonfiction; *Areas:*
Autobiography; Cookery; *Markets:* Adult

Former fiction publisher now relaunched as a
nonfiction publisher. Publishes cookery and
memoir, and looking to extend this list.
Submit online using online submission
system.

Parthian Books
426 Grove Extension
Swansea University
Singleton Park
Swansea
SA2 8PP
Tel: +44 (0) 1792 606605
Email: susieparthian@gmail.com
Website: http://www.parthianbooks.co.uk

Publishes: Fiction; Poetry; Scripts; *Areas:*
Drama; Short Stories; Translations; *Markets:*
Adult

Contact: Susie Wild

Publisher of poetry, drama, and fiction, of
Welsh origin, in the English language. Also
publishes English language translations of
Welsh language work. Not accepting poetry
submissions as at June 2015 (check website
for current situation). Send query with SAE,
one-page synopsis, and first 30 pages. No
email submissions. See website for full
submission guidelines.

Pavilion Publishing
Rayford House
School Road
Hove
East Sussex
BN3 5HX
Tel: +44 (0) 1273 434943
Fax: +44 (0) 1273 227308
Email: info@pavpub.com
Website: http://www.pavpub.com

Publishes: Nonfiction; Reference; *Areas:*
Health; Sociology; *Markets:* Professional

Publishes books and resources for public,
private and voluntary workers in the health,
social care, education and community safety
sectors. Welcomes submissions from both
new and established authors, and
organisations that are developing training
materials.

Pearson UK
Edinburgh Gate
Harlow
CM20 2JE
Tel: +44 (0) 845 313 6666

Fax: +44 (0) 845 313 7777
Website: http://www.pearsoned.co.uk

Publishes: Nonfiction; *Markets:* Academic;
Professional

World's largest publisher of educational
material, inclusing books for primary school
pupils through to professionals. See website
for appropriate imprint to approach, and
specific submission guidelines.

Persephone Books
59 Lamb's Conduit Street
London
WC1N 3NB
Tel: +44 (0) 20 7242 9292
Fax: +44 (0) 20 7242 9272
Email: info@persephonebooks.co.uk
Website: http://www.persephonebooks.co.uk

Publishes: Fiction; Nonfiction; *Areas:*
Women's Interests; *Markets:* Adult

Publishes mainly forgotten fiction and nonfiction by women, for women and about
women. Publishes reprints, so no unsolicited
material.

Phaidon Press Limited
Regent's Wharf
All Saints Street
London
N1 9PA
Tel: +44 (0) 20 7843 1000
Fax: +44 (0) 20 7843 1010
Email: submissions@phaidon.com
Website: http://www.phaidon.com

Publishes: Nonfiction; *Areas:* Architecture;
Arts; Beauty and Fashion; Cookery; Culture;
Design; Film; Historical; Music;
Photography; Travel; *Markets:* Academic;
Adult; Children's

Publishes books in the areas of art,
architecture, design, photography, film,
fashion, contemporary culture, decorative
arts, music, performing arts, cultural history,
food and cookery, travel and books for
children. No fiction or approaches by post.
Send query by email only, with CV and short

description of the project. Response only if interested.

Phoenix Yard Books

65 King's Cross Road
London
WC1X 9LW
Tel: +44 (0) 20 7239 4968
Email: submissions@phoenixyardbooks.com
Website: http://www.phoenixyardbooks.com

Publishes: Fiction; Nonfiction; Poetry;
Markets: Children's; Youth; *Treatments:*
Literary

Contact: Emma Langley

Publishes picture books, fiction, poetry, nonfiction and illustration for children aged around three to thirteen. Considers books of all genres, but leans more towards the literary and of the fiction spectrum. Particularly interested in character-based series, and fiction appealing to boys aged 6-9. Does not concentrate on young adult fiction, but will consider older fiction as part of epic series, sagas or trilogies. Send query by email only – no exceptions. See website for full submission guidelines. Replies to email queries only if interested.

Piccadilly Press

5 Castle Road
London
NW1 8PR
Tel: +44 (0) 20 7267 4492
Fax: +44 (0) 20 7267 4493
Email: books@piccadillypress.co.uk
Website: http://www.piccadillypress.co.uk

Publishes: Fiction; Nonfiction; *Areas:*
Humour; *Markets:* Children's; Youth;
Treatments: Contemporary; Light

Publishes a range of titles, including parental books, but for new titles focuses on three main Areas: picture books for children aged 2 to 5; teen fiction; and teen nonfiction.

Picture books should be character led and between 500 and 1,000 words. No novelty books. Prefers authors to be familiar with other books published before submitting – a

catalogue is available upon request.

Publishes teen fiction and nonfiction which is contemporary, humorous, and deals with the issues faced by teenagers. Usually 25,000-35,000 words.

Send query by email with Word or Doc attachments of up to 5MB only.

Pluto Publishing Ltd

345 Archway Road
London
N6 5AA
Tel: +44 (0) 20 8348 2724
Fax: +44 (0) 20 8340 8252
Email: pluto@plutobooks.com
Website: http://www.plutobooks.com

Publishes: Nonfiction; *Areas:* Anthropology;
Culture; Current Affairs; Finance; Historical;
Legal; Media; Nature; Politics; Sociology;
Markets: Academic

Contact: Anne Beech; David Castle; David
Shulman

Academic press publishing books for students and academics in higher education. Consult website for appropriate commissioning editor to submit your proposal to, then contact by email giving outline of book, synopsis and table of contents, format and delivery estimate, plus market info (see website for more information).

The Policy Press

1-9 Old Park Hill
Bristol
BS2 8BB
Tel: +44 (0) 1179 545940
Email: pp-info@bristol.ac.uk
Website: http://www.policypress.co.uk

Publishes: Nonfiction; *Areas:* Politics;
Sociology; *Markets:* Academic; Professional

Publishes monographs, texts and journals for scholars internationally; reports for policy makers, professionals and researchers; and practice guides for practitioners and user groups. Aims to publish the latest policy research for the whole policy studies community, including academics, policy makers, practitioners and students. Welcomes proposals for books, reports, guides or journals. Author guidelines available on website.

Polity Press

65 Bridge Street
Cambridge
CB2 1UR
Tel: +44 (0) 1223 324315
Fax: +44 (0) 1223 461385
Email: editorial@politybooks.com
Website: http://www.polity.co.uk

Publishes: Nonfiction; Reference; *Areas:* Anthropology; Archaeology; Business; Crime; Culture; Finance; Health; Historical; Literature; Media; Medicine; Nature; Philosophy; Politics; Psychology; Religious; Sociology; Women's Interests; *Markets:* Adult

Contact: Appropriate commissioning editor (see website)

Describes itself as one of the world's leading publishers of social sciences and humanities. Welcomes synopses and ideas for books. See website for appropriate commissioning editor to contact, and details of what your proposal should include.

Princeton University Press Europe

3 Market Place
Woodstock
Oxfordshire
OX20 1SY
Tel: +44 (0) 1993 814500
Fax: +44 (0) 1993 814504
Email: admin@pupress.co.uk
Website: http://www.pupress.co.uk

Publishes: Nonfiction; Reference; *Areas:* Anthropology; Archaeology; Architecture; Arts; Film; Finance; Historical; Legal; Literature; Media; Medicine; Music; Nature; Philosophy; Photography; Politics; Religious; Science; Self-Help; Sociology; *Markets:* Academic

Contact: Richard Baggaley, Publishing Director, Europe

European office of US academic publisher.

Professional and Higher Partnership

4 The Links
Cambridge Road
Newmarket
Suffolk
CB8 0TG
Tel: +44 (0) 1638 663456
Email: info@frontinus.org.uk
Website: http://pandhp.com

Publishes: Nonfiction; *Markets:* Academic; Professional

Publishes nonfiction for the academic and professional markets, including books on higher education and creative writing studies.

Psychology Press

2 Park Square
Milton Park
Abingdon
Oxford
OX14 4RN
Tel: +44 (0) 1235 400400
Fax: +44 (0) 1235 400401
Email: russell.george@tandf.co.uk
Website: https://www.routledge.com/psychology

Publishes: Nonfiction; *Areas:* Psychology; *Markets:* Academic; Professional

Contact: Russell George

Publishes academic and professional books and journals on psychology. Send query by email to appropriate editor (see website for specific addresses).

Pure Indigo Limited

Publishing Department
17 The Herons
Cottenham
Cambridge
CB24 8XX

Tel: +44 (0) 7981 395258
Email: submissions@pureindigo.co.uk
Website: http://www.pureindigo.co.uk/
publishing

Publishes: Fiction; Nonfiction; *Areas:*
Fantasy; Sci-Fi; *Markets:* Children's

Publishes books for children, including
single-player role-playing gamebooks and
books designed to support early readers.
Prefers submissions by email. See website
for guidelines.

Pushkin Press
71-75 Shelton Street
London
WC2H 9JQ
Tel: +44 (0) 20 7470 8830
Email: books@pushkinpress.com
Website: http://pushkinpress.com

Publishes: Fiction; Nonfiction; *Areas:*
Autobiography; *Markets:* Adult; Children's;
Treatments: Contemporary; Traditional

Publishes novels, essays, memoirs,
children's books, including timeless classics
and contemporary.

Quadrille Publishing Ltd
Pentagon House
52-54 Southwark Street
London
SE1 1UN
Tel: +44 (0) 20 7601 7500
Email: enquiries@quadrille.co.uk
Website: http://www.quadrille.co.uk

Publishes: Nonfiction; *Areas:* Beauty and
Fashion; Cookery; Crafts; Design;
Gardening; Health; Humour; *Markets:* Adult

Publishes quality illustrated nonfiction. No
fiction or books for children.

Quarto Publishing Group UK
The Old Brewery
6 Blundell Street
London
N7 9BH
Tel: +44 (0) 20 7700 6700

Fax: +44 (0) 20 7700 8066
Email: info@quarto.com
Website: http://www.quarto.com

Publishes: Nonfiction; *Areas:* Arts; Beauty
and Fashion; Cookery; Crafts; Design;
Entertainment; Gardening; Health;
Historical; Hobbies; How-to; Lifestyle;
Sport; *Markets:* Adult; Children's

Publisher of illustrated nonfiction books for
adults and children.

Radcliffe Publishing Ltd
5 Thomas More Square
London
E1W 1YW
Tel: +44 (0) 844 887 1380
Email: jonathan.mckenna@
radcliffepublishing.com
Website: http://www.radcliffehealth.com

Publishes: Nonfiction; *Areas:* Health;
Medicine; *Markets:* Professional

Contact: Jonathan McKenna; Katrina
Hulme-Cross

Publishes books on medicine, including
health care policy and management, and also
training materials. Welcomes synopses,
ideas, and unsolicited MSS.

Ragged Bears Limited
Unit 14A
Bennett's Field Trading Estate
Southgate Road
Wincanton
Somerset
BA9 9DT
Tel: +44 (0) 1963 34300
Email: books@ragged-bears.co.uk
Website: http://www.ragged-bears.co.uk

Publishes: Fiction; *Markets:* Children's;
Youth

Publishes picture books and novelty books,
up to young teen fiction. Accepts
submissions by post with SAE (no original
artwork), but prefers submissions by email.

Ransom Publishing Ltd
Radley House
8 St Cross Road
Winchester
Hampshire
SO23 9HX
Tel: +44 (0) 1962 862307
Fax: +44 (0) 5601 148881
Email: ransom@ransom.co.uk
Website: http://www.ransom.co.uk

Publishes: Fiction; Nonfiction; *Markets:*
Adult; Children's; Professional; Youth

An independent specialist publisher of high
quality, inspirational books that encourage
and help children, young adults, and adults to
develop their reading skills. Books are
intended to have content which is age
appropriate and engaging, but reading levels
that would normally be appropriate for
younger readers. Also publishes resources
for both the library and classroom. Will
consider unsolicited mss. Email in first
instance.

Reader's Digest Association Ltd
PO Box 7853
Ringwood
BH24 9FH
Tel: +44 (0) 330 333 2220
Email: customer_service@
readersdigest.co.uk
Website: http://www.readersdigest.co.uk

Publishes: Nonfiction; *Markets:* Adult

Publishes monthly magazine and condensed
and series books. See website for more
details.

Reaktion Books
33 Great Sutton Street
London
EC1V 0DX
Tel: +44 (0) 20 7253 1071
Fax: +44 (0) 20 7253 1208
Email: info@reaktionbooks.co.uk
Website: http://www.reaktionbooks.co.uk

Publishes: Nonfiction; *Areas:* Architecture;
Arts; Beauty and Fashion; Biography;

Culture; Current Affairs; Design; Film;
Finance; Gardening; Historical; Literature;
Medicine; Music; Nature; Philosophy;
Photography; Science; Sport; Travel;
Markets: Adult; *Treatments:* Popular

Send 4-5 page book proposal by post or
email, including title, synopsis, outline,
details of illustrations, your CV, details of
the market and competition, and your
anticipated date of data delivery. See website
for more details.

Reality Street Editions
63 All Saints Street
Hastings
East Sussex
TN34 3BN
Tel: +44 (0) 7706 189253
Email: info@realitystreet.co.uk
Website: http://www.realitystreet.co.uk

Publishes: Fiction; Poetry; *Markets:* Adult;
Treatments: Experimental; Literary

Contact: Ken Edwards

**Not planning to publish any new titles
after 2016, when existing commitments
are fulfilled. Not accepting any new
material.**

Small poetry press which in recent years
also published experimental prose, both
narrative and non-narrative. Publishes only a
few books each year, so usually heavily
committed: "if you are not familiar with any
of those writers we have published and/or are
unwilling to research further by buying and
reading our books, then it's highly unlikely
you have anything to interest us."

Red Rattle Books
Email: editor@redrattlebooks.co.uk
Website: http://www.redrattlebooks.co.uk

Publishes: Fiction; Nonfiction; *Areas:*
Crime; Horror; *Markets:* Adult

Independent, family run company,
publishing new crime, horror and nonfiction
books. Submit via website using online
submission form.

Richard Dennis Publications

The New Chapel
Shepton Beauchamp
Ilminster
Somerset
TA19 0JT
Tel: +44 (0) 1460 240044
Email: books@
richarddennispublications.com
Website: http://www.
richarddennispublications.com

Publishes: Nonfiction; *Areas:* Arts; Crafts;
Design; *Markets:* Adult

Publisher of arts and crafts books, including
books on ceramics, glass, sculpture, etc.

Robert Hale Publishers

The Crowood Press
The Stable Block
Crowood Lane
Ramsbury
Wiltshire
SN8 2HR
Tel: +44 (0) 20 7251 2661
Fax: +44 (0) 20 7490 4958
Email: enquiries@crowood.com
Website: http://www.halebooks.com

Publishes: Fiction; Nonfiction; Reference;
Areas: Arts; Biography; Crime; Design;
Health; Historical; Leisure; Lifestyle;
Nature; Romance; Spiritual; Sport;
Westerns; *Markets:* Adult

Contact: Editorial Department

See website for full submission guidelines,
and list of material not currently being
accepted. Send query with synopsis and three
sample chapters.

Rose and Crown Books

36 Salmons Leap
Calne
Wiltshire
SN11 9EU
Tel: +44 (0) 1508 480087
Email: query@roseandcrownbooks.com
Website: http://www.
roseandcrownbooks.com/

Publishes: Fiction; *Areas:* Historical;
Military; Religious; Romance; Travel;
Markets: Adult; Family; *Treatments:*
Commercial; Contemporary; Light; Literary;
Mainstream; Niche; Popular; Positive;
Serious; Traditional

Imprint with launch date in 2009. Our focus
is on romance with an inspirational flavour.
Intended to complement American brands
such as the Steeple Hill, Thorndike and
Bethany House imprints, we would seem to
be the first publisher in the United Kingdom
to take up the banner for this genre.

We believe strongly that Inspirational
Romance has a role to play in the lives of
today's women, of all ages, races and creeds
around the world – a role of pure reading
enjoyment as well as food for their
imaginations and their feminine spirits and
minds. We are concentrating on strong
writing and intelligent stories that speak to
women across the board, with characters and
situations they can identify with – tales that
fit many age groups and categories: tender
young love, later life meetings, families, and
romance for the more senior of us, too.

Some will have more Christian influence
than others; some will be contemporary,
others historical, with locations all around
the world. They will vary in style from
straight romance to historical fiction,
contemporary novels, humour, travel,
adventure, crime/detective, Western,
military, etc. As long as they have a romance
at their heart and Christian characters, with a
greater or lesser Christian implication, they
fit what we are looking for.

Query first please, with single para
description of book, brief author bio, email
address and postal address, and synopsis. For
full guidelines and more information on how
we work as a company, please visit the web
site, and please take the time to read and
follow the guidelines. If you want us to show
interest in you, please show enough interest
in us to submit correctly; we thank you!

RotoVision

Sheridan House
112-116A Western Road

Hove
East Sussex
BN3 1DD
Tel: +44 (0) 1273 727268
Fax: +44 (0) 1273 727269
Email: alison.morris@quarto.com
Website: http://www.rotovision.com

Publishes: Nonfiction; *Areas:* Architecture; Arts; Design; Film; Photography; *Markets:* Adult

Contact: Alison Morris (Commissioning Editor)

Publisher of books on the visual arts.

Roundhouse Group

Unit B
18 Marine Gardens
Brighton
BN2 1AH
Tel: +44 (0) 1273 603717
Fax: +44 (0) 1273 697494
Email: sandy@roundhousegroup.co.uk
Website: https://www.
roundhousegroup.co.uk

Publishes: Nonfiction; Reference; *Areas:* Architecture; Arts; Business; Cookery; Crafts; Design; Film; Health; Historical; Lifestyle; Literature; Medicine; Music; Nature; Photography; Self-Help; Spiritual; Sport; Travel; *Markets:* Adult; Children's; Youth

Publisher of nonfiction and reference for adults, children, and young adults.

Route Publishing

PO Box 167
Pontefract
WF8 4WW
Tel: +44 (0) 845 158 1565
Email: info@route-online.com
Website: http://www.route-online.com

Publishes: Fiction; Poetry; *Areas:* Culture; Short Stories; *Markets:* Adult; *Treatments:* Contemporary

Contact: Ian Daley; Isabel Galan

Publisher of novels, short stories, and poetry. Open door for new writing submissions is currently unsupported. Any new books considered must be self-supporting. This consideration must be addressed in any proposals.

Saffron Books

EAPGROUP
PO Box 13666
London
SW14 8WF
Tel: +44 (0) 20 8392 1122
Fax: +44 (0) 20 8392 1422
Email: info@eapgroup.com
Website: http://www.saffronbooks.com

Publishes: Fiction; Nonfiction; *Areas:* Archaeology; Arts; Business; Culture; Current Affairs; Finance; Historical; Sociology; *Markets:* Adult

Publishes books on art, archaeology and architecture, art history, current affairs and linguistics, with a particular emphasis on Asia, Africa, and the Middle East. Also publishes fiction. Welcomes proposals for books and monongraphs from new or established authors. Send query by email, post, or fax (not preferred for long documents). See website for full guidelines.

The Salariya Book Company

25 Marlborough Place
Brighton
East Sussex
BN1 1UB
Tel: +44 (0) 1273 603306
Fax: +44 (0) 1273 621619
Email: salariya@salariya.com
Website: http://www.salariya.com

Publishes: Fiction; Nonfiction; *Areas:* Adventure; Fantasy; Historical; Nature; Science; *Markets:* Children's

Publishes books of fiction and nonfiction for children.

Salt Publishing Ltd

12 Norwich Road
CROMER

Norfolk
NR27 0AX
Tel: +44 (0) 1263 511011
Email: submissions@saltpublishing.com
Website: http://www.saltpublishing.com

Publishes: Fiction; *Areas:* Crime; Gothic;
Literature; Thrillers; *Markets:* Adult;
Treatments: Dark; Literary; Mainstream;
Traditional

Accepts print fiction submissions via agents
only. Accepts direct submissions from
authors for ebooks – novellas 20,000 to
30,000 words long, dealing explicitly with
lives of young people in modern Britain and
the US. Full submission guidelines on
website. No poetry (adult or children's),
biography or autobiography, plays or
nonfiction.

Samuel French Ltd

Performing Rights Department
52 Fitzroy Street
London
W1T 5JR
Tel: +44 (0) 20 7387 9373
Fax: +44 (0) 20 7387 2161
Email: submissions@samuelfrench-
london.co.uk
Website: http://www.samuelfrench-
london.co.uk

Publishes: Scripts; *Areas:* Drama; *Markets:*
Adult

Publishes plays only. Send query by email
only, following the guidelines in the FAQ
section of the website. No unsolicited MSS.

Sandstone Press Ltd

PO Box 5725
One High Street
Dingwall
Ross-shire
IV15 9WJ
Tel: +44 (0) 1349 862583
Fax: +44 (0) 1349 862583
Email: moira@sandstonepress.com
Website: http://www.sandstonepress.com

Publishes: Fiction; Nonfiction; *Areas:*
Crime; Thrillers; *Markets:* Adult;

Treatments: Literary

Contact: Moira Forsyth, Commissioning
Editor

Publishes fiction and nonfiction and adults.
Interested in literary fiction, crime novels,
and thrillers, set in the past, present, or
future. Welcomes proposals – send
introductory email query in first instance,
including outline and bio, including
publishing history. No children's, young
adult, poetry, short story collections, science
fiction, fantasy, general historical fiction, or
horror. See website for more details and
submission form.

Scala Arts & Heritage Publishers

21 Queen Anne's Gate
London
SW1H 9BU
Tel: +44 (0) 20 7808 1550
Email: info@scalapublishers.com
Website: http://www.scalapublishers.com

Publishes: Nonfiction; *Areas:* Antiques;
Architecture; Arts; Historical; *Markets:*
Adult

Specialises in producing books for museums,
galleries, libraries, heritage organisations,
cathedrals and other religious sites.

Scripture Union

Queensway House
207-209 Queensway
Bletchley
Milton Keynes
MK2 2EB
Email: info@scriptureunion.org.uk
Website: http://www.scriptureunion.org.uk

Publishes: Fiction; Nonfiction; *Areas:*
Religious; *Markets:* Adult; Children's;
Family; Youth

Publishes Christian nonfiction books for
people of all ages. Also Christian fiction for
children only.

Seren Books

57 Nolton Street
Bridgend
Wales
CF31 3AE
Tel: +44 (0) 1656 663018
Fax: +44 (0) 1656 649226
Email: Seren@SerenBooks.com
Website: http://www.serenbooks.com

Publishes: Fiction; Nonfiction; Poetry;
Areas: Anthropology; Arts; Biography;
Criticism; Current Affairs; Drama;
Historical; Music; Photography; Politics;
Sport; Translations; Travel; *Markets:* Adult;
Children's; *Treatments:* Literary

Contact: Penny Thomas (Fiction Editor);
Amy Wack (Poetry Editor); Mick Felton
(Nonfiction Editor)

Publishes fiction, nonfiction, and poetry.
Specialises in English-language writing from
Wales and aims to bring Welsh culture, art,
literature, and politics to a wider audience.
Accepts nonfiction submissions only by
email; no poetry or fiction submissions by
email. See website for complete submission
guidelines.

Severn House Publishers

Salatin House
19 Cedar Road
Sutton
Surrey
SM2 5DA
Tel: +44 (0) 20 8770 3930
Fax: +44 (0) 20 8770 3850
Email: sales@severnhouse.com
Website: http://severnhouse.com

Publishes: Fiction; *Areas:* Crime; Historical;
Horror; Mystery; Romance; Sci-Fi; Thrillers;
Markets

Accepts submissions via literary agents only.
Targets the UK and US fiction library
markets, and considers only authors with a
significant background in these markets.

Shearsman Books

50 Westons Hill Drive
Emersons Green

Bristol
BS16 7DF
Tel: +44 (0) 1179 572957
Email: editor@shearsman.com
Website: http://www.shearsman.com

Publishes: Nonfiction; Poetry; *Areas:*
Autobiography; Criticism; Literature;
Translations; *Markets:* Adult

Contact: Tony Frazer

Publishes poetry books of at least 64 A5
pages. Publishes mainly poetry by British,
Irish, North American and Australian/New
Zealand poets, plus poetry in translation
from any language—although particular
interest in German, Spanish and Latin
American poetry.

Submit only if MS is of appropriate length
and most of it has already appeared in UK or
US magazines of some repute. Send
selection of 6-10 pages by post with SASE
or by email with material embedded in the
text or as PDF attachment. No other kind of
attachments accepted.

Also sometimes publishes literary criticism
on poetry, and essays or memoirs by poets.

Shire Publications Ltd

Editorial Department
Shire & Old House
Midland House
West Way
Botley,
Oxford
OX2 0PH
Tel: +44 (0) 1865 811332
Fax: +44 (0) 1865 242009
Email: shireeditorial@shirebooks.co.uk
Website: http://www.shirebooks.co.uk

Publishes: Nonfiction; *Areas:* Antiques;
Archaeology; Architecture; Beauty and
Fashion; Biography; Crafts; Design; Film;
Gardening; Historical; Hobbies; Military;
Music; Photography; Sociology; Sport;
Technology; Theatre; Travel; *Markets:* Adult

Send query by post or by email, with short
synopsis up to 2,000 words. Publishes
inexpensive, nonfiction paperbacks on a

wide range of subjects: the obscure, the unusual, the collectable, the historical; main subject areas include, but are not limited, to. Archaeology; Architecture; Biographies; Canals; Ceramics; Church History; Coins and Medals; Costume and Fashion Accessories; Egyptology; Ephemera; Ethnography; Furniture and Furnishings; Garden History; Genealogy and local history; Glass; Guide and Walking Books; Household Bygones; Industrial History; London; Maritime; Mechanical & Electrical Bygones; Military History; Motoring; Music; Natural History; Needlecrafts and Accessories; Photography; Railways & Steam; Rural Crafts; Scottish Heritage; Social History; Textile History; Toys and Sporting Collectables...

Short Books

Unit 316
ScreenWorks
22 Highbury Grove
London
N5 2EF
Tel: +44 (0) 20 7833 9429
Email: info@shortbooks.co.uk
Website: http://shortbooks.co.uk

Publishes: Fiction; Nonfiction; *Markets:* Adult

Send submissions via literary agent only. Send cover letter with synopsis and first three chapters / roughly 30 pages.

Sigma Press

Stobart House
Pontyclerc
Penybanc Road
Ammanford
Carmarthenshire
SA18 3HP
Tel: +44 (0) 1269 593100
Fax: +44 (0) 1269 596116
Email: info@sigmapress.co.uk
Website: http://www.sigmapress.co.uk

Publishes: Nonfiction; *Areas:* Adventure; Biography; Historical; Leisure; Travel; *Markets:* Adult

Contact: Nigel Evans; Jane Evans

Publishes books mainly in the leisure area, including the outdoors, adventure, local heritage and biography. No poetry or fiction.

Singing Dragon

73 Collier Street
London
N1 9BE
Tel: +44 (0) 20 7833 2307
Email: hello@singingdragon.com
Website: http://singingdragon.com

Publishes: Nonfiction; *Areas:* Health; Leisure; Medicine; Self-Help; Spiritual; *Markets:* Academic; Adult; Professional

Publishes authoritative books on complementary and alternative health, Tai Chi, Qigong and ancient wisdom traditions for health, wellbeing, and professional and personal development, for parents, professionals, academics and the general reader. Welcomes ideas for new books. Send query by email with CV and completed proposal form (available on website).

Society for Promoting Christian Knowledge (SPCK)

36 Causton Street
London
SW1P 4ST
Tel: +44 (0) 20 7592 3900
Fax: +44 (0) 20 7592 3939
Email: submissions@spck.org.uk
Website: http://www.spck.org.uk

Publishes: Nonfiction; *Areas:* Health; Lifestyle; Medicine; Psychology; Religious; Self-Help; Sociology; Spiritual; *Markets:* Academic; Adult

Publisher of Christian books, including liturgy, prayer, biblical studies, educational resources, etc. Imprints handle general spirituality and topics such as popular medicine, self-help, health, etc. Send query by post with SAE or by email. See website for full guidelines.

Souvenir Press Ltd

43 Great Russell Street
London

WC1B 3PA
Tel: +44 (0) 20 7580 9307 / +44 (0) 20 7637 5711
Fax: +44 (0) 20 7580 5064
Email: souvenirpress@souvenirpress.co.uk
Website: http://www.souvenirpress.co.uk

Publishes: Fiction; Nonfiction; *Areas:* Antiques; Archaeology; Autobiography; Beauty and Fashion; Biography; Business; Cookery; Crafts; Crime; Gardening; Health; Historical; Hobbies; Humour; Lifestyle; Literature; Medicine; Military; Music; Mystery; Nature; Philosophy; Politics; Psychology; Religious; Science; Self-Help; Sociology; Spiritual; Sport; Theatre; Travel; Women's Interests; *Markets:* Academic; Adult

Contact: Ernest Hecht

Independent publisher publishing an eclectic mixture of bestsellers and books intended for more limited audiences. Send query letter with outline in first instance.

St David's Press

PO Box 733
Cardiff
CF14 7ZY
Tel: +44 (0) 2920 218187
Email: post@welsh-academic-press.com
Website: http://www.welsh-academic-press.com

Publishes: Nonfiction; Reference; *Areas:* Historical; Leisure; Sport; Travel; *Markets:* Adult

Publisher focussing primarily on books for the Welsh market. Publishes books on sport, including boxing, cricket, football, and rugby; books on walking; reference; and local history and Celtic interest titles. Proposal submission form available on website.

Stainer & Bell Ltd

PO Box 110
Victoria House
23 Gruneisen Road
London, England
N3 1DZ

Tel: +44 (0) 20 8343 3303
Fax: +44 (0) 20 8343 3024
Email: post@stainer.co.uk
Website: http://www.stainer.co.uk

Publishes: Nonfiction; *Areas:* Music; Religious; *Markets:* Adult

Independent, family run business, specialising in the publication of printed music and books on music and religious communication, including hymns.

Stairwell Books

Email: rose@stairwellbooks.com
Website: http://www.stairwellbooks.co.uk

Publishes: Fiction; Poetry; *Areas:* Short Stories; *Markets:* Adult

Contact: Rose Drew

Small press publisher specialising in poetry anthologies, short stories, and novels from new writers. Send query by email. See website for full details.

Stenlake Publishing

54-58 Mill Square
Catrine
Ayrshire
KA5 6RD
Tel: +44 (0) 1290 552233
Fax: +44 (0) 1290 551122
Email: info@stenlake.co.uk
Website: http://stenlake.co.uk

Publishes: Nonfiction; *Areas:* Architecture; Arts; Cookery; Crafts; Historical; Hobbies; Literature; Travel; *Markets:* Adult; Children's

Publishes books of local interest, highly illustrated with old photographs, and usually accompanied by informative text. Also publishes industrial and transport-related titles – railways, canals, road transport, coastal shipping, mining, and aviation, covering Scotland, Wales, Northern Ireland, England, the Isle of Man and the Republic of Ireland. Also publishes books on Robert Burns, ceramics, horticulture, bee-keeping, building conservation, and china painting. Send outline by email in first instance.

Stripes Publishing
1 The Coda Centre
189 Munster Road
London
SW6 6AW
Tel: +44 (0) 20 7385 6333
Email: editorial@stripespublishing.co.uk
Website: http://www.stripespublishing.co.uk

Publishes: Fiction; *Markets:* Children's

Publishes fiction for children aged 6-12 and teendagers. No books for adults, educational books, poetry, graphic novels, comics, multimedia, scripts, screenplays, short stories, nonfiction or picture books for babies and toddlers. No longer accepting submissions by post. Send queries by email only, with one-page synopsis and 1,000-word extract.

Sweet & Maxwell
Friars House
160 Blackfriars Road
London
SE1 8EZ
Tel: +44 (0) 20 7542 6664
Email: TRLUKI.CS@thomsonreuters.com
Website: http://www.sweetandmaxwell.co.uk

Publishes: Nonfiction; Reference; *Areas:* Legal; *Markets:* Academic; Professional

Contact: Tania Quan; Katherine Brewer; Steven Warriner; Nicola Thurlow; Simon Smith; Cassi Waddy

Publishes legal material only, for professionals, academics, and students. Products include looseleafs, CDs, books, newsletters, and online services. Ideas from writers for legal / professional projects are welcomed. See website for list of managers for different subject areas, and their email addresses.

Sweet Cherry Publishing
Unit E Vulcan Business Complex
Vulcan Road

Leicester
LE5 3EB
Email: submissions@
sweetcherrypublishing.com
Website: http://www.
sweetcherrypublishing.com

Publishes: Fiction; *Markets:* Children's; Youth

Contact: Abdul Thadha

Publishes books for children of all ages and young adults. Send submissions by post or by email, or through online form. Postal submissions accepted from UK authors only. See website for full submission guidelines.

Tarquin
Suite 74
17 Holywell Hill
St Albans
Hertfordshire
AL1 1DT
Tel: +44 (0) 1727 833866
Fax: +44 (0) 8454 566385
Email: info@tarquinbooks.com
Website: http://www.tarquinbooks.com

Publishes: Nonfiction; *Markets:* Children's

Publishes books for children on mathematical models, puzzles, and paper engineering. Aims to combine fun with education. Send query by email.

The Templar Company Limited
Deepdene Lodge
Deepdene Avenue
Dorking
Surrey
RH5 4AT
Tel: +44 (0) 1306 876361
Fax: +44 (0) 1306 889097
Email: submissions@templarco.co.uk
Website: http://www.templarco.co.uk

Publishes: Fiction; Nonfiction; *Markets:* Children's

Publishes children's fiction and picture and novelty books. Currently closed to fiction submissions, but welcomes novelty and picture book submissions, in hard copy by post only. Include SAE if return of work required. Artwork submissions accepted by email.

Templar Poetry

58 Dale Road
Matlock
Derbyshire
DE4 3NB
Tel: +44 (0) 1629 582500
Email: info@templarpoetry.com
Website: http://templarpoetry.com

Publishes: Poetry; *Markets:* Adult; *Treatments:* Contemporary; Literary

Publishes poetry acquired through a numebr of competitions, ranging from short selections of poems up to a full collection. See website for guidelines and to submit online. Note that entering the competitions requires the payment of an entry fee.

Top That! Publishing

Marine House
Tide Mill Way
Woodbridge
Suffolk
IP12 1AP
Tel: +44 (0) 1394 386651
Email: dan@topthatpublishing.com
Website: http://topthatpublishing.com

Publishes: Fiction; Nonfiction; Reference; *Areas:* Cookery; Humour; *Markets:* Adult; Children's

Contact: Dan Graham, Editorial Director

Publishes Activity Books, Character Books, Cookery Books, Felt Books, Fiction, Humour, Magnetic Books, Novelty Books, Phonics Books, Picture Storybooks, Pop-Up Books, Press Out & Play, Reference Books, and Sticker Books. Does not currently publish "regular" children's or adults fiction. See online book catalogue for the kinds of books published. If suitable for the list, send submissions by email (preferred), ideally under 1MB, or by post (mss not returned). See website for full guidelines. Responds

within 8 weeks if interested. No simultaneous submissions.

Trentham Books Limited

Institute of Education
University of London
20 Bedford Way
London
WC1H 0AL
Tel: +44 (0) 20 7911 5563
Email: g.klein@ioe.ac.uk
Website: http://www.trentham-books.co.uk

Publishes: Nonfiction; *Areas:* Culture; Humour; Legal; Sociology; Women's Interests; *Markets:* Academic; Professional

Contact: Dr Gillian Klein

Publishes academic and professional books. No fiction, biography, or poetry. No unsolicited MSS, but accepts queries by post with SASE, or by email. See website for full guidelines.

Ulverscroft Large Print Books Ltd

The Green
Bradgate Road
Anstey
Leicester
LE7 7FU
Tel: +44 (0) 1162 364325
Fax: +44 (0) 1162 340205
Email: m.merrill@ulverscroft.co.uk
Website: http://www.ulverscroft.com

Publishes: Fiction; Nonfiction; *Markets:* Adult

Contact: Mark Merrill

Publishes a wide variety of large print titles in hard and soft cover formats, as well as abridged and unabridged audio books. Many titles are written by the world's favourite authors.

Unthank Books

PO Box 3506
Norwich
Norfolk

NR7 7QP
Tel: +44 (0) 1603 471300
Email: robin.jones@unthankbooks.com
Website: http://www.unthankbooks.com

Publishes: Fiction; Nonfiction; *Markets:*
Adult; *Treatments:* Literary

Contact: Robin Jones (Publisher); Ashley
Stokes (Editorial Director)

Publishes adult literary fiction and
nonfiction. Send query with SAE, synopsis,
and 50 double spaced pages.

Vallentine Mitchell & Co., Limited

Catalyst House
720 Centennial Court
Centennial Park
Elstree
Herts
WD6 3SY
Tel: +44 (0) 20 8736 4596
Email: editor@vmbooks.com
Website: http://www.vmbooksuk.com

Publishes: Nonfiction; *Areas:* Culture;
Historical; Philosophy; Religious; *Markets:*
Academic; Adult

Publishes books on Jewish history, culture
and heritage, Jewish thought, Middle Eastern
history, politics and culture and the
Holocaust, for both academic and general
readerships. Offices in London and Portland,
Oregon. Send proposals by email.

Virago Press

Carmelite House
50 Victoria Embankment
LONDON
EC4Y 0DZ
Tel: +44 (0) 20 3122 7000
Email: virago@littlebrown.co.uk
Website: http://www.virago.co.uk

Publishes: Fiction; Nonfiction; *Areas:*
Literature; Women's Interests; *Markets:*
Adult; *Treatments:* Literary

Publishes fiction and nonfiction women's

literature. No poetry. Accepts approaches via
literary agents only.

Virtue Books

Edward House
Tenter Street
Rotherham
S60 1LB
Tel: +44 (0) 845 094 2030
Fax: +44 (0) 845 094 2060
Email: info@russums.co.uk
Website: http://www.virtuebooks.co.uk

Publishes: Nonfiction; *Areas:* Cookery;
Markets: Professional

Publishes books for professional chefs.

W.W. Norton & Company Ltd

75-76 Wells Street
London
W1T 3QT
Tel. +44 (0) 20 7323 1379
Fax: +44 (0) 20 7436 4553
Email: office@wwnorton.co.uk
Website: http://wwnorton.co.uk

Publishes: Fiction; Nonfiction; Poetry;
Areas: Adventure; Anthropology;
Archaeology; Architecture; Autobiography;
Biography; Business; Crafts; Crime; Current
Affairs; Design; Drama; Film; Finance;
Health; Historical; Hobbies; Humour; Legal;
Leisure; Lifestyle; Literature; Medicine;
Music; Nature; Philosophy; Politics;
Psychology; Religious; Science; Self-Help;
Sociology; Sport; Technology; Travel;
Women's Interests; *Markets:* Academic;
Adult; Professional

UK branch of a US publisher. No editorial
office in the UK – contact the main office in
New York (see separate listing).

Waverley Books

Academy Park
Building 4000
Glasgow
G51 1PR
Email: info@waverley-books.co.uk
Website: http://www.waverley-books.co.uk

Publishes: Fiction; Nonfiction; *Areas:*
Cookery; Historical; Humour; *Markets:*
Adult; Children's

Publishes history, fiction, nostalgia, food and
drink, humour, children's, graphic novels,
and Scottish interest.

Welsh Academic Press
PO Box 733
Caerdydd
Cardiff
CF14 7ZY
Tel: +44 (0) 29 2021 8187
Email: post@welsh-academic-press.com
Website: http://www.welsh-academic-press.com

Publishes: Nonfiction; *Areas:* Historical;
Politics; *Markets:* Academic

Publishes academic monographs, reference
works, text books and popular scholarly titles
in the fields of education, history, political
studies, Scandinavian and Baltic studies,
contemporary work and employment, and
medieval Wales. Complete questionnaire
available on website.

Philip Wilson Publishers Ltd
6 Salem Road
London
W2 4BU
Tel: +44 (0) 20 7243 1225
Fax: +44 (0) 20 7243 1226
Email: philipwilso@gmail.com
Website: http://www.philip-wilson.co.uk

Publishes: Nonfiction; *Areas:* Architecture;
Arts; Design; Historical; *Markets:* Adult

Contact: Philip Wilson; Anne Jackson

Publishes books on art, art history, andtiques,
and collectibles. See website and contact for
further details.

Wolters Kluwer (UK) Ltd
145 London Road
Kingston upon Thames
Surrey
KT2 6SR

Tel: +44 (0) 20 8547 3333
Fax: +44 (0) 20 8547 2637
Email: info@croner.co.uk
Website: http://www.wolterskluwer.co.uk

Publishes: Nonfiction; Reference; *Areas:*
Business; Finance; Health; Legal; *Markets:*
Professional

Publishes books, looseleafs, and online
services for professionals. Areas of expertise
include: Human Resources, Health and
Safety, Tax and Accountancy, Education and
Healthcare, Manufacturing and Construction.

The X Press
PO Box 25694
London
N17 6FP
Tel: +44 (0) 20 8801 2100
Fax: +44 (0) 20 8885 1322
Email: vibes@xpress.co.uk
Website: http://www.xpress.co.uk

Publishes: Fiction; *Areas:* Culture; *Markets:*
Adult; Children's; *Treatments:*
Contemporary; Literary; Popular

Contact: Dotun Adebayo (Editorial
Director); Steve Pope (Marketing Director)

Europe's largest publisher of Black interest
books. Publishes popular contemporary
fiction, children's fiction, and black classics,
though scope is expanding. Send SAE with
MS, rather than synopses or ideas. No
poetry.

Yale University Press (London)
47 Bedford Square
London
WC1B 3DP
Tel: +44 (0) 20 7079 4900
Fax: +44 (0) 20 7079 4901
Email: sales@yaleup.co.uk
Website: http://www.yalebooks.co.uk

Publishes: Nonfiction; Reference; *Areas:*
Architecture; Arts; Autobiography; Beauty
and Fashion; Biography; Business;
Criticism; Current Affairs; Finance; Health;
Historical; Legal; Literature; Medicine;

Music; Philosophy; Politics; Religious; Science; Sociology; Technology; Translations; *Markets:* Adult

Welcomes unsolicited MSS and synopses in specified subject areas.

Zambezi Publishing Ltd
PO Box 221
Plymouth
PL2 2YJ
Tel: +44 (0) 1752 367300

Fax: +44 (0) 1752 350453
Email: pubscripts@zampub.com
Website: http://www.zampub.com

Publishes: Nonfiction; *Areas:* Business; Finance; Health; Lifestyle; New Age; Self-Help; Spiritual; *Markets:* Adult

Publisher of books on mind, body, and spirit, including self-publishing division. Send synopsis and sample chapter by mail, or brief email query. No attachments.

Canadian Publishers

For the most up-to-date listings of these and hundreds of other publishers, visit http://www.firstwriter.com/publishers

*To claim your **free** access to the site, please see the back of this book.*

Annick Press

15 Patricia Avenue
Toronto, ON
M2M 1H9
Email: annickpress@annickpress.com
Website: http://www.annickpress.com

Publishes: Fiction; Nonfiction; *Markets:* Children's; Youth

Canadian publisher committed to publishing Canadian authors. Publishes fiction and nonfiction for children aged six months to twelve years and young adults. Not currently accepting picture book submissions. No submissions by fax or email. See website for full submission guidelines.

The Brucedale Press

Box 2259
Port Elgin, Ontario N0H 2C0
Tel: +1 (519) 832-6025
Email: info@brucedalepress.ca
Website: http://www.brucedalepress.ca

Publishes: Fiction; Nonfiction; *Areas:* Historical; *Markets:* Adult; *Treatments:* Literary

Publishes literary, historical, and pictorial works focusing on the Bruce Peninsula and Queen's Bush area of Ontario. Publishes books by Canadian authors only. Query by

post in first instance. See website for full details.

Carswell

One Corporate Plaza
2075 Kennedy Road
Toronto, ON
M1T 3V4
Tel: +1 (416) 298-5007
Email: jayne.jackson@thomsonreuters.com
Website: http://www.carswell.com

Publishes: Nonfiction; Reference; *Areas:* Finance; Legal; *Markets:* Professional

Publishes material for legal, tax, and accounting professionals.

Dragon Moon Press

Email: dmpsubmissions@gmail.com
Website: http://dragonmoonpress.com

Publishes: Fiction; Nonfiction; *Areas:* Fantasy; Horror; How-to; Romance; Sci-Fi; *Markets:* Adult; Youth

Publishes novel-length fantasy, science fiction, and gentle horror for adults and the upper end of the YA spectrum. No middle grade or children's, or short story collections. Particularly interested in traditional fantasy (quests / dragons rather than werewolves and vampires). Also publishes how-to titles on how to write / sell writing. See website for submission guidelines.

ECW Press
665 Gerrard Street East
Toronto, ON M4M 1Y2
Tel: +1 (416) 694-3348
Fax: +1 (416) 698-9906
Email: info@ecwpress.com
Website: http://www.ecwpress.com

Publishes: Fiction; Nonfiction; Poetry; *Areas:* Autobiography; Biography; Business; Culture; Finance; Health; Historical; Humour; Literature; Mystery; Politics; Religious; Sport; Suspense; TV; Women's Interests; *Markets:* Adult; *Treatments:* Commercial; Literary; Mainstream

Publishes only Canadian-authored fiction and poetry. Non-fiction proposals accepted from anywhere. Proposal should be made by post and include: cover letter; biog; sample of the manuscript (for poetry, 10-15 pages, for fiction and nonfiction, 15-25 pages); synopsis.

Fitzhenry & Whiteside Ltd
195 Allstate Parkway
Markham, Ontario L3R 4T8
Tel: +1 (905) 477-9700
Fax: +1 (800) 260-9777
Email: godwit@fitzhenry.ca
Website: http://www.fitzhenry.ca

Publishes: Fiction; Nonfiction; *Markets:* Adult; Children's; Youth

Contact: Sharon Fitzhenry (Adult); Cheryl Chen (Children's)

Publishes fiction and nonfiction for adults, children, and young adults. See website for submission guidelines.

Groundwood Books
Attention: Submissions
110 Spadina Avenue, Suite 801
Toronto, Ontario
M5V 2K4
Email: submissions@
groundwoodbooks.com

Website: http://www.houseofanansi.com

Publishes: Fiction; Nonfiction; *Markets:* Children's; Youth; *Treatments:* Literary

Publishes picture books and novel-length fiction and nonfiction for children of all ages. Publishes character-driven literary fiction; no stories with obvious moral messages, or genre fiction such as thrillers or fantasy. Closed to approaches for picture books. Send query with brief synopsis and several sample chapters. See website for full guidelines.

On The Mark Press
15 Dairy Avenue
Napanee, ON, K7R 1M4
Tel: +1 (800) 463-6367
Email: productdevelopment@
onthemarkpress.com
Website: http://www.onthemarkpress.com

Publishes: Nonfiction; *Markets:* Academic; Professional

Publishes workbooks and resources to support teachers in the classroom. Send samples with resume by post or by email.

Pedlar Press
113 Bond Street
St John's NL
A1C 1T6
Email: feralgrl@interlog.com
Website: http://www.pedlarpress.com

Publishes: Fiction; Poetry; *Markets:* Adult; *Treatments:* Contemporary; Experimental; Literary

Publishes innovative contemporary Canadian poetry and fiction. Particularly interested in work that preserves and extends the literary tradition that values experimentation in style and form. Send query by email in first instance. No attachments.

Penguin Canada
Penguin Group (Canada)
90 Eglinton Avenue East, Suite 700
Toronto, Ontario M4P 2Y3

Tel: +1 (416) 925-2249
Fax: +1 (416) 925-0068
Email: customerservicescanada@
penguinrandomhouse.com
Website: http://penguinrandomhouse.ca

Publishes: Fiction; Nonfiction; *Markets:*
Adult

Publishes fiction and nonfiction by Canadian
authors on Canadian subjects. Accepts
submissions through literary agents only.

Red Deer Press

195 Allstate Parkway
Markham, Ontario
L3R 4T8
Tel: +1 (905) 477-9700
Fax: +1 (905) 477-9179
Email: rdp@reddeerpress.com
Website: http://www.reddeerpress.com

Publishes: Fiction; Nonfiction; *Areas:*
Biography; Drama; Fantasy; Historical; Sci-
Fi; *Markets:* Adult; Children's; Youth;
Treatments: Contemporary

Publishes fiction and nonfiction for adults
and children of all ages, though currently
less interested in picture books and more
interested in middle grade and young adult
fiction. See website for full submission
guidelines.

Ronsdale Press

3350 West 21st Avenue
Vancouver, B.C.
V6S 1G7
Tel: +1 (604) 738-4688
Fax: +1 (604) 731-4548
Email: ronsdale@shaw.ca
Website: http://www.ronsdalepress.com

Publishes: Fiction; Nonfiction; Poetry;
Areas: Biography; Historical; Short Stories;
Theatre; *Markets:* Adult; Children's;
Treatments: Literary

Contact: Ronald B. Hatch (General
Acquisition Editor); Veronica Hatch
(Children's Acquisition Editor)

Literary publishing house, publishing fiction,

poetry, biography, regional history, and
children's literature. Particularly interested in
young adult historical novels. No mass-
market, pulp, mystery stories, or fiction that
is entirely plot-driven. MSS considered only
from writers who have had work published
in literary magazines. See website for full
submission guidelines.

All prospective authors are encouraged to
familiarise themselves with the list (perusing
the catalogue; reading published titles) to
assess suitability before submitting. Send
query with sample or full MS with SASE for
response, with brief bio and list of writing
credits (if any).

Stonehouse Publishing

PO Box 68092
Bonnie Doon Shopping Centre
Edmonton, Alberta
T6C 4N6
Email: editor@stonehousepublishing.ca
Website: http://www.stonehousepublishing.
ca

Publishes: Fiction; *Markets:* Adult;
Treatments: Commercial; Literary

Contact: Julie Yerex, Editor; Netta Johnson,
Publisher

Publishes literary fiction with commercial
appeal, and non-formulaic fiction in general
– initially by Canadian authors only, but with
the intention of opening to international
writers in future. No nonfiction, formulaic
genre fiction, sci-fi, horror, mysteries,
thrillers, erotica, picture books, or children's
books. Send query by post only with 30
sample pages. No submissions by email –
these will not be read or responded to. See
website for full guidelines.

Thistledown Press

410 2nd Avenue North
Saskatoon, SK S7K 2C3
Tel: +1 (306) 244-1722
Fax: +1 (306) 244-1762
Email: editorial@thistledownpress.com
Website: http://www.thistledownpress.com

Publishes: Fiction; Poetry; *Areas:* Short

Stories; *Markets:* Adult

Contact: Allan Forrie

Accepts work by Canadian citizens or landed immigrants only. Publishes novels, poetry, and short story collections, but no romance, science fiction, horror, westerns, or fiction in verse. Not currently accepting juvenile fiction or children's manuscripts. Reading period from August 1 to November 30. See website for full submission guidelines.

Turnstone Press

Artspace Building
206-100 Arthur Street
Winnipeg, Manitoba
Canada R3B 1H3
Tel: +1 (204) 947-1555
Fax: +1 (204) 947-1556
Email: editor@turnstonepress.com

Website: http://www.turnstonepress.com

Publishes: Fiction; Nonfiction; Poetry; *Areas:* Criticism; Fantasy; Literature; Mystery; Short Stories; Thrillers; *Markets:* Adult; *Treatments:* Literary

Contact: Submissions Assistant

Literary publisher publishing the work of Canadian authors or landed immigrants only. Publishes literary fiction, literary non-fiction – including literary criticism – and poetry. Publishes literary mysteries, thrillers, noir, speculative fiction, and fantasy under imprint. No contact by email. All submissions must be by post with SASE. Mss without SASE will be recycled without response, as will submissions requesting response by email. See website for full guidelines.

Irish Publishers

For the most up-to-date listings of these and hundreds of other publishers, visit http://www.firstwriter.com/publishers

*To claim your **free** access to the site, please see the back of this book.*

CJ Fallon
Ground Floor – Block B
Liffey Valley Office Campus
Dublin 22
Tel: 01 6166400
Fax: 01 6166499
Email: editorial@cjfallon.ie
Website: http://www.cjfallon.ie

Publishes: Nonfiction; Reference; Business; Finance; Historical; Literature; Music; Religious; Science; Technology; *Markets:* Academic; Children's; Professional; Youth

Publishes teaching resources written by teachers, for teachers. Send proposal to the Managing Editor in the first instance.

Columba Press
55a Spruce Avenue
Stillorgan Industrial Park
Blackrock
Co. Dublin
Tel: +353 (1) 2942556
Email: Fearghal@columba.ie
Website: http://www.columba.ie

Publishes: Nonfiction; *Areas:* Arts; Biography; Historical; Music; Nature; Religious; Spiritual; *Markets:* Adult

Religious publisher publishing across a broad range of areas, including pastoral resources, spirituality, theology, the arts, and history.

Flyleaf Press
4 Spencer Villas
Glenageary
Co. Dublin
Tel: +353 1 2854658
Email: books@flyleaf.ie
Website: http://flyleaf.ie

Publishes: Nonfiction; Reference; *Areas:* Historical; How-to; *Markets:* Adult

Publishes family history and genealogy titles, how-to guides for researching family history, and reference workds on Church Records, Census records and wills.

The Gallery Press
Loughcrew
Oldcastle
County Meath
Tel: +353 (0) 49 8541779
Fax: +353 (0) 49 8541779
Email: gallery@indigo.ie
Website: http://www.gallerypress.com

Publishes: Fiction; Nonfiction; Poetry; Scripts; *Areas:* Theatre; *Markets:* Adult; *Treatments:* Literary

Contact: Peter Fallon

Publishes poetry, drama, and prose by Ireland's leading contemporary writers. See website for submission guidelines. No submissions by fax or email. Accepts work from Irish or Irish-based authors only.

Gill & Macmillan

Hume Avenue
Park West
Dublin 12
Tel: +353 (01) 500 9500
Email: dmarsh@gillmacmillan.ie
Website: http://www.gillmacmillanbooks.ie

Publishes: Fiction; Nonfiction; Reference; *Areas:* Biography; Cookery; Crime; Current Affairs; Historical; Hobbies; Humour; Leisure; Lifestyle; Nature; Sport; *Markets:* Adult; Children's

Contact: Deborah Marsh, Editorial Administrator

Publishes adult nonfiction and children's fiction and nonfiction. No adult fiction, poetry, short stories or plays. Prefers proposals by email, but will also accept proposals by post. See website for full submission guidelines.

Institute of Public Administration (IPA)

57-61 Lansdowne Road
Ballsbridge
Dublin 4
Tel: +353 1 240 3600
Fax: +353 1 668 9135
Email: information@ipa.ie

Publishes: Nonfiction; *Areas:* Current Affairs; Finance; Health; Legal; Politics; Sociology; *Markets:* Academic; Professional

Irish publisher specialising in texts on public service administration and management.

Liberties Press

140 Terenure Road North
Terenure
Dublin 6W
Tel: +353 01 405 5703
Email: editorial@libertiespress.com

Website: http://www.libertiespress.com

Publishes: Fiction; Nonfiction; Poetry; *Areas:* Architecture; Arts; Autobiography; Biography; Business; Cookery; Crime; Current Affairs; Finance; Health; Historical; Hobbies; Humour; Lifestyle; Music; Politics; Sport; *Markets:* Adult; *Treatments:* Literary

Publishes fiction, nonfiction, and poetry primarily for the Irish market. Focusses on Irish interest nonfiction in such areas as history, memoir, politics, current affairs, sport and lifestyle. Accepts submissions between January 1 and March 31 each year only. Prefers hard copy submissions (include SAE if return required) but will also accept email submissions. See website for full details.

The Lilliput Press

62-63 Sitric Road
Arbour Hill
Dublin 7
Tel: +353 (01) 671 16 47
Fax: +353 (01) 671 12 33
Email: info@lilliputpress.ie
Website: http://www.lilliputpress.ie

Publishes: Fiction; Nonfiction; Poetry; Reference; Scripts; *Areas:* Architecture; Arts; Autobiography; Biography; Business; Cookery; Criticism; Culture; Current Affairs; Drama; Historical; Literature; Music; Nature; Philosophy; Photography; Politics; Sociology; Sport; Travel; *Markets:* Adult; *Treatments:* Literary; Popular

Contact: Submissions Editor

Publishes books broadly focused on Irish themes. Send query by post with one-page synopsis and complete ms or three sample chapters. Include SASE if response required. No submissions by email. See website for full guidelines.

Mentor Books

43 Furze Road
Sandyford Industrial Estate
Dublin 18
Tel: 01 2952112
Fax: 01 295 2114

Email: admin@mentorbooks.ie
Website: http://www.mentorbooks.ie

Publishes: Nonfiction; *Areas:* Biography;
Business; Crime; Historical; Humour;
Politics; Science; Sport; *Markets:* Academic;
Adult

Publishes educational books and general
nonfiction of Irish interest.

New Island
16 Priory Hall Office Park
Stillorgan
County Dublin
Tel: + 353 1 278 42 25
Email: editor@newisland.ie
Website: http://www.newisland.ie

Publishes: Fiction; Nonfiction; Poetry;
Scripts; *Areas:* Autobiography; Biography;
Cookery; Crime; Criticism; Current Affairs;
Drama; Historical; Humour; Literature;
Politics; Short Stories; Sociology; Travel;
Women's Interests; *Markets:* Adult;
Treatments: Literary; Popular

Contact: Editorial Manager

Committed to literature and literary
publishing. Publishes in all literary areas,
from fiction to drama to poetry. Also
publishes nonfiction of Irish interest,
especially social affairs and biographies. No
children's books. Not currently accepting
drama and poetry. Seeking submissions of
literary fiction, general fiction, crime fiction,
short stories, history, biography, memoir,
autobiography, and food and drink. Accepts
submissions by email only. Send query with
one-page synopsis and sample of the text as
Word .doc or .docx attachments. Include
details of any previous publications. No
submissions by post. See website for full
details.

The O'Brien Press
12 Terenure Road East
Rathgar
Dublin 6
Tel: +353-1-4923333
Fax: +353-1-4922777
Email: books@obrien.ie

Website: http://www.obrien.ie

Publishes: Fiction; Nonfiction; Reference;
Areas: Architecture; Arts; Autobiography;
Biography; Business; Cookery; Crafts;
Crime; Drama; Historical; Humour;
Lifestyle; Literature; Music; Nature;
Photography; Politics; Religious; Sport;
Travel; *Markets:* Adult; Children's; Youth

Mainly publishes children's fiction,
children's nonfiction and adult nonfiction.
Generally doesn't publish poetry, academic
works or adult fiction. Send synopsis and
two or three sample chapters. If fewer than
1,000 words, send complete ms. See website
for full guidelines.

Oak Tree Press
33 Rochestown Rise
Rochestown
Cork
Tel: +353 86 244 1633
Fax: +353 86 330 7694
Email: info@oaktreepress.com
Website: http://oaktreepress.eu

Publishes: Nonfiction; *Areas:* Business;
Finance; Legal; *Markets:* Professional

Publishes books on business, particularly for
small business owners and managers.

Onstream Publications Ltd
Currabaha
Cloghroe
Blarney
Co. Cork
Tel: +353 21 4385798
Email: info@onstream.ie
Website: http://www.onstream.ie

Publishes: Fiction; Nonfiction; *Areas:*
Cookery; Historical; Travel; *Markets:*
Academic; Adult

Publisher of mainly nonfiction, although
some fiction published. Also offers services
to authors.

Poolbeg
123 Grange Hill

Baldoyle Industrial Estate
Baldoyle
Dublin 13
Tel: +353 1 832 1477
Email: info@poolbeg.com
Website: http://www.poolbeg.com

Publishes: Fiction; Nonfiction; *Areas:*
Cookery; Gardening; Travel; *Markets:*
Adult; Children's

Contact: Paula Campbell, publisher

Accepts submissions of nonfiction, and
fiction up to 100,000 words. Send query by
post with SASE, CV, short bio, first six
chapters in hard copy, and full ms as Word
file on CD. See website for full submission
guidelines.

Round Hall

43 Fitzwilliam Place
Dublin 2
Tel: + 353 1 662 5301
Fax: + 353 1 662 5302
Email: frieda.donohue@thomsonreuters.com
Website: http://www.roundhall.ie

Publishes: Nonfiction; Reference; *Areas:*
Legal; *Markets:* Academic; Professional

Publishes information on Irish law in the
form of books, journals, periodicals,
looseleaf services, CD-ROMs and online
services. See website for submission
guidelines and appropriate contacts /
proposal forms to complete.

Somerville Press

Dromore
Bantry
Co. Cork
Tel: 353 (0) 28 32873
Fax: 353 (0) 28 328
Email: somervillepress@eircom.net
Website: http://www.somervillepress.com

Publishes: Fiction; Nonfiction; *Markets:*
Adult

Publishes fiction and nonfiction of Irish
interest.

University College Dublin (UCD) Press

UCD Humanities Institute Room H103
Belfield
Dublin 4

Tel: + 353 1 4716 4680
Email: ucdpress@ucd.ie
Website: http://www.ucdpress.ie

Publishes: Nonfiction; *Areas:* Historical;
Literature; Music; Nature; Politics; Science;
Sociology; *Markets:* Academic

Contact: Noelle Moran, Executive Editor

Peer-reviewed publisher of contemporary
scholarship with a reputation for publications
relating to historic and contemporary Ireland.
Send synopsis with market description, a
paragraph about the career and publications
of the author(s), and two specimen chapters
in hard copy (not email attachments). See
website for full guidelines.

Publishers Subject Index

*This section lists publishers by their subject matter, with directions to the
section of the book where the full listing can be found.*

*You can create your own customised lists of publishers using different
combinations of these subject areas, plus over a dozen other criteria,
instantly online at http://www.firstwriter.com.*

*To claim your **free** access to the site, please see the back of this book.*

Adventure
Amakella Publishing (*US*)
Arcade Publishing (*US*)
Arrow Publications, LLC (*US*)
Black Lyon Publishing, LLC (*US*)
Bold Strokes Books (*US*)
Capstone (*US*)
Carina UK (*UK*)
Cave Books (*US*)
Children's Brains are Yummy (CBAY) Books
(*US*)
Covenant Communications Inc. (*US*)
Cricket Books (*US*)
Crystal Spirit Publishing, Inc. (*US*)
Curious Fox (*UK*)
Ex-L-Ence Publishing (*UK*)
FalconGuides (*US*)
Geostar Publishing & Services LLC (*US*)
Goosebottom Books LLC (*US*)
Lost Tower Publications (*UK*)
M P Publishing USA (*US*)
Maverick Reads (*UK*)
Papercutz (*US*)
Pen Books (*US*)
Red Empress Publishing (*US*)
The Salariya Book Company (*UK*)
Sidestreet Cookie Publishing (*US*)
Sigma Press (*UK*)
Sunscribe (*US*)
Tate Publishing and Enterprises, LLC (*US*)
Top Cow Productions, Inc (*US*)
Tsaba House (*US*)
W.W. Norton & Company Ltd (*UK*)

Anthropology
Alondra Press (*US*)
Amakella Publishing (*US*)
American Press (*US*)
Bucknell University Press (*US*)
Cave Books (*US*)
Eagle's View Publishing (*US*)
Ex-L-Ence Publishing (*UK*)
Fordham University Press (*US*)
Geostar Publishing & Services LLC (*US*)
Marion Boyars Publishers (*UK*)
New York University (NYU) Press (*US*)
Pen Books (*US*)
Pluto Publishing Ltd (*UK*)
Polity Press (*UK*)
Princeton University Press Europe (*UK*)
Seren Books (*UK*)
Sidestreet Cookie Publishing (*US*)
Sunscribe (*US*)
University of Alabama Press (*US*)
University of Chicago Press (*US*)
Utah State University Press (*US*)
Vanderbilt University Press (*US*)
W.W. Norton & Company Ltd (*UK*)
Wannabee Books (*US*)
Waveland Press, Inc. (*US*)

Antiques
Astragal Press (*US*)
Ex-L-Ence Publishing (*UK*)
Geostar Publishing & Services LLC (*US*)
Goss & Crested China Club (*UK*)
New Cavendish Books (*UK*)
Octopus Publishing Group Limited (*UK*)
Scala Arts & Heritage Publishers (*UK*)

Shire Publications Ltd (*UK*)
Souvenir Press Ltd (*UK*)
Sunscribe (*US*)
Archaeology
Alondra Press (*US*)
Boydell & Brewer Ltd (*UK*)
Cave Books (*US*)
Eagle's View Publishing (*US*)
Ex-L-Ence Publishing (*UK*)
Fonthill Media LLC (*US*)
Fonthill Media Ltd (*UK*)
Geostar Publishing & Services LLC (*US*)
The History Press (*UK*)
Liverpool University Press (*UK*)
Logaston Press (*UK*)
National Museum Wales (*UK*)
Polity Press (*UK*)
Princeton University Press Europe (*UK*)
Saffron Books (*UK*)
Shire Publications Ltd (*UK*)
Souvenir Press Ltd (*UK*)
Sunscribe (*US*)
University of Alabama Press (*US*)
University of Chicago Press (*US*)
Utah State University Press (*US*)
Vanderbilt University Press (*US*)
W.W. Norton & Company Ltd (*UK*)
Wannabee Books (*US*)
Waveland Press, Inc. (*US*)
Architecture
American Press (*US*)
ASCE Press (*US*)
Bucknell University Press (*US*)
Carlton Publishing Group (*UK*)
David R. Godine, Publisher (*US*)
Ex-L-Ence Publishing (*UK*)
Floris Books (*UK*)
Fordham University Press (*US*)
Geostar Publishing & Services LLC (*US*)
Gibbs Smith, Publisher (*US*)
Gingko Library (*UK*)
Guild of Master Craftsman (GMC) Publications
Ltd (*UK*)
Harry N. Abrams, Inc. (*US*)
Liberties Press (*Ire*)
The Lilliput Press (*Ire*)
Frances Lincoln Ltd (*UK*)
Liverpool University Press (*UK*)
McFarland & Company, Inc. (*US*)
Merrell Publishers Limited (*UK*)
The O'Brien Press (*Ire*)
Octopus Publishing Group Limited (*UK*)
Paul Dry Books, Inc. (*US*)
Phaidon Press Limited (*UK*)
Princeton University Press Europe (*UK*)
Professional Publications, Inc. (PPI) (*US*)
Quill Driver Books (*US*)
Reaktion Books (*UK*)
Reference Service Press (*US*)
RotoVision (*UK*)
Roundhouse Group (*UK*)
Scala Arts & Heritage Publishers (*UK*)
Shire Publications Ltd (*UK*)

Stenlake Publishing (*UK*)
Sunscribe (*US*)
University of Chicago Press (*US*)
University of South Carolina Press (*US*)
W.W. Norton & Company Ltd (*UK*)
Wannabee Books (*US*)
Waveland Press, Inc. (*US*)
John Wiley & Sons, Inc. (*US*)
Philip Wilson Publishers Ltd (*UK*)
Yale University Press (*US*)
Yale University Press (London) (*UK*)
Arts
Alma Classics (*UK*)
American Press (*US*)
Anness Publishing Ltd (*UK*)
Arcade Publishing (*US*)
Arch Street Press (*US*)
Barron's Educational Series, Inc. (*US*)
Beacon Press (*US*)
Bick Publishing House (*US*)
Bloomsbury Publishing Plc (*UK*)
Bodleian Library (*UK*)
Boydell & Brewer Ltd (*UK*)
Bucknell University Press (*US*)
Carlton Publishing Group (*UK*)
Columba Press (*Ire*)
Continental (*US*)
Crescent Moon Publishing (*UK*)
David R. Godine, Publisher (*US*)
Enitharmon Press (*UK*)
Ex-L-Ence Publishing (*UK*)
Fantagraphics (*US*)
Finney Company (*US*)
Floris Books (*UK*)
Fordham University Press (*US*)
Geostar Publishing & Services LLC (*US*)
Gibbs Smith, Publisher (*US*)
Gibson Square Books Ltd (*UK*)
Gingko Library (*UK*)
Gomer Press (*UK*)
Guild of Master Craftsman (GMC) Publications
Ltd (*UK*)
Halsgrove (*UK*)
Harry N. Abrams, Inc. (*US*)
Haus Publishing (*UK*)
Heyday Books (*US*)
HOW Books (*US*)
IBEX Publishers, Inc. (*US*)
Icon Books Ltd (*UK*)
The Ilex Press (*UK*)
Interlink Publishing Group, Inc. (*US*)
Jacaranda Books Art Music Ltd (*UK*)
Liberties Press (*Ire*)
The Lilliput Press (*Ire*)
Frances Lincoln Ltd (*UK*)
Liverpool University Press (*UK*)
Luath Press Ltd (*UK*)
Mainstream Publishing Co. (Edinburgh) Ltd
(*UK*)
Manchester University Press (*UK*)
Mandrake of Oxford (*UK*)
McFarland & Company, Inc. (*US*)
Merrell Publishers Limited (*UK*)

Mitchell Lane Publishers, Inc. (*US*)
National Museum Wales (*UK*)
Natural History Museum Publishing (*UK*)
New Cavendish Books (*UK*)
New Holland Publishers (UK) Ltd (*UK*)
The O'Brien Press (*Ire*)
Octopus Publishing Group Limited (*UK*)
Peter Owen Publishers (*UK*)
Phaidon Press Limited (*UK*)
Princeton University Press Europe (*UK*)
Quarto Publishing Group UK (*UK*)
Quarto Publishing Group USA (*US*)
Quill Driver Books (*US*)
Reaktion Books (*UK*)
Reference Service Press (*US*)
Richard Dennis Publications (*UK*)
Robert Hale Publishers (*UK*)
The Rosen Publishing Group, Inc. (*US*)
RotoVision (*UK*)
Roundhouse Group (*UK*)
Running Press (*US*)
Saffron Books (*UK*)
Scala Arts & Heritage Publishers (*UK*)
Seren Books (*UK*)
Soft Skull Press (*US*)
Stenlake Publishing (*UK*)
Sunscribe (*US*)
Swan Isle Press (*US*)
Tate Publishing and Enterprises, LLC (*US*)
University of Chicago Press (*US*)
University of South Carolina Press (*US*)
University of Tampa Press (*US*)
Vernon Press (an imprint of Vernon Art and
Science Inc.) (*US*)
Wannabee Books (*US*)
Waveland Press, Inc. (*US*)
Williamson Books (*US*)
Philip Wilson Publishers Ltd (*UK*)
Yale University Press (*US*)
Yale University Press (London) (*UK*)
Autobiography
Akasha Publishing Ltd (*UK*)
Alma Classics (*UK*)
Arcade Publishing (*US*)
Arch Street Press (*US*)
Beacon Press (*US*)
BenBella Books (*US*)
John Blake Publishing (*UK*)
Blink Publishing (*UK*)
Canongate Books (*UK*)
Canterbury House Publishing, Ltd (*US*)
Capstone (*US*)
Chicago Review Press (*US*)
ECW Press (*Can*)
Enete Enterprises (*US*)
Ex-L-Ence Publishing (*UK*)
Familius (*US*)
Fantagraphics (*US*)
Geostar Publishing & Services LLC (*US*)
Gomer Press (*UK*)
Granta Books (*UK*)
Halban Publishers (*UK*)
HarperCollins Publishers Ltd (*UK*)

Headline Publishing Group (*UK*)
Hesperus Press Limited (*UK*)
Honno Welsh Women's Press (*UK*)
IBEX Publishers, Inc. (*US*)
Jacaranda Books Art Music Ltd (*UK*)
Liberties Press (*Ire*)
The Lilliput Press (*Ire*)
Lion Hudson Plc (*UK*)
Lost Tower Publications (*UK*)
The Lyons Press Inc. (*US*)
Macmillan (*UK*)
Mainstream Publishing Co. (Edinburgh) Ltd
(*UK*)
Marion Boyars Publishers (*UK*)
Merlin Unwin Books (*UK*)
Milo Books Ltd (*UK*)
New Island (*Ire*)
The O'Brien Press (*Ire*)
PaperBooks (*UK*)
Paul Dry Books, Inc. (*US*)
Pen Books (*US*)
Persea Books (*US*)
Pushkin Press (*UK*)
Reading Harbor (*US*)
Shearsman Books (*UK*)
Soft Skull Press (*US*)
Souvenir Press Ltd (*UK*)
St. Johann Press (*US*)
Sunscribe (*US*)
Triumph Books (*US*)
Tsaba House (*US*)
Turn the Page Publishing LLC (*US*)
W.W. Norton & Company Ltd (*UK*)
Whitaker House (*US*)
Yale University Press (London) (*UK*)
Beauty and Fashion
Barron's Educational Series, Inc. (*US*)
Carlton Publishing Group (*UK*)
Ex-L-Ence Publishing (*UK*)
Geostar Publishing & Services LLC (*US*)
Harry N. Abrams, Inc. (*US*)
Jacaranda Books Art Music Ltd (*UK*)
Kyle Books (*UK*)
Luath Press Ltd (*UK*)
Merrell Publishers Limited (*UK*)
Octopus Publishing Group Limited (*UK*)
Phaidon Press Limited (*UK*)
Quadrille Publishing Ltd (*UK*)
Quarto Publishing Group UK (*UK*)
Reaktion Books (*UK*)
Running Press (*US*)
Shire Publications Ltd (*UK*)
Souvenir Press Ltd (*UK*)
Sunscribe (*US*)
Tsaba House (*US*)
Yale University Press (London) (*UK*)
Biography
Akasha Publishing Ltd (*UK*)
Alma Classics (*UK*)
Alpine Publications, Inc. (*US*)
Amakella Publishing (*US*)
Arch Street Press (*US*)
Authentic Media (*UK*)

Beacon Press (*US*)
BenBella Books (*US*)
John Blake Publishing (*UK*)
Bowker (UK) Ltd (*UK*)
Canongate Books (*UK*)
Capstone (*US*)
Carlton Publishing Group (*UK*)
Cave Books (*US*)
Centerstream Publishing (*US*)
Chicago Review Press (*US*)
Columba Press (*Ire*)
Covenant Communications Inc. (*US*)
David R. Godine, Publisher (*US*)
Dufour Editions (*US*)
Dynasty Press (*UK*)
Eakin Press (*US*)
ECW Press (*Can*)
Ex-L-Ence Publishing (*UK*)
Faber & Faber Ltd (*UK*)
Fleming Publications (*UK*)
Floris Books (*UK*)
Fonthill Media LLC (*US*)
Fonthill Media Ltd (*UK*)
Fordham University Press (*US*)
Frederic C. Beil, Publisher (*US*)
Geostar Publishing & Services LLC (*US*)
Gibson Square Books Ltd (*UK*)
Gill & Macmillan (*Ire*)
Gingko Library (*UK*)
Gomer Press (*UK*)
Granta Books (*UK*)
Halban Publishers (*UK*)
Halsgrove (*UK*)
HarperCollins Publishers Ltd (*UK*)
Haus Publishing (*UK*)
Hay House Publishers (*UK*)
Head of Zeus (*UK*)
Headland Publications (*UK*)
Headline Publishing Group (*UK*)
Hesperus Press Limited (*UK*)
The History Press (*UK*)
House of Lochar (*UK*)
Hymns Ancient & Modern Ltd (*UK*)
Independent Music Press (*UK*)
Jacaranda Books Art Music Ltd (*UK*)
Kube Publishing (*UK*)
Liberties Press (*Ire*)
The Lilliput Press (*Ire*)
Lion Hudson Plc (*UK*)
Logaston Press (*UK*)
Luath Press Ltd (*UK*)
Macmillan (*UK*)
Mainstream Publishing Co. (Edinburgh) Ltd (*UK*)
Marion Boyars Publishers (*UK*)
Mentor Books (*Ire*)
Milo Books Ltd (*UK*)
Mitchell Lane Publishers, Inc. (*US*)
Neil Wilson Publishing Ltd (*UK*)
New Holland Publishers (UK) Ltd (*UK*)
New Island (*Ire*)
The O'Brien Press (*Ire*)
Michael O'Mara Books Ltd (*UK*)

Omnibus Press (*UK*)
Oneworld Publications (*UK*)
Owen Press (*UK*)
Peter Owen Publishers (*UK*)
Paragon House (*US*)
Paul Dry Books, Inc. (*US*)
Pauline Books and Media (*US*)
Pen Books (*US*)
Persea Books (*US*)
Quill Driver Books (*US*)
Reaktion Books (*UK*)
Red Deer Press (*Can*)
Robert Hale Publishers (*UK*)
Ronsdale Press (*Can*)
The Rosen Publishing Group, Inc. (*US*)
Seren Books (*UK*)
Shire Publications Ltd (*UK*)
Sigma Press (*UK*)
Soft Skull Press (*US*)
Souvenir Press Ltd (*UK*)
St. Johann Press (*US*)
Sunscribe (*US*)
Tate Publishing and Enterprises, LLC (*US*)
Triumph Books (*US*)
Tsaba House (*US*)
University of Alabama Press (*US*)
University of Chicago Press (*US*)
Vernon Press (an imprint of Vernon Art and Science Inc.) (*US*)
W.W. Norton & Company Ltd (*UK*)
Whitaker House (*US*)
Yale University Press (London) (*UK*)

Business
Amakella Publishing (*US*)
American Press (*US*)
Arcade Publishing (*US*)
Arch Street Press (*US*)
Barron's Educational Series, Inc. (*US*)
BenBella Books (*US*)
Bennion Kearny (*UK*)
John Blake Publishing (*UK*)
Bowker (UK) Ltd (*UK*)
CJ Fallon (*Ire*)
Crystal Spirit Publishing, Inc. (*US*)
Eakin Press (*US*)
ECW Press (*Can*)
Edward Elgar Publishing Inc. (*US*)
Edward Elgar Publishing Ltd (*UK*)
Euromonitor (*UK*)
Ex-L-Ence Publishing (*UK*)
Fordham University Press (*US*)
Geostar Publishing & Services LLC (*US*)
Hay House Publishers (*UK*)
International Foundation of Employee Benefit Plans (*US*)
JIST Publishing (*US*)
Legend Business (*UK*)
Liberties Press (*Ire*)
The Lilliput Press (*Ire*)
Macmillan (*UK*)
Management Books 2000 Ltd (*UK*)
Manchester University Press (*UK*)
Mentor Books (*Ire*)

Stone Bridge Press (*US*)
Storey Publishing (*US*)
Sunscribe (*US*)
W.W. Norton & Company Ltd (*UK*)
Williamson Books (*US*)
Crime
Ankerwycke (*US*)
Arrow Publications, LLC (*US*)
John Blake Publishing (*UK*)
Bold Strokes Books (*US*)
Carina UK (*UK*)
Curiosity Quills Press (*US*)
Curious Fox (*UK*)
Darkhouse Books (*US*)
Ex-L-Ence Publishing (*UK*)
Geostar Publishing & Services LLC (*US*)
Ghostwoods Books (*UK*)
Gill & Macmillan (*Ire*)
Harlequin Mills & Boon Ltd (*UK*)
HarperCollins Publishers Ltd (*UK*)
Head of Zeus (*UK*)
Hesperus Press Limited (*UK*)
The History Press (*UK*)
Honno Welsh Women's Press (*UK*)
Jacaranda Books Art Music Ltd (*UK*)
Joffe Books Ltd (*UK*)
Liberties Press (*Ire*)
Lost Tower Publications (*UK*)
Luath Press Ltd (*UK*)
M P Publishing USA (*US*)
Macmillan (*UK*)
Mandrake of Oxford (*UK*)
Mentor Books (*Ire*)
Milo Books Ltd (*UK*)
Neil Wilson Publishing Ltd (*UK*)
New Island (*Ire*)
New York University (NYU) Press (*US*)
The O'Brien Press (*Ire*)
Pen Books (*US*)
Polity Press (*UK*)
Quill Driver Books (*US*)
Red Rattle Books (*UK*)
Robert Hale Publishers (*UK*)
Salt Publishing Ltd (*UK*)
Sandstone Press Ltd (*UK*)
Severn House Publishers (*UK*)
Soft Skull Press (*US*)
Souvenir Press Ltd (*UK*)
Strategic Media Books (*US*)
Sunscribe (*US*)
SynergEbooks (*US*)
Tyrus Books (*US*)
W.W. Norton & Company Ltd (*UK*)
Criticism
Arch Street Press (*US*)
BlazeVOX [books] (*US*)
Bucknell University Press (*US*)
Crescent Moon Publishing (*UK*)
David R. Godine, Publisher (*US*)
Enitharmon Press (*UK*)
Ex-L-Ence Publishing (*UK*)
Geostar Publishing & Services LLC (*US*)
Gibson Square Books Ltd (*UK*)

Granta Books (*UK*)
Halban Publishers (*UK*)
IBEX Publishers, Inc. (*US*)
Imprint Academic (*UK*)
The Lilliput Press (*Ire*)
Manchester University Press (*UK*)
Marion Boyars Publishers (*UK*)
Maverick Reads (*UK*)
New Island (*Ire*)
Peter Owen Publishers (*UK*)
Paul Dry Books, Inc. (*US*)
Persea Books (*US*)
Presa Press (*US*)
Seren Books (*UK*)
Shearsman Books (*UK*)
Sunscribe (*US*)
Turnstone Press (*Can*)
University of Alabama Press (*US*)
Vernon Press (an imprint of Vernon Art and
Science Inc.) (*US*)
Wannabee Books (*US*)
Yale University Press (London) (*UK*)
Culture
Akasha Publishing Ltd (*UK*)
Amakella Publishing (*US*)
Arch Street Press (*US*)
BenBella Books (*US*)
Blink Publishing (*UK*)
Blue Guides Limited (*UK*)
Blue River Press (*US*)
Bucknell University Press (*US*)
By Light Unseen Media (*US*)
Canongate Books (*UK*)
Carlton Publishing Group (*UK*)
Chicago Review Press (*US*)
Concordia Publishing House (*US*)
Crescent Moon Publishing (*UK*)
Eagle's View Publishing (*US*)
Eakin Press (*US*)
ECW Press (*Can*)
Edward Elgar Publishing Ltd (*UK*)
Ex-L-Ence Publishing (*UK*)
Fantagraphics (*US*)
Finney Company (*US*)
Fordham University Press (*US*)
Frances Lincoln Children's Books (*UK*)
Geostar Publishing & Services LLC (*US*)
GEY Books (*UK*)
Gibson Square Books Ltd (*UK*)
Gival Press, LLC (*US*)
Gomer Press (*UK*)
Granta Books (*UK*)
Harry N. Abrams, Inc. (*US*)
Hesperus Press Limited (*UK*)
Heyday Books (*US*)
Hipso Media (*US*)
HOW Books (*US*)
Ig Publishing (*US*)
The Ilex Press (*UK*)
Independent Music Press (*UK*)
Kube Publishing (*UK*)
The Lilliput Press (*Ire*)
Liverpool University Press (*UK*)

The Lyons Press Inc. (*US*)
Macmillan (*UK*)
Mainstream Publishing Co. (Edinburgh) Ltd (*UK*)
Manchester University Press (*UK*)
Mandrake of Oxford (*UK*)
Marion Boyars Publishers (*UK*)
Maverick Reads (*UK*)
McFarland & Company, Inc. (*US*)
Merrell Publishers Limited (*UK*)
Milo Books Ltd (*UK*)
Neil Wilson Publishing Ltd (*UK*)
New York University (NYU) Press (*US*)
Octopus Publishing Group Limited (*UK*)
Paul Dry Books, Inc. (*US*)
Pen Books (*US*)
Phaidon Press Limited (*UK*)
Pluto Publishing Ltd (*UK*)
Polity Press (*UK*)
Reading Harbor (*US*)
Reaktion Books (*UK*)
Red Empress Publishing (*US*)
Reference Service Press (*US*)
The Rosen Publishing Group, Inc. (*US*)
Route Publishing (*UK*)
Running Press (*US*)
Saffron Books (*UK*)
Scarecrow Press Inc. (*US*)
Soft Skull Press (*US*)
Stone Bridge Press (*US*)
Sunscribe (*US*)
Swan Isle Press (*US*)
Trentham Books Limited (*UK*)
Tu Books (*US*)
University of South Carolina Press (*US*)
Utah State University Press (*US*)
Vallentine Mitchell & Co., Limited (*UK*)
Vanderbilt University Press (*US*)
Vernon Press (an imprint of Vernon Art and Science Inc.) (*US*)
Voyageur Press (*US*)
Westminster John Knox Press (WJK) (*US*)
The X Press (*UK*)
Zenith Press (*US*)
Current Affairs
Amakella Publishing (*US*)
Arcade Publishing (*US*)
Beacon Press (*US*)
Divertir Publishing LLC (*US*)
Ex-L-Ence Publishing (*UK*)
Fabian Society (*UK*)
Geostar Publishing & Services LLC (*US*)
Gibson Square Books Ltd (*UK*)
Gill & Macmillan (*Ire*)
Hay House Publishers (*UK*)
Institute of Public Administration (IPA) (*Ire*)
Liberties Press (*Ire*)
The Lilliput Press (*Ire*)
Luath Press Ltd (*UK*)
The Lyons Press Inc. (*US*)
Macmillan (*UK*)
Mainstream Publishing Co. (Edinburgh) Ltd (*UK*)

McFarland & Company, Inc. (*US*)
Milo Books Ltd (*UK*)
New Island (*Ire*)
Oneworld Publications (*UK*)
Paragon House (*US*)
Pen Books (*US*)
Pluto Publishing Ltd (*UK*)
Prometheus Books (*US*)
Quarto Publishing Group USA (*US*)
Reading Harbor (*US*)
Reaktion Books (*UK*)
Saffron Books (*UK*)
Seren Books (*UK*)
Soft Skull Press (*US*)
Strategic Media Books (*US*)
Sunscribe (*US*)
Tsaba House (*US*)
Vernon Press (an imprint of Vernon Art and Science Inc.) (*US*)
W.W. Norton & Company Ltd (*UK*)
Yale University Press (*US*)
Yale University Press (London) (*UK*)
Design
Anness Publishing Ltd (*UK*)
ASCE Press (*US*)
Carlton Publishing Group (*UK*)
Ex-L-Ence Publishing (*UK*)
Frontinus (*UK*)
Geostar Publishing & Services LLC (*US*)
Gibbs Smith, Publisher (*US*)
Harry N. Abrams, Inc. (*US*)
HOW Books (*US*)
Kansas City Star Books (*US*)
Frances Lincoln Ltd (*UK*)
Manchester University Press (*UK*)
Merrell Publishers Limited (*UK*)
New Holland Publishers (UK) Ltd (*UK*)
Octopus Publishing Group Limited (*UK*)
Phaidon Press Limited (*UK*)
Professional Publications, Inc. (PPI) (*US*)
Quadrille Publishing Ltd (*UK*)
Quarto Publishing Group UK (*UK*)
Quarto Publishing Group USA (*US*)
Reaktion Books (*UK*)
Richard Dennis Publications (*UK*)
Robert Hale Publishers (*UK*)
RotoVision (*UK*)
Roundhouse Group (*UK*)
Shire Publications Ltd (*UK*)
Stone Bridge Press (*US*)
Sunscribe (*US*)
W.W. Norton & Company Ltd (*UK*)
Waveland Press, Inc. (*US*)
John Wiley & Sons, Inc. (*US*)
Philip Wilson Publishers Ltd (*UK*)
Drama
American Press (*US*)
Bronze Man Books (*US*)
Capstone (*US*)
Chapman Publishing (*UK*)
Cressrelles Publishing Co. Ltd (*UK*)
Ex-L-Ence Publishing (*UK*)
Faber & Faber Ltd (*UK*)

Geostar Publishing & Services LLC (*US*)
GEY Books (*UK*)
Gomer Press (*UK*)
The Lilliput Press (*Ire*)
Luath Press Ltd (*UK*)
Marion Boyars Publishers (*UK*)
New Island (*Ire*)
New Playwrights' Network (NPN) (*UK*)
The O'Brien Press (*Ire*)
Oberon Books (*UK*)
Parthian Books (*UK*)
Pen Books (*US*)
Red Deer Press (*Can*)
Samuel French Ltd (*UK*)
Seren Books (*UK*)
Sidestreet Cookie Publishing (*US*)
Sunscribe (*US*)
W.W. Norton & Company Ltd (*UK*)
Entertainment
John Blake Publishing (*UK*)
Carlton Publishing Group (*UK*)
Ex-L-Ence Publishing (*UK*)
Geostar Publishing & Services LLC (*US*)
GEY Books (*UK*)
HarperCollins Publishers Ltd (*UK*)
Harry N. Abrams, Inc. (*US*)
Pen Books (*US*)
Quarto Publishing Group UK (*UK*)
Reading Harbor (*US*)
Sidestreet Cookie Publishing (*US*)
Sunscribe (*US*)
Tate Publishing and Enterprises, LLC (*US*)
Erotic
Amira Press (*US*)
Bold Strokes Books (*US*)
Carina UK (*UK*)
Crystal Spirit Publishing, Inc. (*US*)
Geostar Publishing & Services LLC (*US*)
GEY Books (*UK*)
HarperImpulse (*UK*)
Hesperus Press Limited (*UK*)
Hipso Media (*US*)
Mandrake of Oxford (*UK*)
Sidestreet Cookie Publishing (*US*)
Fantasy
Akasha Publishing Ltd (*UK*)
AMG Publishers (*US*)
Amira Press (*US*)
Arrow Publications, LLC (*US*)
BelleBooks (*US*)
Bethany House Publishers (*US*)
Bold Strokes Books (*US*)
By Light Unseen Media (*US*)
Capstone (*US*)
Carina UK (*UK*)
Children's Brains are Yummy (CBAY) Books (*US*)
Chipping Norton Publishers (*UK*)
Cricket Books (*US*)
Curiosity Quills Press (*US*)
Curious Fox (*UK*)
Dark Horse Comics (*US*)
Divertir Publishing LLC (*US*)

Dragon Moon Press (*Can*)
Ellysian Press (*US*)
Entangled Teen (*US*)
Ex-L-Ence Publishing (*UK*)
Geostar Publishing & Services LLC (*US*)
GEY Books (*UK*)
Ghostwoods Books (*UK*)
Harken Media (*US*)
Harmony Ink Press (*US*)
HarperCollins Publishers Ltd (*UK*)
Head of Zeus (*UK*)
Hesperus Press Limited (*UK*)
Honno Welsh Women's Press (*UK*)
Lost Tower Publications (*UK*)
Luna Press Publishing (*UK*)
M P Publishing USA (*US*)
Macmillan (*UK*)
Maverick Reads (*UK*)
Pen Books (*US*)
Pure Indigo Limited (*UK*)
Red Deer Press (*Can*)
Red Empress Publishing (*US*)
Roberts Press (*US*)
The Salariya Book Company (*UK*)
Sidestreet Cookie Publishing (*US*)
Soft Skull Press (*US*)
Sunscribe (*US*)
SynergEbooks (*US*)
Tate Publishing and Enterprises, LLC (*US*)
Top Cow Productions, Inc (*US*)
Tsaba House (*US*)
Tu Books (*US*)
Turnstone Press (*Can*)
Twilight Times Books (*US*)
Fiction
A Swift Exit (*UK*)
Abrams ComicArts (*US*)
Akasha Publishing Ltd (*UK*)
Alma Books Ltd (*UK*)
Alma Classics (*UK*)
Alondra Press (*US*)
Amakella Publishing (*US*)
American Quilter's Society (*US*)
AMG Publishers (*US*)
Amira Press (*US*)
Ankerwycke (*US*)
Annick Press (*Can*)
Arbordale Publishing (*US*)
Arcade Publishing (*US*)
Arch Street Press (*US*)
Arrow Publications, LLC (*US*)
Bailiwick Press (*US*)
Barefoot Books Ltd (*UK*)
Barron's Educational Series, Inc. (*US*)
BelleBooks (*US*)
Bellevue Literary Press (*US*)
Bethany House Publishers (*US*)
Bick Publishing House (*US*)
Bilingual Review Press (*US*)
Black Lyon Publishing, LLC (*US*)
Black Rose Writing (*US*)
John Blake Publishing (*UK*)
BlazeVOX [books] (*US*)

Bloomsbury Publishing Plc (*UK*)
Bold Strokes Books (*US*)
BookFish Books (*US*)
Boyds Mills Press (*US*)
Bronze Man Books (*US*)
The Brucedale Press (*Can*)
Bullitt Publishing (*US*)
By Light Unseen Media (*US*)
Canongate Books (*UK*)
Canterbury House Publishing, Ltd (*US*)
Capstone (*US*)
Carina UK (*UK*)
Cave Books (*US*)
Cave Hollow Press (*US*)
Chapman Publishing (*UK*)
Chicago Review Press (*US*)
Children's Brains are Yummy (CBAY) Books (*US*)
Chipping Norton Publishers (*UK*)
Cinco Puntos Press (*US*)
Classical Comics Limited (*UK*)
Continental (*US*)
Corazon Books (*UK*)
Covenant Communications Inc. (*US*)
Craigmore Creations (*US*)
Creative With Words (CWW) (*US*)
Crescent Moon Publishing (*UK*)
Creston Books (*US*)
Cricket Books (*US*)
Crimson Romance (*US*)
Crystal Spirit Publishing, Inc. (*US*)
Cup of Tea Books (*US*)
Curiosity Quills Press (*US*)
Curious Fox (*UK*)
Dark Horse Comics (*US*)
Darkhouse Books (*US*)
David R. Godine, Publisher (*US*)
DC Thomson (*UK*)
Dedalus Ltd (*UK*)
Divertir Publishing LLC (*US*)
Dragon Moon Press (*Can*)
Dufour Editions (*US*)
Eakin Press (*US*)
ECW Press (*Can*)
Egmont UK Ltd (*UK*)
Ellysian Press (*US*)
The Emma Press Ltd (*UK*)
Enitharmon Press (*UK*)
Entangled Teen (*US*)
Ex-L-Ence Publishing (*UK*)
Faber & Faber Ltd (*UK*)
Familius (*US*)
Fantagraphics (*US*)
Farrar, Straus & Giroux, Inc. (*US*)
Farrar, Straus and Giroux Books for Younger Readers (*US*)
Fiction Collective Two (FC2) (*US*)
Filbert Publishing (*US*)
Fingerpress UK (*UK*)
Fisherton Press (*UK*)
Fitzhenry & Whiteside Ltd (*Can*)
Fitzrovia Press Limited (*UK*)
Fleming Publications (*UK*)

Floris Books (*UK*)
Folded Word LLC (*US*)
Frances Lincoln Children's Books (*UK*)
Frederic C. Beil, Publisher (*US*)
Free Spirit Publishing (*US*)
The Gallery Press (*Ire*)
Galley Beggar Press (*UK*)
GEY Books (*UK*)
Ghostwoods Books (*UK*)
Gibson Square Books Ltd (*UK*)
Gill & Macmillan (*Ire*)
Gival Press, LLC (*US*)
Gomer Press (*UK*)
Goosebottom Books LLC (*US*)
Granta Books (*UK*)
Groundwood Books (*Can*)
Hachai Publishing (*US*)
Halban Publishers (*UK*)
Harken Media (*US*)
Harlequin American Romance (*US*)
Harlequin Mills & Boon Ltd (*UK*)
Harmony Ink Press (*US*)
HarperCollins Publishers Ltd (*UK*)
HarperImpulse (*UK*)
Harry N. Abrams, Inc. (*US*)
Harvest House Publishers (*US*)
Haus Publishing (*UK*)
Head of Zeus (*UK*)
Headland Publications (*UK*)
Headline Publishing Group (*UK*)
Hearts 'N Tummies Cookbook Co. / Quixote Press (*US*)
Helicon Nine Editions (*US*)
Hesperus Press Limited (*UK*)
Heyday Books (*US*)
Hipso Media (*US*)
Holiday House, Inc. (*US*)
Honno Welsh Women's Press (*UK*)
House of Lochar (*UK*)
Ig Publishing (*US*)
Igloo Books Limited (*UK*)
Illusio & Baqer (*US*)
Image Comics (*US*)
Influx Press (*UK*)
Interlink Publishing Group, Inc. (*US*)
Iron Press (*UK*)
Jacaranda Books Art Music Ltd (*UK*)
Joffe Books Ltd (*UK*)
Kathy Dawson Books (*US*)
Kind of a Hurricane Press (*US*)
Kube Publishing (*UK*)
Legend Press (*UK*)
Liberties Press (*Ire*)
The Lilliput Press (*Ire*)
Limitless Publishing (*US*)
Frances Lincoln Ltd (*UK*)
Lion Hudson Plc (*UK*)
Lost Tower Publications (*UK*)
Luath Press Ltd (*UK*)
Luna Press Publishing (*UK*)
M P Publishing USA (*US*)
Macmillan (*UK*)
Mandrake of Oxford (*UK*)

Scarecrow Press Inc. (*US*)
Shire Publications Ltd (*UK*)
Soft Skull Press (*US*)
Stone Bridge Press (*US*)
Sunscribe (*US*)
Teachers College Press (*US*)
University of Chicago Press (*US*)
W.W. Norton & Company Ltd (*UK*)

Finance

Akasha Publishing Ltd (*UK*)
American Press (*US*)
Arch Street Press (*US*)
Barron's Educational Series, Inc. (*US*)
Carswell (*Can*)
Chelsea Green Publishing, Inc. (*US*)
CJ Fallon (*Ire*)
Eakin Press (*US*)
ECW Press (*Can*)
Edward Elgar Publishing Inc. (*US*)
Edward Elgar Publishing Ltd (*UK*)
Ex-L-Ence Publishing (*UK*)
Fabian Society (*UK*)
Familius (*US*)
Fordham University Press (*US*)
Geostar Publishing & Services LLC (*US*)
Gingko Library (*UK*)
Hay House Publishers (*UK*)
Institute of Public Administration (IPA) (*Ire*)
Liberties Press (*Ire*)
Macmillan (*UK*)
Management Books 2000 Ltd (*UK*)
Manchester University Press (*UK*)
Nolo (*US*)
Oak Tree Press (*Ire*)
Paragon House (*US*)
Pen Books (*US*)
Pluto Publishing Ltd (*UK*)
Polity Press (*UK*)
Possibility Press (*US*)
Princeton University Press Europe (*UK*)
Reaktion Books (*UK*)
Saffron Books (*UK*)
Sunscribe (*US*)
Tsaba House (*US*)
Turn the Page Publishing LLC (*US*)
Vernon Press (an imprint of Vernon Art and Science Inc.) (*US*)
Verso (*US*)
W.W. Norton & Company Ltd (*UK*)
Waveland Press, Inc. (*US*)
John Wiley & Sons, Inc. (*US*)
Wolters Kluwer (UK) Ltd (*UK*)
Yale University Press (London) (*UK*)
Zambezi Publishing Ltd (*UK*)

Gardening

Anness Publishing Ltd (*UK*)
Ball Publishing (*US*)
Chelsea Green Publishing, Inc. (*US*)
Chicago Review Press (*US*)
David R. Godine, Publisher (*US*)
Ex-L-Ence Publishing (*UK*)
Finney Company (*US*)
Geostar Publishing & Services LLC (*US*)

Guild of Master Craftsman (GMC) Publications Ltd (*UK*)
HarperCollins Publishers Ltd (*UK*)
Harry N. Abrams, Inc. (*US*)
Headline Publishing Group (*UK*)
Kyle Books (*UK*)
Frances Lincoln Ltd (*UK*)
Macmillan (*UK*)
New Holland Publishers (UK) Ltd (*UK*)
Octopus Publishing Group Limited (*UK*)
Poolbeg (*Ire*)
Quadrille Publishing Ltd (*UK*)
Quarto Publishing Group UK (*UK*)
Reaktion Books (*UK*)
Shire Publications Ltd (*UK*)
Souvenir Press Ltd (*UK*)
Storey Publishing (*US*)
Sunscribe (*US*)
University of Chicago Press (*US*)
University of South Carolina Press (*US*)
Wannabee Books (*US*)

Gothic

Carina UK (*UK*)
Chipping Norton Publishers (*UK*)
Corazon Books (*UK*)
Ex-L-Ence Publishing (*UK*)
Geostar Publishing & Services LLC (*US*)
Ghostwoods Books (*UK*)
Lost Tower Publications (*UK*)
M P Publishing USA (*US*)
Maverick Reads (*UK*)
Red Empress Publishing (*US*)
Salt Publishing Ltd (*UK*)
Sidestreet Cookie Publishing (*US*)
Sunscribe (*US*)

Health

American Counseling Association (*US*)
American Press (*US*)
Anness Publishing Ltd (*UK*)
Barron's Educational Series, Inc. (*US*)
BenBella Books (*US*)
Bick Publishing House (*US*)
John Blake Publishing (*UK*)
Blue River Press (*US*)
Conari Press (*US*)
Connections Book Publishing Ltd (*UK*)
ECW Press (*Can*)
Ex-L-Ence Publishing (*UK*)
Familius (*US*)
Filbert Publishing (*US*)
Floris Books (*UK*)
Geostar Publishing & Services LLC (*US*)
Grub Street Publishing (*UK*)
Haldane Mason Ltd (*UK*)
HarperCollins Publishers Ltd (*UK*)
Harvest House Publishers (*US*)
Hay House Publishers (*UK*)
Hipso Media (*US*)
Hodder Education (*UK*)
Institute of Public Administration (IPA) (*Ire*)
International Foundation of Employee Benefit Plans (*US*)
Kyle Books (*UK*)

Liberties Press (*Ire*)
Lion Hudson Plc (*UK*)
Macmillan (*UK*)
Mainstream Publishing Co. (Edinburgh) Ltd (*UK*)
Mandrake of Oxford (*UK*)
McFarland & Company, Inc. (*US*)
Mitchell Lane Publishers, Inc. (*US*)
New Holland Publishers (UK) Ltd (*UK*)
NursesBooks (*US*)
Octopus Publishing Group Limited (*UK*)
Pavilion Publishing (*UK*)
Pen Books (*US*)
Polity Press (*UK*)
Possibility Press (*US*)
Prometheus Books (*US*)
Quadrille Publishing Ltd (*UK*)
Quarto Publishing Group UK (*UK*)
Quarto Publishing Group USA (*US*)
Quill Driver Books (*US*)
Radcliffe Publishing Ltd (*UK*)
Reference Service Press (*US*)
Robert Hale Publishers (*UK*)
The Rosen Publishing Group, Inc. (*US*)
Roundhouse Group (*UK*)
Running Press (*US*)
Singing Dragon (*UK*)
Society for Promoting Christian Knowledge (SPCK) (*UK*)
Soft Skull Press (*US*)
Souvenir Press Ltd (*UK*)
Storey Publishing (*US*)
Sunscribe (*US*)
Tate Publishing and Enterprises, LLC (*US*)
Vanderbilt University Press (*US*)
W.W. Norton & Company Ltd (*UK*)
Wannabee Books (*US*)
Waveland Press, Inc. (*US*)
Wolters Kluwer (UK) Ltd (*UK*)
World Book, Inc. (*US*)
Yale University Press (London) (*UK*)
Zambezi Publishing Ltd (*UK*)

Historical
Akasha Publishing Ltd (*UK*)
Alma Books Ltd (*UK*)
Alondra Press (*US*)
Amakella Publishing (*US*)
American Press (*US*)
Amira Press (*US*)
Anness Publishing Ltd (*UK*)
Arcade Publishing (*US*)
Arch Street Press (*US*)
Astragal Press (*US*)
Atlantic Europe Publishing (*UK*)
Beacon Press (*US*)
BelleBooks (*US*)
Bethany House Publishers (*US*)
Black Lyon Publishing, LLC (*US*)
John Blake Publishing (*UK*)
Blink Publishing (*UK*)
Bloomsbury Publishing Plc (*UK*)
Bodleian Library (*UK*)
Bold Strokes Books (*US*)

Boydell & Brewer Ltd (*UK*)
The Brucedale Press (*Can*)
Bucknell University Press (*US*)
By Light Unseen Media (*US*)
Canongate Books (*UK*)
Capstone (*US*)
Carina UK (*UK*)
Carlton Publishing Group (*UK*)
The Catholic University of America Press (*US*)
Cave Books (*US*)
Chicago Review Press (*US*)
CJ Fallon (*Ire*)
Columba Press (*Ire*)
Corazon Books (*UK*)
Covenant Communications Inc. (*US*)
CQ Press (*US*)
Cricket Books (*US*)
Crimson Romance (*US*)
Curious Fox (*UK*)
David R. Godine, Publisher (*US*)
Divertir Publishing LLC (*US*)
Dufour Editions (*US*)
Dynasty Press (*UK*)
Eagle's View Publishing (*US*)
Eakin Press (*US*)
ECW Press (*Can*)
William B. Eerdmans Publishing Co. (*US*)
Entangled Teen (*US*)
Ex-L-Ence Publishing (*UK*)
Fingerpress UK (*UK*)
Finney Company (*US*)
Fleming Publications (*UK*)
Floris Books (*UK*)
Flyleaf Press (*Ire*)
Fonthill Media LLC (*US*)
Fonthill Media Ltd (*UK*)
Fordham University Press (*US*)
Foreign Policy Association (*US*)
Frederic C. Beil, Publisher (*US*)
Geostar Publishing & Services LLC (*US*)
Ghostwoods Books (*UK*)
Gibson Square Books Ltd (*UK*)
Gill & Macmillan (*Ire*)
Gingko Library (*UK*)
Gomer Press (*UK*)
Goosebottom Books LLC (*US*)
Granta Books (*UK*)
Grub Street Publishing (*UK*)
Gun Digest Books (*US*)
Hachai Publishing (*US*)
Halban Publishers (*UK*)
Haldane Mason Ltd (*UK*)
Halsgrove (*UK*)
Harken Media (*US*)
Harlequin Mills & Boon Ltd (*UK*)
HarperCollins Publishers Ltd (*UK*)
HarperImpulse (*UK*)
Harvest House Publishers (*US*)
Haus Publishing (*UK*)
Head of Zeus (*UK*)
Headline Publishing Group (*UK*)
Hesperus Press Limited (*UK*)
Heyday Books (*US*)

Hill and Wang (*US*)
The History Press (*UK*)
House of Lochar (*UK*)
IBEX Publishers, Inc. (*US*)
Icon Books Ltd (*UK*)
Interlink Publishing Group, Inc. (*US*)
IWM (Imperial War Museums) (*UK*)
Kube Publishing (*UK*)
Liberties Press (*Ire*)
The Lilliput Press (*Ire*)
Liverpool University Press (*UK*)
Logaston Press (*UK*)
Luath Press Ltd (*UK*)
The Lyons Press Inc. (*US*)
Macmillan (*UK*)
Mainstream Publishing Co. (Edinburgh) Ltd
(*UK*)
Manchester University Press (*UK*)
Maverick Reads (*UK*)
McBooks Press (*US*)
McFarland & Company, Inc. (*US*)
Mentor Books (*Ire*)
The Merlin Press (*UK*)
Mitchell Lane Publishers, Inc. (*US*)
Museum of Northern Arizona (*US*)
National Museum Wales (*UK*)
Neil Wilson Publishing Ltd (*UK*)
New Holland Publishers (UK) Ltd (*UK*)
New Island (*Ire*)
New York University (NYU) Press (*US*)
The O'Brien Press (*Ire*)
Michael O'Mara Books Ltd (*UK*)
Octopus Publishing Group Limited (*UK*)
Oneworld Publications (*UK*)
Onstream Publications Ltd (*Ire*)
Osprey Publishing Ltd (*UK*)
The Overmountain Press (*US*)
Peter Owen Publishers (*UK*)
Paragon House (*US*)
Paul Dry Books, Inc. (*US*)
Pen Books (*US*)
Phaidon Press Limited (*UK*)
Picton Press (*US*)
Pluto Publishing Ltd (*UK*)
Polity Press (*UK*)
Princeton University Press Europe (*UK*)
Quarto Publishing Group UK (*UK*)
Quarto Publishing Group USA (*US*)
Reaktion Books (*UK*)
Red Deer Press (*Can*)
Red Empress Publishing (*US*)
Reference Service Press (*US*)
Robert Hale Publishers (*UK*)
Ronsdale Press (*Can*)
Rose and Crown Books (*UK*)
The Rosen Publishing Group, Inc. (*US*)
Roundhouse Group (*UK*)
Saffron Books (*UK*)
The Salariya Book Company (*UK*)
Scala Arts & Heritage Publishers (*UK*)
Scarecrow Press Inc. (*US*)
Seren Books (*UK*)
Seriously Good Books (*US*)

Severn House Publishers (*UK*)
Shire Publications Ltd (*UK*)
Sidestreet Cookie Publishing (*US*)
Sigma Press (*UK*)
Soft Skull Press (*US*)
Souvenir Press Ltd (*UK*)
St David's Press (*UK*)
Stenlake Publishing (*UK*)
Sunscribe (*US*)
Tate Publishing and Enterprises, LLC (*US*)
Teachers College Press (*US*)
Twilight Times Books (*US*)
University College Dublin (UCD) Press (*Ire*)
University of Alabama Press (*US*)
University of Chicago Press (*US*)
University of South Carolina Press (*US*)
University of Tampa Press (*US*)
Utah State University Press (*US*)
Vallentine Mitchell & Co., Limited (*UK*)
Vanderbilt University Press (*US*)
Vernon Press (an imprint of Vernon Art and
Science Inc.) (*US*)
Verso (*US*)
Voyageur Press (*US*)
W.W. Norton & Company Ltd (*UK*)
Waveland Press, Inc. (*US*)
Waverley Books (*UK*)
Welsh Academic Press (*UK*)
Whitaker House (*US*)
Williamson Books (*US*)
Philip Wilson Publishers Ltd (*UK*)
World Book, Inc. (*US*)
Yale University Press (*US*)
Yale University Press (London) (*UK*)
Zenith Press (*US*)
Hobbies
Alpine Publications, Inc. (*US*)
Amakella Publishing (*US*)
American Quilter's Society (*US*)
Anness Publishing Ltd (*UK*)
Barron's Educational Series, Inc. (*US*)
Bloomsbury Publishing Plc (*UK*)
Divertir Publishing LLC (*US*)
Eagle's View Publishing (*US*)
Ex-L-Ence Publishing (*UK*)
Familius (*US*)
4th Level Indie (*US*)
Geostar Publishing & Services LLC (*US*)
Gill & Macmillan (*Ire*)
Guild of Master Craftsman (GMC) Publications
Ltd (*UK*)
Gun Digest Books (*US*)
Harry N. Abrams, Inc. (*US*)
Igloo Books Limited (*UK*)
Kansas City Star Books (*US*)
Leisure Arts, Inc. (*US*)
Liberties Press (*Ire*)
New Cavendish Books (*UK*)
Picton Press (*US*)
Quarto Publishing Group UK (*UK*)
Quarto Publishing Group USA (*US*)
Quill Driver Books (*US*)
Running Press (*US*)

Legal
American Press (*US*)
Ankerwycke (*US*)
Arch Street Press (*US*)
Barron's Educational Series, Inc. (*US*)
John Blake Publishing (*UK*)
Bucknell University Press (*US*)
Carswell (*Can*)
Edward Elgar Publishing Inc. (*US*)
Edward Elgar Publishing Ltd (*UK*)
Fordham University Press (*US*)
Foreign Policy Association (*US*)
Geostar Publishing & Services LLC (*US*)
Hart Publishing Ltd (*UK*)
Institute of Public Administration (IPA) (*Ire*)
Jordan Publishing (*UK*)
LexisNexis (*US*)
Manchester University Press (*UK*)
New York University (NYU) Press (*US*)
Nolo (*US*)
Oak Tree Press (*Ire*)
Pen Books (*US*)
Pluto Publishing Ltd (*UK*)
Princeton University Press Europe (*UK*)
Round Hall (*Ire*)
Sunscribe (*US*)
Sweet & Maxwell (*UK*)
Tower Publishing (*US*)
Trentham Books Limited (*UK*)
University of Chicago Press (*US*)
W.W. Norton & Company Ltd (*UK*)
Wannabee Books (*US*)
Waveland Press, Inc. (*US*)
William S. Hein & Co., Inc. (*US*)
Wolters Kluwer (UK) Ltd (*UK*)
Yale University Press (*US*)
Yale University Press (London) (*UK*)
Leisure
AA Publishing (*UK*)
Amakella Publishing (*US*)
Anness Publishing Ltd (*UK*)
Cave Books (*US*)
Connections Book Publishing Ltd (*UK*)
Ex-L-Ence Publishing (*UK*)
Finney Company (*US*)
Geostar Publishing & Services LLC (*US*)
Gill & Macmillan (*Ire*)
Gomer Press (*UK*)
HarperCollins Publishers Ltd (*UK*)
Harry N. Abrams, Inc. (*US*)
Haynes Publishing (*UK*)
Interlink Publishing Group, Inc. (*US*)
Frances Lincoln Ltd (*UK*)
Lost Tower Publications (*UK*)
Luath Press Ltd (*UK*)
McFarland & Company, Inc. (*US*)
Merlin Unwin Books (*UK*)
Pen Books (*US*)
Robert Hale Publishers (*UK*)
Running Press (*US*)
Sigma Press (*UK*)
Singing Dragon (*UK*)
St David's Press (*UK*)

Sunscribe (*US*)
Tsaba House (*US*)
W.W. Norton & Company Ltd (*UK*)
Lifestyle
AA Publishing (*UK*)
Amakella Publishing (*US*)
AMG Publishers (*US*)
Anness Publishing Ltd (*UK*)
Barron's Educational Series, Inc. (*US*)
Beacon Press (*US*)
BenBella Books (*US*)
Blink Publishing (*UK*)
Chelsea Green Publishing, Inc. (*US*)
Chicago Review Press (*US*)
Conari Press (*US*)
Concordia Publishing House (*US*)
Connections Book Publishing Ltd (*UK*)
Ex-L-Ence Publishing (*UK*)
Familius (*US*)
Ferguson Publishing (*US*)
Filbert Publishing (*US*)
Free Spirit Publishing (*US*)
Geostar Publishing & Services LLC (*US*)
Gill & Macmillan (*Ire*)
Haldane Mason Ltd (*UK*)
HarperCollins Publishers Ltd (*UK*)
Harry N. Abrams, Inc. (*US*)
Harvest House Publishers (*US*)
Hawthorn Press (*UK*)
Hay House Publishers (*UK*)
Hipso Media (*US*)
Igloo Books Limited (*UK*)
Kube Publishing (*UK*)
Kyle Books (*UK*)
Leisure Arts, Inc. (*US*)
Liberties Press (*Ire*)
Frances Lincoln Ltd (*UK*)
Lost Tower Publications (*UK*)
Luath Press Ltd (*UK*)
Management Books 2000 Ltd (*UK*)
Mandrake of Oxford (*UK*)
New Holland Publishers (UK) Ltd (*UK*)
Nightingale Press (*UK*)
The O'Brien Press (*Ire*)
Octopus Publishing Group Limited (*UK*)
Pen Books (*US*)
Possibility Press (*US*)
Quarto Publishing Group UK (*UK*)
Quill Driver Books (*US*)
Robert Hale Publishers (*UK*)
Roundhouse Group (*UK*)
Running Press (*US*)
Society for Promoting Christian Knowledge
(SPCK) (*UK*)
Soft Skull Press (*US*)
Souvenir Press Ltd (*UK*)
Stone Bridge Press (*US*)
Sunscribe (*US*)
Tate Publishing and Enterprises, LLC (*US*)
Tsaba House (*US*)
Turn the Page Publishing LLC (*US*)
Voyageur Press (*US*)
W.W. Norton & Company Ltd (*UK*)

Whitaker House (*US*)
Zambezi Publishing Ltd (*UK*)
Literature
Alma Books Ltd (*UK*)
Alma Classics (*UK*)
Amakella Publishing (*US*)
Arch Street Press (*US*)
Beacon Press (*US*)
BlazeVOX [books] (*US*)
Bodleian Library (*UK*)
Boydell & Brewer Ltd (*UK*)
Bucknell University Press (*US*)
Carina UK (*UK*)
The Catholic University of America Press (*US*)
CJ Fallon (*Ire*)
Classical Comics Limited (*UK*)
Crescent Moon Publishing (*UK*)
David R. Godine, Publisher (*US*)
Dedalus Ltd (*UK*)
Duquesne University Press (*US*)
ECW Press (*Can*)
Ex-L-Ence Publishing (*UK*)
Floris Books (*UK*)
Folded Word LLC (*US*)
Fordham University Press (*US*)
Galley Beggar Press (*UK*)
Geostar Publishing & Services LLC (*US*)
Gingko Library (*UK*)
Gomer Press (*UK*)
Halban Publishers (*UK*)
Hesperus Press Limited (*UK*)
Heyday Books (*US*)
House of Lochar (*UK*)
IBEX Publishers, Inc. (*US*)
Influx Press (*UK*)
Interlink Publishing Group, Inc. (*US*)
The Lilliput Press (*Ire*)
Liverpool University Press (*UK*)
M P Publishing USA (*US*)
Manchester University Press (*UK*)
Marion Boyars Publishers (*UK*)
Maverick Reads (*UK*)
McFarland & Company, Inc. (*US*)
Mitchell Lane Publishers, Inc. (*US*)
New Island (*Ire*)
New York University (NYU) Press (*US*)
The O'Brien Press (*Ire*)
Peter Owen Publishers (*UK*)
Pen Books (*US*)
Polity Press (*UK*)
Presa Press (*US*)
Princeton University Press Europe (*UK*)
Reading Harbor (*US*)
Reaktion Books (*UK*)
Roundhouse Group (*UK*)
Salt Publishing Ltd (*UK*)
Scarecrow Press Inc. (*US*)
Shearsman Books (*UK*)
Sidestreet Cookie Publishing (*US*)
Soft Skull Press (*US*)
Souvenir Press Ltd (*UK*)
Stenlake Publishing (*UK*)
Stone Bridge Press (*US*)

Sunscribe (*US*)
Swan Isle Press (*US*)
Tsaba House (*US*)
Turnstone Press (*Can*)
University College Dublin (UCD) Press (*Ire*)
University of Alabama Press (*US*)
University of South Carolina Press (*US*)
Vanderbilt University Press (*US*)
Vernon Press (an imprint of Vernon Art and
Science Inc.) (*US*)
Virago Press (*UK*)
W.W. Norton & Company Ltd (*UK*)
Wannabee Books (*US*)
Waveland Press, Inc. (*US*)
Yale University Press (*US*)
Yale University Press (London) (*UK*)
Media
Amakella Publishing (*US*)
Crescent Moon Publishing (*UK*)
Ex-L-Ence Publishing (*UK*)
Fordham University Press (*US*)
Geostar Publishing & Services LLC (*US*)
HarperCollins Publishers Ltd (*UK*)
Manchester University Press (*UK*)
Maverick Reads (*UK*)
New York University (NYU) Press (*US*)
Pen Books (*US*)
Pluto Publishing Ltd (*UK*)
Polity Press (*UK*)
Princeton University Press Europe (*UK*)
Soft Skull Press (*US*)
Sunscribe (*US*)
Medicine
Beacon Press (*US*)
Bucknell University Press (*US*)
Ex-L-Ence Publishing (*UK*)
Familius (*US*)
Fordham University Press (*US*)
Geostar Publishing & Services LLC (*US*)
Hay House Publishers (*UK*)
Hipso Media (*US*)
Hodder Education (*UK*)
McFarland & Company, Inc. (*US*)
Polity Press (*UK*)
Princeton University Press Europe (*UK*)
Radcliffe Publishing Ltd (*UK*)
Reaktion Books (*UK*)
Reference Service Press (*US*)
Roundhouse Group (*UK*)
Singing Dragon (*UK*)
Society for Promoting Christian Knowledge
(SPCK) (*UK*)
Souvenir Press Ltd (*UK*)
Sunscribe (*US*)
University of Chicago Press (*US*)
Vanderbilt University Press (*US*)
W.W. Norton & Company Ltd (*UK*)
Wannabee Books (*US*)
John Wiley & Sons, Inc. (*US*)
Yale University Press (*US*)
Yale University Press (London) (*UK*)
Men's Interests
Amakella Publishing (*US*)

Carina UK (*UK*)
Connections Book Publishing Ltd (*UK*)
Ex-L-Ence Publishing (*UK*)
Geostar Publishing & Services LLC (*US*)
GEY Books (*UK*)
Harvest House Publishers (*US*)
Hay House Publishers (*UK*)
Sunscribe (*US*)
Tsaba House (*US*)
Whitaker House (*US*)
Military
Anness Publishing Ltd (*UK*)
Arcade Publishing (*US*)
John Blake Publishing (*UK*)
Blink Publishing (*UK*)
Boydell & Brewer Ltd (*UK*)
Capstone (*US*)
Eakin Press (*US*)
Ex-L-Ence Publishing (*UK*)
Fonthill Media LLC (*US*)
Fonthill Media Ltd (*UK*)
Geostar Publishing & Services LLC (*US*)
Grub Street Publishing (*UK*)
HarperCollins Publishers Ltd (*UK*)
The History Press (*UK*)
IWM (Imperial War Museums) (*UK*)
Limitless Publishing (*US*)
Macmillan (*UK*)
McBooks Press (*US*)
McFarland & Company, Inc. (*US*)
Osprey Publishing Ltd (*UK*)
Quarto Publishing Group USA (*US*)
Rose and Crown Books (*UK*)
Shire Publications Ltd (*UK*)
Sidestreet Cookie Publishing (*US*)
Souvenir Press Ltd (*UK*)
Sunscribe (*US*)
Tate Publishing and Enterprises, LLC (*US*)
Turn the Page Publishing LLC (*US*)
University of Alabama Press (*US*)
University of South Carolina Press (*US*)
Zenith Press (*US*)
Music
Amadeus Press (*US*)
American Press (*US*)
Anness Publishing Ltd (*UK*)
Arc Publications (*UK*)
Arch Street Press (*US*)
John Blake Publishing (*UK*)
Blink Publishing (*UK*)
Bloomsbury Publishing Plc (*UK*)
Boydell & Brewer Ltd (*UK*)
Carlton Publishing Group (*UK*)
Centerstream Publishing (*US*)
Chicago Review Press (*US*)
CJ Fallon (*Ire*)
Columba Press (*Ire*)
Crescent Moon Publishing (*UK*)
Ex-L-Ence Publishing (*UK*)
Faber & Faber Ltd (*UK*)
Fordham University Press (*US*)
Geostar Publishing & Services LLC (*US*)
Gingko Library (*UK*)

Gomer Press (*UK*)
Harry N. Abrams, Inc. (*US*)
Haus Publishing (*UK*)
Hymns Ancient & Modern Ltd (*UK*)
IBEX Publishers, Inc. (*US*)
Independent Music Press (*UK*)
Interlink Publishing Group, Inc. (*US*)
Liberties Press (*Ire*)
The Lilliput Press (*Ire*)
Macmillan (*UK*)
Marion Boyars Publishers (*UK*)
Maverick Reads (*UK*)
McFarland & Company, Inc. (*US*)
Mitchell Lane Publishers, Inc. (*US*)
Neil Wilson Publishing Ltd (*UK*)
The O'Brien Press (*Ire*)
Octopus Publishing Group Limited (*UK*)
Omnibus Press (*UK*)
Phaidon Press Limited (*UK*)
Piano Press (*US*)
Princeton University Press Europe (*UK*)
Quarto Publishing Group USA (*US*)
Reaktion Books (*UK*)
Roundhouse Group (*UK*)
Scarecrow Press Inc. (*US*)
Seren Books (*UK*)
Shire Publications Ltd (*UK*)
Souvenir Press Ltd (*UK*)
Stainer & Bell Ltd (*UK*)
Sunscribe (*US*)
SynergEbooks (*US*)
University College Dublin (UCD) Press (*Ire*)
University of Chicago Press (*US*)
Vanderbilt University Press (*US*)
Vernon Press (an imprint of Vernon Art and Science Inc.) (*US*)
Voyageur Press (*US*)
W.W. Norton & Company Ltd (*UK*)
Wannabee Books (*US*)
Waveland Press, Inc. (*US*)
Yale University Press (London) (*UK*)
Mystery
American Quilter's Society (*US*)
Arrow Publications, LLC (*US*)
BelleBooks (*US*)
Bethany House Publishers (*US*)
Bold Strokes Books (*US*)
Canterbury House Publishing, Ltd (*US*)
Capstone (*US*)
Carina UK (*UK*)
Children's Brains are Yummy (CBAY) Books (*US*)
Chipping Norton Publishers (*UK*)
Covenant Communications Inc. (*US*)
Cricket Books (*US*)
Cup of Tea Books (*US*)
Curiosity Quills Press (*US*)
Darkhouse Books (*US*)
Divertir Publishing LLC (*US*)
ECW Press (*Can*)
Ex-L-Ence Publishing (*UK*)
Geostar Publishing & Services LLC (*US*)
Harken Media (*US*)

Harmony Ink Press (*US*)
Harvest House Publishers (*US*)
Head of Zeus (*UK*)
Hipso Media (*US*)
Joffe Books Ltd (*UK*)
Limitless Publishing (*US*)
Lost Tower Publications (*UK*)
M P Publishing USA (*US*)
Mandrake of Oxford (*UK*)
Maverick Reads (*UK*)
Papercutz (*US*)
Pen Books (*US*)
Red Empress Publishing (*US*)
Roberts Press (*US*)
Severn House Publishers (*UK*)
Sidestreet Cookie Publishing (*US*)
Soft Skull Press (*US*)
Souvenir Press Ltd (*UK*)
Sunscribe (*US*)
SynergEbooks (*US*)
Tate Publishing and Enterprises, LLC (*US*)
The Poisoned Pencil (*US*)
Tsaba House (*US*)
Tu Books (*US*)
Turnstone Press (*Can*)
Twilight Times Books (*US*)
Nature
Alpine Publications, Inc. (*US*)
Amakella Publishing (*US*)
Arcade Publishing (*US*)
Arch Street Press (*US*)
Beacon Press (*US*)
John Blake Publishing (*UK*)
Bloomsbury Publishing Plc (*UK*)
Cave Books (*US*)
Chelsea Green Publishing, Inc. (*US*)
Columba Press (*Ire*)
Craigmore Creations (*US*)
Curious Fox (*UK*)
David R. Godine, Publisher (*US*)
Dawn Publications (*US*)
Dog-Eared Publications (*US*)
Edward Elgar Publishing Ltd (*UK*)
Ex-L-Ence Publishing (*UK*)
Fabian Society (*UK*)
FalconGuides (*US*)
Finney Company (*US*)
Folded Word LLC (*US*)
Geostar Publishing & Services LLC (*US*)
Gill & Macmillan (*Ire*)
Gomer Press (*UK*)
Granta Books (*UK*)
Harry N. Abrams, Inc. (*US*)
Hay House Publishers (*UK*)
Heyday Books (*US*)
The Lilliput Press (*Ire*)
Frances Lincoln Ltd (*UK*)
Luath Press Ltd (*UK*)
The Lyons Press Inc. (*US*)
Macmillan (*UK*)
Maverick Reads (*UK*)
Merlin Unwin Books (*UK*)
Museum of Northern Arizona (*US*)

National Museum Wales (*UK*)
Natural History Museum Publishing (*UK*)
Neil Wilson Publishing Ltd (*UK*)
New Holland Publishers (UK) Ltd (*UK*)
The O'Brien Press (*Ire*)
Oneworld Publications (*UK*)
Pluto Publishing Ltd (*UK*)
Polity Press (*UK*)
Princeton University Press Europe (*UK*)
Reaktion Books (*UK*)
Robert Hale Publishers (*UK*)
Roundhouse Group (*UK*)
The Salariya Book Company (*UK*)
Sierra Club Books (*US*)
Souvenir Press Ltd (*UK*)
Storey Publishing (*US*)
Sunscribe (*US*)
Tsaba House (*US*)
University College Dublin (UCD) Press (*Ire*)
University of South Carolina Press (*US*)
Utah State University Press (*US*)
Vanderbilt University Press (*US*)
Voyageur Press (*US*)
W.W. Norton & Company Ltd (*UK*)
Wannabee Books (*US*)
Waveland Press, Inc. (*US*)
Yale University Press (*US*)
New Age
Anness Publishing Ltd (*UK*)
Barron's Educational Series, Inc. (*US*)
Chelsea Green Publishing, Inc. (*US*)
Connections Book Publishing Ltd (*UK*)
Ex-L-Ence Publishing (*UK*)
Geostar Publishing & Services LLC (*US*)
Maverick Reads (*UK*)
Sunscribe (*US*)
SynergEbooks (*US*)
Turn the Page Publishing LLC (*US*)
Twilight Times Books (*US*)
Zambezi Publishing Ltd (*UK*)
Nonfiction
A Swift Exit (*UK*)
AA Publishing (*UK*)
Abrams ComicArts (*US*)
ACTA Publications (*US*)
Akasha Publishing Ltd (*UK*)
J.A. Allen (*UK*)
Alma Books Ltd (*UK*)
Alondra Press (*US*)
Alpine Publications, Inc. (*US*)
Amadeus Press (*US*)
Amakella Publishing (*US*)
American Counseling Association (*US*)
American Press (*US*)
American Quilter's Society (*US*)
AMG Publishers (*US*)
Ankerwycke (*US*)
Anness Publishing Ltd (*UK*)
Annick Press (*Can*)
Appletree Press Ltd (*UK*)
Arbordale Publishing (*US*)
Arcade Publishing (*US*)
Arch Street Press (*US*)

Persea Books (*US*)
Persephone Books (*UK*)
Pflaum Publishing Group (*US*)
Phaidon Press Limited (*UK*)
Phoenix Yard Books (*UK*)
Piano Press (*US*)
Picador USA (*US*)
Piccadilly Press (*UK*)
Picton Press (*US*)
Pluto Publishing Ltd (*UK*)
The Policy Press (*UK*)
Polity Press (*UK*)
Poolbeg (*Ire*)
Possibility Press (*US*)
Presa Press (*US*)
Princeton University Press Europe (*UK*)
Professional and Higher Partnership (*UK*)
Professional Publications, Inc. (PPI) (*US*)
Prometheus Books (*US*)
Psychology Press (*UK*)
Pure Indigo Limited (*UK*)
Pushkin Press (*UK*)
Quadrille Publishing Ltd (*UK*)
Quarto Publishing Group UK (*UK*)
Quarto Publishing Group USA (*US*)
Quill Driver Books (*US*)
Radcliffe Publishing Ltd (*UK*)
Rainbow Publishers (*US*)
Ransom Publishing Ltd (*UK*)
Reader's Digest Association Ltd (*UK*)
Reading Harbor (*US*)
Reaktion Books (*UK*)
Red Deer Press (*Can*)
Red Rattle Books (*UK*)
Redleaf Press (*US*)
Reference Service Press (*US*)
Richard Dennis Publications (*UK*)
Robert Hale Publishers (*UK*)
Ronsdale Press (*Can*)
The Rosen Publishing Group, Inc. (*US*)
RotoVision (*UK*)
Round Hall (*Ire*)
Roundhouse Group (*UK*)
Running Press (*US*)
Saffron Books (*UK*)
Sakura Publishing & Technologies (*US*)
The Salariya Book Company (*UK*)
Sandstone Press Ltd (*UK*)
Scala Arts & Heritage Publishers (*UK*)
Scarecrow Press Inc. (*US*)
School Guide Publications (*US*)
Scripture Union (*UK*)
Seren Books (*UK*)
Shearsman Books (*UK*)
Shire Publications Ltd (*UK*)
Short Books (*UK*)
Sierra Club Books (*US*)
Sigma Press (*UK*)
Singing Dragon (*UK*)
Society for Promoting Christian Knowledge (SPCK) (*UK*)
Soft Skull Press (*US*)
Somerville Press (*Ire*)

Souvenir Press Ltd (*UK*)
St David's Press (*UK*)
St. Johann Press (*US*)
Stainer & Bell Ltd (*UK*)
Standard Publishing (*US*)
STC Craft (*US*)
Stenlake Publishing (*UK*)
Stone Bridge Press (*US*)
Storey Publishing (*US*)
Strategic Media Books (*US*)
Sunscribe (*US*)
Swan Isle Press (*US*)
Swedenborg Foundation (*US*)
Sweet & Maxwell (*UK*)
SynergEbooks (*US*)
Tarquin (*UK*)
Tate Publishing and Enterprises, LLC (*US*)
Teachers College Press (*US*)
The Templar Company Limited (*UK*)
Top That! Publishing (*UK*)
Tower Publishing (*US*)
Trentham Books Limited (*UK*)
Triumph Books (*US*)
Tsaba House (*US*)
Turn the Page Publishing LLC (*US*)
Turnstone Press (*Can*)
Ulverscroft Large Print Books Ltd (*UK*)
University College Dublin (UCD) Press (*Ire*)
University of Alabama Press (*US*)
University of Chicago Press (*US*)
University of South Carolina Press (*US*)
University of Tampa Press (*US*)
Unthank Books (*UK*)
Urban Ministries, Inc. (*US*)
Utah State University Press (*US*)
Vallentine Mitchell & Co., Limited (*UK*)
Vanderbilt University Press (*US*)
Veritas Publications (*US*)
Vernon Press (an imprint of Vernon Art and Science Inc.) (*US*)
Verso (*US*)
Virago Press (*UK*)
Virtue Books (*UK*)
Voyageur Press (*US*)
W.W. Norton & Company Ltd (*UK*)
Wannabee Books (*US*)
Waveland Press, Inc. (*US*)
Waverley Books (*UK*)
Welsh Academic Press (*UK*)
Wesleyan Publishing House (*US*)
Western Psychological Services (*US*)
Westminster John Knox Press (WJK) (*US*)
Whitaker House (*US*)
John Wiley & Sons, Inc. (*US*)
William S. Hein & Co., Inc. (*US*)
Williamson Books (*US*)
Wilshire Book Company (*US*)
Philip Wilson Publishers Ltd (*UK*)
Wolters Kluwer (UK) Ltd (*UK*)
World Book, Inc. (*US*)
Yale University Press (*US*)
Yale University Press (London) (*UK*)
Zambezi Publishing Ltd (*UK*)

Zenith Press (*US*)
Philosophy
  Alondra Press (*US*)
  American Press (*US*)
  Arch Street Press (*US*)
  Bick Publishing House (*US*)
  Bucknell University Press (*US*)
  The Catholic University of America Press (*US*)
  CATO Institute (*US*)
  Connections Book Publishing Ltd (*UK*)
  Crescent Moon Publishing (*UK*)
  Duquesne University Press (*US*)
  William B. Eerdmans Publishing Co. (*US*)
  Ex-L-Ence Publishing (*UK*)
  Fitzrovia Press Limited (*UK*)
  Floris Books (*UK*)
  Fordham University Press (*US*)
  Geostar Publishing & Services LLC (*US*)
  Gibson Square Books Ltd (*UK*)
  Gingko Library (*UK*)
  Gival Press, LLC (*US*)
  Halban Publishers (*UK*)
  Hay House Publishers (*UK*)
  Head of Zeus (*UK*)
  IBEX Publishers, Inc. (*US*)
  Icon Books Ltd (*UK*)
  Imprint Academic (*UK*)
  The Lilliput Press (*Ire*)
  Macmillan (*UK*)
  Mandrake of Oxford (*UK*)
  Marion Boyars Publishers (*UK*)
  Maverick Reads (*UK*)
  The Merlin Press (*UK*)
  Methodist Publishing (*UK*)
  Oneworld Publications (*UK*)
  Paragon House (*US*)
  Paul Dry Books, Inc. (*US*)
  Pen Books (*US*)
  Polity Press (*UK*)
  Princeton University Press Europe (*UK*)
  Prometheus Books (*US*)
  Reading Harbor (*US*)
  Reaktion Books (*UK*)
  Scarecrow Press Inc. (*US*)
  Soft Skull Press (*US*)
  Souvenir Press Ltd (*UK*)
  Sunscribe (*US*)
  Swedenborg Foundation (*US*)
  Tate Publishing and Enterprises, LLC (*US*)
  Teachers College Press (*US*)
  University of Chicago Press (*US*)
  Vallentine Mitchell & Co., Limited (*UK*)
  Vanderbilt University Press (*US*)
  Vernon Press (an imprint of Vernon Art and
    Science Inc.) (*US*)
  Verso (*US*)
  W.W. Norton & Company Ltd (*UK*)
  Waveland Press, Inc. (*US*)
  Yale University Press (*US*)
  Yale University Press (London) (*UK*)
Photography
  Anness Publishing Ltd (*UK*)
  Barron's Educational Series, Inc. (*US*)

Cave Books (*US*)
David R. Godine, Publisher (*US*)
Enitharmon Press (*UK*)
Ex-L-Ence Publishing (*UK*)
Fleming Publications (*UK*)
Fordham University Press (*US*)
Geostar Publishing & Services LLC (*US*)
Guild of Master Craftsman (GMC) Publications
  Ltd (*UK*)
Halsgrove (*UK*)
Harry N. Abrams, Inc. (*US*)
Haus Publishing (*UK*)
The Ilex Press (*UK*)
Interlink Publishing Group, Inc. (*US*)
Jacaranda Books Art Music Ltd (*UK*)
The Lilliput Press (*Ire*)
Luath Press Ltd (*UK*)
Merrell Publishers Limited (*UK*)
New Holland Publishers (UK) Ltd (*UK*)
The O'Brien Press (*Ire*)
Phaidon Press Limited (*UK*)
Princeton University Press Europe (*UK*)
Reaktion Books (*UK*)
RotoVision (*UK*)
Roundhouse Group (*UK*)
Seren Books (*UK*)
Shire Publications Ltd (*UK*)
Sunscribe (*US*)
Voyageur Press (*US*)
Wannabee Books (*US*)
Poetry
  A Swift Exit (*UK*)
  Ahsahta Press (*US*)
  Alma Classics (*UK*)
  Arc Publications (*UK*)
  Arrowhead Press (*UK*)
  The Backwater Press (*US*)
  Bilingual Review Press (*US*)
  Black Ocean (*US*)
  BlazeVOX [books] (*US*)
  Blue Light Press (*US*)
  Boyds Mills Press (*US*)
  Bronze Man Books (*US*)
  Capstone (*US*)
  Chapman Publishing (*UK*)
  Cinco Puntos Press (*US*)
  Cleveland State University Poetry Center (*US*)
  Creative With Words (CWW) (*US*)
  Crescent Moon Publishing (*UK*)
  Crystal Spirit Publishing, Inc. (*US*)
  David R. Godine, Publisher (*US*)
  Divertir Publishing LLC (*US*)
  Dufour Editions (*US*)
  ECW Press (*Can*)
  Eland Publishing Ltd (*UK*)
  The Emma Press Ltd (*UK*)
  Enitharmon Press (*UK*)
  Ex-L-Ence Publishing (*UK*)
  Faber & Faber Ltd (*UK*)
  Farrar, Straus & Giroux, Inc. (*US*)
  Fleming Publications (*UK*)
  Floating Bridge Press (*US*)
  Folded Word LLC (*US*)

Frances Lincoln Children's Books (*UK*)
FutureCycle Press (*US*)
The Gallery Press (*Ire*)
GEY Books (*UK*)
Gival Press, LLC (*US*)
Gomer Press (*UK*)
Grayson Books (*US*)
Green Bottle Press (*UK*)
Headland Publications (*UK*)
Helicon Nine Editions (*US*)
Hesperus Press Limited (*UK*)
Heyday Books (*US*)
Hippopotamus Press (*UK*)
Honno Welsh Women's Press (*UK*)
IBEX Publishers, Inc. (*US*)
Indigo Dreams Publishing (*UK*)
Influx Press (*UK*)
Iron Press (*UK*)
Kind of a Hurricane Press (*US*)
Kube Publishing (*UK*)
Liberties Press (*Ire*)
The Lilliput Press (*Ire*)
Frances Lincoln Ltd (*UK*)
Lost Tower Publications (*UK*)
Luath Press Ltd (*UK*)
Macmillan (*UK*)
Maverick Reads (*UK*)
Mudfog Press (*UK*)
Neon (*UK*)
New Island (*Ire*)
Oversteps Books (*UK*)
Parthian Books (*UK*)
Paul Dry Books, Inc. (*US*)
Pedlar Press (*Can*)
Persea Books (*US*)
Phoenix Yard Books (*UK*)
Piano Press (*US*)
Plan B Press (*US*)
Presa Press (*US*)
Press 53 (*US*)
Ragged Sky Press (*US*)
Reality Street Editions (*UK*)
Ronsdale Press (*Can*)
Route Publishing (*UK*)
Sakura Publishing & Technologies (*US*)
Saturnalia Books (*US*)
Seren Books (*UK*)
Shape & Nature Press (*US*)
Shearsman Books (*UK*)
Silverfish Review Press (*US*)
St. Johann Press (*US*)
Stairwell Books (*UK*)
Steel Toe Books (*US*)
Sunscribe (*US*)
Swan Isle Press (*US*)
Swan Scythe Press (*US*)
SynergEbooks (*US*)
Tarpaulin Sky Press (*US*)
Tate Publishing and Enterprises, LLC (*US*)
Tebot Bach (*US*)
Templar Poetry (*UK*)
Thistledown Press (*Can*)
Tia Chucha Press (*US*)

Turnstone Press (*Can*)
University of South Carolina Press (*US*)
University of Tampa Press (*US*)
W.W. Norton & Company Ltd (*UK*)
WordSong (*US*)
Yale University Press (*US*)
Politics
American Press (*US*)
AMG Publishers (*US*)
Arch Street Press (*US*)
Beacon Press (*US*)
BenBella Books (*US*)
John Blake Publishing (*UK*)
Bucknell University Press (*US*)
Canongate Books (*UK*)
The Catholic University of America Press (*US*)
CATO Institute (*US*)
Chelsea Green Publishing, Inc. (*US*)
Chicago Review Press (*US*)
CQ Press (*US*)
Crescent Moon Publishing (*UK*)
Divertir Publishing LLC (*US*)
ECW Press (*Can*)
Edward Elgar Publishing Ltd (*UK*)
Ex-L-Ence Publishing (*UK*)
Faber & Faber Ltd (*UK*)
Fabian Society (*UK*)
Fordham University Press (*US*)
Foreign Policy Association (*US*)
Geostar Publishing & Services LLC (*US*)
Gibson Square Books Ltd (*UK*)
Gingko Library (*UK*)
Granta Books (*UK*)
Halban Publishers (*UK*)
Haus Publishing (*UK*)
Hill and Wang (*US*)
IBEX Publishers, Inc. (*US*)
Icon Books Ltd (*UK*)
Imprint Academic (*UK*)
Institute of Public Administration (IPA) (*Ire*)
Interlink Publishing Group, Inc. (*US*)
Kube Publishing (*UK*)
Liberties Press (*Ire*)
The Lilliput Press (*Ire*)
Liverpool University Press (*UK*)
Luath Press Ltd (*UK*)
Macmillan (*UK*)
Mainstream Publishing Co. (Edinburgh) Ltd
(*UK*)
Manchester University Press (*UK*)
Mentor Books (*Ire*)
The Merlin Press (*UK*)
Mitchell Lane Publishers, Inc. (*US*)
Monarch Books (*UK*)
New Island (*Ire*)
New York University (NYU) Press (*US*)
The O'Brien Press (*Ire*)
Oneworld Publications (*UK*)
Paragon House (*US*)
Pen Books (*US*)
Pluto Publishing Ltd (*UK*)
The Policy Press (*UK*)
Polity Press (*UK*)

Princeton University Press Europe (*UK*)
Quarto Publishing Group USA (*US*)
Seren Books (*UK*)
Soft Skull Press (*US*)
Souvenir Press Ltd (*UK*)
Strategic Media Books (*US*)
Sunscribe (*US*)
Tate Publishing and Enterprises, LLC (*US*)
Teachers College Press (*US*)
University College Dublin (UCD) Press (*Ire*)
University of Alabama Press (*US*)
University of Chicago Press (*US*)
Vanderbilt University Press (*US*)
Vernon Press (an imprint of Vernon Art and
Science Inc.) (*US*)
Verso (*US*)
W.W. Norton & Company Ltd (*UK*)
Waveland Press, Inc. (*US*)
Welsh Academic Press (*UK*)
Yale University Press (*US*)
Yale University Press (London) (*UK*)

Psychology
Alondra Press (*US*)
Amakella Publishing (*US*)
American Press (*US*)
Bick Publishing House (*US*)
Bucknell University Press (*US*)
Connections Book Publishing Ltd (*UK*)
Duquesne University Press (*US*)
Ex-L-Ence Publishing (*UK*)
Geostar Publishing & Services LLC (*US*)
Gibson Square Books Ltd (*UK*)
Hay House Publishers (*UK*)
Icon Books Ltd (*UK*)
Impact Publishers (*US*)
Imprint Academic (*UK*)
Macmillan (*UK*)
Marion Boyars Publishers (*UK*)
Maverick Reads (*UK*)
Monarch Books (*UK*)
New York University (NYU) Press (*US*)
Octopus Publishing Group Limited (*UK*)
Oneworld Publications (*UK*)
Paragon House (*US*)
Pen Books (*US*)
Polity Press (*UK*)
Possibility Press (*US*)
Psychology Press (*UK*)
Reading Harbor (*US*)
Society for Promoting Christian Knowledge
(SPCK) (*UK*)
Souvenir Press Ltd (*UK*)
Sunscribe (*US*)
Swedenborg Foundation (*US*)
Tsaba House (*US*)
University of Chicago Press (*US*)
Veritas Publications (*US*)
Vernon Press (an imprint of Vernon Art and
Science Inc.) (*US*)
W.W. Norton & Company Ltd (*UK*)
Wannabee Books (*US*)
Waveland Press, Inc. (*US*)
Western Psychological Services (*US*)

John Wiley & Sons, Inc. (*US*)
Wilshire Book Company (*US*)
Yale University Press (*US*)
Radio
Geostar Publishing & Services LLC (*US*)
Sunscribe (*US*)
Reference
AA Publishing (*UK*)
AMG Publishers (*US*)
Anness Publishing Ltd (*UK*)
Berlitz Publishing (*UK*)
Bloomsbury Publishing Plc (*UK*)
Bowker (UK) Ltd (*UK*)
Carlton Publishing Group (*UK*)
Carswell (*Can*)
Centerstream Publishing (*US*)
Churchwarden Publications Ltd (*UK*)
CJ Fallon (*Ire*)
Connections Book Publishing Ltd (*UK*)
Covenant Communications Inc. (*US*)
CQ Press (*US*)
William B. Eerdmans Publishing Co. (*US*)
Euromonitor (*UK*)
Ex-L-Ence Publishing (*UK*)
Facts on File, Inc. (*US*)
Ferguson Publishing (*US*)
Flyleaf Press (*Ire*)
Geostar Publishing & Services LLC (*US*)
Gill & Macmillan (*Ire*)
Gomer Press (*UK*)
Goss & Crested China Club (*UK*)
Grub Street Publishing (*UK*)
Guild of Master Craftsman (GMC) Publications
Ltd (*UK*)
Gun Digest Books (*US*)
HarperCollins Publishers Ltd (*UK*)
Harry N. Abrams, Inc. (*US*)
Haynes Publishing (*UK*)
Hesperus Press Limited (*UK*)
Hodder Education (*UK*)
Hymns Ancient & Modern Ltd (*UK*)
IBEX Publishers, Inc. (*US*)
Igloo Books Limited (*UK*)
The Ilex Press (*UK*)
Interlink Publishing Group, Inc. (*US*)
JIST Publishing (*US*)
Kirkbride Bible Company (*US*)
Kyle Books (*UK*)
LexisNexis (*US*)
The Lilliput Press (*Ire*)
Lion Hudson Plc (*UK*)
Lonely Planet Publications (*US*)
The Lyons Press Inc. (*US*)
Macmillan (*UK*)
Manchester University Press (*UK*)
Maverick Reads (*UK*)
McFarland & Company, Inc. (*US*)
Michelin Maps and Guides (*UK*)
Neil Wilson Publishing Ltd (*UK*)
New Cavendish Books (*UK*)
New Holland Publishers (UK) Ltd (*UK*)
Nolo (*US*)
The O'Brien Press (*Ire*)

Octopus Publishing Group Limited (*UK*)
Paragon House (*US*)
Pavilion Publishing (*UK*)
Picton Press (*US*)
Polity Press (*UK*)
Princeton University Press Europe (*UK*)
Professional Publications, Inc. (PPI) (*US*)
Quarto Publishing Group USA (*US*)
Reference Service Press (*US*)
Robert Hale Publishers (*UK*)
Round Hall (*Ire*)
Roundhouse Group (*UK*)
Scarecrow Press Inc. (*US*)
School Guide Publications (*US*)
St David's Press (*UK*)
Stone Bridge Press (*US*)
Sunscribe (*US*)
Sweet & Maxwell (*UK*)
SynergEbooks (*US*)
Top That! Publishing (*UK*)
Tower Publishing (*US*)
University of Chicago Press (*US*)
Vernon Press (an imprint of Vernon Art and
Science Inc.) (*US*)
Western Psychological Services (*US*)
John Wiley & Sons, Inc. (*US*)
William S. Hein & Co., Inc. (*US*)
Wolters Kluwer (UK) Ltd (*UK*)
World Book, Inc. (*US*)
Yale University Press (London) (*UK*)

Religious
ACTA Publications (*US*)
American Press (*US*)
AMG Publishers (*US*)
Authentic Media (*UK*)
Baker Publishing Group (*US*)
Beacon Press (*US*)
Bethany House Publishers (*US*)
Boydell & Brewer Ltd (*UK*)
Bryntirion Press (*UK*)
Bucknell University Press (*US*)
The Catholic University of America Press (*US*)
Christian Education (*UK*)
Church Publishing Incorporated (*US*)
Churchwarden Publications Ltd (*UK*)
CJ Fallon (*Ire*)
Columba Press (*Ire*)
Concordia Publishing House (*US*)
Connections Book Publishing Ltd (*UK*)
Covenant Communications Inc. (*US*)
Crystal Spirit Publishing, Inc. (*US*)
CTS (Catholic Truth Society) (*UK*)
Divertir Publishing LLC (*US*)
Duquesne University Press (*US*)
ECW Press (*Can*)
William B. Eerdmans Publishing Co. (*US*)
Ex-L-Ence Publishing (*UK*)
Floris Books (*UK*)
Fordham University Press (*US*)
Geostar Publishing & Services LLC (*US*)
Gingko Library (*UK*)
Gomer Press (*UK*)
Hachai Publishing (*US*)

Halban Publishers (*UK*)
Harry N. Abrams, Inc. (*US*)
Harvest House Publishers (*US*)
Hay House Publishers (*UK*)
Hymns Ancient & Modern Ltd (*UK*)
IBEX Publishers, Inc. (*US*)
Icon Books Ltd (*UK*)
Kirkbride Bible Company (*US*)
Kube Publishing (*UK*)
Lion Hudson Plc (*UK*)
Maverick Reads (*UK*)
Methodist Publishing (*UK*)
Monarch Books (*UK*)
New York University (NYU) Press (*US*)
The O'Brien Press (*Ire*)
Oneworld Publications (*UK*)
Paragon House (*US*)
Pauline Books and Media (*US*)
Pflaum Publishing Group (*US*)
Polity Press (*UK*)
Possibility Press (*US*)
Princeton University Press Europe (*UK*)
Rainbow Publishers (*US*)
Reference Service Press (*US*)
Rose and Crown Books (*UK*)
The Rosen Publishing Group, Inc. (*US*)
Scarecrow Press Inc. (*US*)
Scripture Union (*UK*)
Society for Promoting Christian Knowledge
(SPCK) (*UK*)
Soft Skull Press (*US*)
Souvenir Press Ltd (*UK*)
St. Johann Press (*US*)
Stainer & Bell Ltd (*UK*)
Standard Publishing (*US*)
Sunscribe (*US*)
Swedenborg Foundation (*US*)
SynergEbooks (*US*)
Tate Publishing and Enterprises, LLC (*US*)
Tsaba House (*US*)
University of Alabama Press (*US*)
University of Chicago Press (*US*)
University of South Carolina Press (*US*)
Urban Ministries, Inc. (*US*)
Vallentine Mitchell & Co., Limited (*UK*)
Veritas Publications (*US*)
W.W. Norton & Company Ltd (*UK*)
Waveland Press, Inc. (*US*)
Wesleyan Publishing House (*US*)
Westminster John Knox Press (WJK) (*US*)
Whitaker House (*US*)
John Wiley & Sons, Inc. (*US*)
Yale University Press (*US*)
Yale University Press (London) (*UK*)

Romance
Amakella Publishing (*US*)
American Quilter's Society (*US*)
Amira Press (*US*)
Arrow Publications, LLC (*US*)
BelleBooks (*US*)
Bethany House Publishers (*US*)
Black Lyon Publishing, LLC (*US*)
Bold Strokes Books (*US*)

Fingerpress UK (*UK*)
Galley Beggar Press (*UK*)
Geostar Publishing & Services LLC (*US*)
Ghostwoods Books (*UK*)
Harken Media (*US*)
Harmony Ink Press (*US*)
HarperCollins Publishers Ltd (*UK*)
Head of Zeus (*UK*)
Hesperus Press Limited (*UK*)
Liverpool University Press (*UK*)
Lost Tower Publications (*UK*)
Luna Press Publishing (*UK*)
M P Publishing USA (*US*)
Macmillan (*UK*)
Mandrake of Oxford (*UK*)
Maverick Reads (*UK*)
Pen Books (*US*)
Pure Indigo Limited (*UK*)
Red Deer Press (*Can*)
Severn House Publishers (*UK*)
Sidestreet Cookie Publishing (*US*)
Small Beer Press (*US*)
Sunscribe (*US*)
SynergEbooks (*US*)
Tate Publishing and Enterprises, LLC (*US*)
Top Cow Productions, Inc (*US*)
Tu Books (*US*)
Twilight Times Books (*US*)
Scripts
Alma Classics (*UK*)
Bilingual Review Press (*US*)
Bronze Man Books (*US*)
Chapman Publishing (*UK*)
Cressrelles Publishing Co. Ltd (*UK*)
Faber & Faber Ltd (*UK*)
The Gallery Press (*Ire*)
Gomer Press (*UK*)
Josef Weinberger Ltd (*UK*)
The Lilliput Press (*Ire*)
New Island (*Ire*)
New Playwrights' Network (NPN) (*UK*)
Nick Hern Books Ltd (*UK*)
Oberon Books (*UK*)
Parthian Books (*UK*)
Samuel French Ltd (*UK*)
Sunscribe (*US*)
Self-Help
ACTA Publications (*US*)
Amakella Publishing (*US*)
BenBella Books (*US*)
Bick Publishing House (*US*)
Black Lyon Publishing, LLC (*US*)
John Blake Publishing (*UK*)
Conari Press (*US*)
Connections Book Publishing Ltd (*UK*)
Crystal Spirit Publishing, Inc. (*US*)
Divertir Publishing LLC (*US*)
Ex-L-Ence Publishing (*UK*)
Familius (*US*)
Ferguson Publishing (*US*)
Filbert Publishing (*US*)
Fleming Publications (*UK*)
Floris Books (*UK*)

Free Spirit Publishing (*US*)
Geostar Publishing & Services LLC (*US*)
Hawthorn Press (*UK*)
Hay House Publishers (*UK*)
Hipso Media (*US*)
Hodder Education (*UK*)
Impact Publishers (*US*)
JIST Publishing (*US*)
Management Books 2000 Ltd (*UK*)
Mandrake of Oxford (*UK*)
Maverick Reads (*UK*)
New Holland Publishers (UK) Ltd (*UK*)
Nolo (*US*)
Oneworld Publications (*UK*)
Pauline Books and Media (*US*)
Possibility Press (*US*)
Princeton University Press Europe (*UK*)
Quarto Publishing Group USA (*US*)
Quill Driver Books (*US*)
Reading Harbor (*US*)
The Rosen Publishing Group, Inc. (*US*)
Roundhouse Group (*UK*)
Running Press (*US*)
Singing Dragon (*UK*)
Society for Promoting Christian Knowledge
(SPCK) (*UK*)
Souvenir Press Ltd (*UK*)
Sunscribe (*US*)
SynergEbooks (*US*)
Tate Publishing and Enterprises, LLC (*US*)
Tsaba House (*US*)
Veritas Publications (*US*)
W.W. Norton & Company Ltd (*UK*)
Whitaker House (*US*)
Wilshire Book Company (*US*)
Zambezi Publishing Ltd (*UK*)
Short Stories
A Swift Exit (*UK*)
Amakella Publishing (*US*)
BelleBooks (*US*)
Bilingual Review Press (*US*)
BlazeVOX [books] (*US*)
Bronze Man Books (*US*)
Carina UK (*UK*)
Chapman Publishing (*UK*)
Children's Brains are Yummy (CBAY) Books
(*US*)
Chipping Norton Publishers (*UK*)
Creative With Words (CWW) (*US*)
Crystal Spirit Publishing, Inc. (*US*)
Darkhouse Books (*US*)
Divertir Publishing LLC (*US*)
Dufour Editions (*US*)
Ex-L-Ence Publishing (*UK*)
Galley Beggar Press (*UK*)
Geostar Publishing & Services LLC (*US*)
GEY Books (*UK*)
Ghostwoods Books (*UK*)
HarperImpulse (*UK*)
Head of Zeus (*UK*)
Headland Publications (*UK*)
Hearts 'N Tummies Cookbook Co. / Quixote
Press (*US*)

Helicon Nine Editions (*US*)
Hipso Media (*US*)
Honno Welsh Women's Press (*UK*)
Influx Press (*UK*)
Iron Press (*UK*)
Kind of a Hurricane Press (*US*)
Luna Press Publishing (*UK*)
M P Publishing USA (*US*)
Maverick Reads (*UK*)
Mudfog Press (*UK*)
Neon (*UK*)
New Island (*Ire*)
Ouen Press (*UK*)
Parthian Books (*UK*)
Paul Dry Books, Inc. (*US*)
Persea Books (*US*)
Press 53 (*US*)
Reading Harbor (*US*)
Roberts Press (*US*)
Ronsdale Press (*Can*)
Route Publishing (*UK*)
Shape & Nature Press (*US*)
Small Beer Press (*US*)
St. Johann Press (*US*)
Stairwell Books (*UK*)
Sunscribe (*US*)
Tate Publishing and Enterprises, LLC (*US*)
Thistledown Press (*Can*)
Torquere Press (*US*)
Turnstone Press (*Can*)
Sociology
Alma Classics (*UK*)
Amakella Publishing (*US*)
American Press (*US*)
Arch Street Press (*US*)
Atlantic Europe Publishing (*UK*)
Beacon Press (*US*)
BenBella Books (*US*)
Bucknell University Press (*US*)
The Catholic University of America Press (*US*)
CATO Institute (*US*)
Continental (*US*)
Duquesne University Press (*US*)
Edward Elgar Publishing Inc. (*US*)
Edward Elgar Publishing Ltd (*UK*)
Ex-L-Ence Publishing (*UK*)
Fabian Society (*UK*)
Floris Books (*UK*)
Fonthill Media LLC (*US*)
Fonthill Media Ltd (*UK*)
Fordham University Press (*US*)
Free Spirit Publishing (*US*)
Geostar Publishing & Services LLC (*US*)
Gival Press, LLC (*US*)
Granta Books (*UK*)
Hay House Publishers (*UK*)
Head of Zeus (*UK*)
Hill and Wang (*US*)
Institute of Public Administration (IPA) (*Ire*)
Kube Publishing (*UK*)
The Lilliput Press (*Ire*)
Liverpool University Press (*UK*)
Logaston Press (*UK*)

Luath Press Ltd (*UK*)
Marion Boyars Publishers (*UK*)
National Museum Wales (*UK*)
New Island (*Ire*)
New York University (NYU) Press (*US*)
Pavilion Publishing (*UK*)
Pen Books (*US*)
Pluto Publishing Ltd (*UK*)
The Policy Press (*UK*)
Polity Press (*UK*)
Princeton University Press Europe (*UK*)
Prometheus Books (*US*)
Reference Service Press (*US*)
The Rosen Publishing Group, Inc. (*US*)
Saffron Books (*UK*)
Shire Publications Ltd (*UK*)
Society for Promoting Christian Knowledge
(SPCK) (*UK*)
Soft Skull Press (*US*)
Souvenir Press Ltd (*UK*)
Sunscribe (*US*)
Teachers College Press (*US*)
Trentham Books Limited (*UK*)
University College Dublin (UCD) Press (*Ire*)
University of Chicago Press (*US*)
Veritas Publications (*US*)
Vernon Press (an imprint of Vernon Art and
Science Inc.) (*US*)
Verso (*US*)
W.W. Norton & Company Ltd (*UK*)
Waveland Press, Inc. (*US*)
Western Psychological Services (*US*)
John Wiley & Sons, Inc. (*US*)
World Book, Inc. (*US*)
Yale University Press (London) (*UK*)
Zenith Press (*US*)
Spiritual
ACTA Publications (*US*)
Akasha Publishing Ltd (*UK*)
Amakella Publishing (*US*)
AMG Publishers (*US*)
Anness Publishing Ltd (*UK*)
Arch Street Press (*US*)
Authentic Media (*UK*)
Chelsea Green Publishing, Inc. (*US*)
Columba Press (*Ire*)
Conari Press (*US*)
Concordia Publishing House (*US*)
Connections Book Publishing Ltd (*UK*)
Covenant Communications Inc. (*US*)
Divertir Publishing LLC (*US*)
Duquesne University Press (*US*)
William B. Eerdmans Publishing Co. (*US*)
Ex-L-Ence Publishing (*UK*)
Fitzrovia Press Limited (*UK*)
Floris Books (*UK*)
Geostar Publishing & Services LLC (*US*)
Hay House Publishers (*UK*)
Hymns Ancient & Modern Ltd (*UK*)
Kube Publishing (*UK*)
Lion Hudson Plc (*UK*)
Lost Tower Publications (*UK*)
Mandrake of Oxford (*UK*)

Twilight Times Books (*US*)
Technology
American Press (*US*)
ASCE Press (*US*)
Astragal Press (*US*)
Atlantic Europe Publishing (*UK*)
Bernard Babani (publishing) Ltd (*UK*)
CJ Fallon (*Ire*)
Continental (*US*)
Ex-L-Ence Publishing (*UK*)
Finney Company (*US*)
Frontinus (*UK*)
Geostar Publishing & Services LLC (*US*)
Gingko Library (*UK*)
Gun Digest Books (*US*)
Haynes Publishing (*UK*)
HOW Books (*US*)
Metal Powder Industries Federation (MPIF) (*US*)
Mitchell Lane Publishers, Inc. (*US*)
Pen Books (*US*)
Possibility Press (*US*)
Quarto Publishing Group USA (*US*)
Quill Driver Books (*US*)
Shire Publications Ltd (*UK*)
Sunscribe (*US*)
Teachers College Press (*US*)
University of Alabama Press (*US*)
University of Chicago Press (*US*)
Vernon Press (an imprint of Vernon Art and Science Inc.) (*US*)
W.W. Norton & Company Ltd (*UK*)
Wannabee Books (*US*)
Waveland Press, Inc. (*US*)
John Wiley & Sons, Inc. (*US*)
Yale University Press (London) (*UK*)
Zenith Press (*US*)
Theatre
American Press (*US*)
Ex-L-Ence Publishing (*UK*)
Faber & Faber Ltd (*UK*)
The Gallery Press (*Ire*)
Geostar Publishing & Services LLC (*US*)
Gomer Press (*UK*)
Haus Publishing (*UK*)
Josef Weinberger Ltd (*UK*)
Macmillan (*UK*)
Manchester University Press (*UK*)
Marion Boyars Publishers (*UK*)
Maverick Reads (*UK*)
New Playwrights' Network (NPN) (*UK*)
Nick Hern Books Ltd (*UK*)
Oberon Books (*UK*)
Pen Books (*US*)
Ronsdale Press (*Can*)
Scarecrow Press Inc. (*US*)
Shire Publications Ltd (*UK*)
Souvenir Press Ltd (*UK*)
Sunscribe (*US*)
Teachers College Press (*US*)
University of Alabama Press (*US*)
Waveland Press, Inc. (*US*)

Thrillers
BelleBooks (*US*)
Carina UK (*UK*)
Chipping Norton Publishers (*UK*)
Corazon Books (*UK*)
Curiosity Quills Press (*US*)
Curious Fox (*UK*)
Entangled Teen (*US*)
Ex-L-Ence Publishing (*UK*)
Fingerpress UK (*UK*)
Geostar Publishing & Services LLC (*US*)
GEY Books (*UK*)
Ghostwoods Books (*UK*)
HarperCollins Publishers Ltd (*UK*)
Head of Zeus (*UK*)
Hesperus Press Limited (*UK*)
Limitless Publishing (*US*)
Lost Tower Publications (*UK*)
Luath Press Ltd (*UK*)
M P Publishing USA (*US*)
Macmillan (*UK*)
Maverick Reads (*UK*)
Pen Books (*US*)
Salt Publishing Ltd (*UK*)
Sandstone Press Ltd (*UK*)
Severn House Publishers (*UK*)
Sidestreet Cookie Publishing (*US*)
Soft Skull Press (*US*)
Sunscribe (*US*)
SynergEbooks (*US*)
Tate Publishing and Enterprises, LLC (*US*)
Tsaba House (*US*)
Turnstone Press (*Can*)
Translations
Alma Classics (*UK*)
Alondra Press (*US*)
Arc Publications (*UK*)
Arch Street Press (*US*)
Bilingual Review Press (*US*)
Black Ocean (*US*)
Canongate Books (*UK*)
David R. Godine, Publisher (*US*)
Dedalus Ltd (*UK*)
Dufour Editions (*US*)
Folded Word LLC (*US*)
Geostar Publishing & Services LLC (*US*)
Gival Press, LLC (*US*)
Hesperus Press Limited (*UK*)
IBEX Publishers, Inc. (*US*)
Interlink Publishing Group, Inc. (*US*)
Peter Owen Publishers (*UK*)
Parthian Books (*UK*)
Paul Dry Books, Inc. (*US*)
Pen Books (*US*)
Persea Books (*US*)
Red Empress Publishing (*US*)
Seren Books (*UK*)
Shearsman Books (*UK*)
Stone Bridge Press (*US*)
Sunscribe (*US*)
Swan Isle Press (*US*)
Swan Scythe Press (*US*)
University of Chicago Press (*US*)

Yale University Press (London) (*UK*)
Travel
  AA Publishing (*UK*)
  Amakella Publishing (*US*)
  Amira Press (*US*)
  Anness Publishing Ltd (*UK*)
  Arcade Publishing (*US*)
  The Armchair Traveller at the bookHaus (*UK*)
  Barron's Educational Series, Inc. (*US*)
  Bennion Kearny (*UK*)
  Berlitz Publishing (*UK*)
  John Blake Publishing (*UK*)
  Blue Guides Limited (*UK*)
  Blue River Press (*US*)
  Canongate Books (*UK*)
  Cave Books (*US*)
  Chicago Review Press (*US*)
  Cyclotour Guide Books (*US*)
  Edward Elgar Publishing Inc. (*US*)
  Eland Publishing Ltd (*UK*)
  Enete Enterprises (*US*)
  Ex-L-Ence Publishing (*UK*)
  Eye Books (*UK*)
  FalconGuides (*US*)
  Finney Company (*US*)
  Fodor's Travel Publications (*US*)
  Folded Word LLC (*US*)
  Fonthill Media LLC (*US*)
  Fonthill Media Ltd (*UK*)
  Geostar Publishing & Services LLC (*US*)
  GEY Books (*UK*)
  Gibson Square Books Ltd (*UK*)
  Gomer Press (*UK*)
  Granta Books (*UK*)
  Haus Publishing (*UK*)
  Hesperus Press Limited (*UK*)
  Hipso Media (*US*)
  House of Lochar (*UK*)
  Interlink Publishing Group, Inc. (*US*)
  The Lilliput Press (*Ire*)
  Frances Lincoln Ltd (*UK*)
  Logaston Press (*UK*)
  Lonely Planet Publications (*US*)
  Luath Press Ltd (*UK*)
  Macmillan (*UK*)
  Michelin Maps and Guides (*UK*)
  Neil Wilson Publishing Ltd (*UK*)
  New Holland Publishers (UK) Ltd (*UK*)
  New Island (*Ire*)
  The O'Brien Press (*Ire*)
  Octopus Publishing Group Limited (*UK*)
  Onstream Publications Ltd (*Ire*)
  Ouen Press (*UK*)
  The Overmountain Press (*US*)
  Paul Dry Books, Inc. (*US*)
  Pen Books (*US*)
  Phaidon Press Limited (*UK*)
  Poolbeg (*Ire*)
  Quarto Publishing Group USA (*US*)
  Quill Driver Books (*US*)
  Reaktion Books (*UK*)
  Rose and Crown Books (*UK*)
  Roundhouse Group (*UK*)

  Seren Books (*UK*)
  Shire Publications Ltd (*UK*)
  Sierra Club Books (*US*)
  Sigma Press (*UK*)
  Soft Skull Press (*US*)
  Souvenir Press Ltd (*UK*)
  St David's Press (*UK*)
  Stenlake Publishing (*UK*)
  Stone Bridge Press (*US*)
  Sunscribe (*US*)
  SynergEbooks (*US*)
  University of Chicago Press (*US*)
  Voyageur Press (*US*)
  W.W. Norton & Company Ltd (*UK*)
  Zenith Press (*US*)
TV
  John Blake Publishing (*UK*)
  ECW Press (*Can*)
  Ex-L-Ence Publishing (*UK*)
  Geostar Publishing & Services LLC (*US*)
  Guild of Master Craftsman (GMC) Publications Ltd (*UK*)
  Headline Publishing Group (*UK*)
  Macmillan (*UK*)
  Manchester University Press (*UK*)
  Soft Skull Press (*US*)
  Sunscribe (*US*)
Westerns
  Amira Press (*US*)
  Carina UK (*UK*)
  Cricket Books (*US*)
  Ex-L-Ence Publishing (*UK*)
  Geostar Publishing & Services LLC (*US*)
  Harlequin American Romance (*US*)
  Harvest House Publishers (*US*)
  Robert Hale Publishers (*UK*)
  Sunscribe (*US*)
  SynergEbooks (*US*)
  Tate Publishing and Enterprises, LLC (*US*)
Women's Interests
  Amakella Publishing (*US*)
  Arch Street Press (*US*)
  Arrow Publications, LLC (*US*)
  Beacon Press (*US*)
  BelleBooks (*US*)
  Bethany House Publishers (*US*)
  Black Lyon Publishing, LLC (*US*)
  Carina UK (*UK*)
  Chicago Review Press (*US*)
  Conari Press (*US*)
  Connections Book Publishing Ltd (*UK*)
  Corazon Books (*UK*)
  Crescent Moon Publishing (*UK*)
  Cup of Tea Books (*US*)
  Curiosity Quills Press (*US*)
  ECW Press (*Can*)
  Ex-L-Ence Publishing (*UK*)
  Fordham University Press (*US*)
  Geostar Publishing & Services LLC (*US*)
  Ghostwoods Books (*UK*)
  Gibson Square Books Ltd (*UK*)
  Gival Press, LLC (*US*)
  Harvest House Publishers (*US*)

Get Free Access to the firstwriter.com Website

To claim your free access to the firstwriter.com website simply go to the website at https://www.firstwriter.com/subscribe and begin the subscription process as normal. On the second page, enter the required details (such as your name and address, etc.) then for "Voucher / coupon number" enter the following promotional code:

- **PF49-V2LB**

This will reduce the cost of creating a subscription by up to $15 / £10 / €15, making it free to create a monthly, quarterly, or combination subscription. Alternatively, you can use the discount to take out an annual or life subscription at a reduced rate.

Continue the process until your account is created. Please note that you will need to provide your payment details, even if there is no up-front payment. This is in case you choose to leave your subscription running after the free initial period, but there is no obligation for you to do so.

When you use this code to take out a free subscription you are under no obligation to make any payments whatsoever and you are free to cancel your account before you make any payments if you wish.

If you need any assistance, please email support@firstwriter.com.

If you have found this book useful, please consider leaving a review on the website where you bought it!

What you get

Once you have set up access to ths site you will be able to benefit from all the following features:

Databases

All our databases are updated almost every day, and include powerful search facilities to help you find exactly what you need. Searches that used to take you hours or even days in print books or on search engines can now be done in seconds, and produce more accurate and up-to-date information. Our agents database also includes independent reports from at least three separate sources, showing you which are the top agencies and helping you avoid the scams that are all over the internet. You can try out any of our databases before you subscribe:

- Search over **100 current competitions**
- Search **over 2,000 magazines**

- Search **over 650 literary agencies**
- Search **over 1,800 book publishers** that **don't** charge fees

PLUS advanced features to help you with your search:

- Save searches and save time – set up to 15 search parameters specific to your work, save them, and then access the search results with a single click whenever you log in. You can even save multiple different searches if you have different types of work you are looking to place.
- Add personal notes to listings, visible only to you and fully searchable – helping you to organise your actions.
- Set reminders on listings to notify you when to submit your work, when to follow up, when to expect a reply, or any other custom action.
- Track which listings you've viewed and when, to help you organise your search – any listings which have changed since you last viewed them will be highlighted for your attention!

Daily email updates

As a subscriber you will be able to take advantage of our email alert service, meaning you can specify your particular interests and we'll send you automatic email updates when we change or add a listing that matches them. So if you're interested in agents dealing in romantic fiction in the United States you can have us send you emails with the latest updates about them – keeping you up to date without even having to log in.

User feedback

Our agent, publisher, and magazine databases all include a user feedback feature that allows our subscribers to leave feedback on each listing – giving you not only the chance to have your say about the markets you contact, but giving a unique authors' perspective on the listings.

Save on copyright protection fees

If you're sending your work away to publishers, competitions, or literary agents, it's vital that you first protect your copyright. As a subscriber to firstwriter.com you can do this through our site and save 10% on the copyright registration fees normally payable for protecting your work internationally through the Intellectual Property Rights Office.

firstwriter.magazine

firstwriter.magazine showcases the best in new poetry and fiction from around the world. If you're interested in writing and want to get published, the most important thing you can do is read contemporary writing that's getting into print now. firstwriter.magazine helps you do that.

Half price competitions

As well as saving money on copyright registration, subscribers to firstwriter.com can also make further savings by entering writing competitions at a special reduced rate. Subscribers can enter the firstwriter.com International Poetry Competition and International Short Story Contest for half price.

Monthly newsletter

When you subscribe to firstwriter.com you also receive our monthly email newsletter – described by one publishing company as "the best in the business" – including articles, news, and interviews for writers. And the best part is that you can continue to receive the newsletter even after you stop your paid subscription – at no cost!

Terms and conditions

The promotional code contained in this publication may be used by the owner of the book only to create one subscription to firstwriter.com at a reduced cost, or for free. It may not be used by or disseminated to third parties. Should the code be misused then the owner of the book will be liable for any costs incurred, including but not limited to payment in full at the standard rate for the subscription in question. The code may be used at any time until the end of the calendar year named in the title of the publication, after which time it will become invalid. The code may be redeemed against the creation of a new account only – it cannot be redeemed against the ongoing costs of keeping a subscription open. In order to create a subscription a method of payment must be provided, but there is no obligation to make any payment. Subscriptions may be cancelled at any time, and if an account is cancelled before any payment becomes due then no payment will be made. Once a subscription has been created, the normal schedule of payments will begin on a monthly, quarterly, or annual basis, unless a life Subscription is selected, or the subscription is cancelled prior to the first payment becoming due. Subscriptions may be cancelled at any time, but if they are left open beyond the date at which the first payment becomes due and is processed then payments will not be refundable.

CPSIA information can be obtained
at www.ICGtesting.com
Printed in the USA
LVOW10s1424160717
541558LV00010B/388/P